STREET FONTS

Claudia Walde

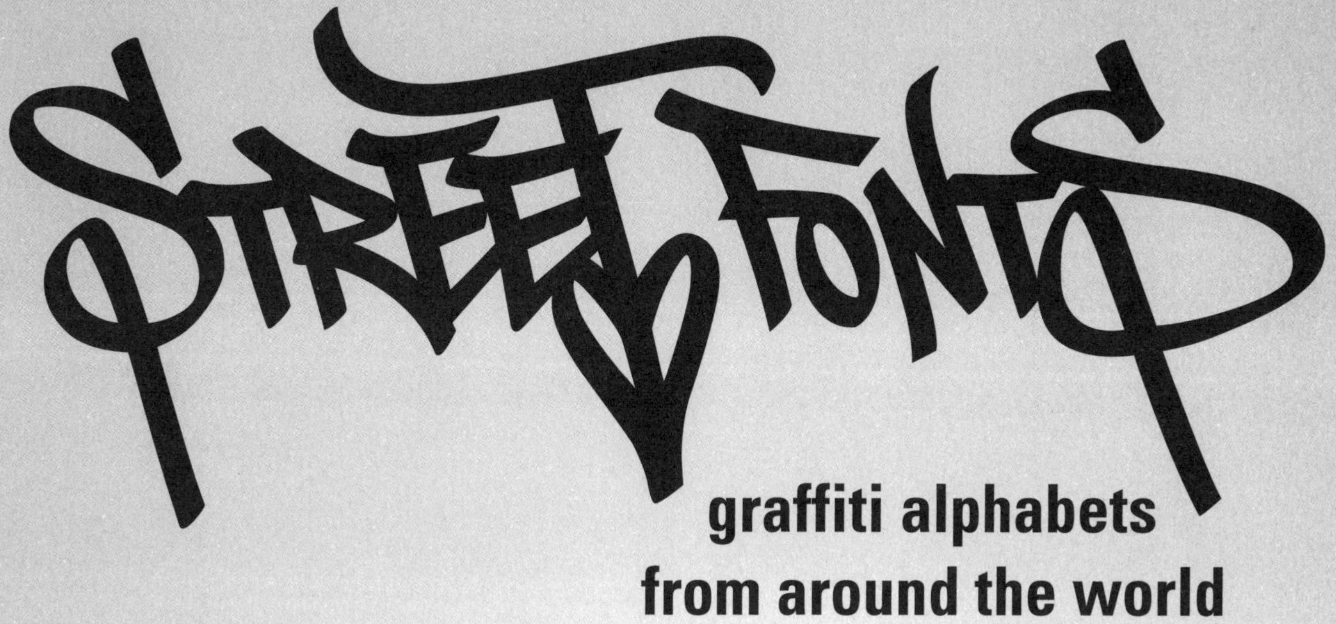

**graffiti alphabets
from around the world**

With over 400 illustrations

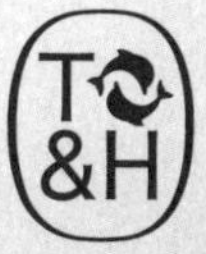

*In loving memory of Sigi 'DARE' von Koeding
who inspired me, believed in me, and without
whom I wouldn't be where I am today.*

Contents

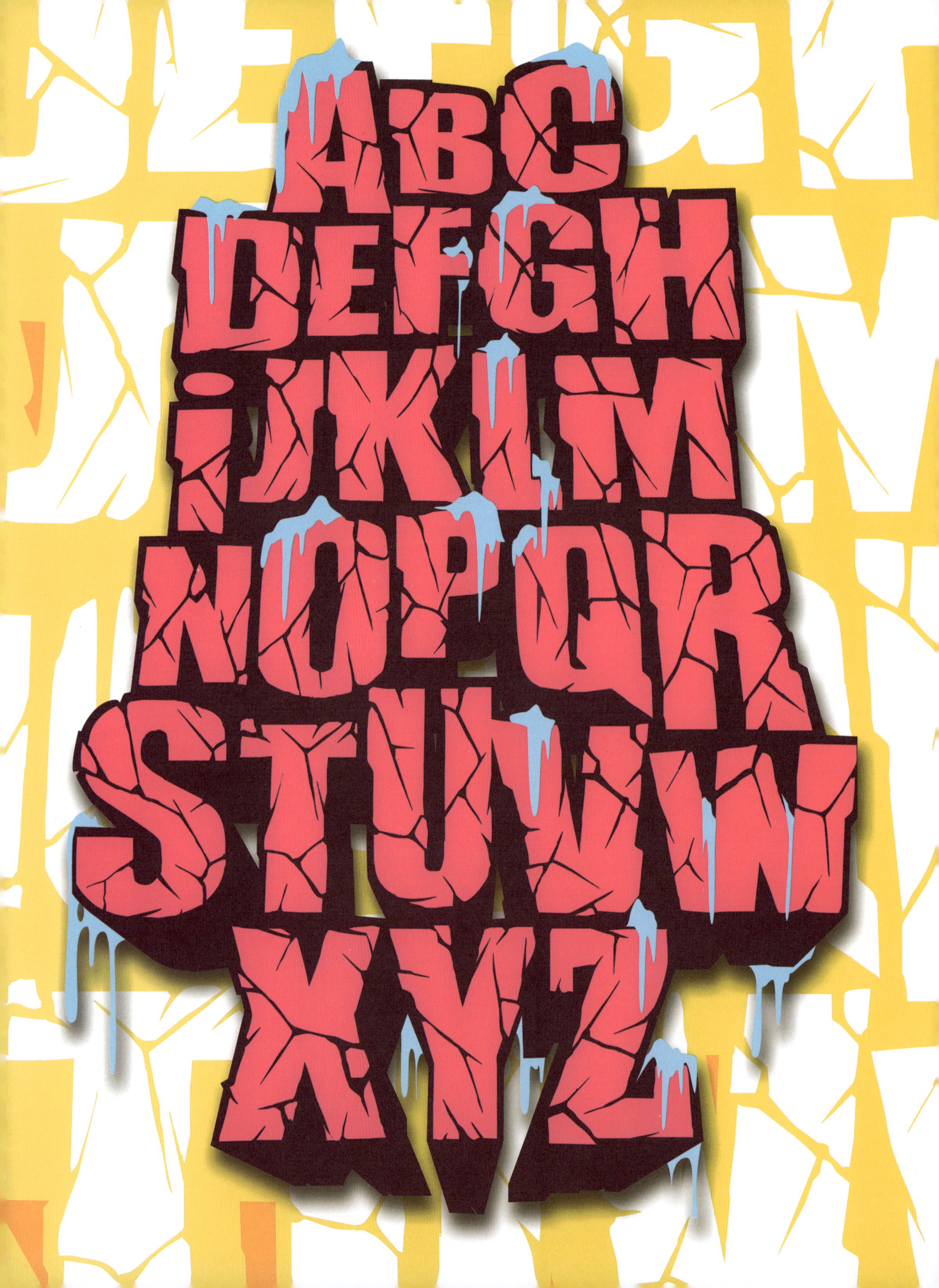

ABC
DEFGH
IJKLM
NOPQR
STUVW
XYZ

Introduction

Contemporary graffiti can take many different forms, each guided by a host of motivations and objectives. This book celebrates the beauty of graffiti writing.

For more than fifty years, graffiti writing has centred around designing the letters of a self-chosen name and bringing it to life. The structure of each letter is predefined and can only be violated to a certain degree if the name is to remain legible to other people. Within these shape guidelines, writers have developed countless styles or style variations, which they continue to redefine.

But a graffiti writer does more than simply communicate a name. Writing is an expression of personality and a reflection of a harmonious physical movement. The letters, and the way in which they are connected, often have their own character. This is usually described as the artist's handwriting or style. These styles are generally variations of the typical writing styles established many years ago, which include wildstyle, semi-wildstyle, bubble style and 3D style.

For over five decades, writers have also influenced traditional type design, advertising and art through the creation of new letter forms in public. All the artists featured in this book have roots in graffiti culture, but many work in design studios and some have moved away from street culture to focus primarily on type design. Nevertheless, the influence of graffiti writing in their work is clearly evident.

Each artist was given the same brief: to design all twenty-six letters of the Latin alphabet. How they approached this task and selected the media with which to express their ideas was entirely up to them. A writer usually designs his name within a connected group of letters rather than bringing single characters together in one piece; and most graffiti artists confine themselves to working with the letters that make up their name. It is therefore no small task to create a complete alphabet.

This book contains alphabets by 154 highly creative writers from around the globe and shows their individual interpretations of the Latin alphabet, with styles ranging from classic old-school graffiti letter forms to modern font designs. It is intended as a beginner's guide for those new to graffiti writing and a timeless collection for experienced writers, as well as a source of inspiration for type designers.

123 Klan

MONTREAL, CANADA
Founded in 1992
Favourite letter: F
www.123klan.com

123 Klan was founded by Scien and Klor in 1992, and they soon
began to develop their signature style – a combination of graffiti
and graphic design – which they have continued to perfect
over the years. They started out in France but are now based in
Montreal, Canada, where they run a design studio that specializes
in character illustration, branding and toy design. Throughout
their work Scien and Klor follow the motto 'style is the message'.
The lack of rules is what they appreciate most about graffiti.

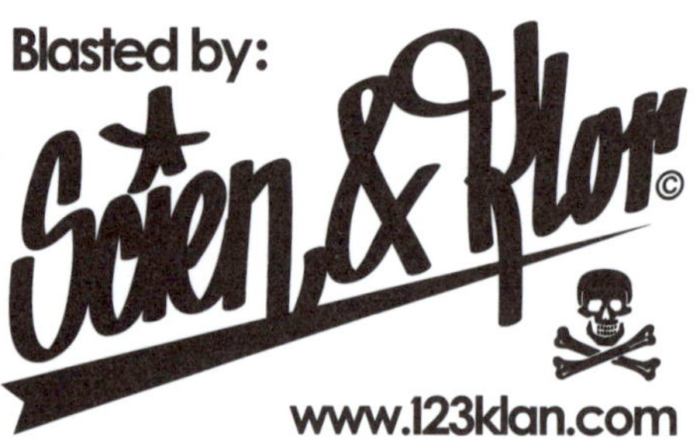

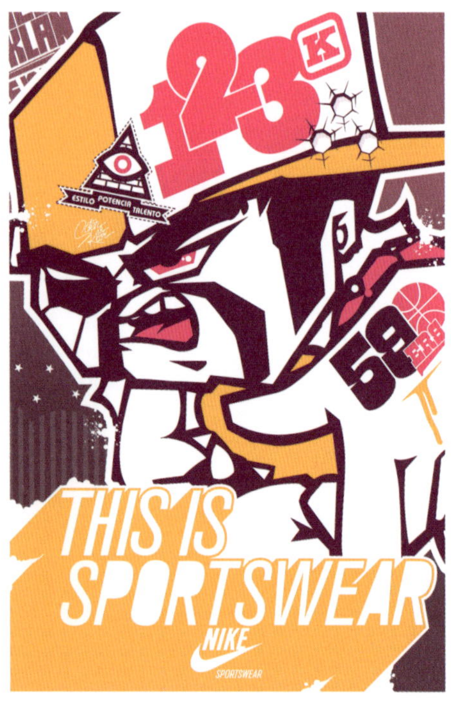

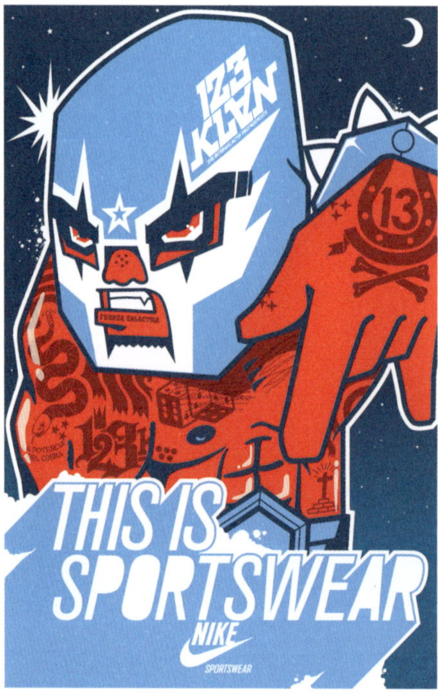

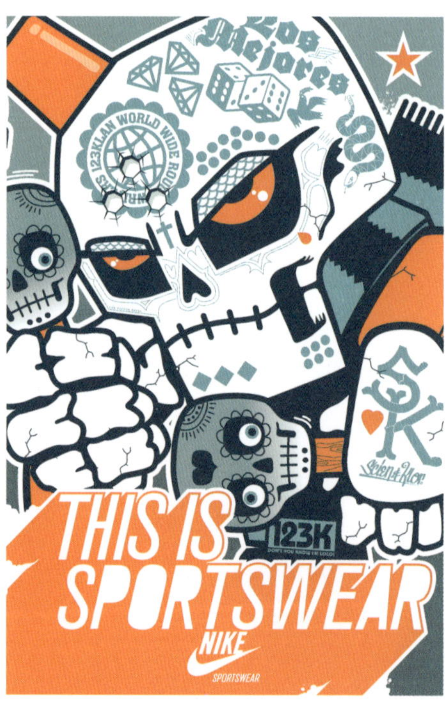

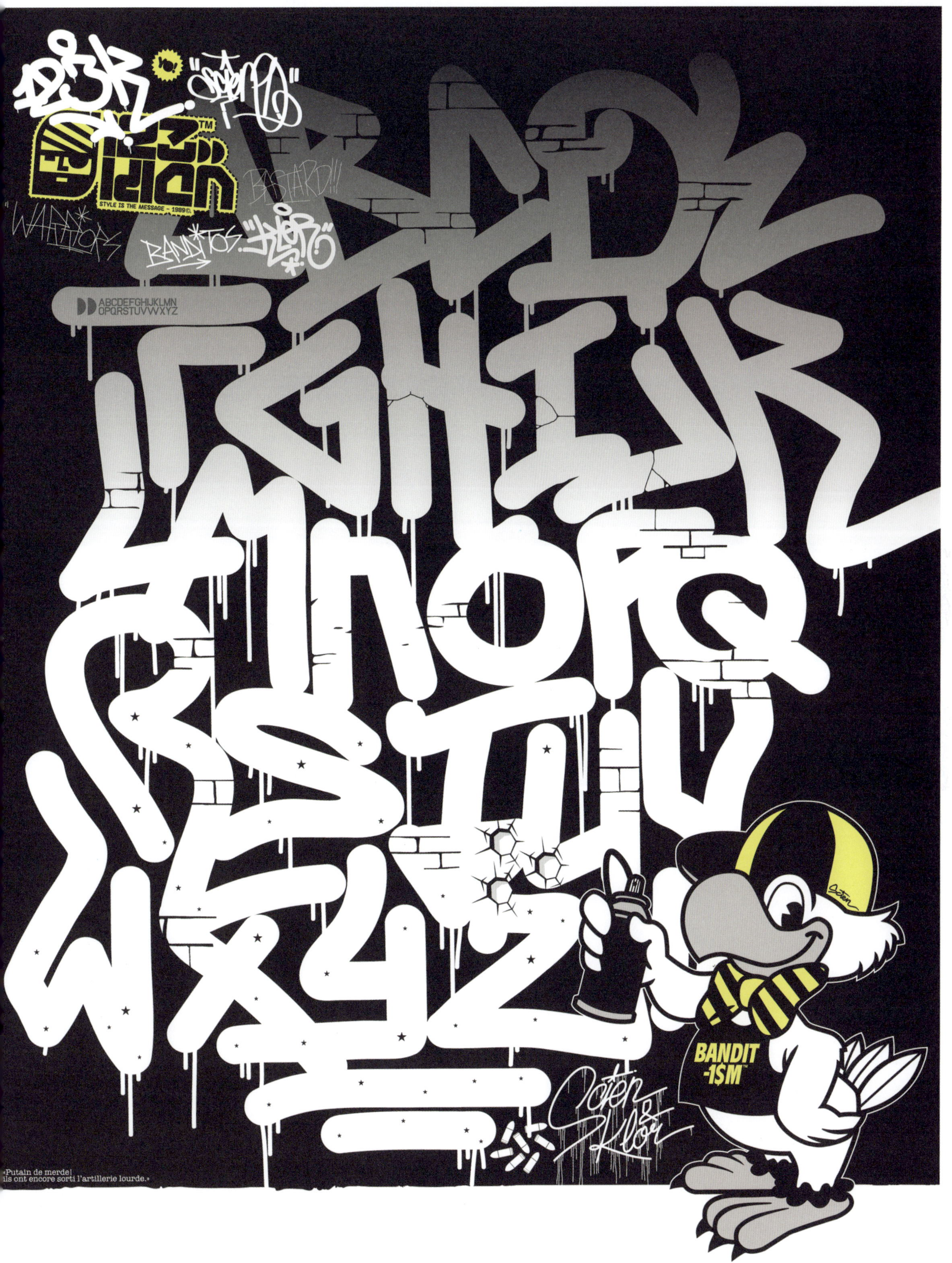

STYLE IS THE MESSAGE ~ 1989©
WARRIORS
BANDITOS
BASTARD!!!
ABCDEFGHIJKLMN
OPQRSTUVWXYZ
BANDIT -1$M
«Putain de merde!
ils ont encore sorti l'artillerie lourde.»

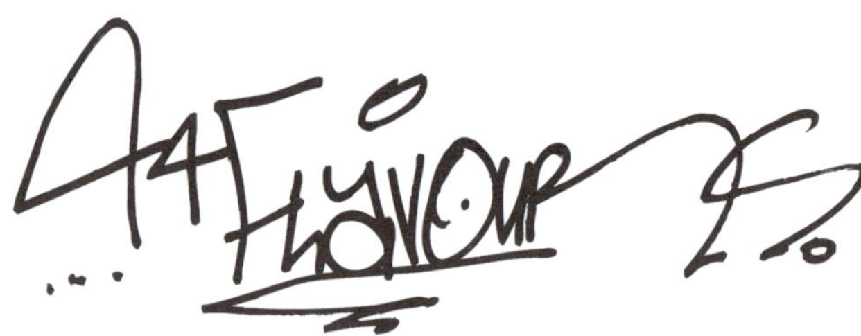

44 Flavours

BERLIN, GERMANY
Writers since 1995
Favourite letter: R
www.44flavours.com

44 Flavours don't limit themselves to one particular medium. They exhibit their work, design magazine layouts and clothes, and have worked on commissions from various recording artists. Graffiti and hip-hop culture influenced them from the very beginning and are reflected in the free spirit of their creations. In their opinion graffiti is, and should be, a passion; if it isn't, you shouldn't do it.

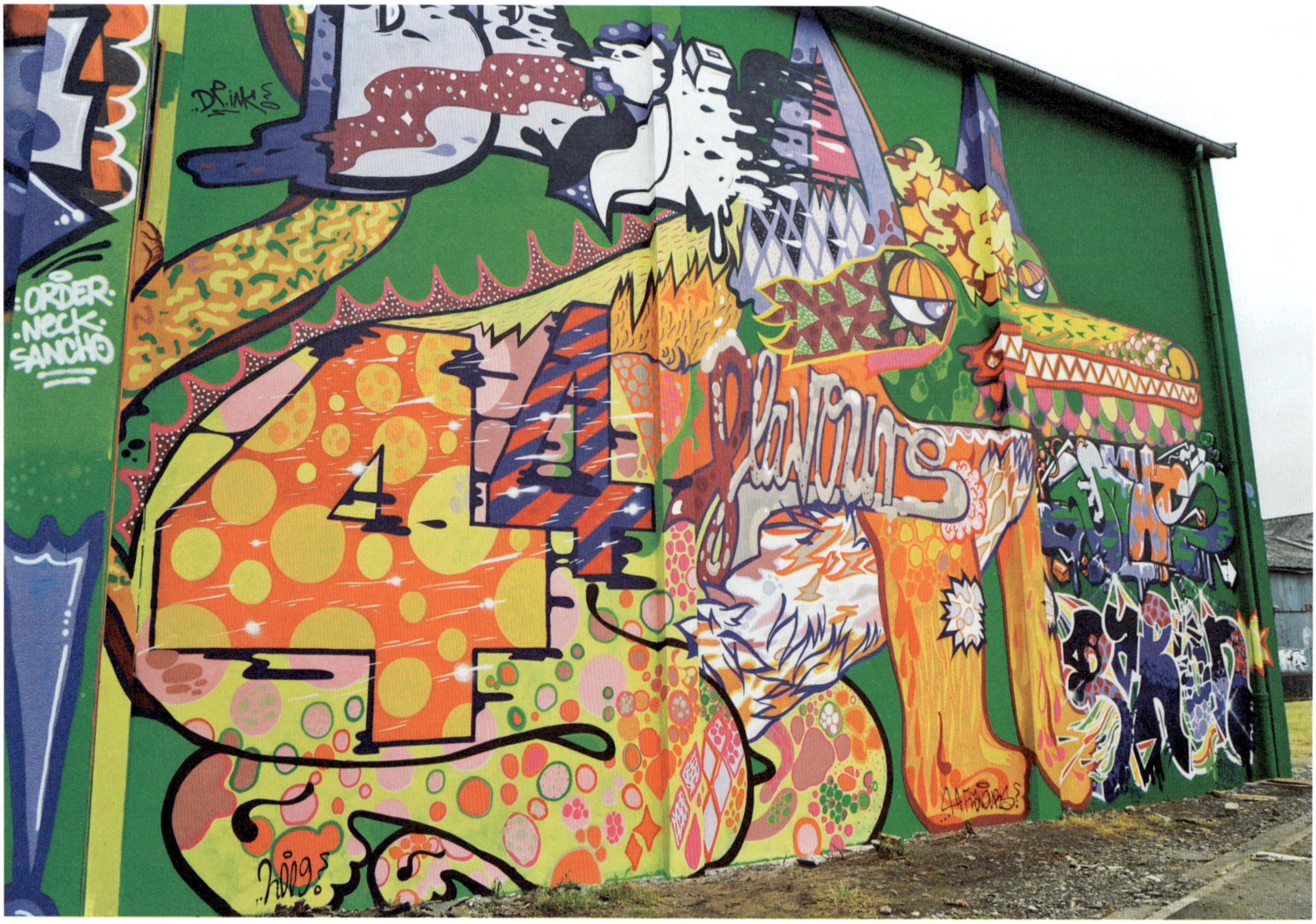

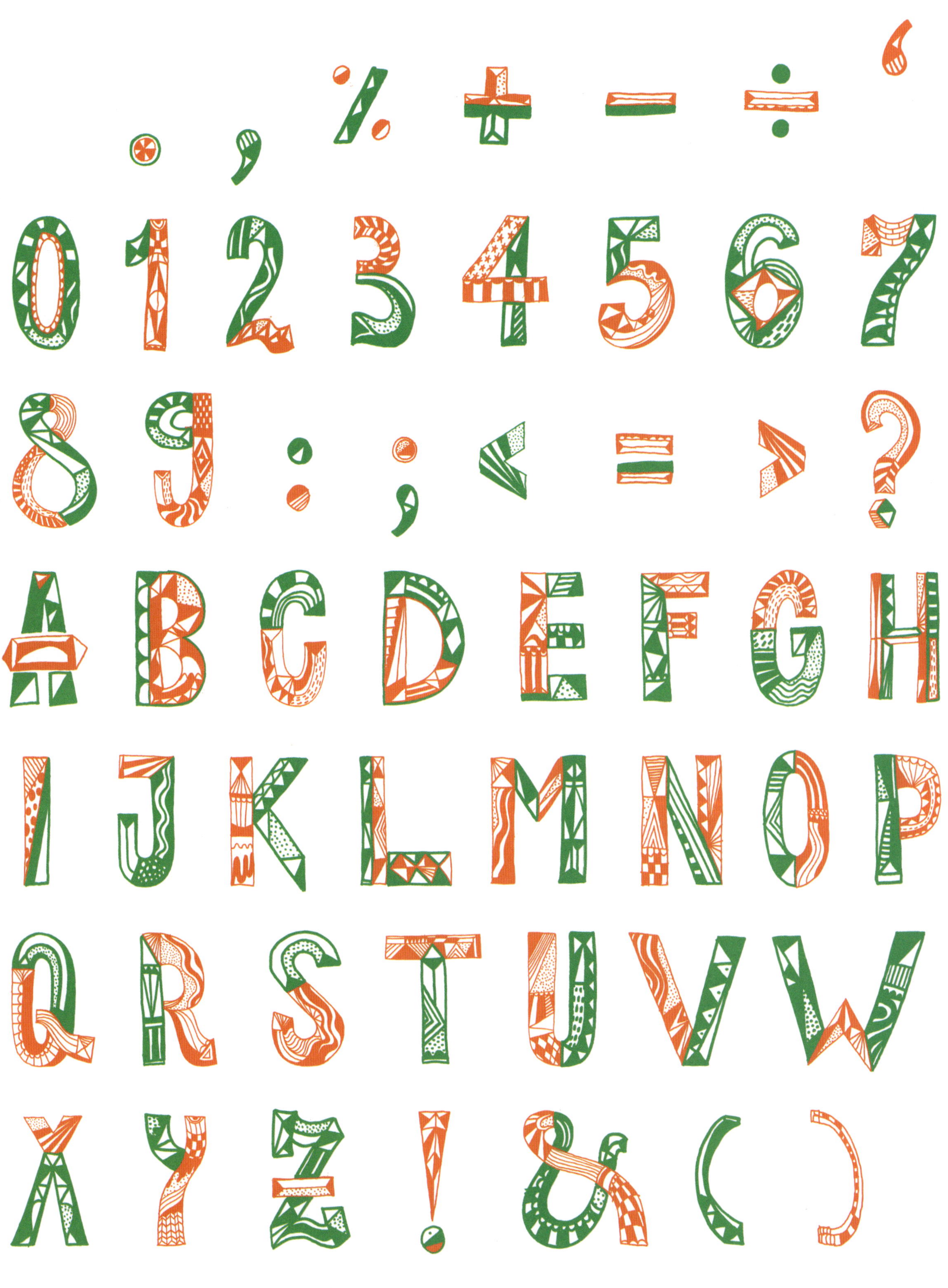

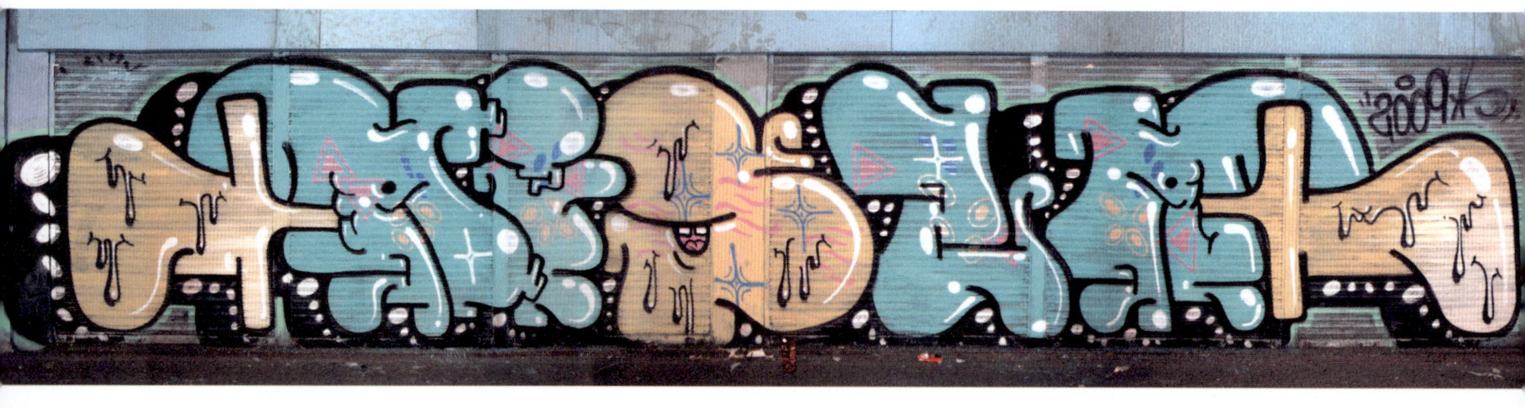

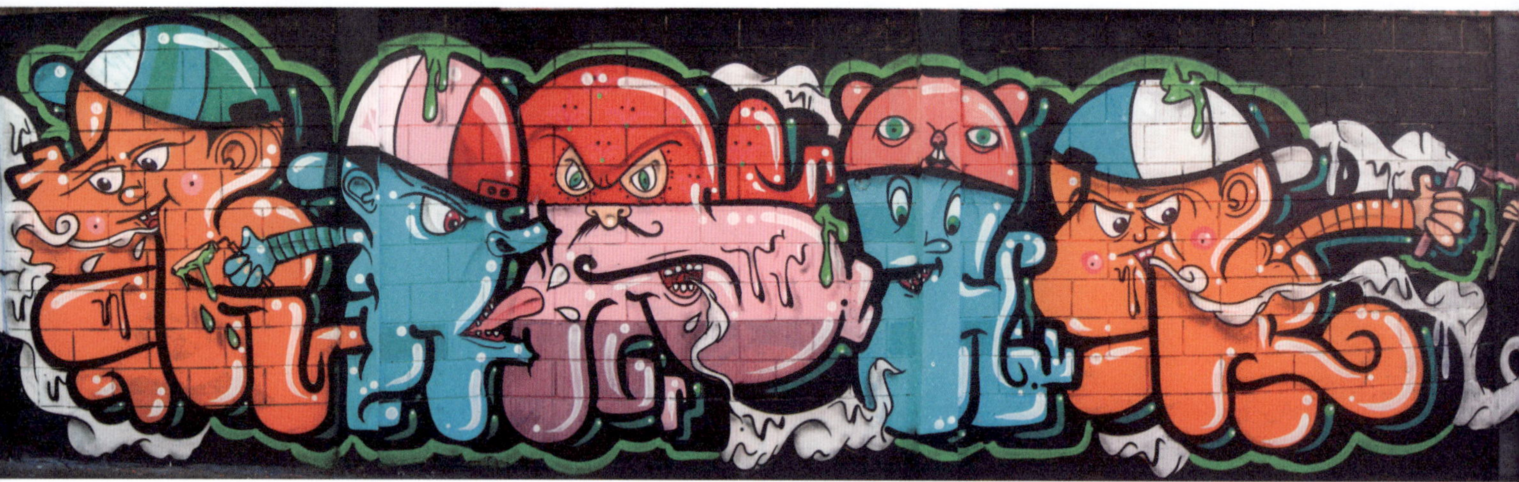

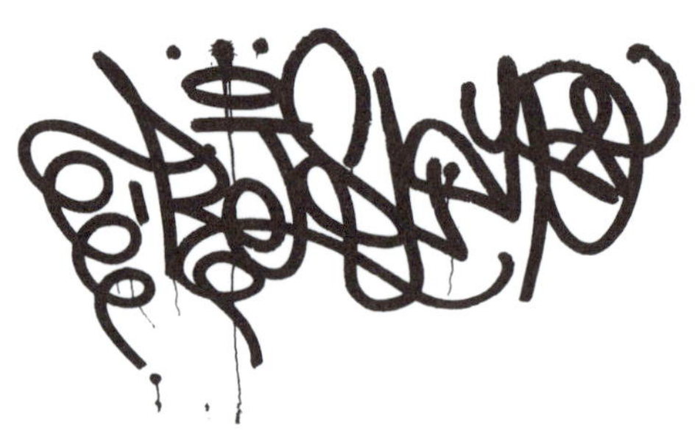

Aislap

SANTIAGO, CHILE
Crew members of ADEP
Writers since 1996
Favourite letter: R

Rounded edges, striking colours and personified letter forms
are all typical of Aislap's style. The choice of medium is not what
matters most to the crew, but rather the desire to create something
and the development of a personal style.

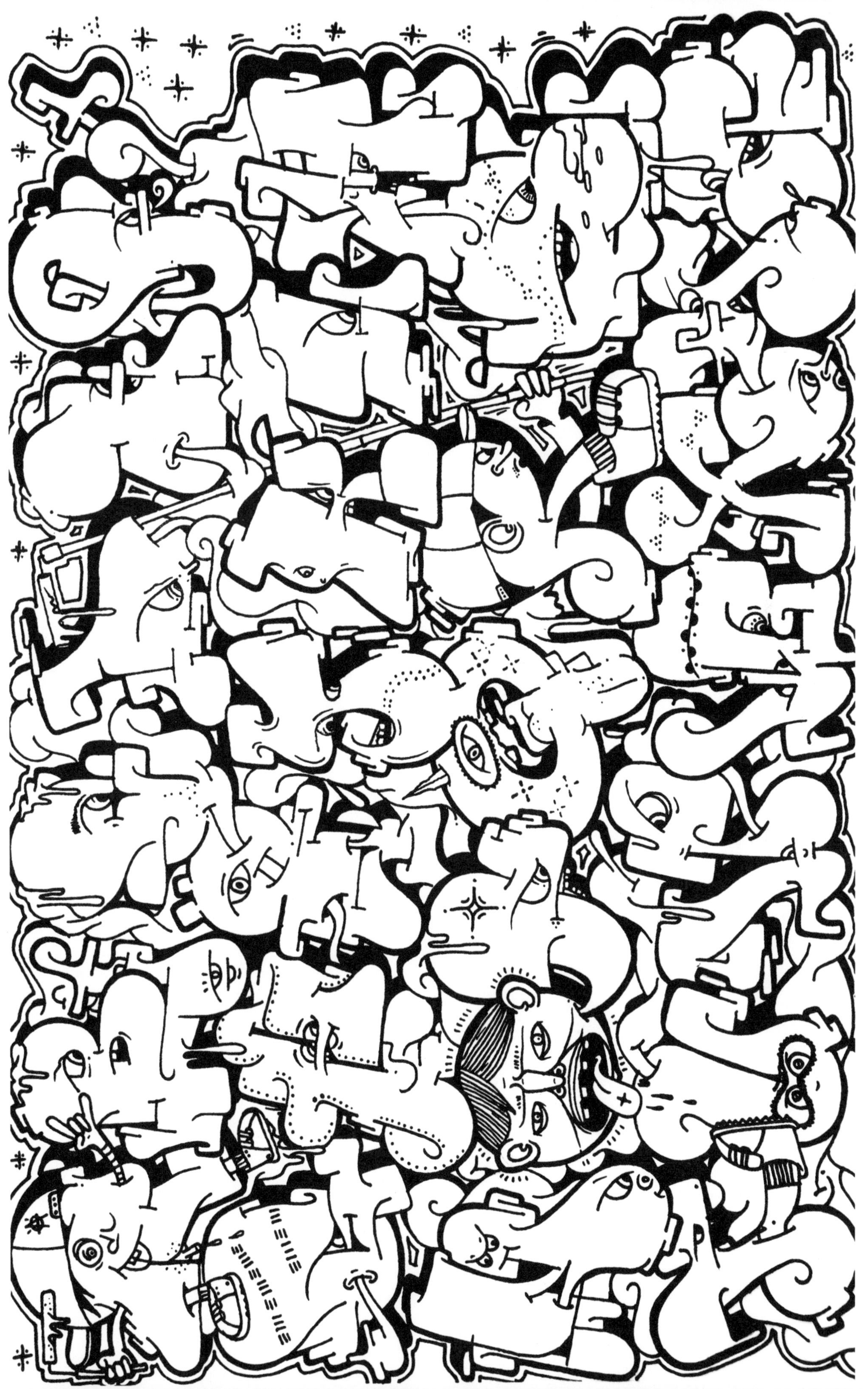

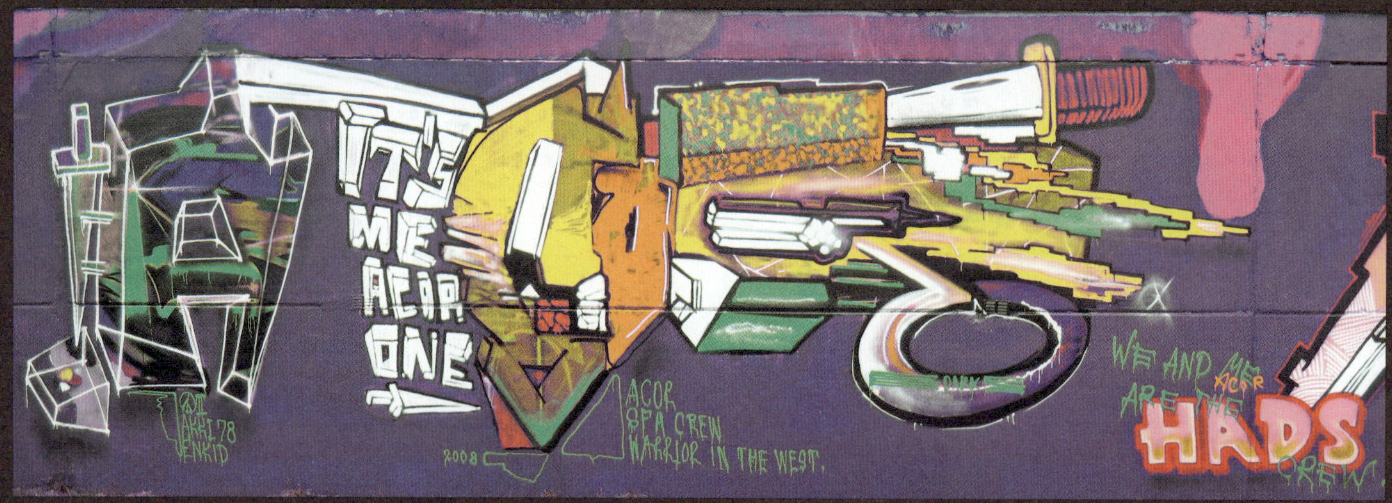

Akor

HALLE, GERMANY
Crew member of SFA, HADS
Writer since 1994
Favourite letter: S

Akor has a strong illustrative style. He set out to design an
alphabet made up of new, simple and expressive shapes; knots
and twisting, overlapping forms that aren't typical of graffiti
letters but are still legible. According to Akor, a good style needs
artistic unity, a connection between the individual letters, as well
as experimental and fresh ideas.

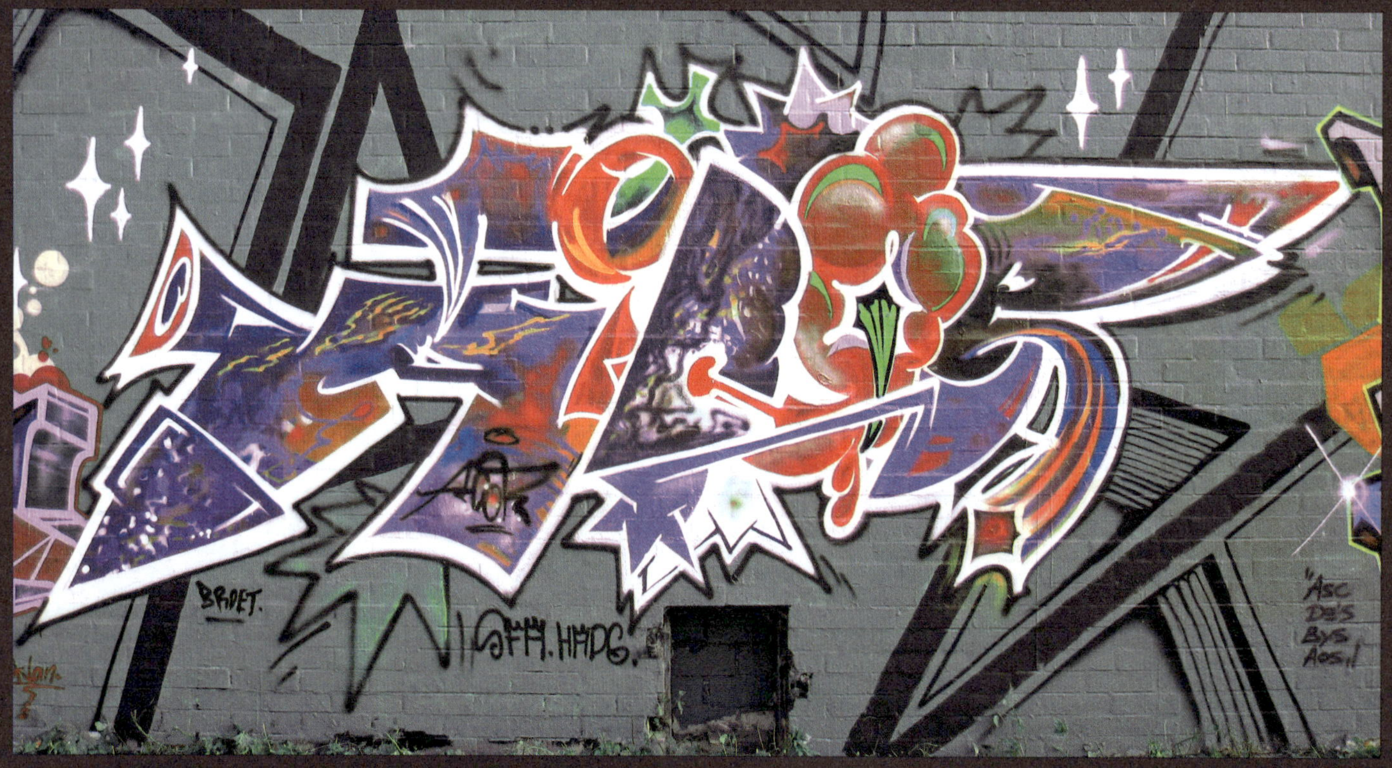

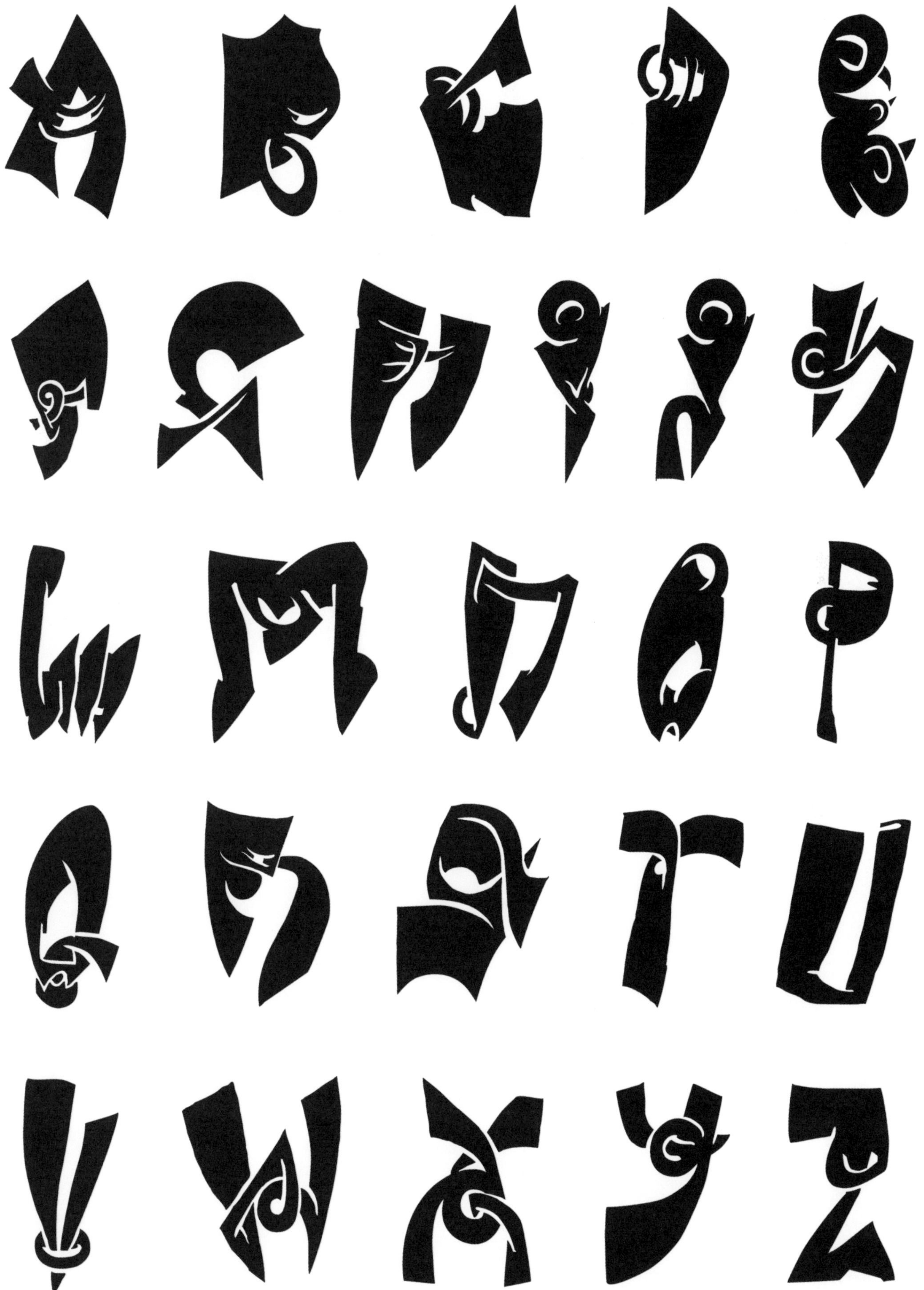

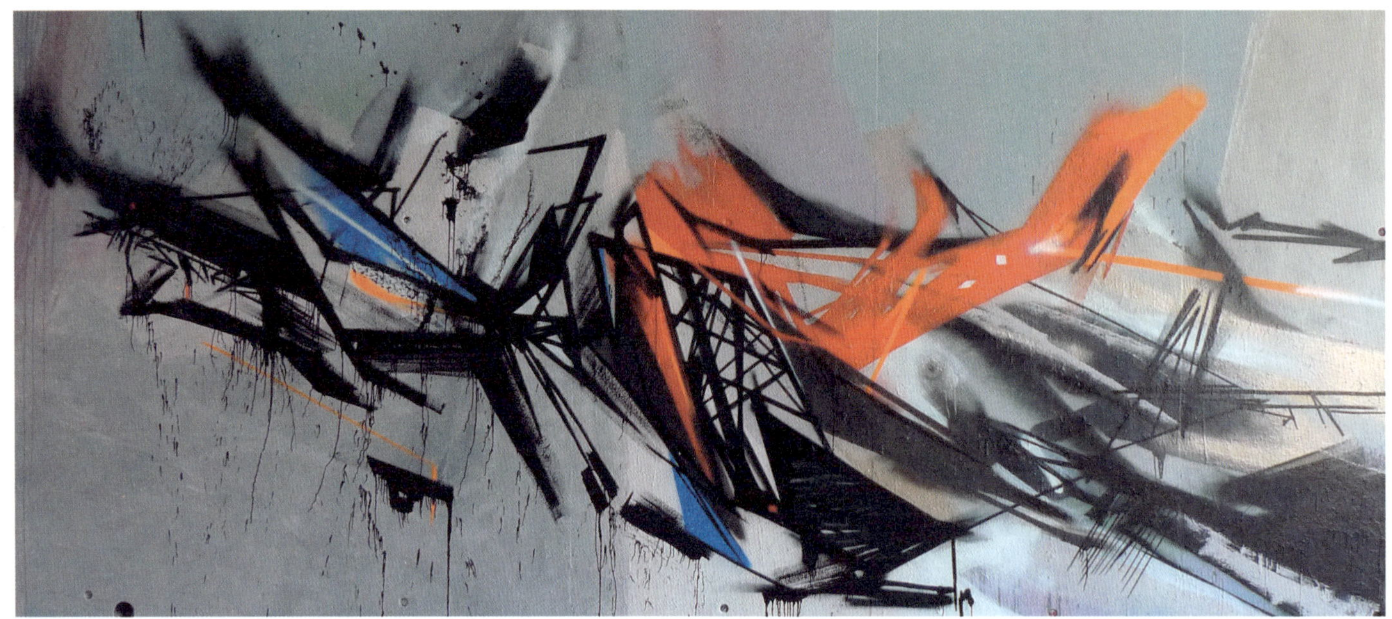

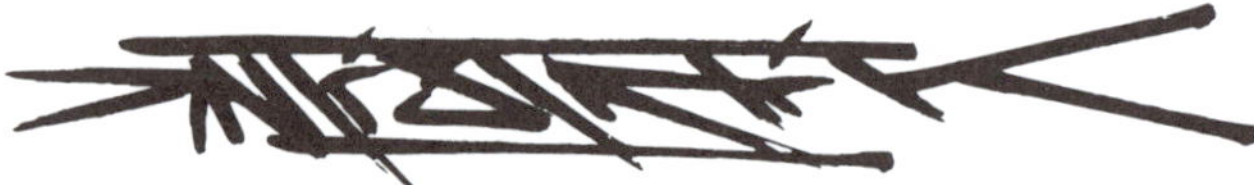

Antistatik
STRASBOURG, FRANCE
Crew member of Orbit119
Favourite letter: T

Whether it's letters or characters, canvases or walls, Antistatik's work is dynamic and incorporates various different techniques and media. His experimental and futuristic style is reflected in his hand-drawn alphabet, which was inspired by the Death Star space station from *Star Wars*.

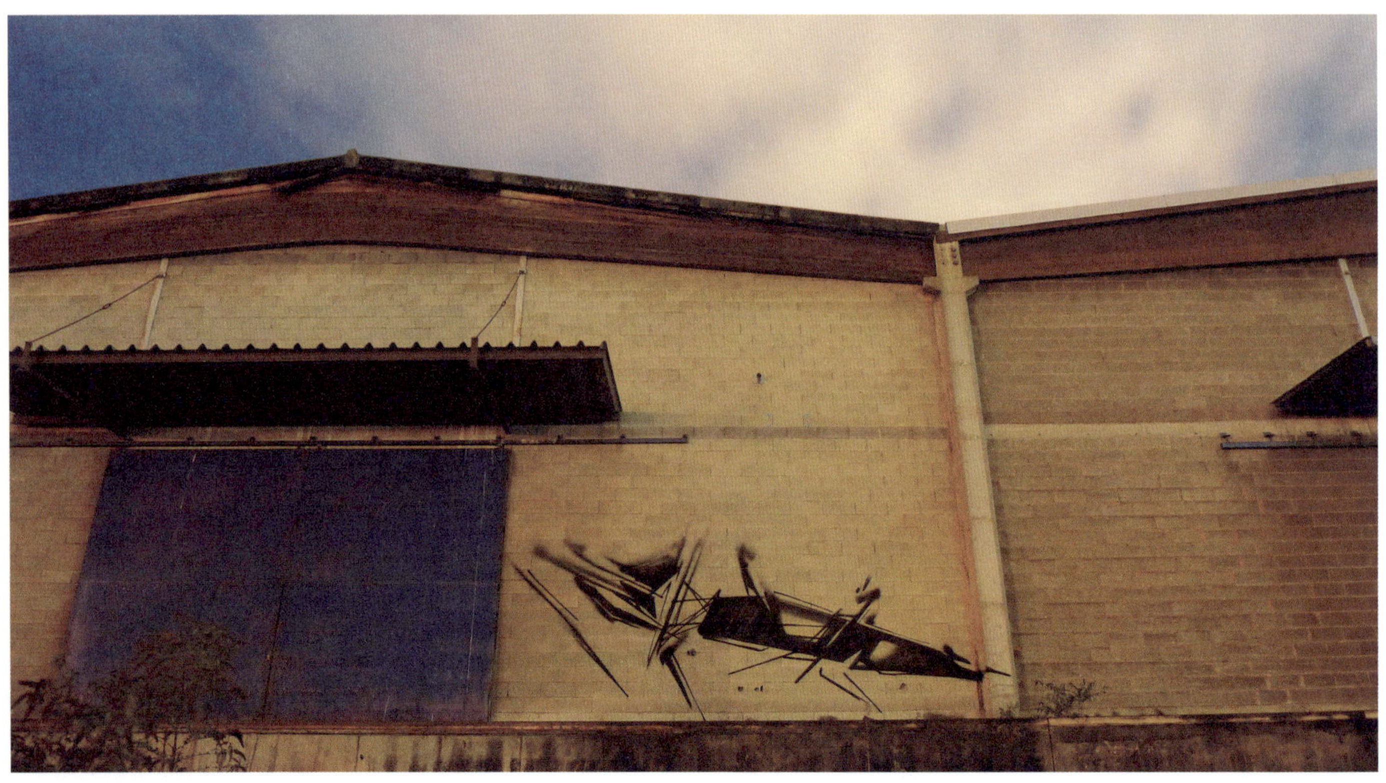

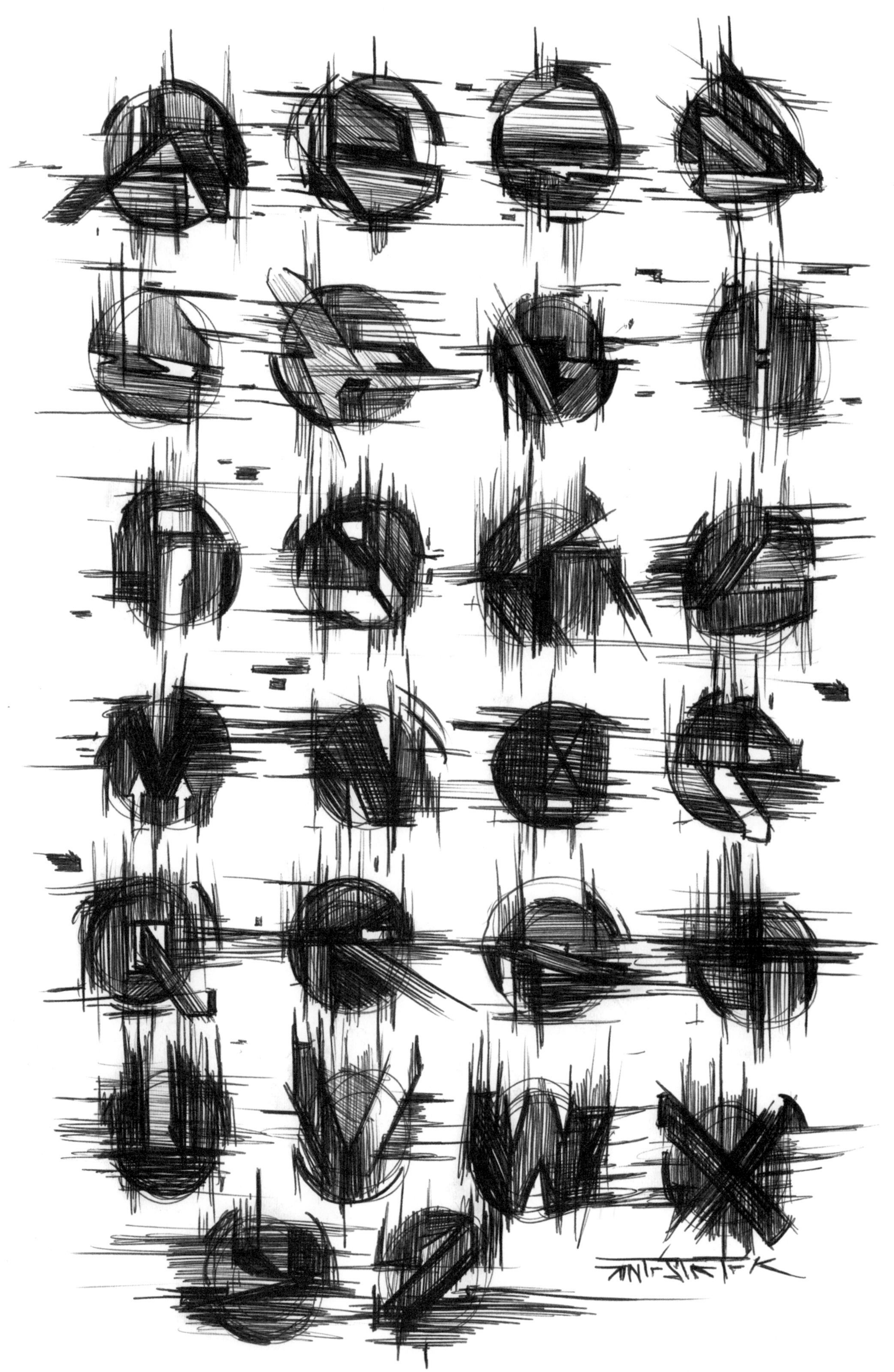

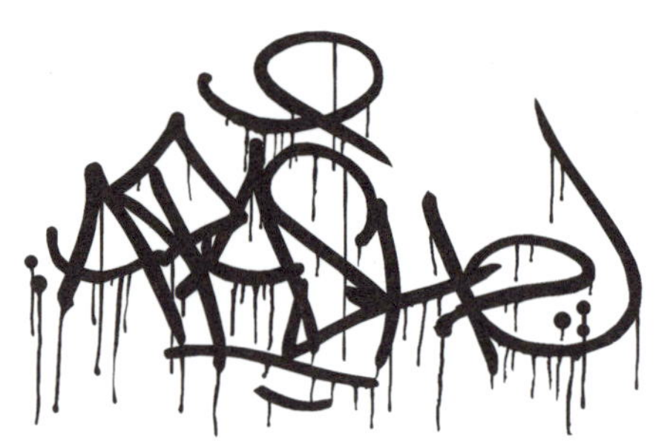

Apashe

TOULOUSE, FRANCE
Crew member of ABS, FWT
Writer since 2000
Favourite letter: E
www.apashoner.com

Straight lines are a defining feature of Apashe's work. According to the French artist, a piece can only be good if it is coherent. His alphabet was drawn by hand and then coloured digitally.

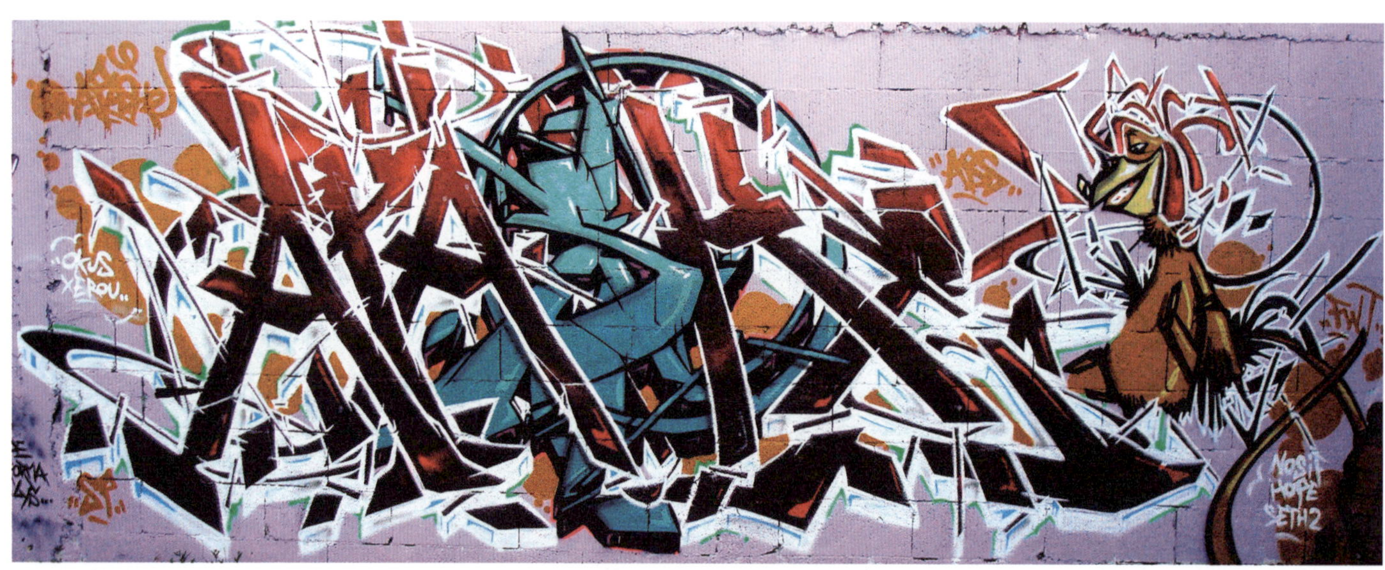

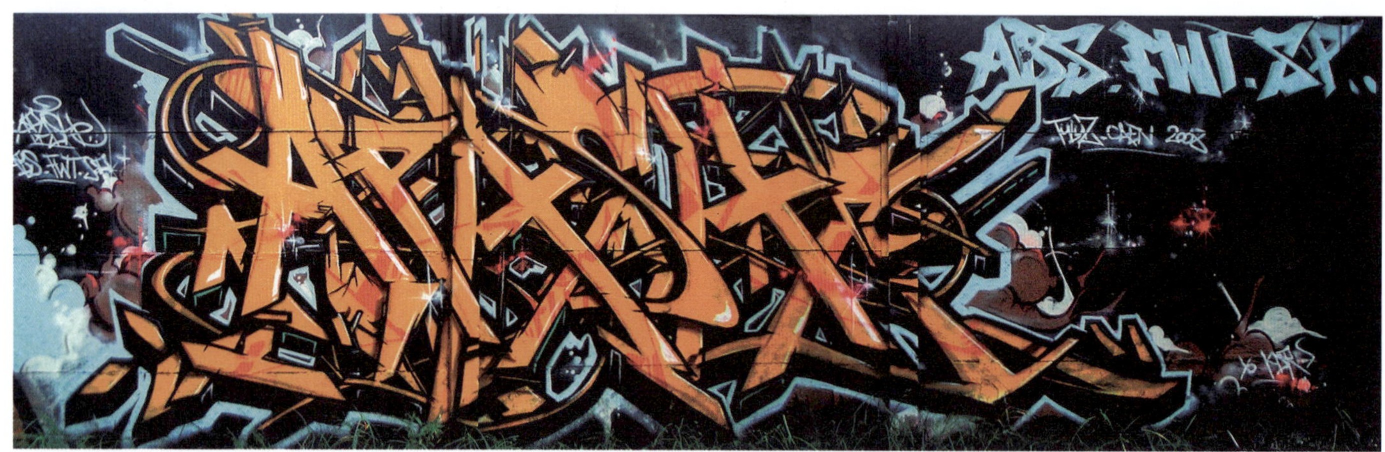

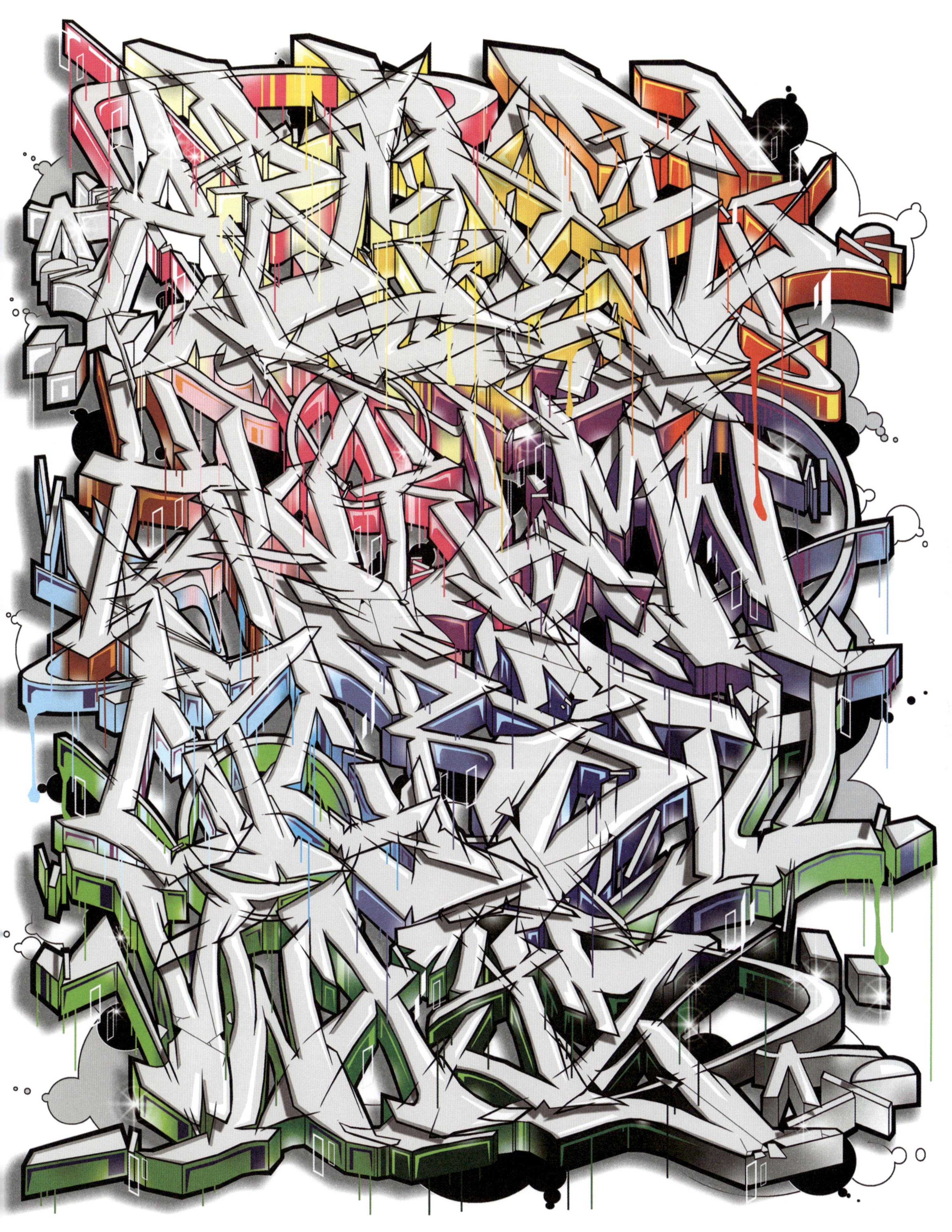

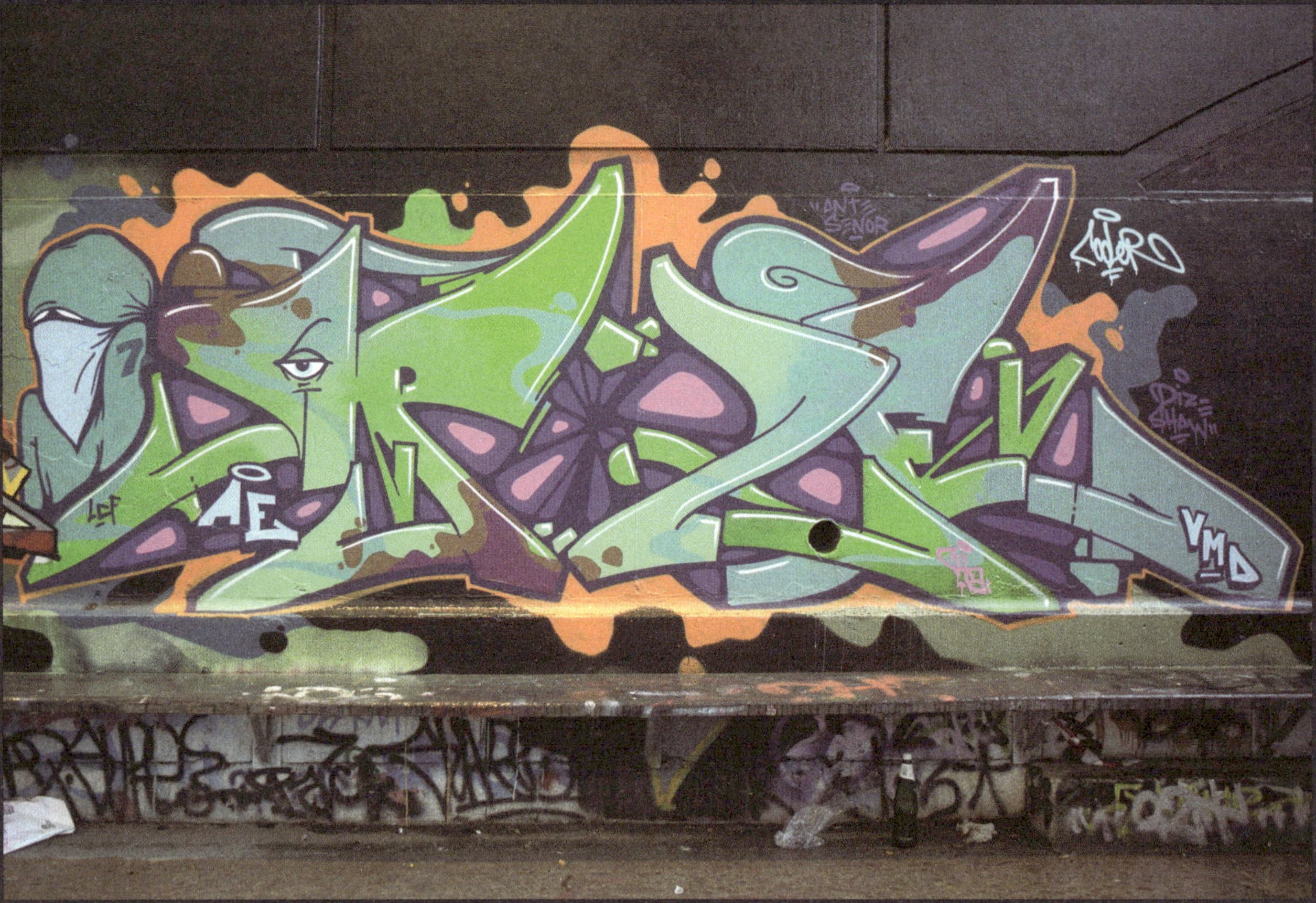

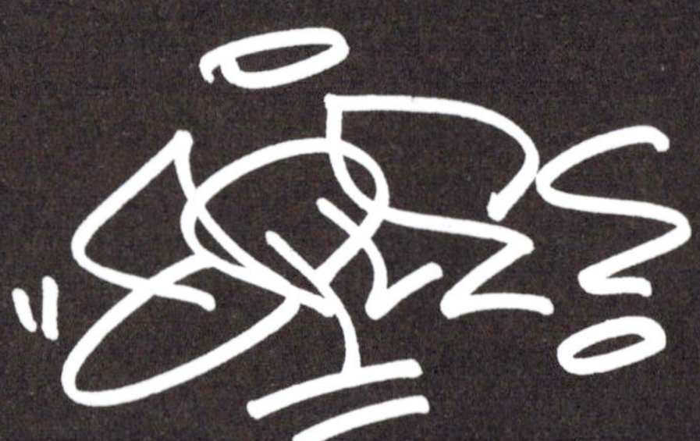

Aple76
GRENOBLE, FRANCE
Crew member of VMD, Adults Entertainment, DFP, LCF, TSH
Writer since 1993
Favourite letter: A
www.a76.fr

Also known as Cooler or Fact, French writer Aple76 is passionate about letters and B-Boy characters and has influenced many European writers through his work. He never uses colour in his sketches. The only tools he needs to create a good piece are cans, a wall and some Marvin Gaye songs.

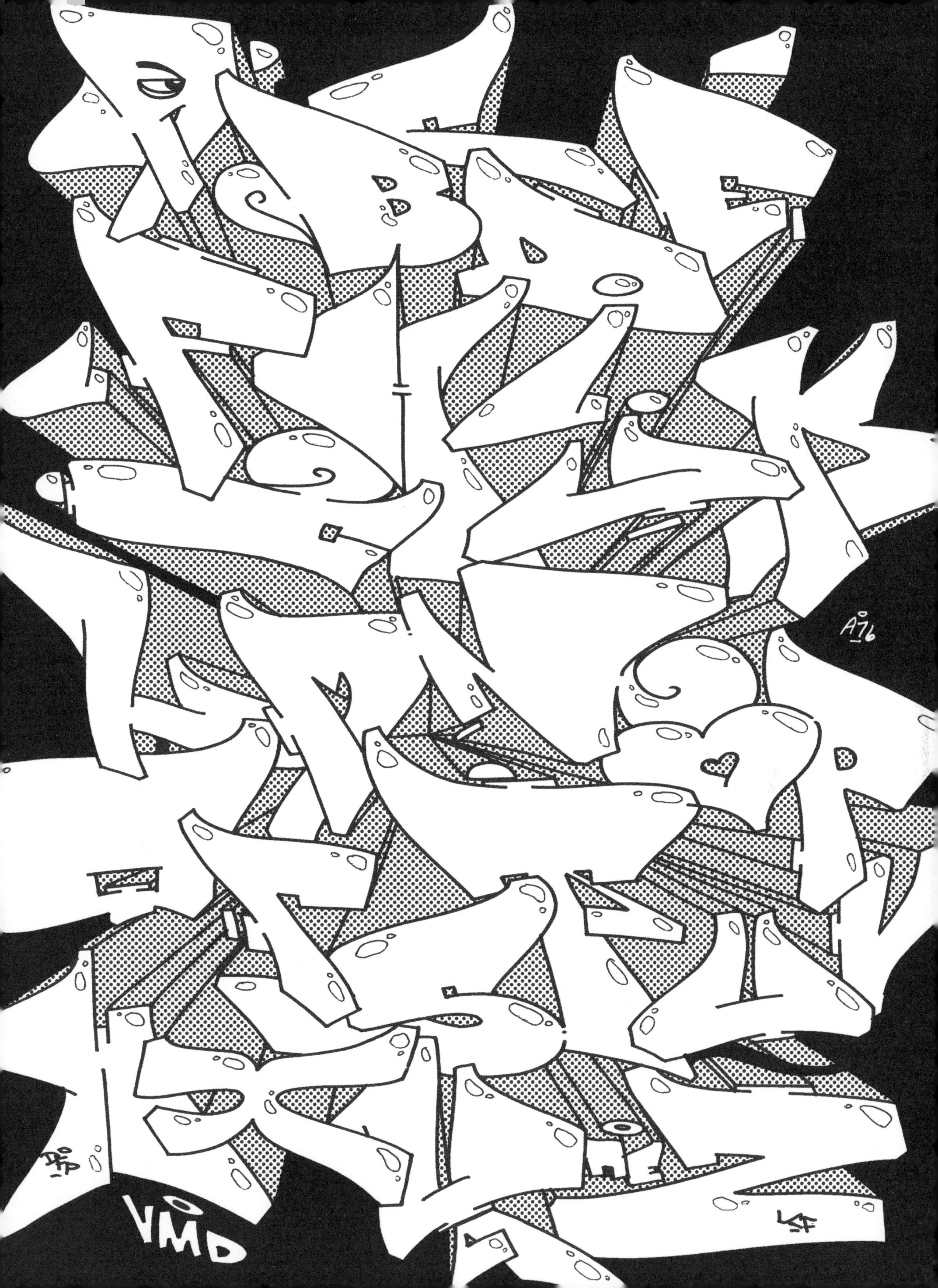

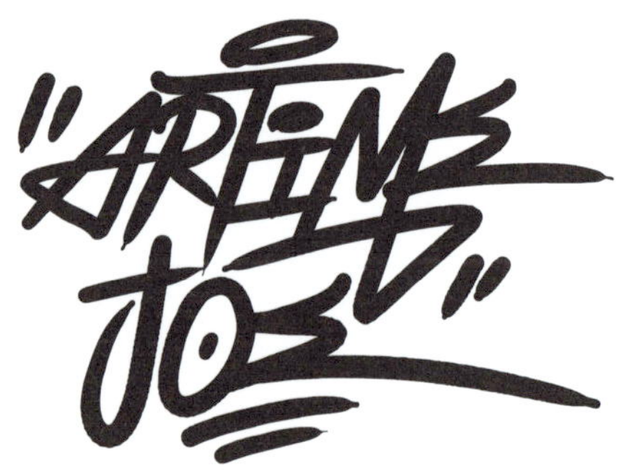

Artime Joe
SEOUL, SOUTH KOREA
Crew member of JNJ Crew, SM8, SUK
Writer since 2001
Favourite letter: A
www.artimejoe.com

Artime Joe has developed a unique illustrative style and use of colour. He pays a lot of attention to detail, and his pieces are full of intricate elements. As he only had basic spray cans at his disposal when he first started out, his technique differs from those typically seen in Europe and North America. He was one of the first South Korean writers to travel extensively, gaining international recognition in the process.

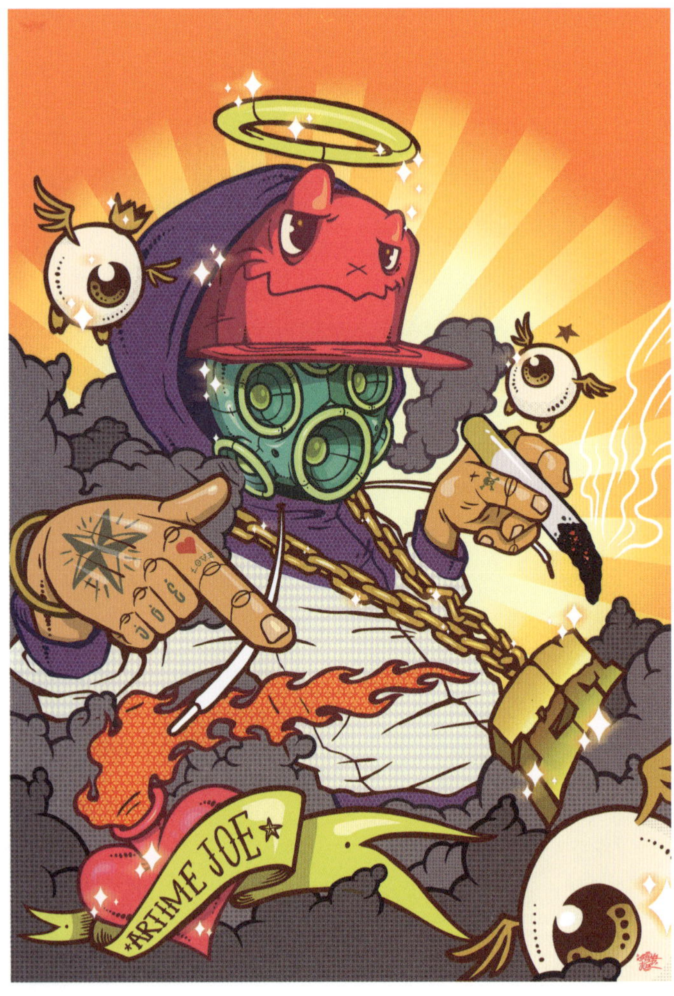

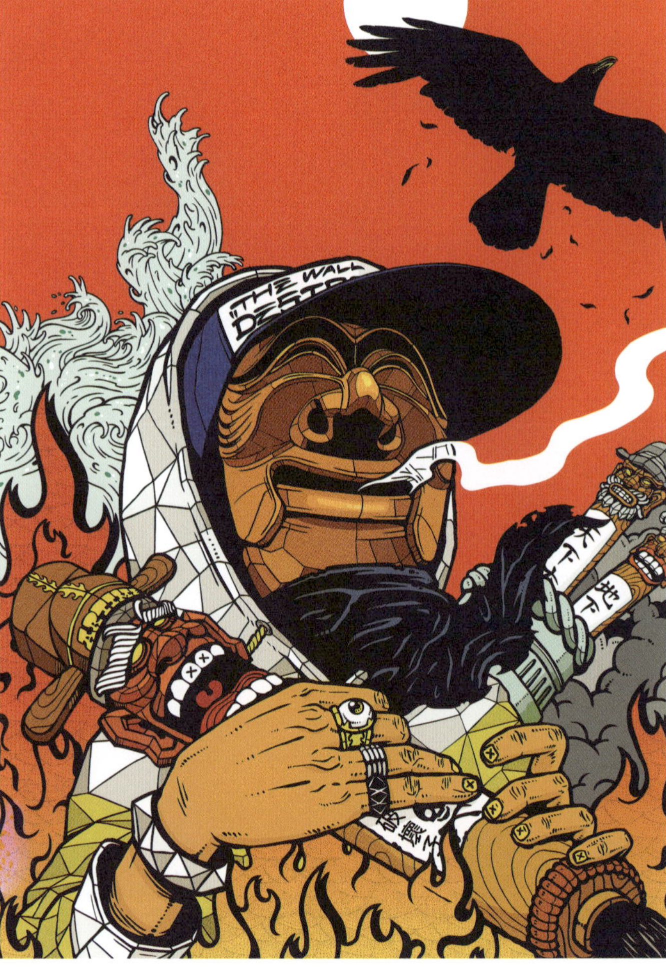

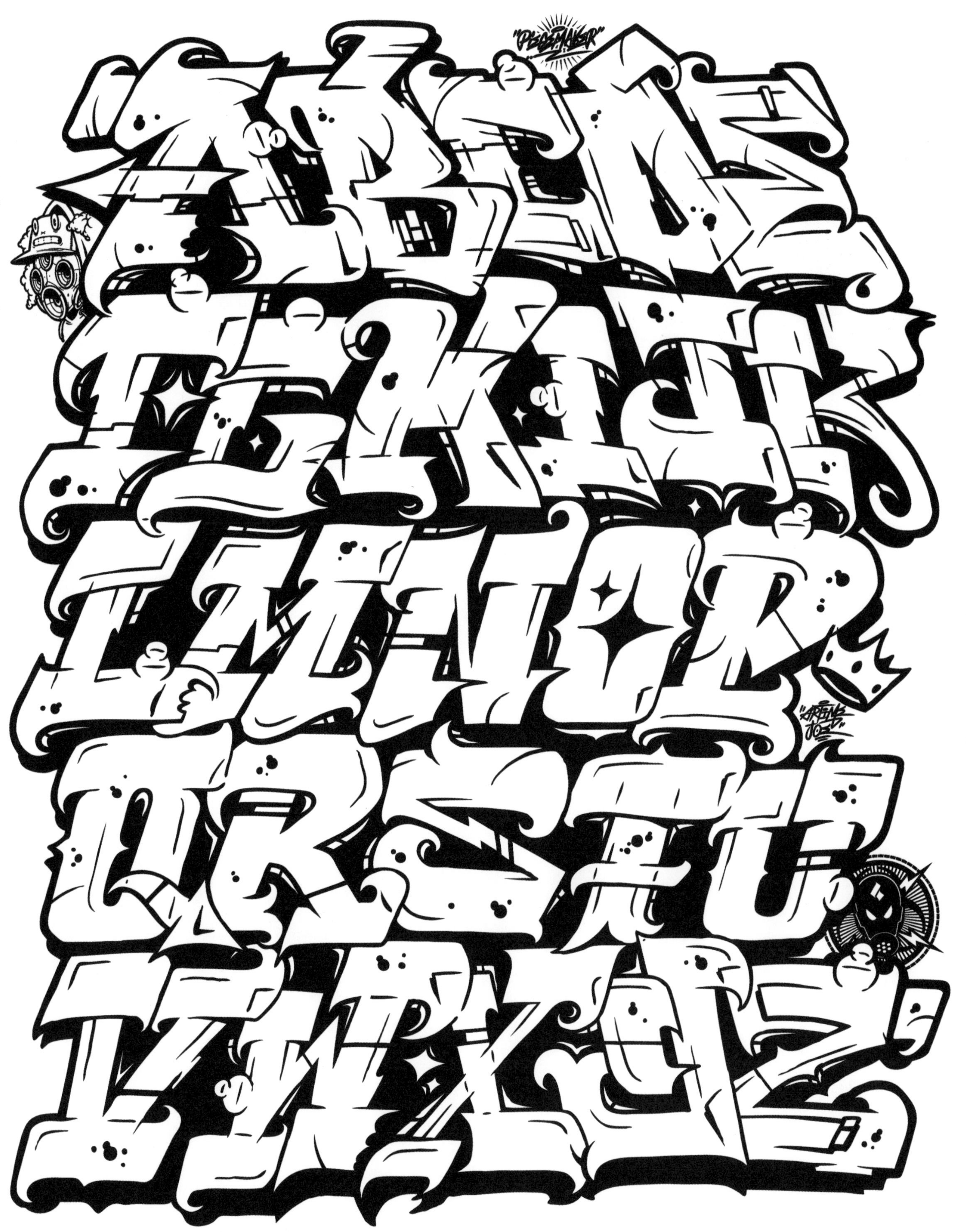

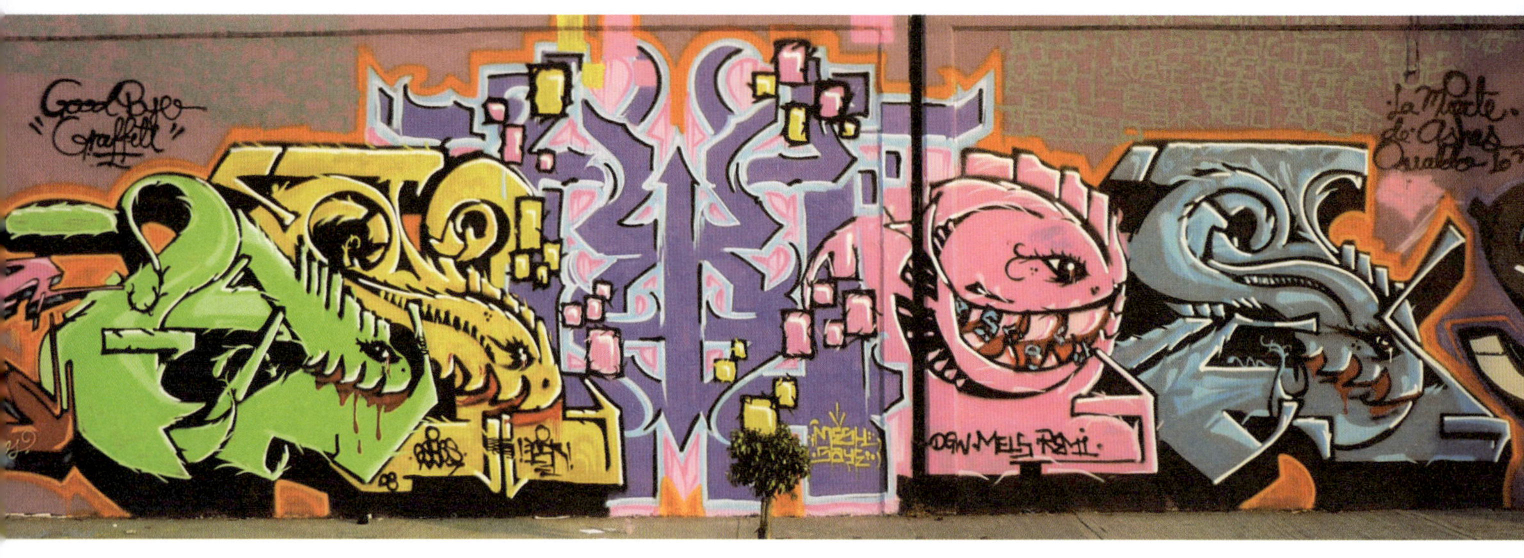

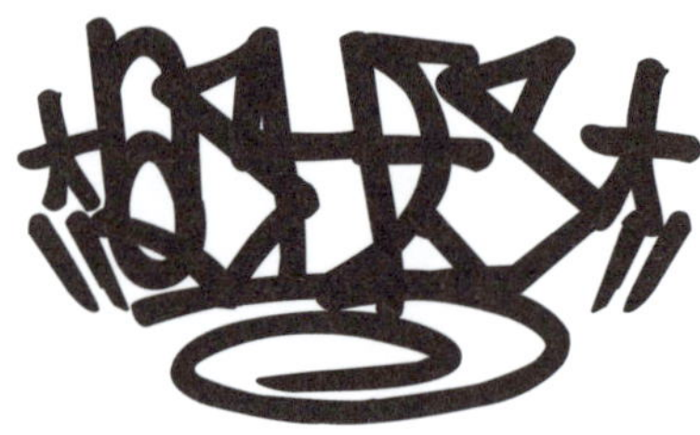

Ashes

MEXICO CITY, MEXICO

Crew member of ICR, MAINTAIN
Writer since 1997
Favourite letter: R
www.ashesgang.blogspot.com

Ashes uses his work to express his feelings and reflect his life. A piece must be sincere and come from the heart; it is very important to him that it is not simply a name. He says: 'Graffiti is able to do what our leaders can't: bring people together, irrespective of who they are, where they come from, the language they speak, and their religious or sexual preferences.'

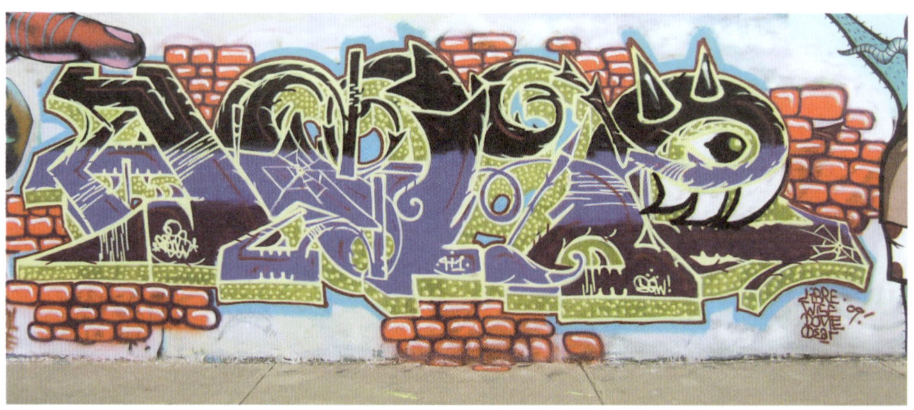

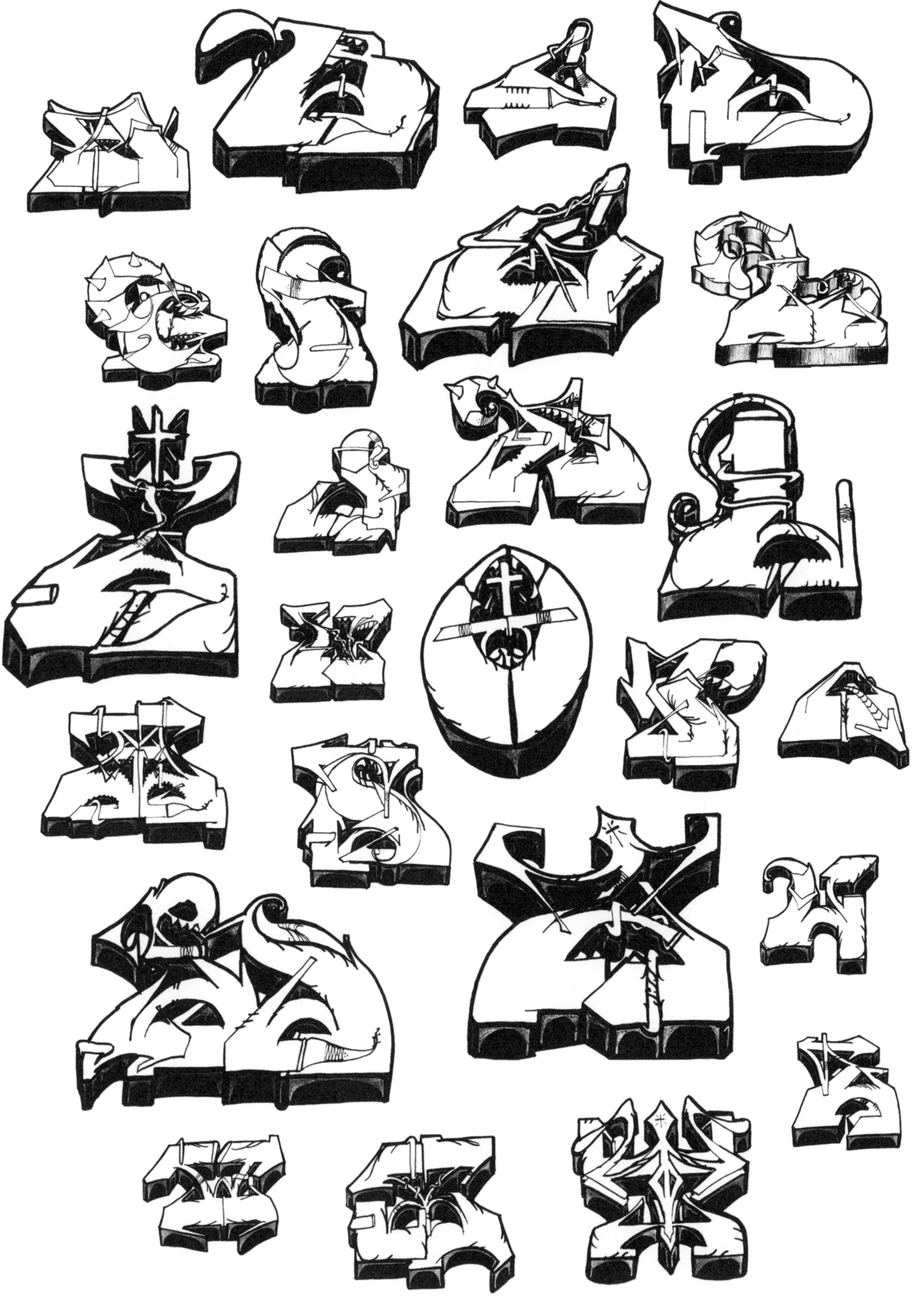

Aske

MOSCOW, RUSSIA
Writer since 2000
Favourite letter: A
www.sicksystems.ru

Sicksystems is an art project by Aske. Initially founded as a graffiti crew, it evolved into an artists' collective and then became founding member Aske's personal project. Although he started out as a graffiti writer, he is now involved in many artistic fields, primarily graphic design. With a passion for colourful, bold, geometric forms, he gives great thought to his creations in public spaces.

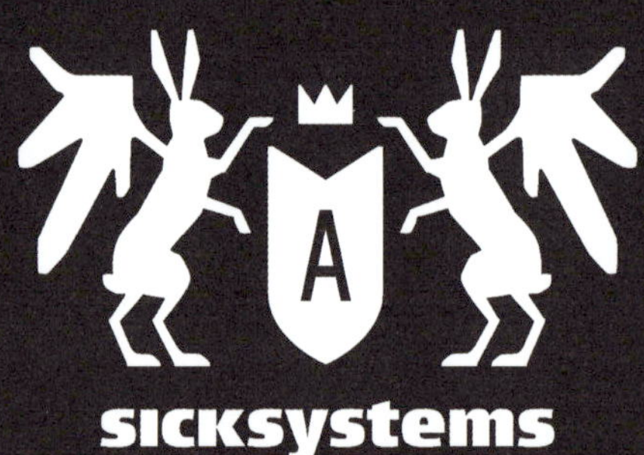

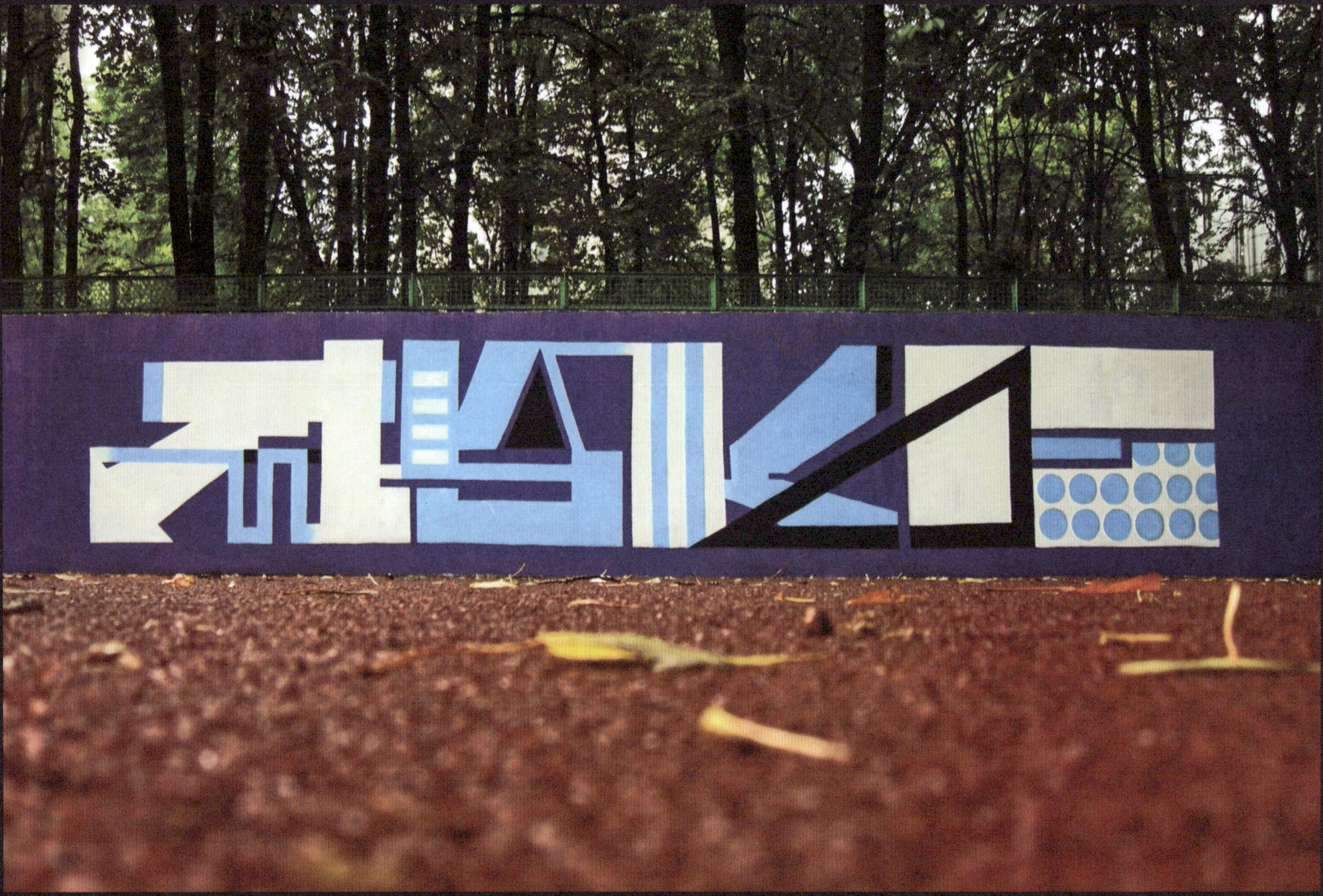

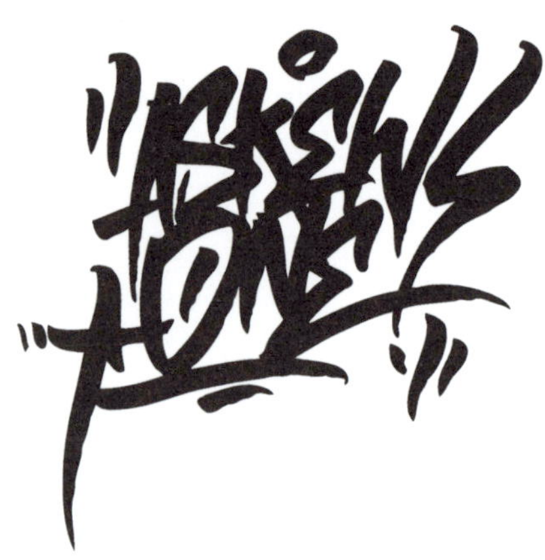

Askew One
AUCKLAND, NEW ZEALAND
Crew member of TMD, SUK, F1C
Writer since 1993
Favourite letter: E
www.askew1.com

Askew One has travelled extensively and painted in countless countries over the years. He has continually pushed his spray-can technique, and can skilfully combine a vast array of colours in a single piece whilst maintaining its legibility. He also works in graphic design, illustration and photography. The most important aspect of graffiti, he says, is the sense of freedom and friendship that it brings.

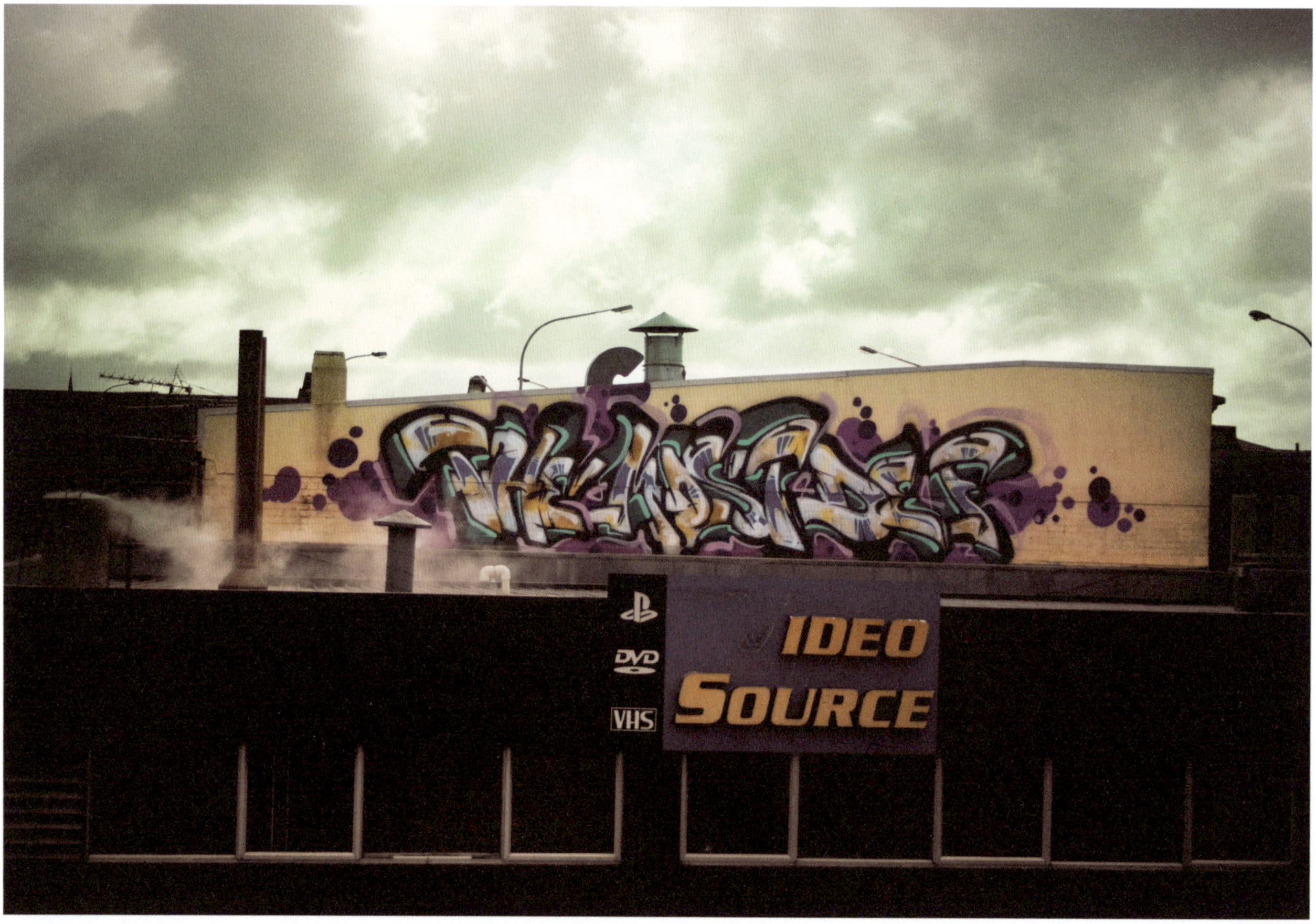

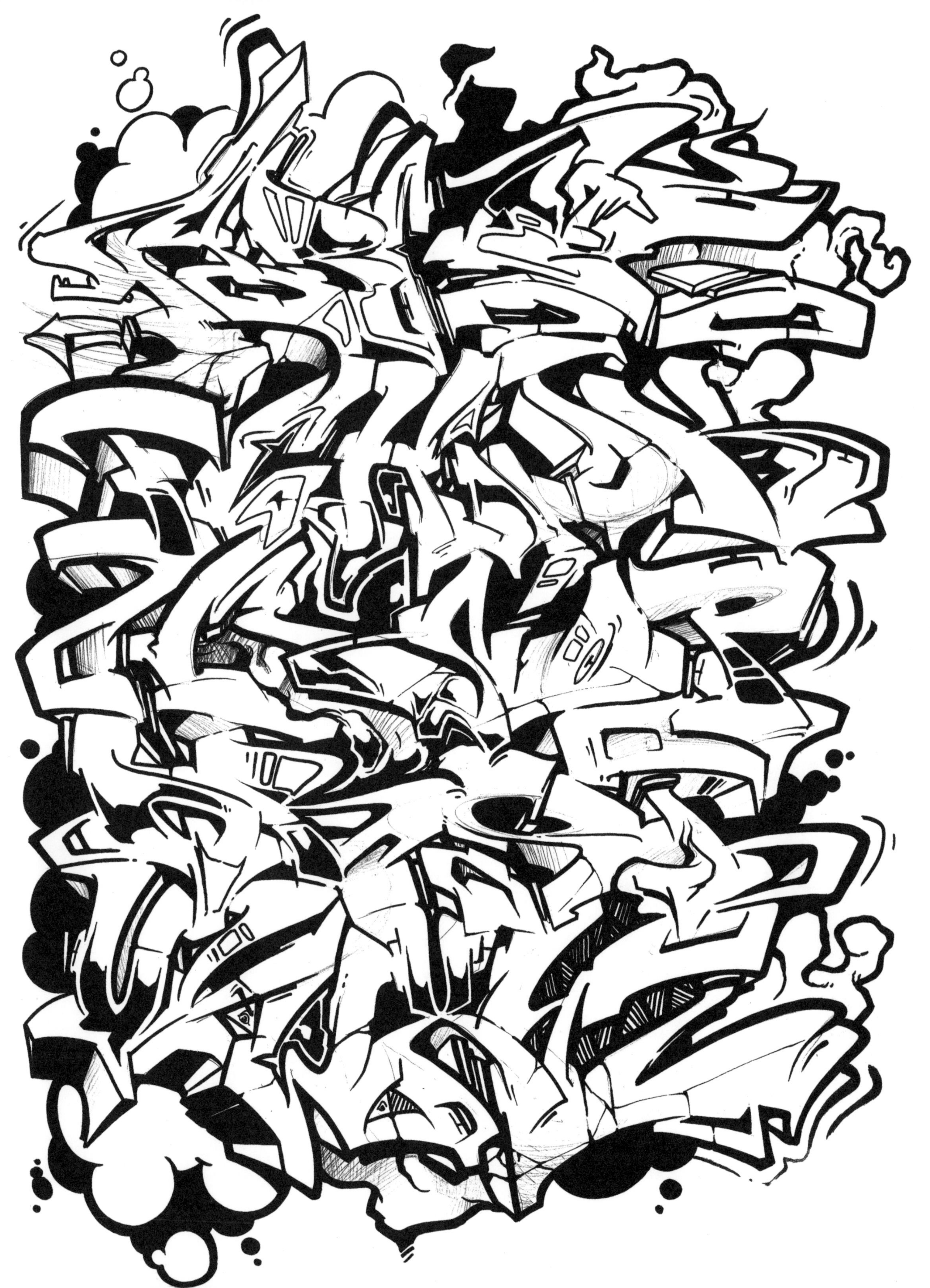

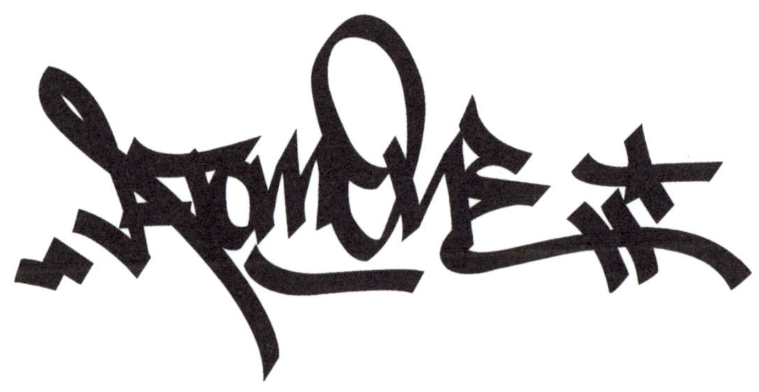

Atom One

DORTMUND, GERMANY

Crew member of MOA, TMD, SUK
Favourite letter: A
www.atomone.de

Atom One is one of those writers who lives and breathes graffiti. He is also known for his rap music in which he talks about his experiences as a writer and the problems that come with this lifestyle. A good piece needs 'swing and funk', he says, and shouldn't be overcrowded with elements that don't make sense. And it should always be legible and reflect the personality or mood of the writer. For Atom, trains are the best thing about graffiti 'because that's what graffiti is for'.

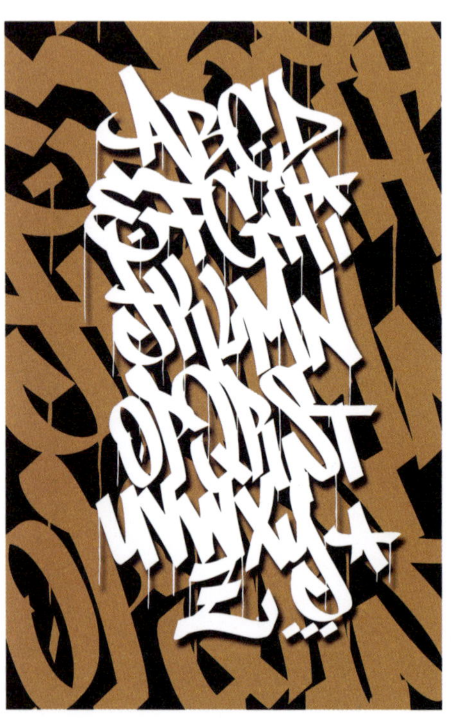
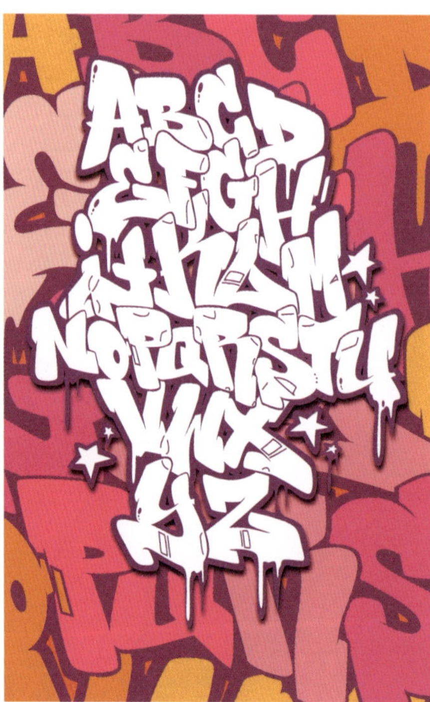
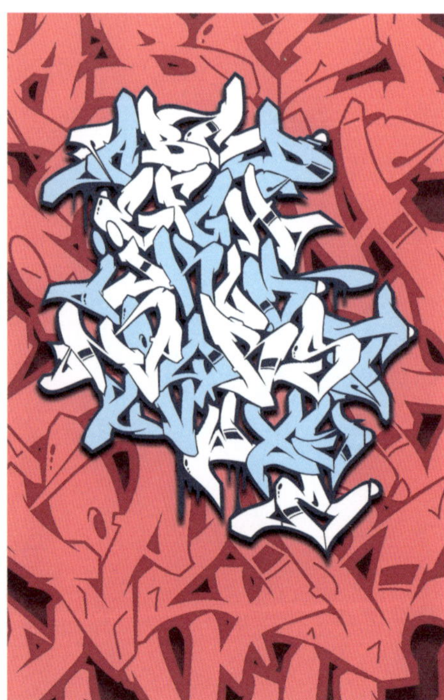

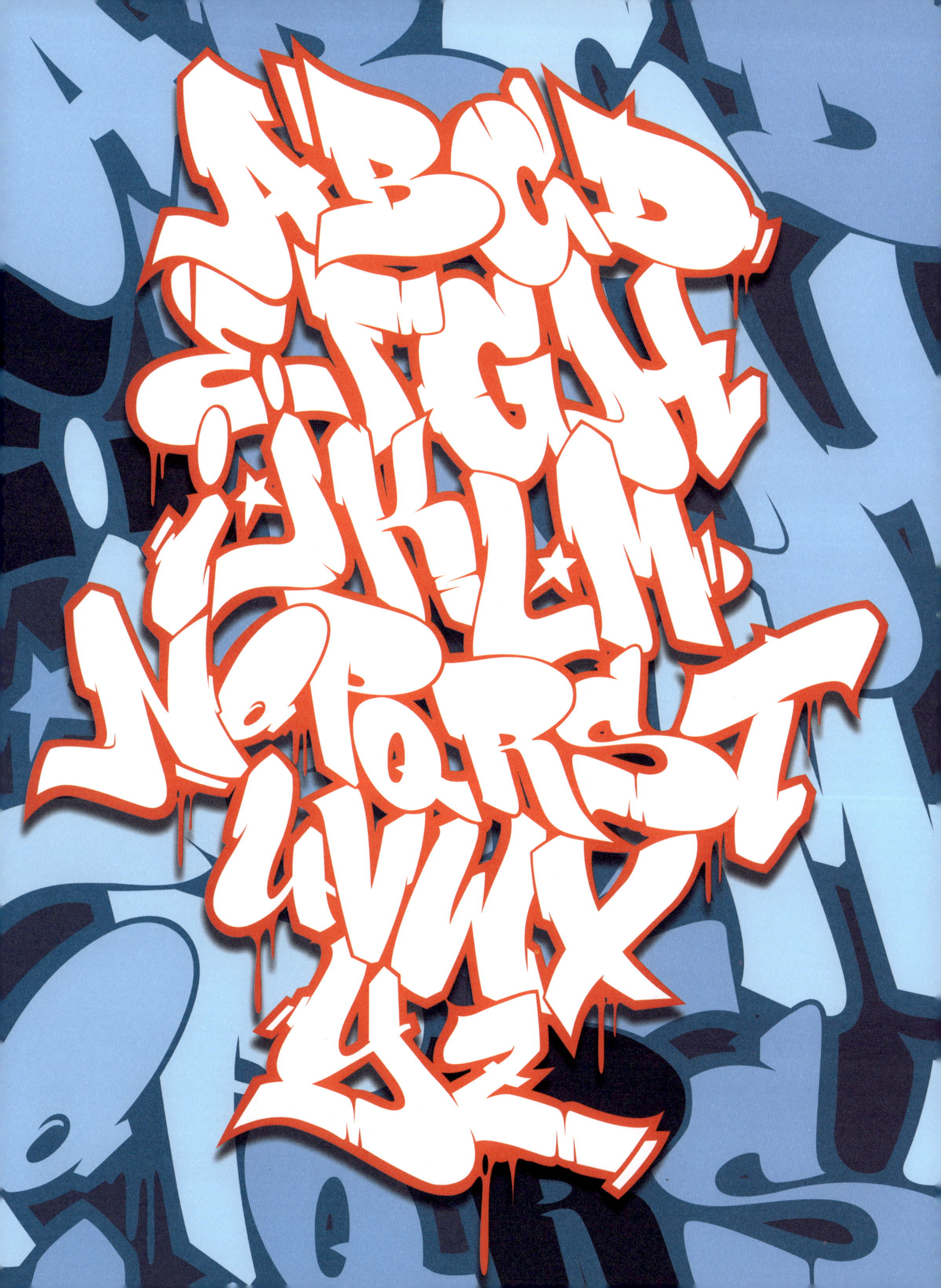

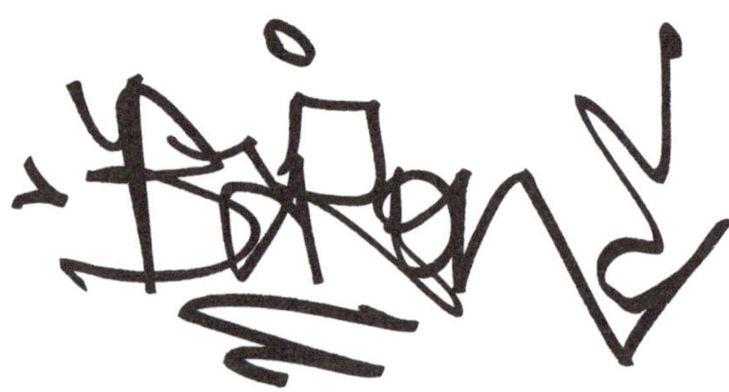

Baron

BERLIN, GERMANY

Crew member of TNC, RDA, LCF
Writer since 1995
Favourite letter: X

Baron likes colourful compositions with clear contrasts and fresh ideas that 'are a departure from the classic path of writing. To create a burner you need a strong, quick and direct line – and to be in a spontaneous mood.' Graffiti gives him opportunities to travel and the freedom to create new styles.

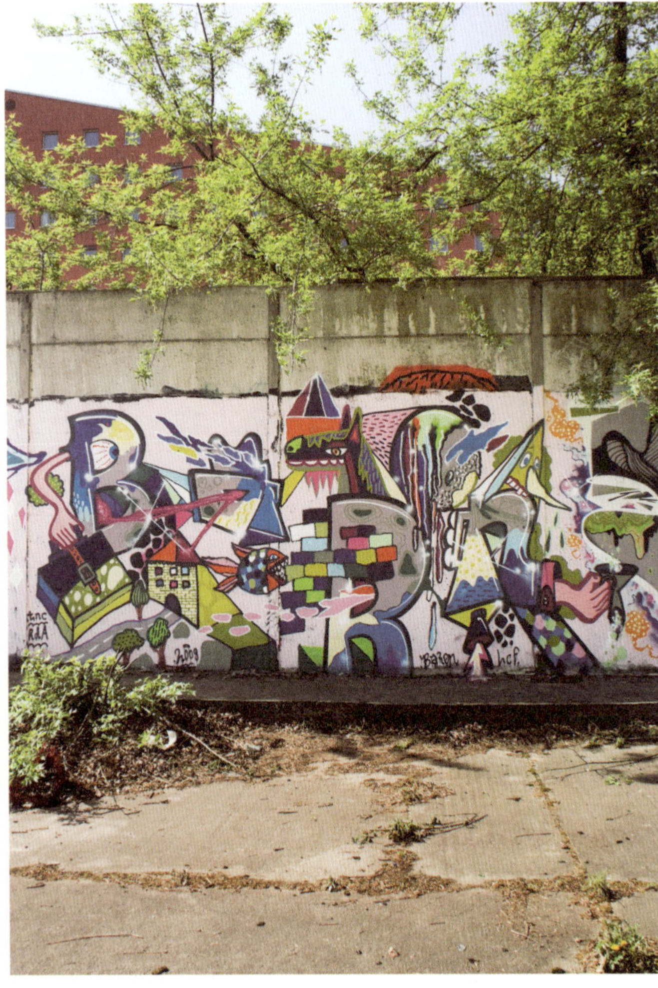

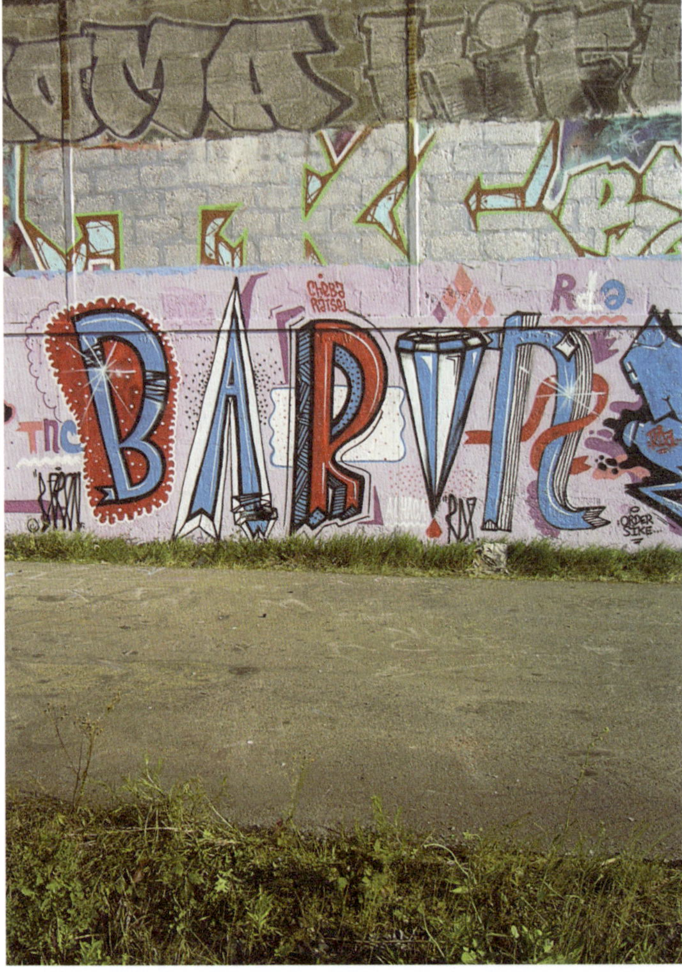

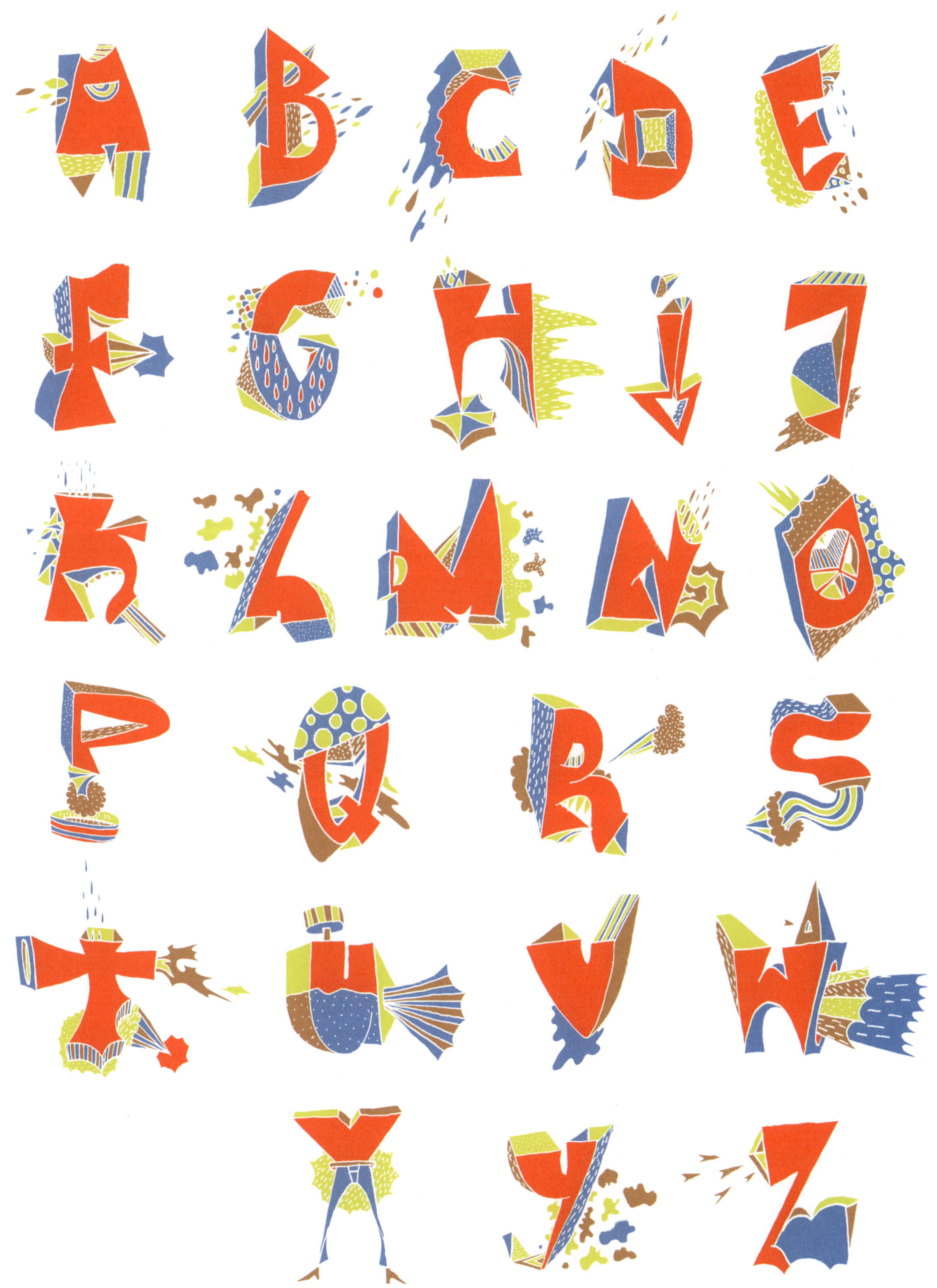

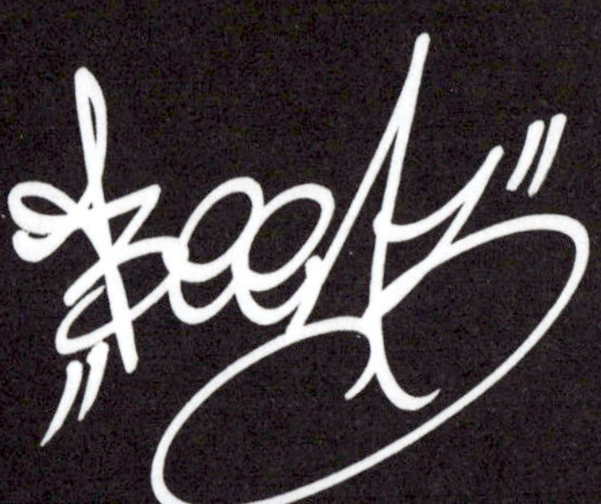

Been3

NEW YORK CITY, USA

Crew member of The Wallnuts, BYB, TDM, TUC
Writer since 1979
Favourite letter: B

Even though Been3 started tagging around 1979, he didn't paint pieces until 1985. With his crew, The Wallnuts, he created huge and detailed murals in New York City. The most important part of the creative process, he says, is letting your imagination go, as too much thinking holds you back. Spending time with the crew, having fun and not taking things too seriously are the aspects of graffiti that he most enjoys.

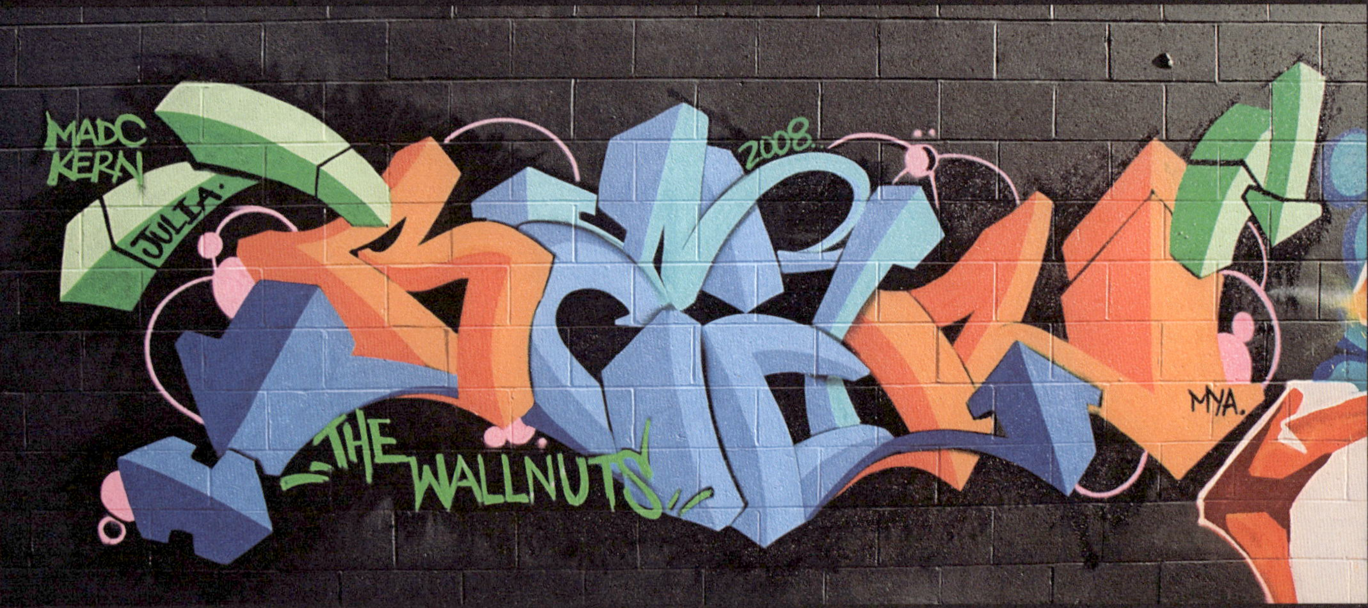

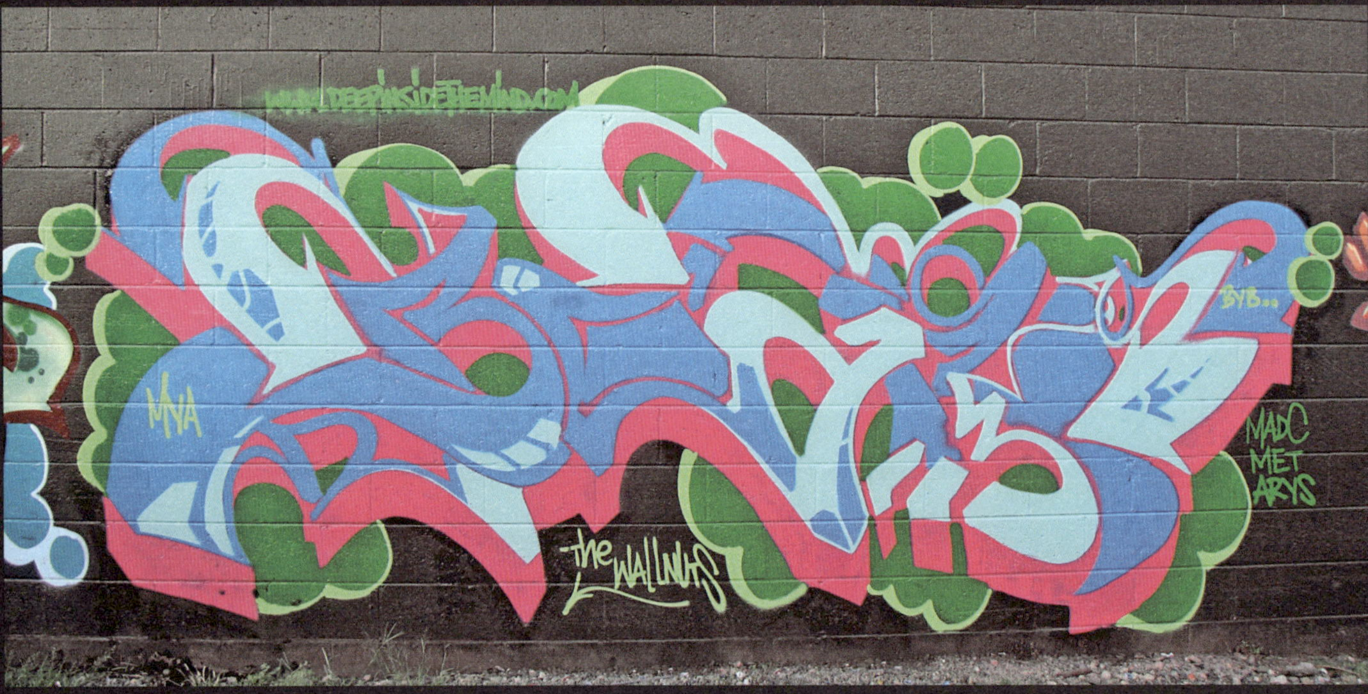

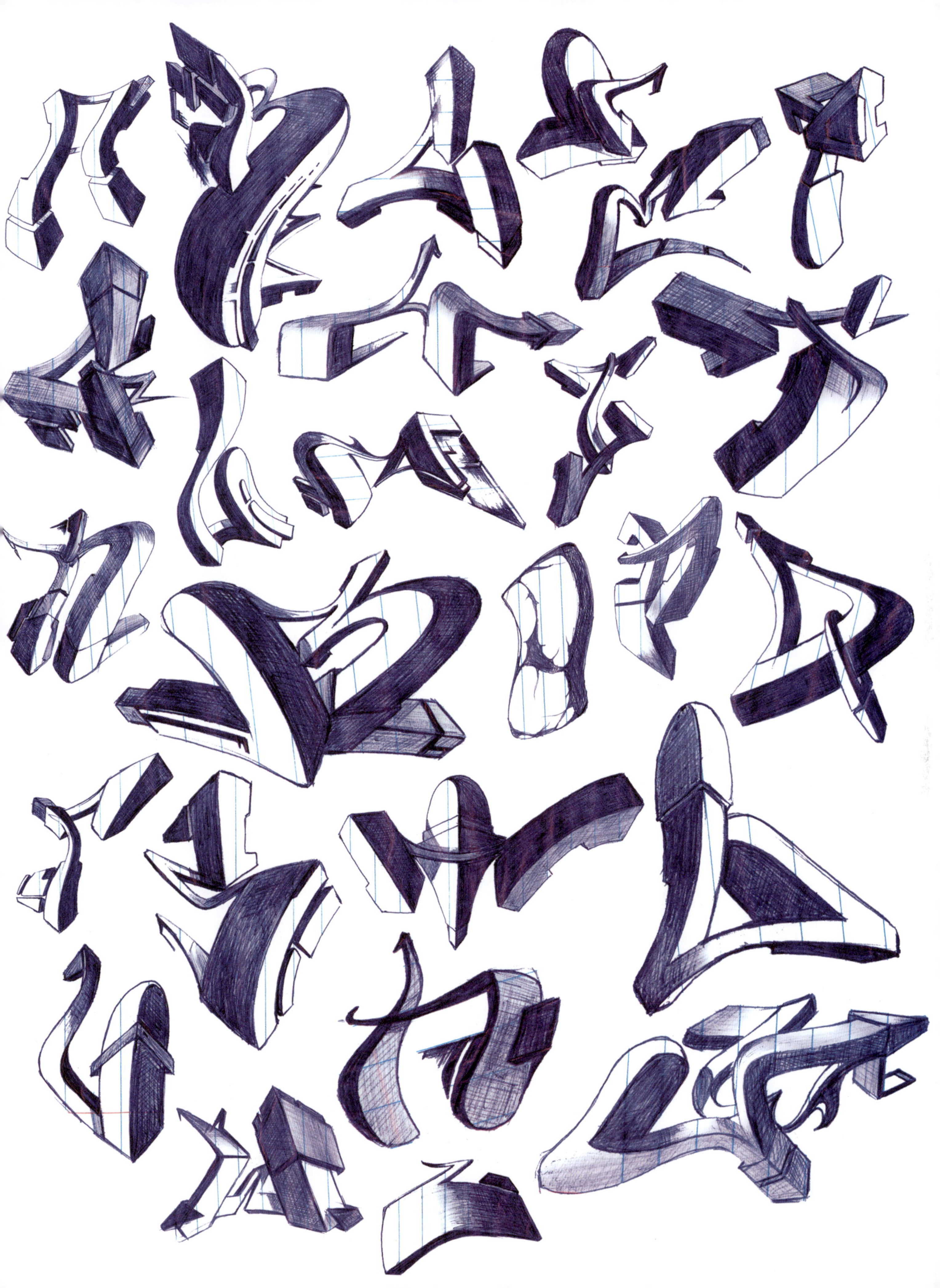

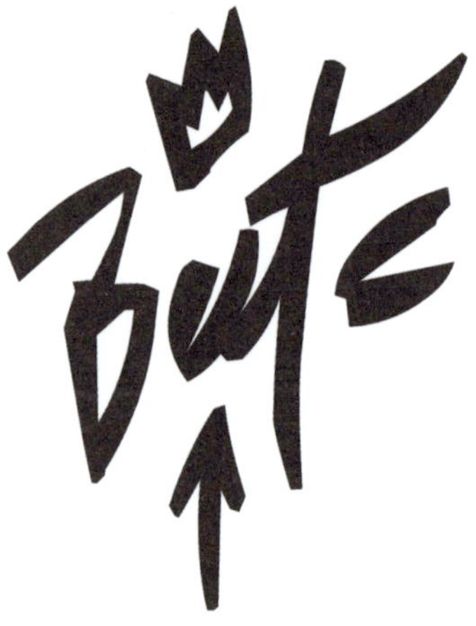

Beet74

BRAUNSCHWEIG, GERMANY
Crew member of GNB, PBS
Favourite letter: 'I like them all'
www.beet74.com

Beet74 created a series called *Living Letters*. This alphabet is number 10 of the series. Whether he is painting a wall or working on a computer, his style is innovative, vibrant and detailed. There is just one thing that he doesn't like about the scene, and that's people flogging graffiti to death by trying to lay down rules for everything.

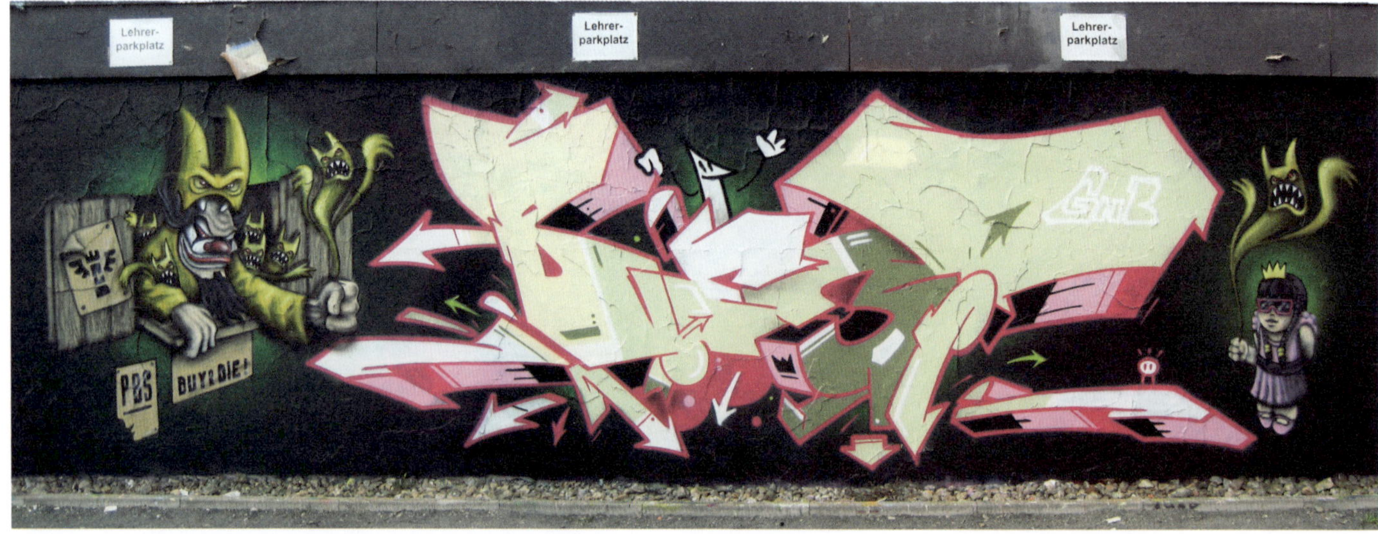

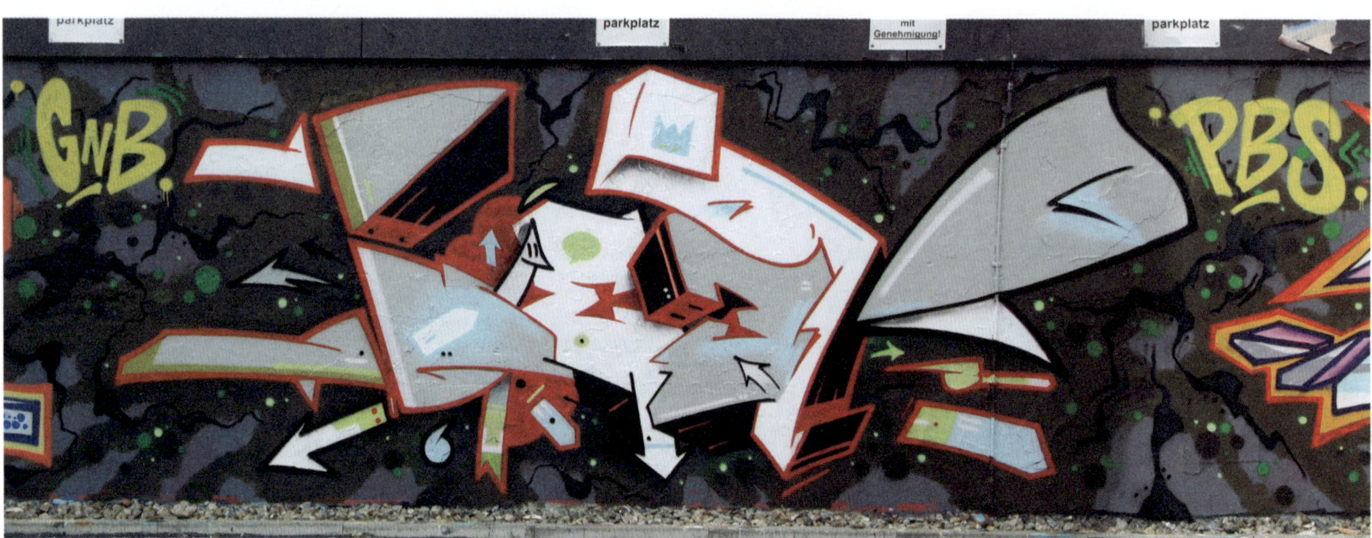

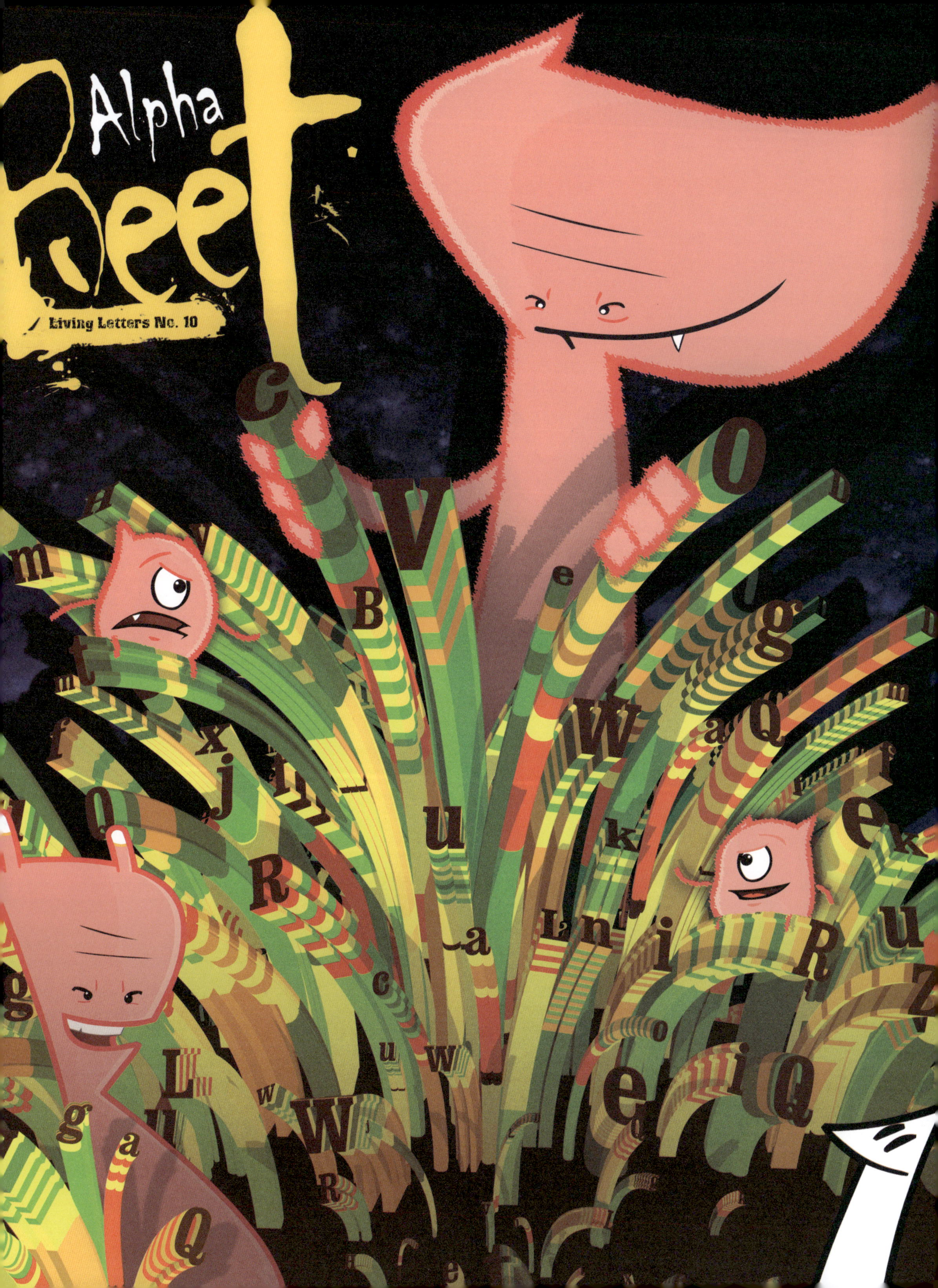
Alpha
beet.
Living Letters No. 10

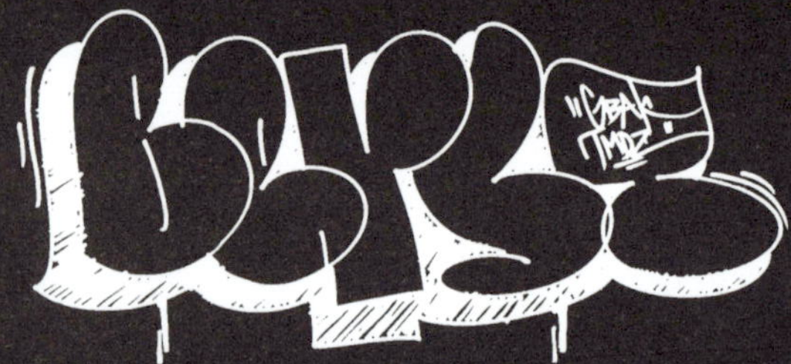

Berst

AUCKLAND, NEW ZEALAND
Crew member of GBAK, TMD
Writer since 2002
Favourite letter: B
www.tmdcrew.com

Berst drew his alphabet in black ink on paper. On walls, however, he prefers to create colourful wildstyles, and tries to put a lot of energy and movement into his pieces. The act of painting a wall and seeing his work develop are what he likes best about writing.

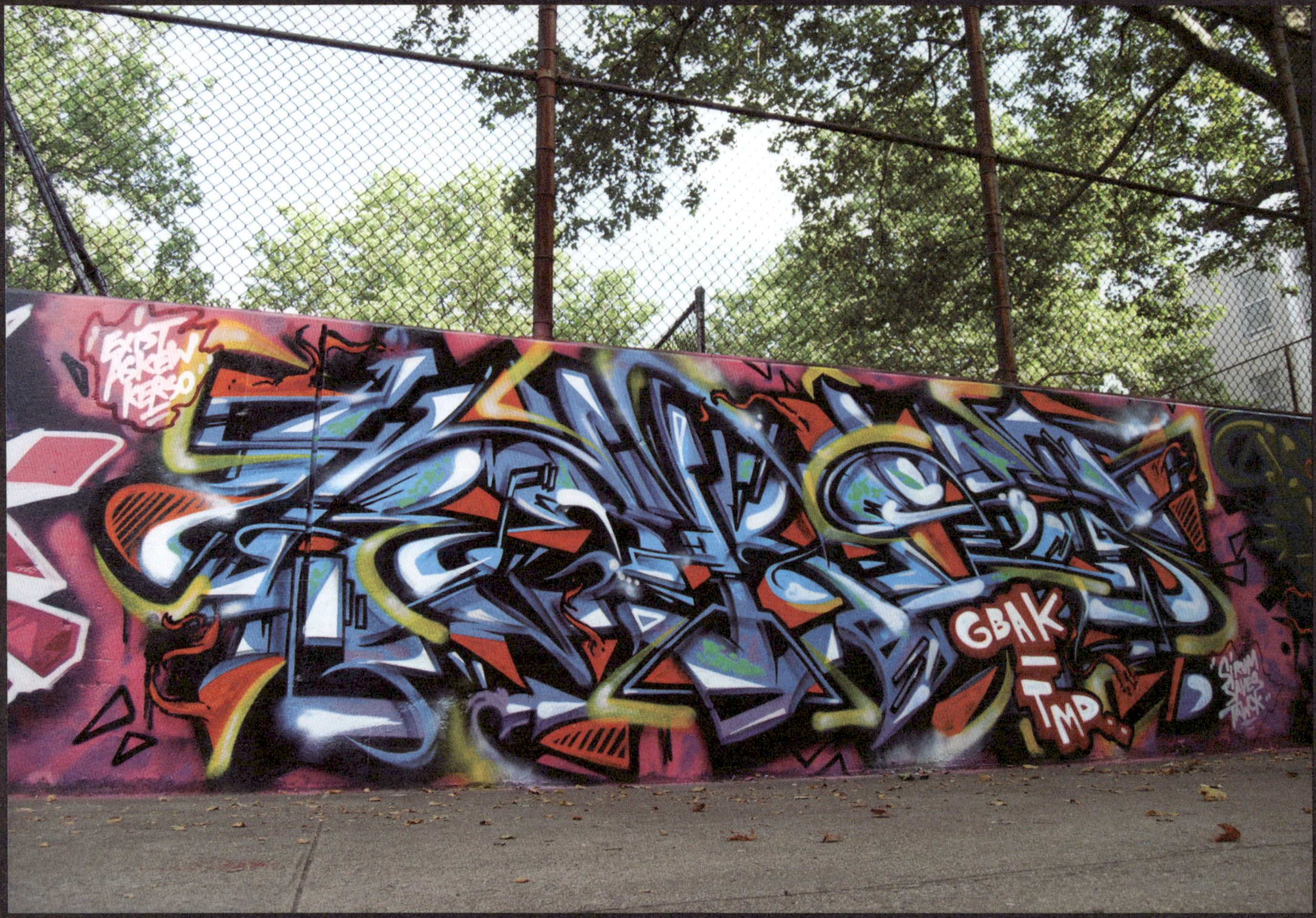

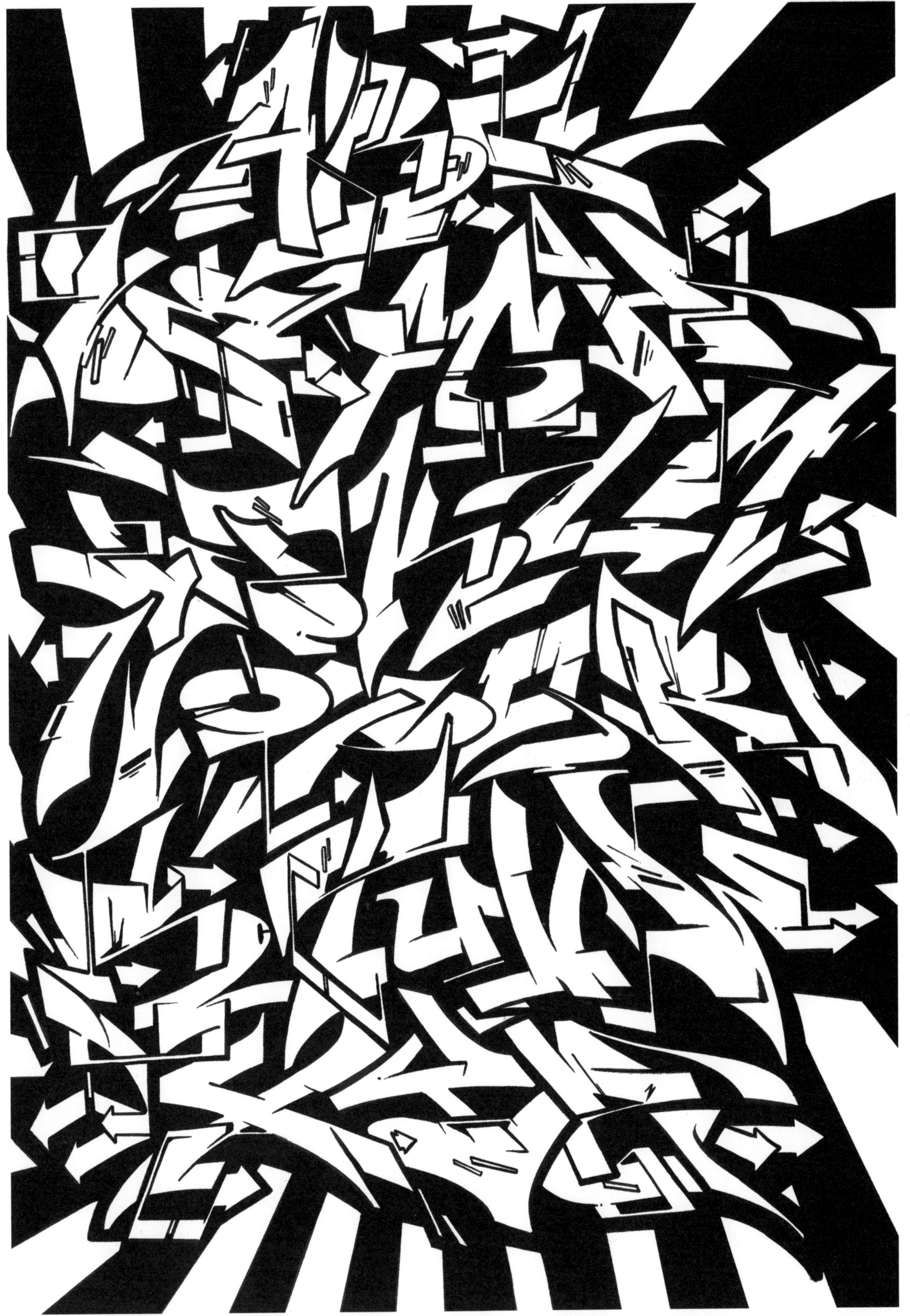

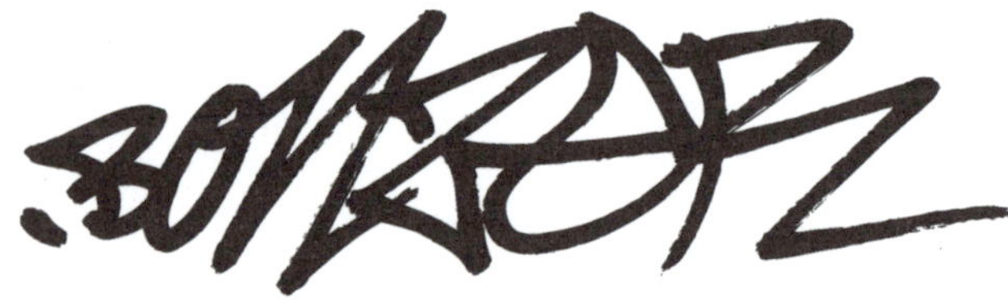

Bonzer
STRASBOURG, FRANCE
Crew member of Macia
Writer since 1987
Favourite letters: B, M
www.macia-crew.com

Bonzer sees his alphabet as the result of his years of experience as a writer. For him, letters must always remain legible. 'On a wall the colours you use have to fit the piece and, wherever possible, a nice B-Boy character should make the wall complete,' he adds.

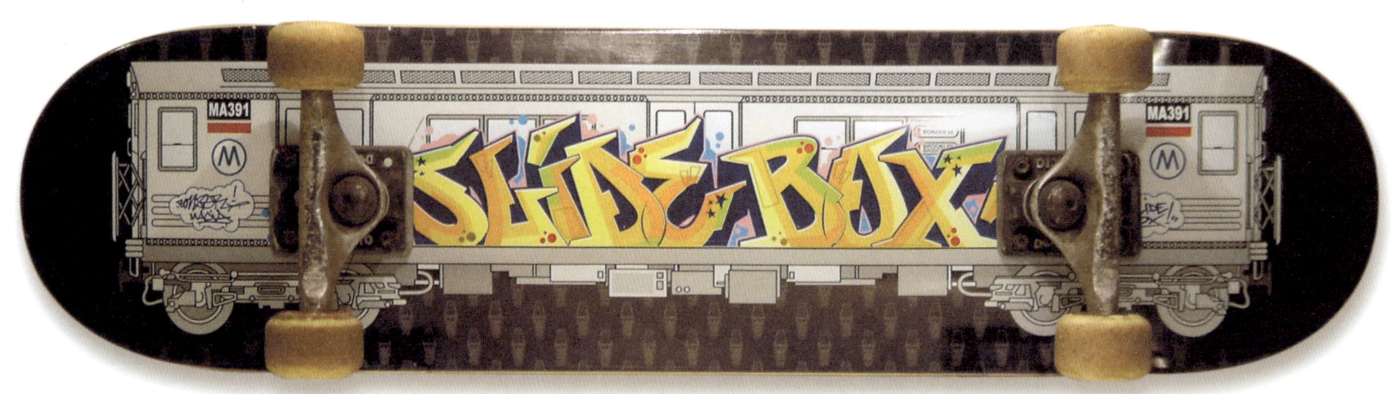

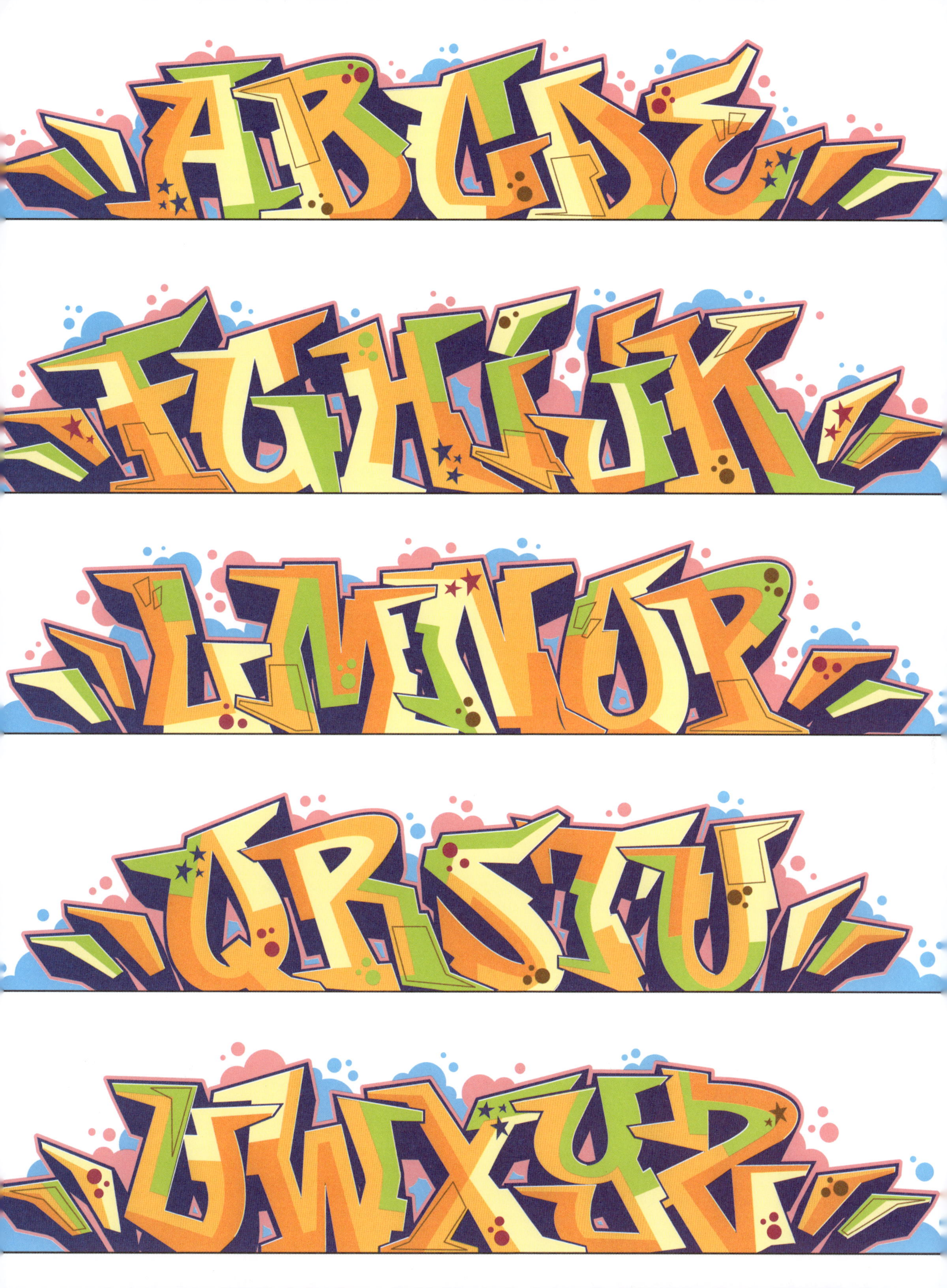

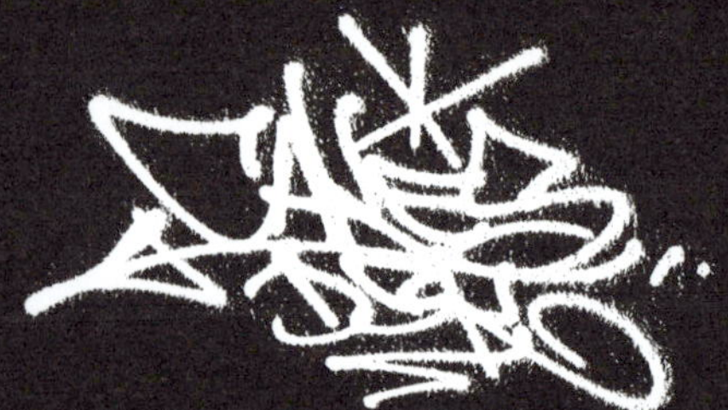

Cakes

PRAGUE, CZECH REPUBLIC
Crew member of DSK
Writer since 1993
Favourite letter: S
www.onepoint.cz

Cakes is one of the foremost representatives of the Czech graffiti scene. For a piece to be good it takes the right combination of style, technique, colours and mood, he says. In terms of what he likes best about graffiti, he adds: 'It is not possible to do the same piece twice, even if you use the same letters and colours.'

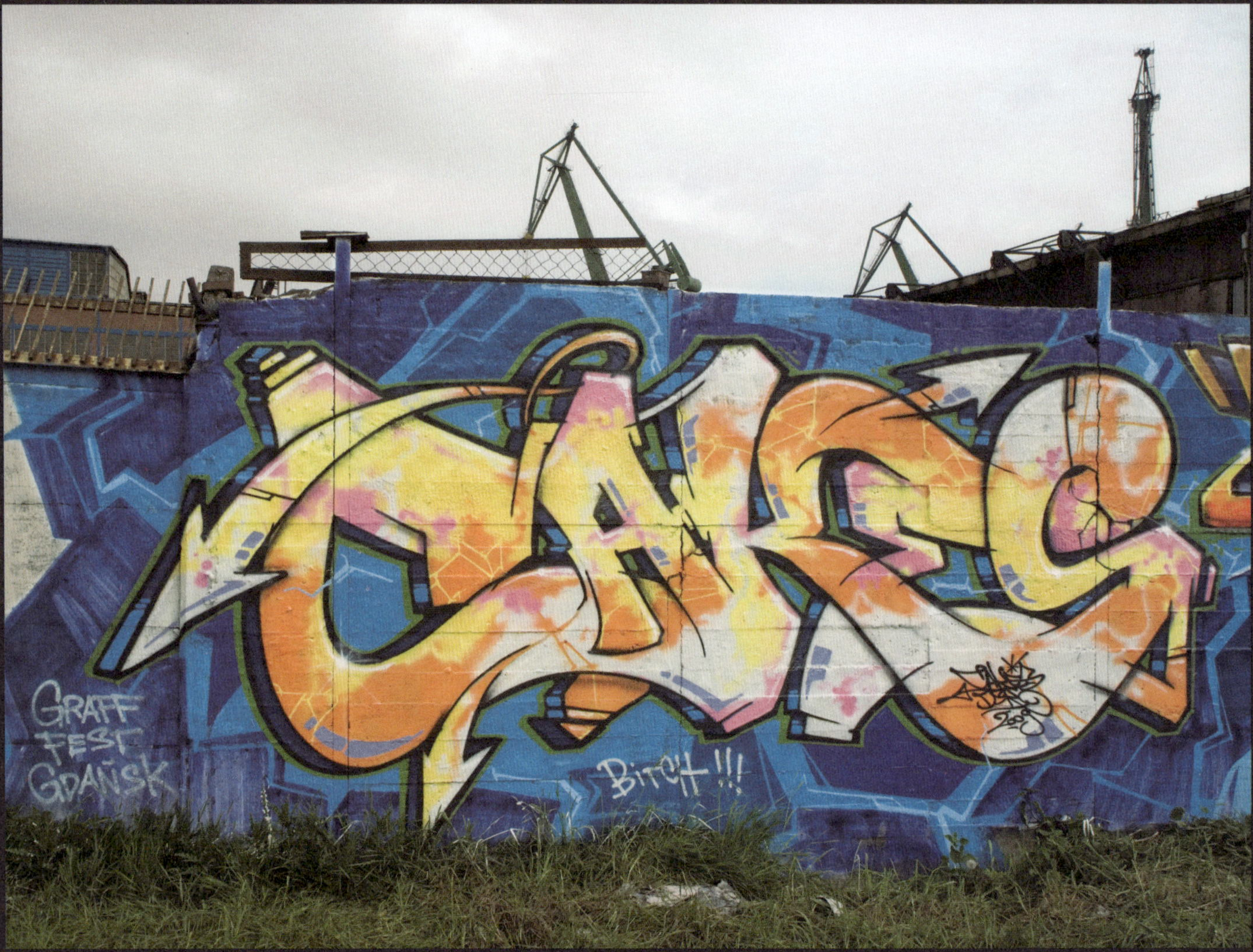

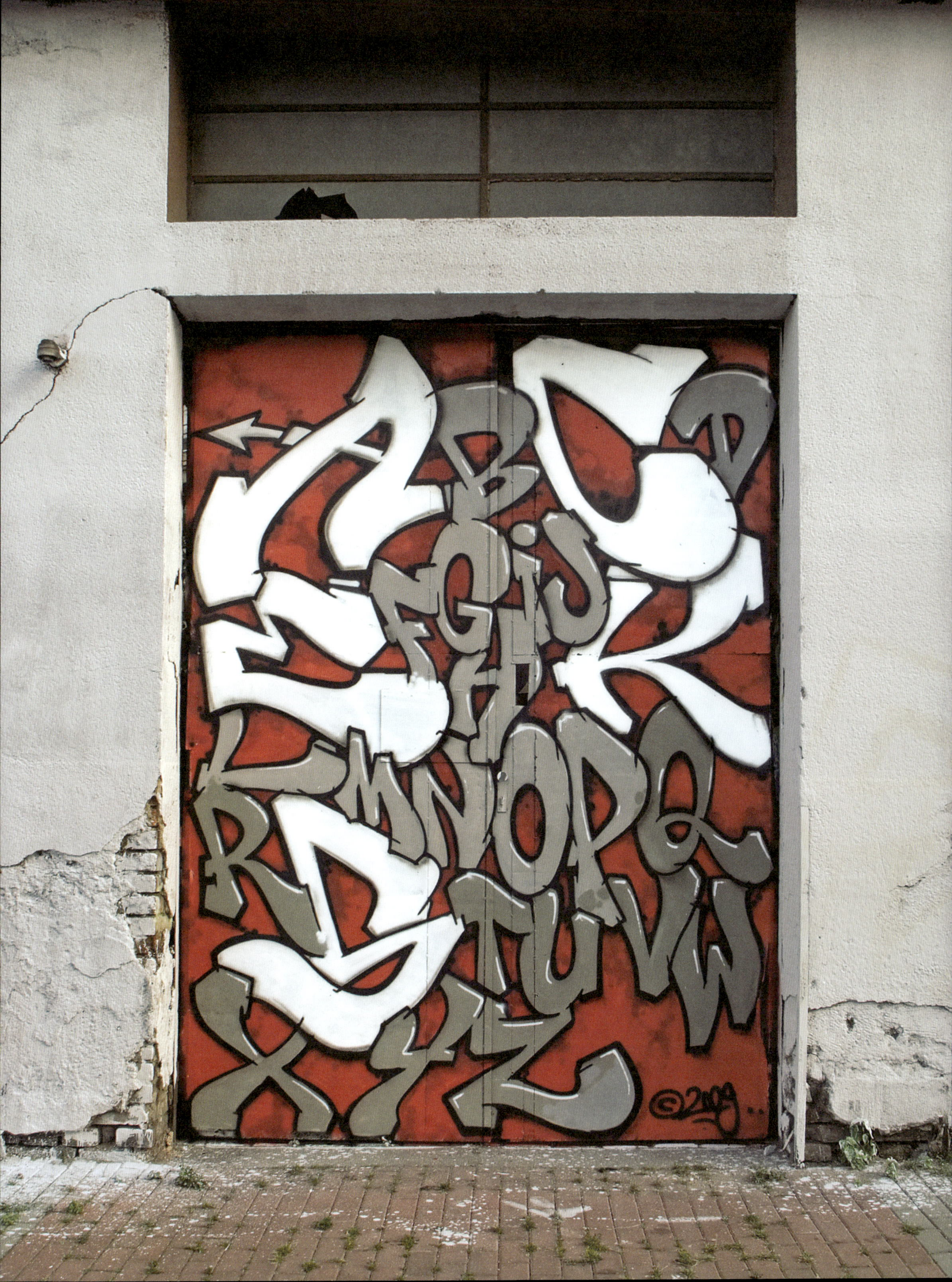

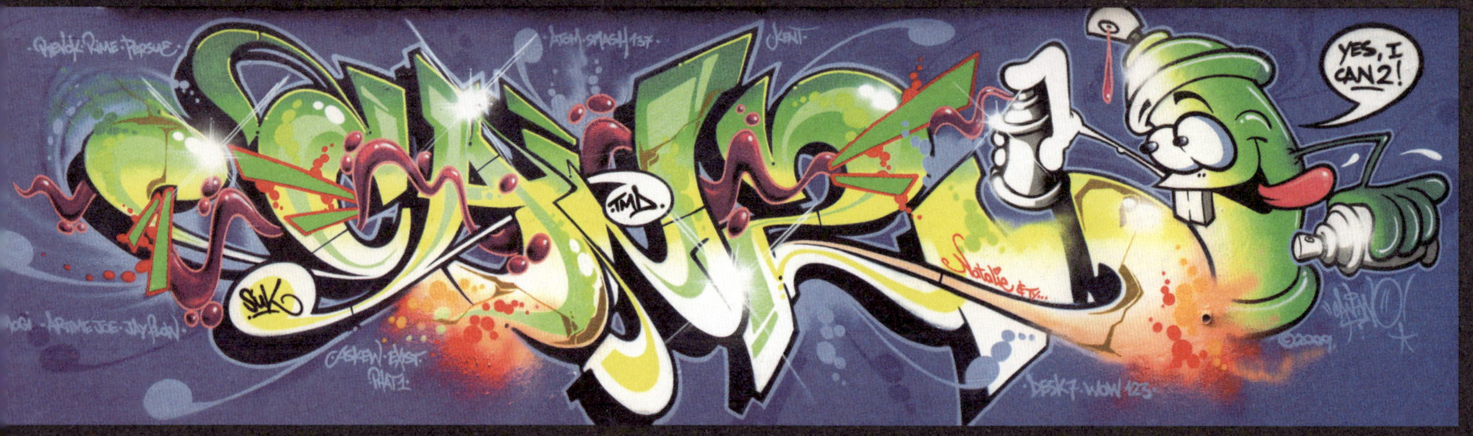

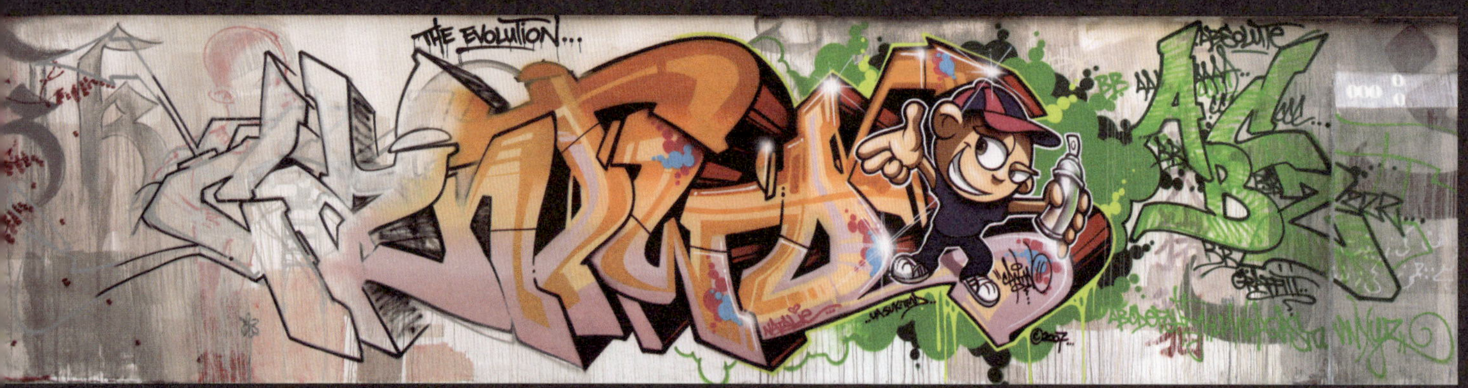

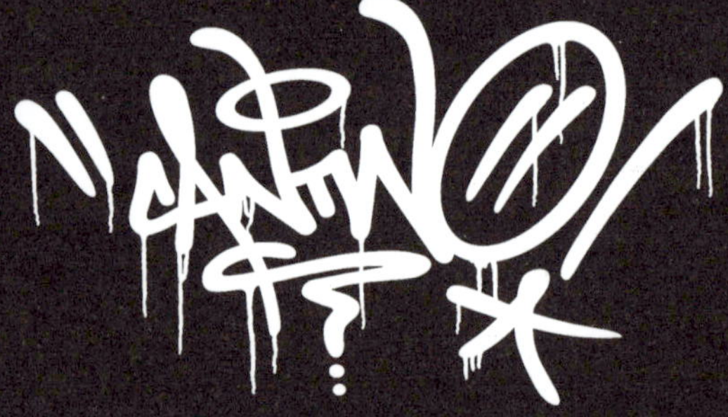

Can Two
MAINZ, GERMANY

Crew member of SUK and TMD
Writer since 1983
Favourite letter: E
www.cantwo.com

Can Two is one of the few writers to have mastered both letters and characters to perfection. For over three decades, he has travelled the globe and left his name in more than thirty countries. During this period, he developed his signature style and use of colours, which he describes as 'def skills, fresh styles, dope colours, mad backgrounds and funky characters'. In his opinion, a perfect piece must have energy and legibility. 'Camouflaged letters with too many elements and excessive use of colour contradict the basic idea of writing – getting up,' he says.

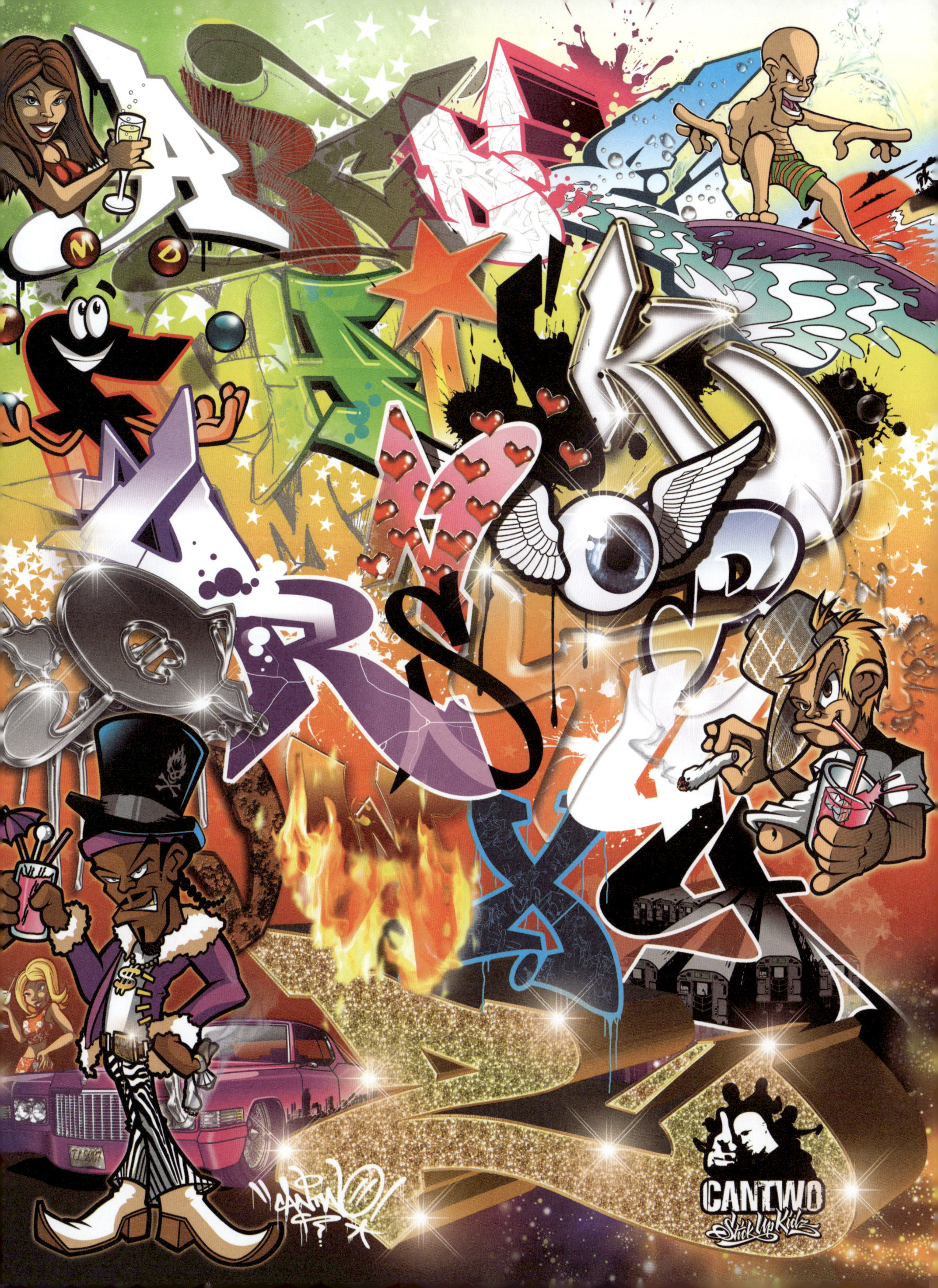
CANTWO
Stick Up Kidz

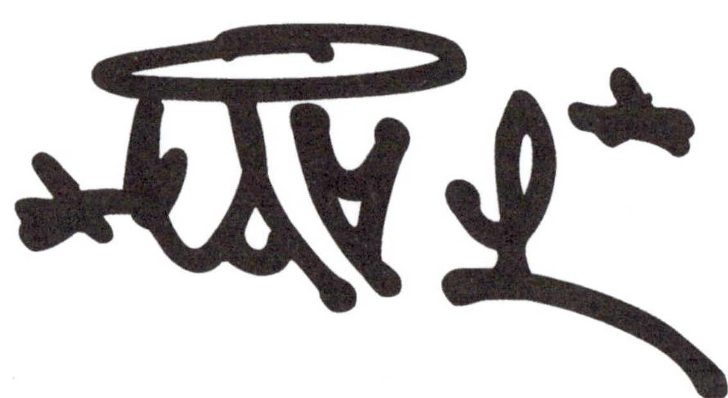

Cap One

NEW YORK CITY, USA
Writer since the 1970s

The notorious Cap One came to worldwide fame through the documentary *Style Wars* in the early 1980s. Everyone in the graffiti scene is familiar with his throw-up (below). While he is known for his aggressive tactics in getting up, he now focuses on the art. His alphabet epitomizes the letters he has used for decades. 'The great span of graffiti is the best,' he says. 'We rock the world!'

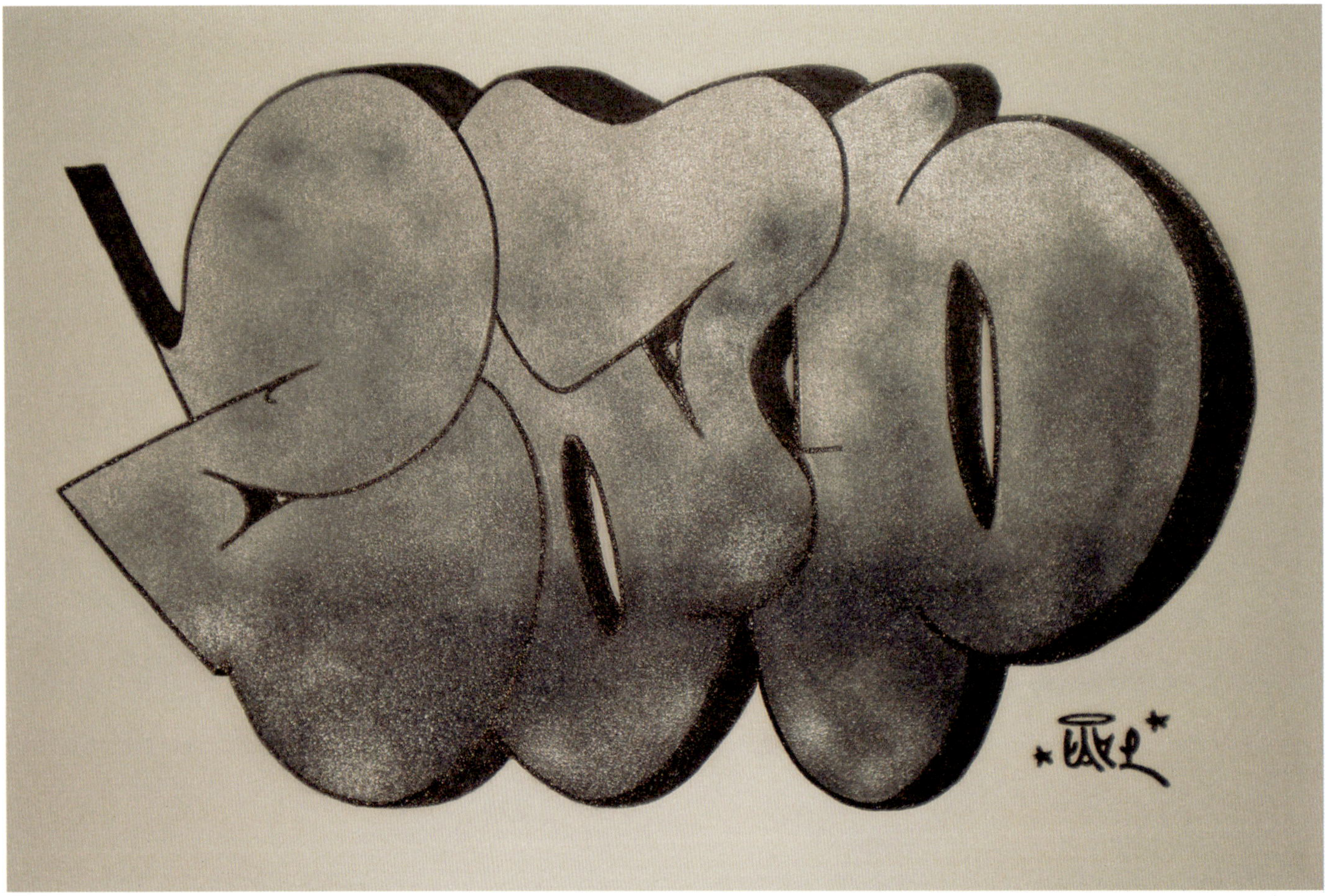

A B C D E

F G H I J

K L M N O

P Q R S

T U V W

X Y Z

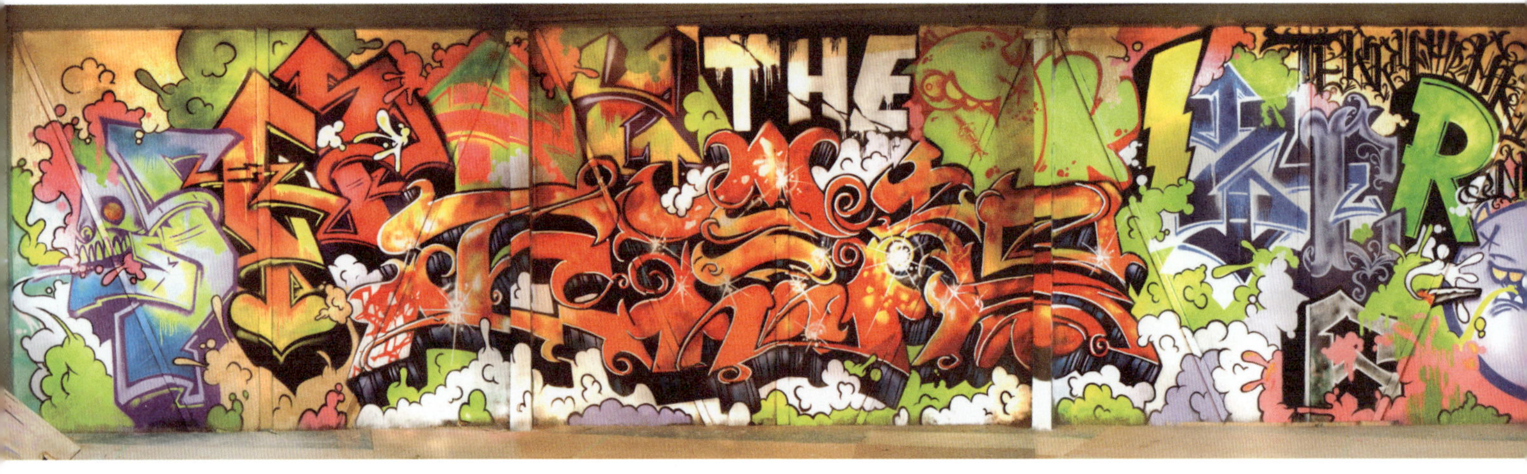

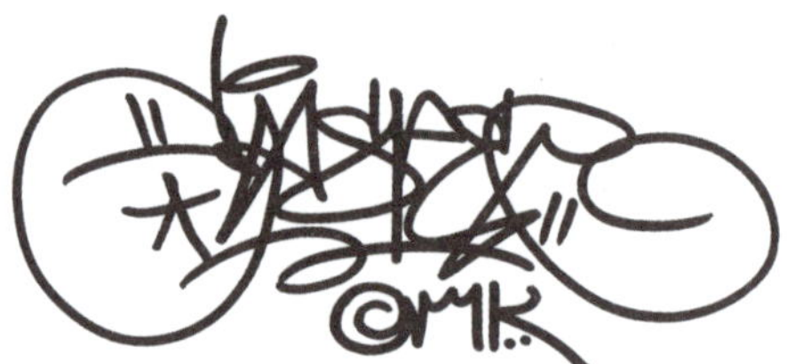

Casper

OSAKA, JAPAN
Crew member of CMK, KTC, EDC,
WOM, AD, DOA, SOC, 420
Favourite letters: C, A, S, P, E, R

Casper's work is greatly influenced by calligraphy. All you need
to create a good piece is a wall and some spray paint, he says.
He loves the freedom of graffiti and its lack of constraints.

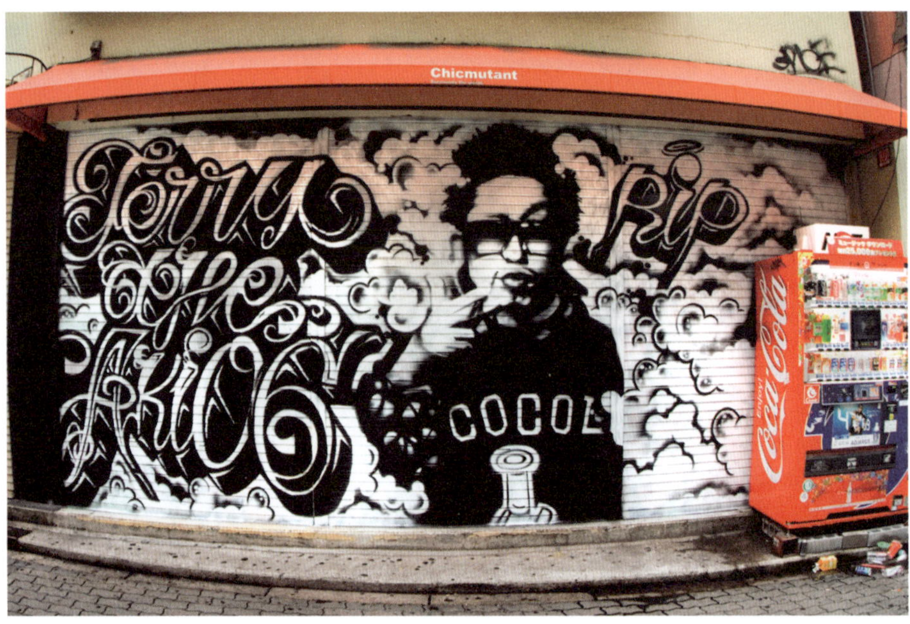

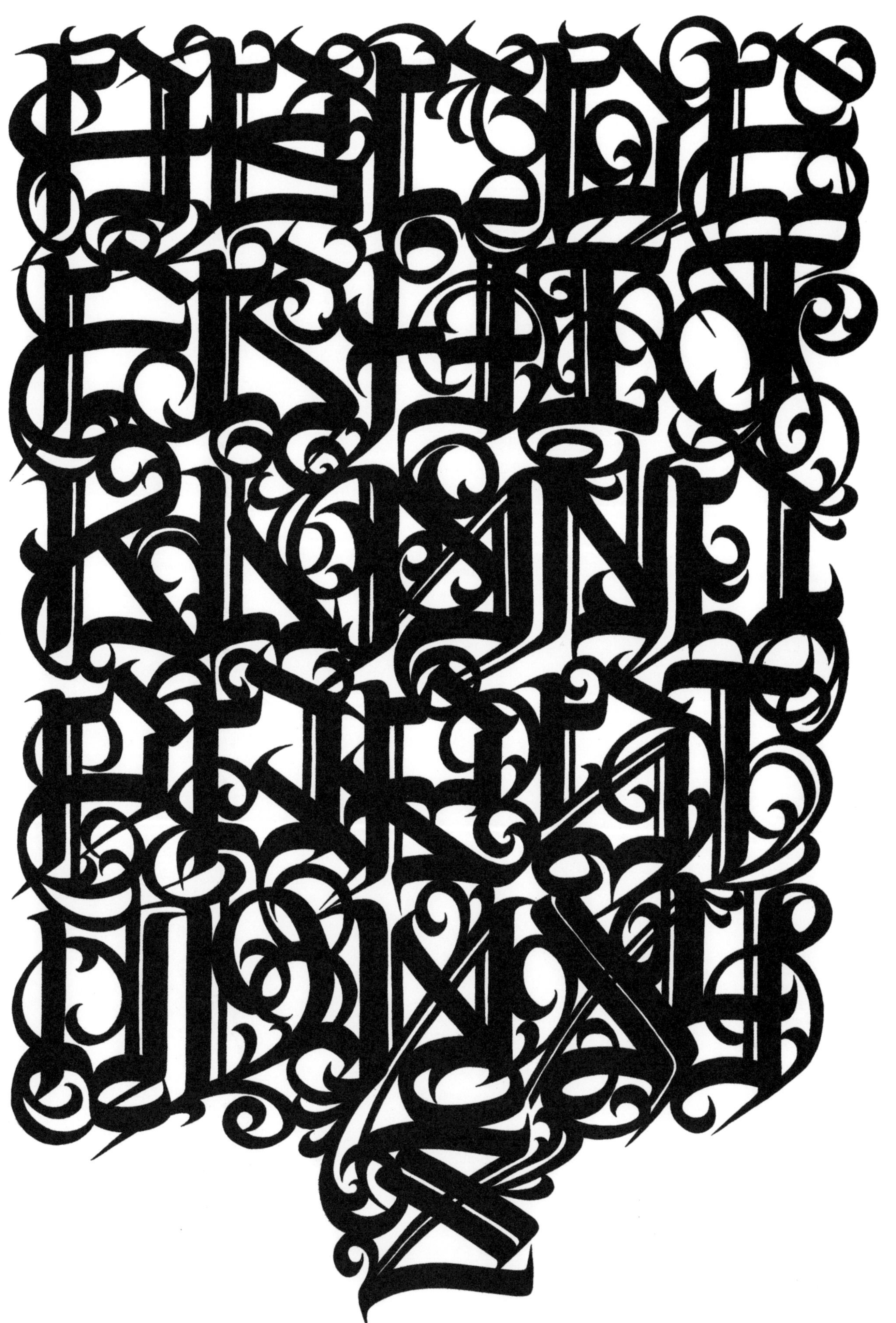

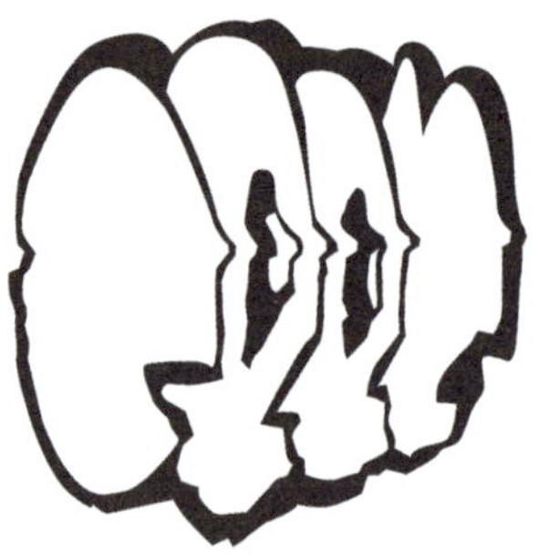

Ceet

HONG KONG, CHINA
Crew member of El Camion, BAD, KD, TNB, CPS
Writer since 1988
Favourite letter: M
www.megaceet.com

Ceet comes from France but has called China home for many years. He still likes to travel and to meet people from around the world. His alphabet consists of Pac-Man-like aluminium balls with cutouts. By adjusting the position of each of the 25cm-diameter balls, he used the cutouts to create letter shapes.

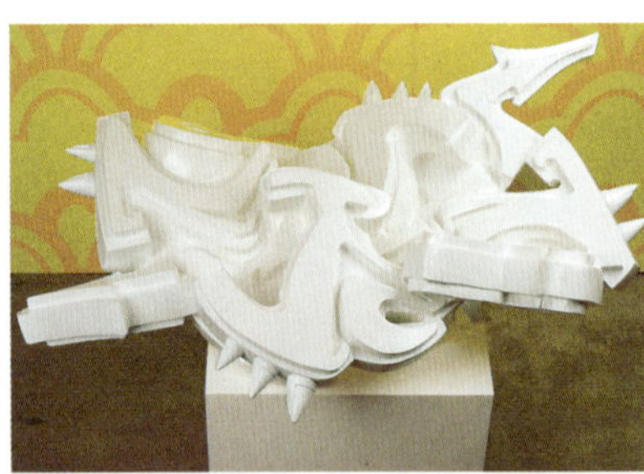

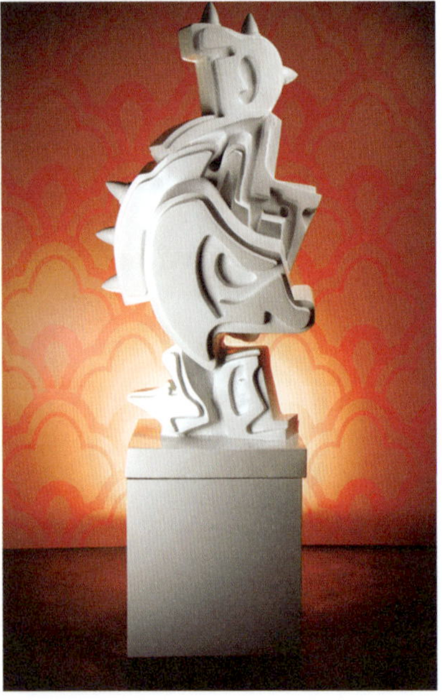

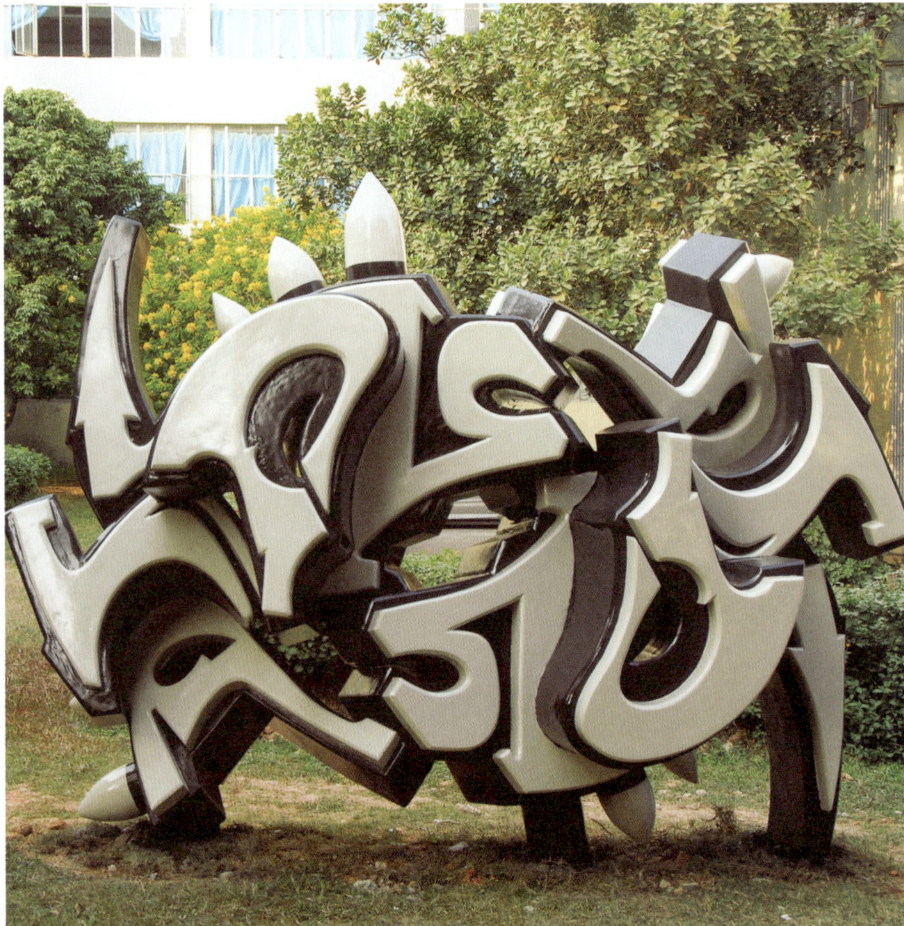

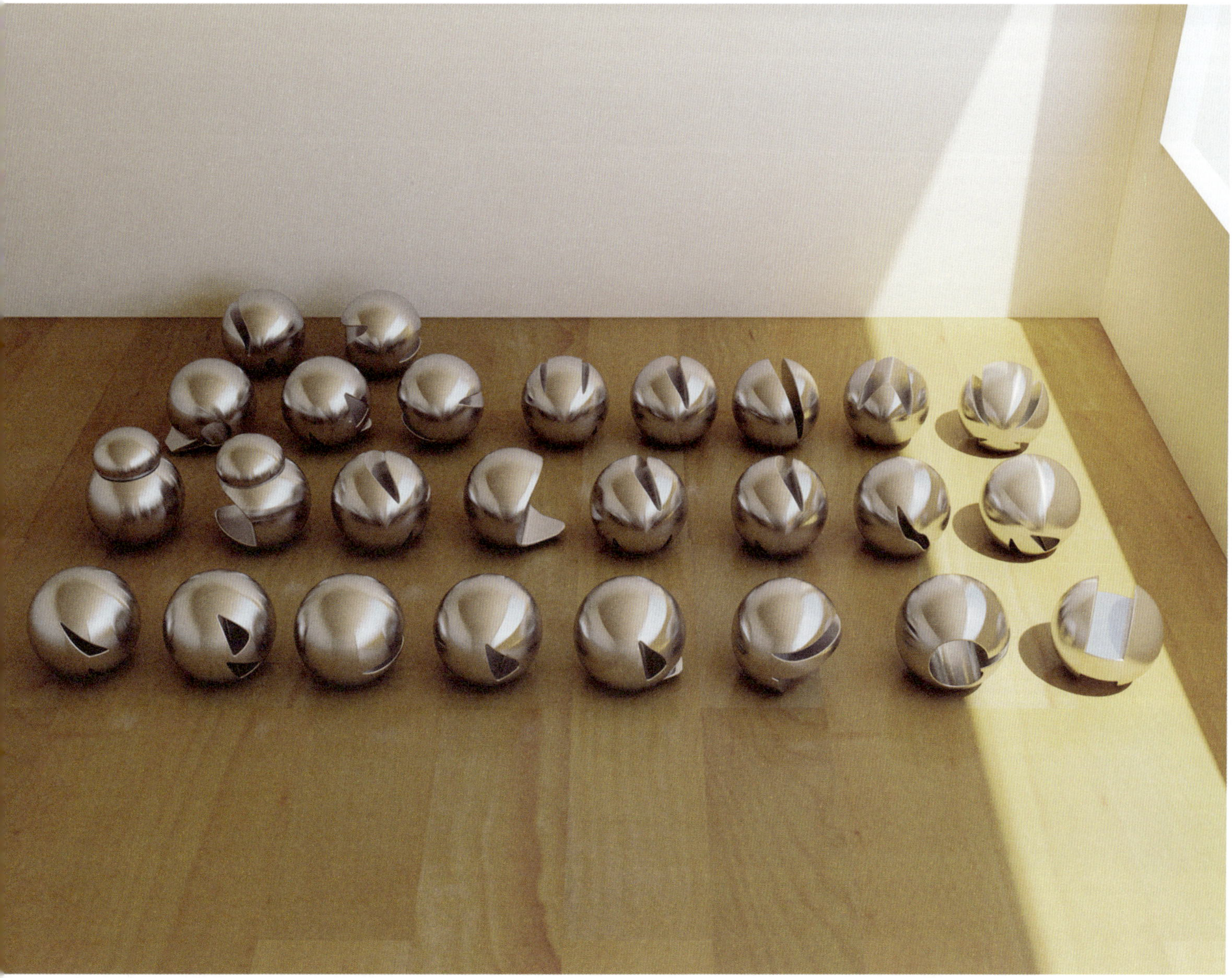

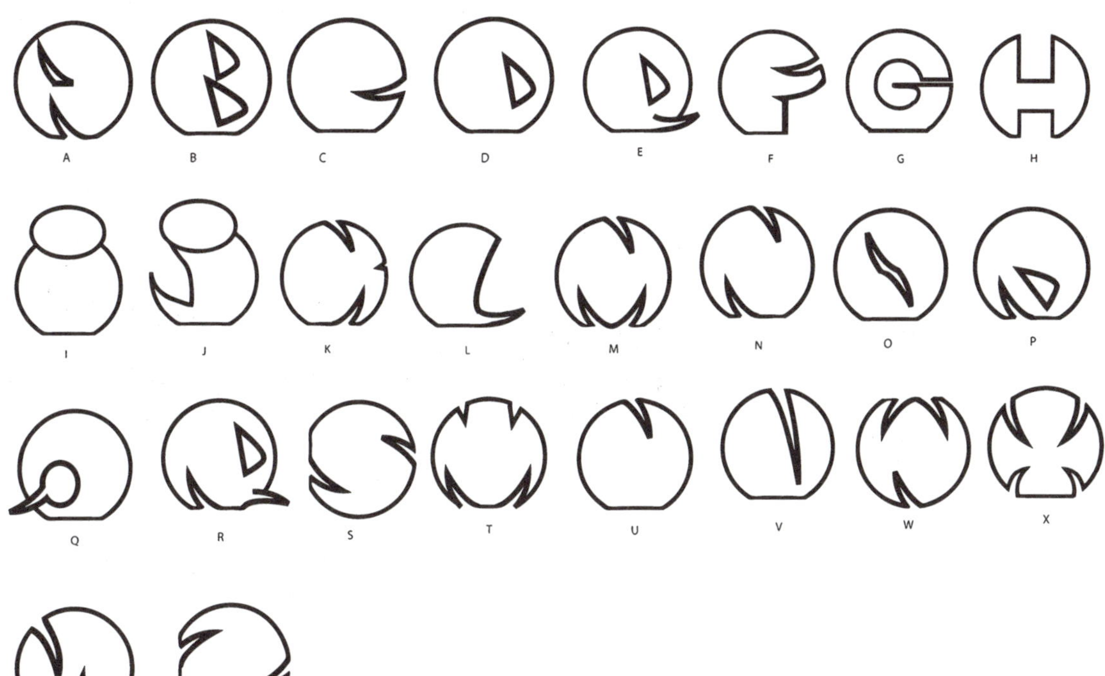

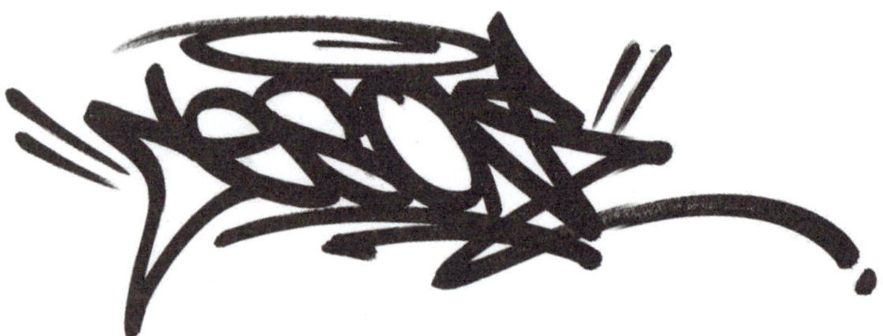

Ces One

NEW YORK CITY, USA
Crew member of TMT, TNB, FC, FBA
Writer since 1983
Favourite letter: 'All of them'

Ces One epitomizes the classic New York graffiti style. Having mastered wildstyle and other forms of graffiti, he doesn't limit himself to walls but applies himself to everything from canvases to tattoos. His alphabet shows the foundation and structure of his work. For him, freedom is the most important aspect of graffiti.

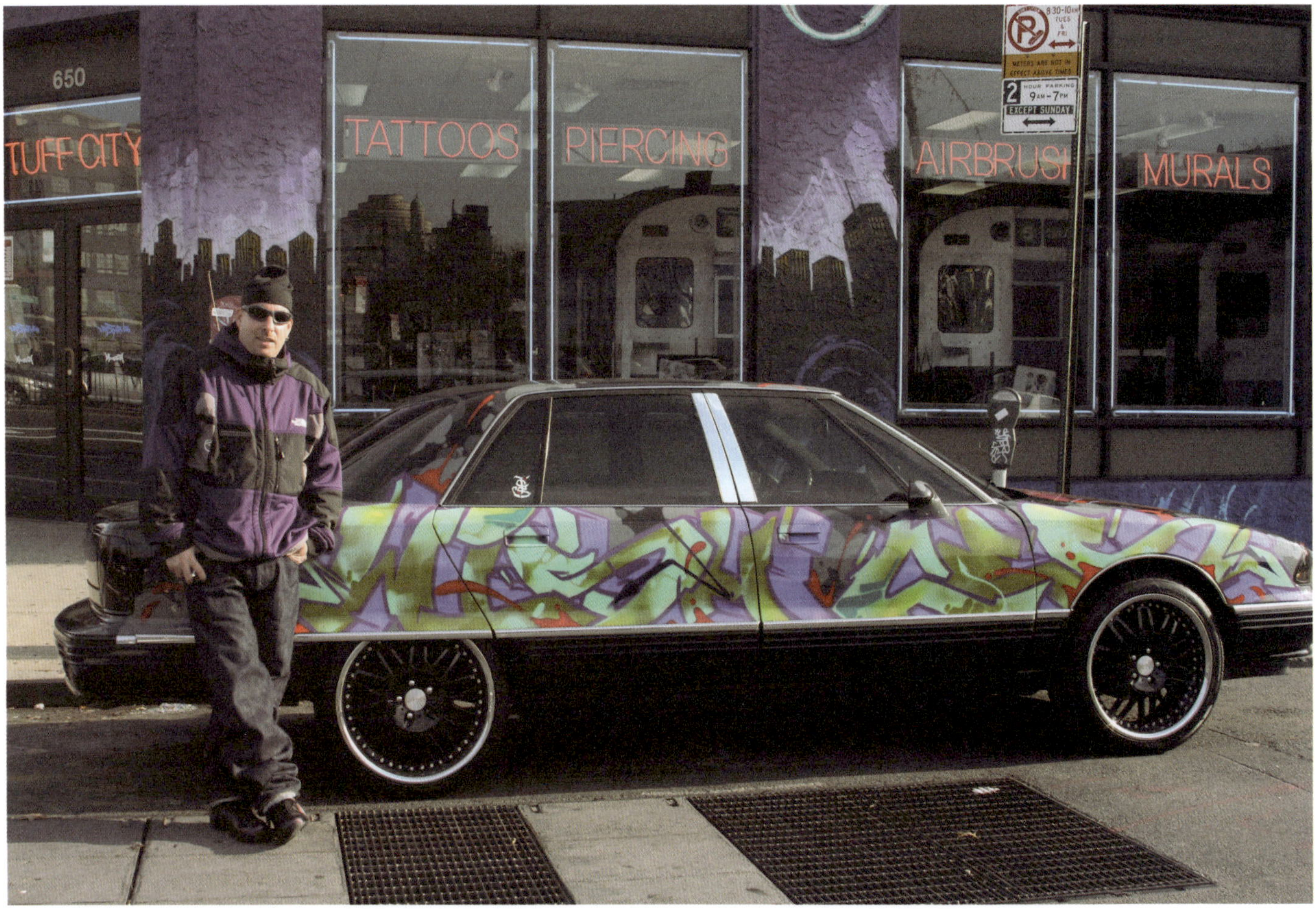

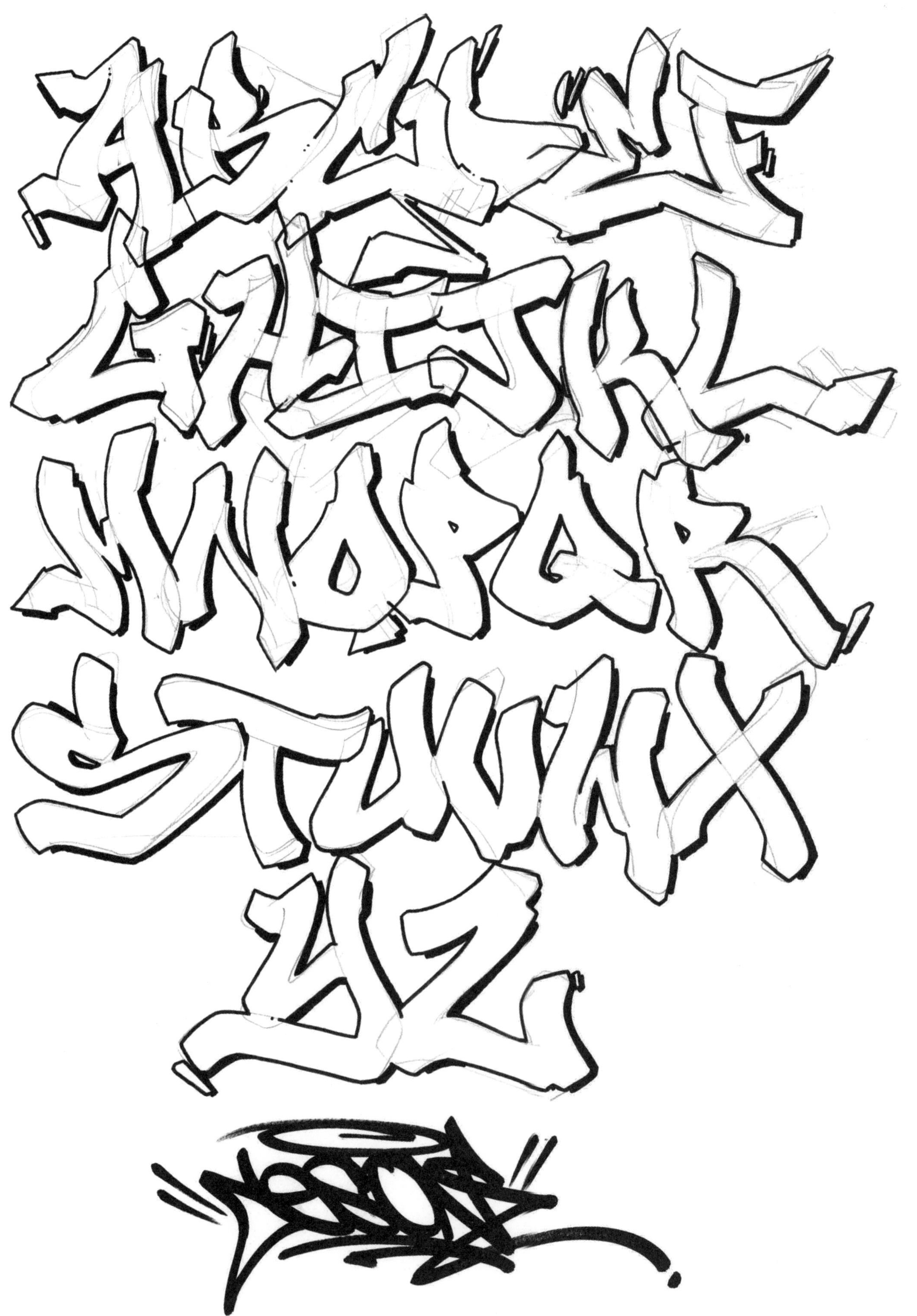

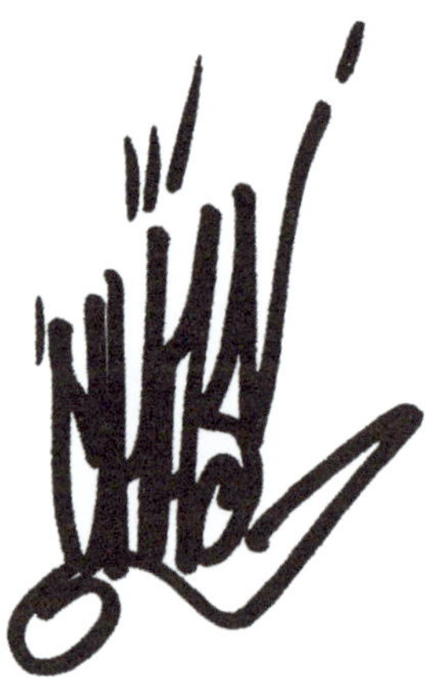

Chas

VENLO, NETHERLANDS
Crew member of LoveLetters
Writer since 1989
Favourite letters: S, A
https://loveletterscollective.tumblr.com

Like the other members of the LoveLetters crew, Chas pays a lot
of attention to detail, flow and balance in his pieces. He came up
with a lot of different ideas for his alphabet, but in the end he
decided that graffiti should be painted on a wall – in this case,
the rooftop of his office. Progress in graffiti is what he values
most, and he hopes to create the perfect style and piece one day.

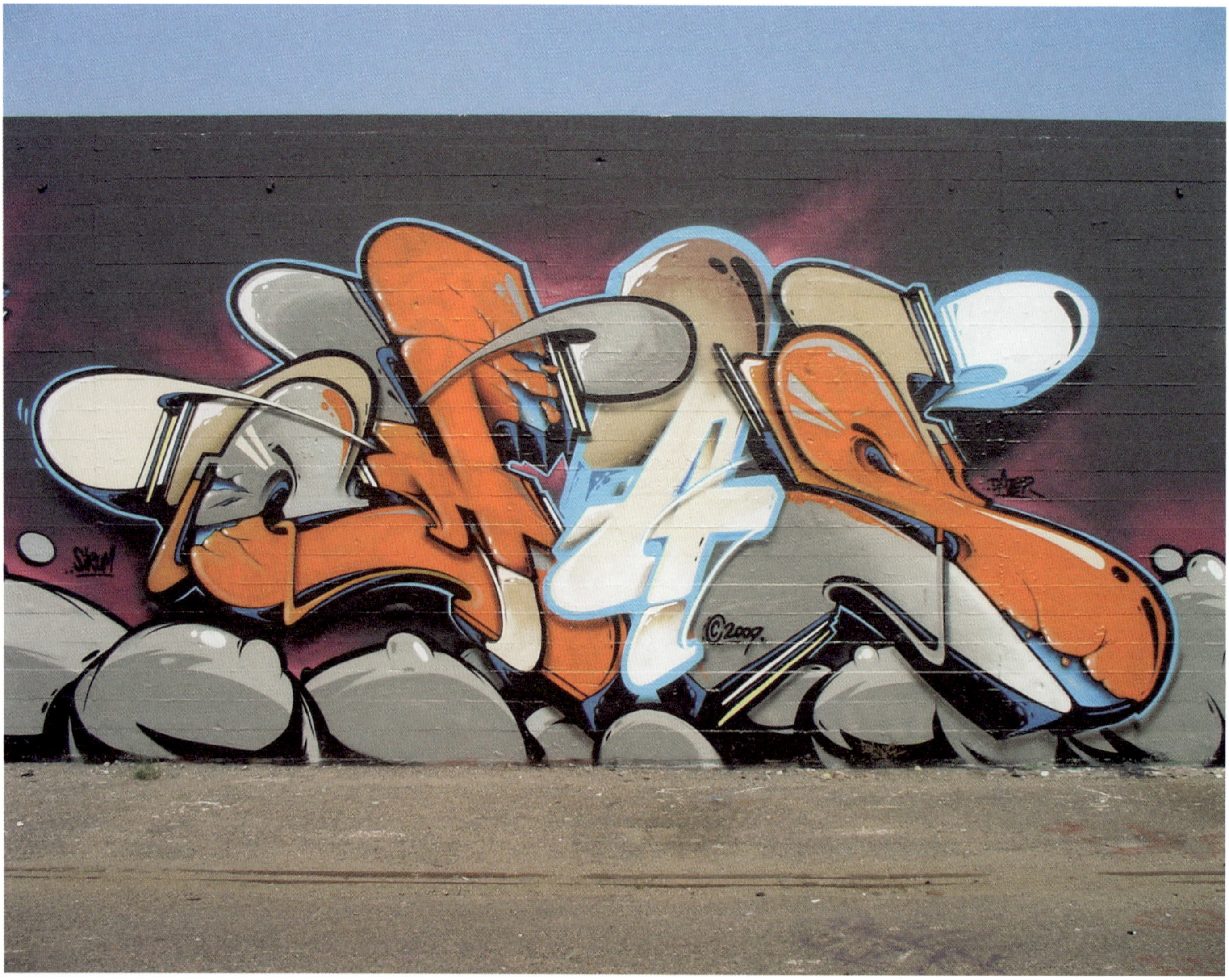

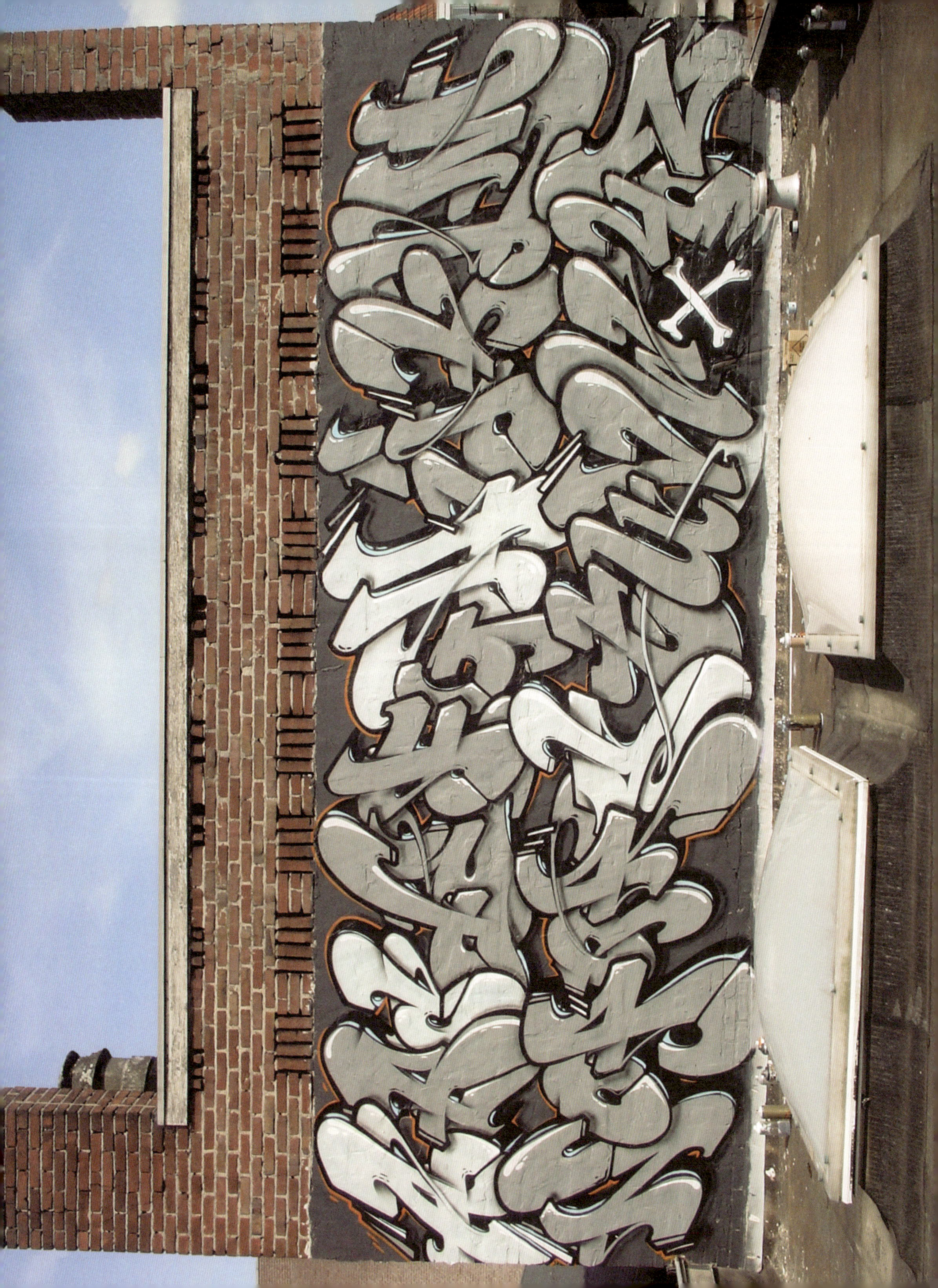

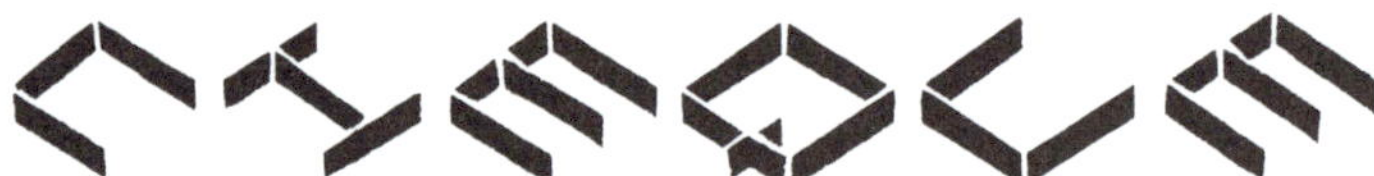

Cheque
INOWROCLAW, POLAND

Crew member of Typoets
Writer since 2000
Favourite letter: A

Cheque's work is influenced by typography, and is experimental and versatile. He came up with the idea for his alphabet after chancing upon an instruction manual for assembling a shelf. He likes 'the pureness of graffiti and the fact that it is not driven by commercial objectives; it can arouse emotions in people who just happen to come across it.'

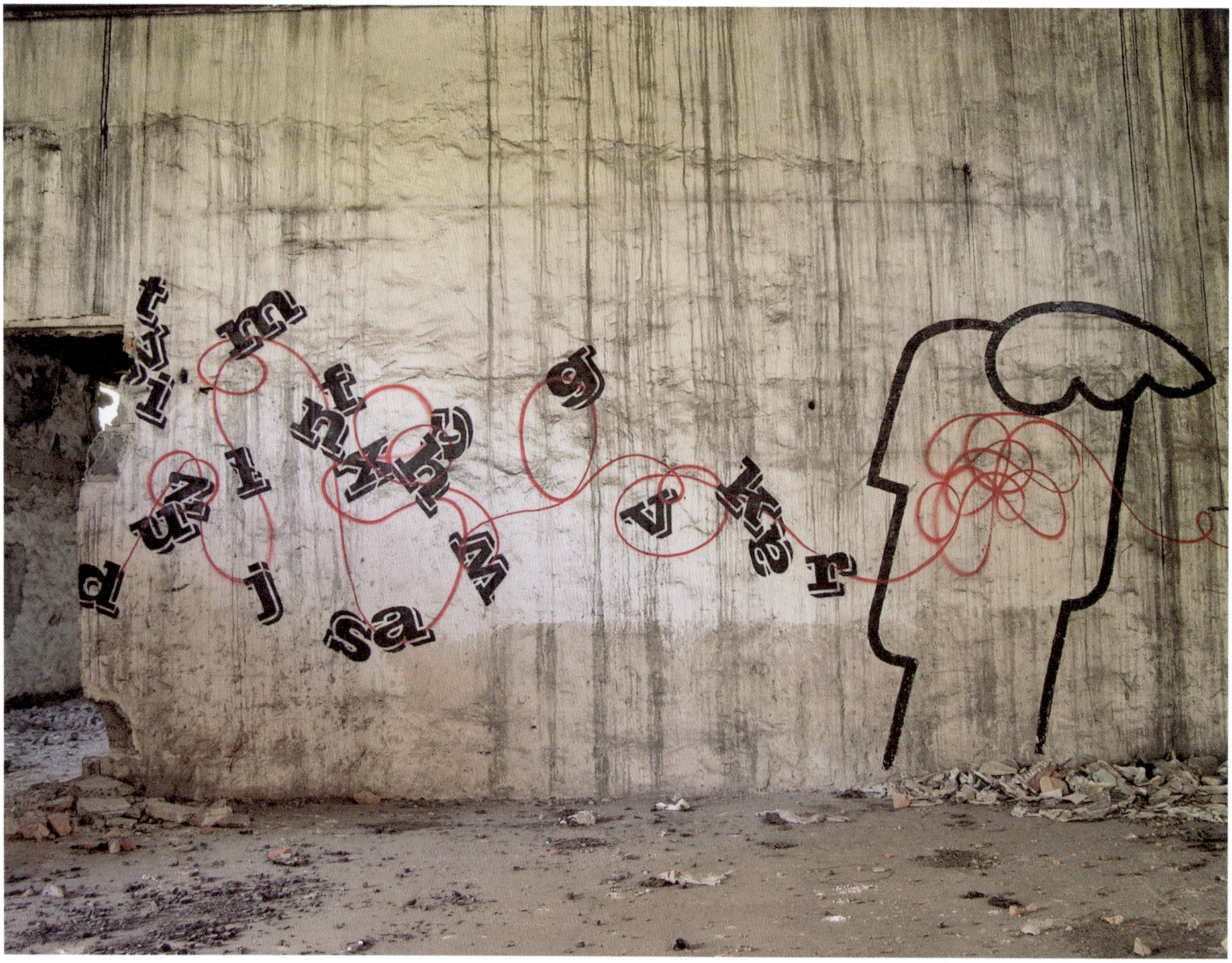

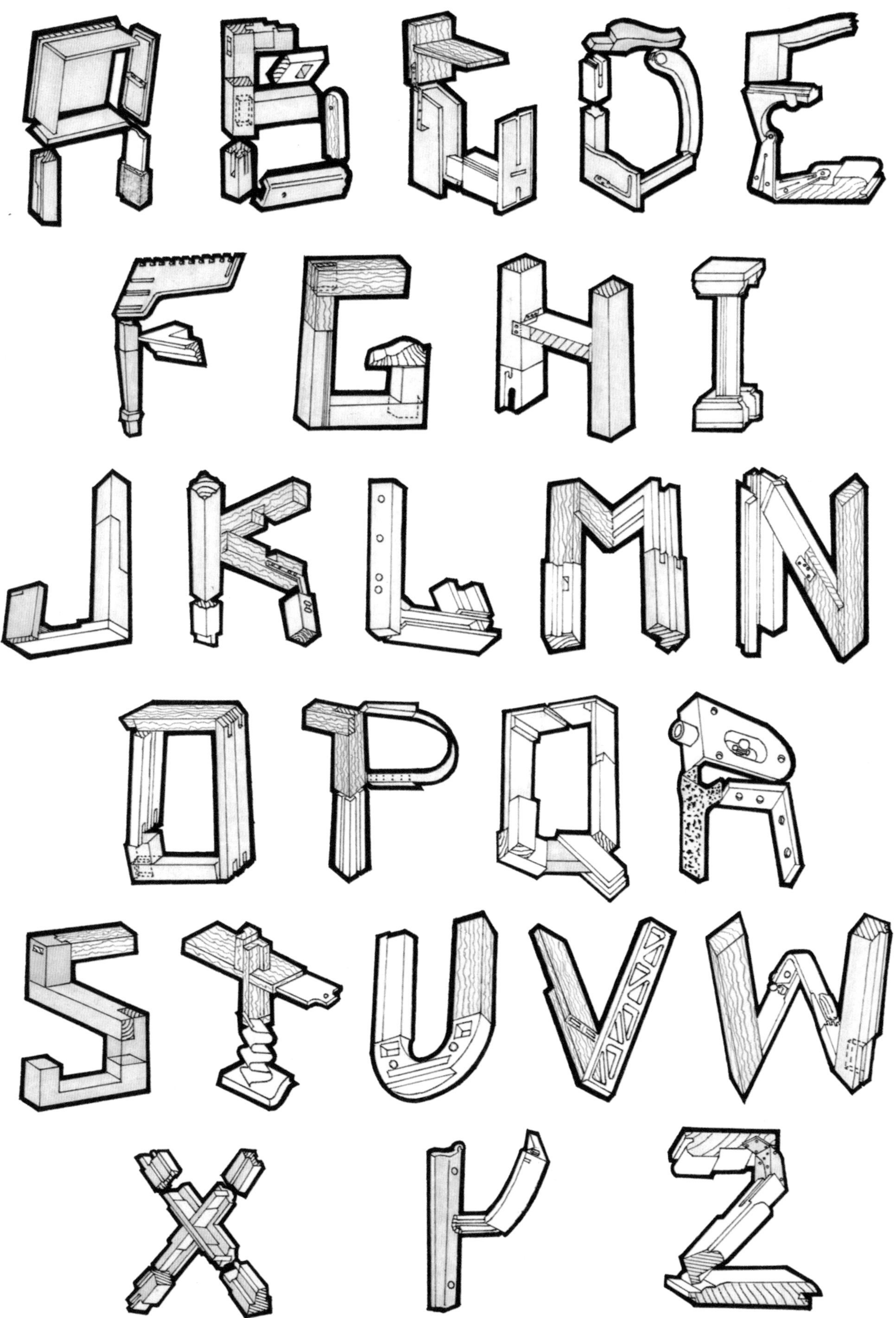

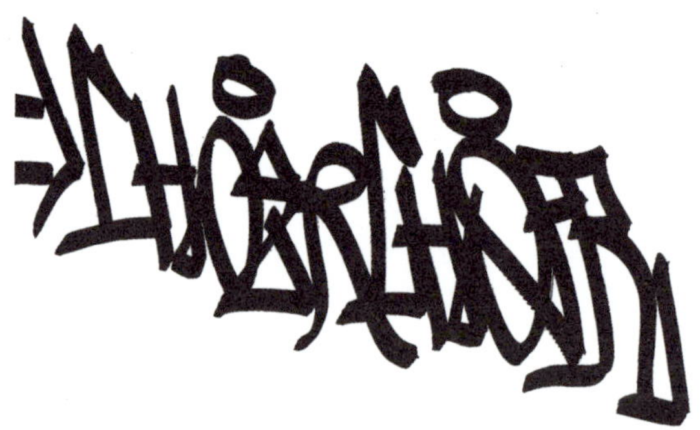

Choer

LONDON, UK
Crew member of RT
Writer since 2001
Favourite letter: R

London-based Choer primarily focuses on letters. He likes styles that are based on traditional letter forms but have their own individual flair and personality. 'If you can look at something without questioning any part of it, then it's usually pretty good!' he says. To get his alphabet done he stayed up until 6 am for three nights, armed with pen and paper, until he drew something he was happy with.

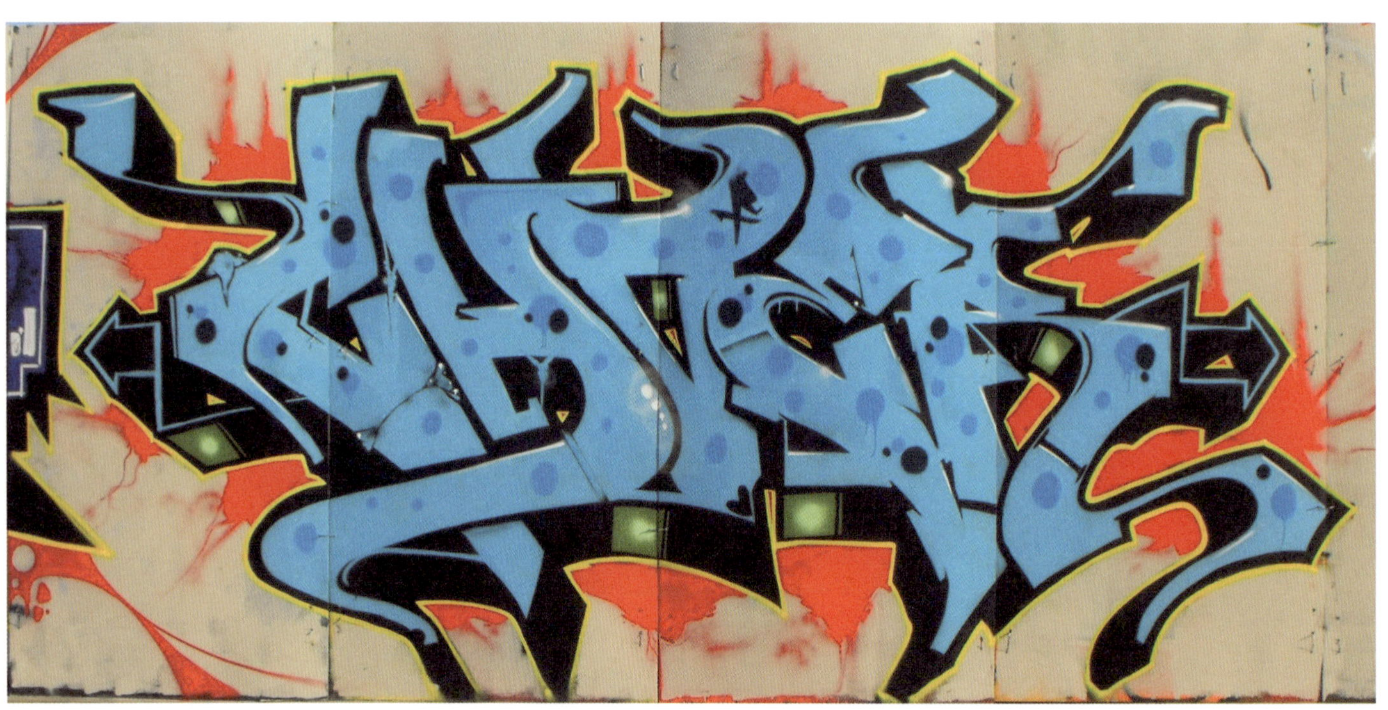

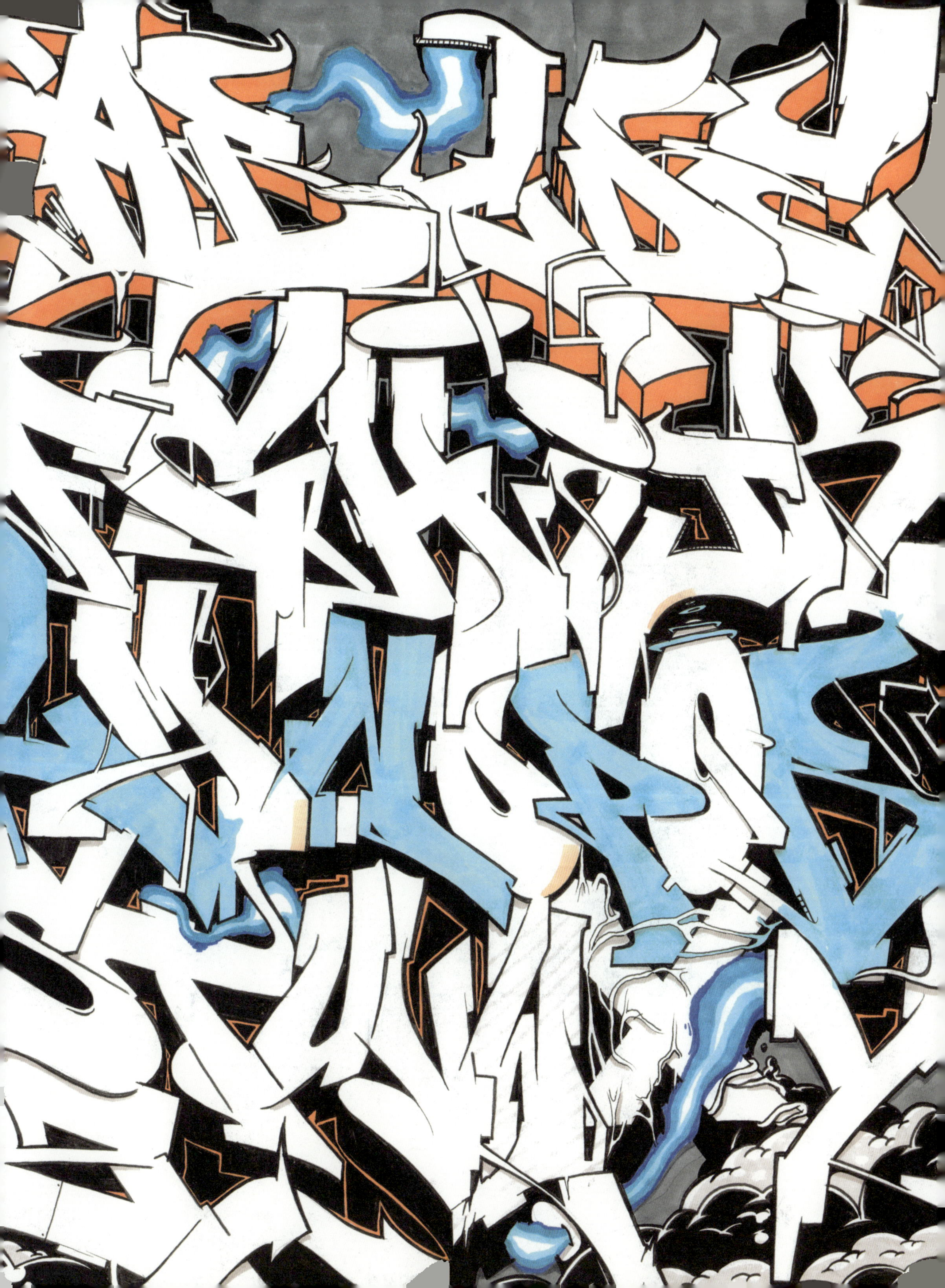

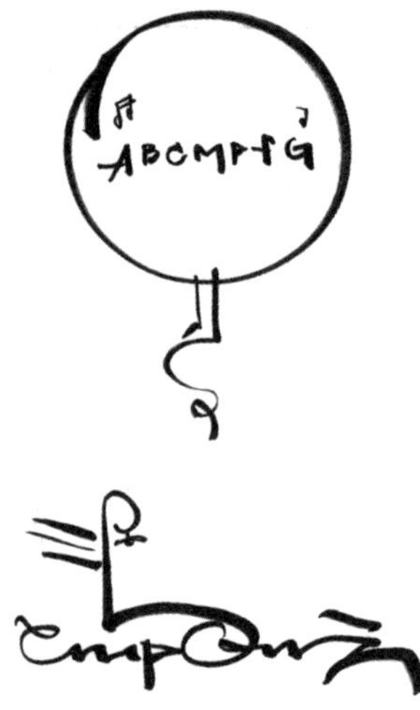

CMP One
NÆSTVED, DENMARK
Crew member of CMPSPIN, The South Side Crew
Writer since 1984
Favourite letter: 'I love most of them'
www.cmpspin.com

CMP One is well known for his powerful drawings of urban scenes, which are reminiscent of film noir and comics. His letters are clearly defined and based on classic shapes. Throughout his work he uses a subdued colour palette, which complements his style perfectly. For him the best thing about graffiti is 'the sense of freedom, and the travelling and friendships pre-internet-era'.

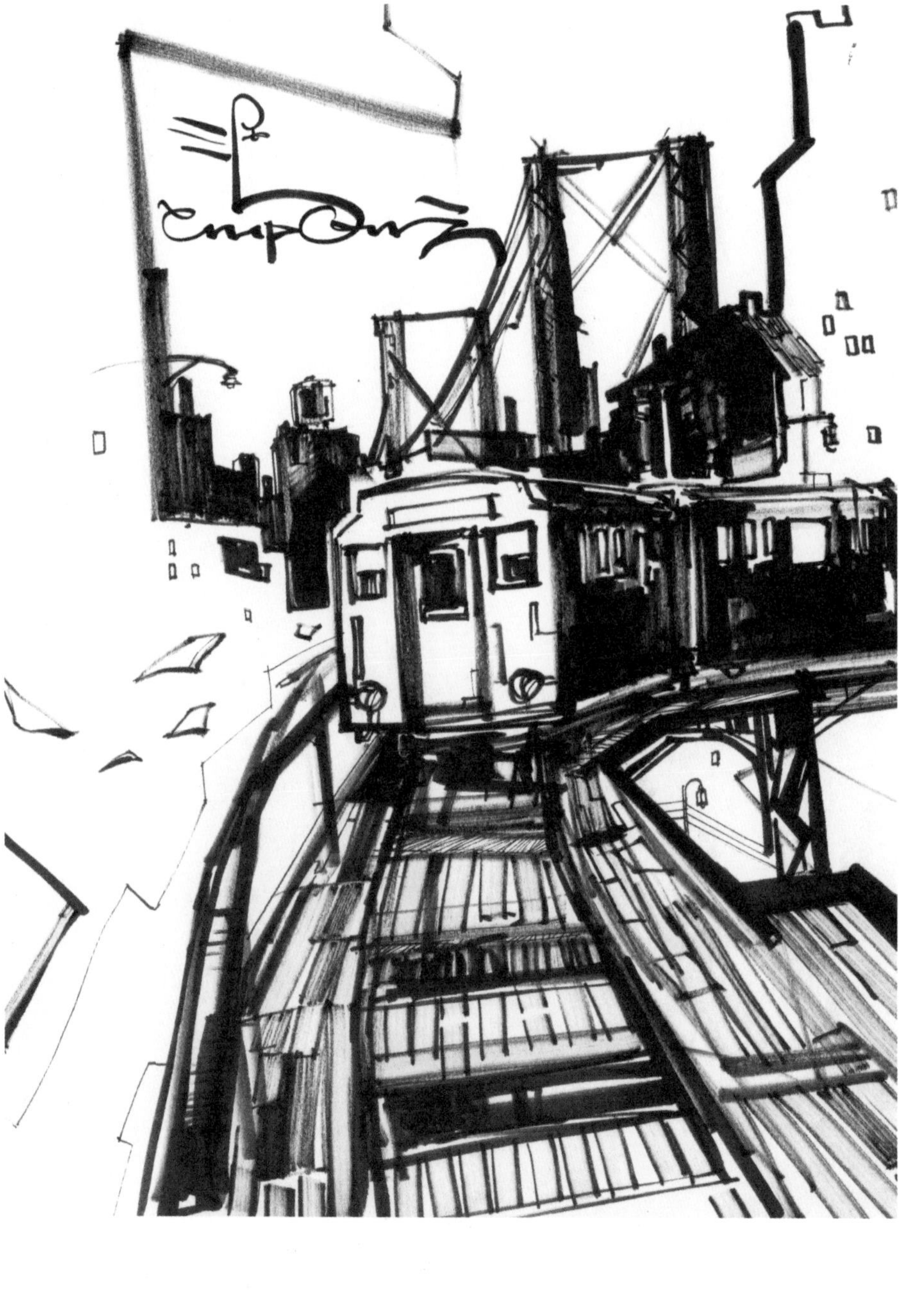

A B C D E F G
H I J K L M N
O P Q R S T U
V W X Y Z

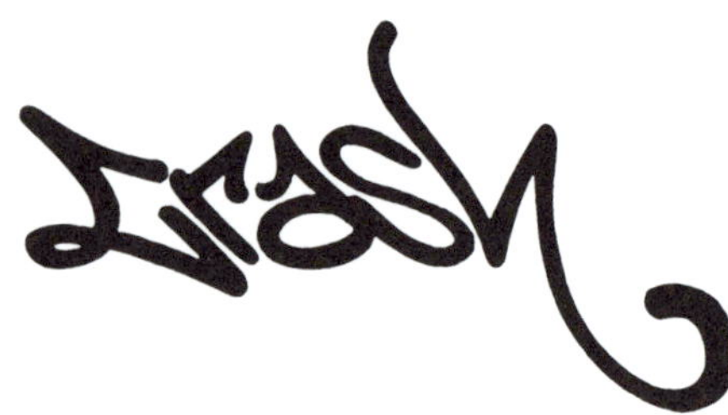

Crash

NEW YORK CITY, USA
Crew member of TDS, CIA, BLS
Writer since 1973
Favourite letter: C
www.crashone.com
www.crashocasters.com

Crash has done everything from wildstyles to straight letters, but he prefers the beauty of bubble style. He achieved recognition within the art world in the 1980s and became especially known for his Signature Stratocaster for Eric Clapton. Crash created five guitars for the musician and was then commissioned by Fender to produce a line of fifty 'graffiti' guitars, which were given the name 'Crashocasters'. Crash says: 'The best thing about graffiti is the freedom that you get from doing what you love most.'

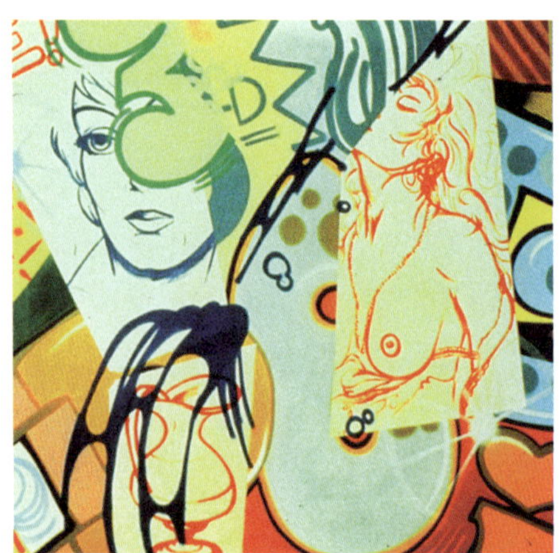

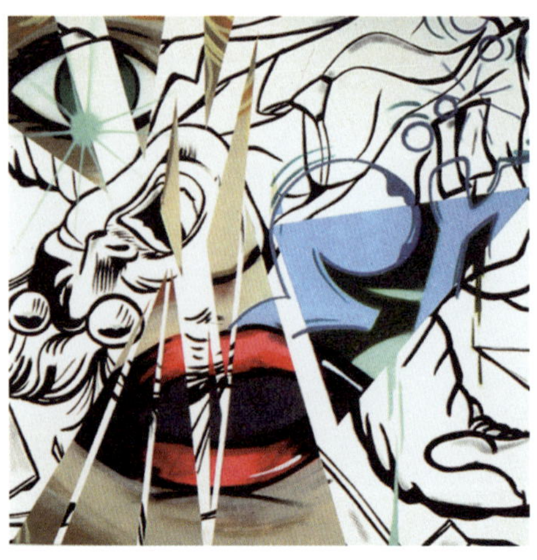

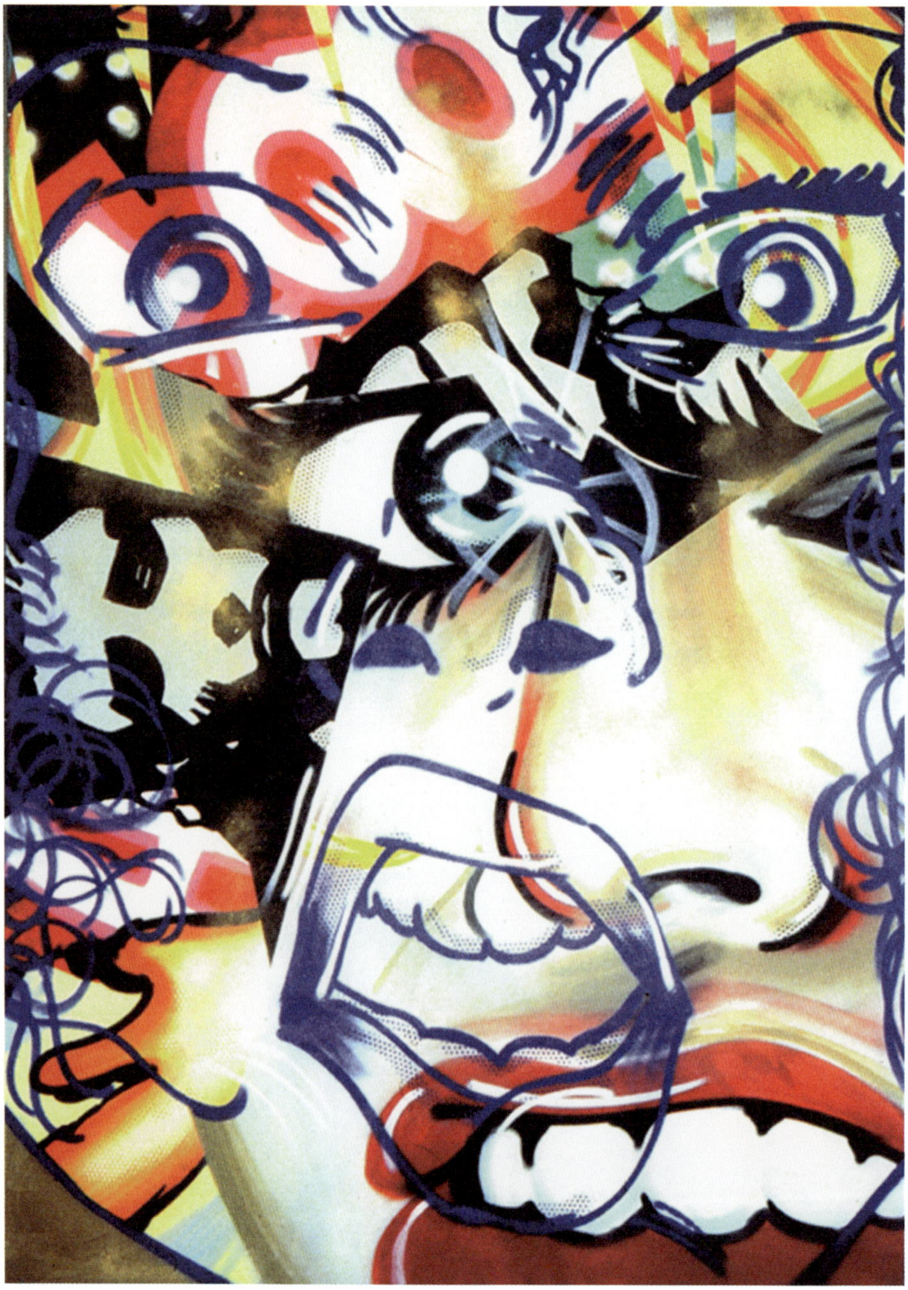

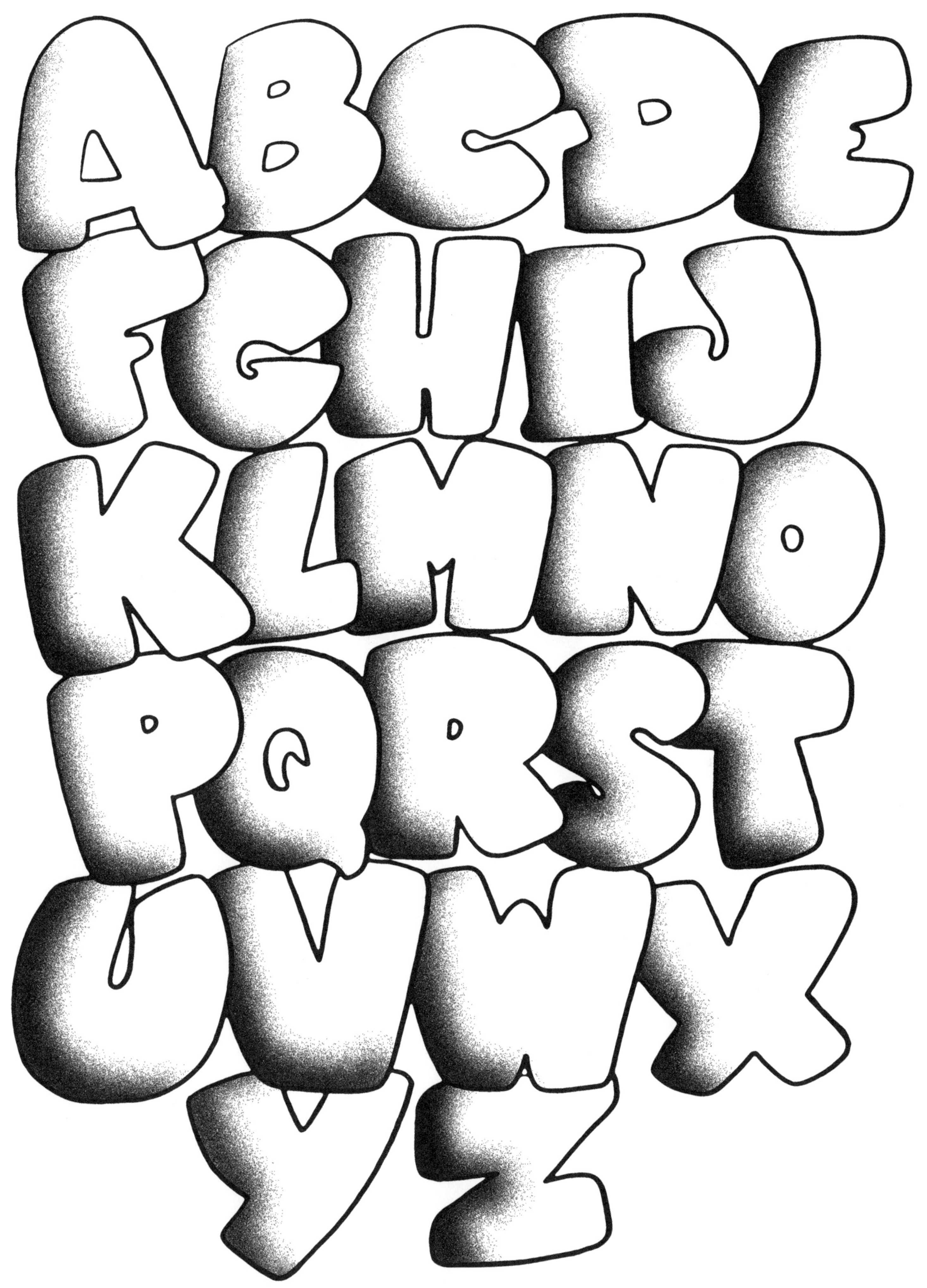

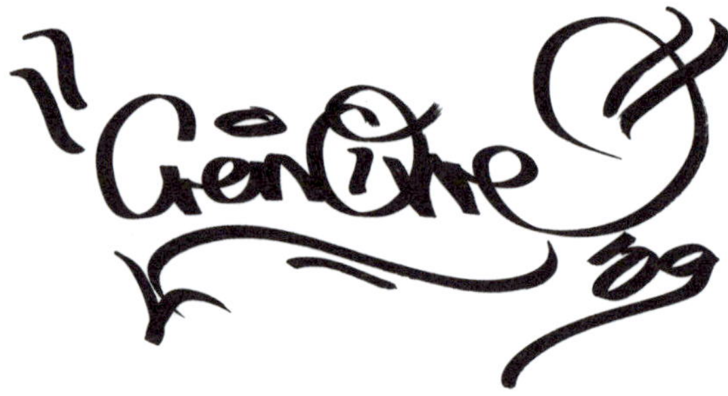

Cren One

BERLIN, GERMANY

Crew member of CBR, HSF, TNB, KD,
TPA, Rock and Roll Inc
Writer since 1989
Favourite letter: E
www.michel-cren-pietsch.de

Cren One was born near Hanover but now lives in Berlin. For
his alphabet he decided to abandon colour so that he could
concentrate on the letters themselves, without camouflaging
them. 'The letters are always the most important element [in
creating a good piece],' he says, 'and making sure that you don't
violate them too much.' However, he does think that the choice
of colour is important in determining whether a piece works,
as is the background.

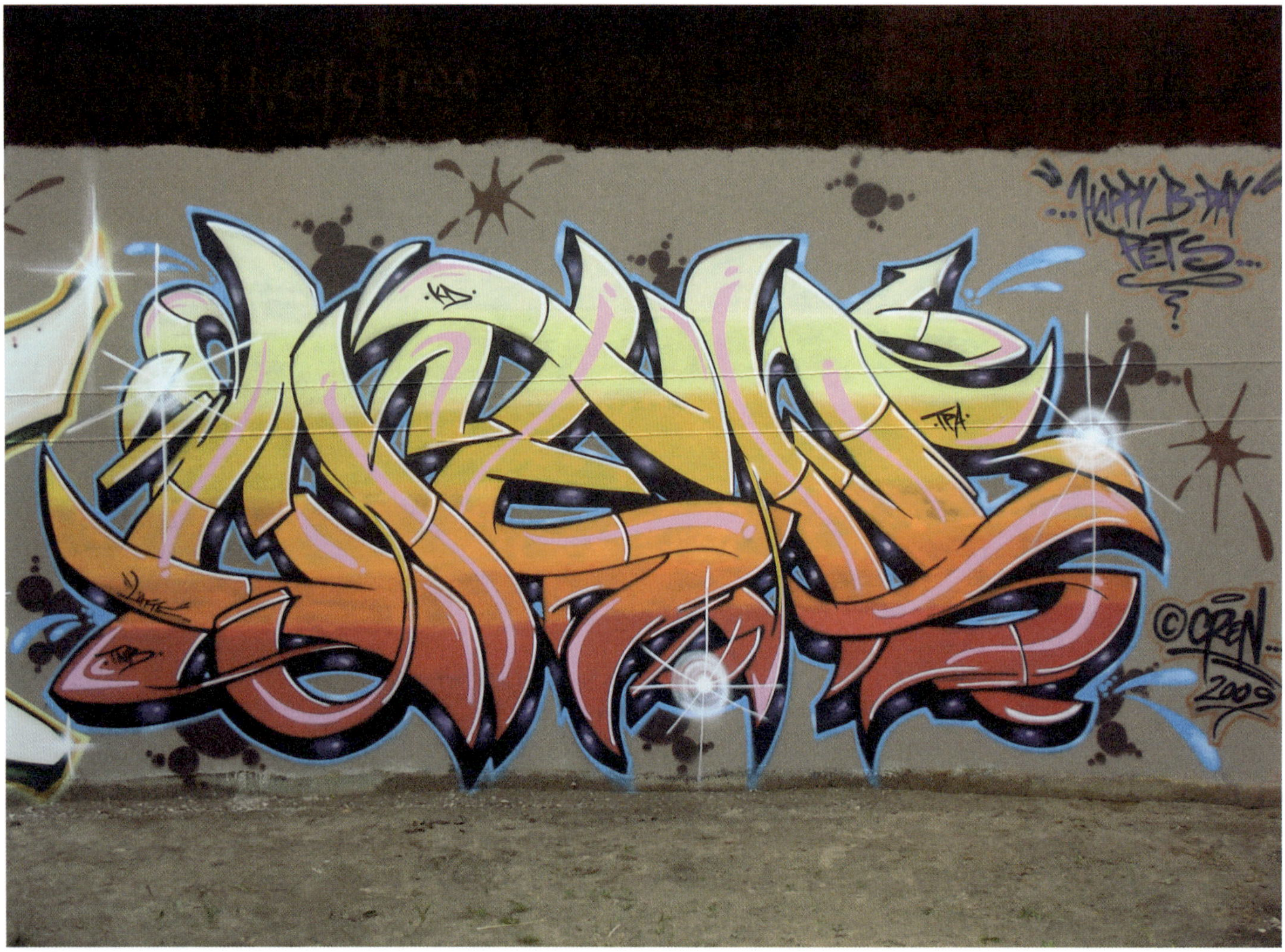

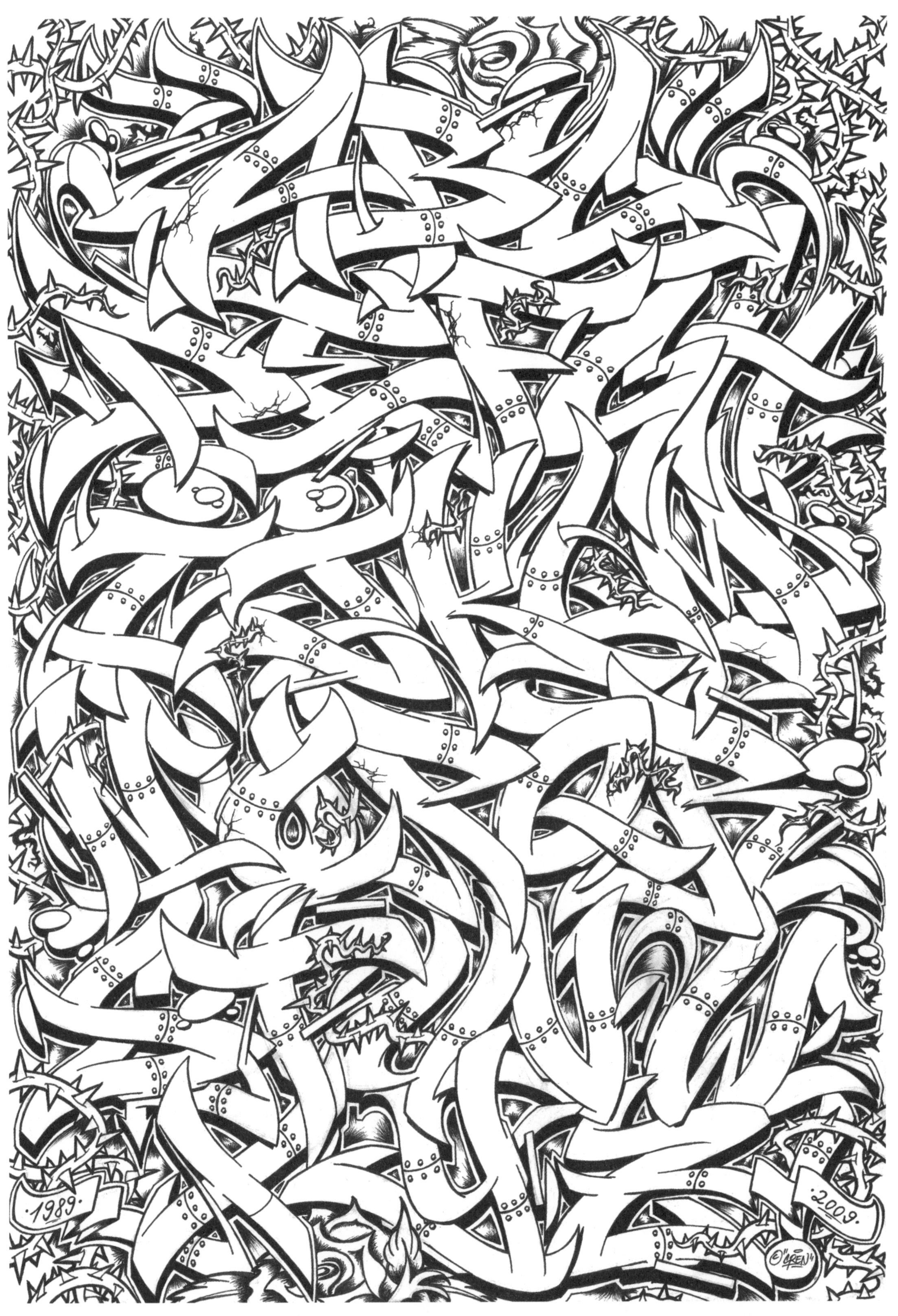

·1989·
·2009·

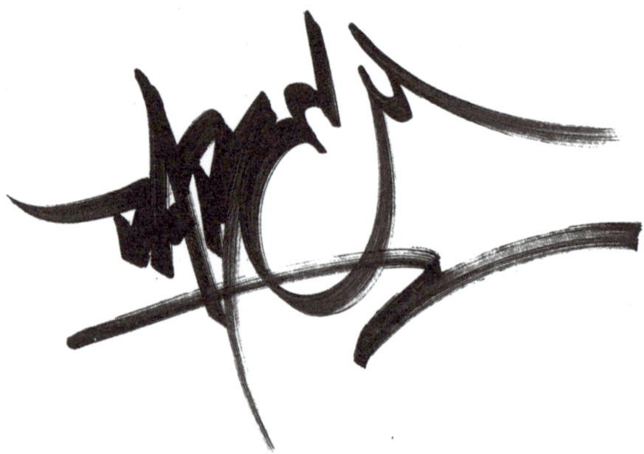

Dare

BASEL, SWITZERLAND

Crew member of TWS, LL, S2R, RDM
Writer since 1986
Favourite letter: 'I love all letters'
www.dare.ch

In his twenty-three years as an artist, Dare influenced many writers around the world with his highly aesthetic and graceful style. He turned the famous Basel line into one of the biggest and most beautiful outdoor galleries in Europe. He would take his friends there at night and execute carefully planned paintings on walls with matching backgrounds and fill-ins, setting a high standard for the writers in his hometown as well as further afield. He was equally successful indoors and showed his work in galleries all over Europe, despite the fact that he only did letters. Through exhibitions and his work as a curator, he paved the way for many like-minded artists to show their work in galleries. About his alphabet Dare said: 'I think there is no alphabet for graffiti.'

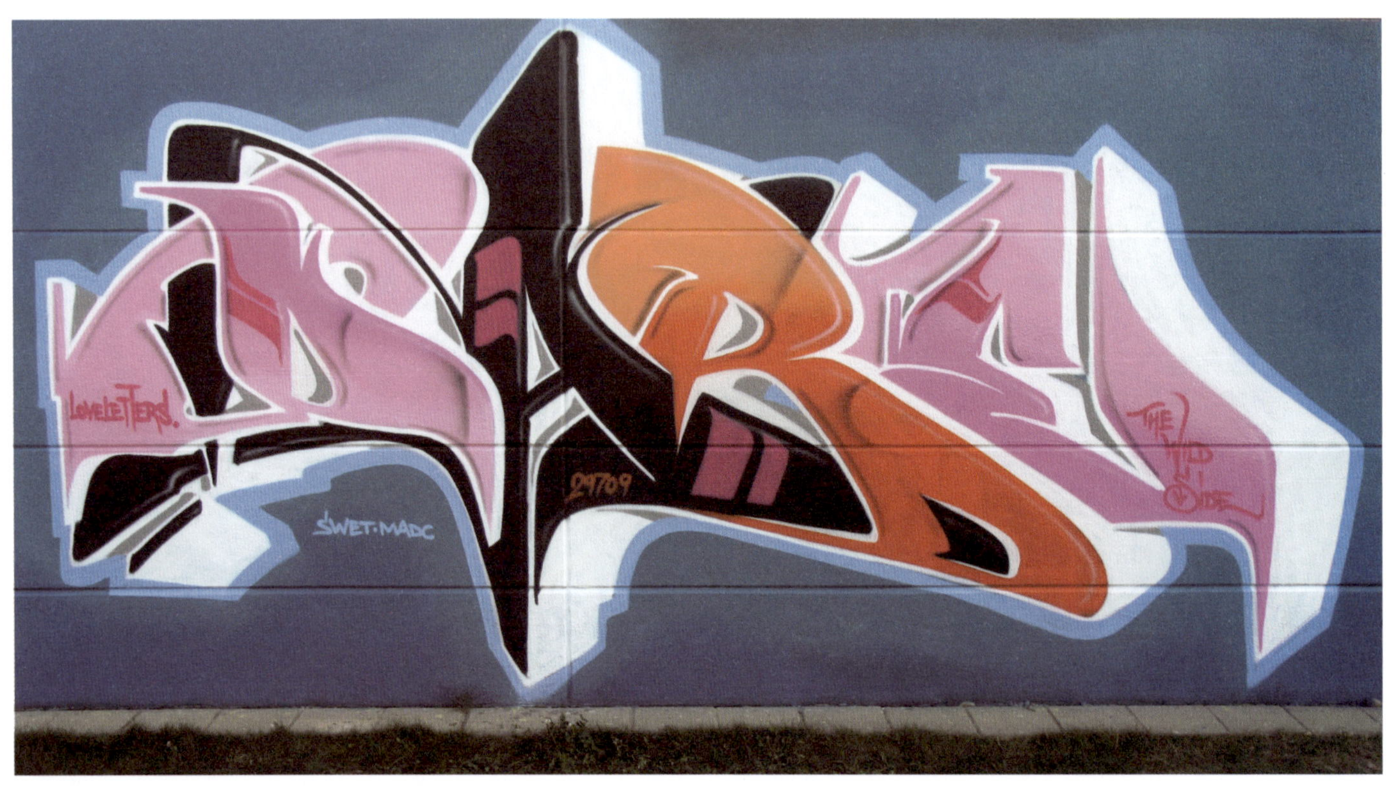

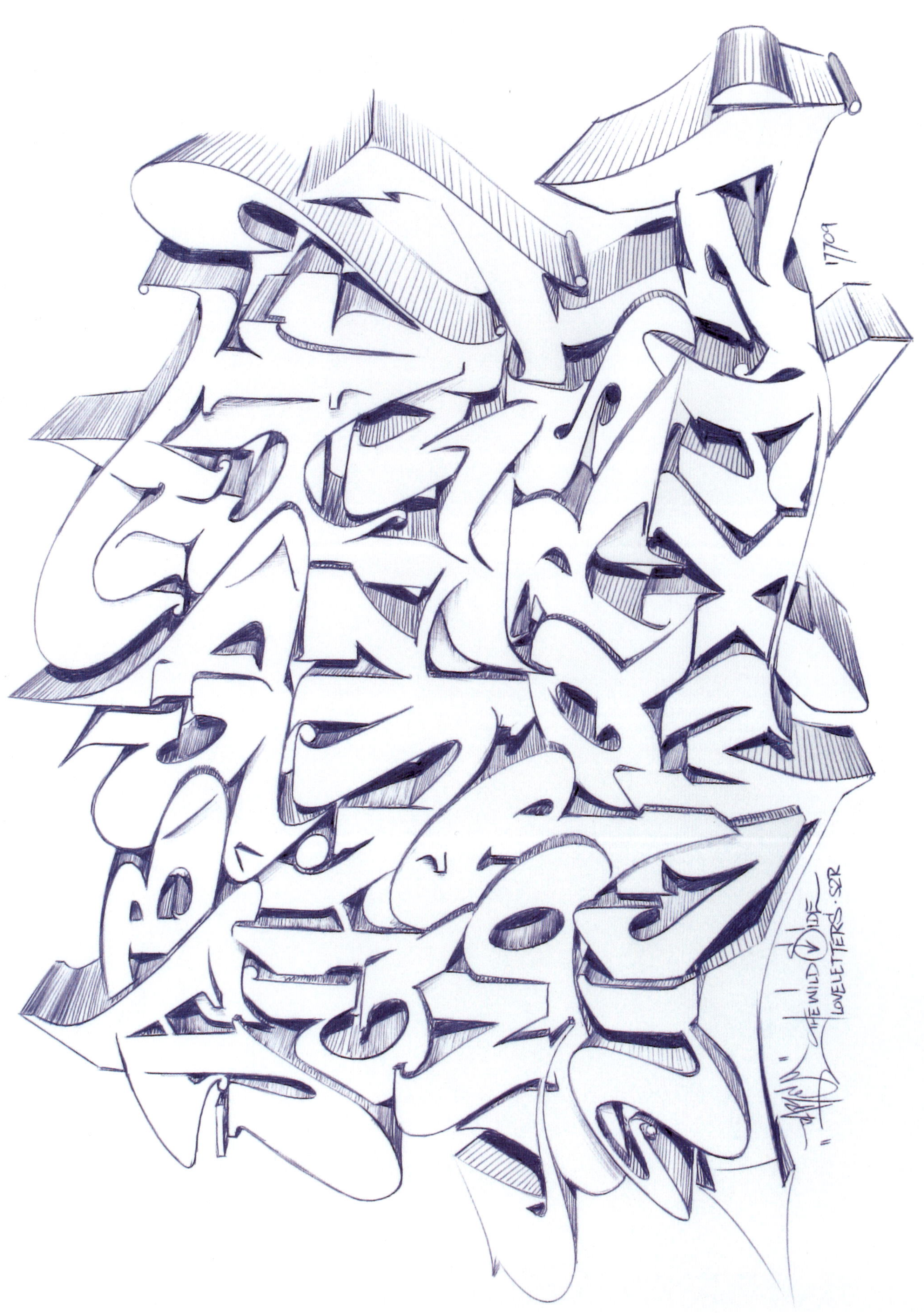

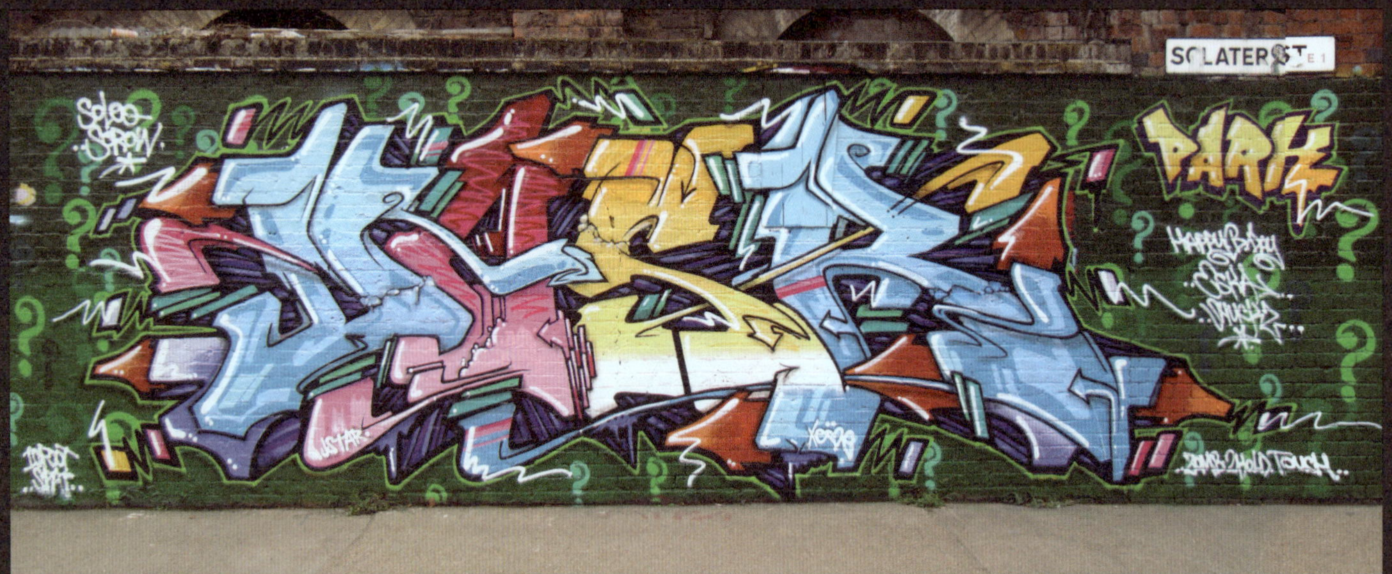

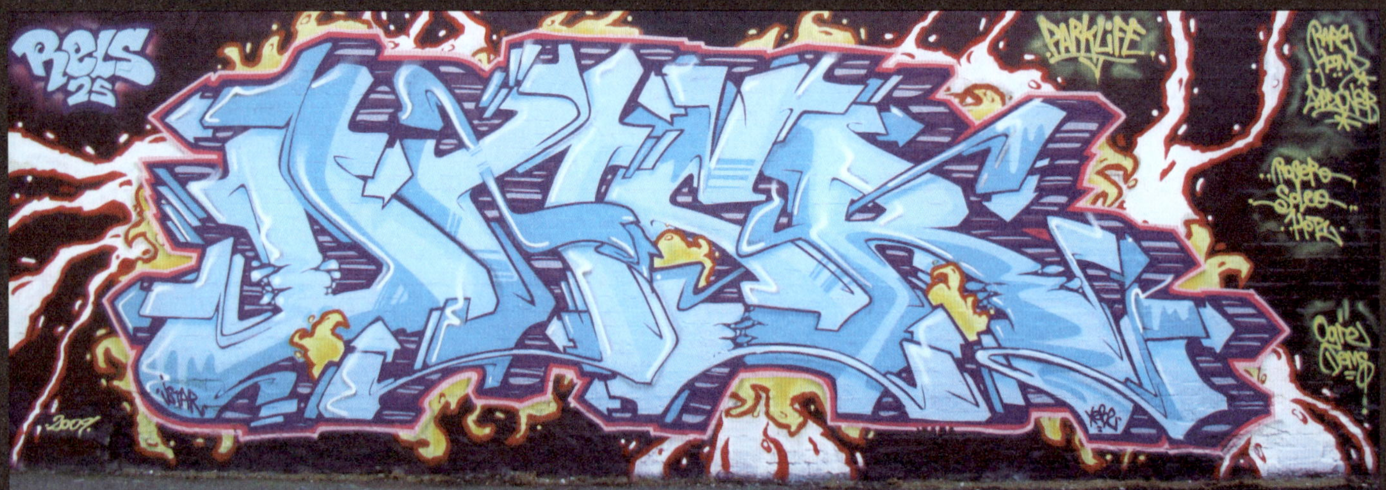

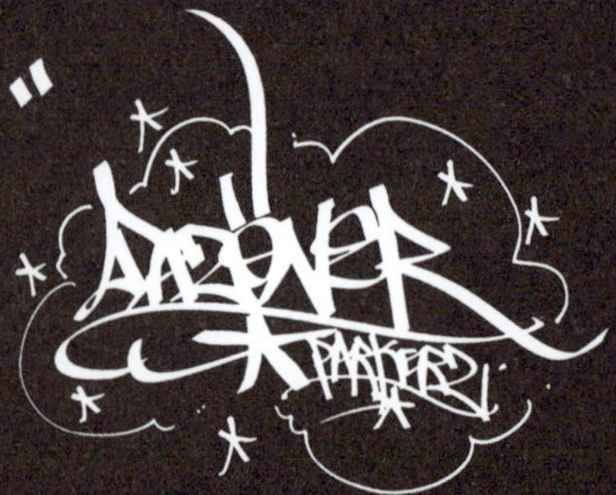

Dasone

LONDON, UK

Crew member of Rarekind, Parkers
Writer since 1995
Favourite letter: R
www.rarekindlondon.com

Dasone is one of the artists behind Rarekind. He has produced
alphabets for several years, and finds it a better way to improve
his style than painting the same three or four letters over and
over again. 'It made me love letters and typefaces,' he says.

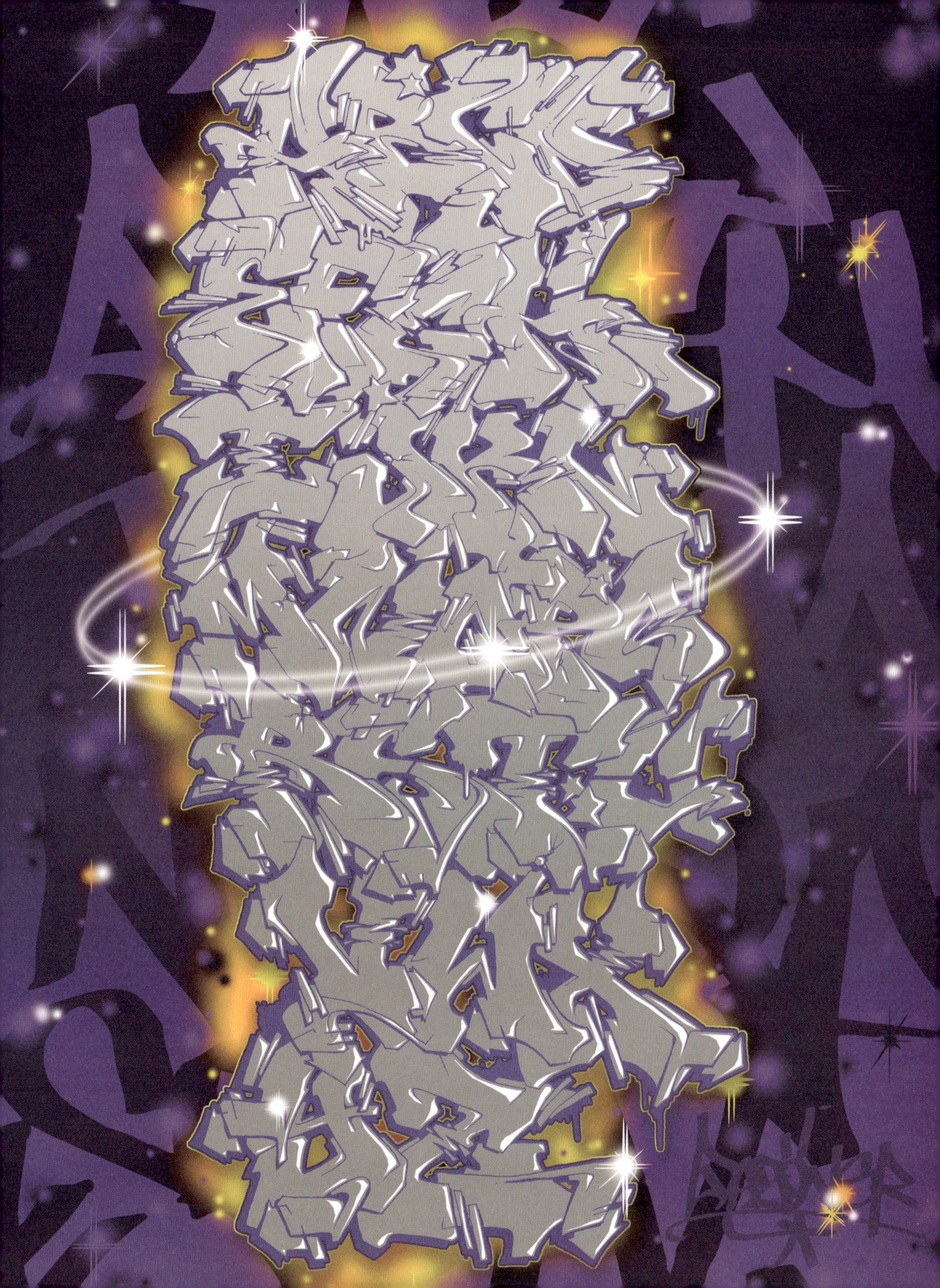

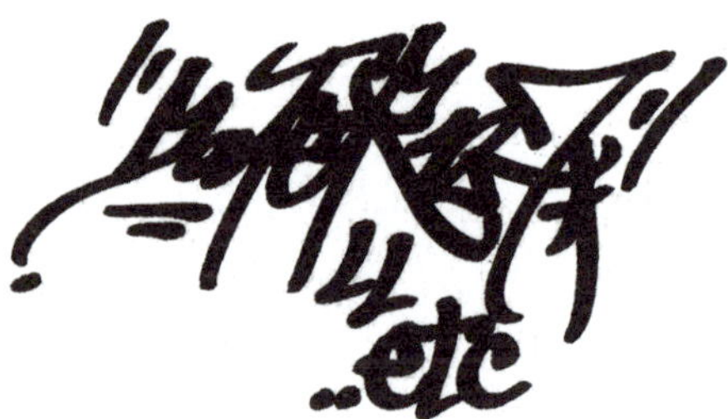

Dater

KOBLENZ, GERMANY

Crew member of LoveLetters, ETC

Favourite letter: D

Dater's style is always legible, executed with clean lines and a carefully considered colour scheme. In his opinion, it takes original letter shapes and colours as well as elegance, dynamism and impact for a piece to be successful.

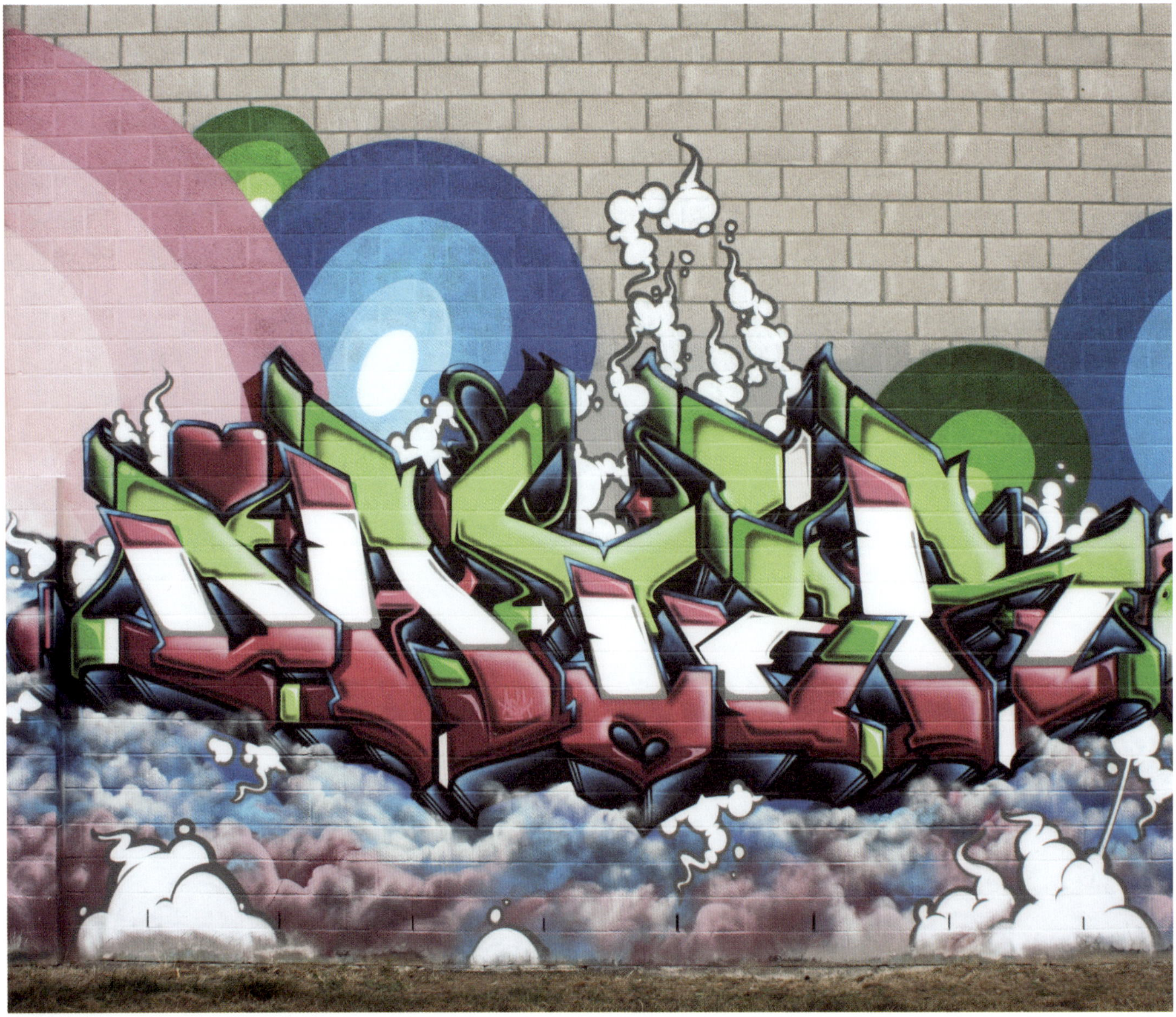

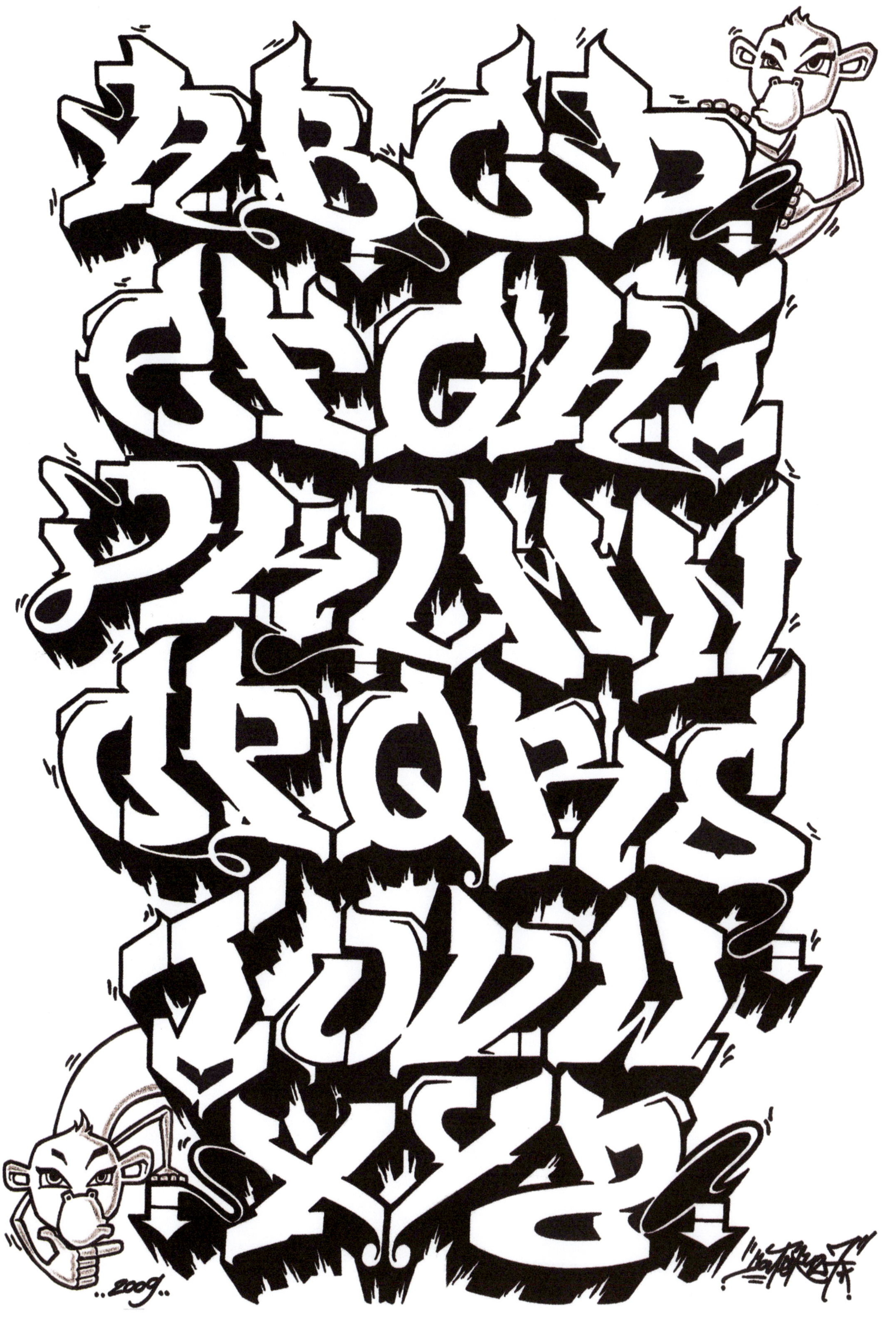

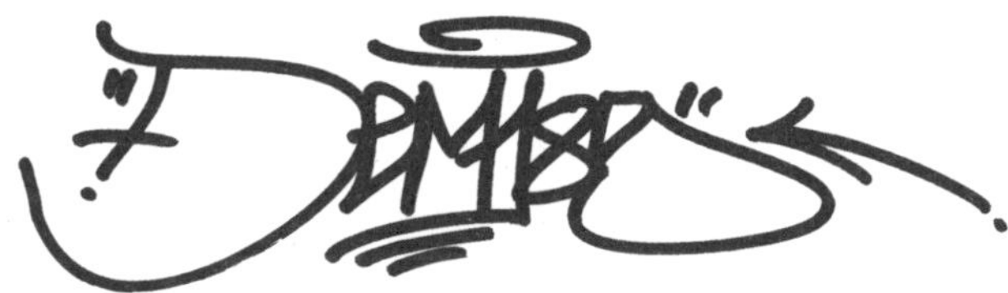

Dem189
PARIS, FRANCE
Crew member of LBD/PCF, 90DBC,
TCP, CKT, CMP, Formula One
Writer since 1991
Favourite letter: S
www.cargocollective.com/dem189

Whenever Dem189 has a spare minute, he draws in one of his
many travel books. Through sketching, he has developed a unique
style and technique with a seemingly endless array of variations.
Sometimes he focuses on letters or characters, and at other times
the letters turn into characters or vice versa. This is why he describes
his style as 'uncoherent'. Dem189 drew his alphabet in ink on paper.

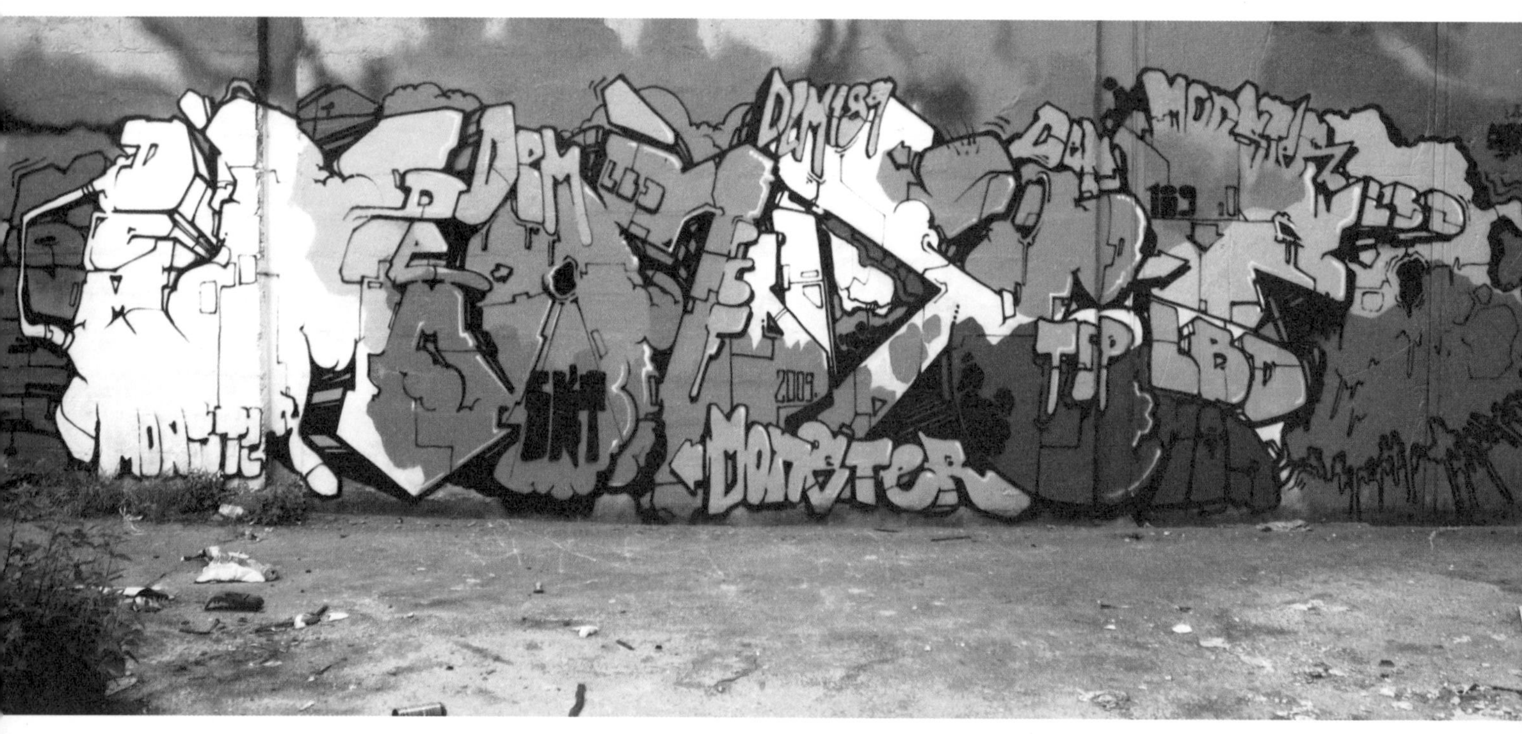

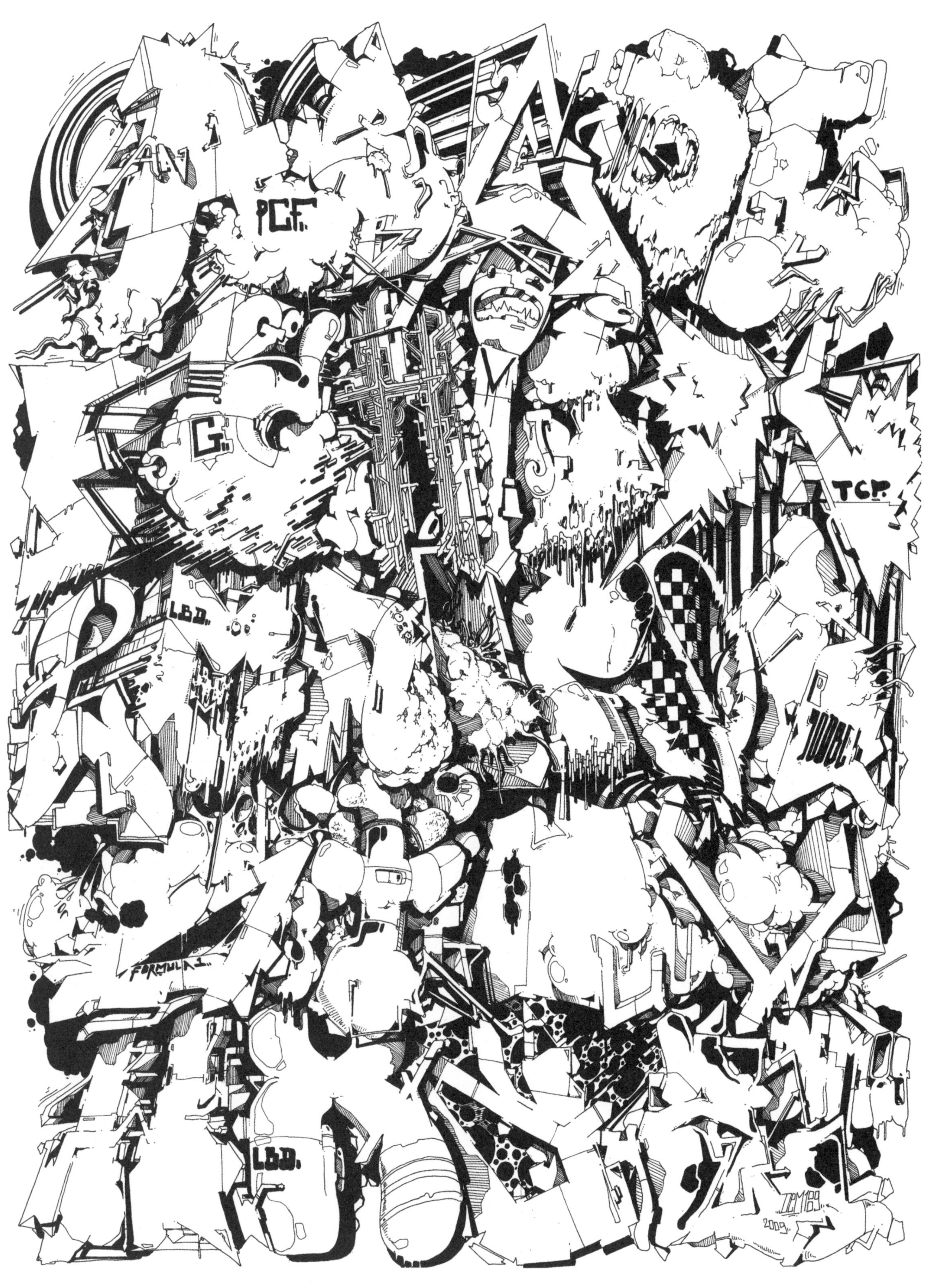
PCF.
TCP.
G.
L.B.D.
FORMULA 1
TODO
L.B.D.
2009.

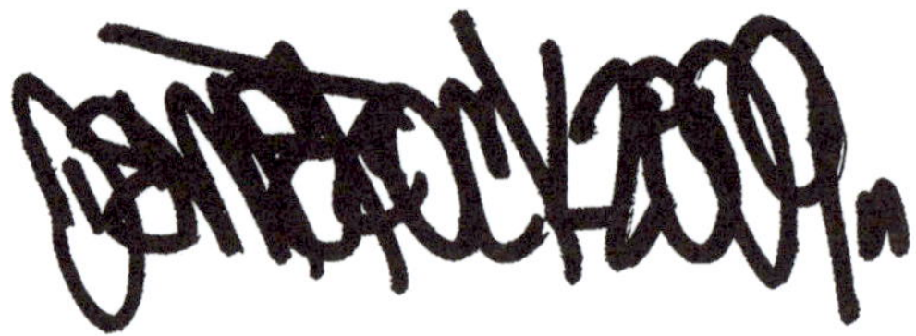

Demer

NEWARK (NEW JERSEY), USA
Crew member of The Wallnuts, Vicious Styles
Writer since 1982
Favourite letter: D
www.viciousstylescrew.com

Demer started writing in New York, and his style is influenced by
the city's old-school graffiti. He is known not only for the walls
he has painted with his crew, The Wallnuts, but also for his freight
train graffiti. 'A wall can have all the pretty colours and characters,
but if the letters are bad, it's a bad wall,' he says. 'If you can burn in
black and white, that says it all.'

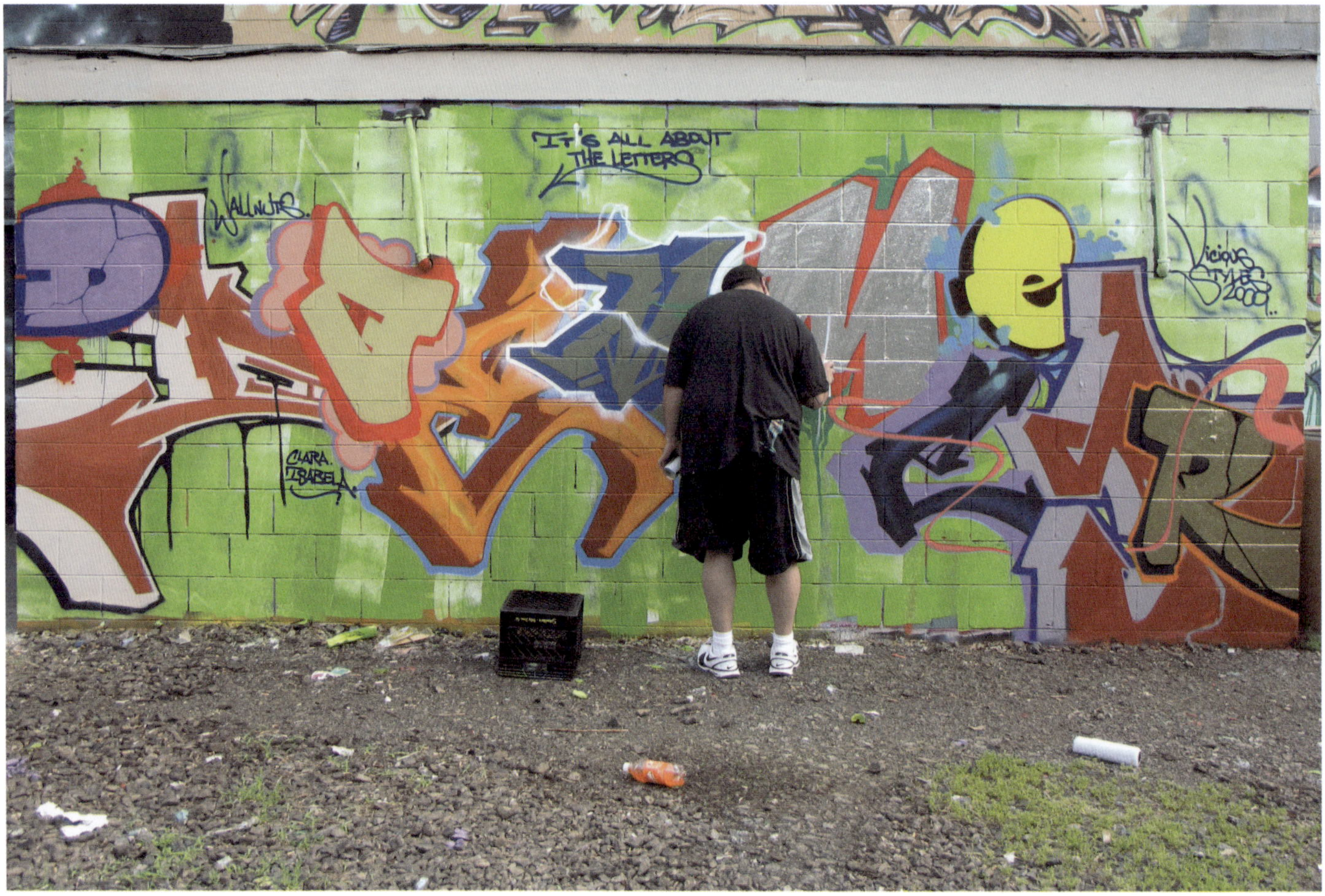

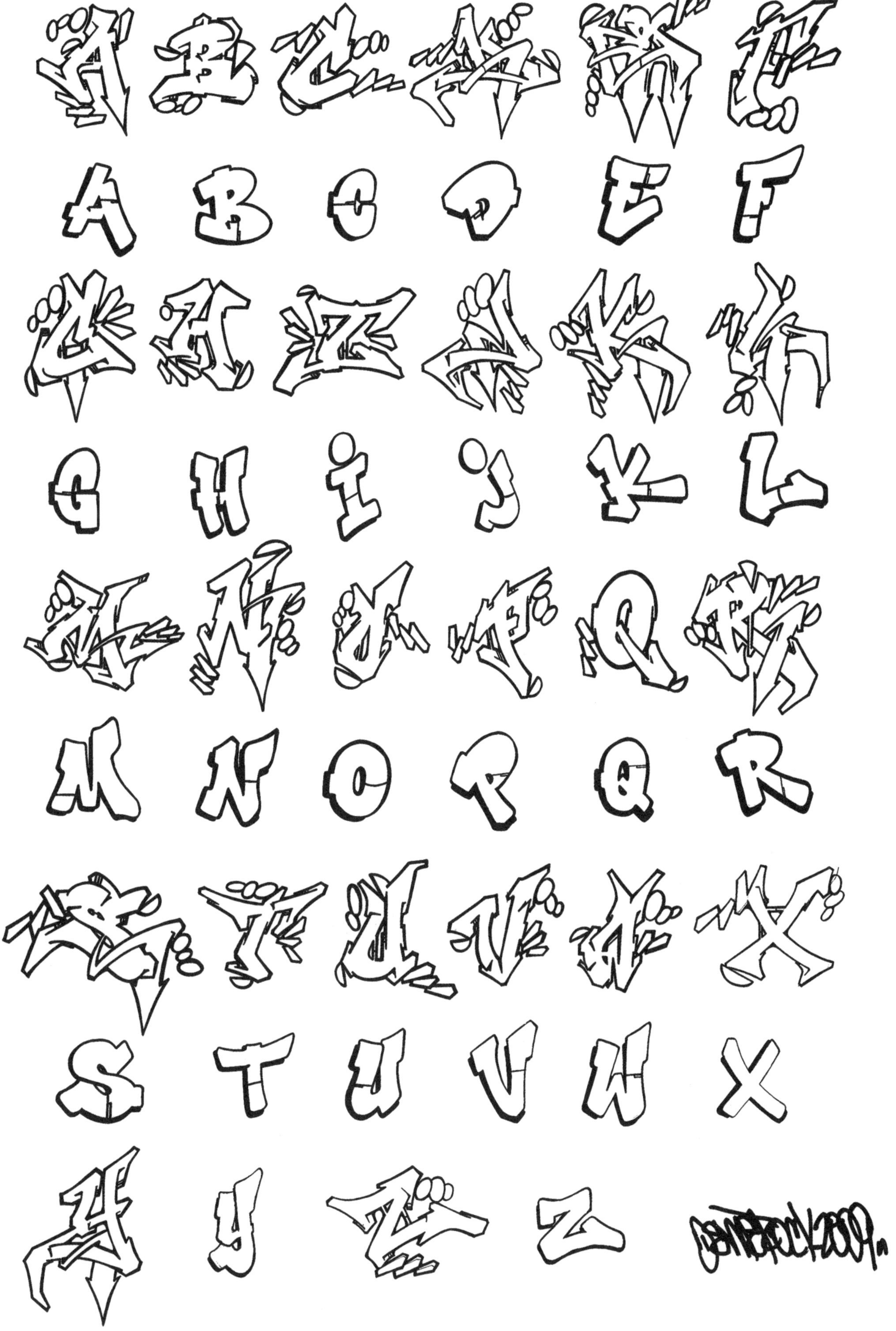

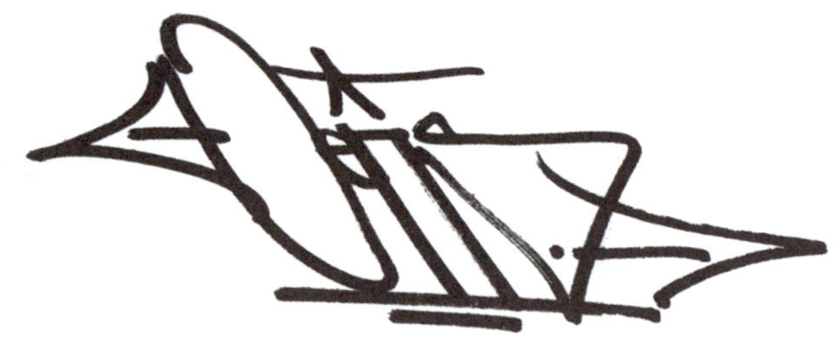

Dems333

ALICANTE, SPAIN

Crew member of 333, Pornostars, Ultraboyz
Writer since the early 1990s
Favourite letters: D, E, M, S
www.jdemsky.com

Dems333 was initially influenced by Spanish writers in cities
such as Elche and Alicante, but in 2000 he started to travel
further afield. He rarely sketches and prefers his letters to take
shape on the wall so that he doesn't repeat himself. Dems333
describes his style as 'galactic fury with digital rock', and likes
the fact that graffiti makes him different from most other people.

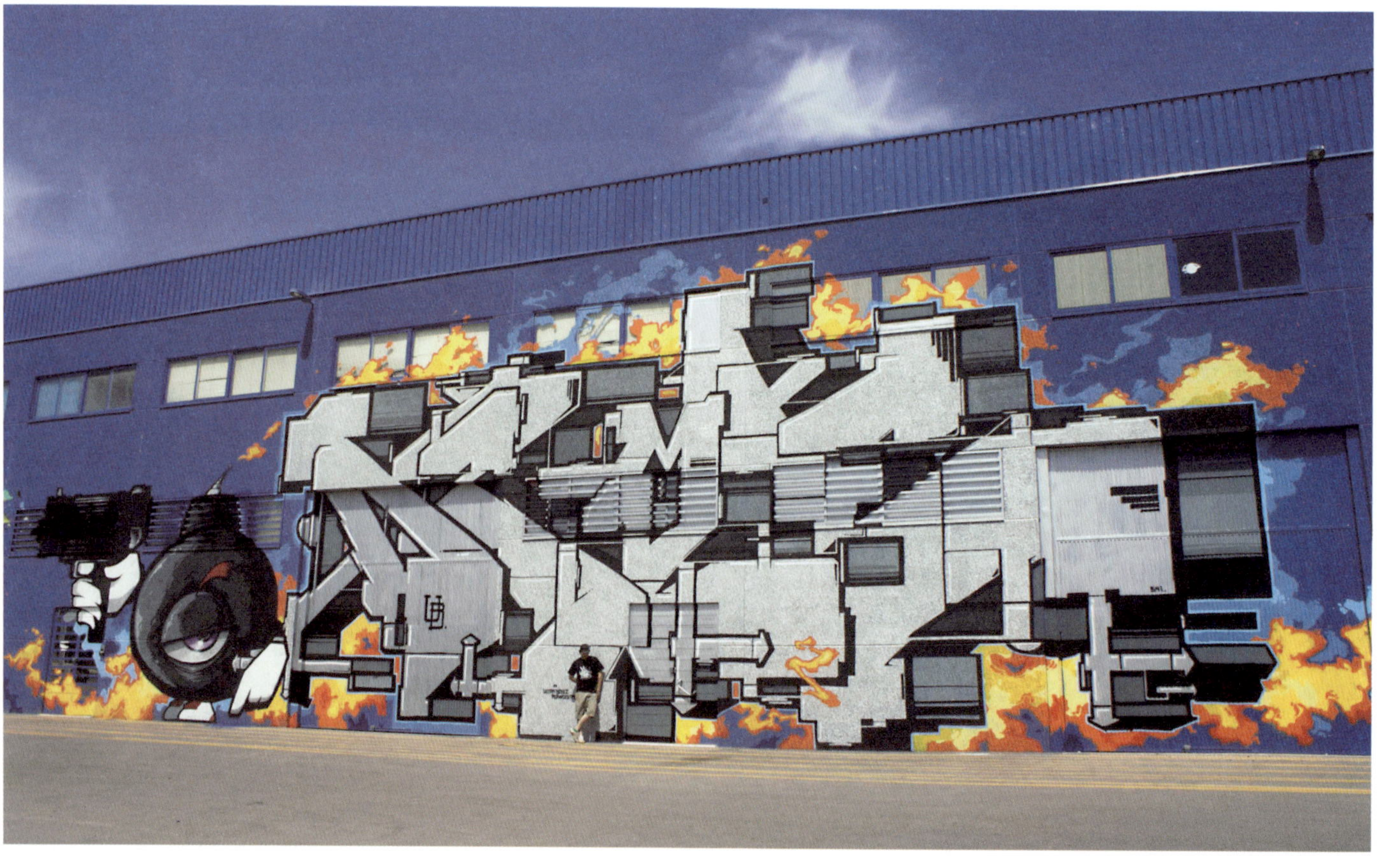

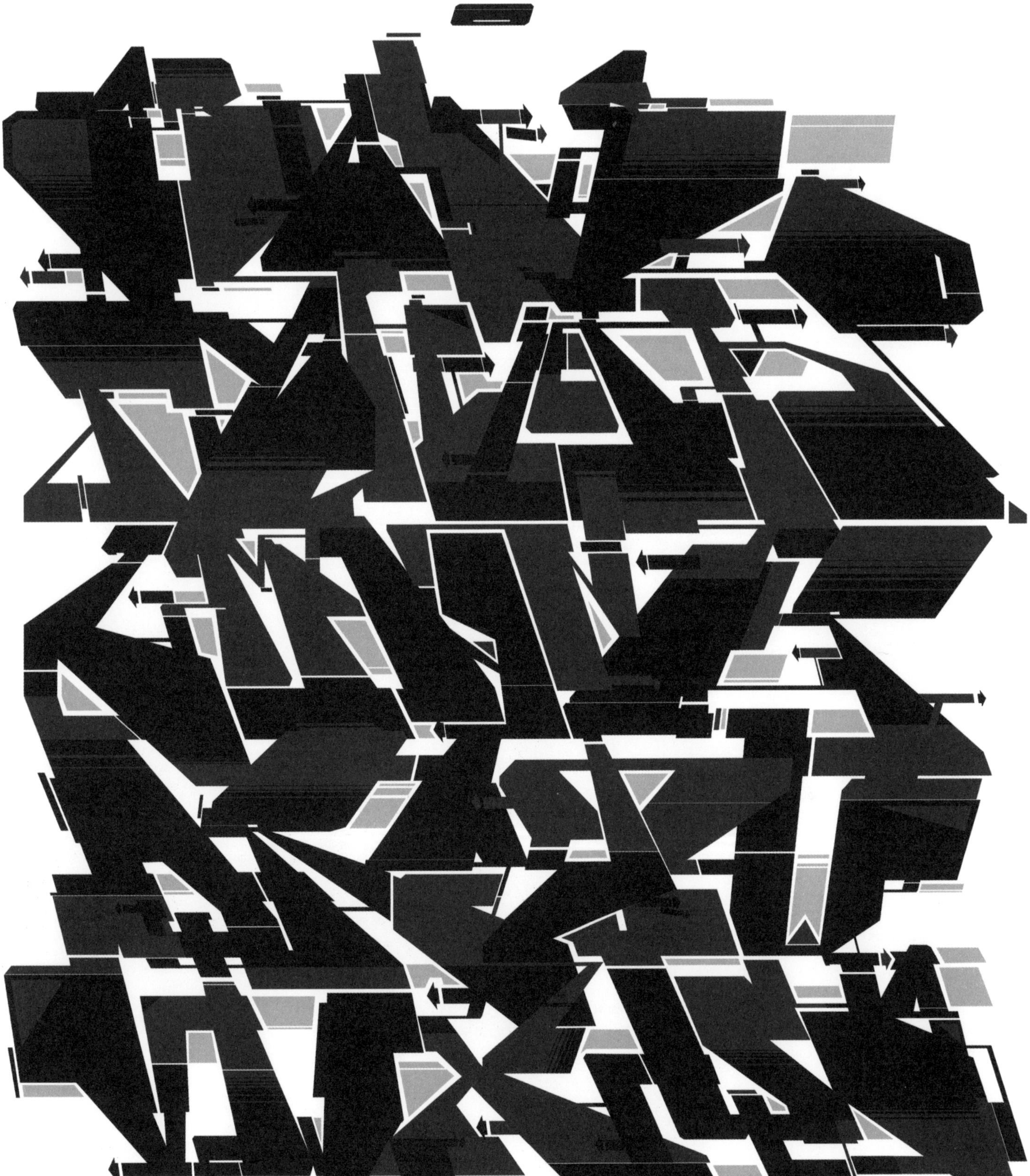

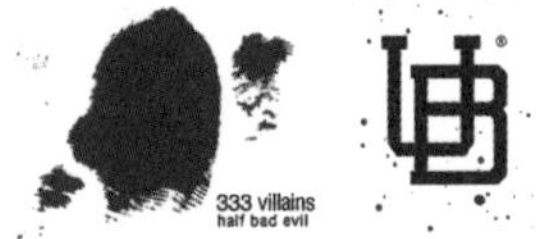
333 villains
half bad evil

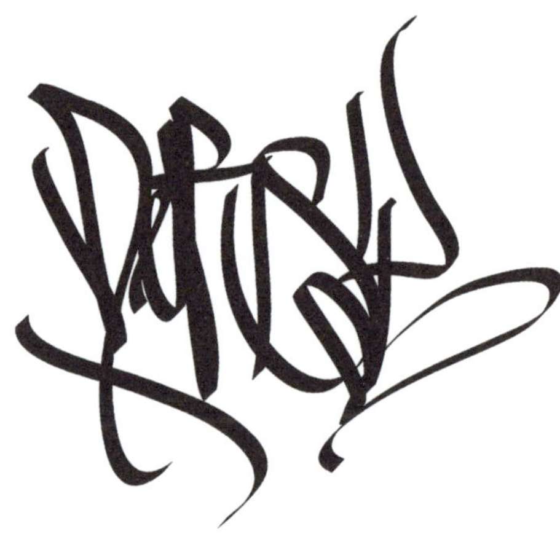

Ders

BASEL, SWITZERLAND
Crew member of GRAFF SUCKS, ETC, M4C, TBT
Writer since 1995
Favourite letter: S
https://streetpins.com/members/ders

Basel has been home to many good writers, but Ders has developed his own style. Rather than following classic graffiti, he likes to experiment with paint and create interesting new styles. A good piece, he says, needs flow, fresh ideas and lines that are full of tension.

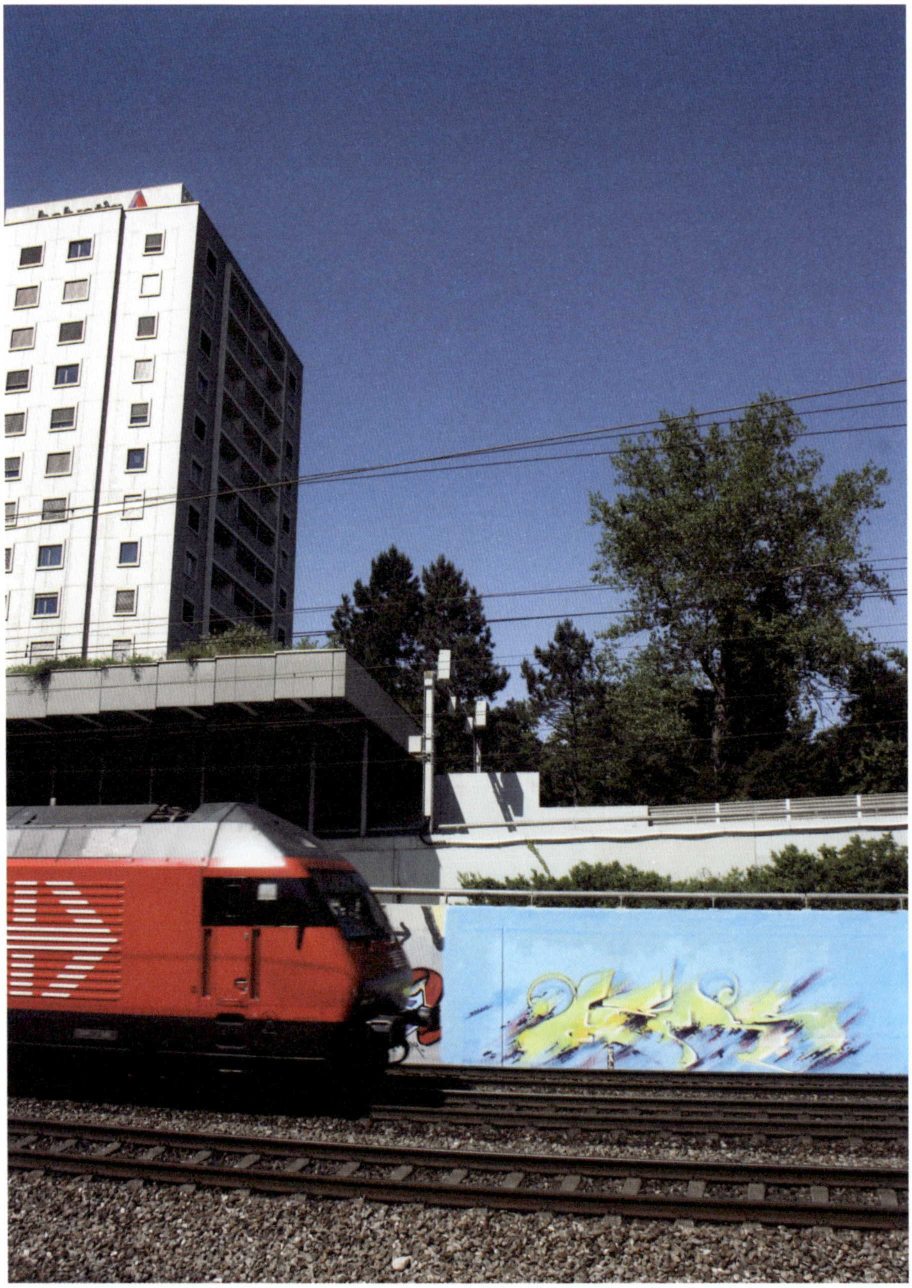

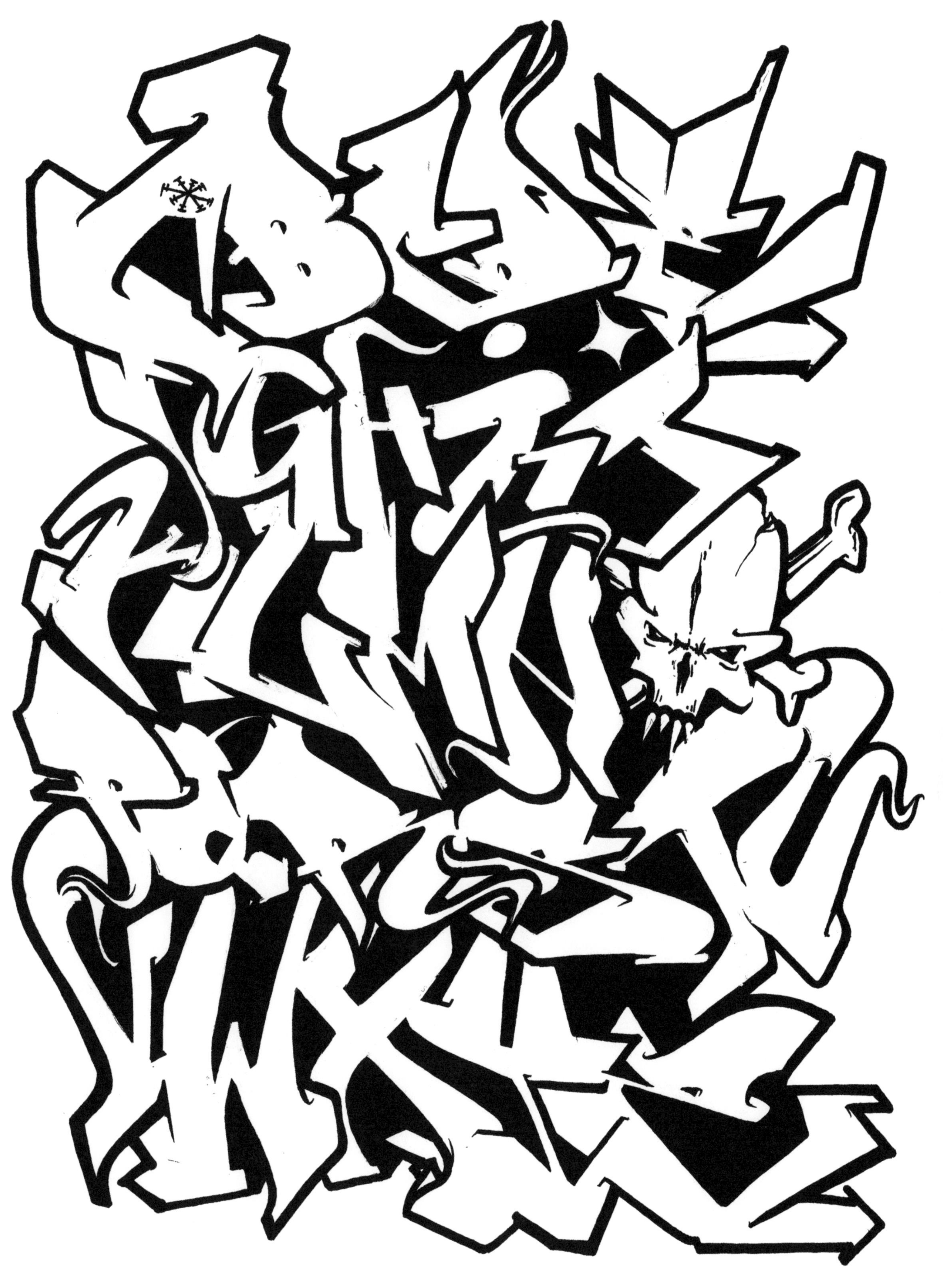

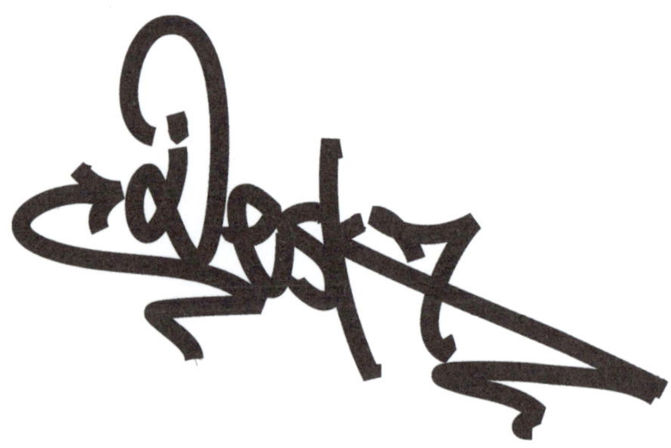

Desk7
HAMBURG, GERMANY
Crew member of SUK, THY
Writer since 1992
Favourite letter: S
www.instagram.com/desk7

Desk7's work will put a smile on your face. He doesn't just paint his name but incorporates characters and objects, or his letters take on personalities of their own. Also typical of his work is a clear, thin outline. Desk7 thinks that you should never do the same piece twice and that every piece should hold something new.

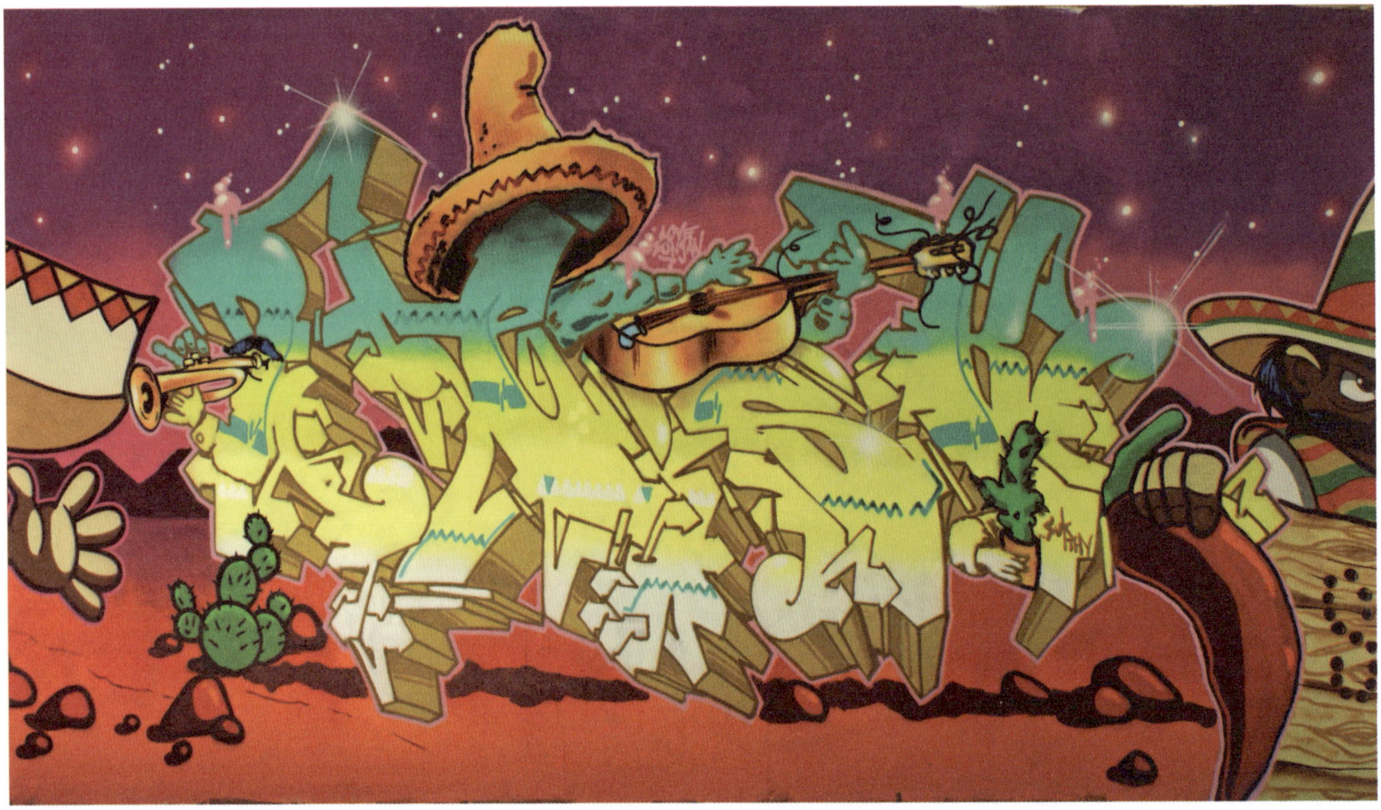

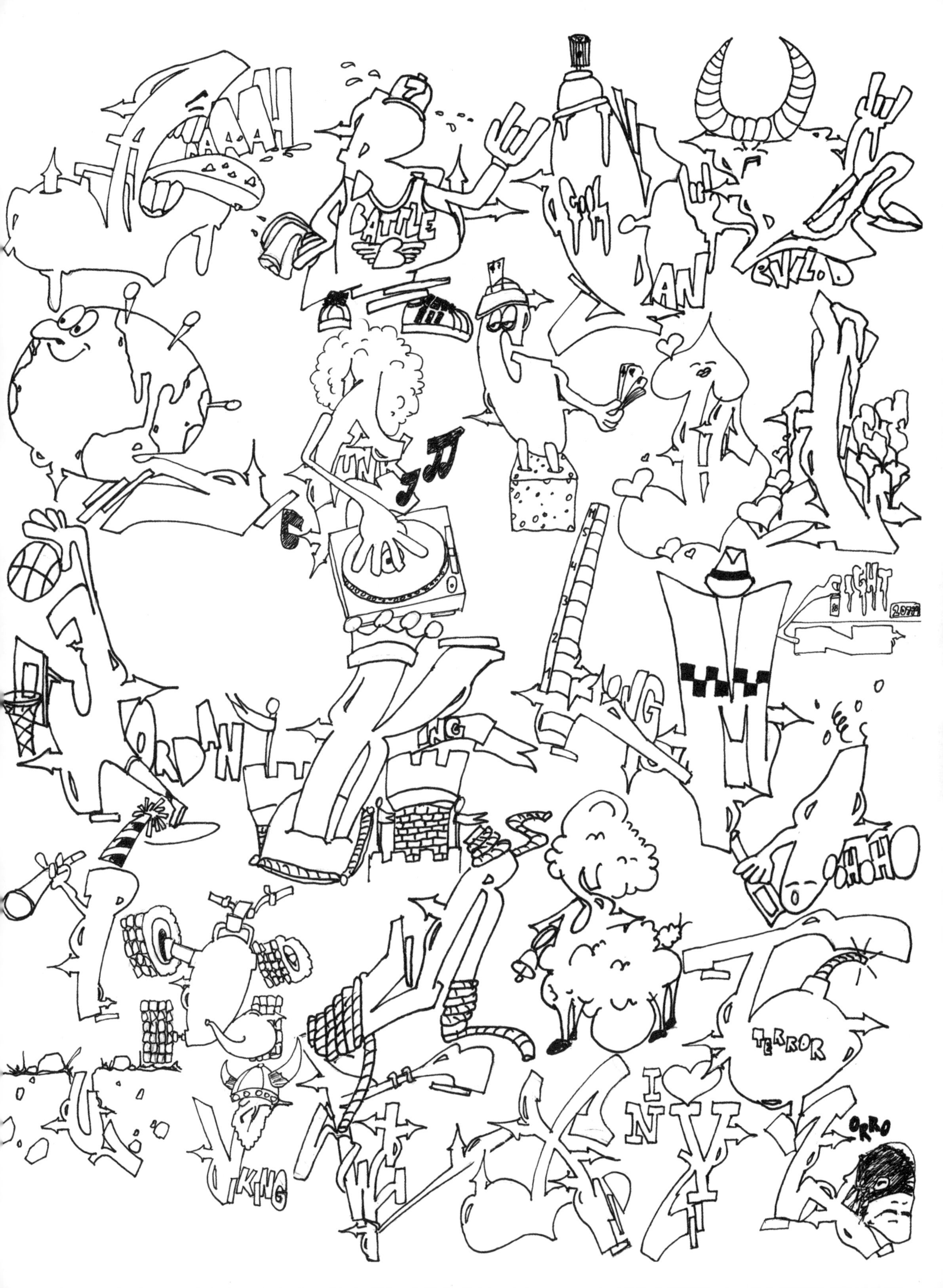

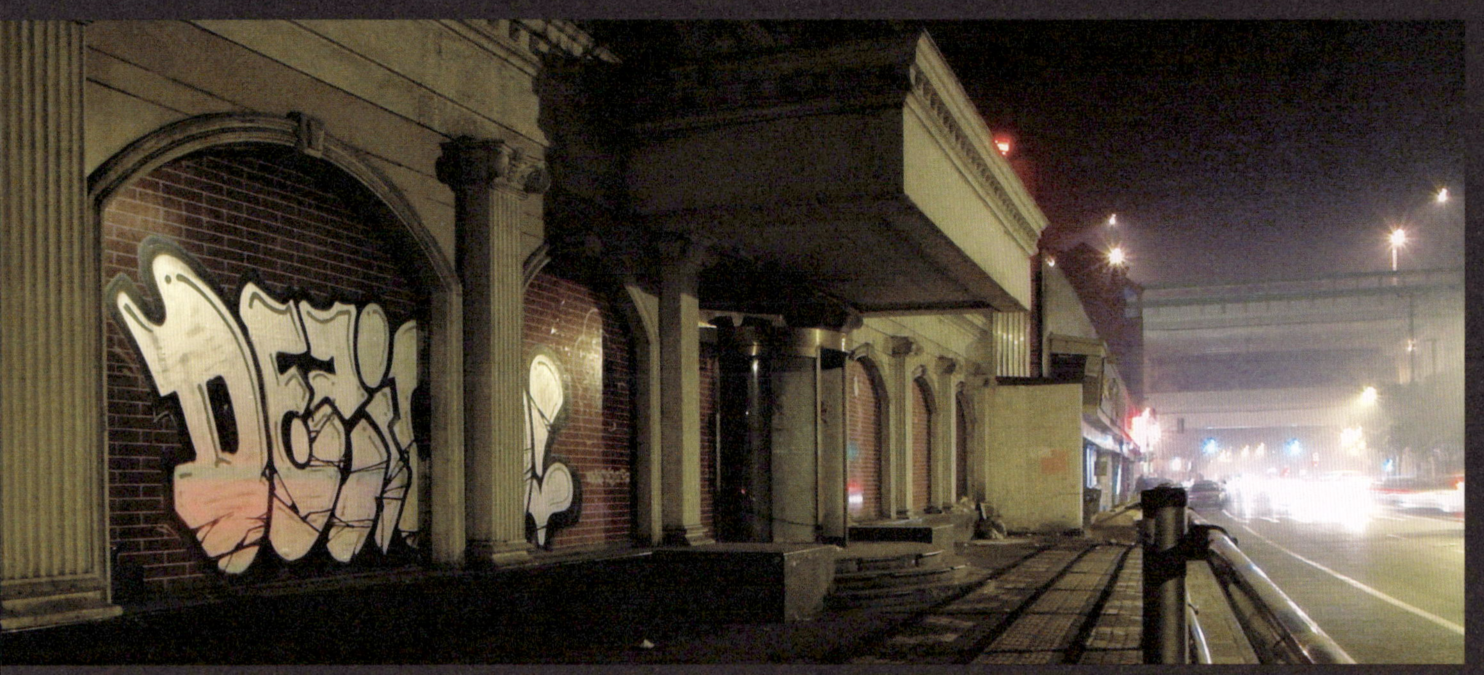

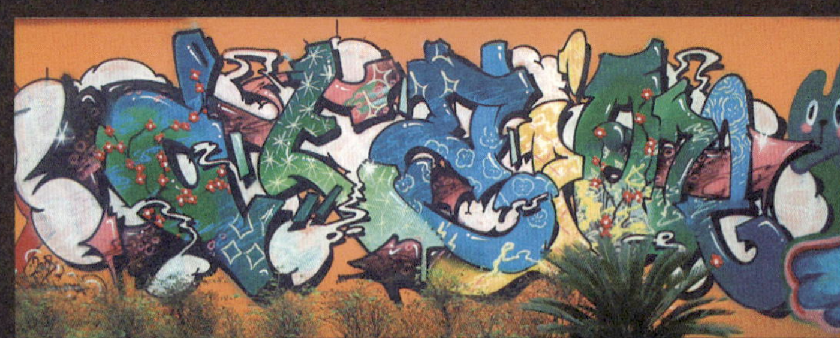

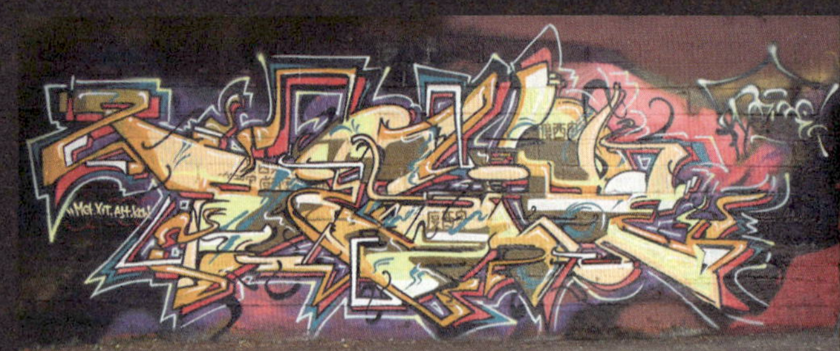

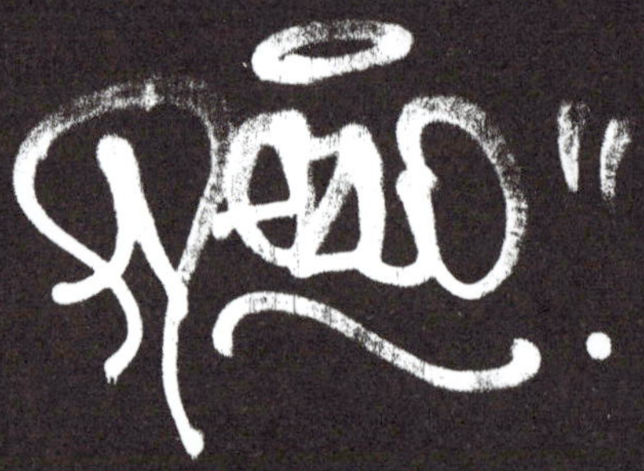

Dezio
PARIS, FRANCE
Crew member of MCT, AJT, XIT, KCW
Writer since 1994–95
www.facebook.com/deziograff

Dezio assembled his alphabet on the streets of Paris and his
adoptive home of Shanghai. His aim was to convey the essence
of graffiti. 'What is written is of little importance compared with
how it looks and where it's written,' he says. He designed the
letters in an improvised manner, painting in as many locations
as possible. 'A letter or piece has to have character. It needs
personality and flow.'

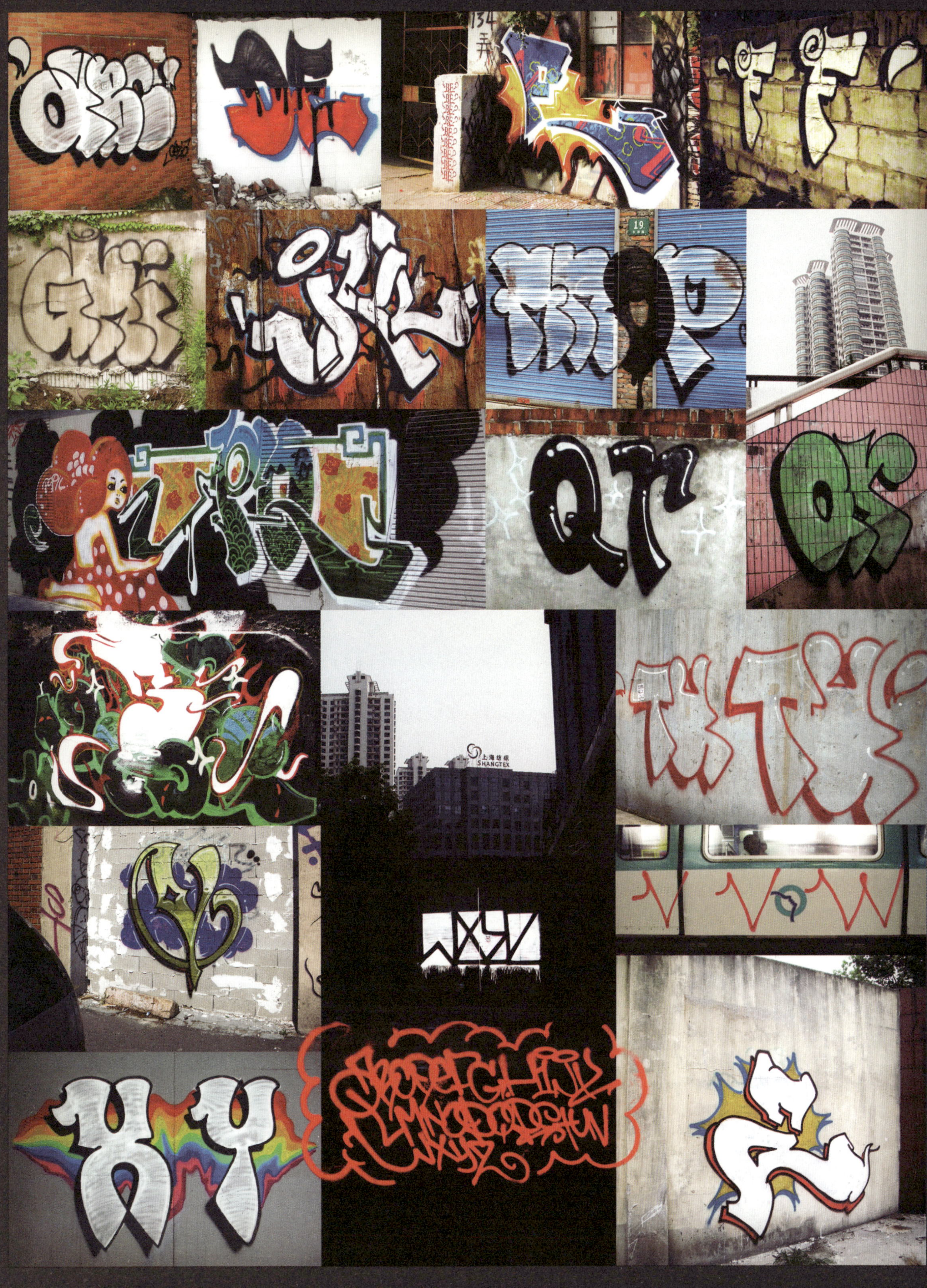

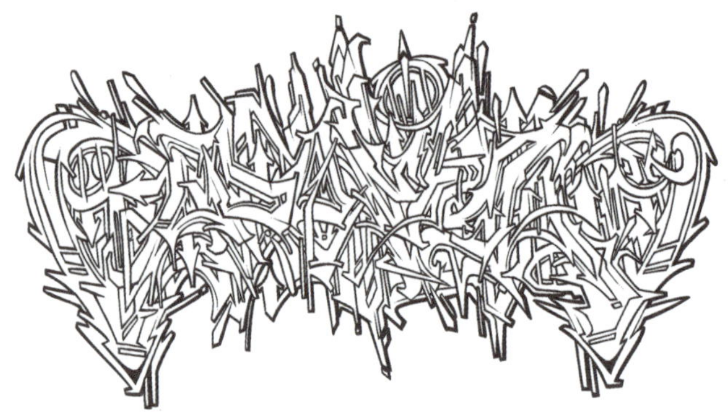

Does

SÃO PAULO, BRAZIL
Crew member of HDV, EC, TK
Writer since 1988
Favourite letters: D, O, E, S
http://doeshdv.wixsite.com/does1

Does started to develop his unique wildstyle in 1988. His complex pieces are easily recognizable, although only an expert eye can decipher them. He has always wanted to design a complete alphabet but this is his first. The act of painting is what Does likes best about graffiti.

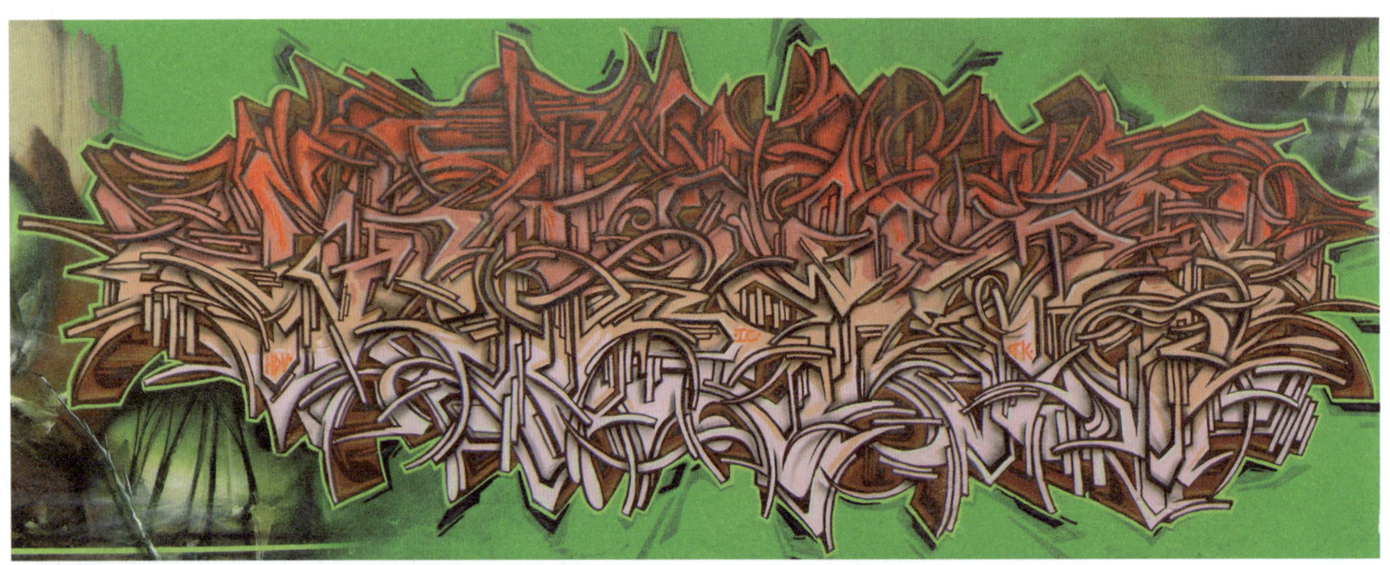

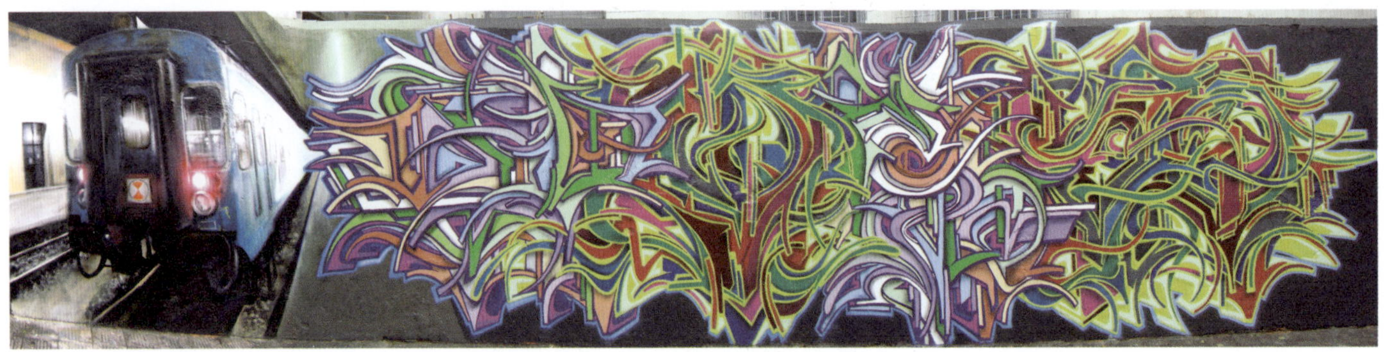

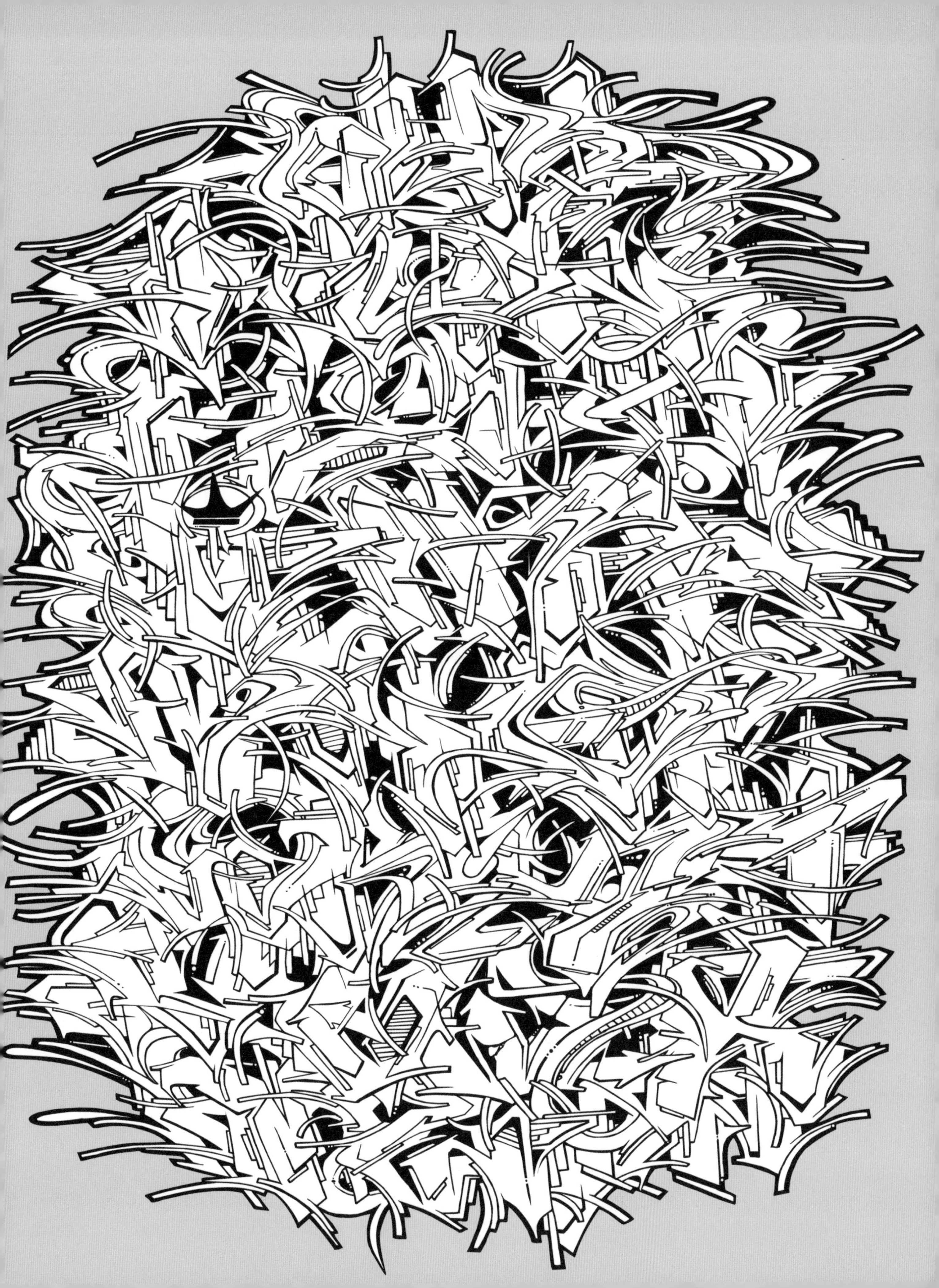

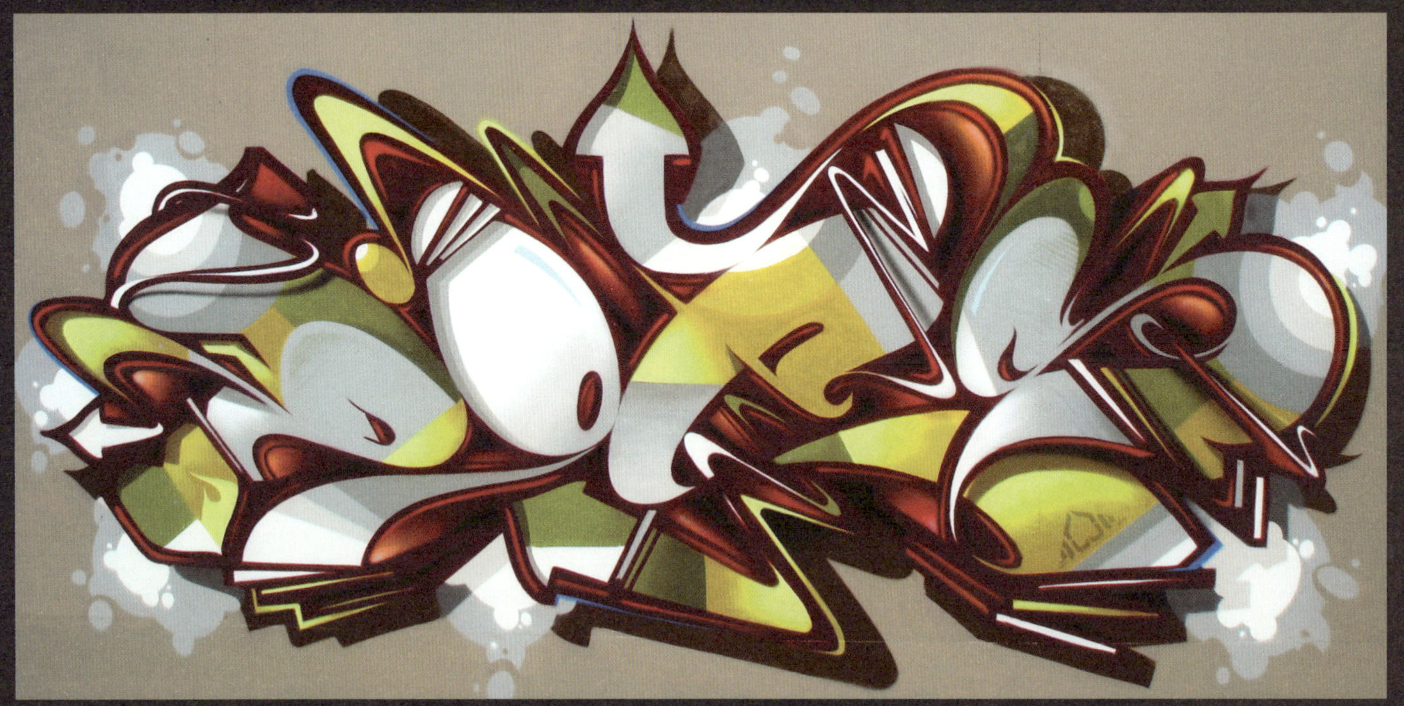

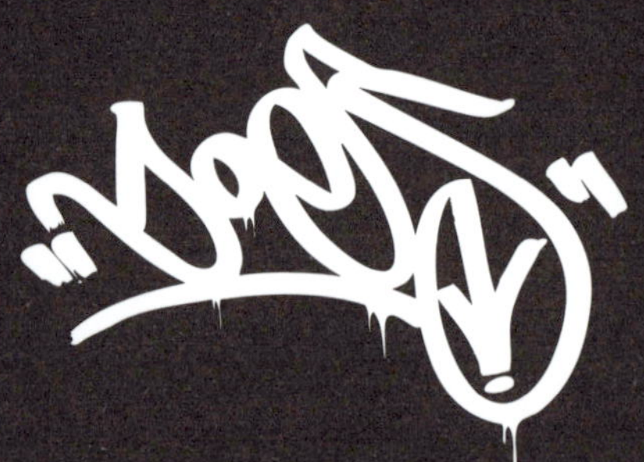

Does

SITTARD, NETHERLANDS
Crew member of LoveLetters
Writer since 1997
Favourite letter: E
www.digitaldoes.com

Does did a few pieces between 1997 and 2000 and then stopped painting for three years. In 2003 he returned to the scene and is now a well-known member of the LoveLetters crew. 'I can enjoy rough lines and drips,' he says, discussing style in general. 'But for me a good piece consists of great letters, a strong use of colours and refinements.'

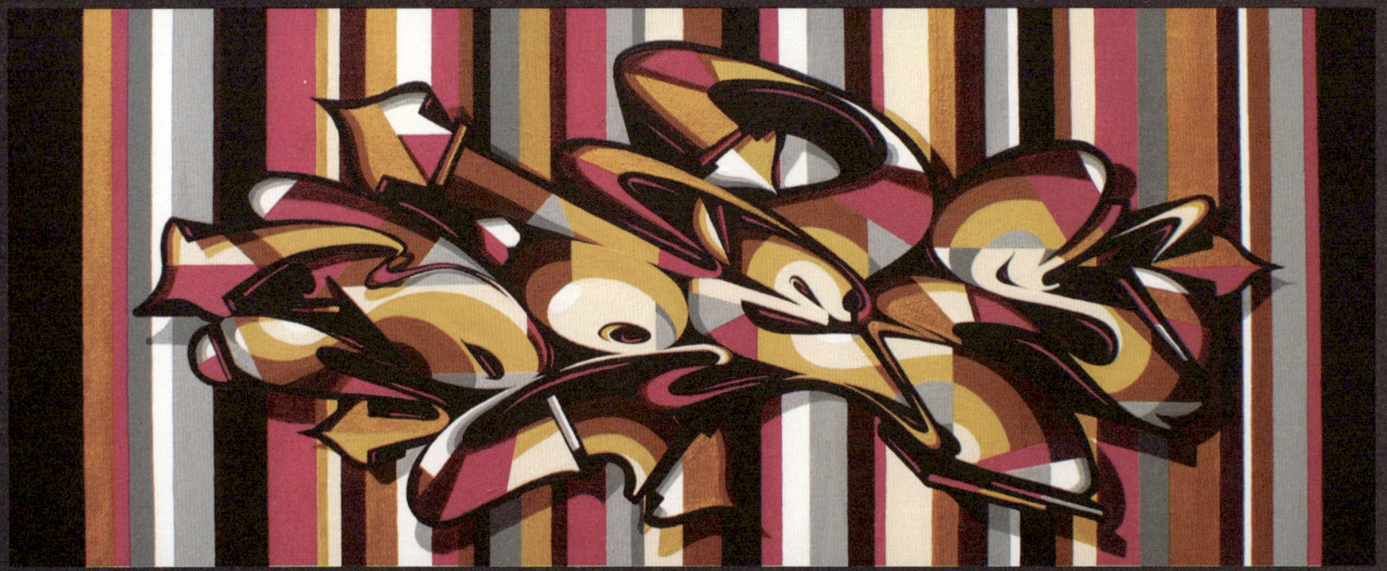

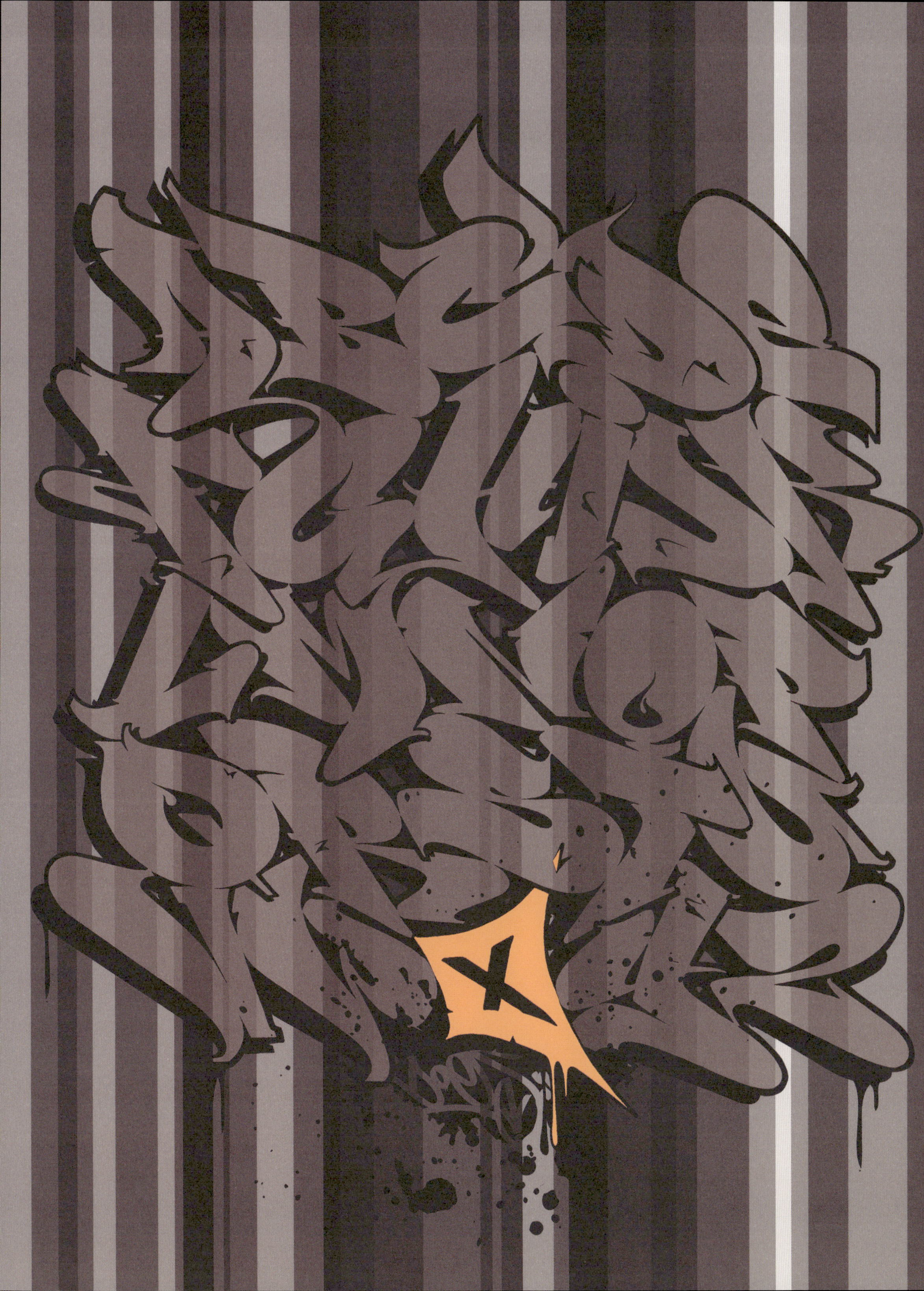

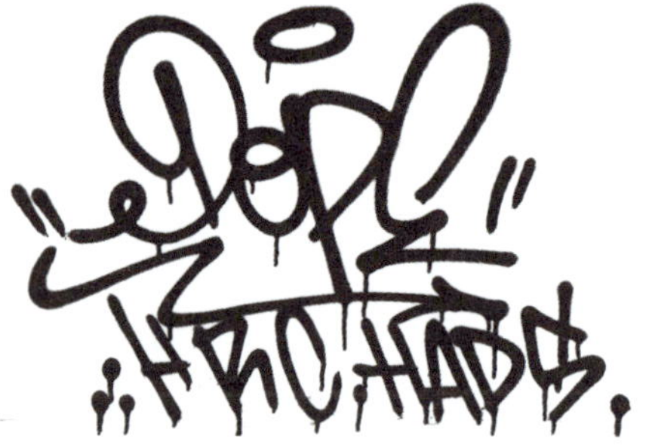

Dope78

HALLE, GERMANY
Crew member of HADS, HRC
Writer since 1992
Favourite letter: E
www.myspace.com/dope78

Dope78's pieces are a combination of straight lines and strong curves. He tends to use a lot of colours in a single piece, but keeps the shapes of his letters defined and legible. He likes pieces to look original but not too experimental. The best thing about graffiti is 'spending a day painting with friends', he says.

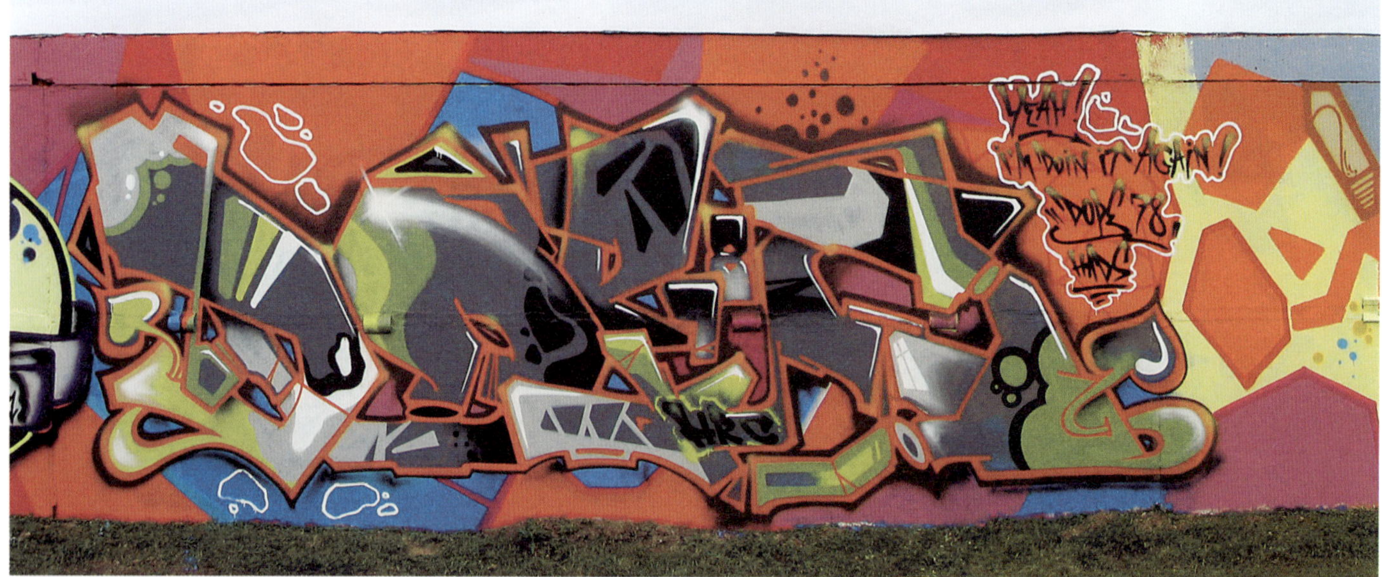

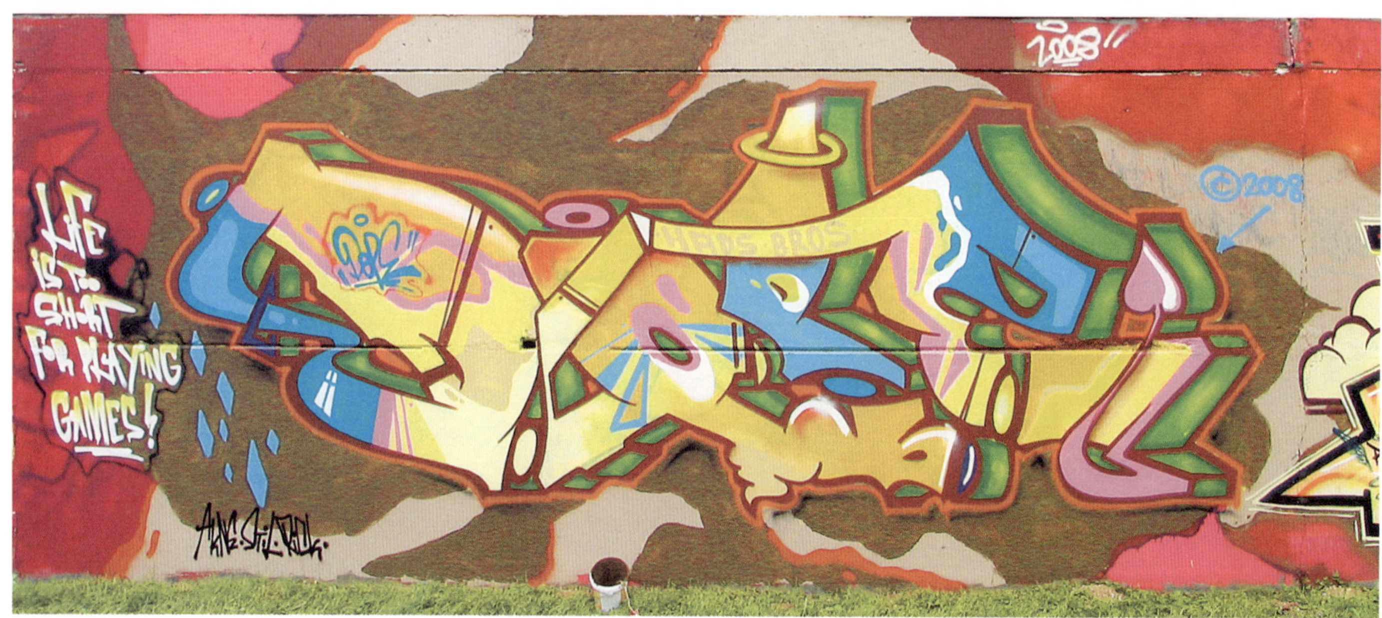

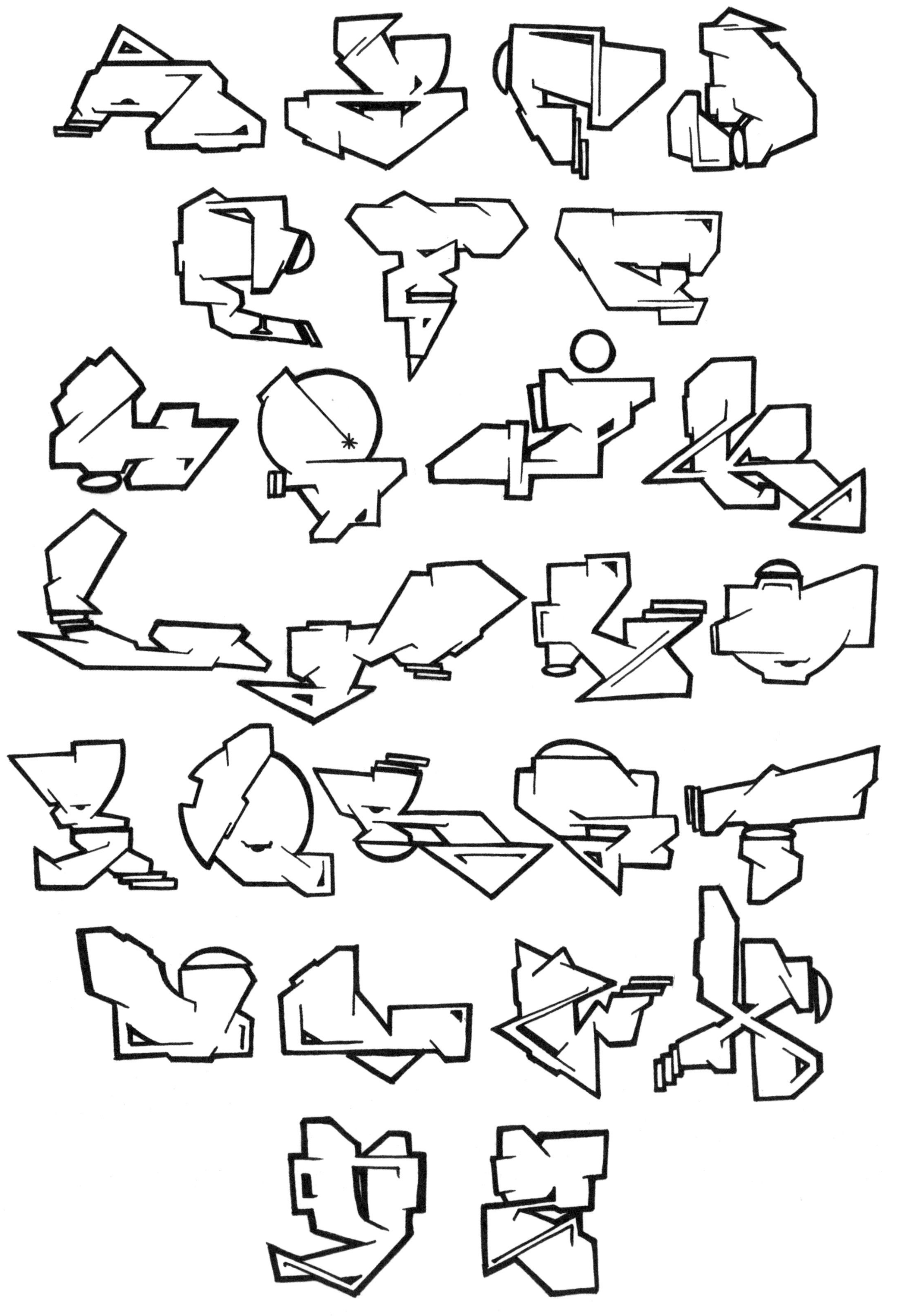

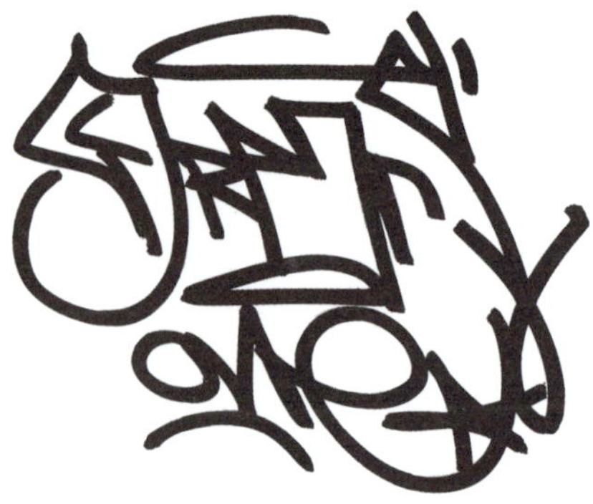

Dream
BASEL, SWITZERLAND
Crew member of TWS, GBF, FTP
Writer since 1989
Favourite letter: D

Dream's pieces are dynamic and legible, with a good choice of colour and technique. Over the past few decades he has created many outstanding pieces, especially along the Basel line. His alphabet is a compilation of selected pieces that were painted on various surfaces between 1990 and 2010. The potential to make a big impression on people is one of the best things about graffiti, he says.

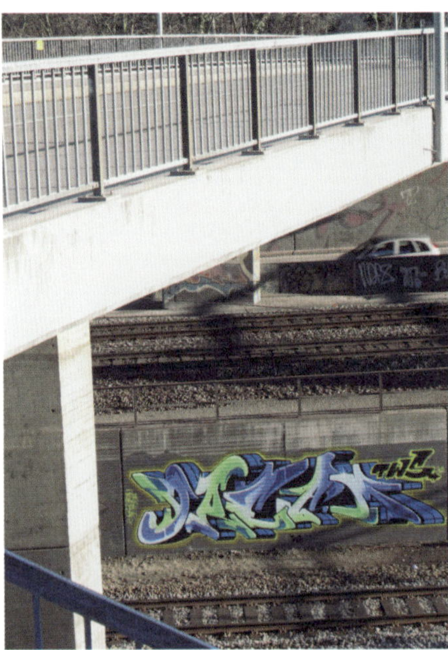

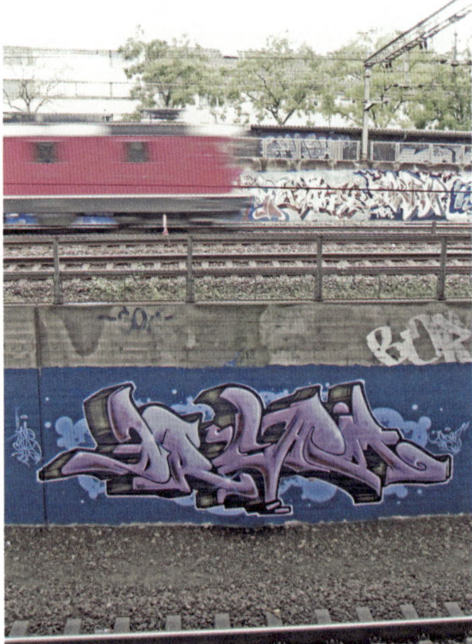

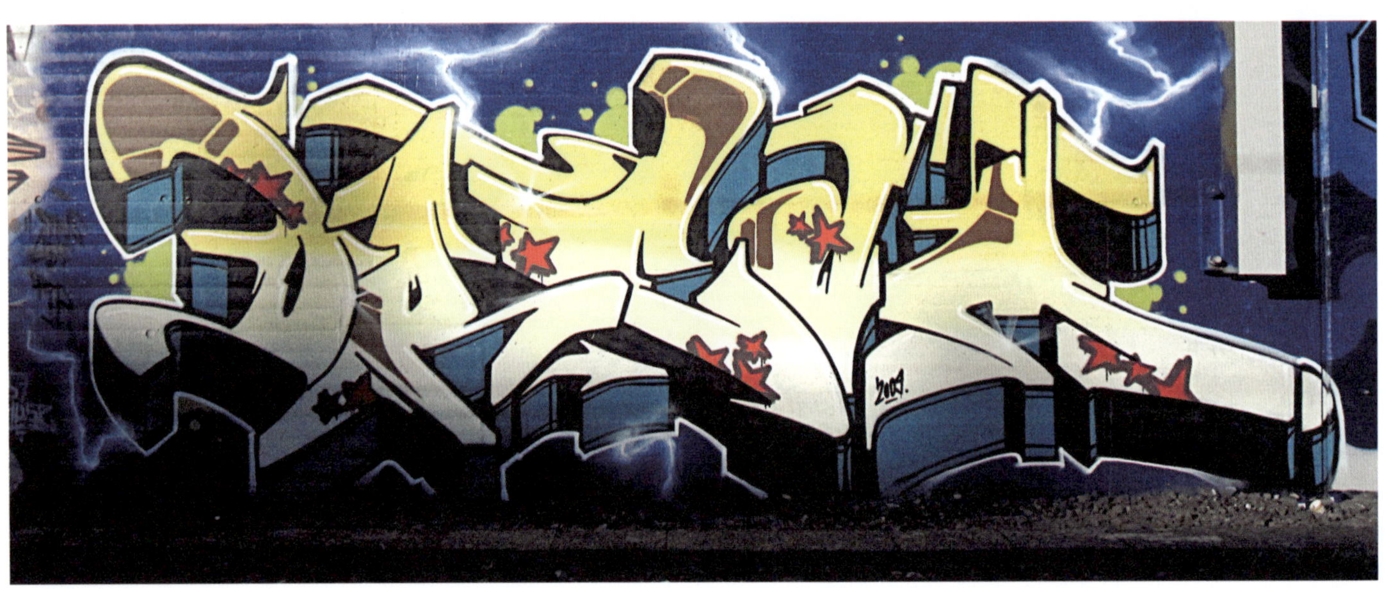

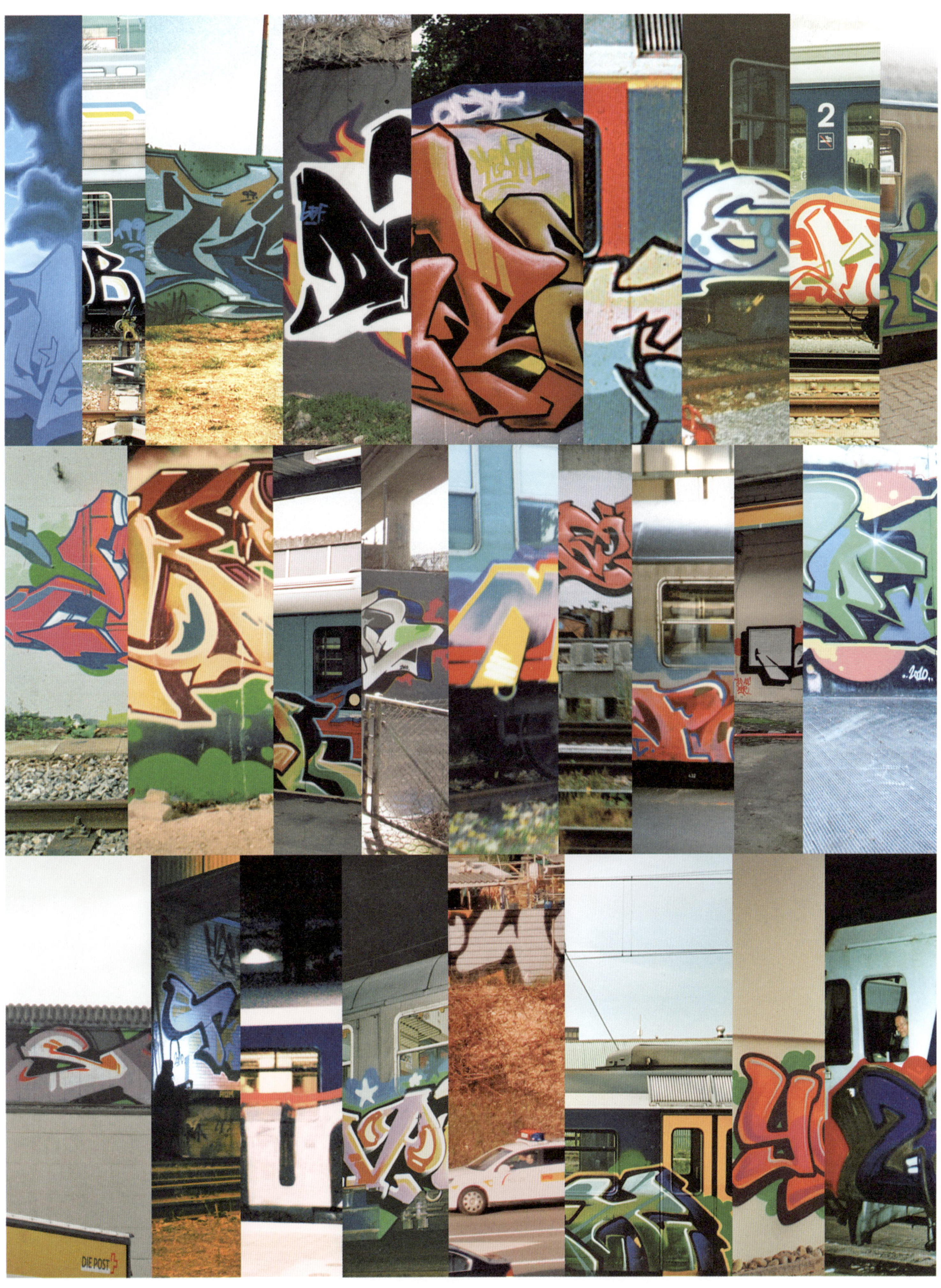

Erni Vales

NEW YORK CITY, USA
Crew member of NewaveCru
Writer since 1981
Favourite letter: E
www.ernidesigns.com

Erni initially sketched the outlines of the letters in his alphabet by hand and added colour in Adobe Photoshop. The design was then transformed into the first of three lines of silver jewelry created by the artist in 2009, in collaboration with Dax Jewellery. 'Balance is the most important element in creating a good piece,' says Erni. He makes a good living from his art and likes to meet people from around the world.

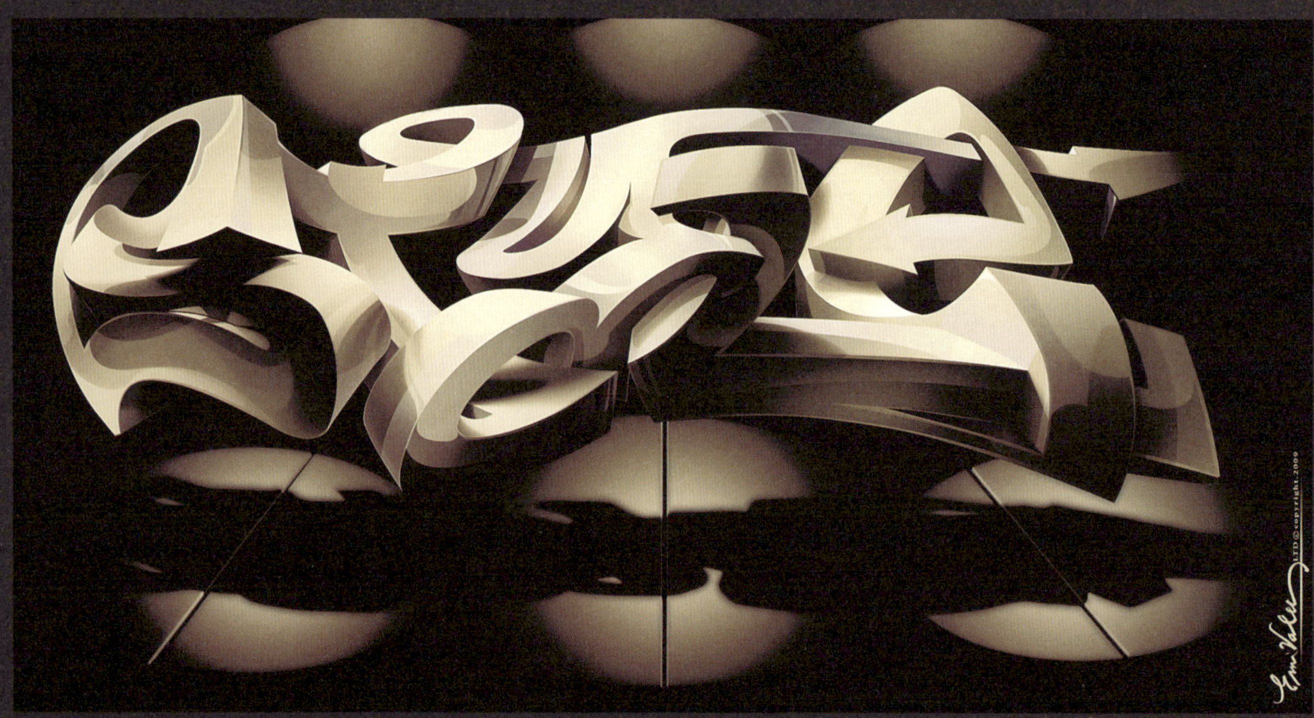

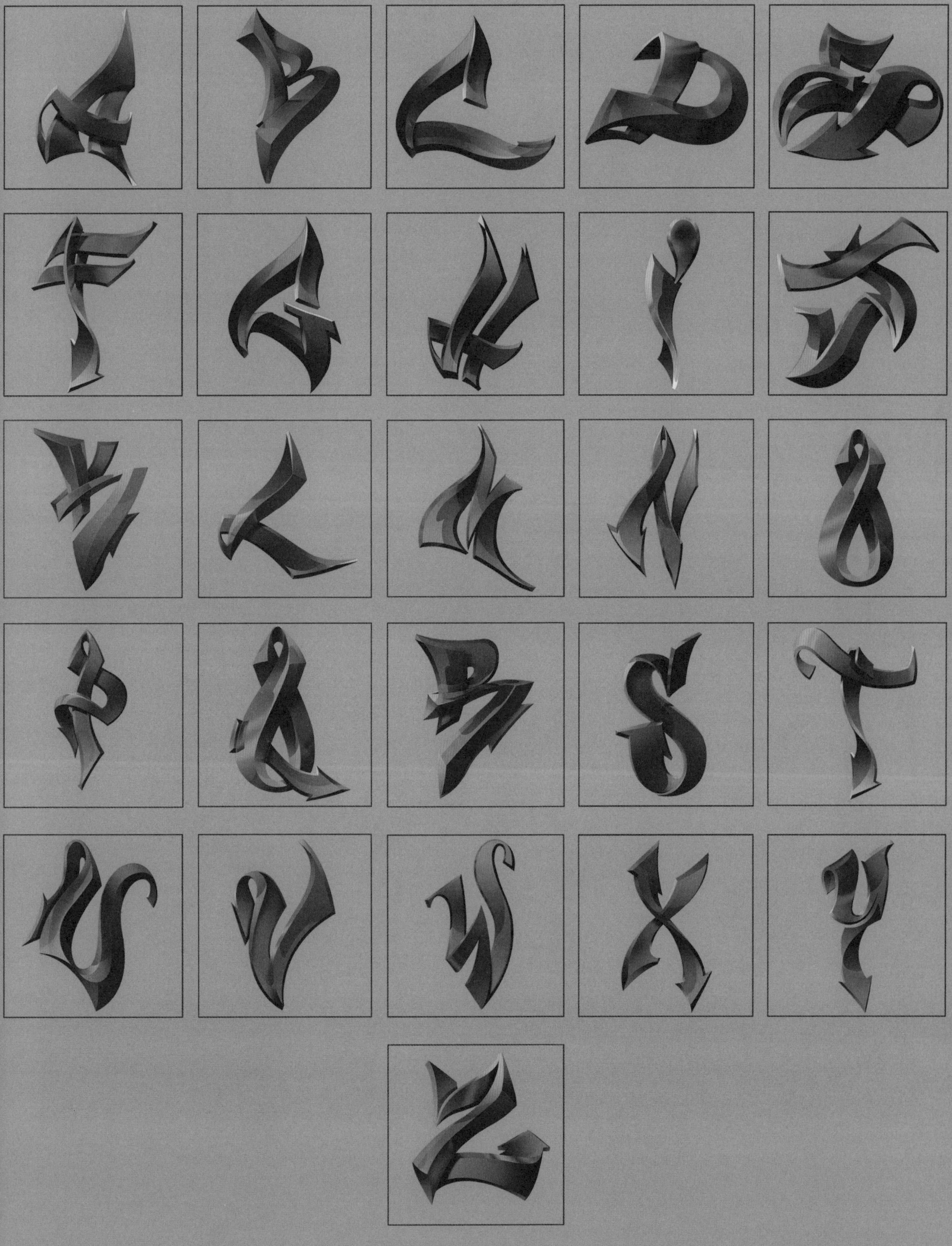

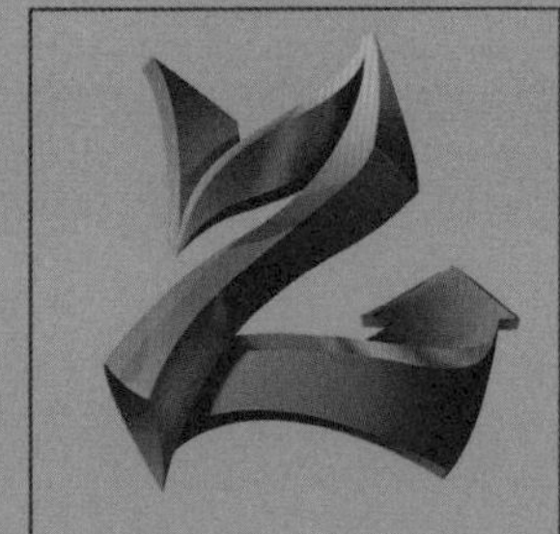

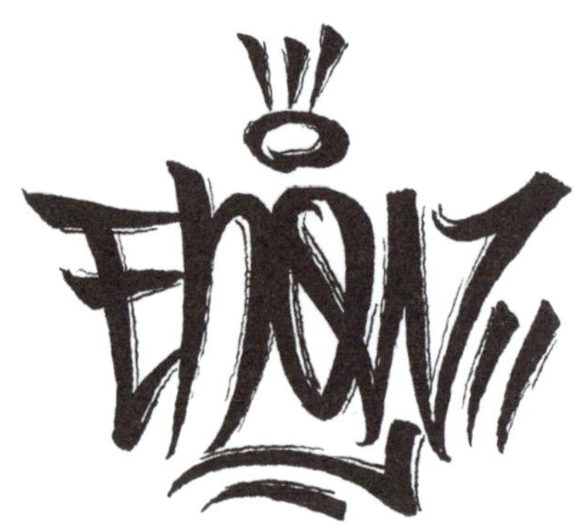

Esow

TOKYO, JAPAN
Crew member of RDK, KTC, DOA
Writer since 1998
Favourite letter: S

Japanese artists and illustrators have been a strong influence
on Esow's work. He mostly works with characters, and therefore
keeps his letters simple and legible.

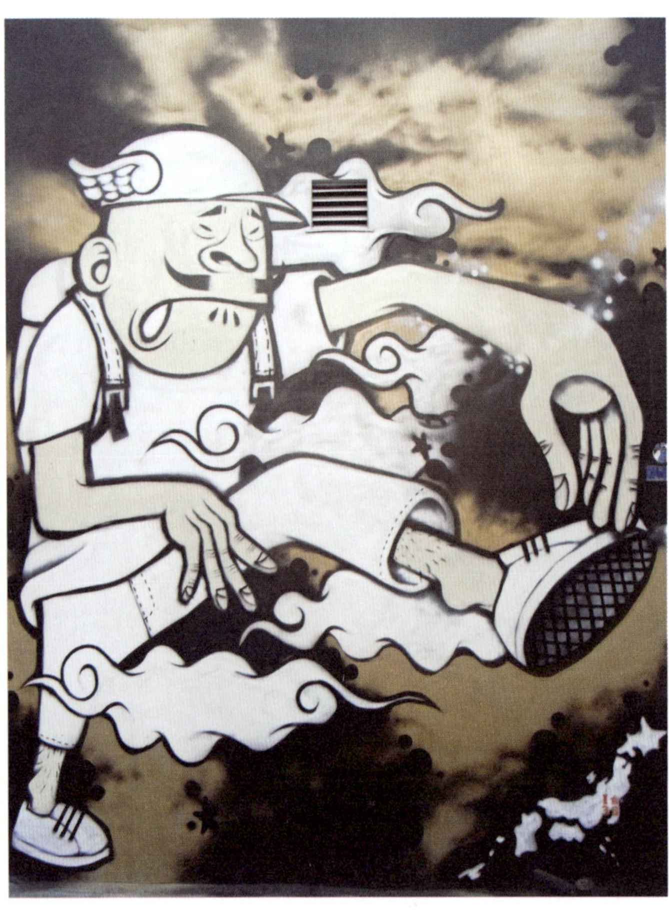

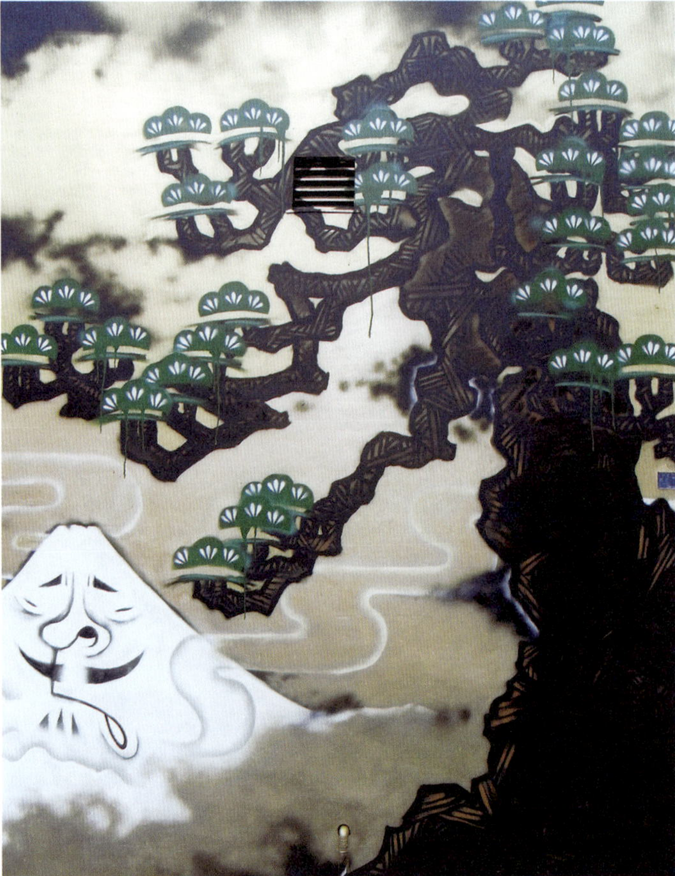

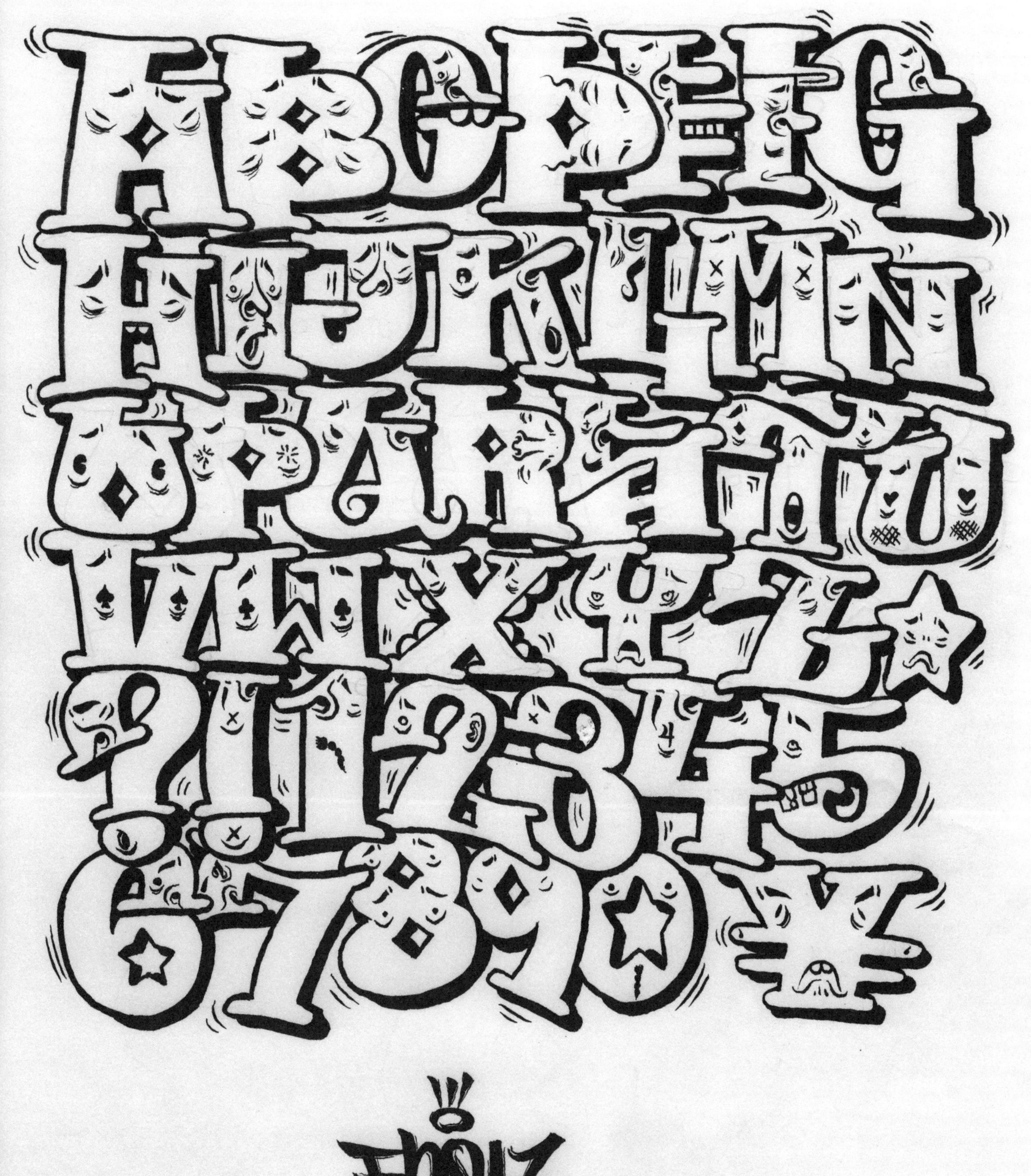

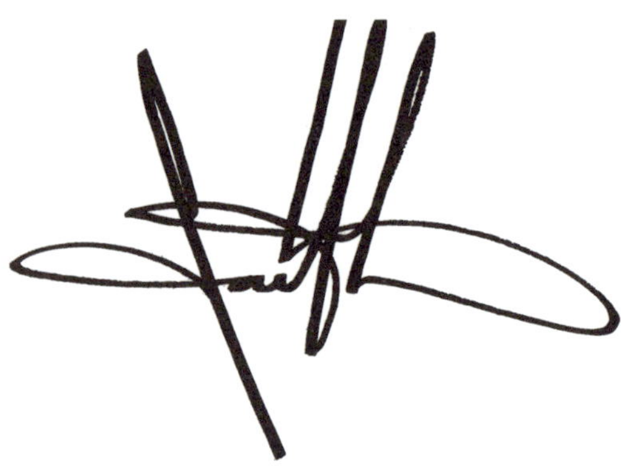

Faith47
CAPE TOWN, SOUTH AFRICA
Writer since 1997
www.faith47.com

Faith47 does not simply write her name, but often explores the issues facing her native South Africa. She paints her characters and typographic pieces in abandoned places, on the shacks of the poor and in the streets of Cape Town. For many years she has followed invitations to paint in countries around the world and has exhibited in galleries. She loves graffiti for 'the physical and emotional experiences of exploring cities, the people you meet on the way and the situations you find yourself in'.

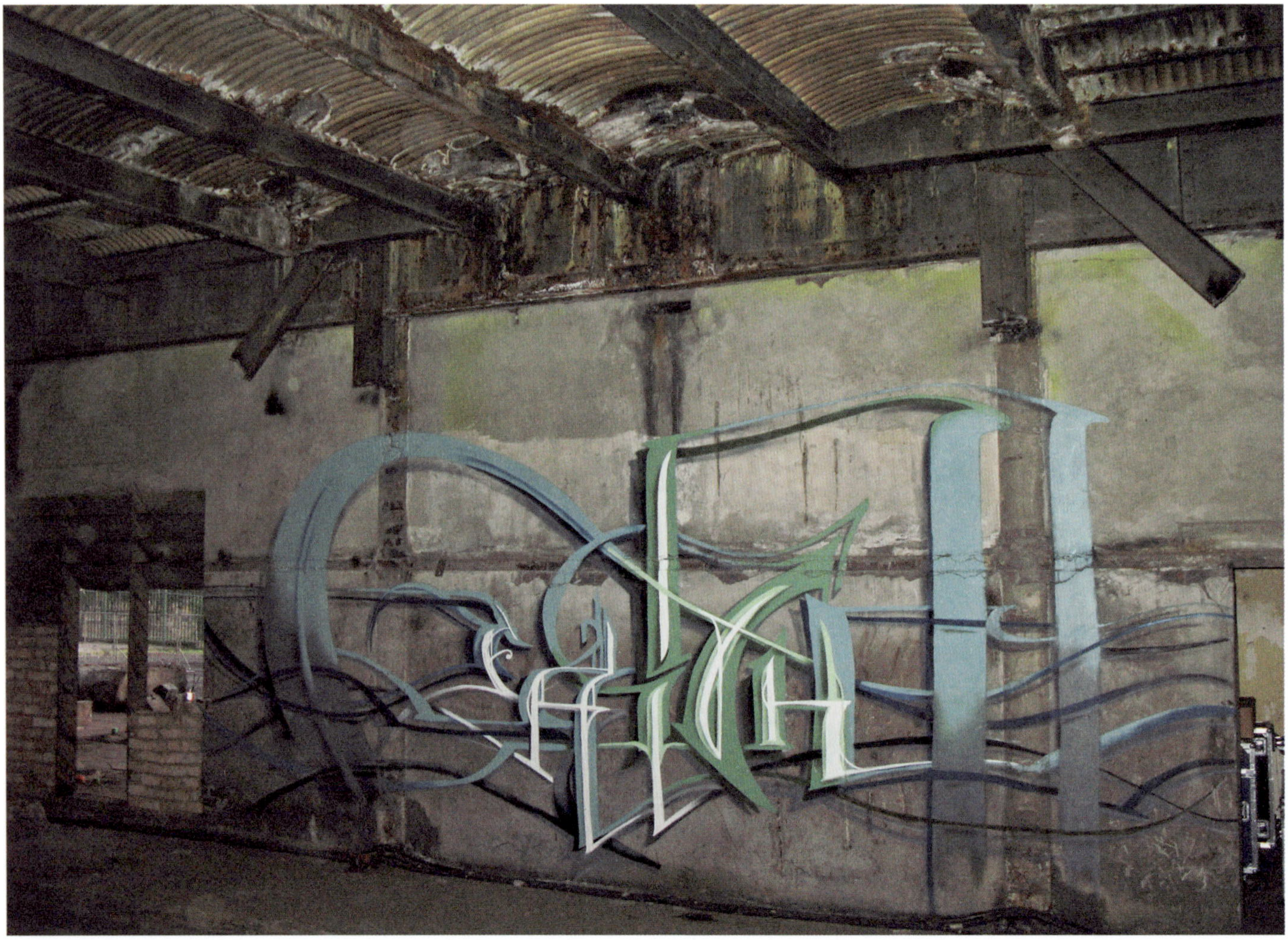

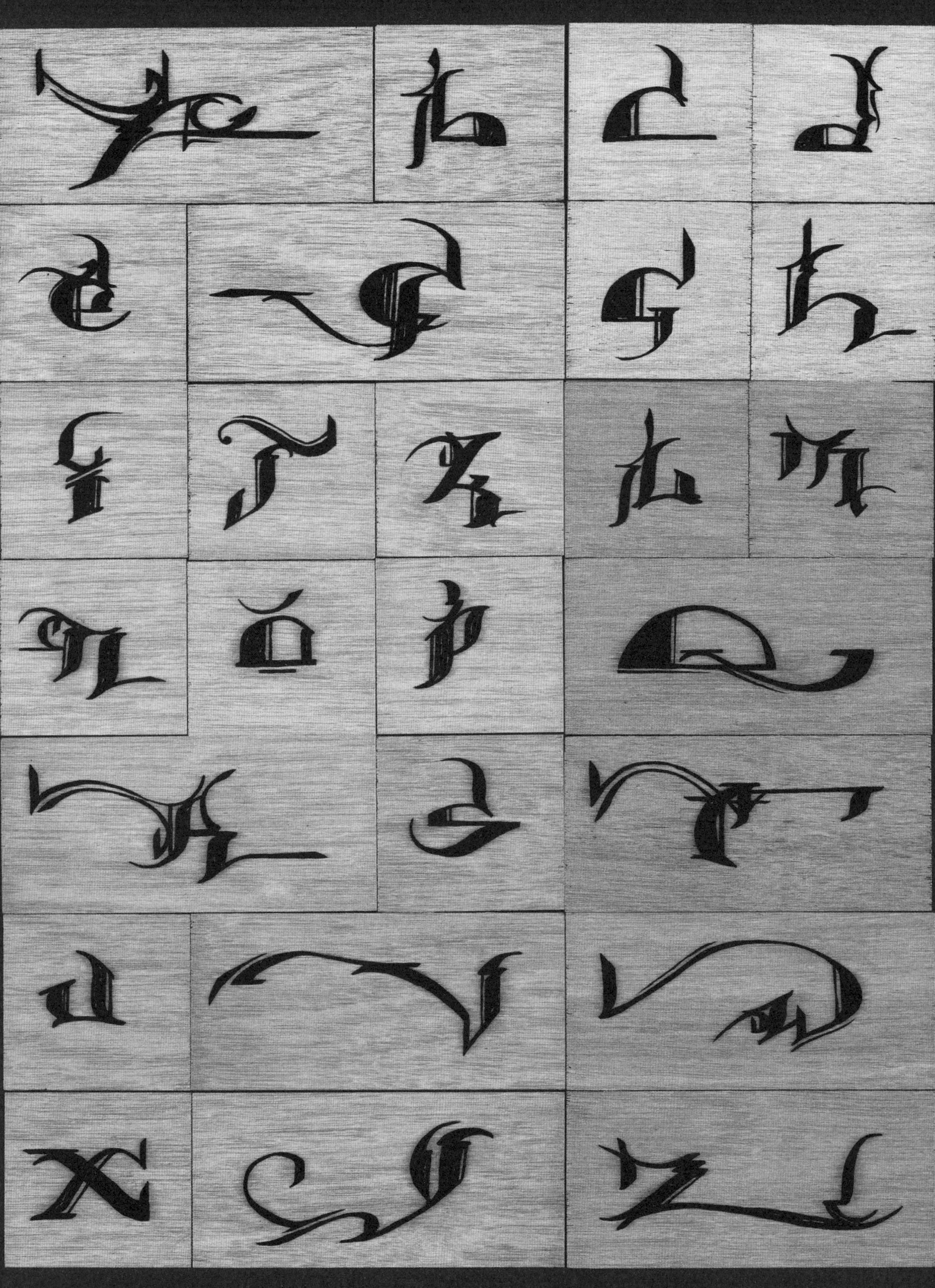

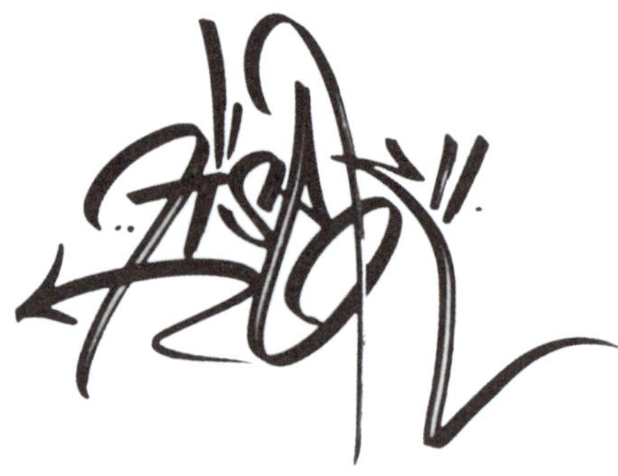

Fisek

SANTIAGO, CHILE
Crew member of CWP, CEC, ELCARTEL, STGOUNDER
Writer since 1992
Favourite letter: F
www.flickr.com/fisek

Fisek is passionate about wildstyle. He decided to apply this style to his alphabet, using the interlocking letters as building blocks within the overall structure of Fisek's favourite letter 'F'. Creating his own style is his main priority, and each letter must have personality – not just the piece as a whole.

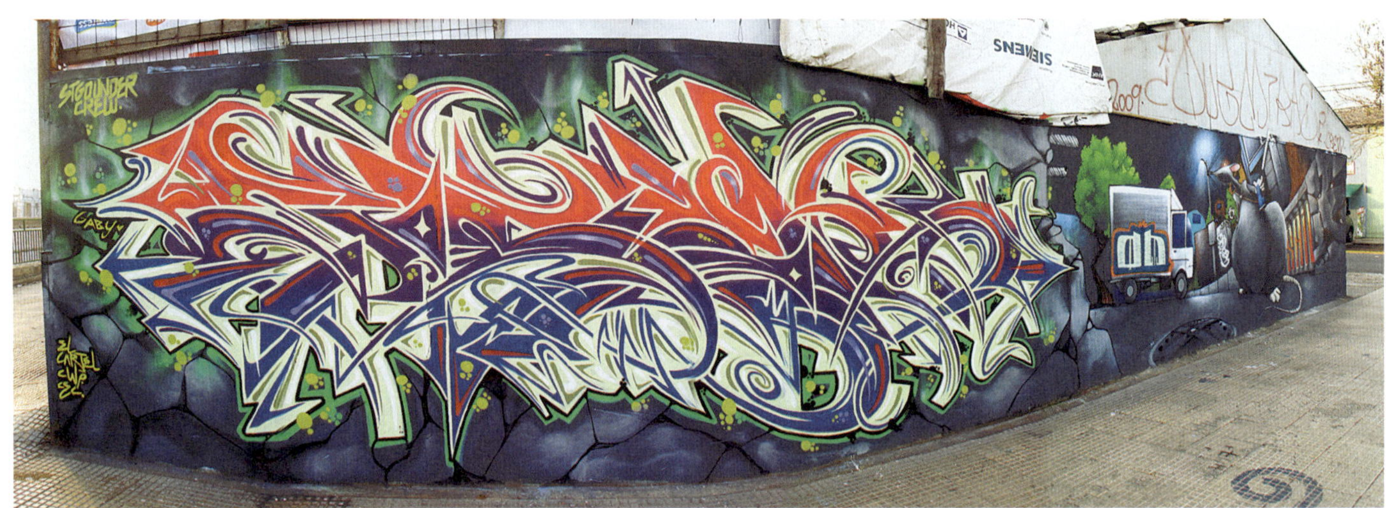

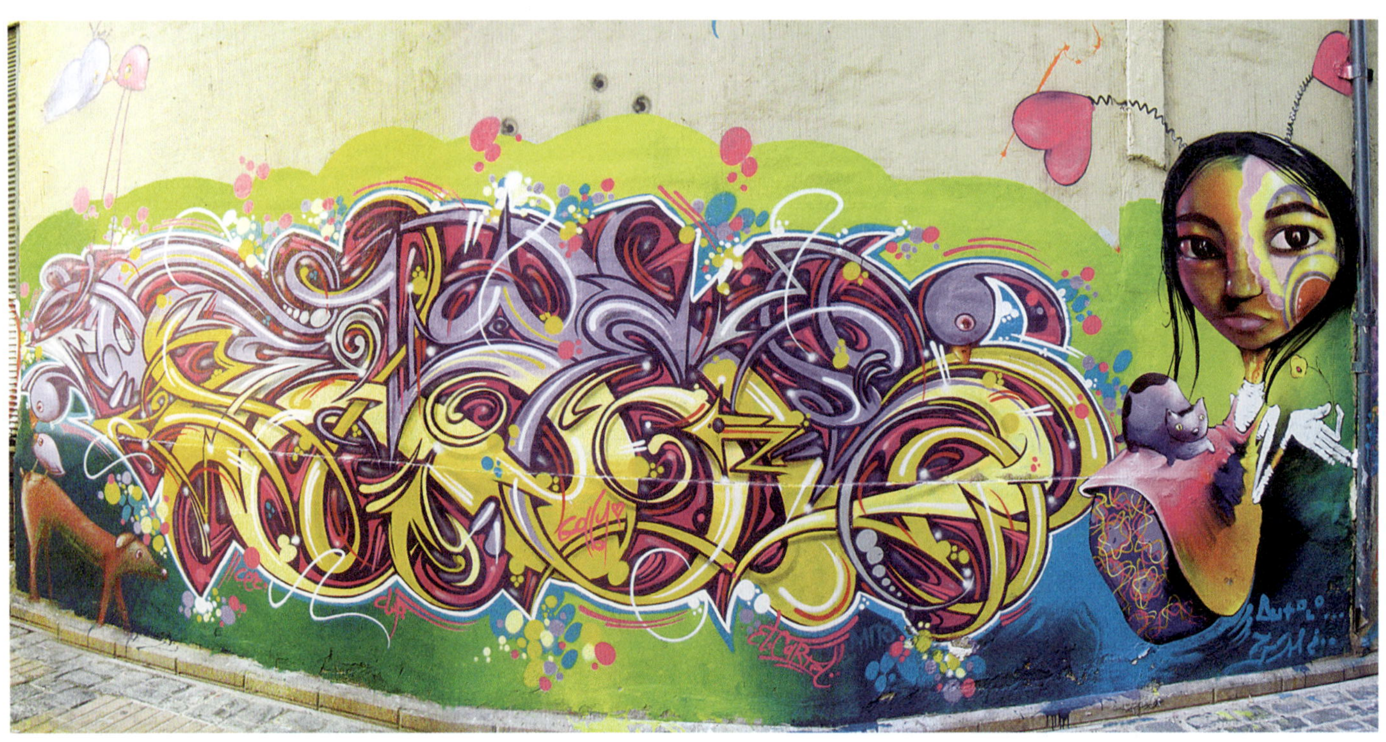

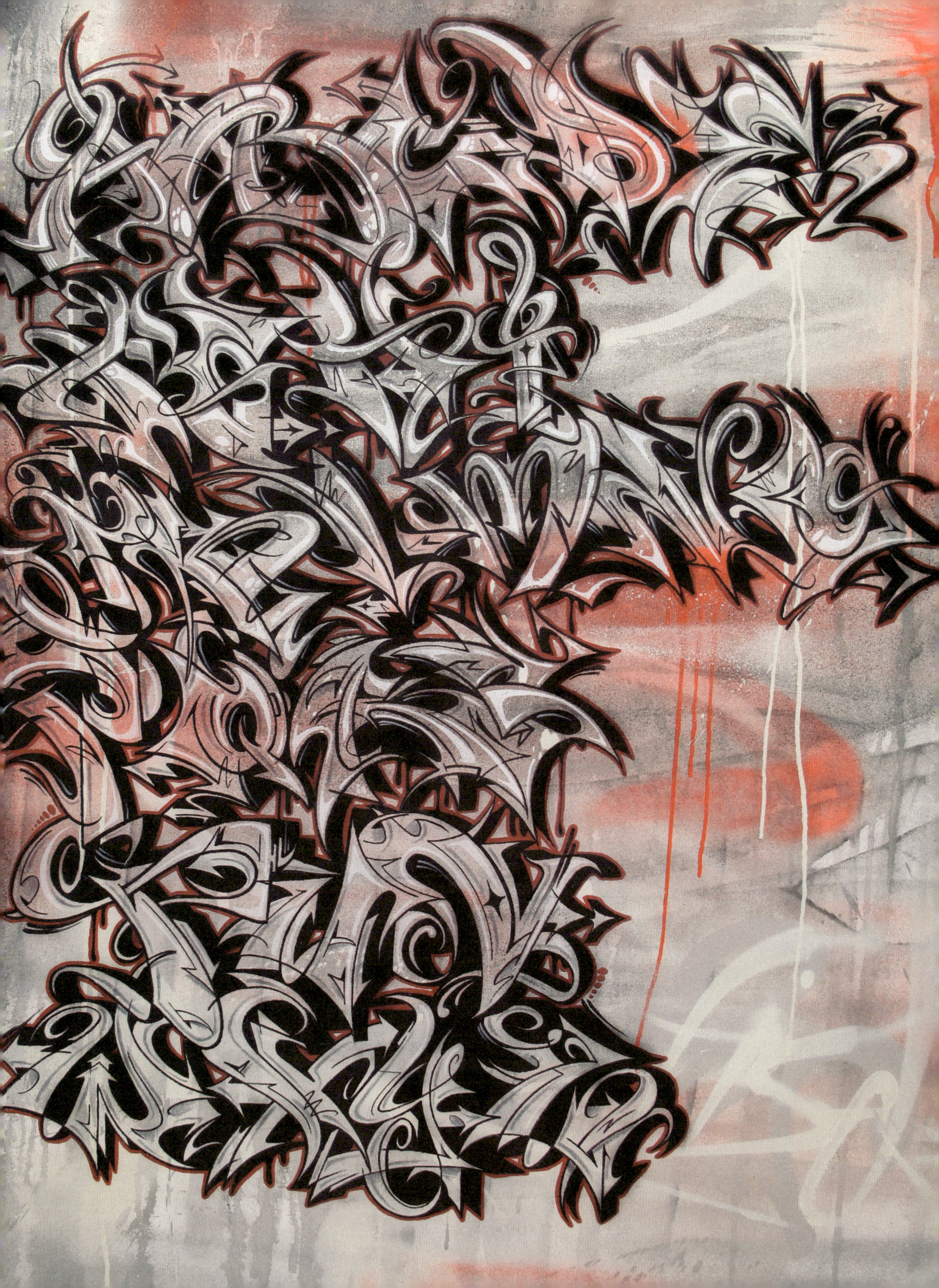

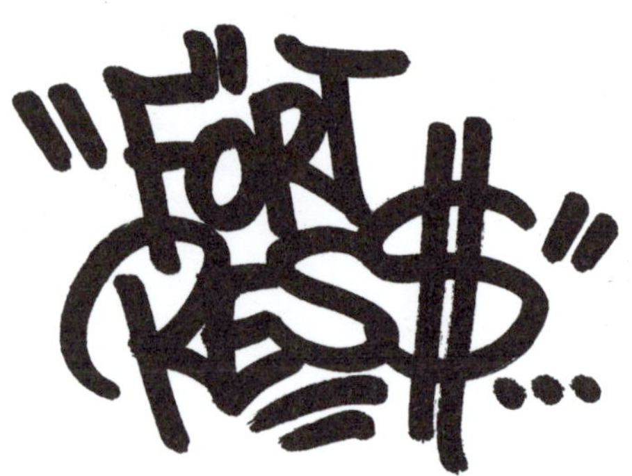

Flying Fortress
HAMBURG, GERMANY
Crew member of 243, VRS, WAB, YCP, RWK, ES
Favourite letter: E
www.flying-fortress.de

Flying Fortress is known for his helmet-clad bear character. He chose the name having assembled a model of the Second World War bomber as a child. It reminded him of the Millennium Falcon from the *Star Wars* movies. The word 'Flying' represents man's ultimate dream of freedom, while 'Fortress' symbolizes our need to feel safe. He designed his alphabet to look like the sticker sheet that is usually included with a kit to complete the model and make it look like the genuine article.

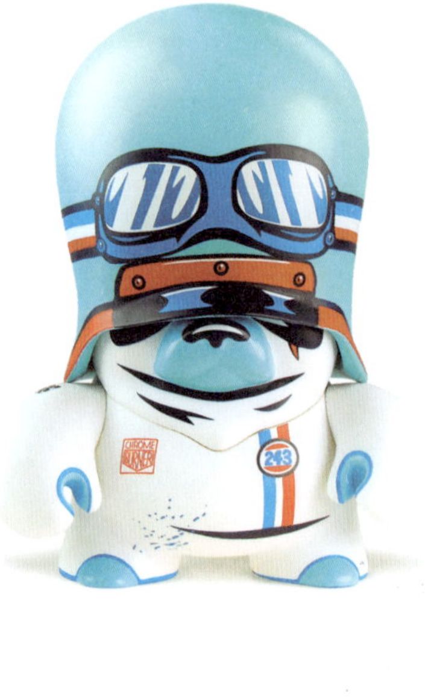

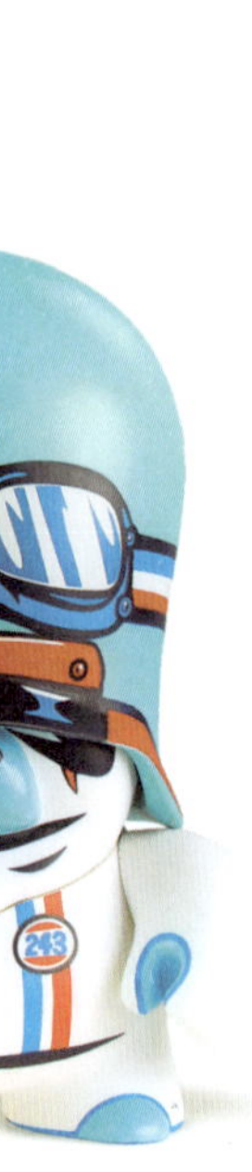

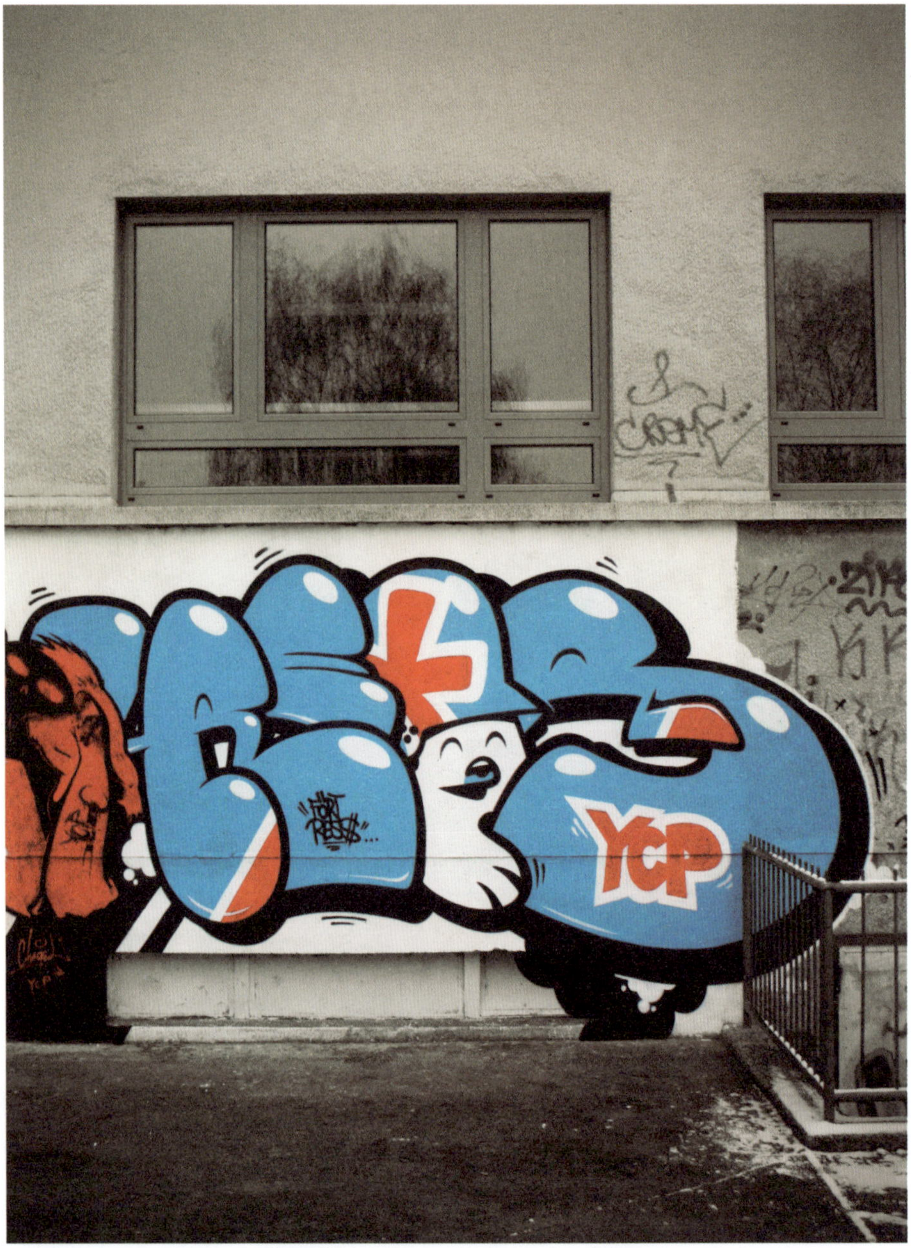

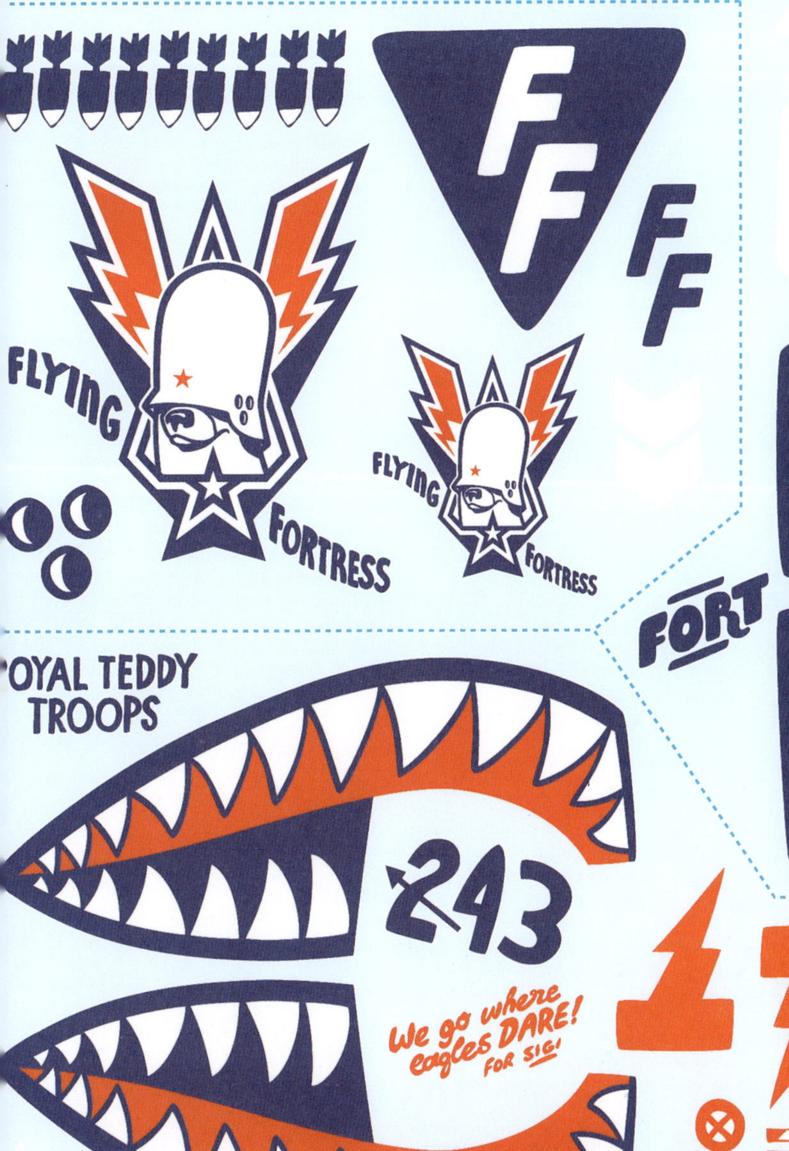

FLYING FORTRESS
FLYING FORTRESS
ROYAL TEDDY TROOPS
243
We go where eagles DARE!
FOR SIG!
FORT

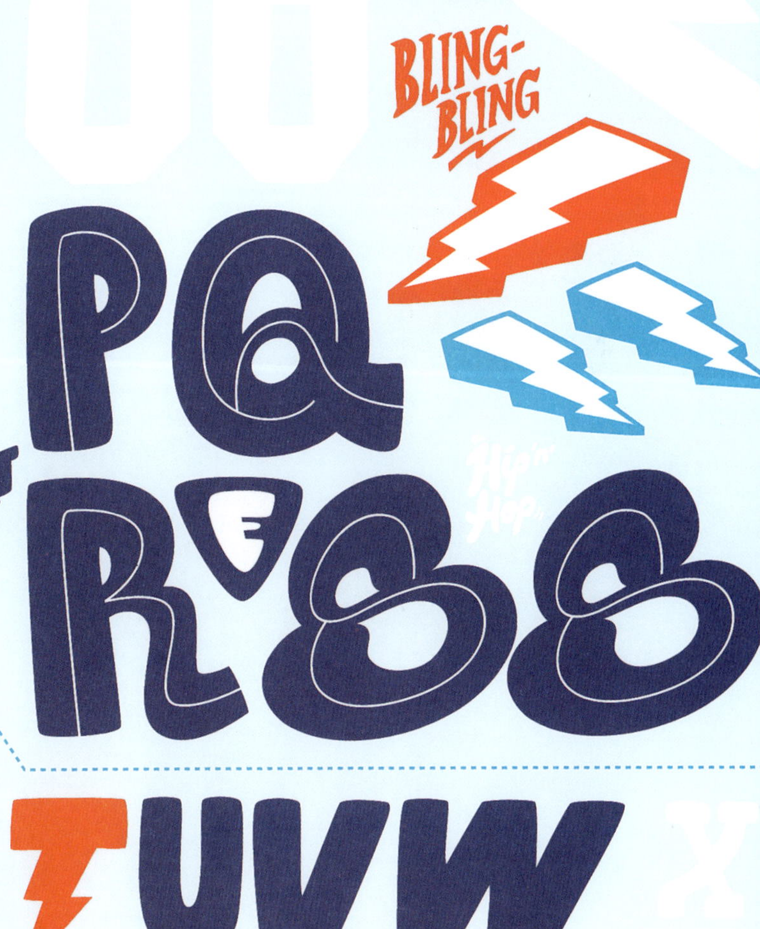

BLING-BLING
FLY1NG FÖRTR3SS

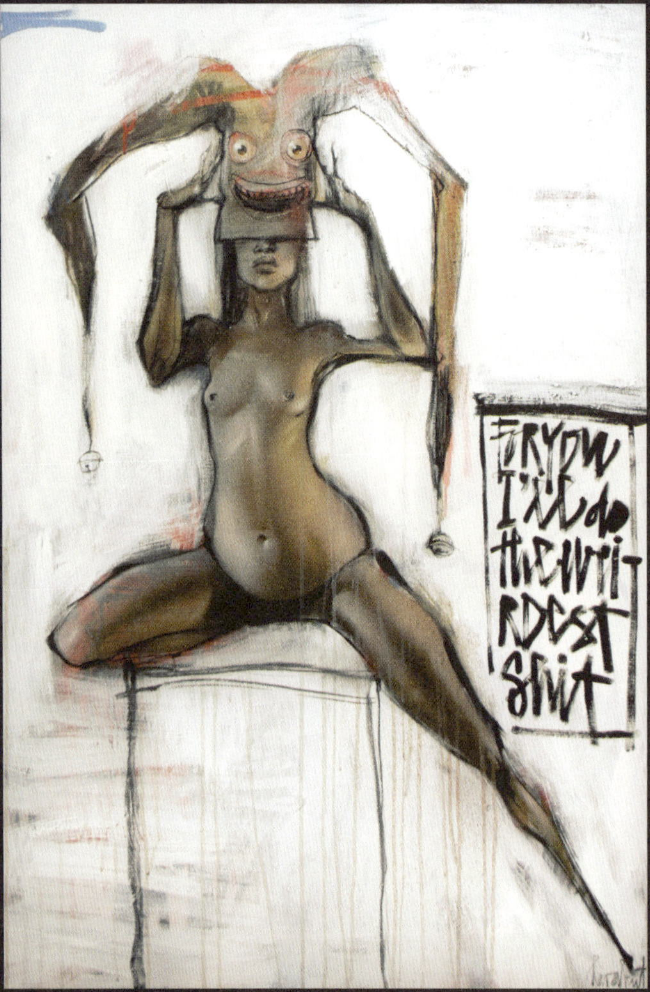

FOR YOU
I'LL DO
THE WEIR-
DEST
SHIT

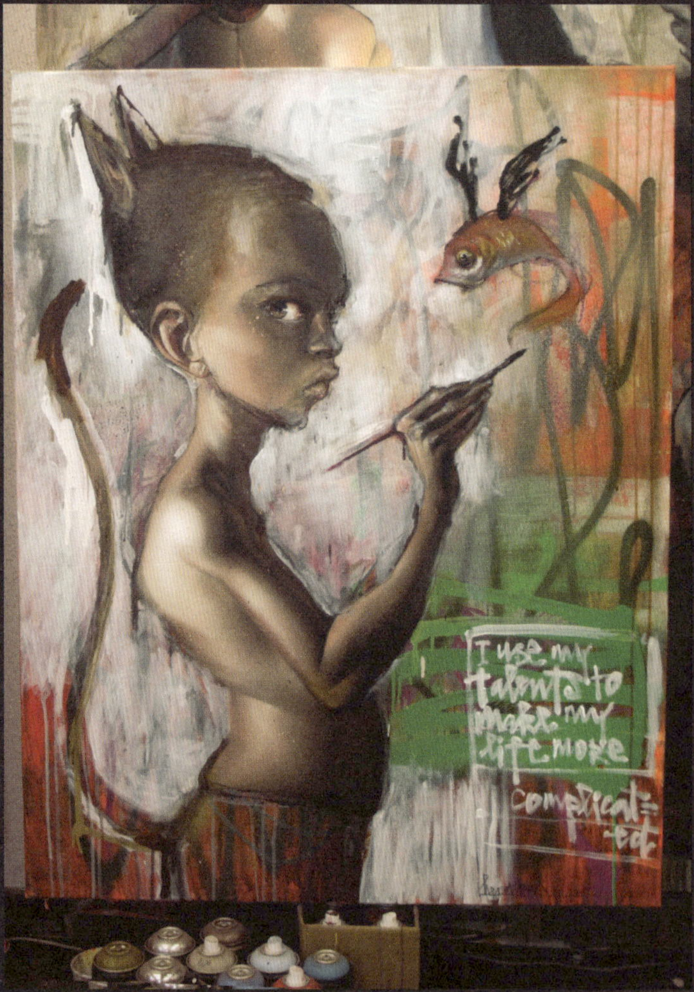

I use my
talents to
make my
life more
complicat-
ed

abcd
efghijkl
mnop
qrstuvw
xyz

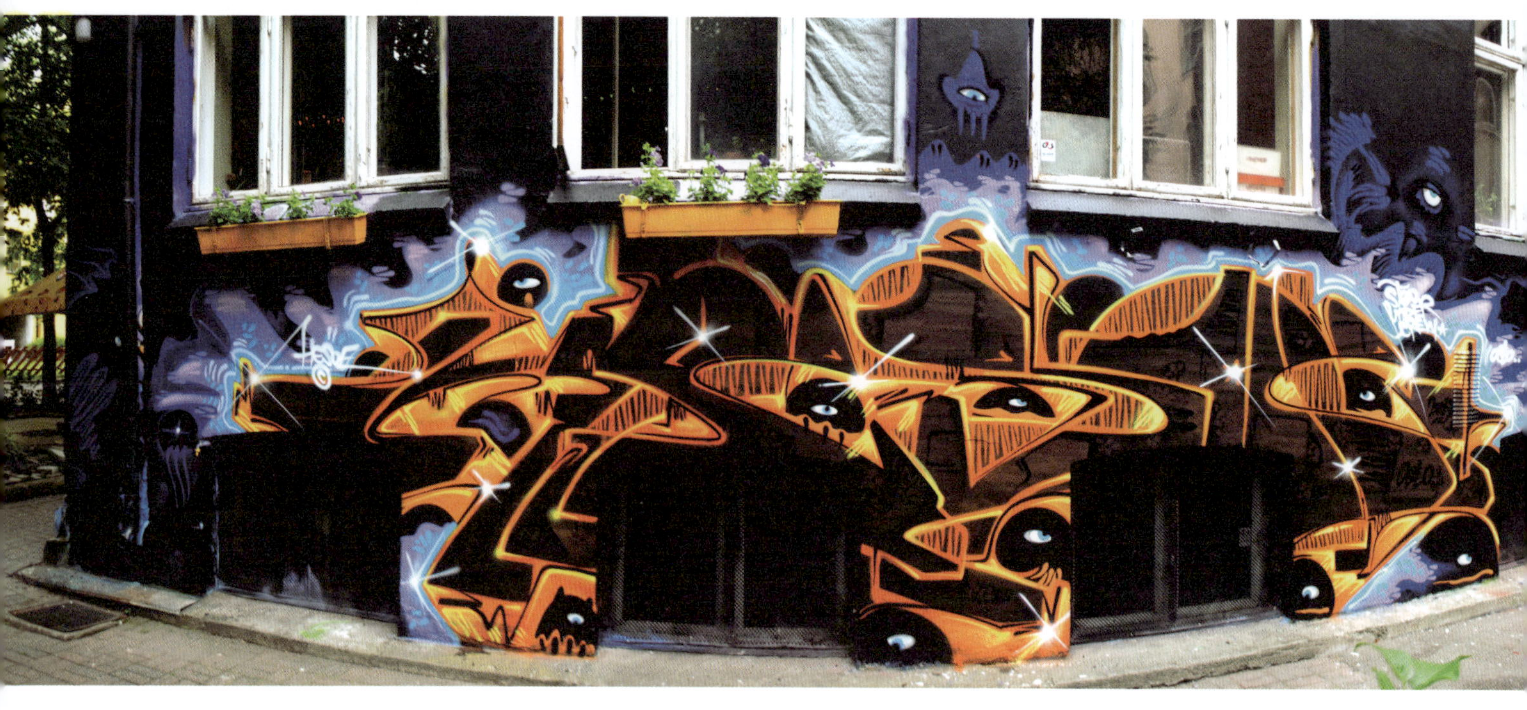

Hesoe

SANTIAGO, CHILE
Crew member of STGOUNDER
Writer since 1997
Favourite letter: S
www.hesoe.com

In order to prepare for his alphabet, Hesoe followed a back-to-basics approach. He did a lot of drawing and studied each letter individually, which helped him to develop a new style. He likes pieces that have new, classic and incongruous elements and are full of movement and contrast. Graffiti gives him the opportunity to travel around, and he finds it a great motivation and a learning process to see what writers in other places are up to.

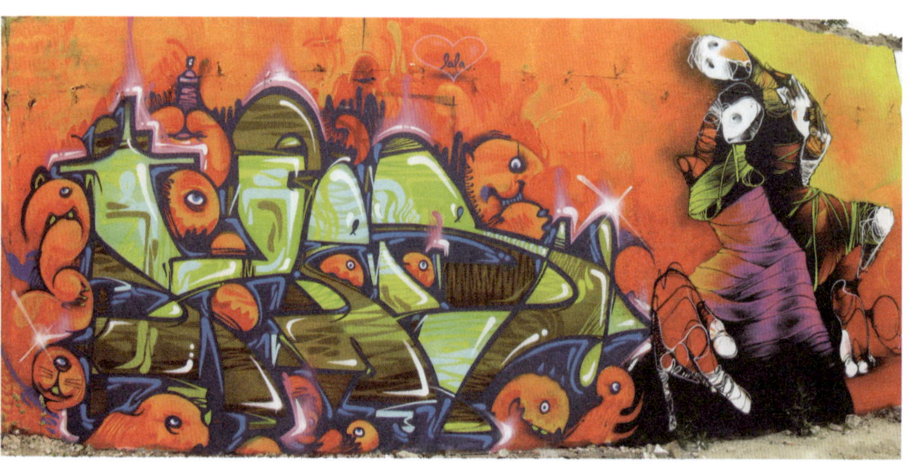

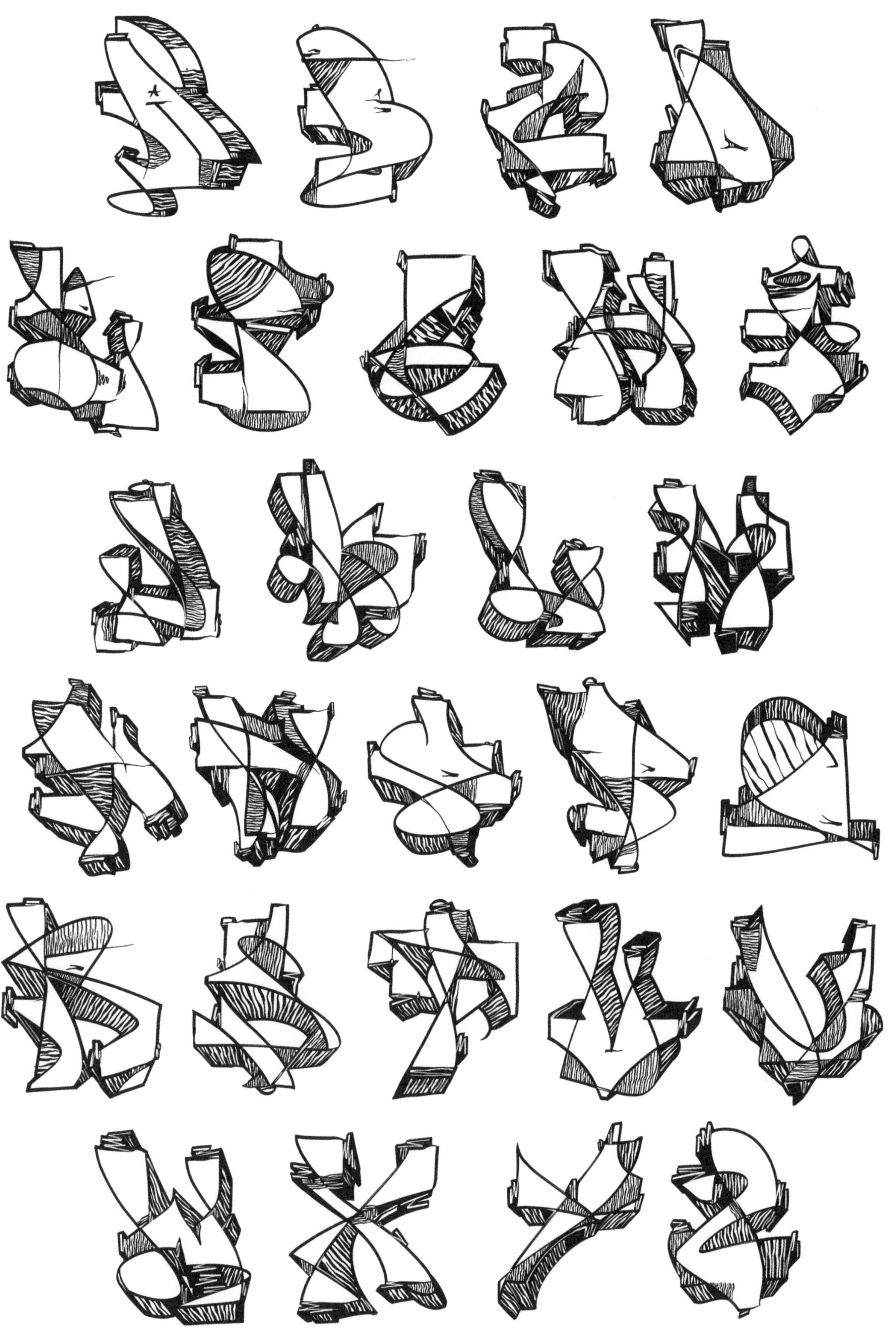

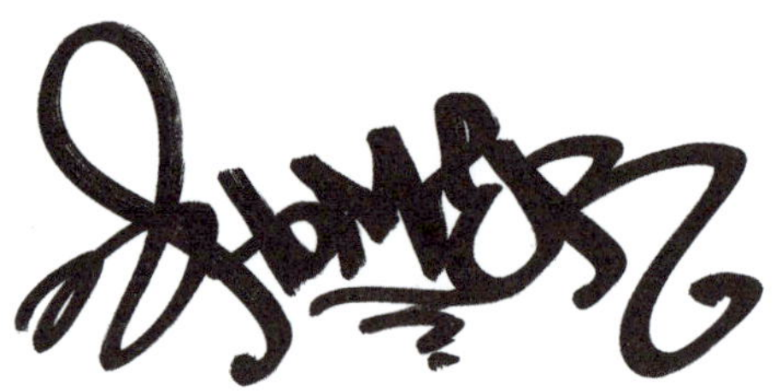

Homer
BRASOV, ROMANIA
Crew member of LDJ, GipsyKings
Writer since 1997
Favourite letter: M
www.flickr.com/homeboyldj

Homer describes his style as 'a trip to wonderland'. For his
alphabet he used regular markers and paint markers on paper
and made sure every single letter has its own story to tell. He
enjoys being part of the graffiti community and sees writing
as the perfect foundation for anything that can be designed
– logos, furniture and even buildings.

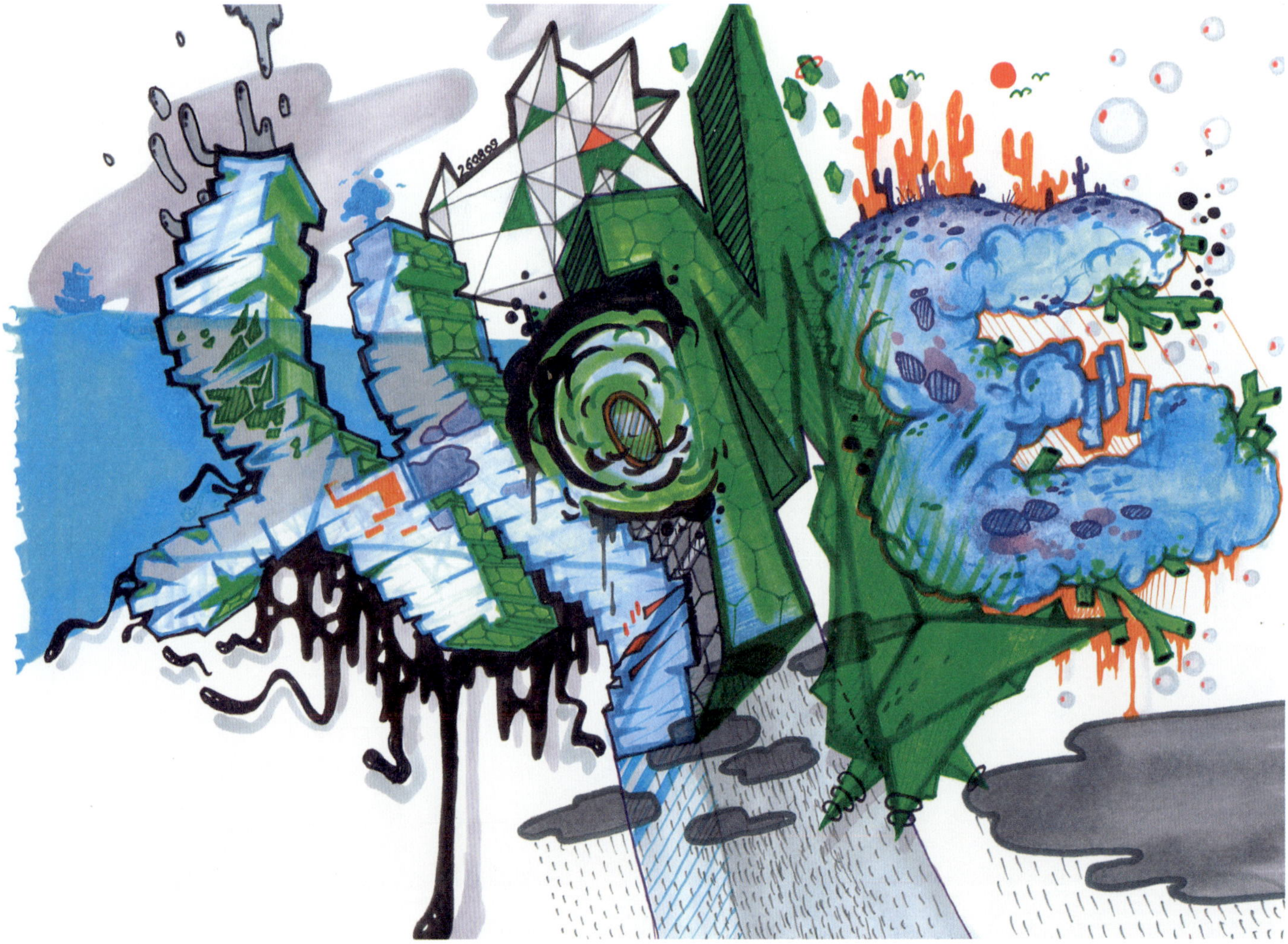

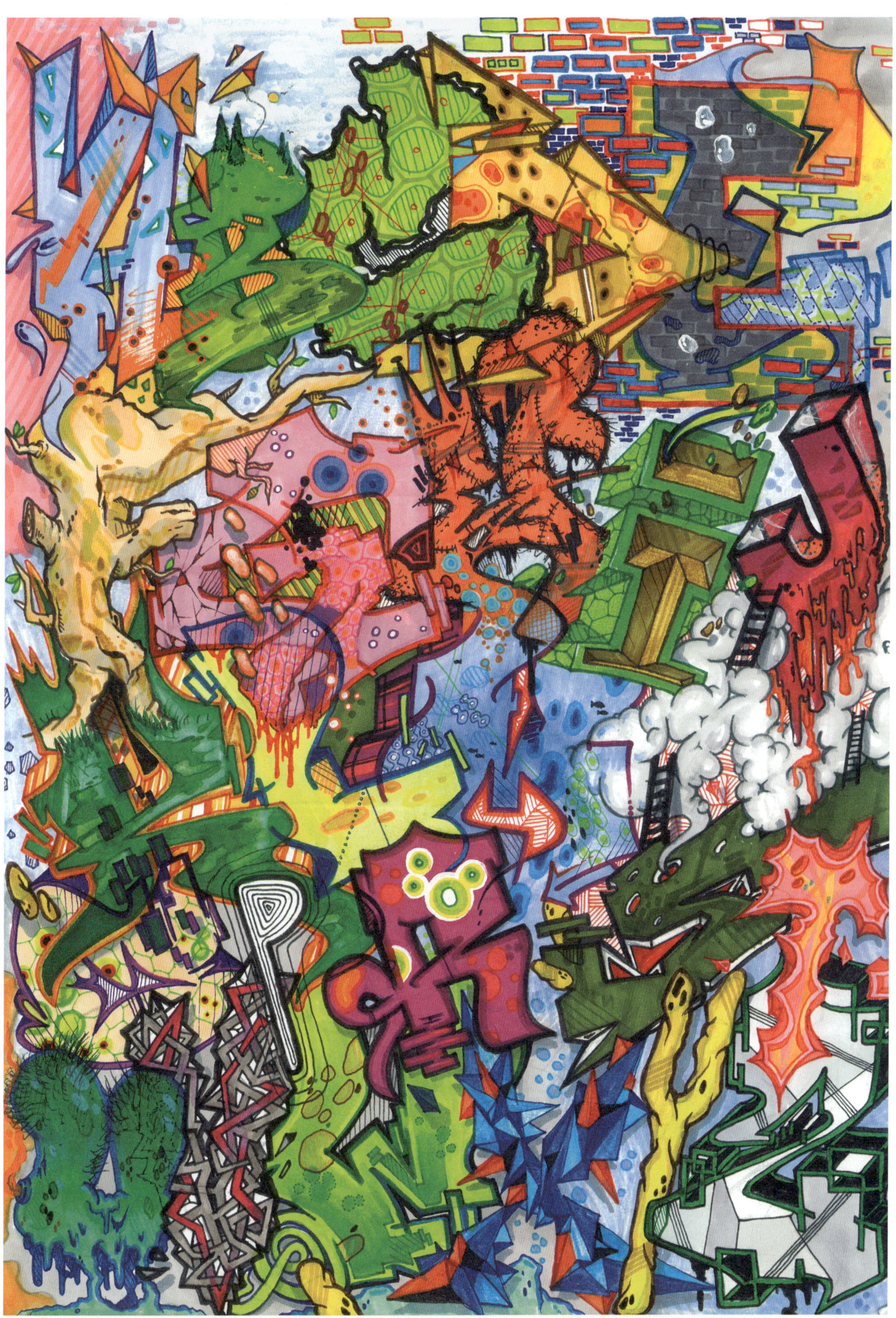

www.aventuresextraordinaires.fr

A B C D
G H I J
K L M N O
P Q R S +
U V W X Y Z

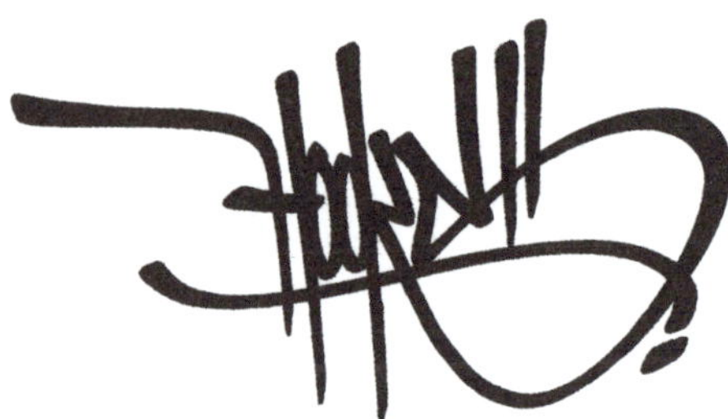

Hooks

MELBOURNE, AUSTRALIA
Crew member of F1
Writer since 2000
Favourite letter: K
www.hooker1.com

Hooks's chunky pieces are characterized by strong outlines and a clean, cut-down, cartoon-like look. He kept his alphabet in black and white to emphasize the letters. Hooks prefers simple, funky styles to wildstyle pieces. There are two things in particular that he likes about graffiti: discovering new ways to represent a letter; and the satisfaction of stepping back to view a freshly painted piece.

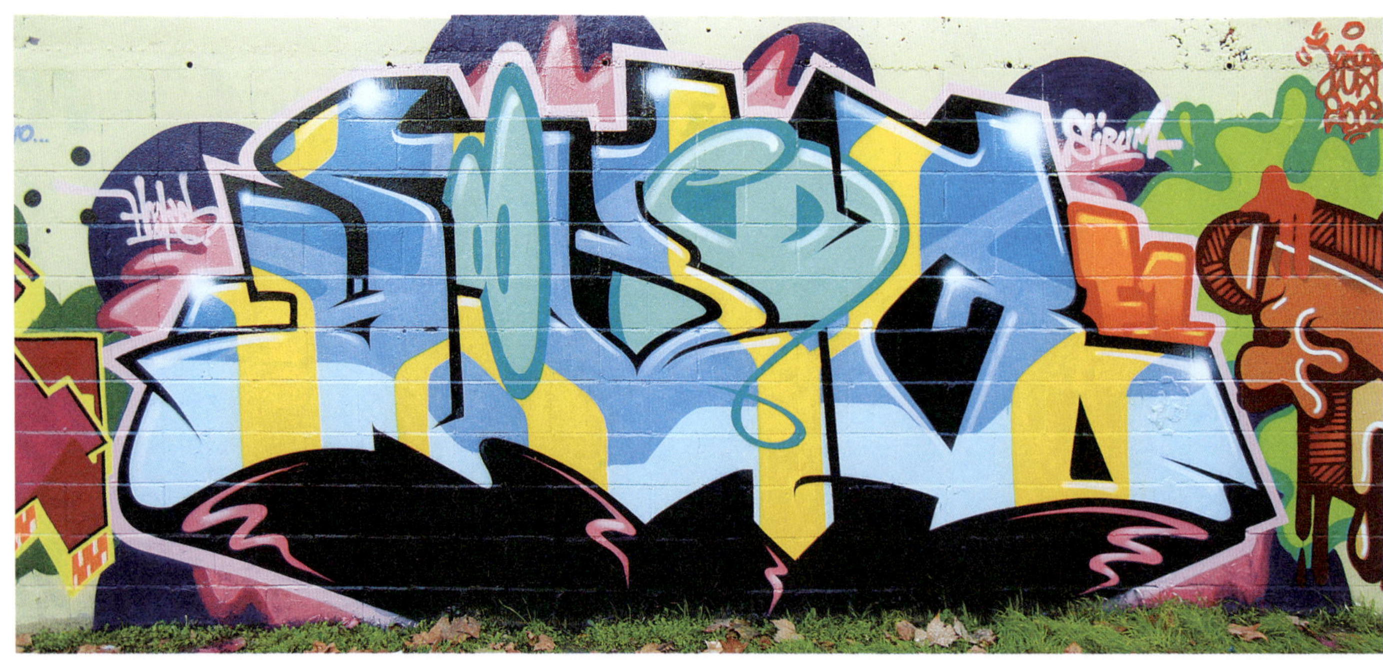

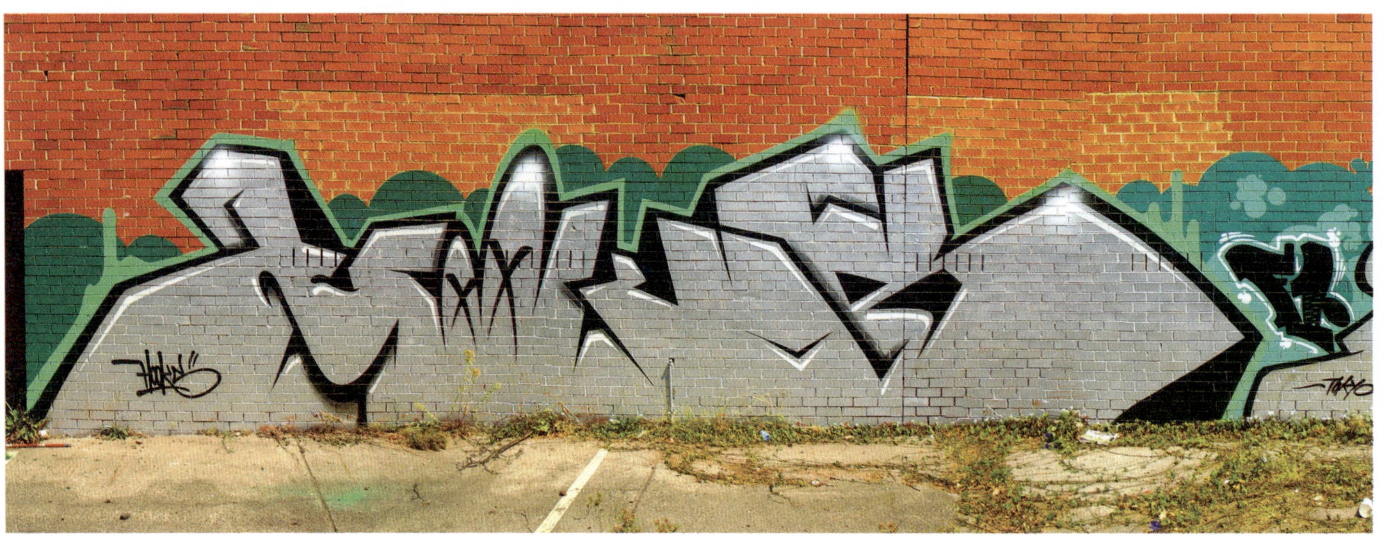

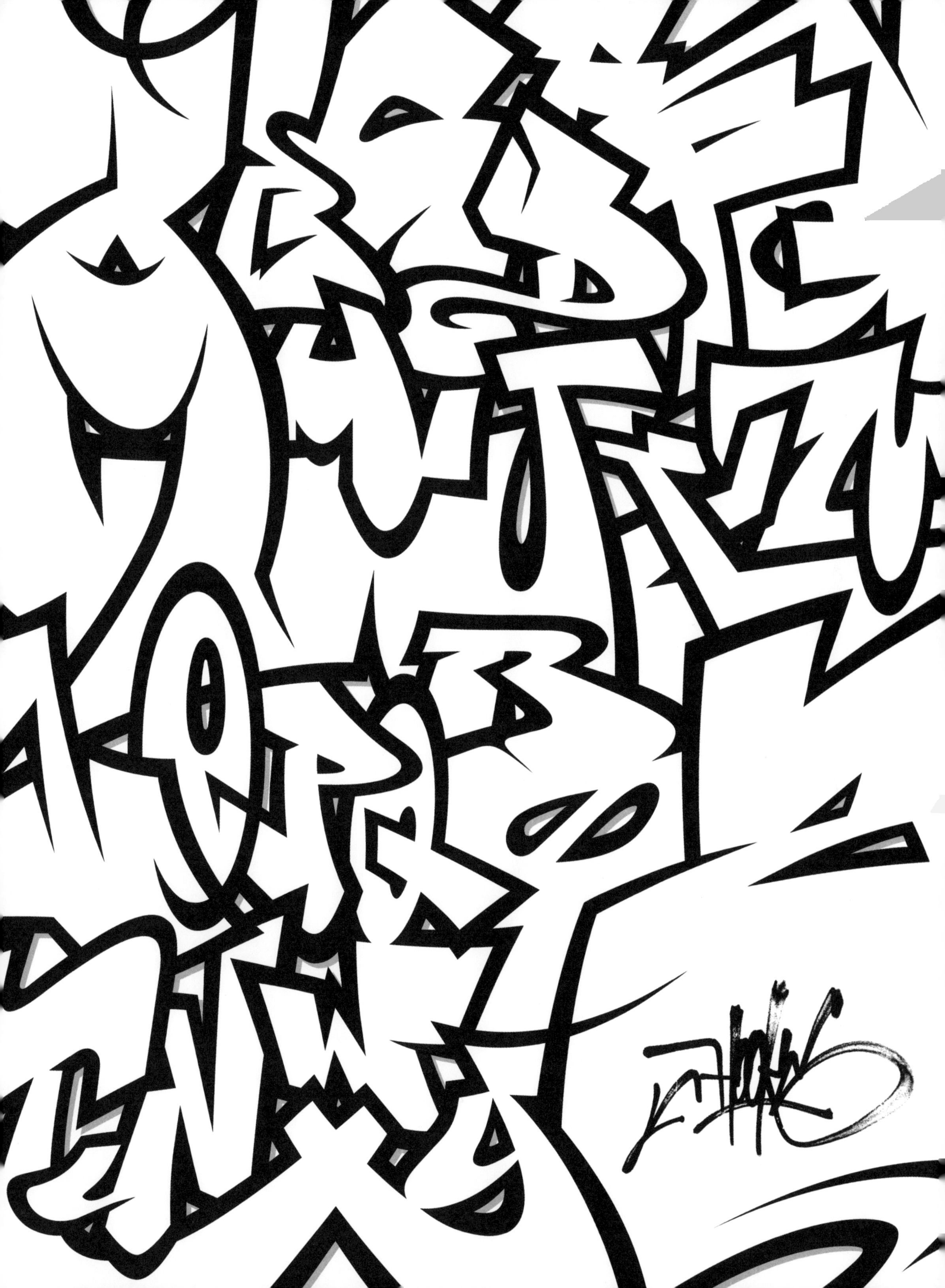

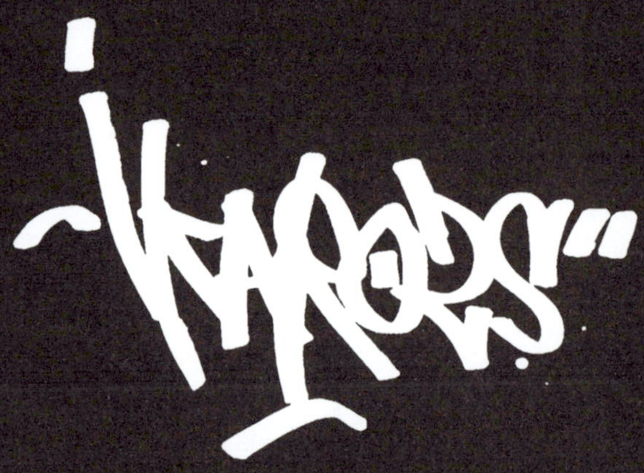

Ikaroz

STOCKHOLM, SWEDEN
Crew member of Norrlands Guld, Top Dogs
Writer since 1990
Favourite letters: K, R
ikaroz.blogspot.com

Ikaroz draws simplified and legible letters. Describing his style
as 'dirty but still clean', he sees graffiti as 'anarchy with rules'.
He used ink, spray paint, acrylic paint and charcoal to create
his alphabet.

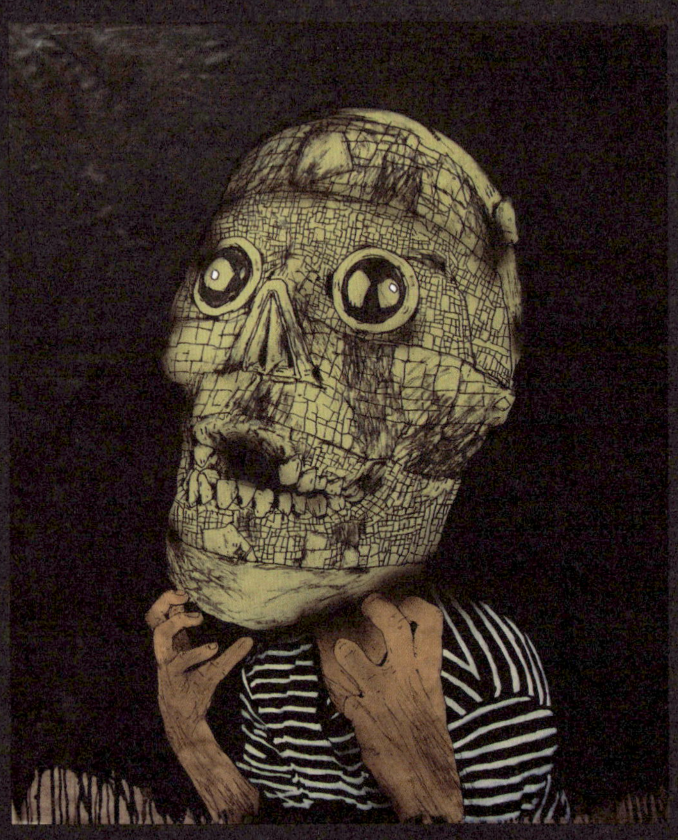

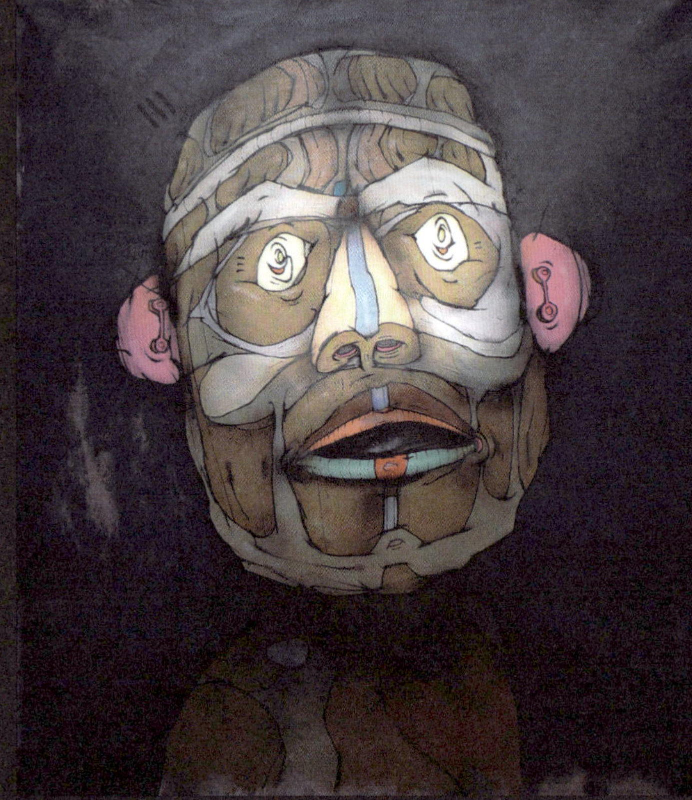

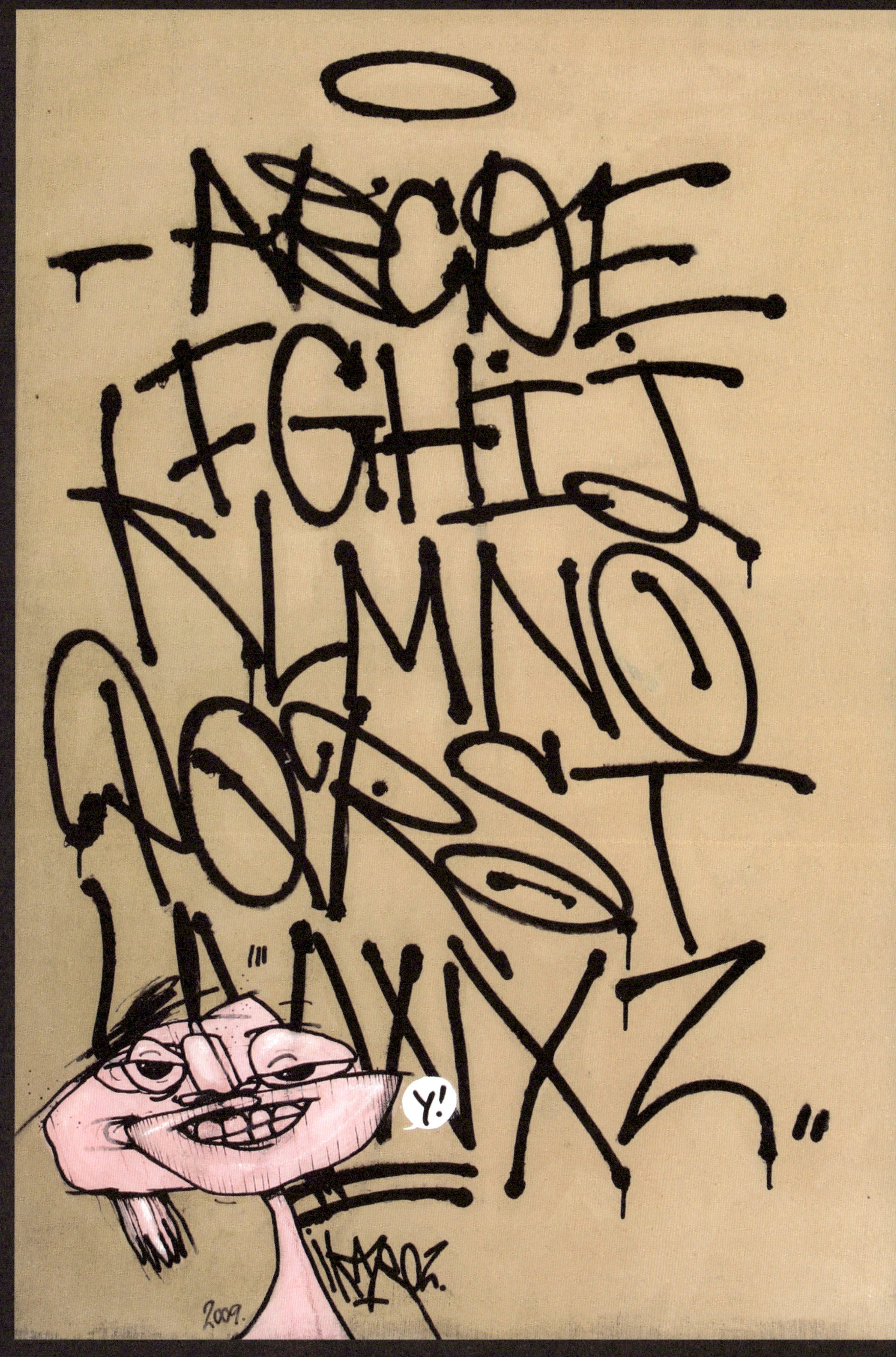
ABCDE
FGHIJ
KLMNO
PQRST
UVWXYZ
Y!
2009.

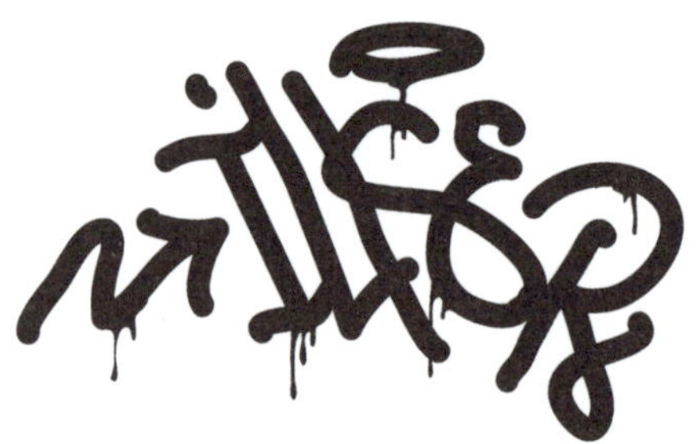

iLK

PARIS, FRANCE
Crew member of AGB
Writer since 1998
Favourite letter: O
www.ilkilkilk.com

iLK is a successful graphic designer living and working in Paris. His illustrations are almost always hand drawn in felt tip and then finalized on a computer using a graphics tablet. His work is characterized by his use of fresh and bright colours as well as a sense of depth. He still paints walls in the streets and especially appreciates the friends he has made through graffiti.

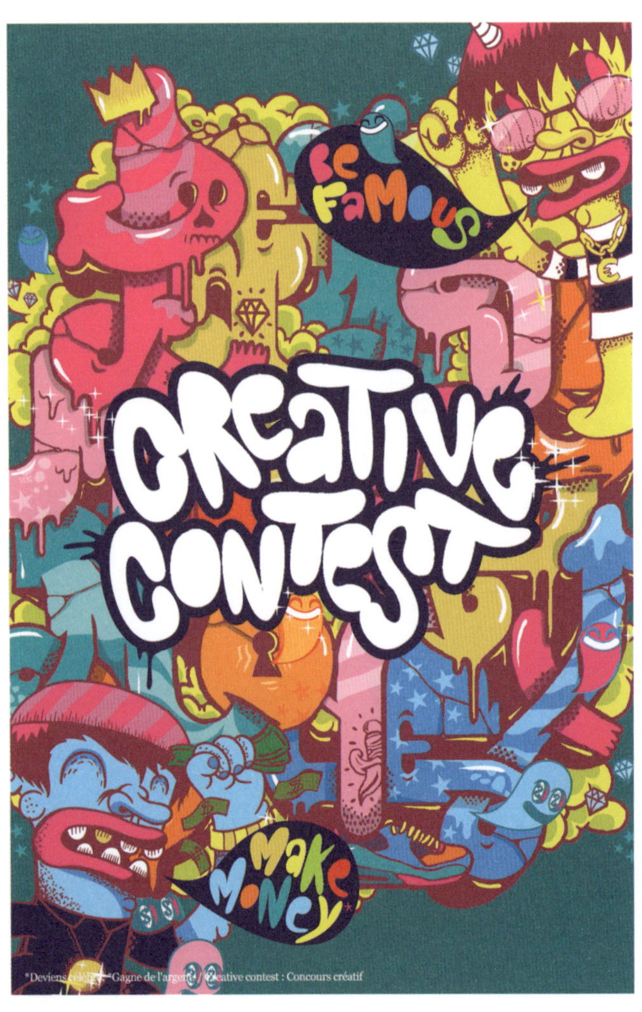

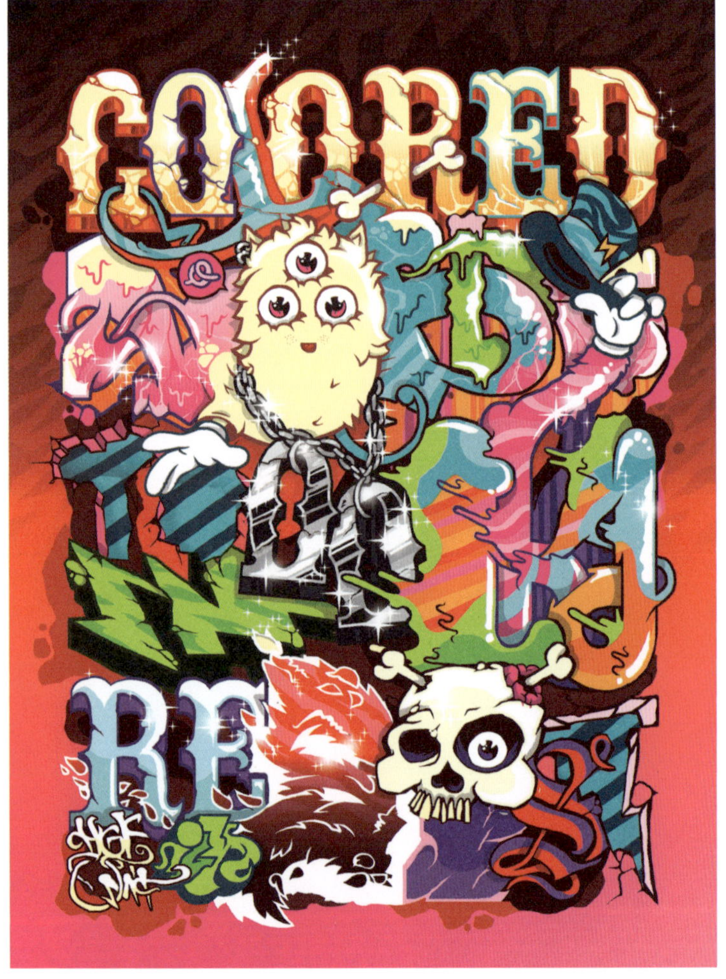

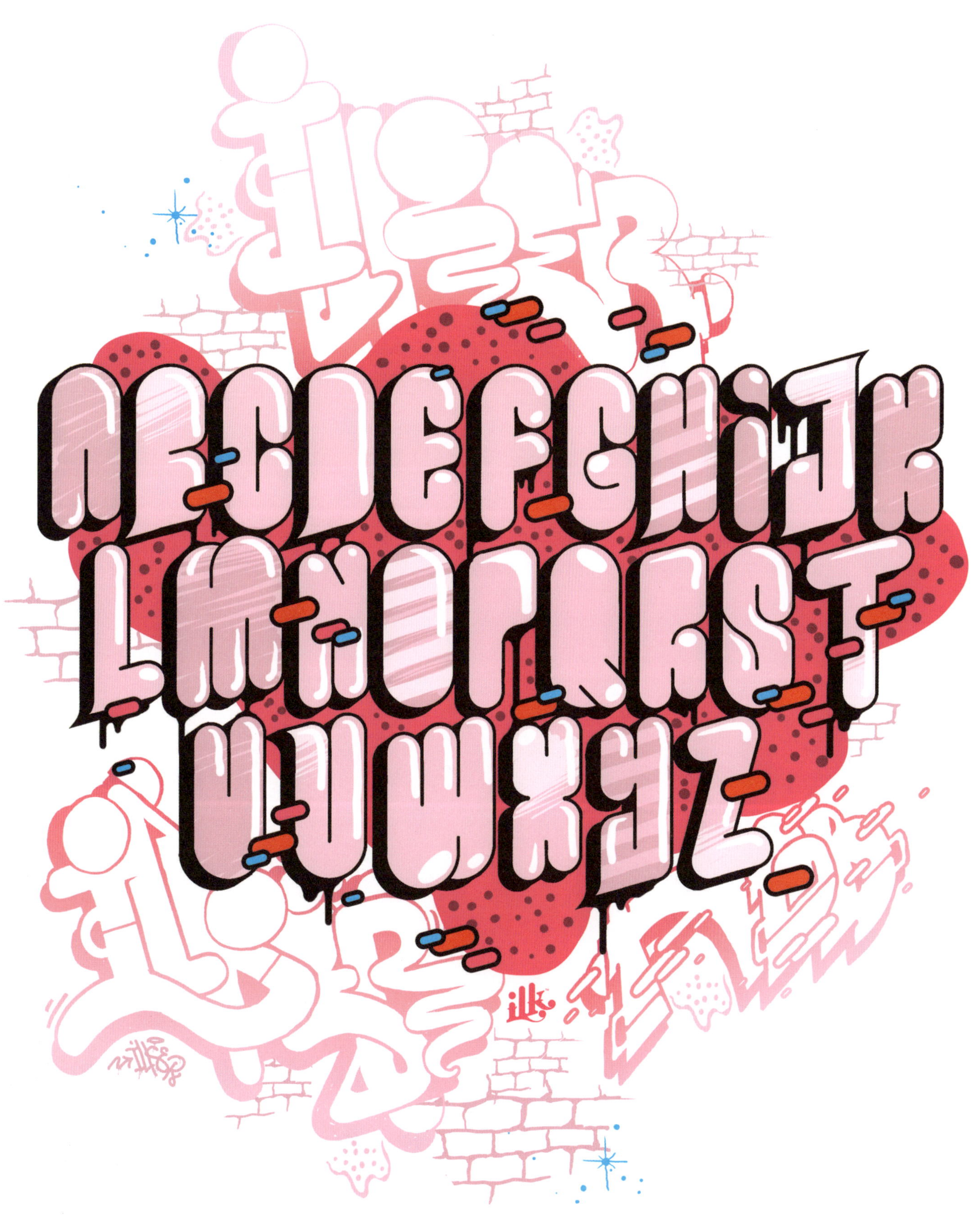

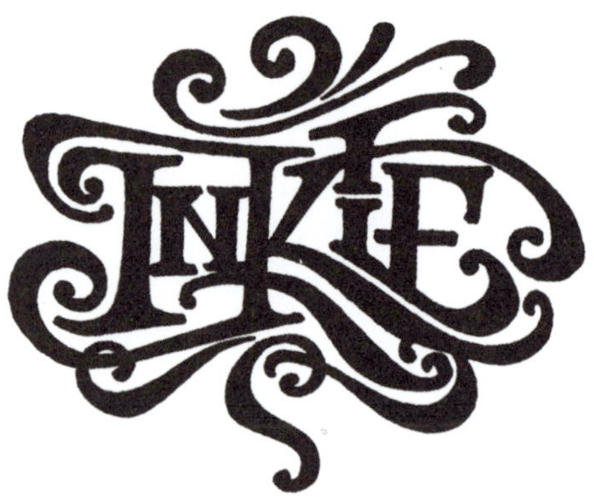

Inkie

LONDON, UK
Crew member of CRIME INC, XXX, NOT, RDA
Writer since 1984
Favourite letter: T
www.inkie.co.uk

Inkie's style is inspired by Art Nouveau and is reminiscent of
cartoon art and the work of Alphonse Mucha. Describing his
style as '21st-century Ink Nouveau', he says: 'A piece should always
be viewed as a whole word and not just individual letters stuck
together. The word needs to have a dynamic flow that gives it the
funk.' After more than twenty-five years of painting, Inkie is still
excited by good lettering.

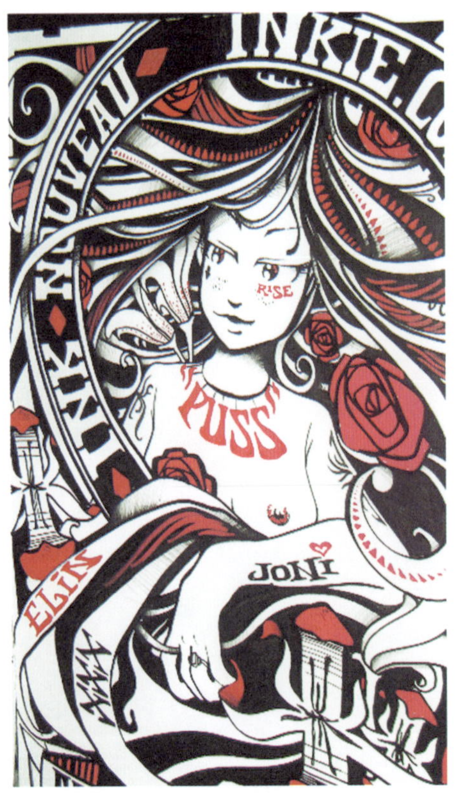

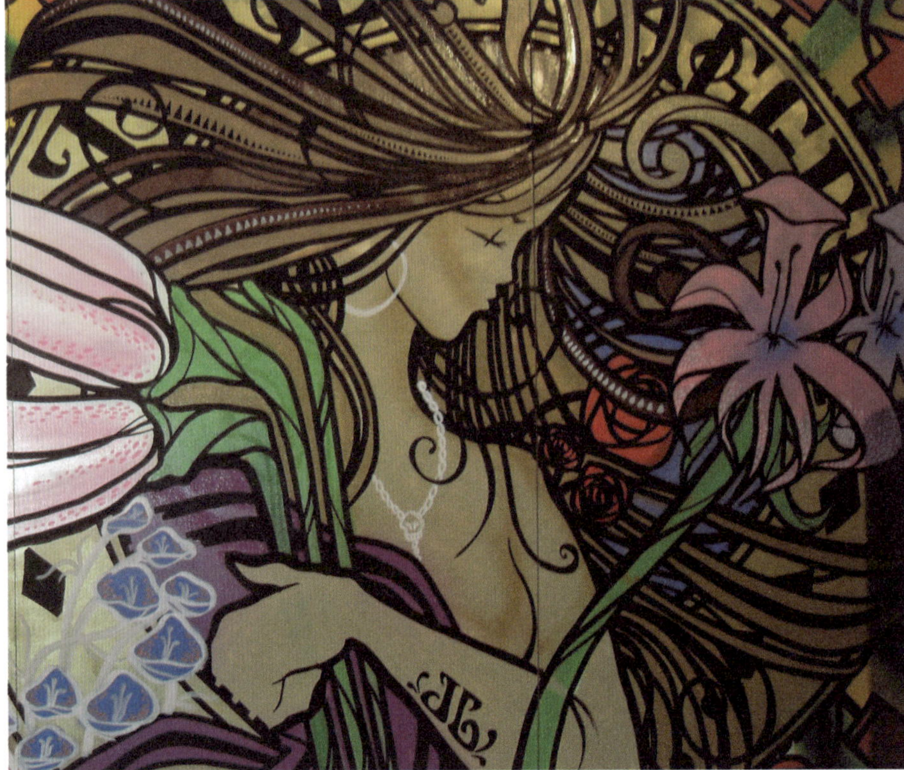

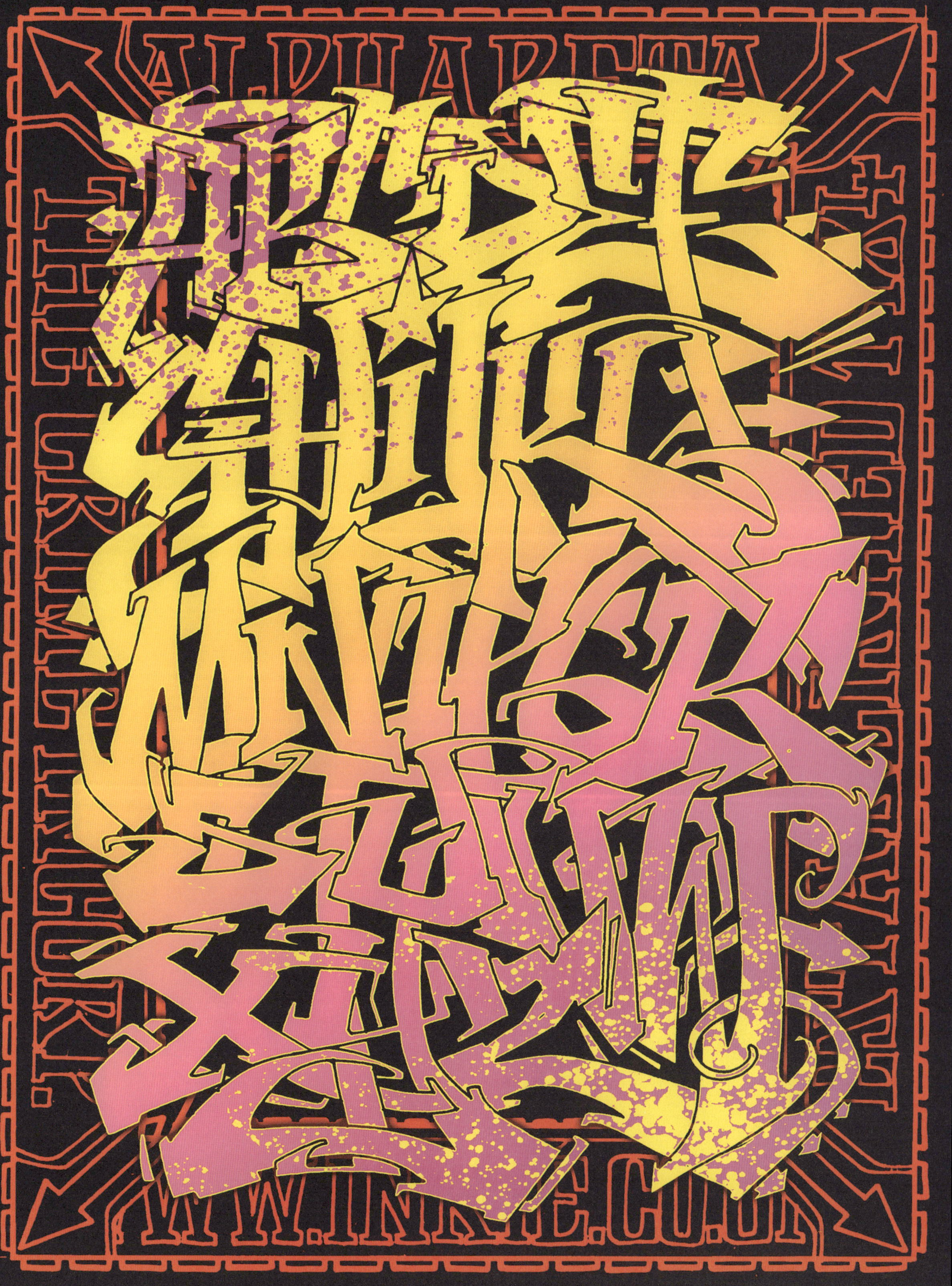

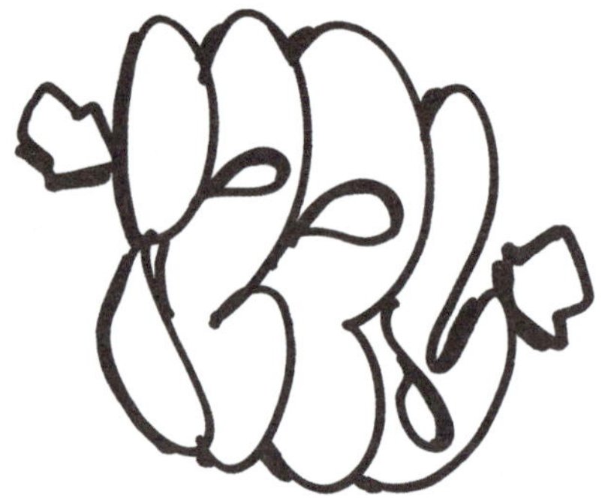

Izzy

LYONS, FRANCE

Crew member of Adult Entertainment, All You Can Eat, Lectrics
Writer since 1996   Favourite letter: E   www.lectrics.fr

Izzy's style is a mixture of modern and traditional. He always tries to include something new in every piece that he does. In his alphabet he wanted to distance himself from classic graffiti and design something slightly illegible, so that people would stop and take a moment to decipher the letters. Izzy says: 'Backgrounds are always part of my sketches, so I had to include some characters and other elements next to the letters of my alphabet.'

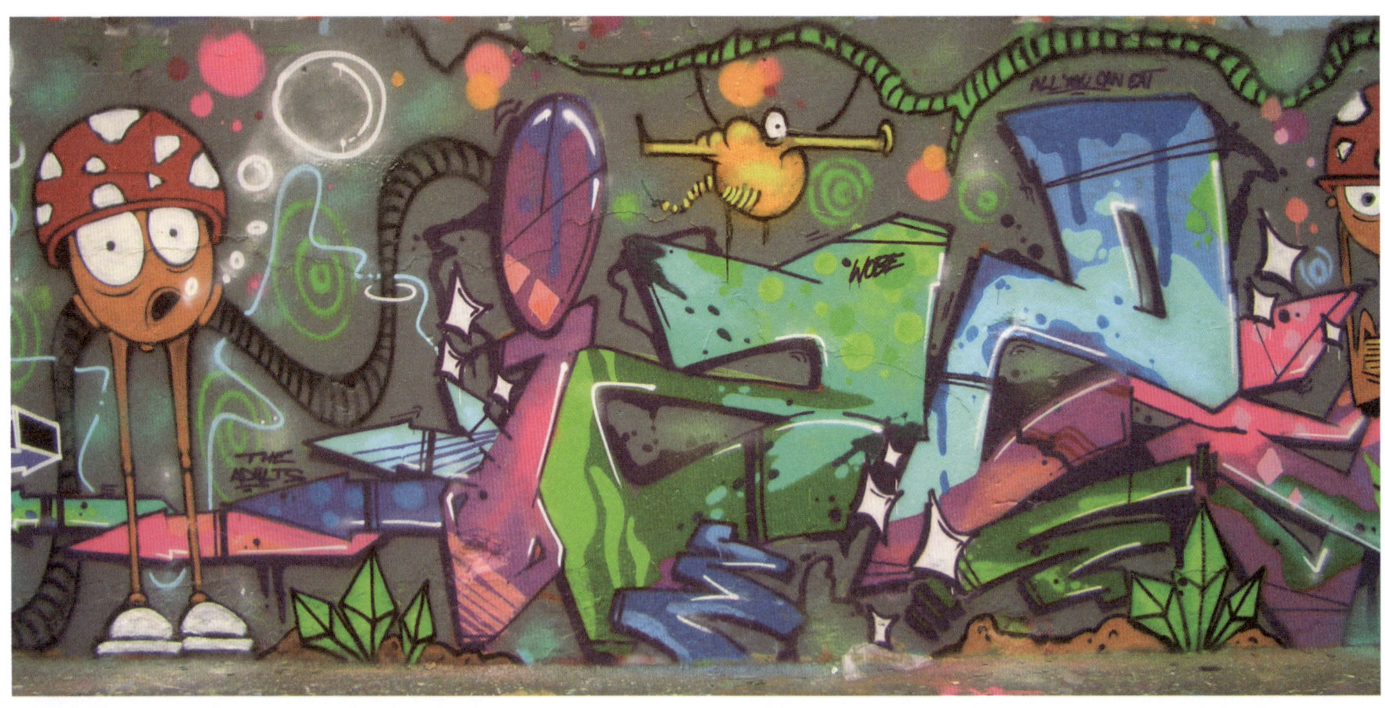

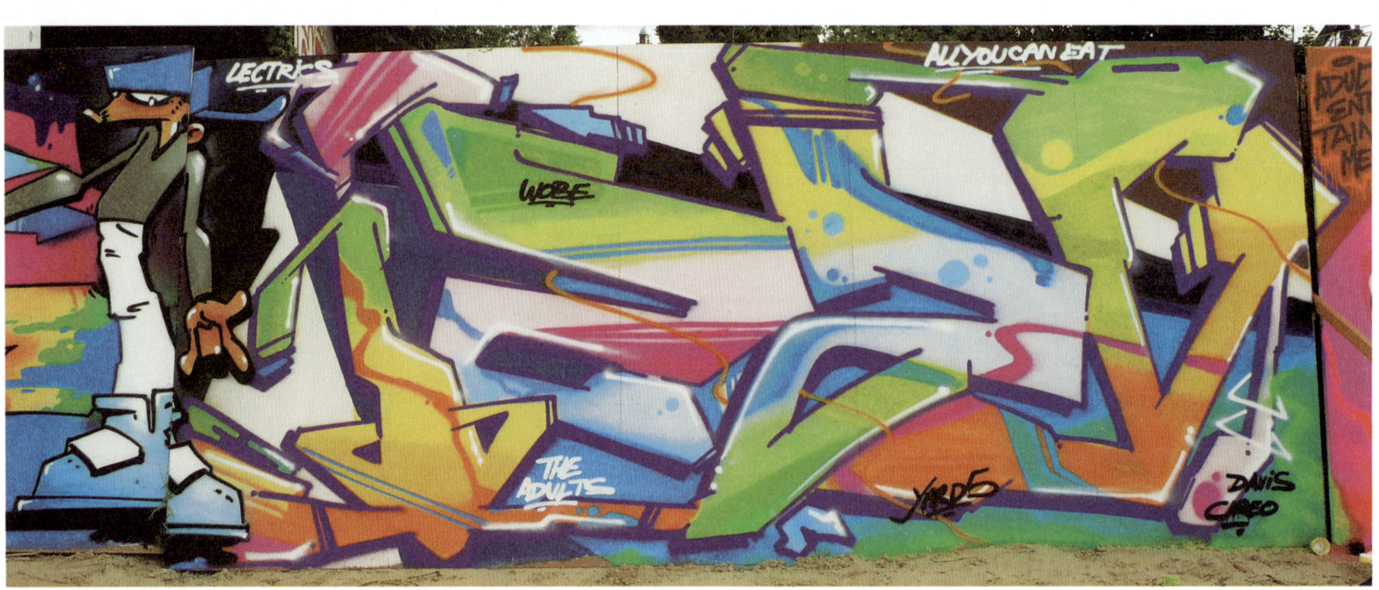

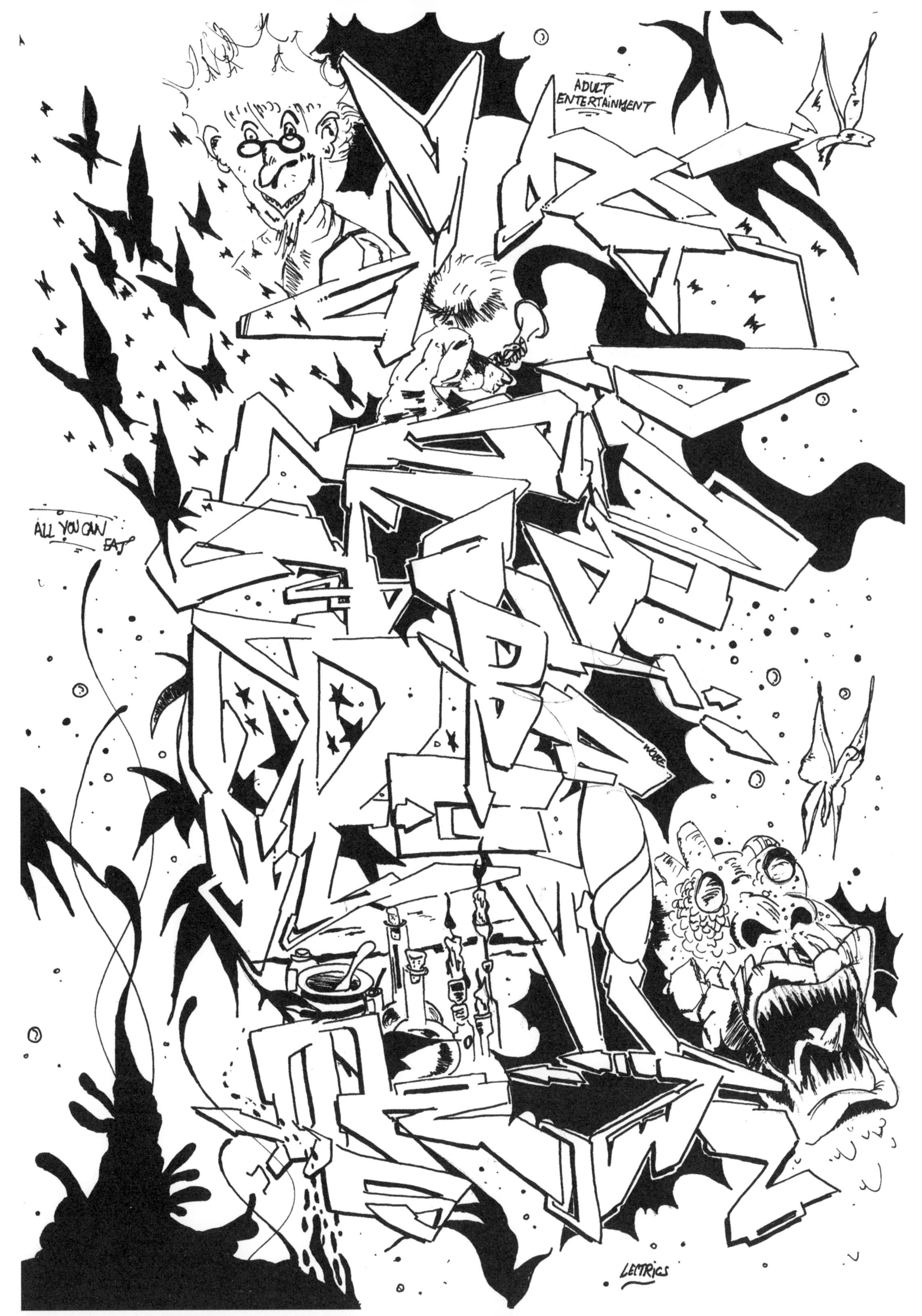

ADULT ENTERTAINMENT
ALL YOU CAN EAT
MORE
LETTRICS

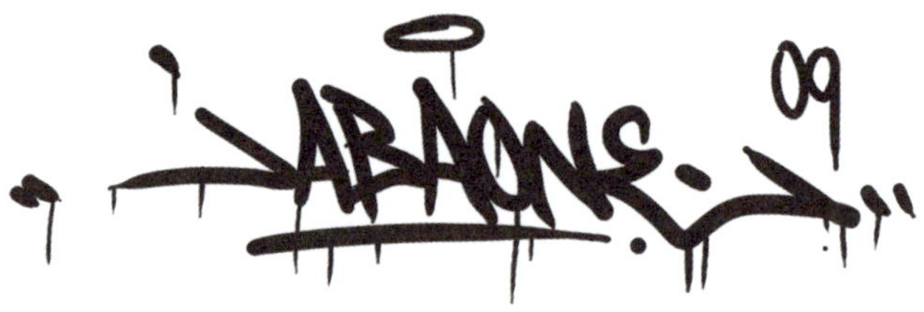

Jaba One
BELGIUM
Crew member of JNC,
Ultraboyz, OAC
Writer since 1990
Favourite letter: J
www.jabaone.com

Jaba One was born and raised in Colombia but fell in love with graffiti when he moved to Belgium. He is currently living in Singapore, where he applies his many talents working as a digital artist for Lucasfilm Animation. Jaba describes his pieces as a mix of 'classic graffiti and futuristic wildstyles'. He designed his alphabet as one big piece, with all the letters connected. It takes 'knowledge about the history of graffiti and years of practice' to create a good piece, he says.

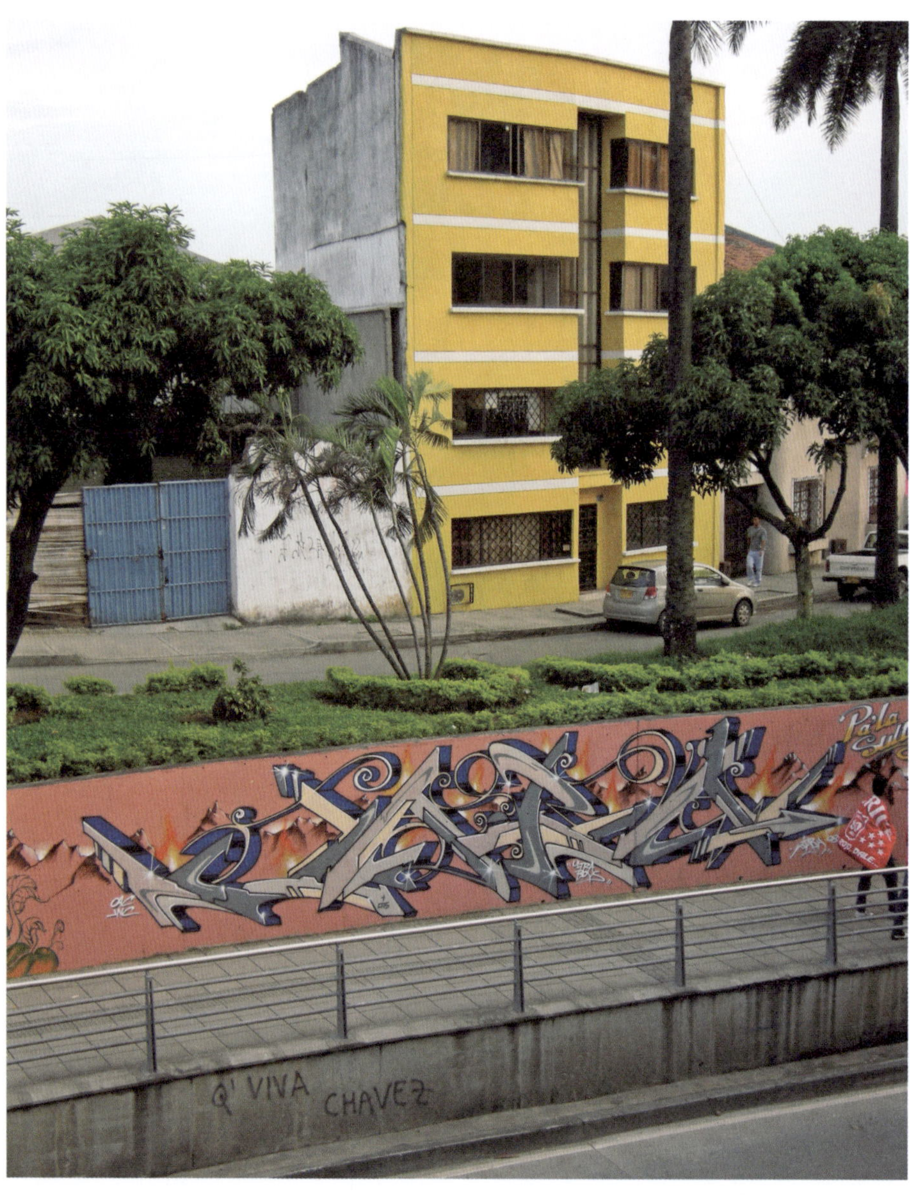

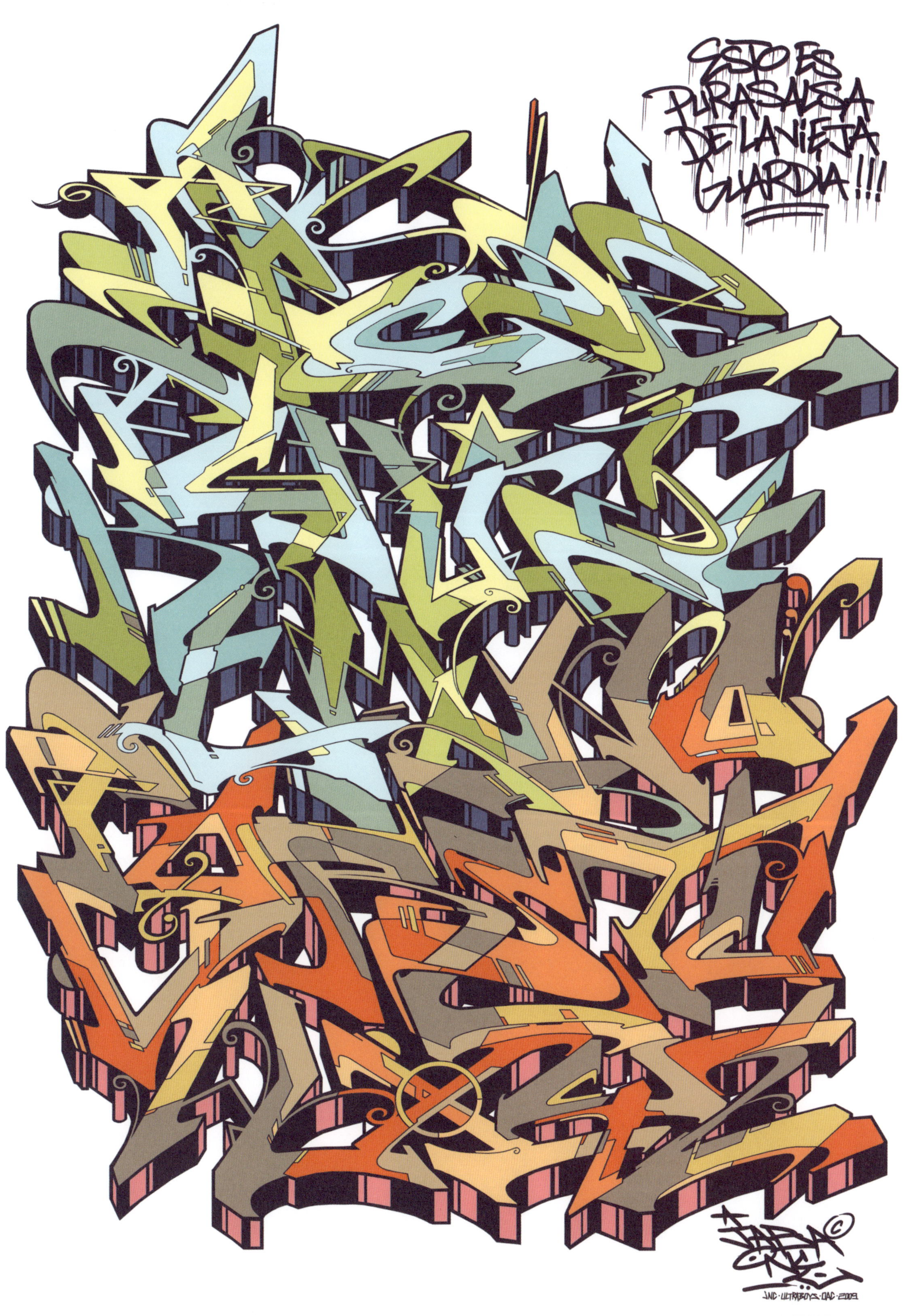

ESTO ES
PURA SALSA
DE LA VIEJA
GUARDIA!!!

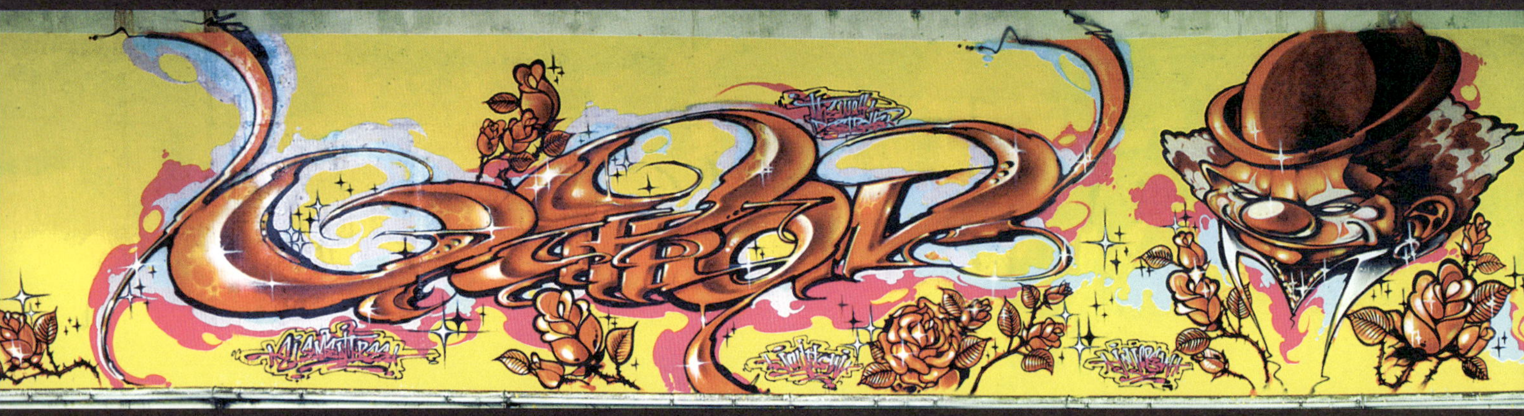

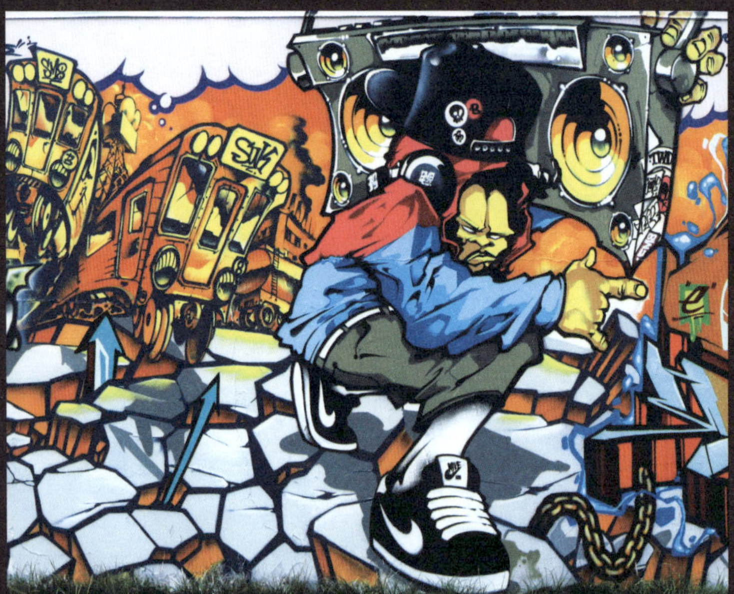

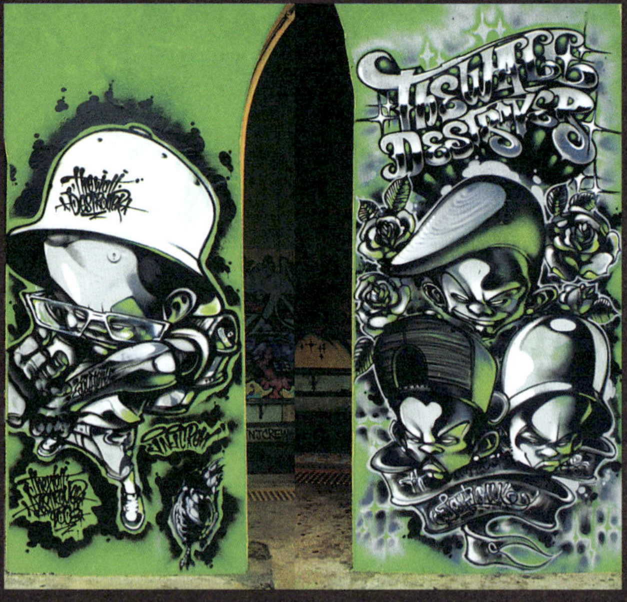

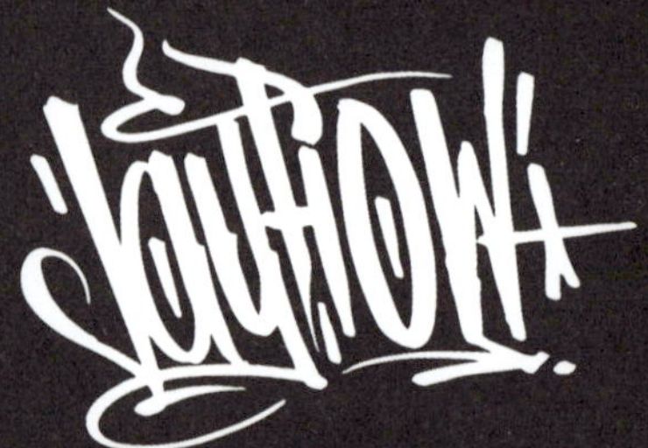

Jay Flow
SEOUL, SOUTH KOREA
Crew member of JNJ, SUK, SM8
Writer since 2001
Favourite letter: B
www.jay-flow.com

Jay Flow's style blends oriental and Asian influences, tattoo art and a general love of detail. He has developed a unique way of giving his characters depth, whether he uses two tones or multiple colours. His sketches are flamboyant but he doesn't need to refer back to them to create his detailed large-scale wall productions, which he usually paints freestyle. In 2009 he travelled around Europe with his crew, the Seoulmates, for the first time and gained recognition outside of his native country.

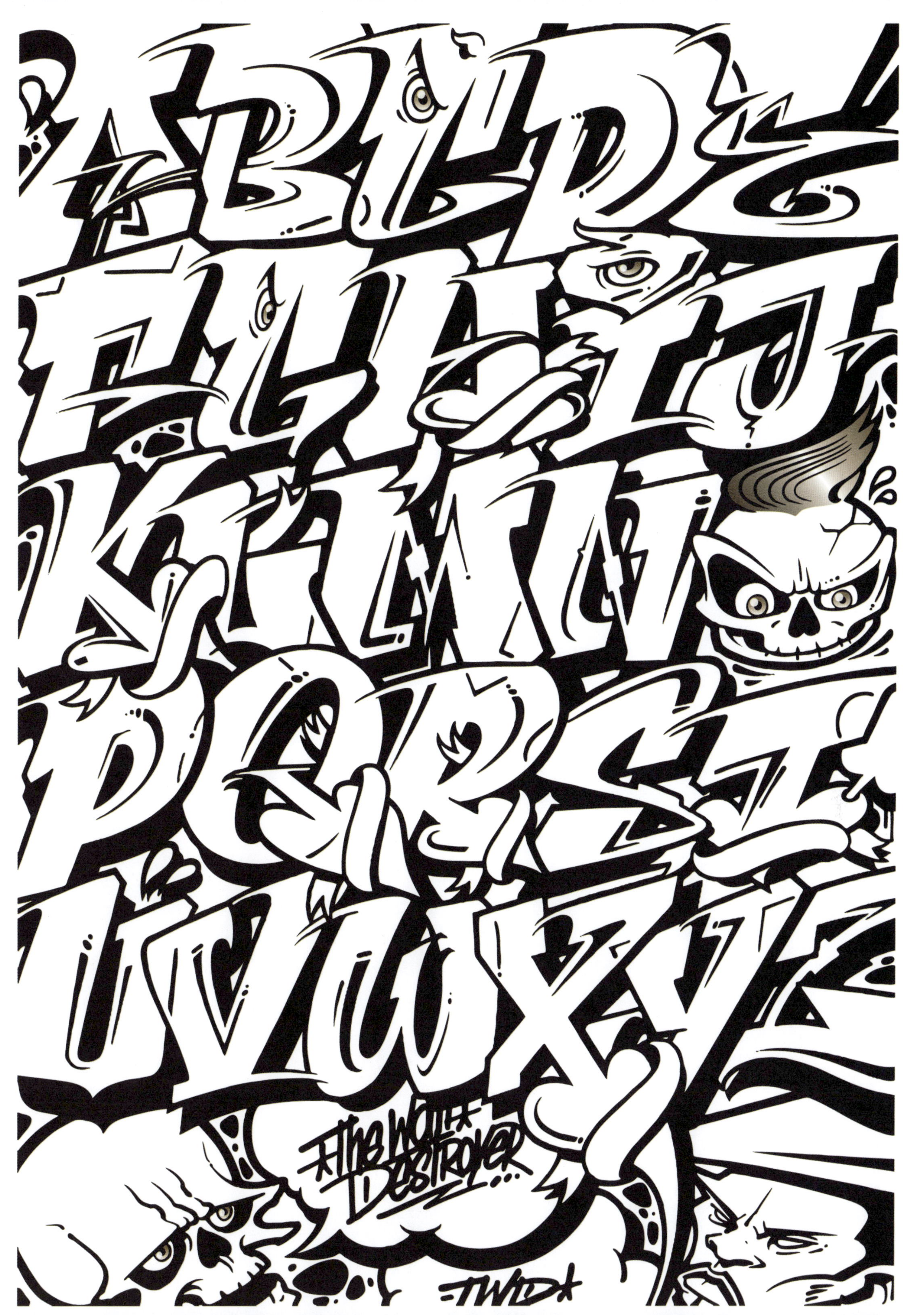

The Wall Destroyer
TWIDX

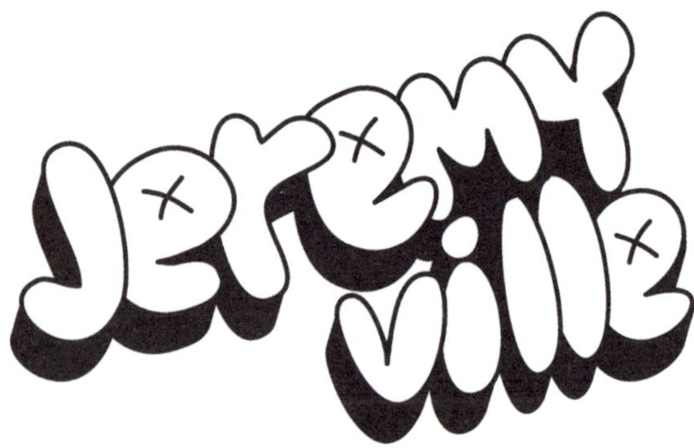

Jeremyville

SYDNEY, AUSTRALIA
Crew member of The Jeremyville 5
Writer since 1993
Favourite letters: J, V
www.jeremyville.com

Jeremyville is active in many different fields. He is an artist, designer, animator and author, and divides his time between Sydney and New York. When he first started out as an artist he mainly used stencils, large pasteups and UV stickers, but not much aerosol. At the time he focused on big murals with house paint and line work in ink. He always wanted to work with new media, not just spray. 'Acid Pop' is how he describes his mellow, graphic style.

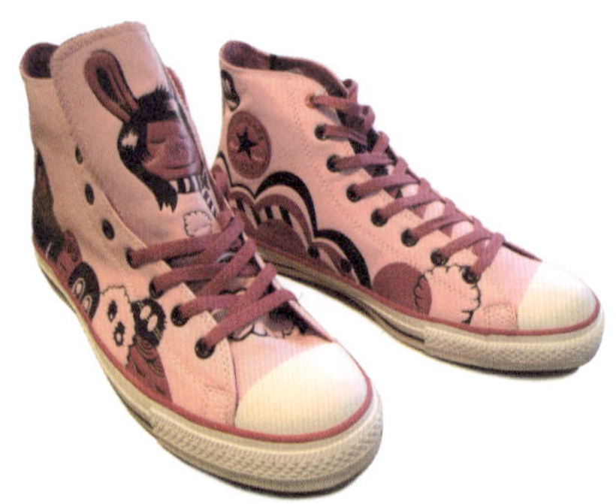

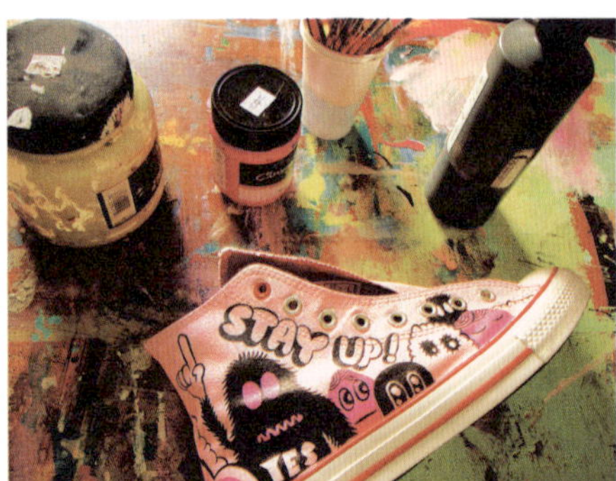

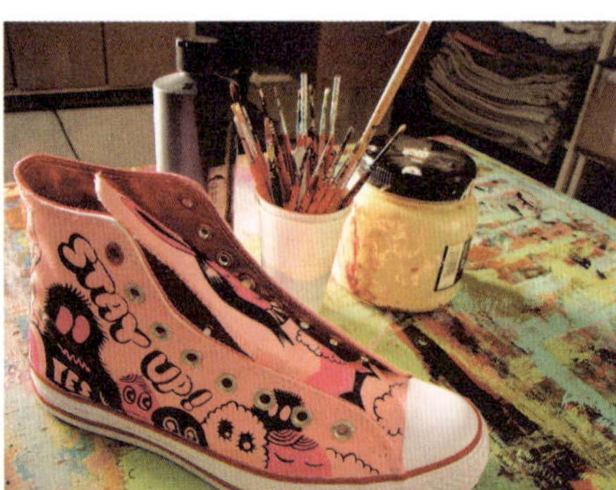

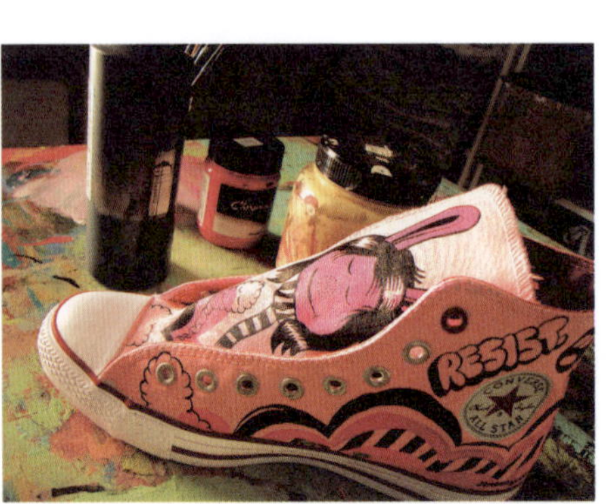

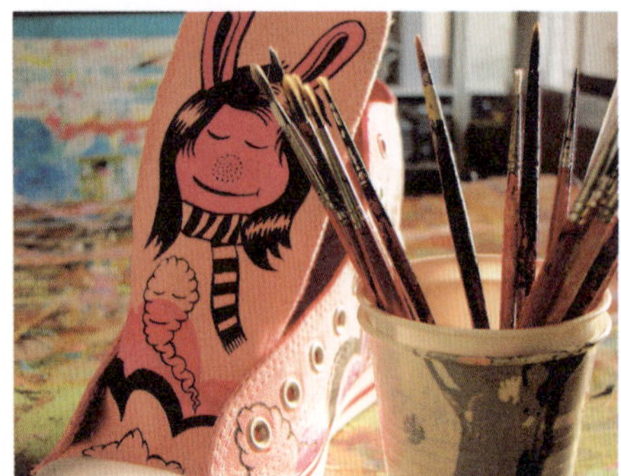

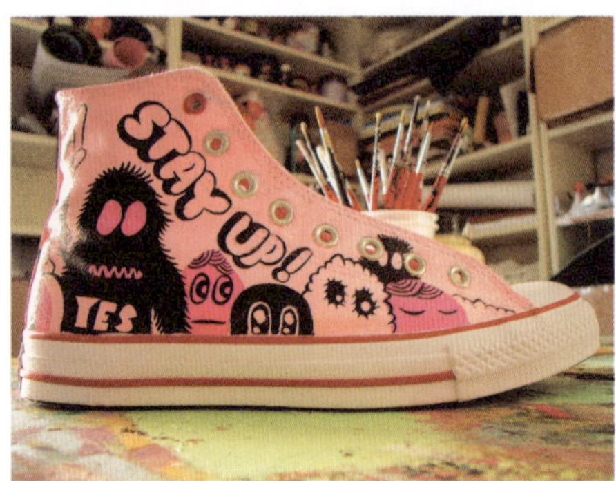

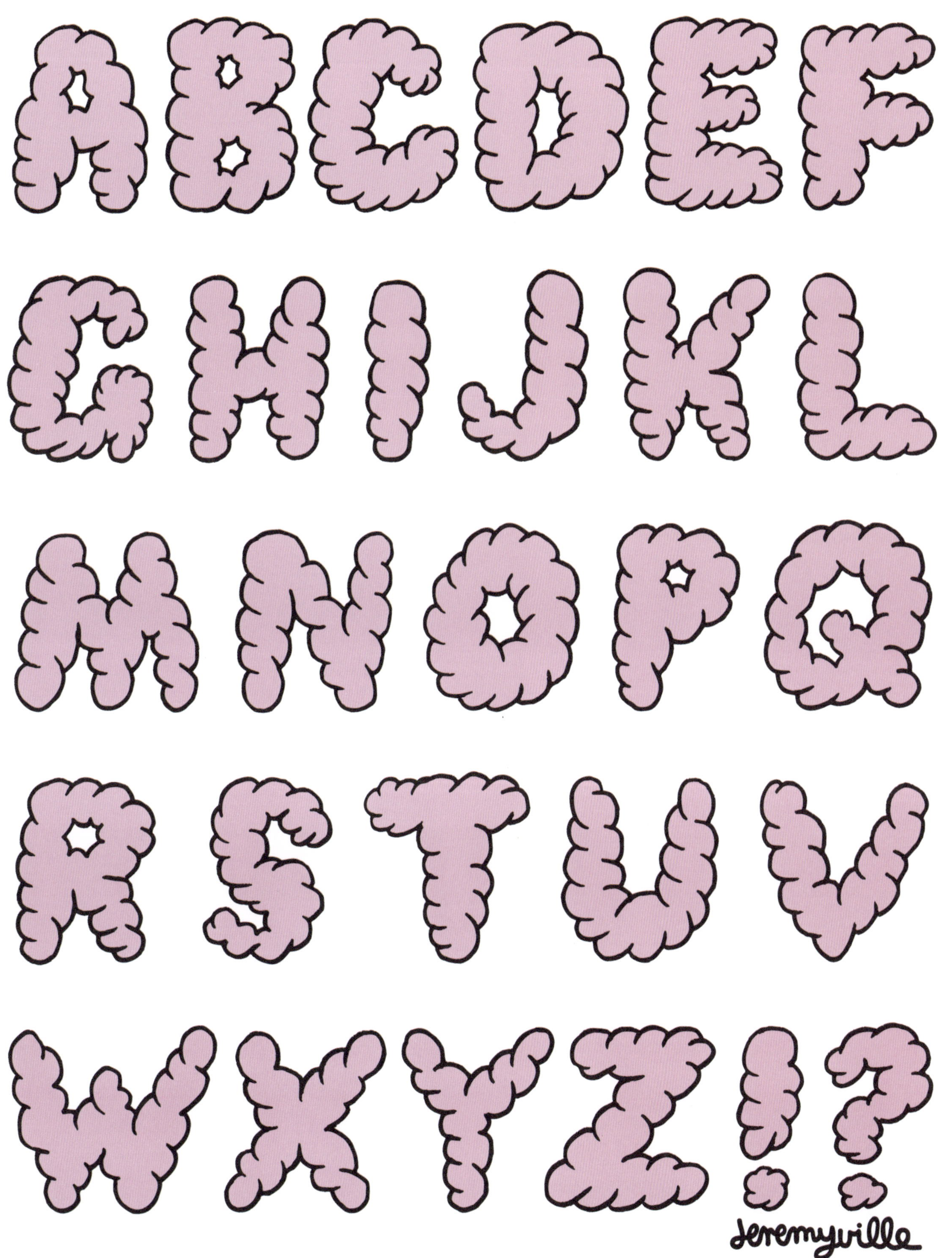

A B C D E F
G H I J K L
M N O P Q
R S T U V
W X Y Z ! ?
Jeremyville

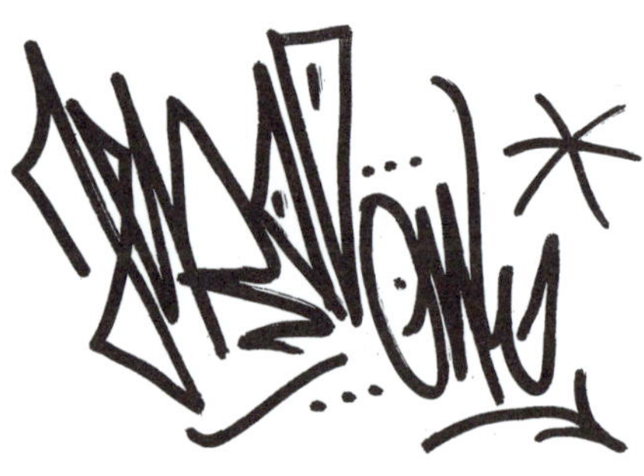

Jeroo

STUTTGART, GERMANY
Crew member of The JDIs
Writer since 1993
Favourite letter: J
www.jeroo.de

Jeroo loves to explore extreme proportions and distortions and likes to connect his letters in funky ways. His alphabet was originally painted with acrylic paint and marker on wood. It takes an open mind, persistence, fascination and a love of detail to create a good piece, he says. Being productive is what he likes best about graffiti.

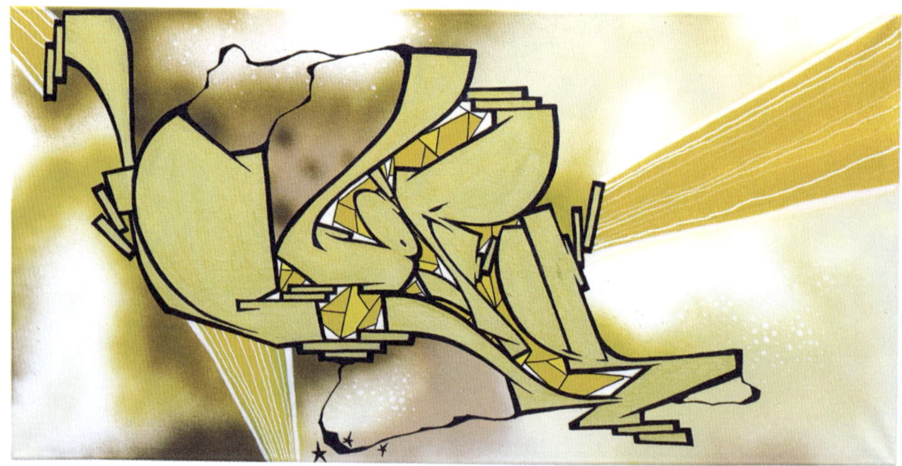

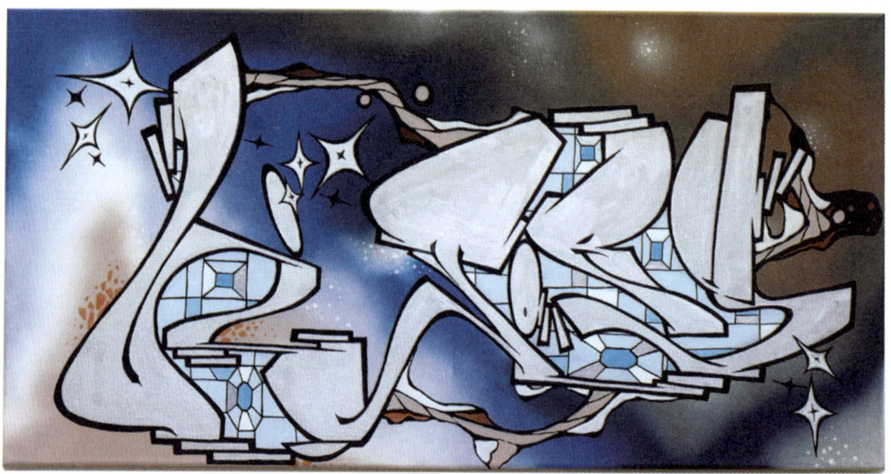

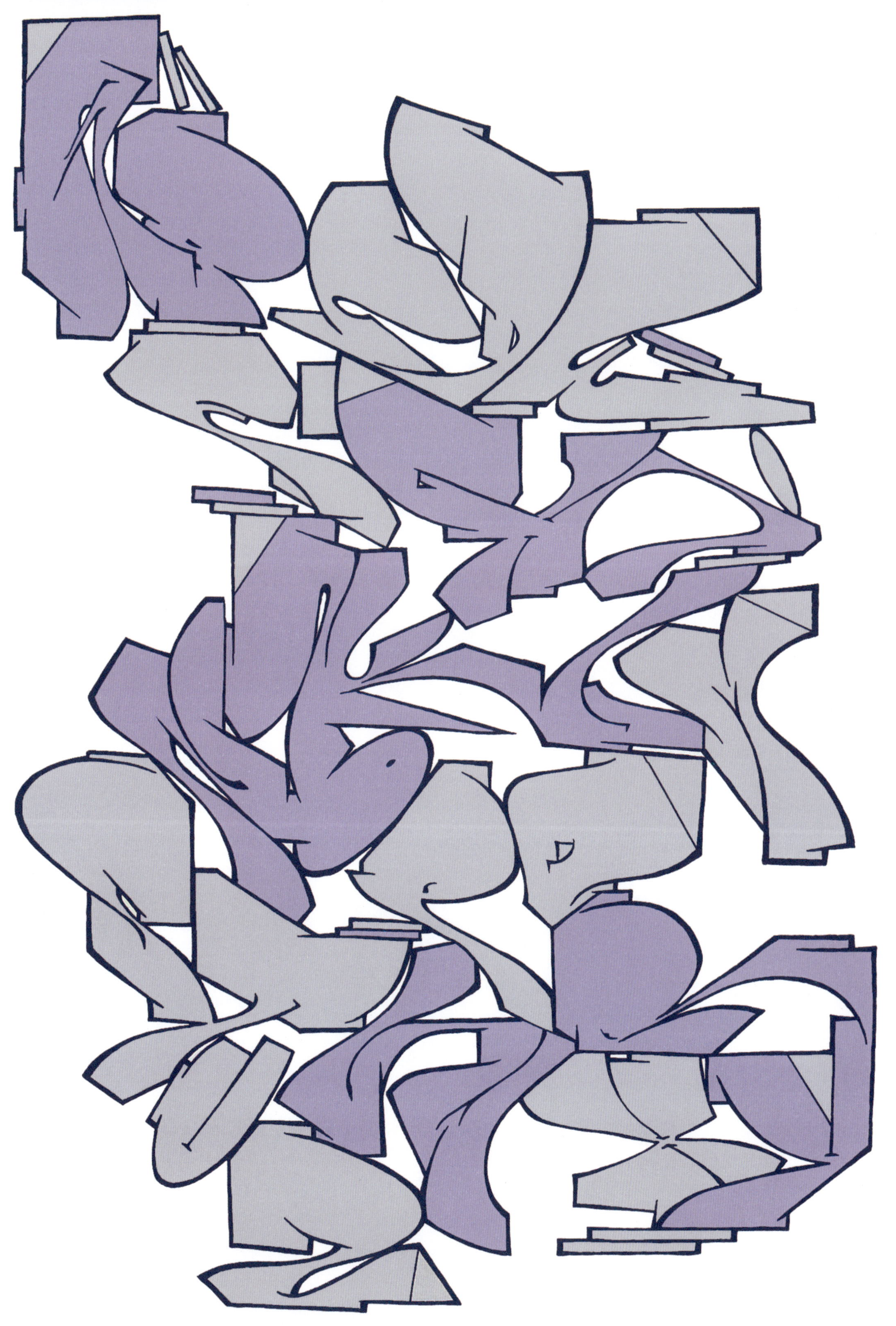

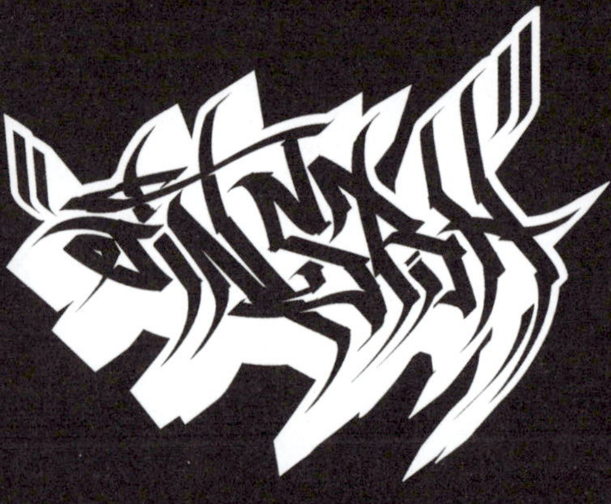

JINSBH

SEOUL, SOUTH KOREA
Crew member of WONTAK
Writer since 2000
Favourite letters: J, S, K, Z, O
www.jinsbh.com

JINSBH is a graffiti artist and graphic designer living and working in Seoul. His alphabet shows the style that he typically uses for his letters, although he often also incorporates characters and other graphic elements into his pieces.

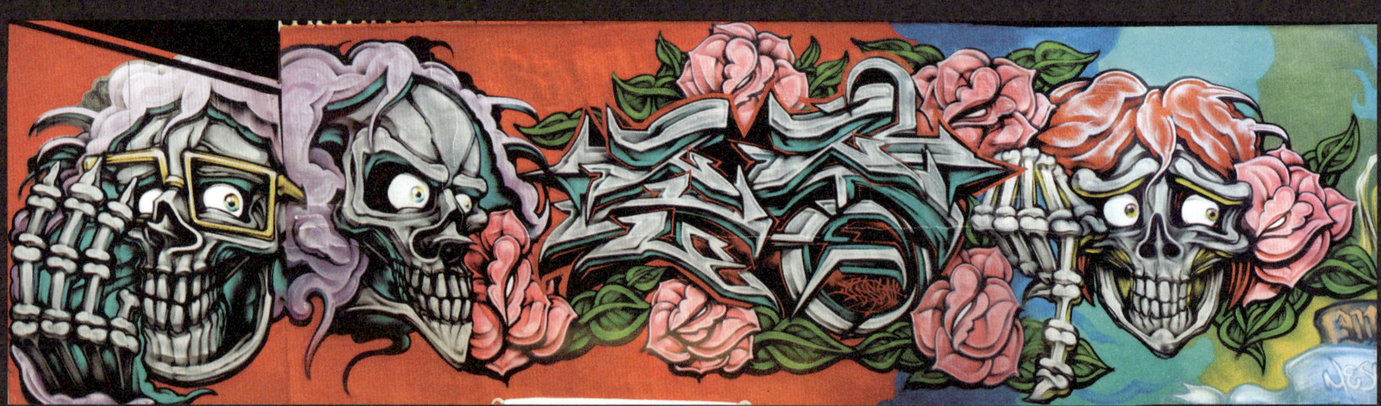

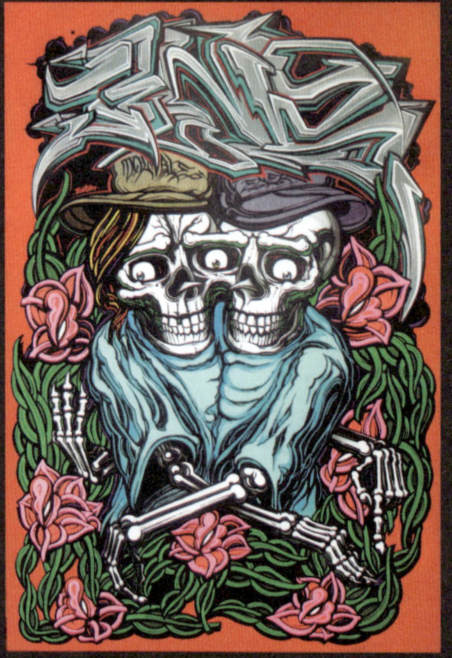

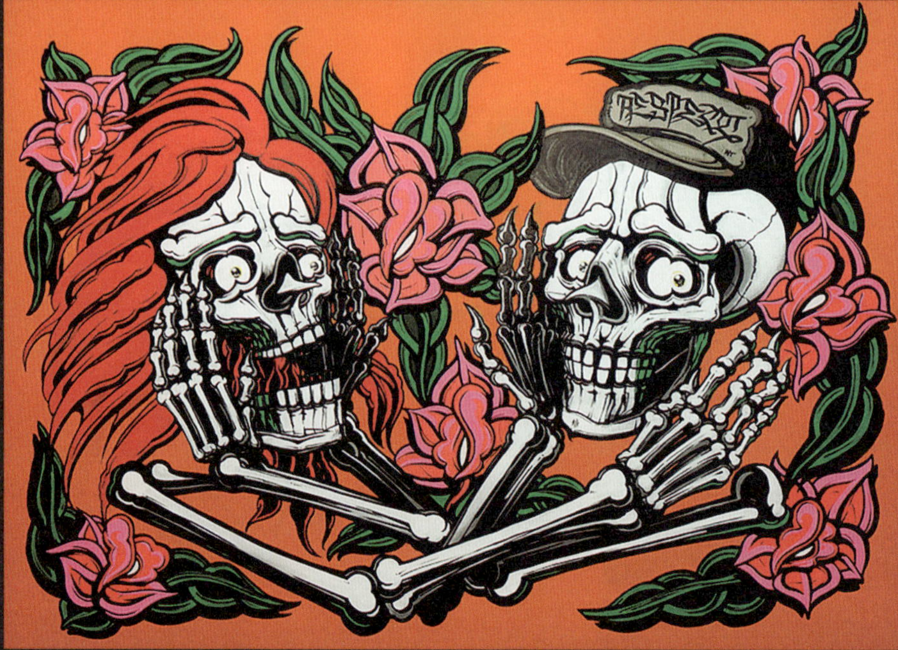

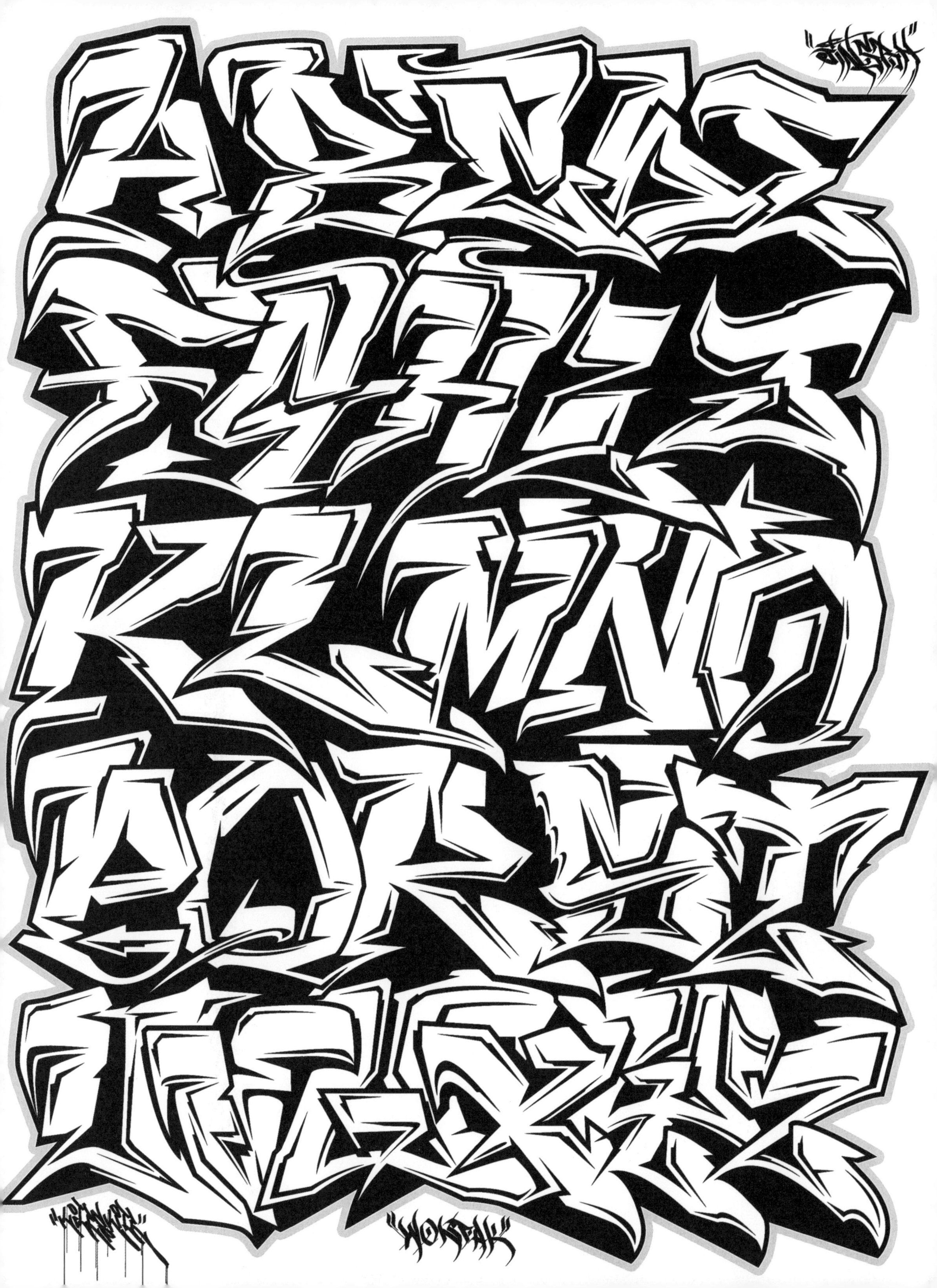

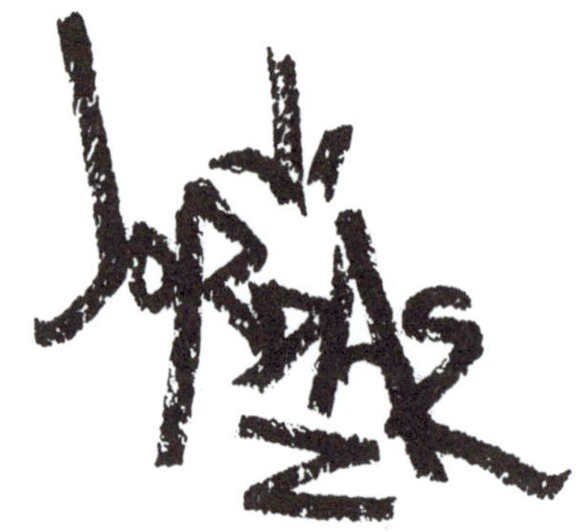

Jordae

Crew member of 667, dothemath
Writer since 1995
Favourite letters: K, Q, R, F
www.jordae.com

Jordae travels around Europe, dividing his time primarily between
Spain, Germany and the Netherlands. His alphabet is based on
classic fonts and was created with acrylic and spray paint and ink
on canvas boards. 'It takes passion and practice to create a good
piece,' Jordae says.

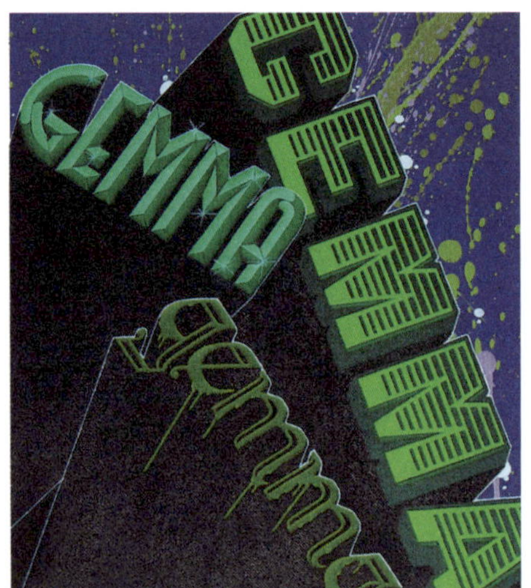

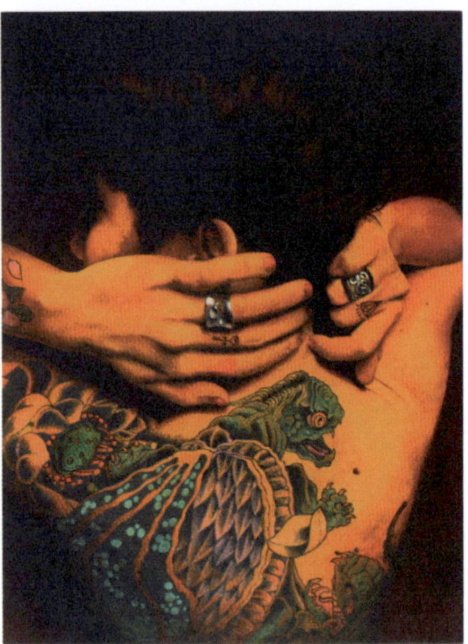

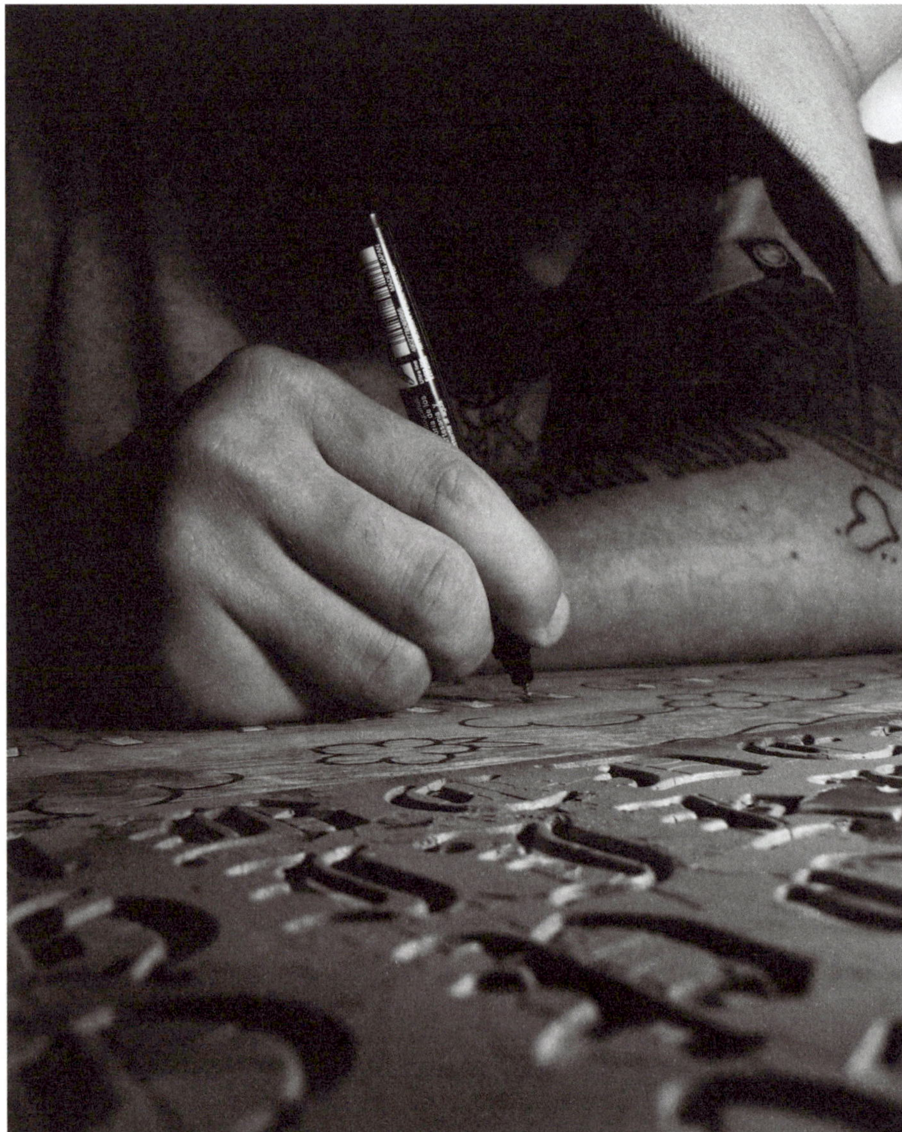

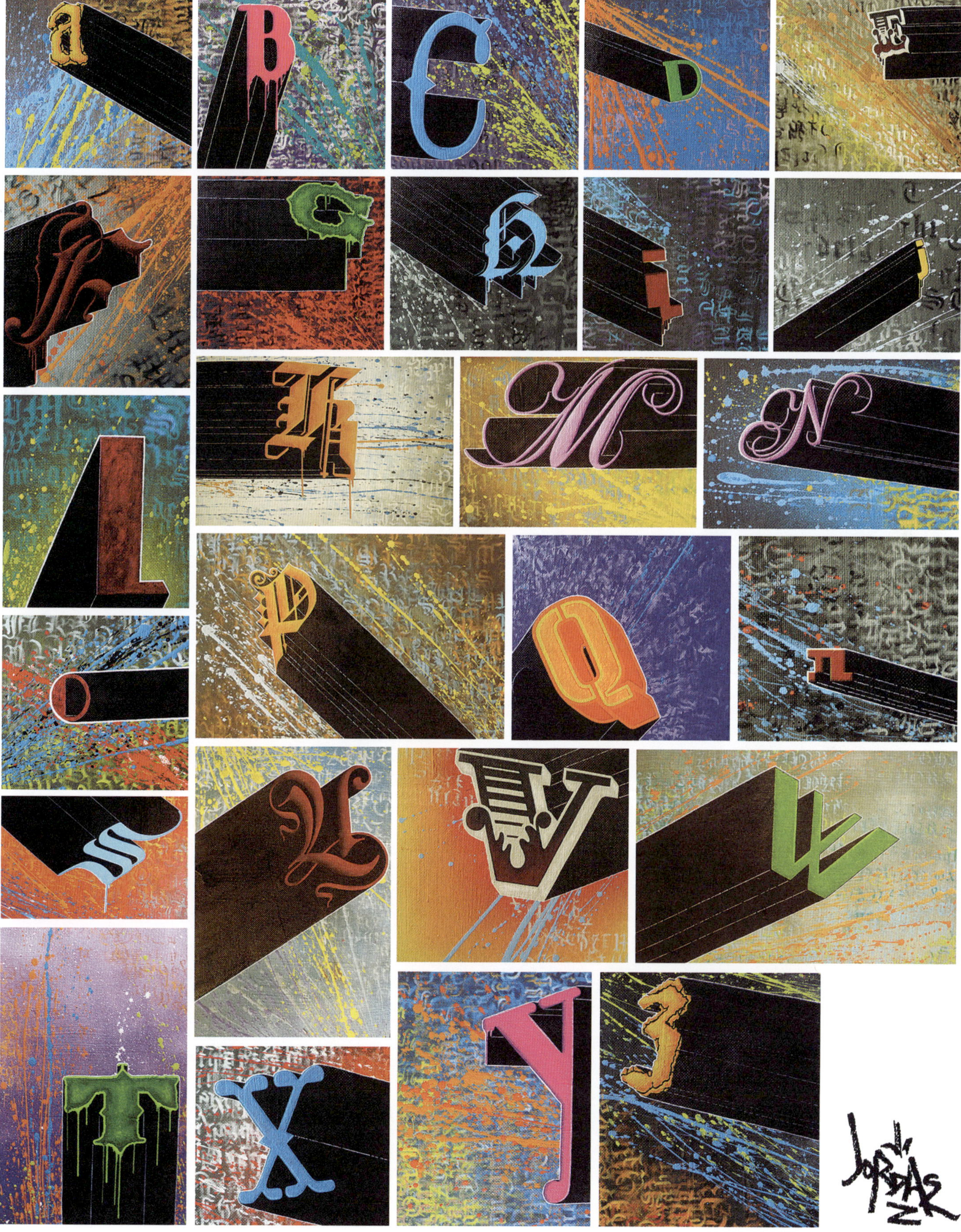
JORDAN
ZK

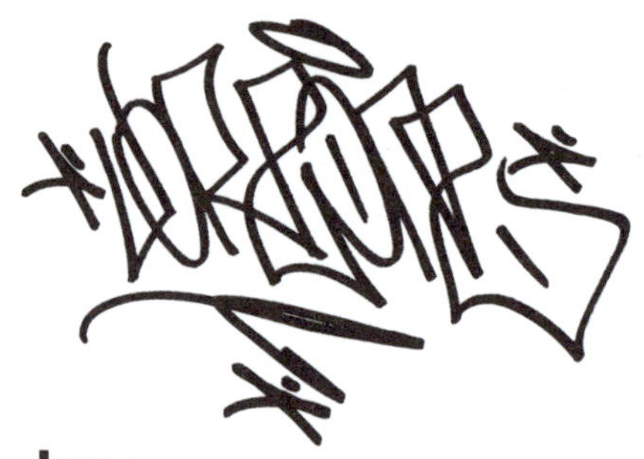

Jorz

MELBOURNE, AUSTRALIA
Crew member of Rock Da City, Majestic Rockers
Writer since 1987
Favourite letter: 'I love all letters'

Jorz is an old-school writer from Melbourne. He drew his alphabet twenty
times before he finally found a version that he was happy with and a true
interpretation of a style that he has studied for more than twenty years. The
interplay of lines suggests different ways of reading his letters. 'Some letters
borrow elements from the previous letters and then merge into the next,' he
explains. Jorz appreciates the satisfaction that he gets from graffiti, as well
as the feeling of elation and the never-ending learning process.

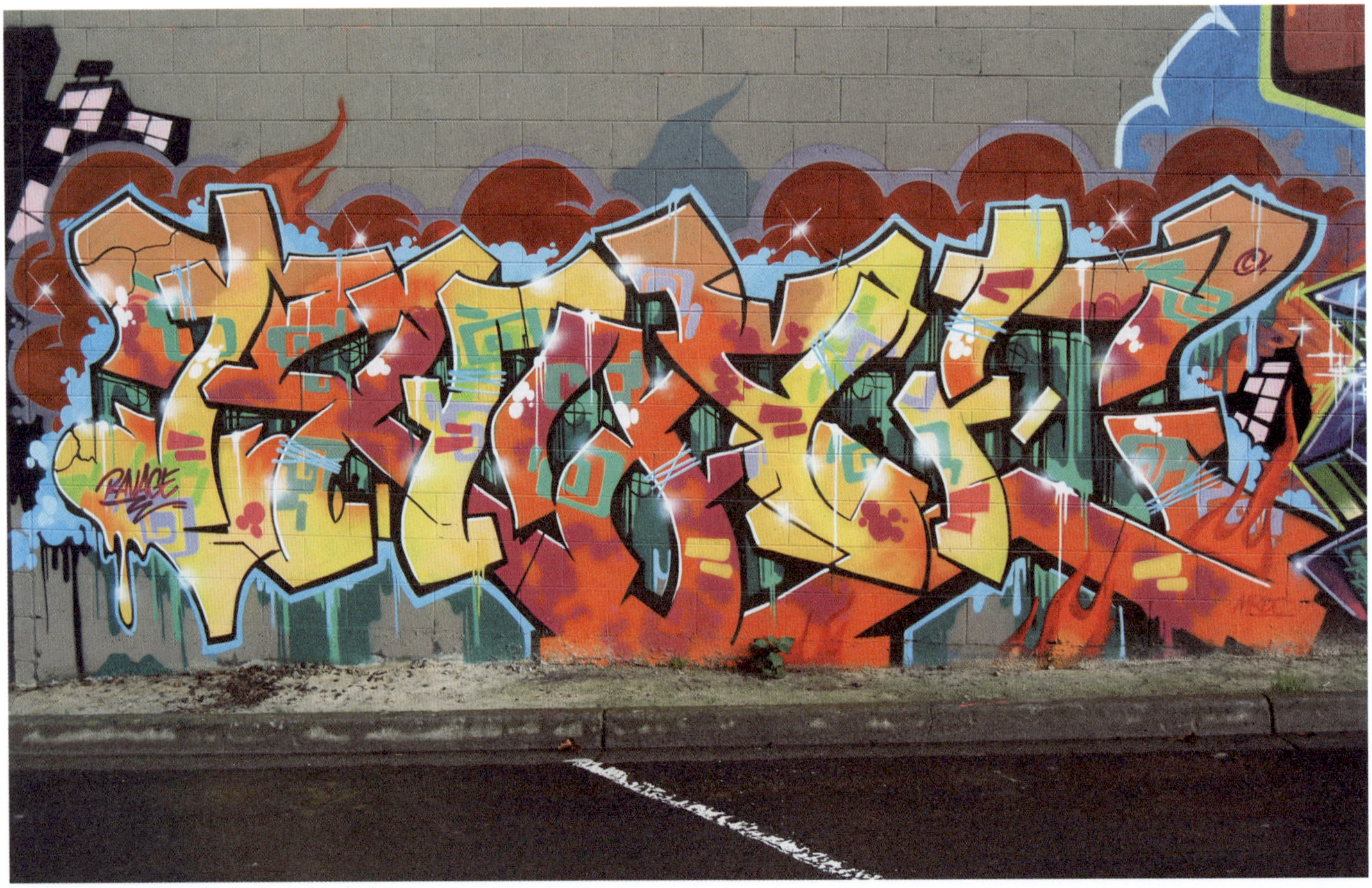

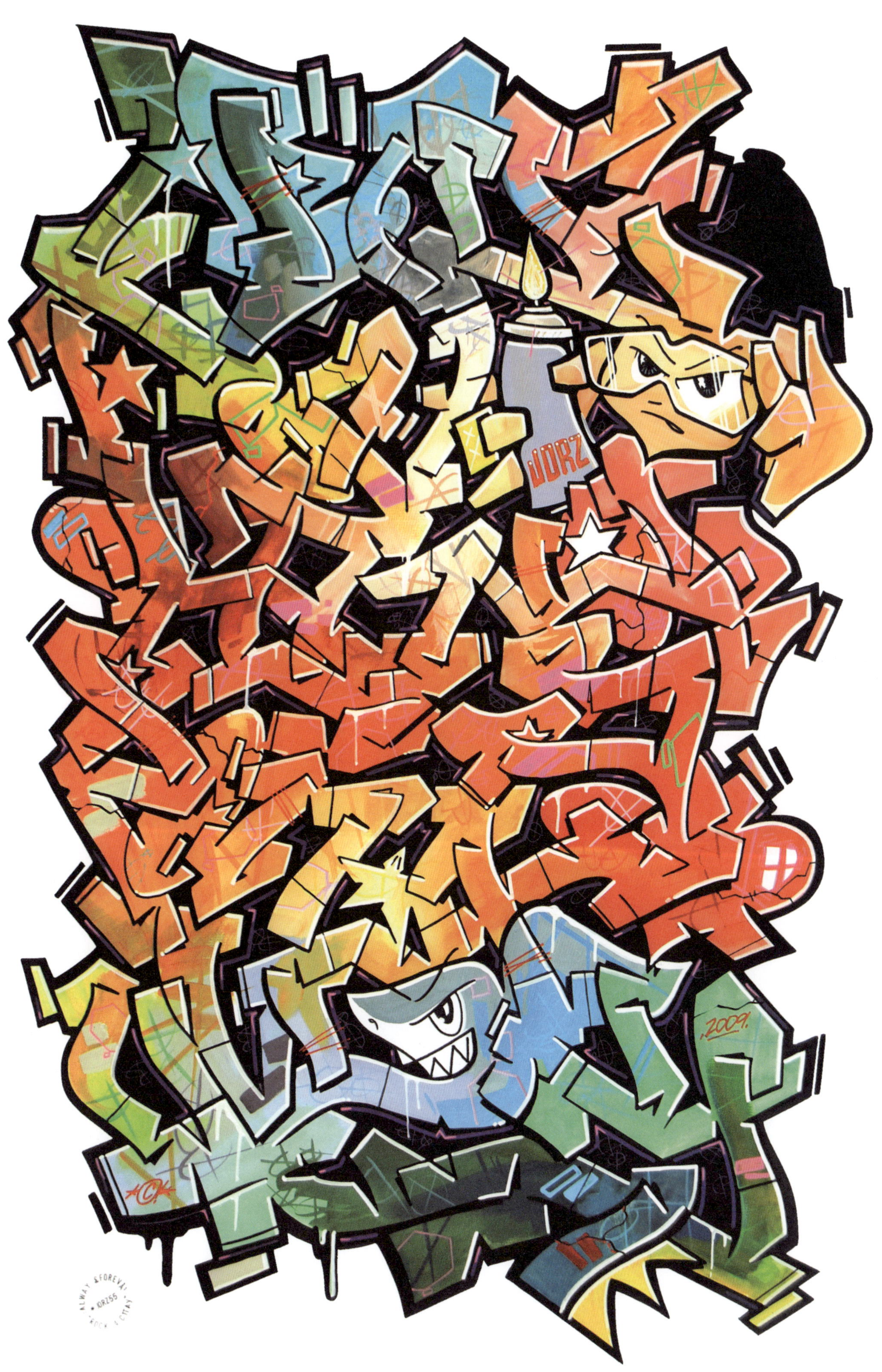

UDRZ
2009.
ACK

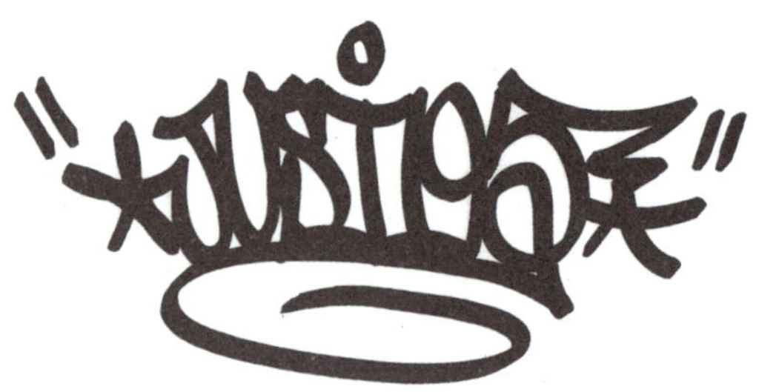

Just195

LOS ANGELES, USA
Crew member of NASA, AWR/MSK, TATS, DF, IBS
Writer since 1984
Favourite letter: 'All of them'

A good piece has to have style, technique and the right colours, according to Just195. What fascinates him most about graffiti is that it's everywhere.

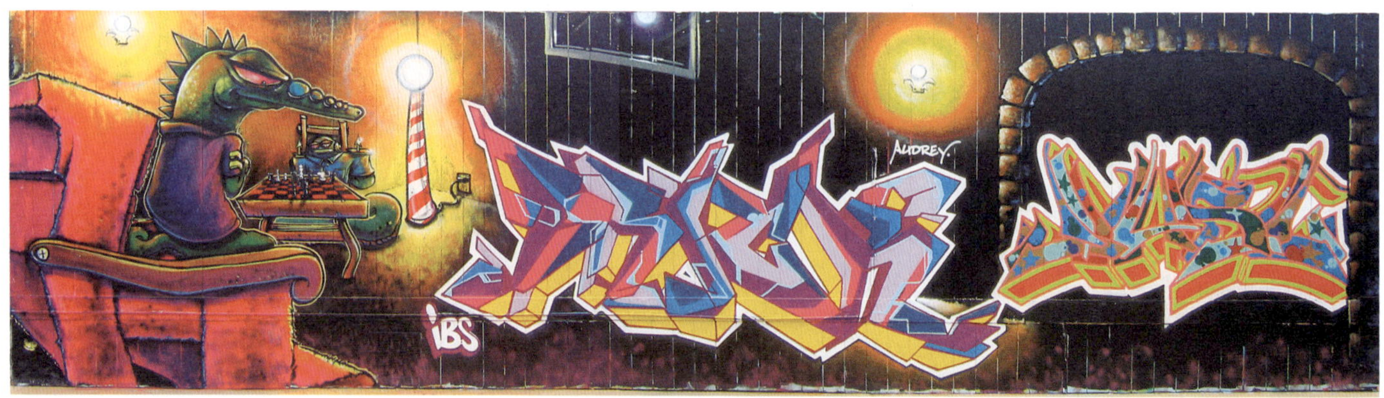

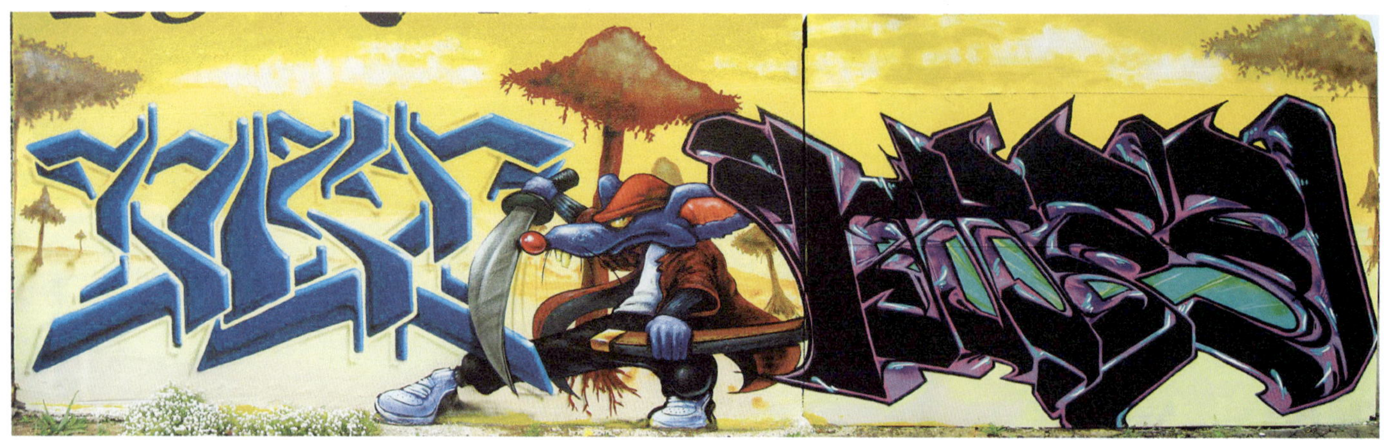

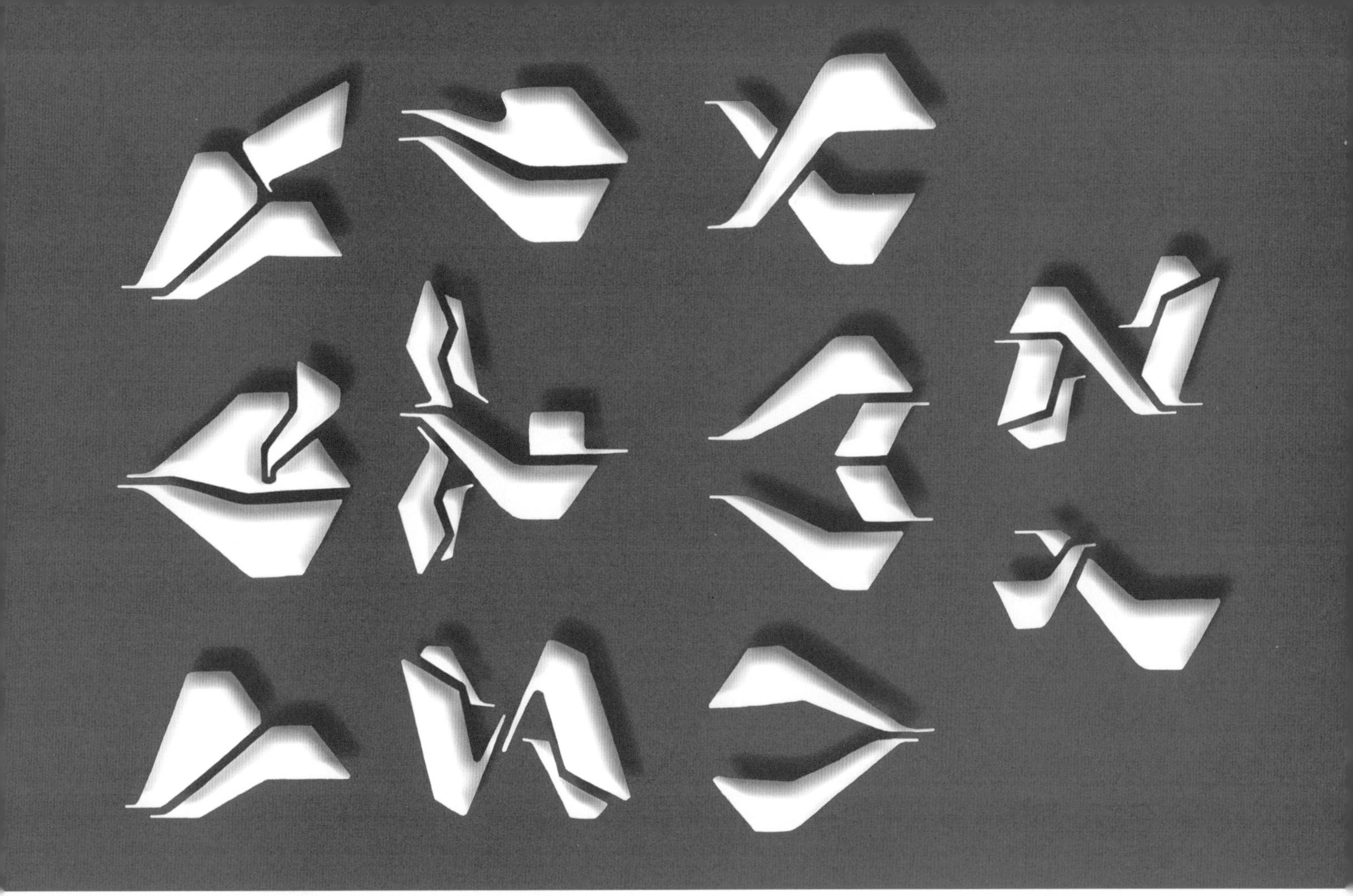

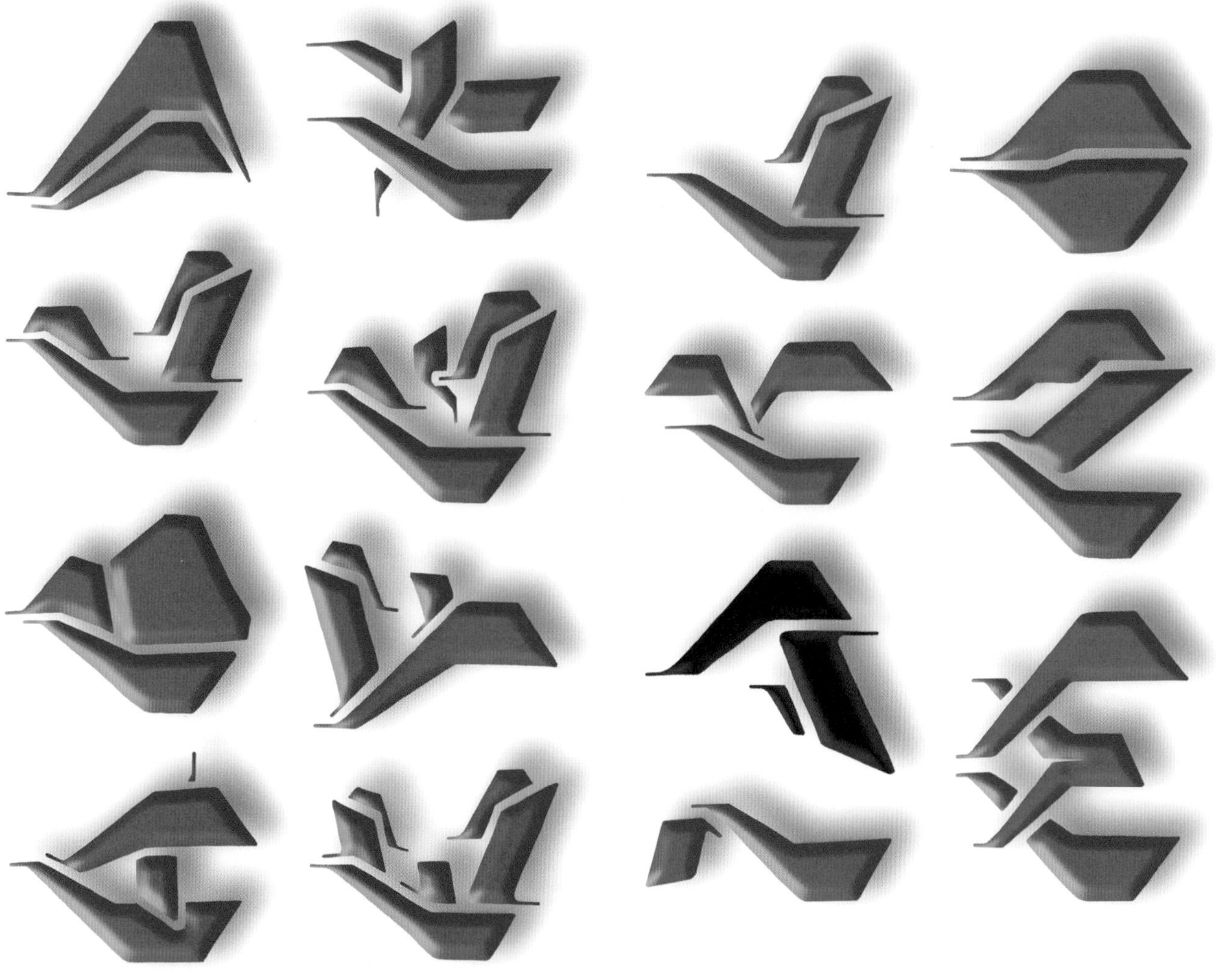

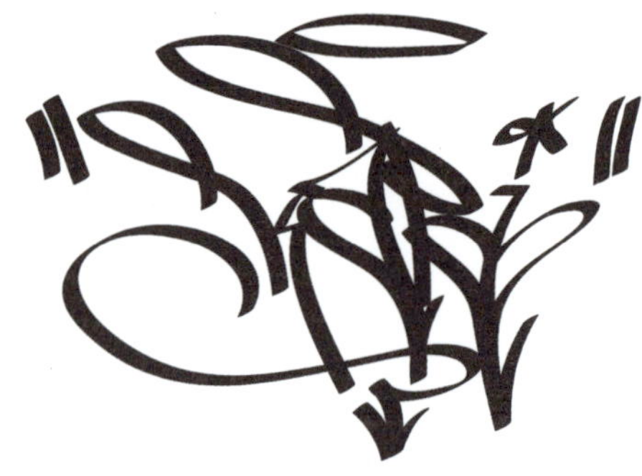

Kapi

BARCELONA, SPAIN
Crew member of The Chosen Few
Writer since 1986
Favourite letter: P
www.kapione.com

Kapi is a well-known writer and musician, and has also initiated various other projects. He started a graffiti magazine in 1992, opened Barcelona's first graffiti shop in 1993 and has advised the spray-paint company Montana Colors Spain. His pieces are influenced by the classic New York wildstyle. It is essential that every single letter looks good, he says, but the different elements in a piece must also work well together. He adds: 'Graffiti has many rules, but they are easily broken. That's what makes this movement so free.'

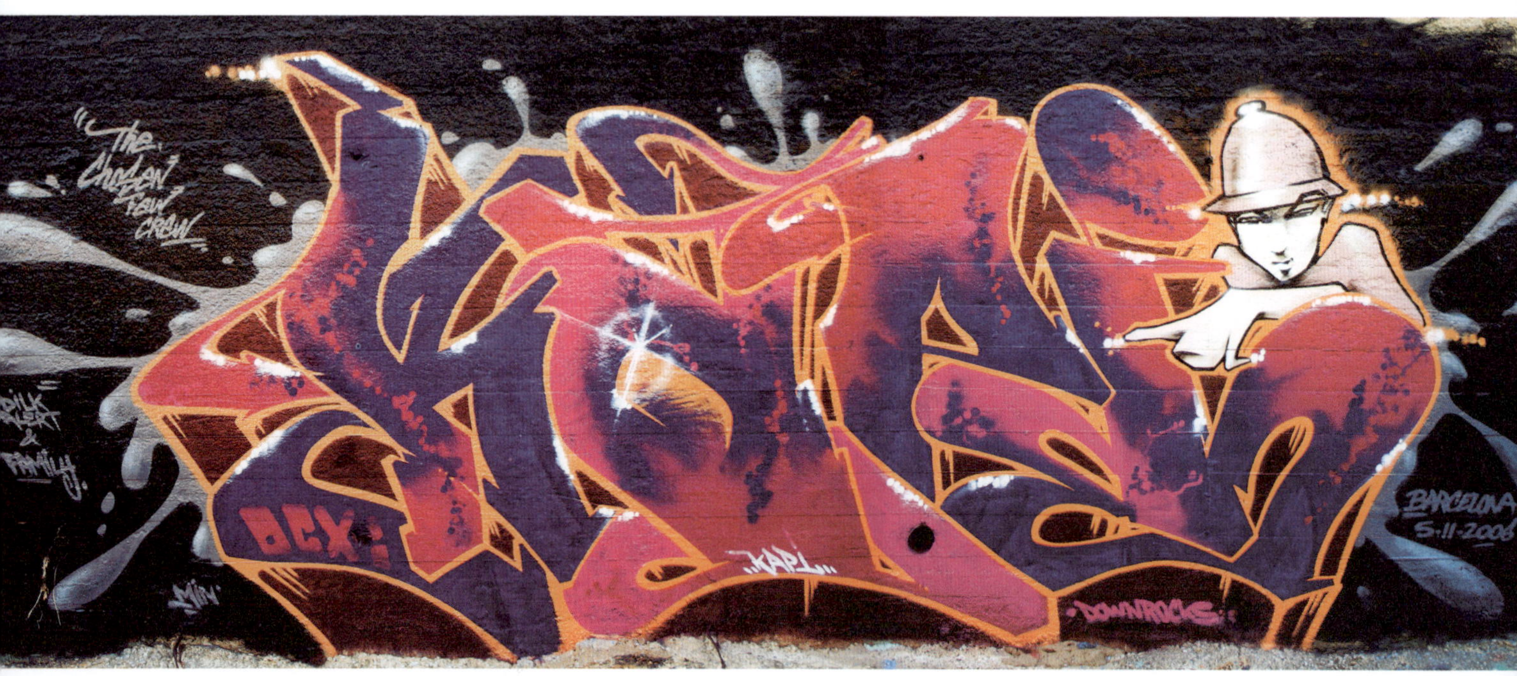

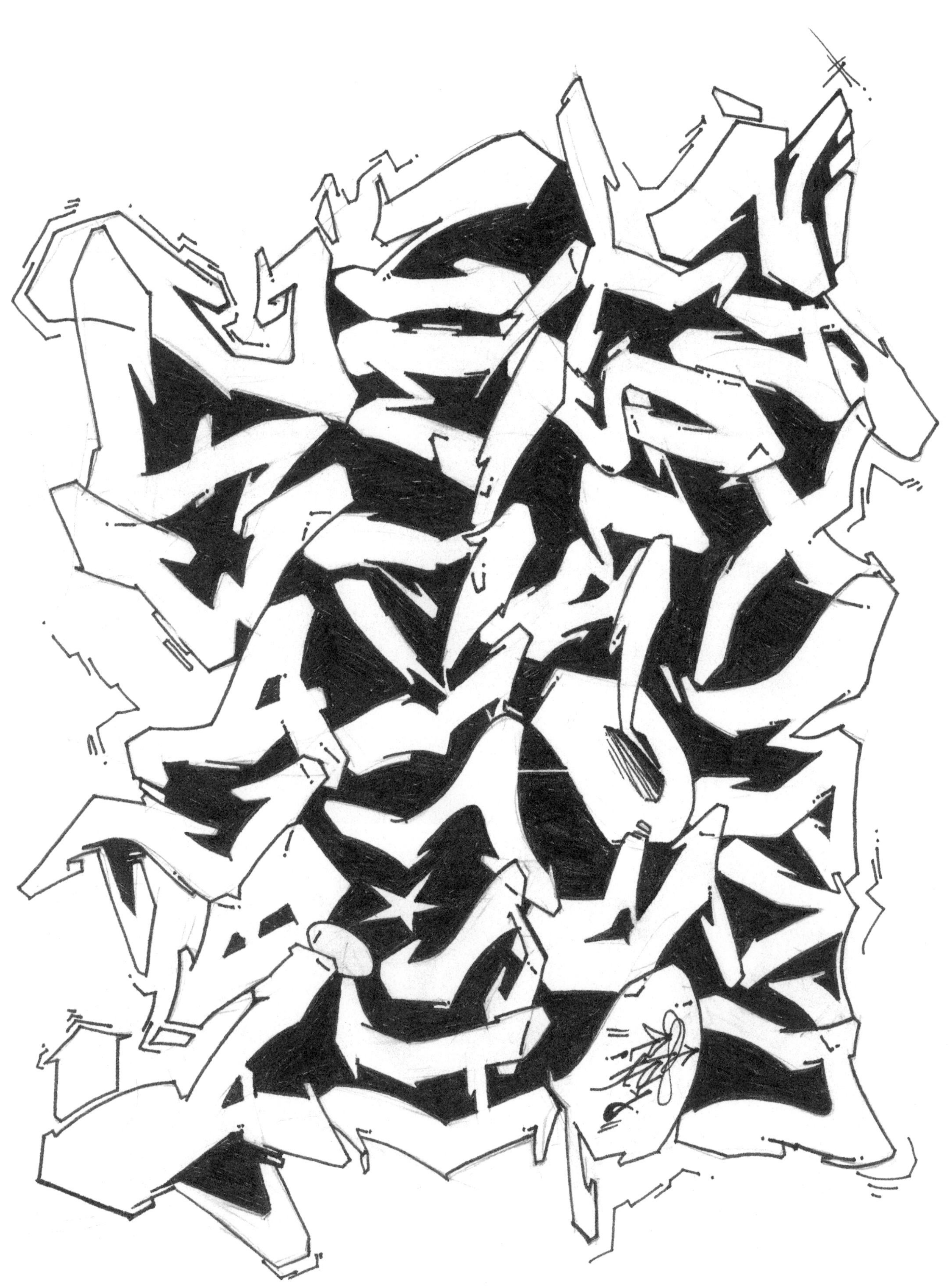

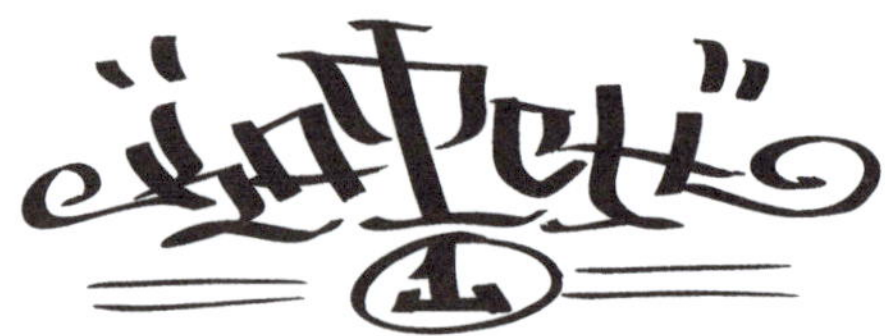

Katch1

HONOLULU, USA

Crew member of NASA
Writer from the age of 13
Favourite letter: K
www.instagram.com/katch1

Katch1 is a Hawaiian graffiti legend. He is known for his illustrations, characters, and carefully planned walls combining letters, characters and backgrounds. His work of the past twenty years was recently published in a book. Describing his alphabet, Katch1 says: 'Over the years my letters have slowly drifted towards a combination of both letters and characters.' Despite living with graffiti for more than two decades, he still loves the adrenalin rush and the stillness and hum of the freight yard.

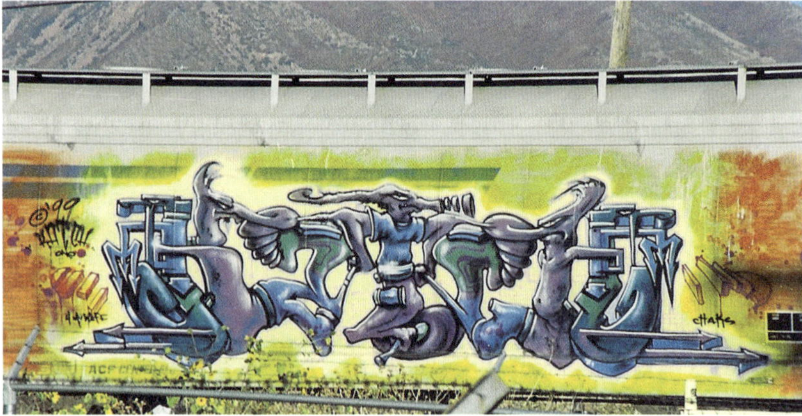

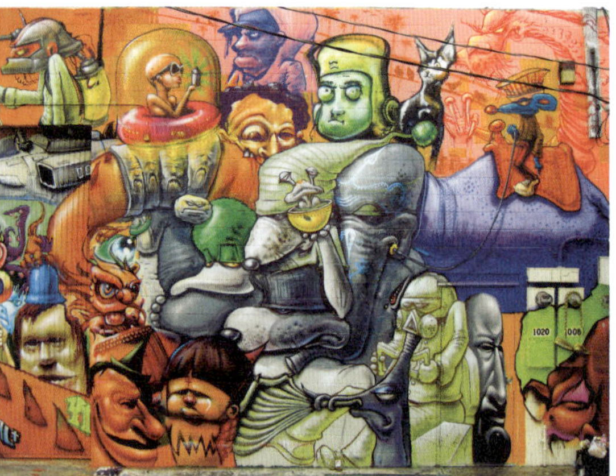

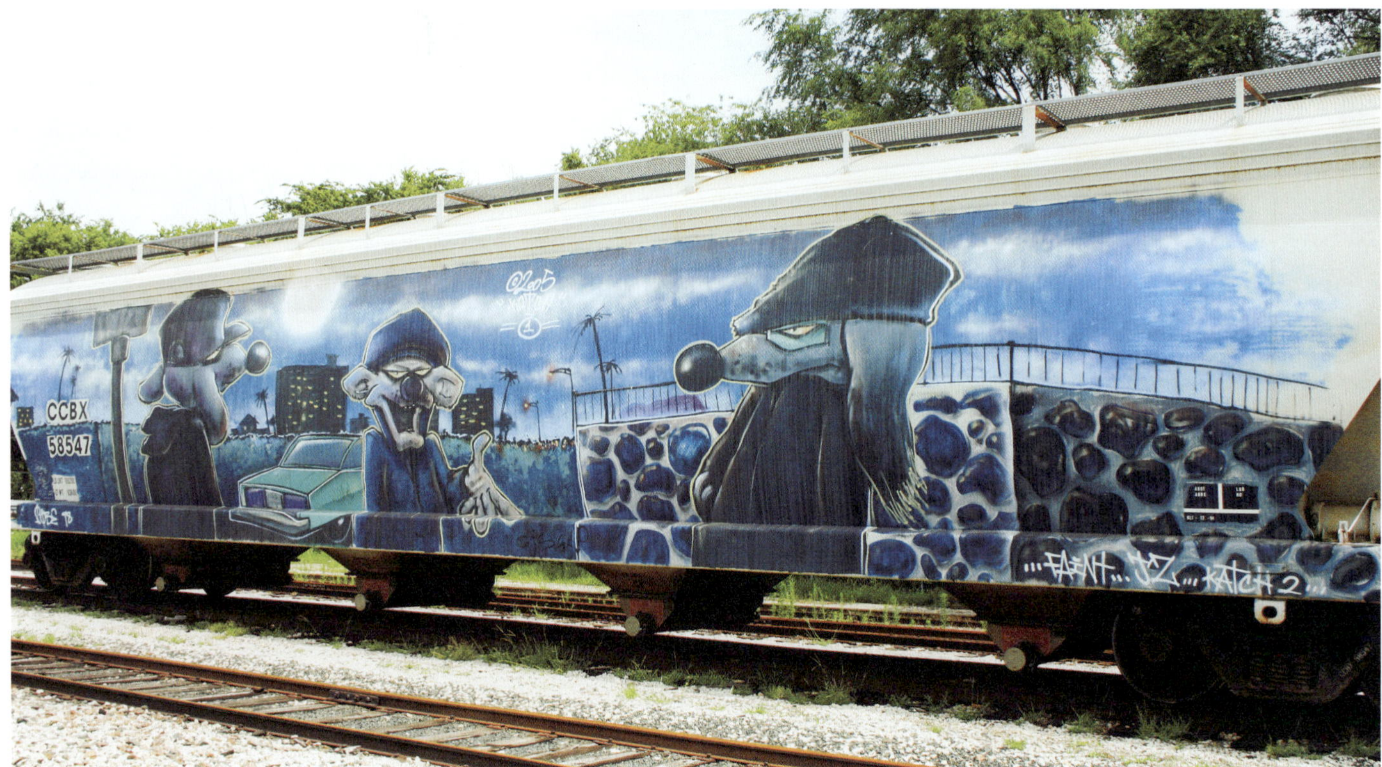

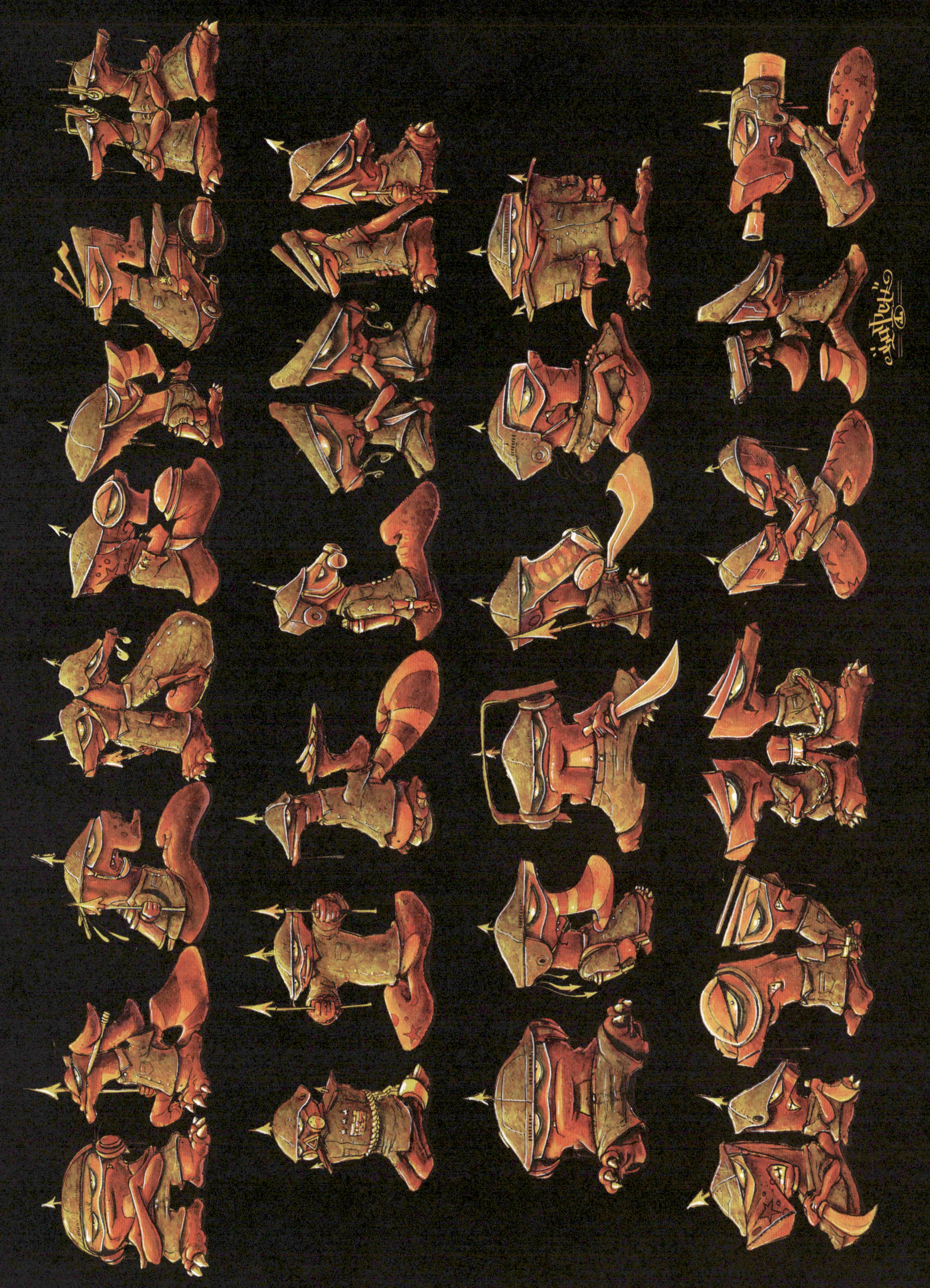

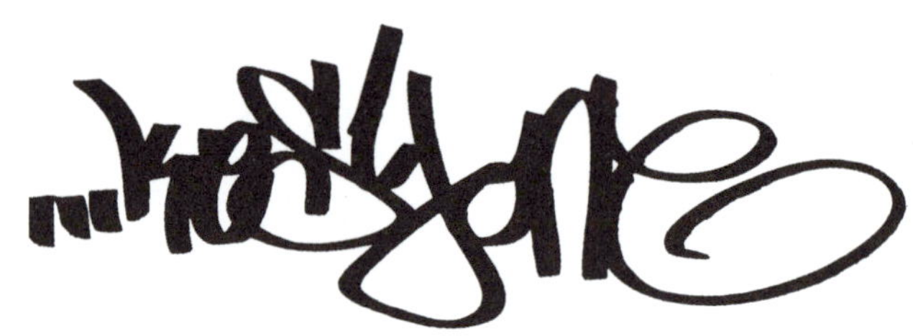

Kesy One

BERN, SWITZERLAND

Crew member of Adult Entertainment, HWS, S2R
Favourite letter: 'None in particular'
www.myspace.com/kesyone

Kesy One developed his semi-wildstyle over several years and
says that he tries to do with letters what mathematicians do with
numbers. Letters need logic and vivacity, he explains, and each
piece should be different from whatever you have done before.

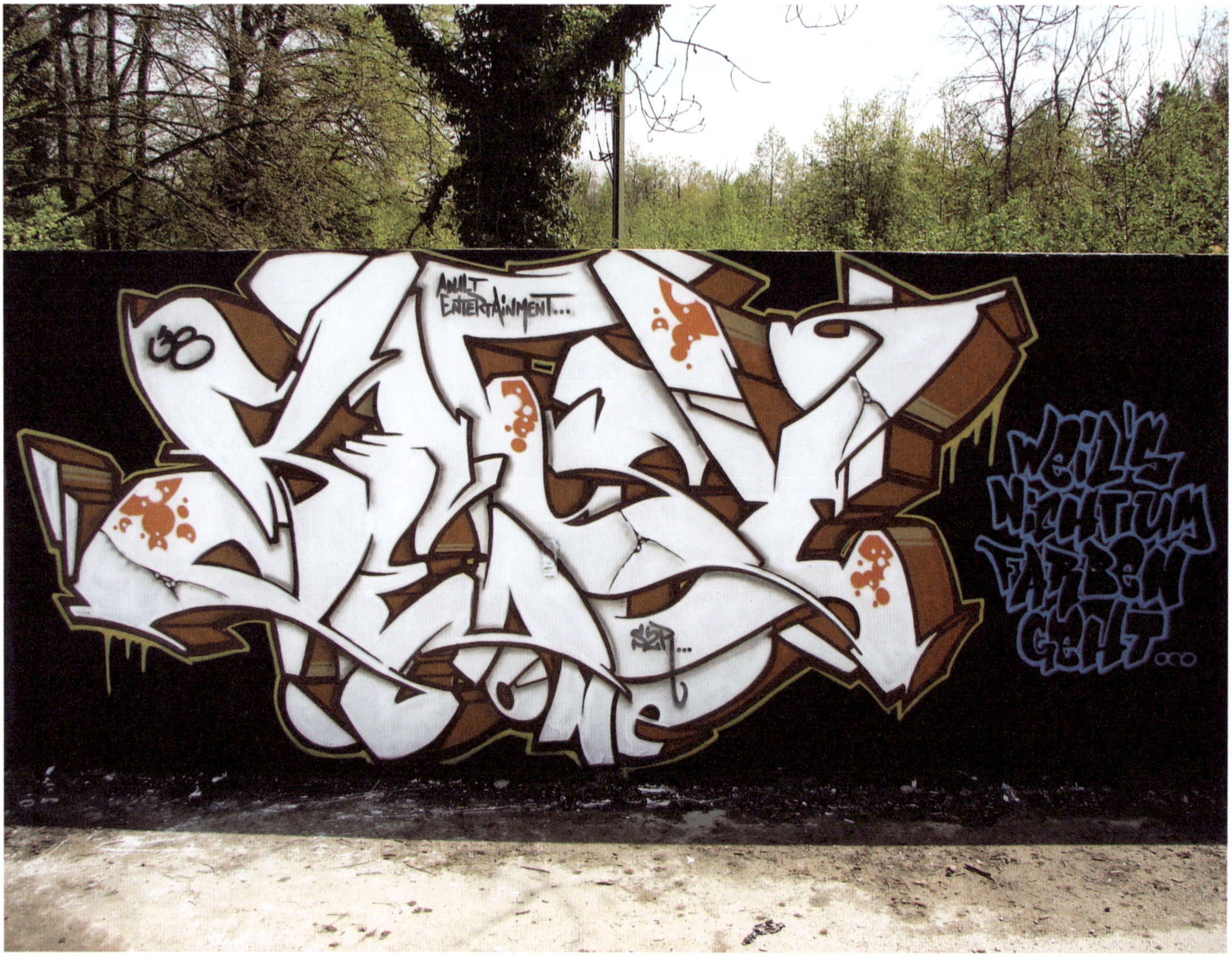

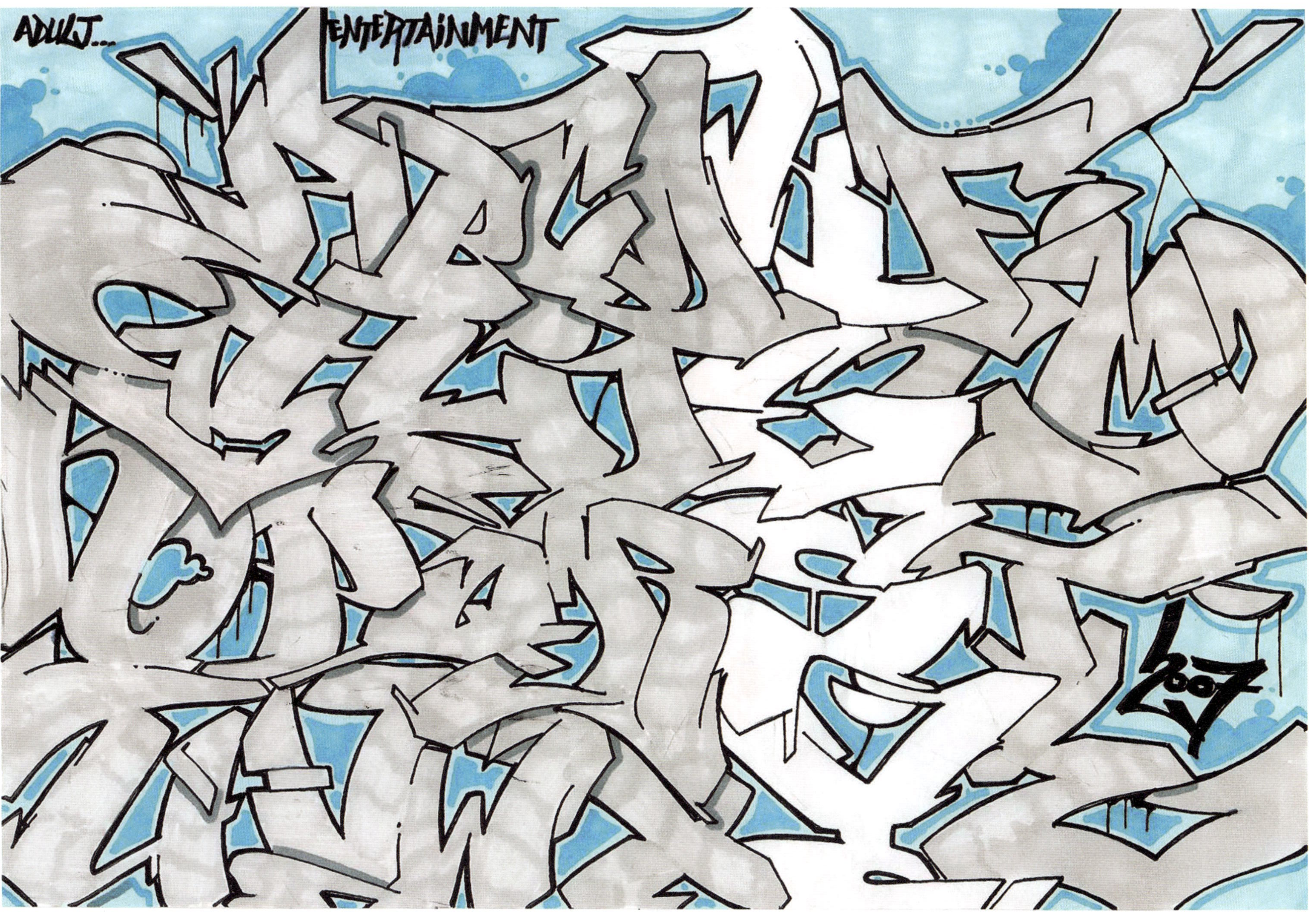

ADULT...
ENTERTAINMENT
2007

Kies

ALCOY, SPAIN
Crew member of Wild Cans, Pornostars
Writer since 1993
Favourite letter: K
www.instagram.com/kies_wildcans

Kies has always wanted to design an alphabet and finally
succeeded in creating one that shows his typical style of heavy
strokes connected by thin joins. As a writer you should always
enjoy what you do, he says; otherwise you will never be able
to paint a good piece.

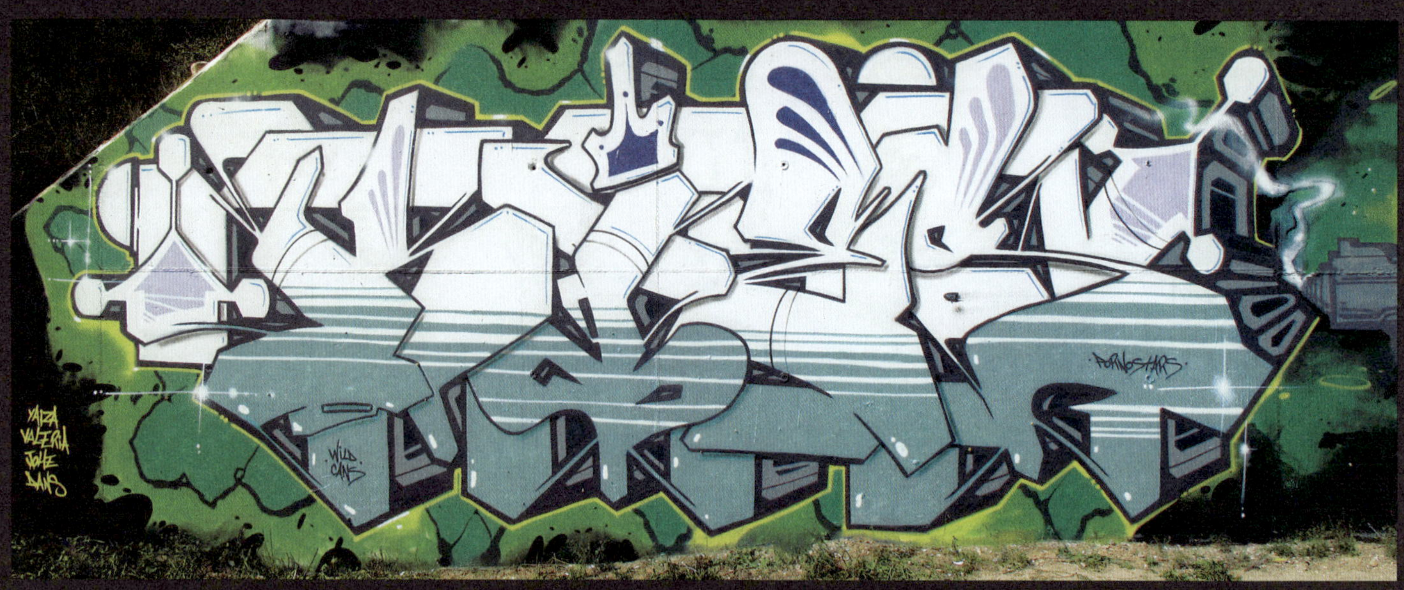

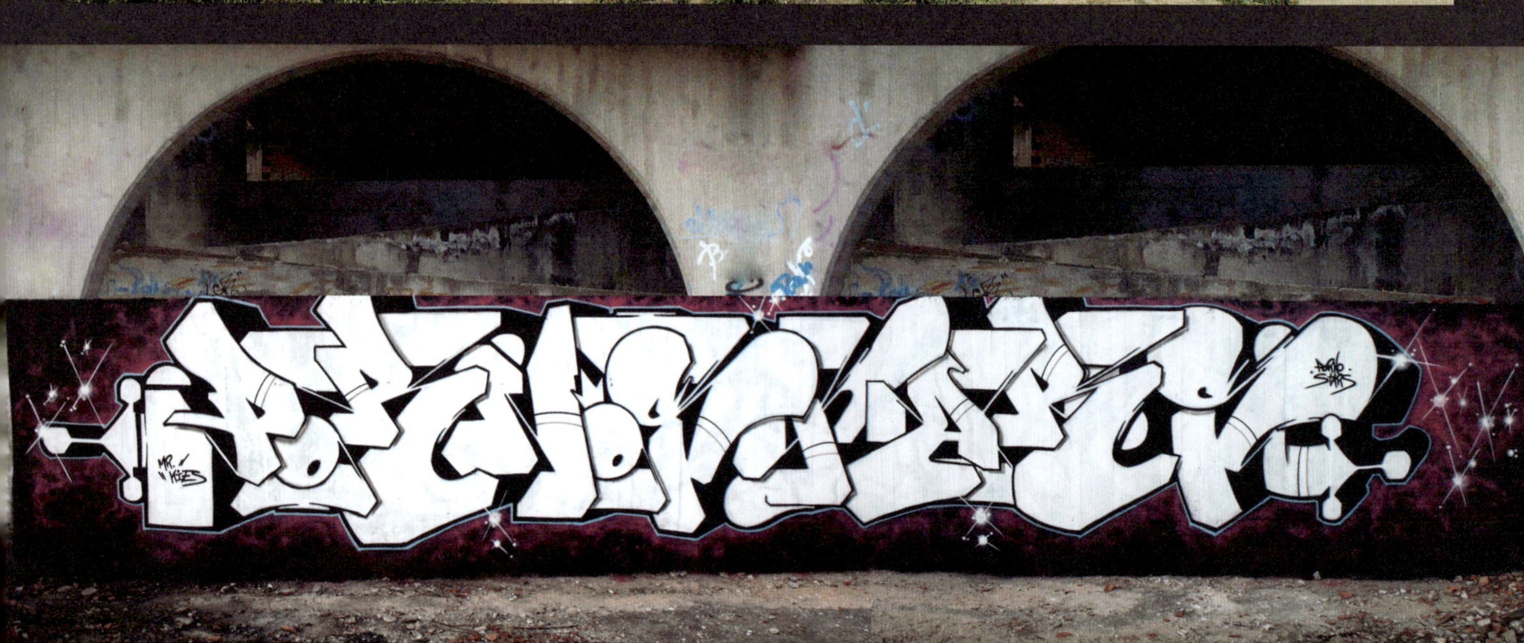

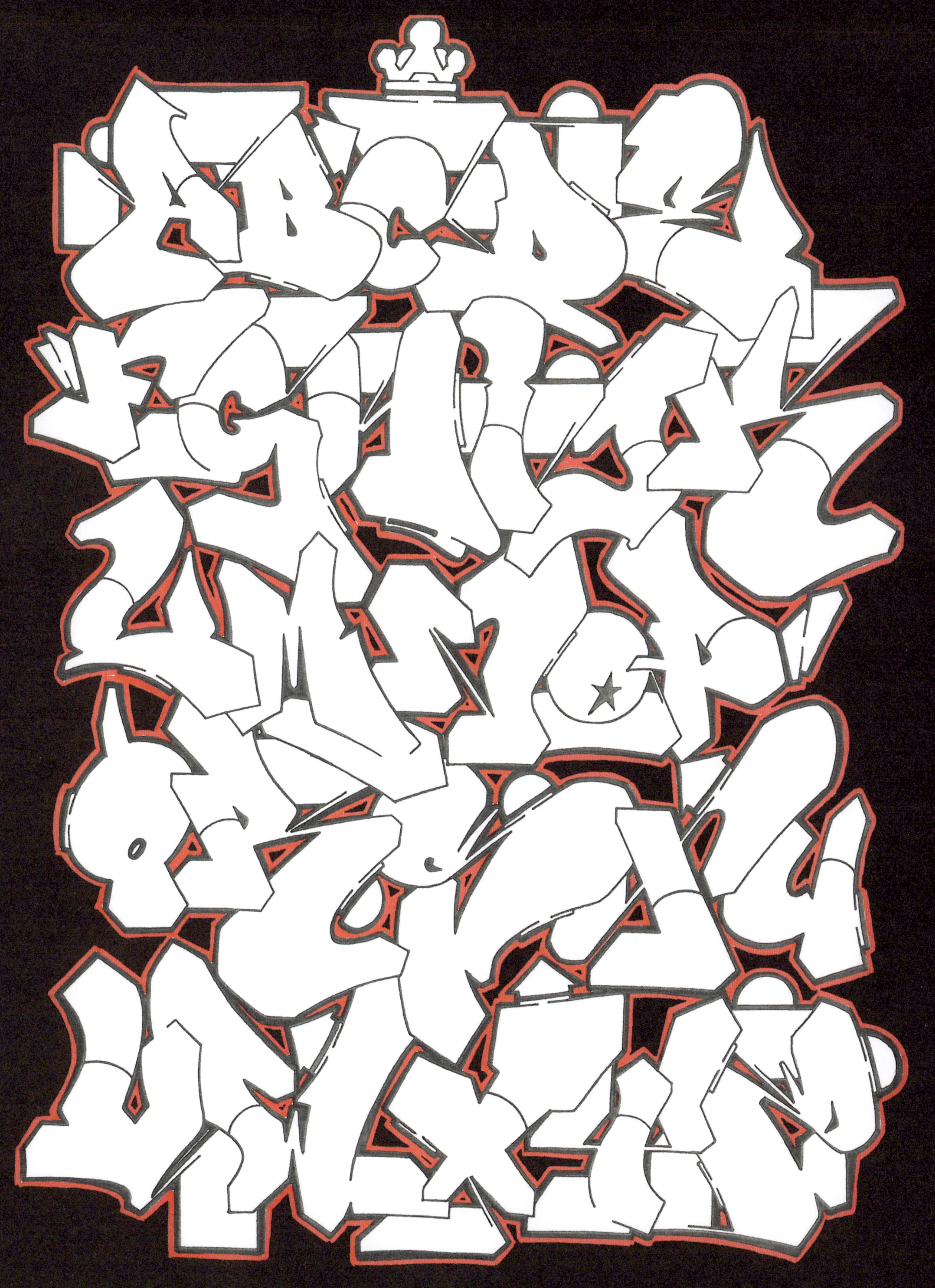

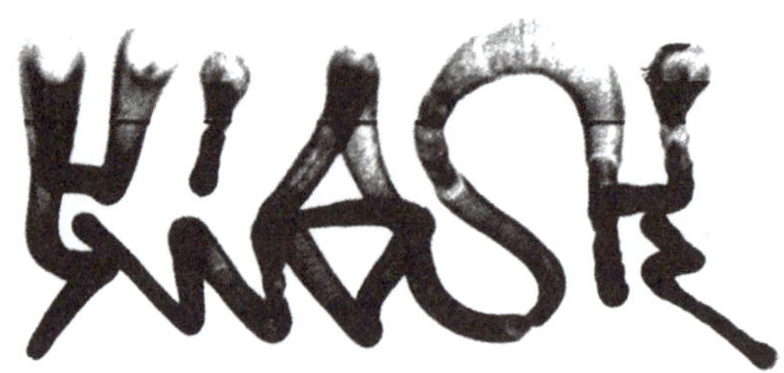

Kio

MOSCOW, RUSSIA
Crew member of Sicksystems (2005–9)
Writer since 2000
Favourite letter: S
www.alexeykio.com

Graphic designer, illustrator and graffiti artist Kio has worked with companies such as Adidas and MTV. Straight lines, angled shapes and contrasting colours characterize his work. Graffiti helps him to free his mind and let his imagination go.

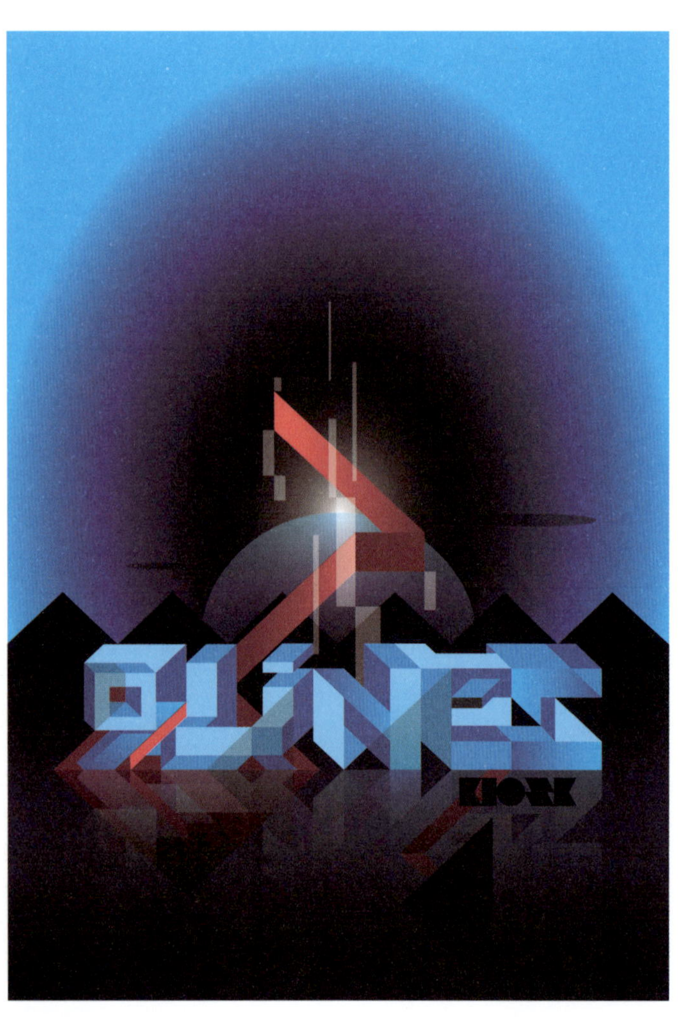

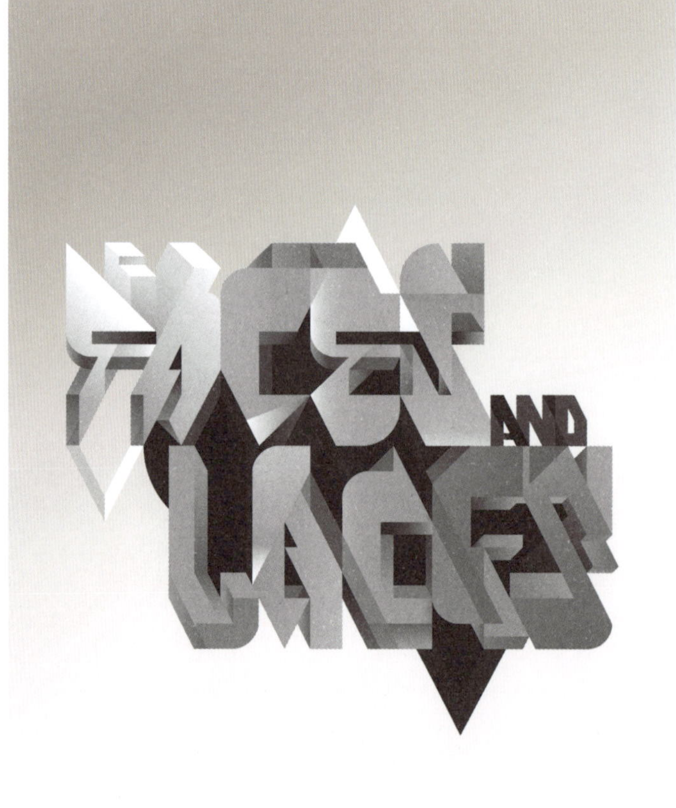

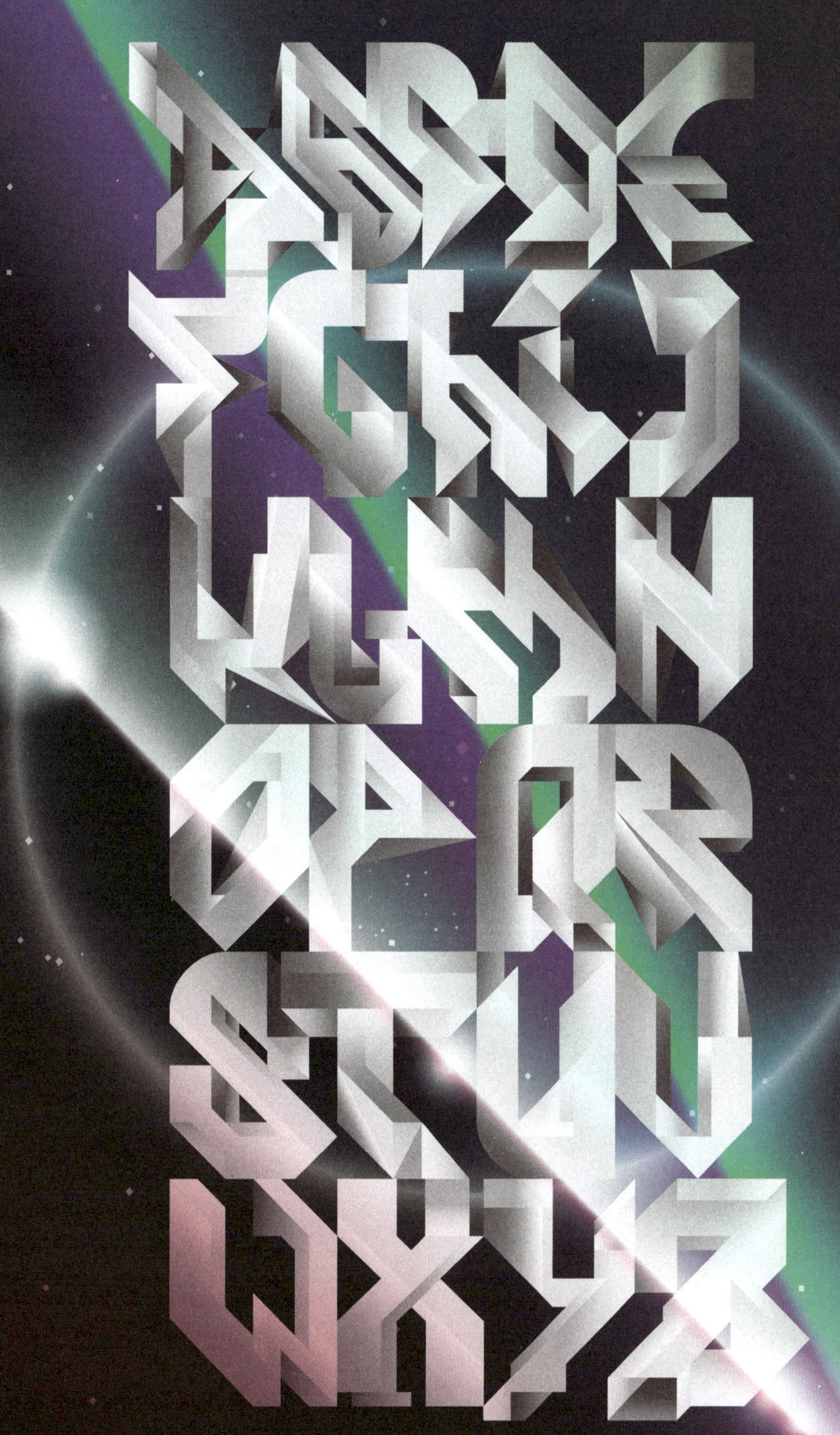

Klark Kent

FRANKFURT, GERMANY
Crew member of SUK, TNB, DBL, GBF, BSQ
Writer since 1989
Favourite letters: K, S
www.klarkkent.de

Klark Kent is a perfectionist with a distinctive style. His striking pieces
stand out for their clean-cut shapes, blazing colours and expertly joined
letters. It takes 'passion, aggression and flow' to create a quality piece,
he says. He has also taken part in many large-scale graffiti productions,
and has travelled around the world as part of the Montana Writer Team.

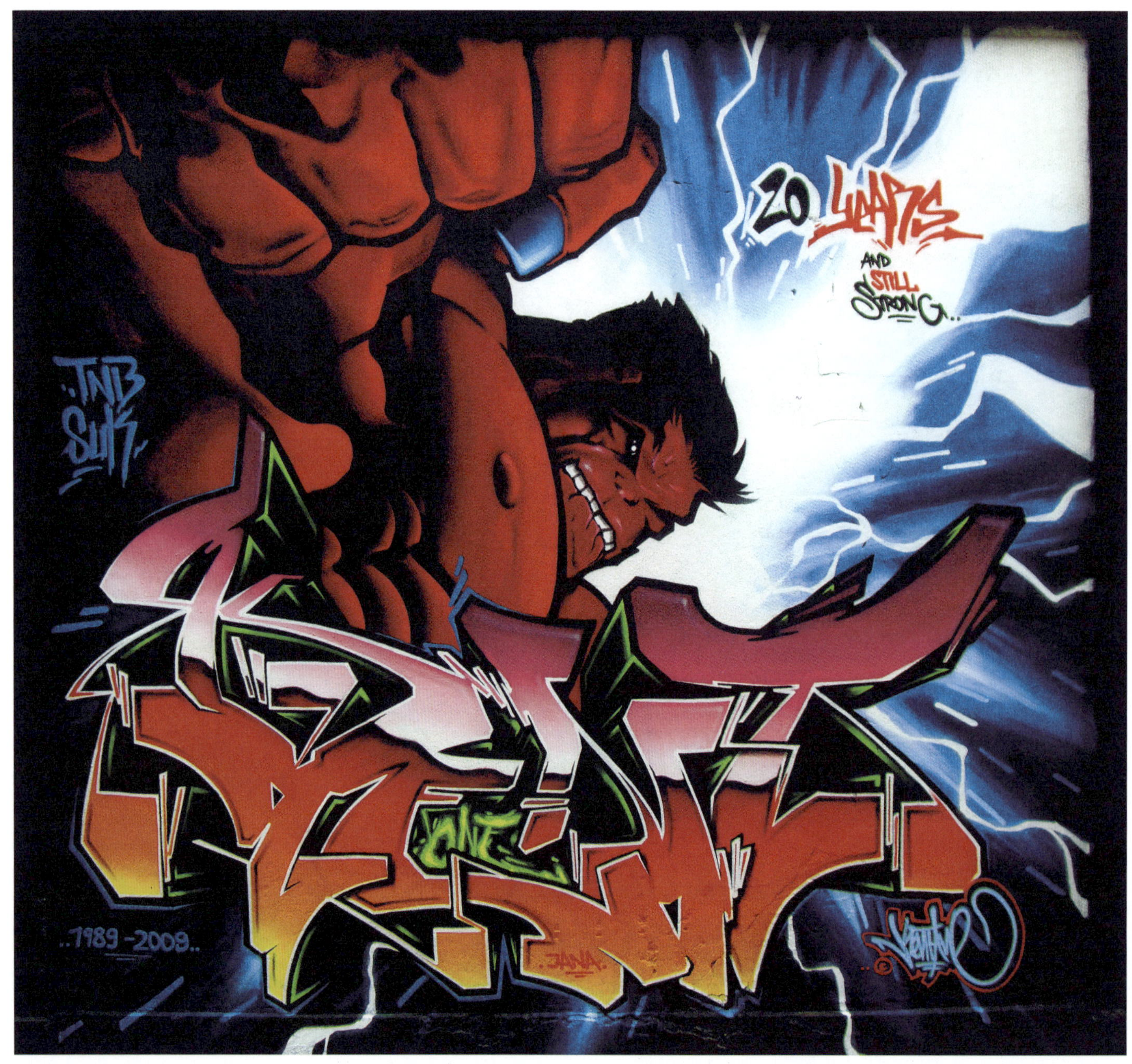

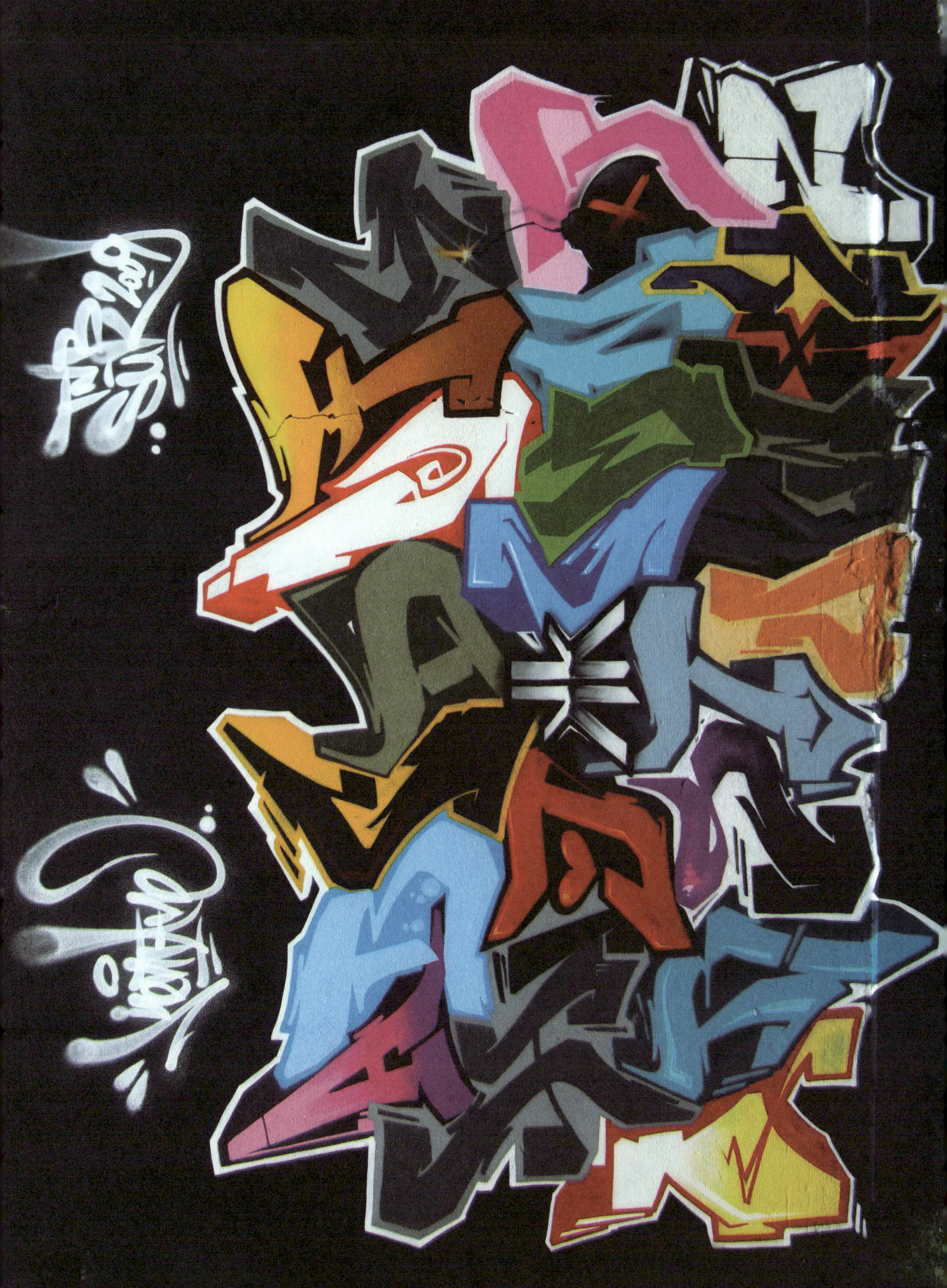

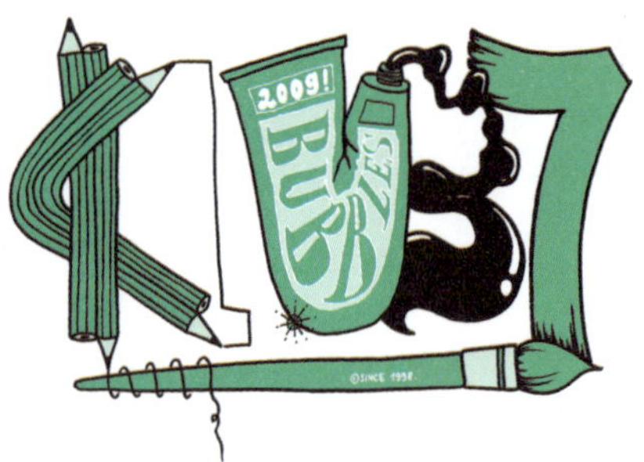

Klub7
BERLIN, GERMANY

Crew members: Dani Daphne,
Diskorobot, Lowskii, Mike Okay,
Kid Cash, Otto Baum
Favourite letter: S
www.klub7.de

Klub7 is a successful creative collective that started out in the German city of Halle and later relocated to Berlin. Their alphabet is a metamorphosis of all twenty-six letters, starting with the 'A' morphing into the 'B' and so on, right up to the letter 'Z'. All kinds of materials were used to create the letters, including acrylic paint, brushes, rollers, markers, spray cans, stencils, cutouts, paper, glue, chalk and sponges. Throughout the process of painting the alphabet, Klub7 took more than 10,000 pictures and made a 6-minute video with those images. The film can be viewed at www.vimeo.com/5855456.

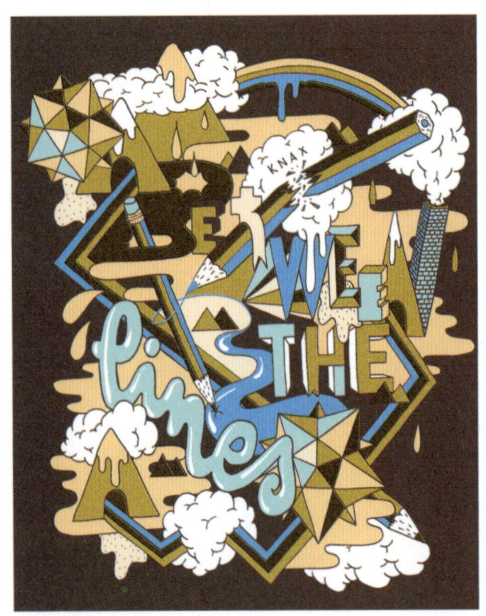

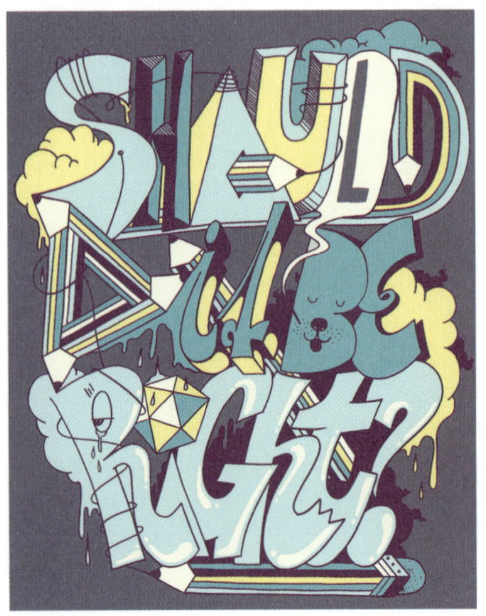

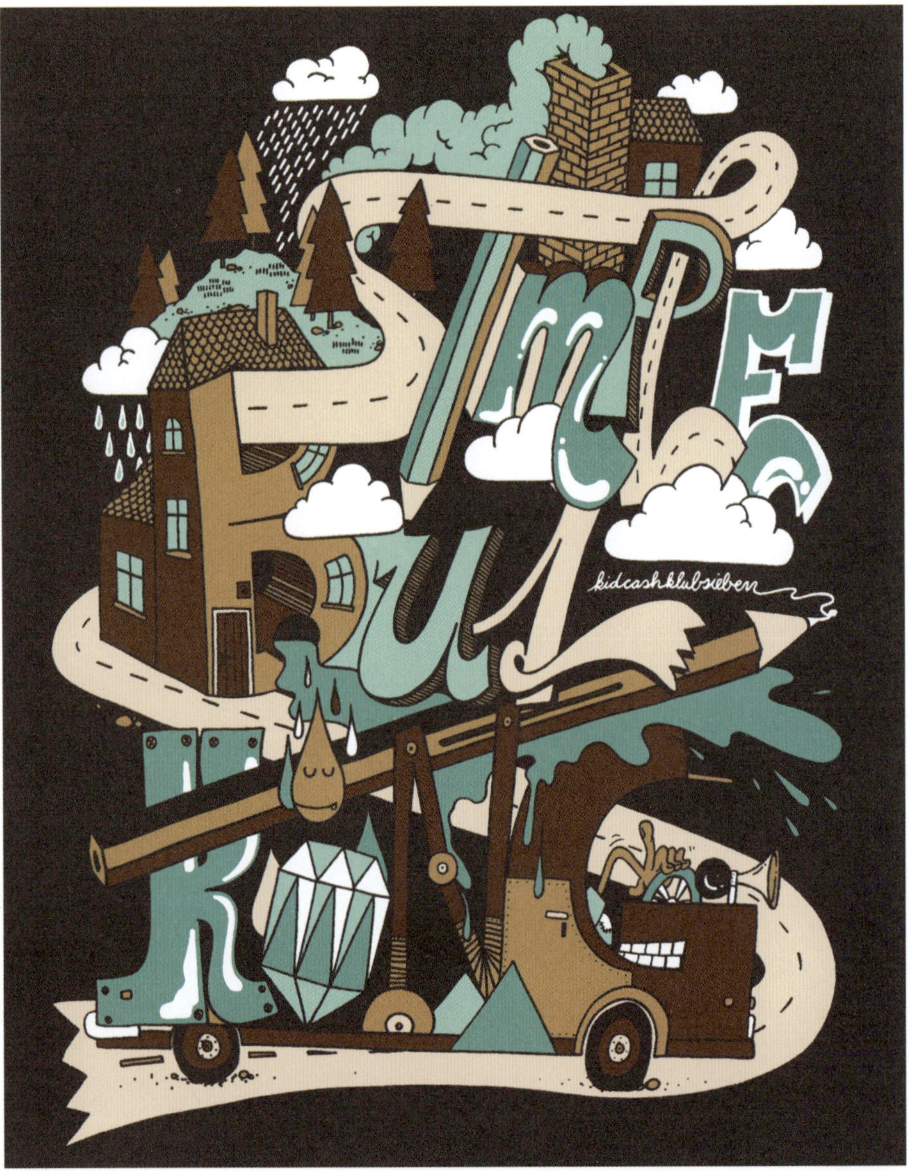

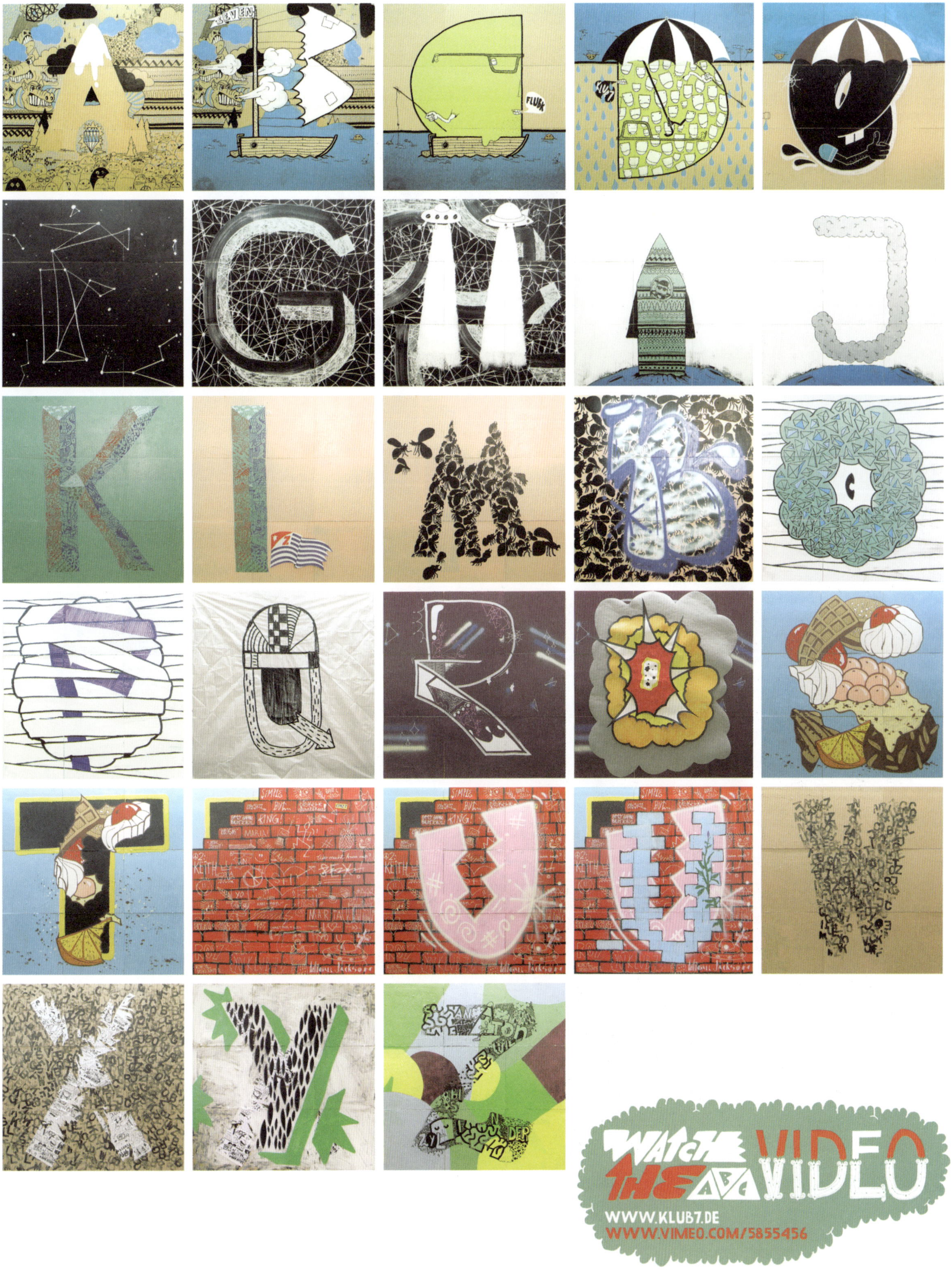

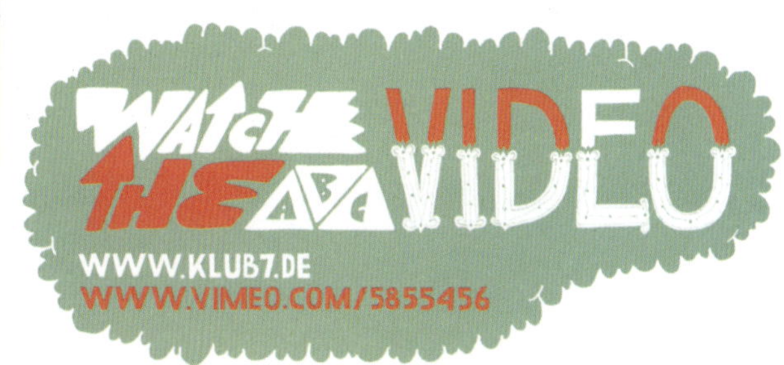

WATCH THE ABC VIDEO
WWW.KLUB7.DE
WWW.VIMEO.COM/5855456

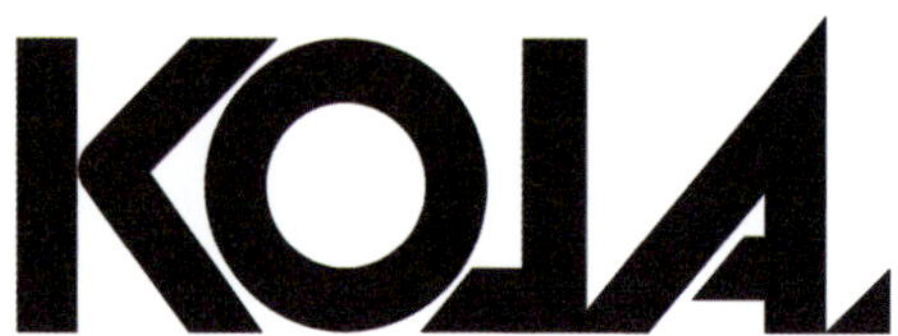

Kola

MOSCOW, RUSSIA
Crew member of Sicksystems (2003–9)
Writer since 2001
Favourite letter: I

Kola is passionate about 3D letters, perfecting them on a computer
to create his 'visual utopia'. Writing is all about ideas, he says, and
he believes that graffiti makes people more open-minded and gives
them a different view of reality.

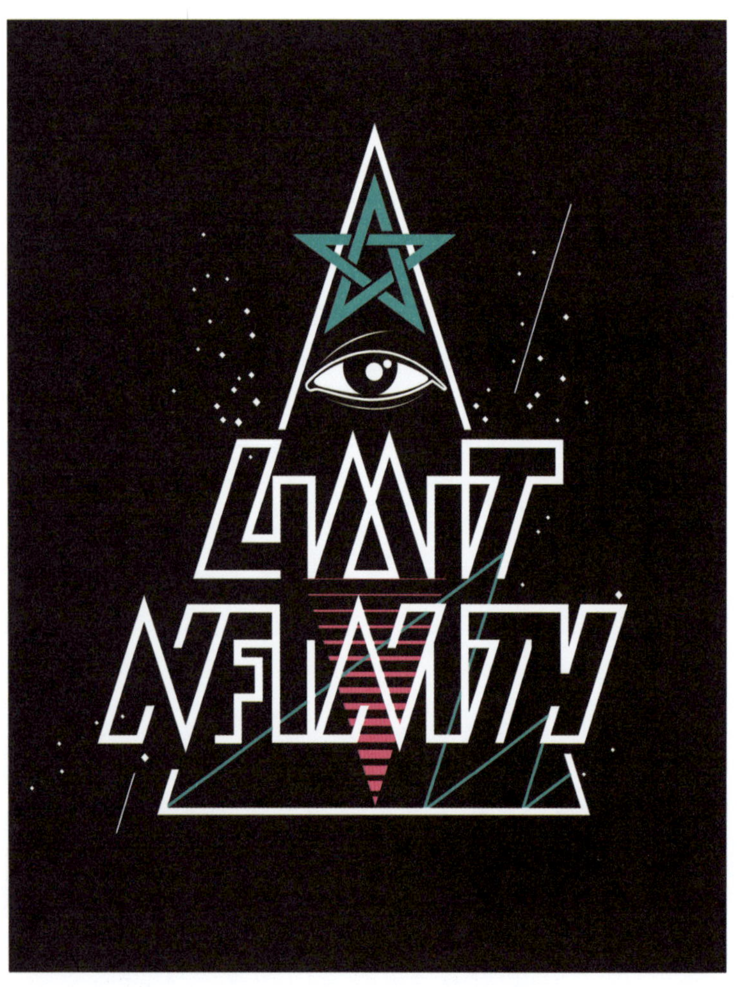

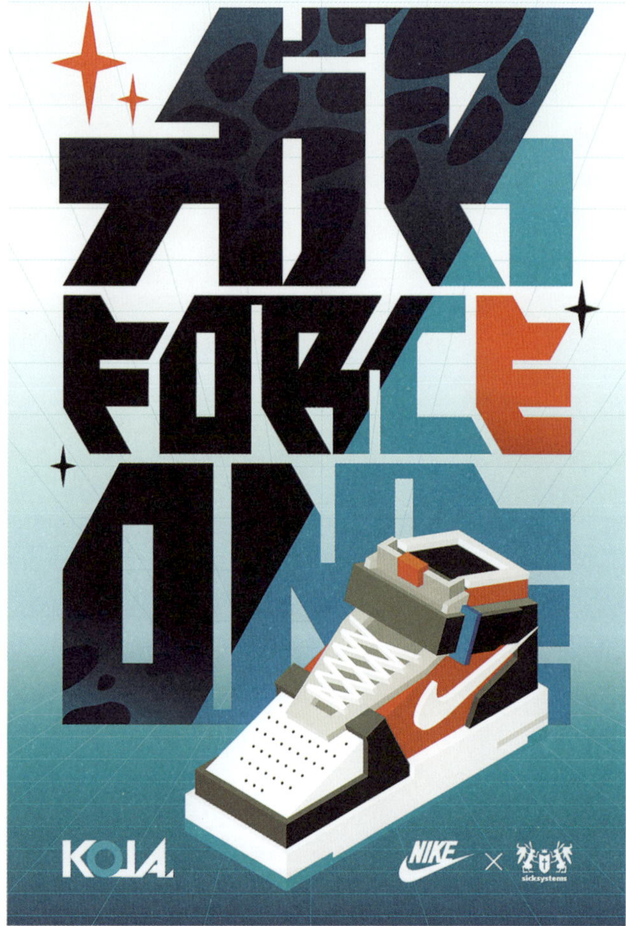

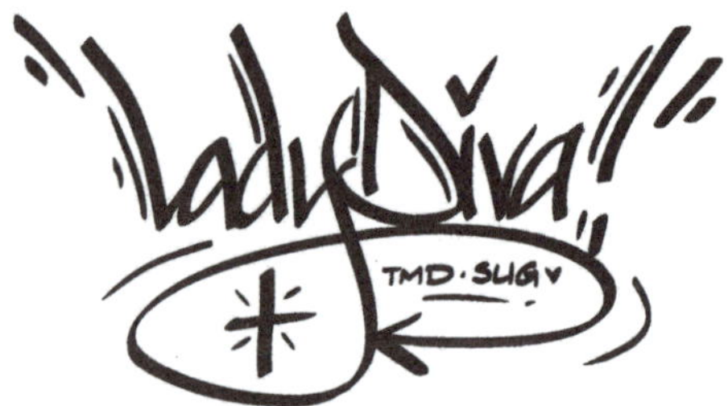

Lady Diva

AUCKLAND, NEW ZEALAND
Crew member of TMD, SUG
Writer since 1998
Favourite letter: B
www.tmdcrew.com

When Lady Diva started out, in 1998, she was one of the first female writers in Auckland. Her accessible, curvy, feminine style is reminiscent of classic calligraphy. She paints regularly with her TMD and SUG crew mates, juggling work and family life. 'A good piece has to look tidy and funky with good colours,' she says.

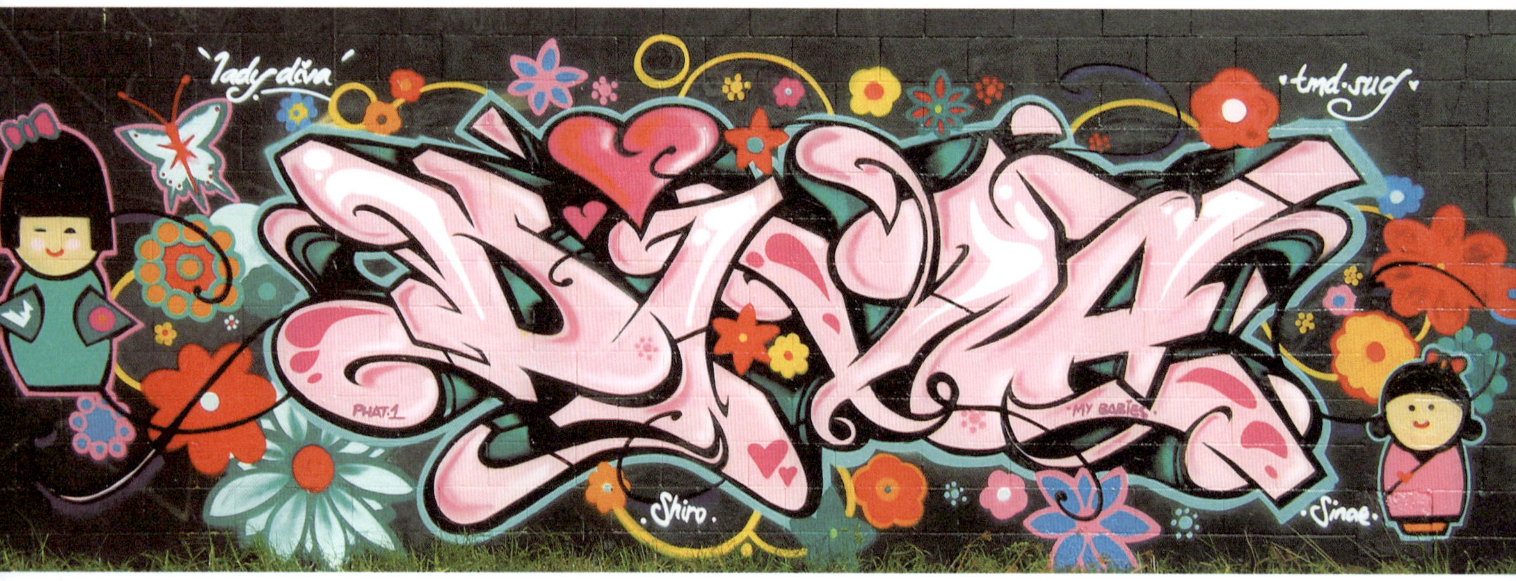

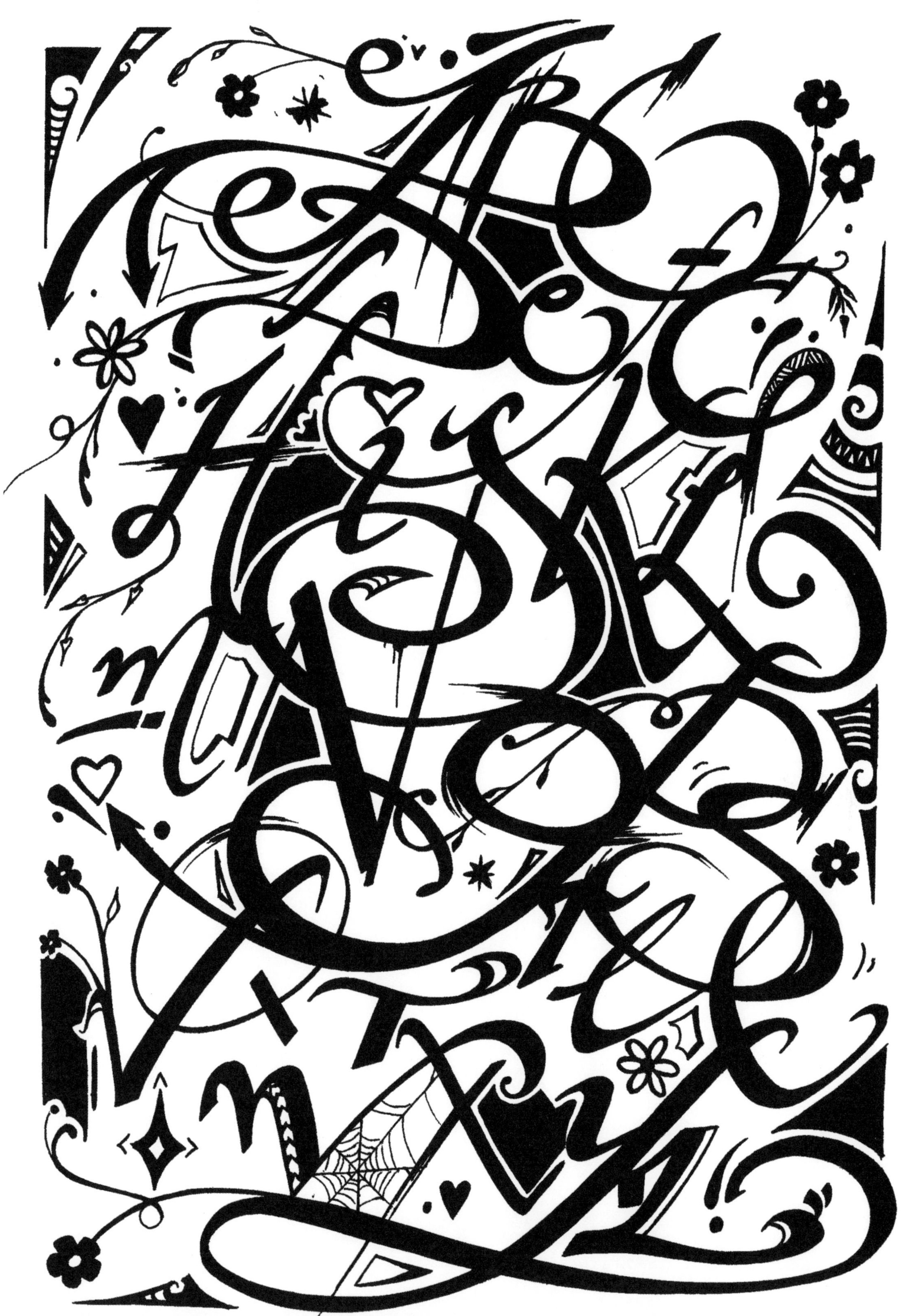

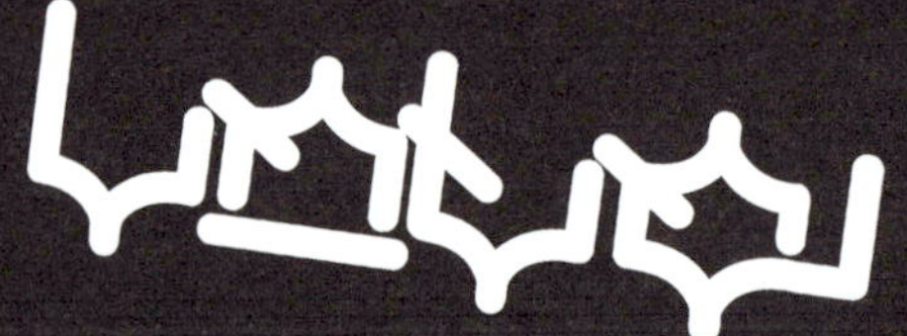

Late

EINDHOVEN, NETHERLANDS
Crew member of SOLCREW
Writer since 1995
Favourite letter: E

Late often works with basic geometric shapes. He describes his style as 'variations on the same theme'. The letter 'E' especially appeals to him because its construction allows him to write it in many different ways; particularly at the end of a tag or a piece, the 'E' can add a lot of energy to the written word. For a whole piece to be considered a success, Late believes that legibility, composition, contrast, a good colour scheme and an authentic style are indispensable.

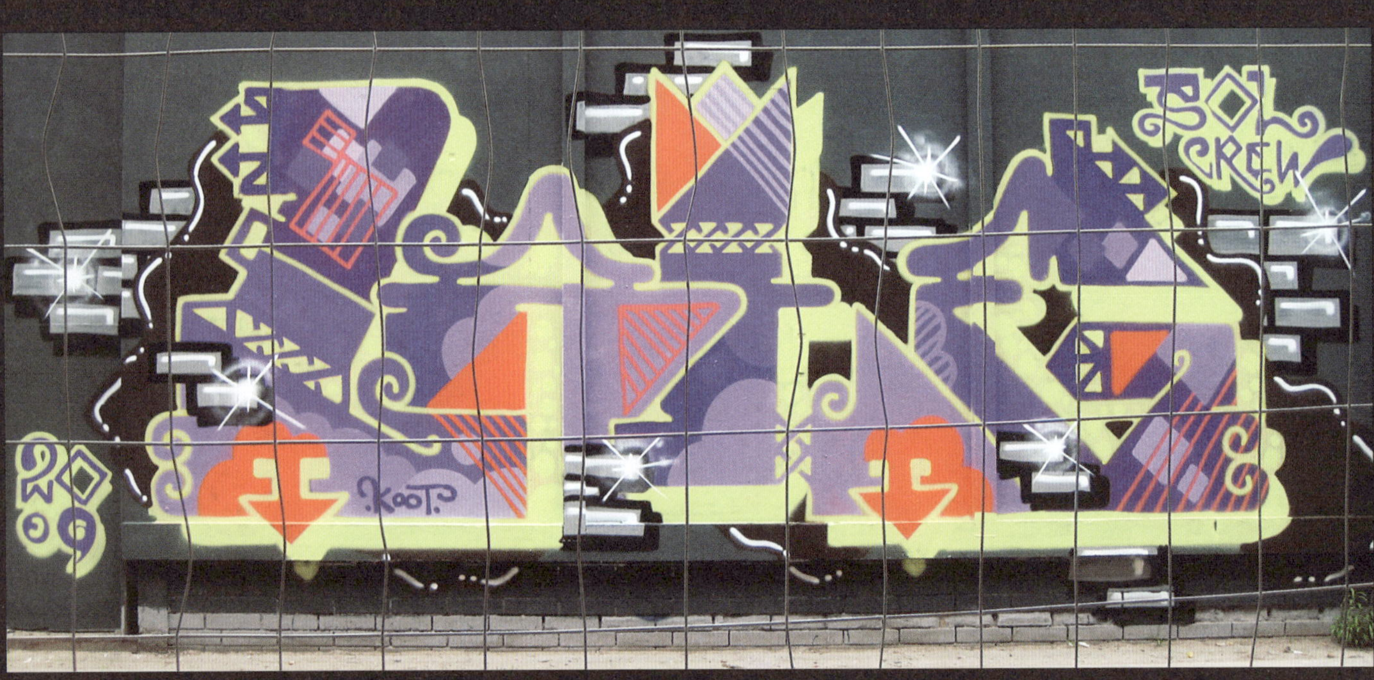

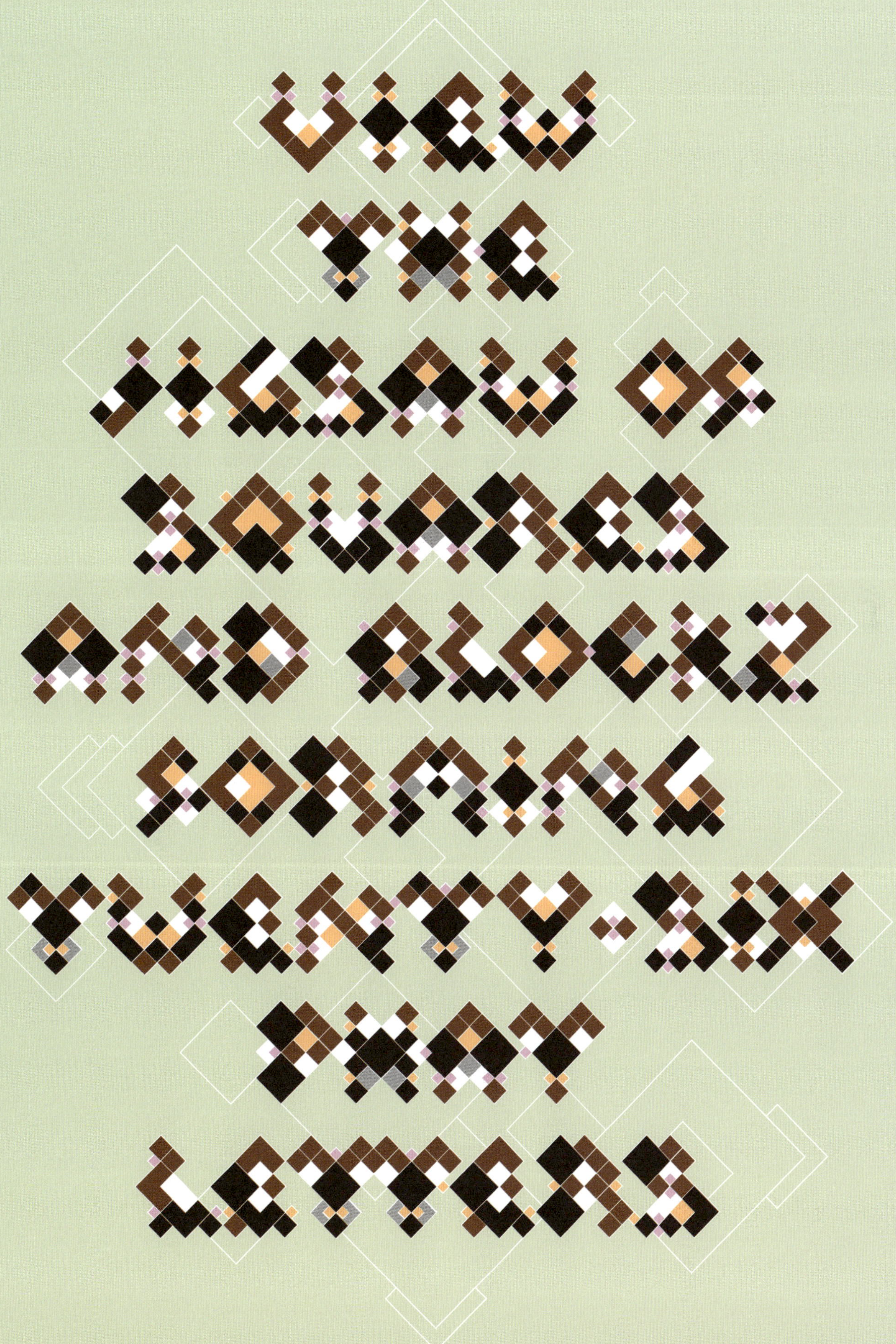

'View the jigsaw of squares and blockz forming twenty-six phat letters.'

L'Atlas
PARIS, FRANCE
Crew member of VAO
Writer since 1990
Favourite letter: 'I can't choose!'
www.latlas.net

L'Atlas limits his work to geometric calligraphic forms in black and white. He spent a long time tagging before he abandoned the spray can in 2001 and discovered gaffer tape as his material of choice. From then on he started writing his name in his signature labyrinthine style. Today he uses various media in his work on the streets and in galleries. He believes that it's important to give your work meaning.

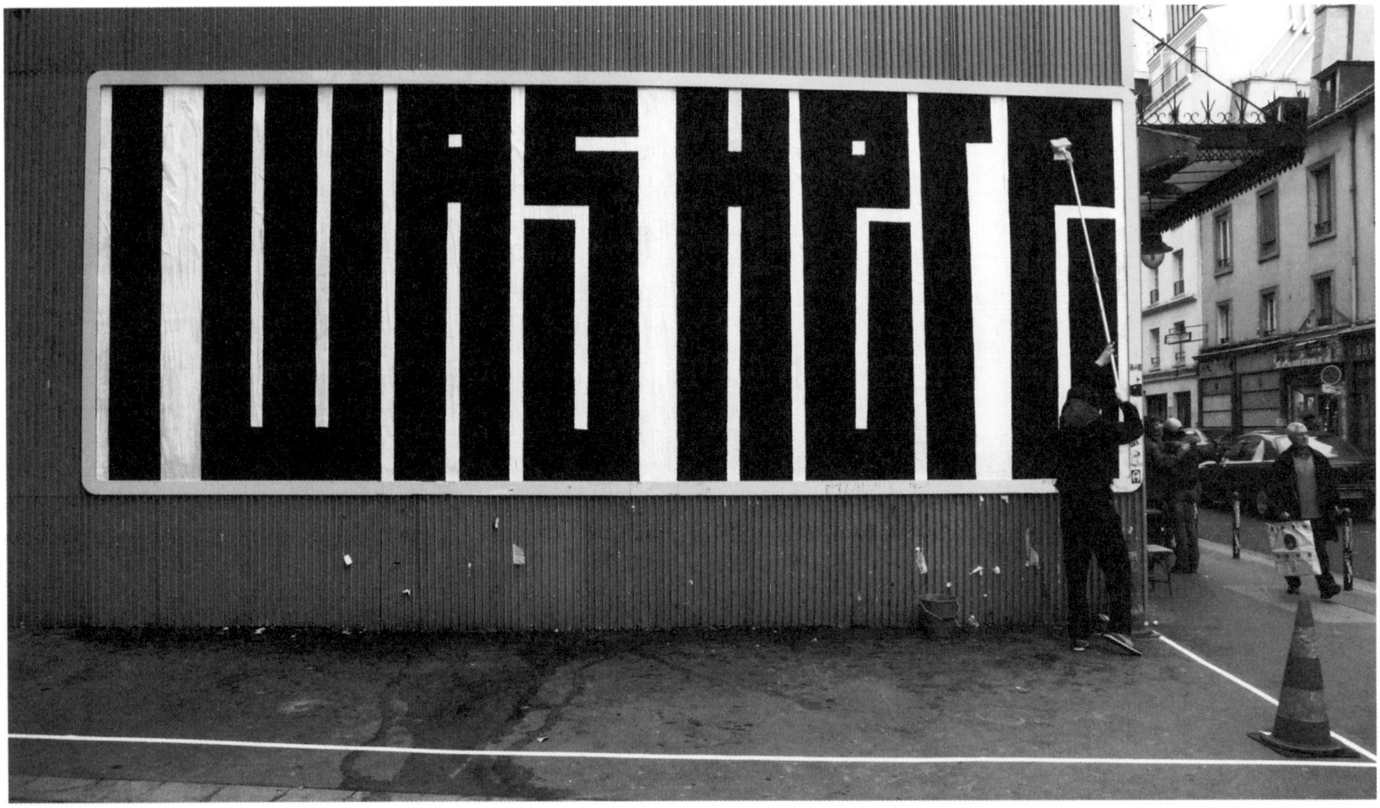

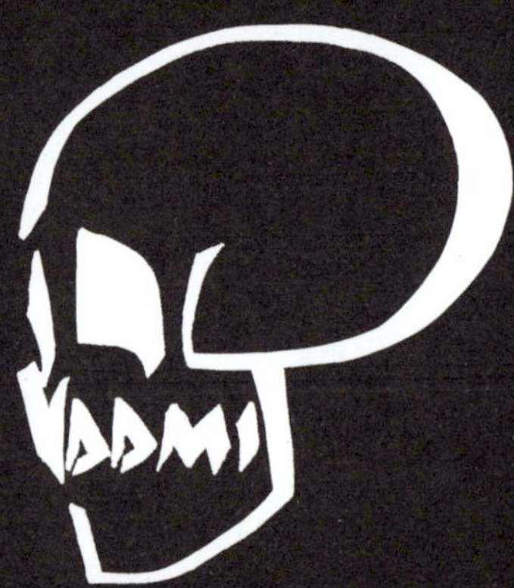

Loomit

MUNICH, GERMANY

Crew member of FBI, UA
Writer since 1983
Favourite letter: W
www.loomit.de

There are very few writers who could compete with Loomit when it comes to large-scale walls. His compositions dwarf regular graffiti lettering. Often you have to step back from the wall to decipher Loomit's name amid the characters and backgrounds of the piece. The outlines and fill-ins of classic graffiti are usually abandoned in favour of light and shadow effects. A good composition and location for the piece are very important to him.

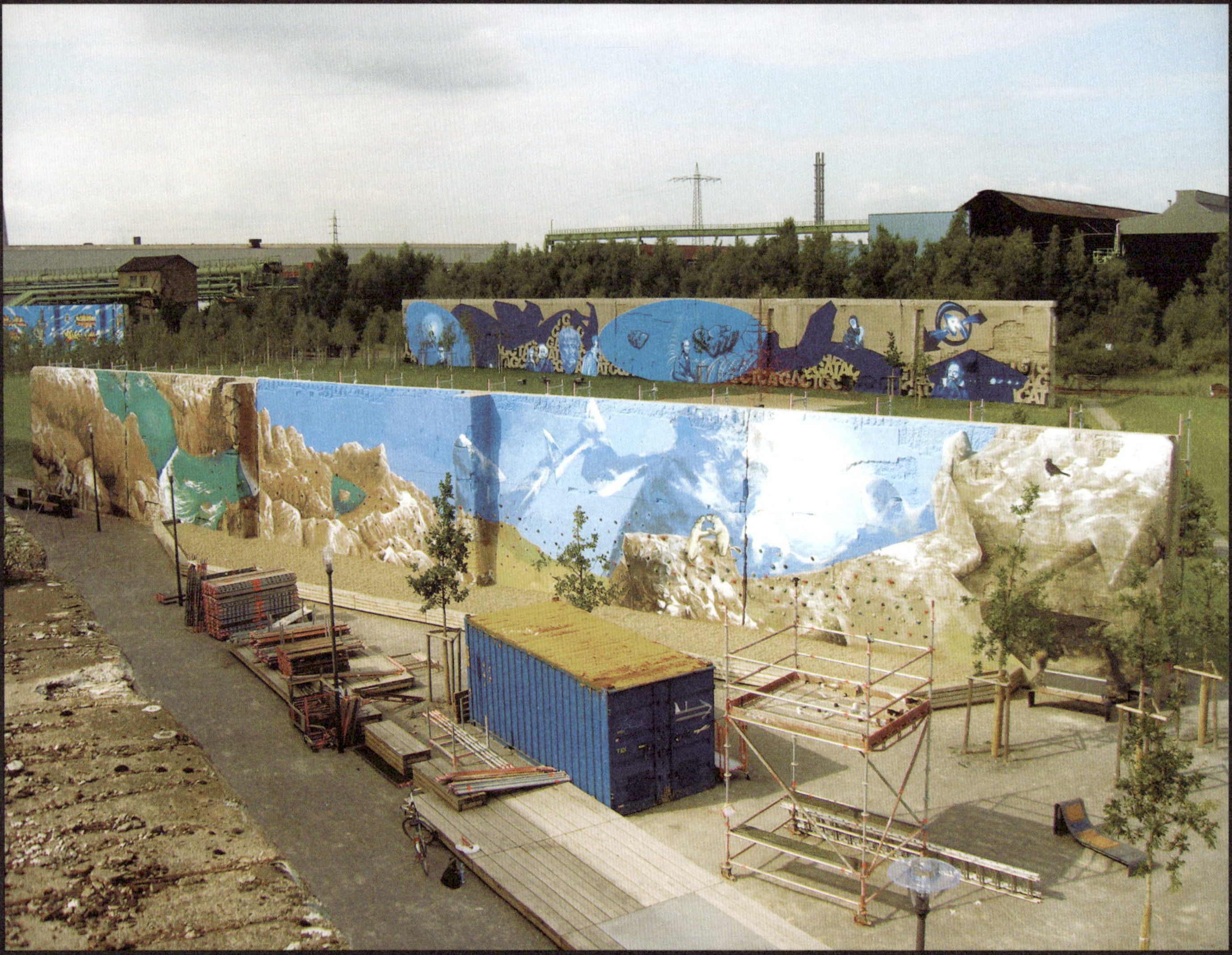

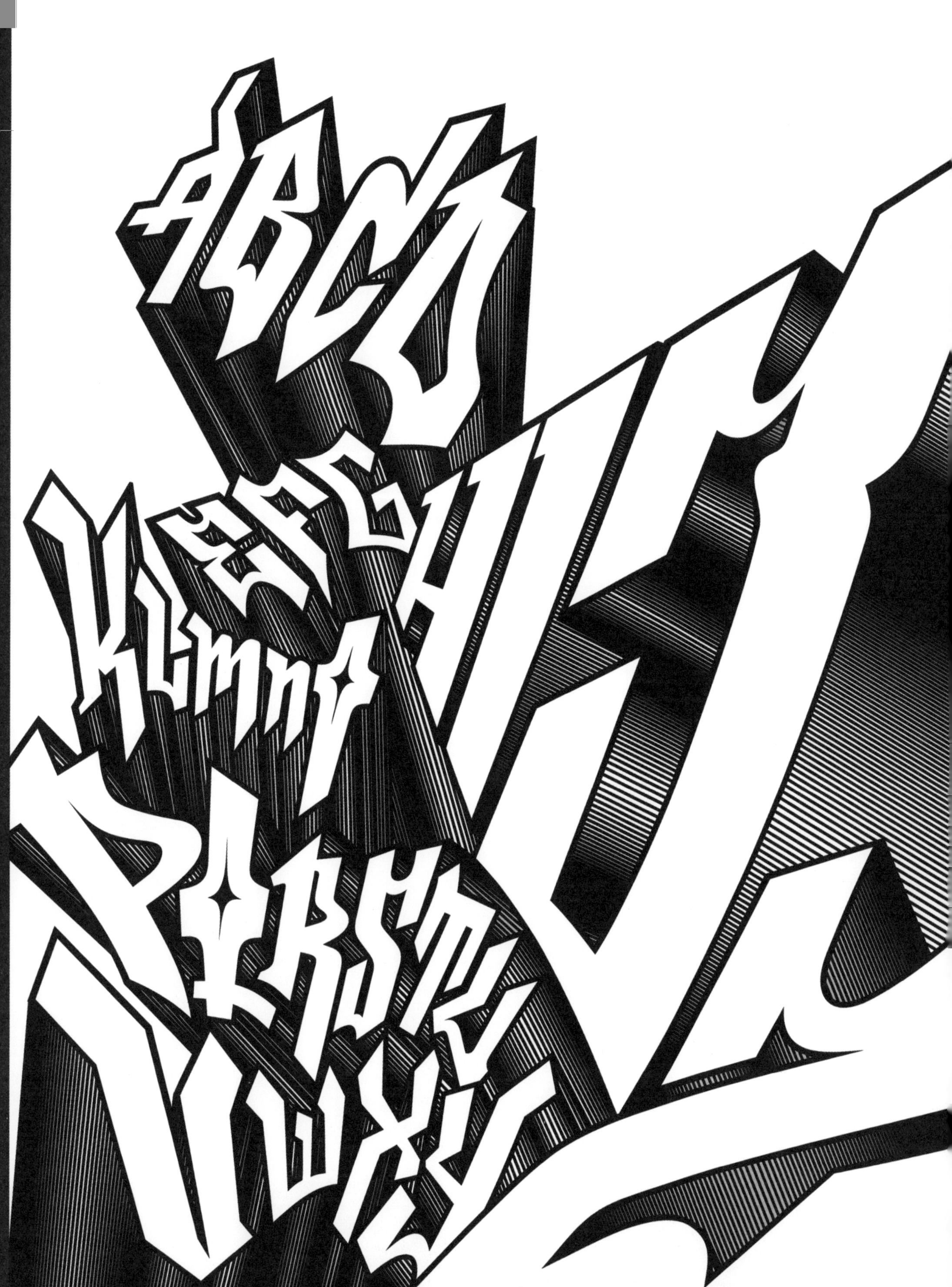

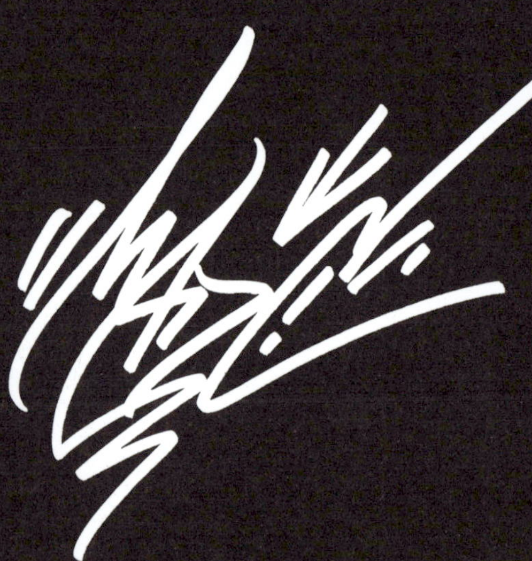

MadC

HALLE, GERMANY

Crew member of Bandits,
The Wallnuts, Stick Up Kids
Writer since 1998
Favourite letter: A
www.madc.tv

MadC likes travelling and large-scale walls. Her murals have a striking three-dimensional quality and a high level of detail throughout all the different elements – the piece, characters, background. She wants her work to show diversity and doesn't limit herself to one particular style. However, she always keeps her letters legible and dynamic. 'Graffiti allows you to see the world through new eyes, and the act of painting gives you a feeling of pure satisfaction and happiness,' she says.

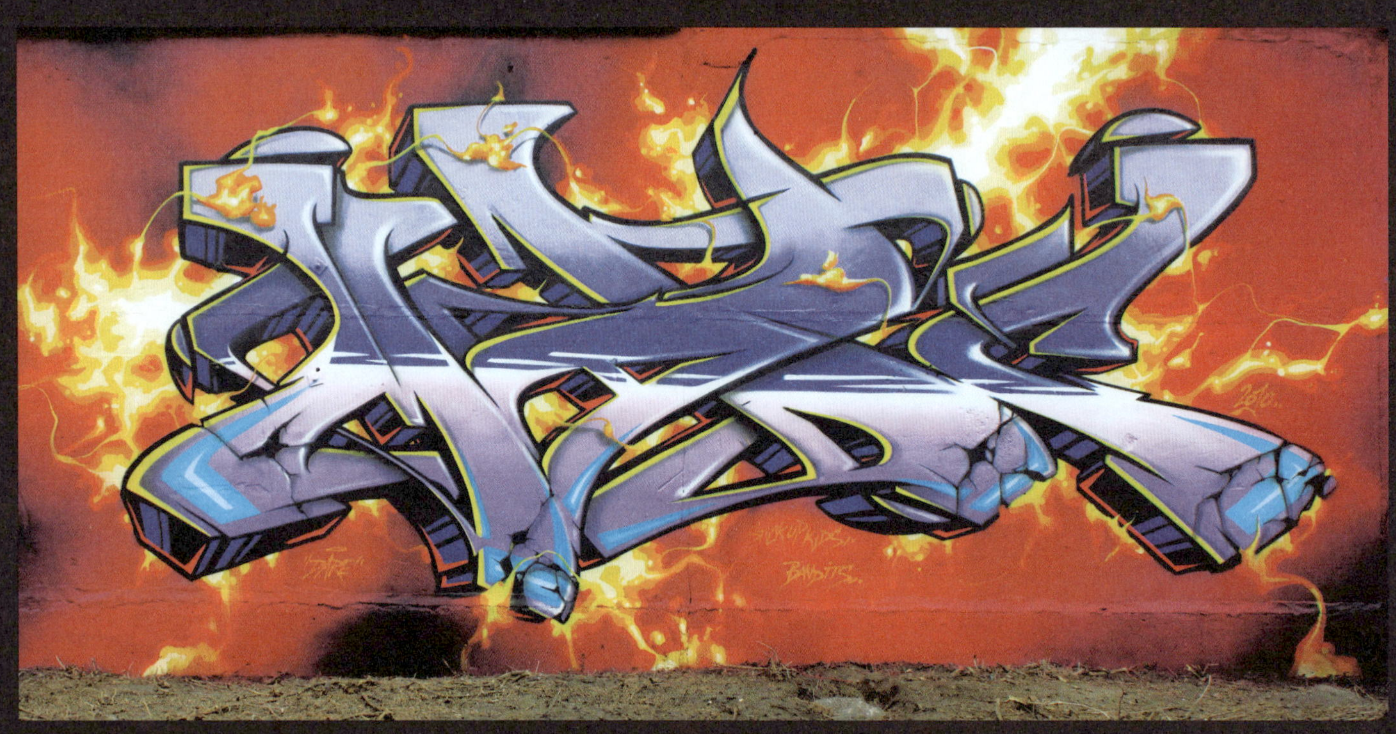

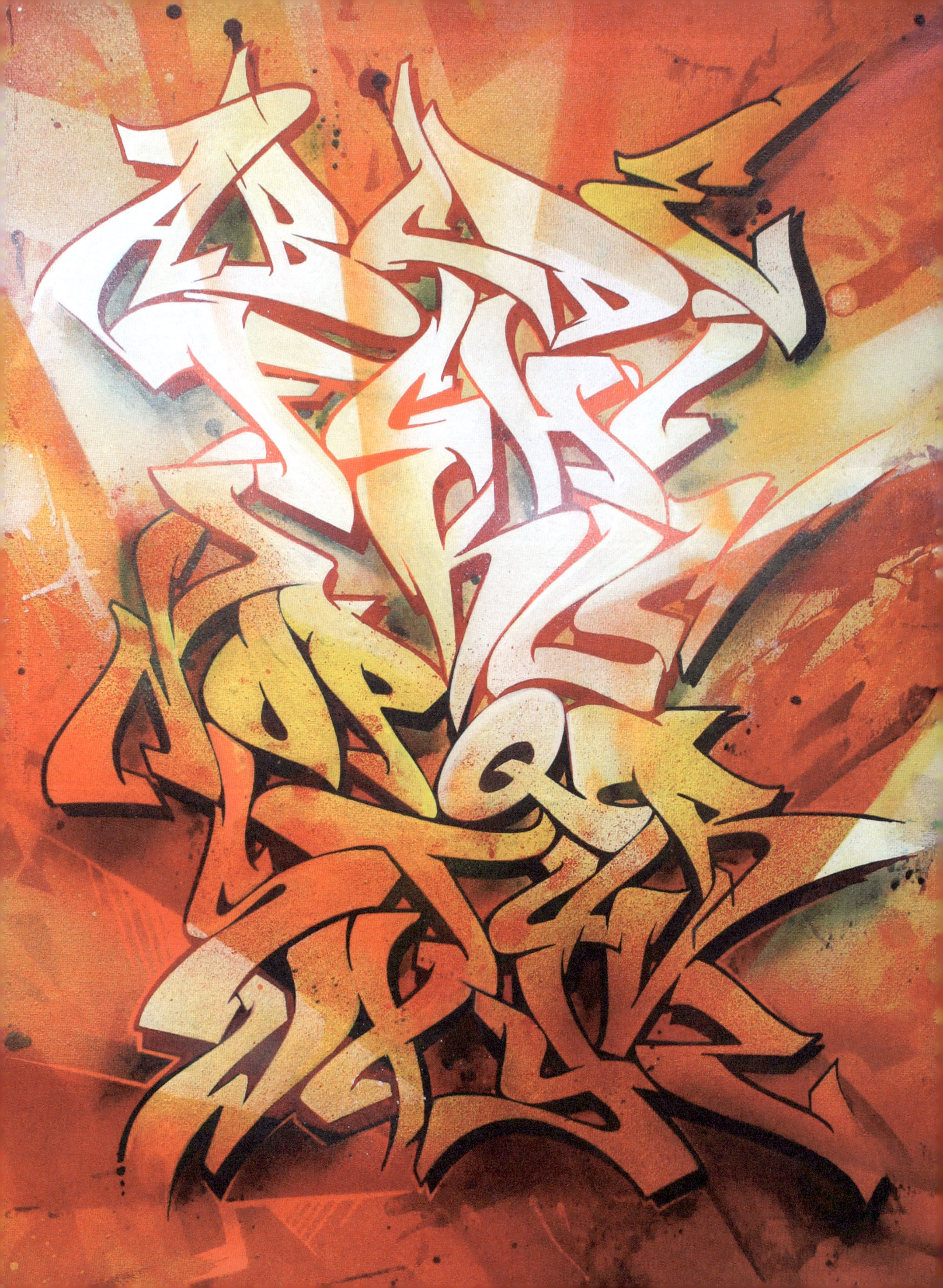

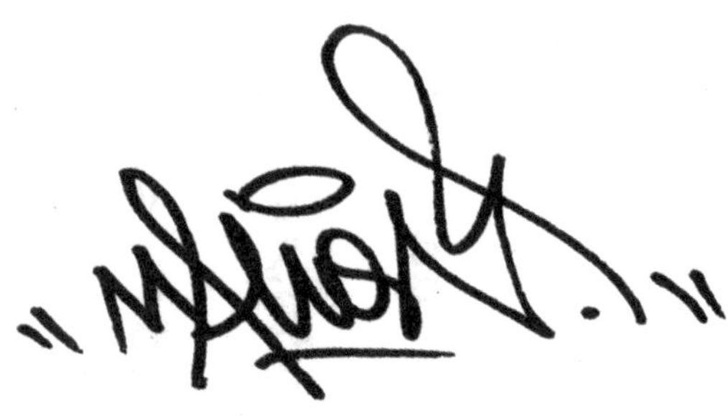

Mahon

STRASBOURG, FRANCE
Crew member of Macia
Writer since 1988
Favourite letter: M
www.smooth-hustler.tumblr.com

Mahon's pieces are characterized by clearly defined letters and a strong focus on character design. As an illustrator and designer, he has worked with companies such as BMW, Adidas, Mars and Puma. 'I like walls where the pieces fit the background and the colour choice,' he says. 'I hate stuff that doesn't make sense, like illegible letters or bad colours.'

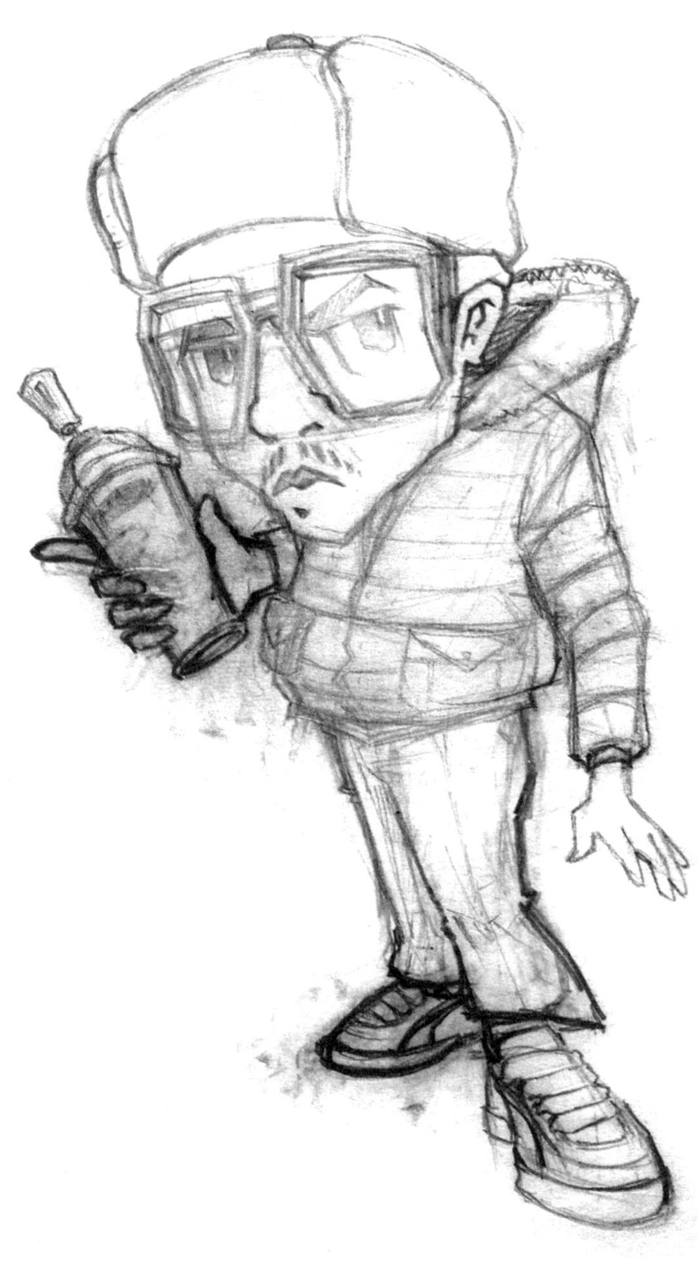

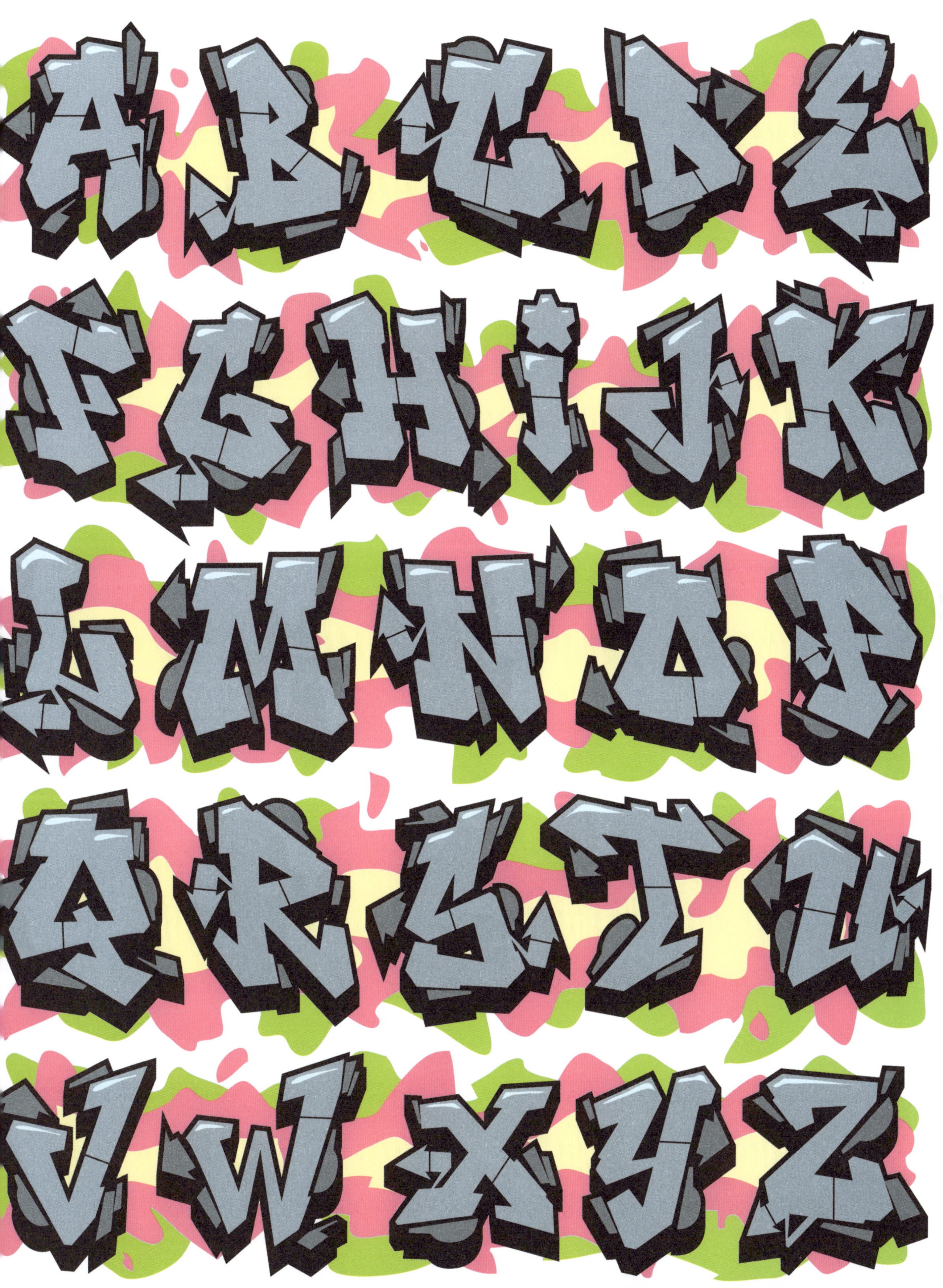

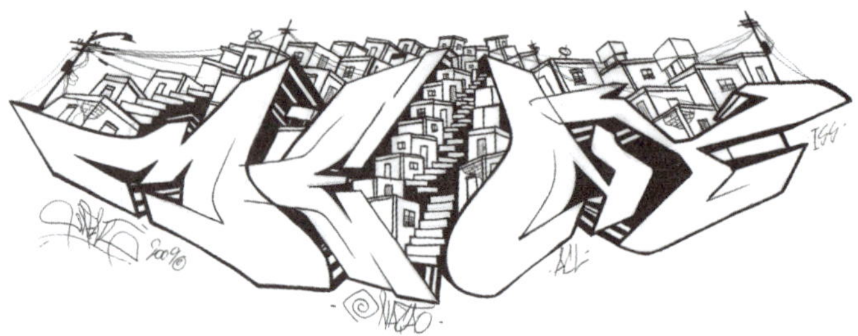

Ment

RIO DE JANEIRO, BRAZIL

Crew member of Nação Crew,
ACL, ISS
Writer since 1998
Favourite letter: M
www.marceloment.com/br

Ment often likes to incorporate the landscapes of Rio de Janeiro into his pieces, as well as those of other places he has visited. His alphabet reflects this way of connecting his experiences with the letters he paints. Ment belongs to Rio's first generation of graffiti writers and is involved with social projects in the favelas and poor neighbourhoods of the city to give the next generation a different perspective through art.

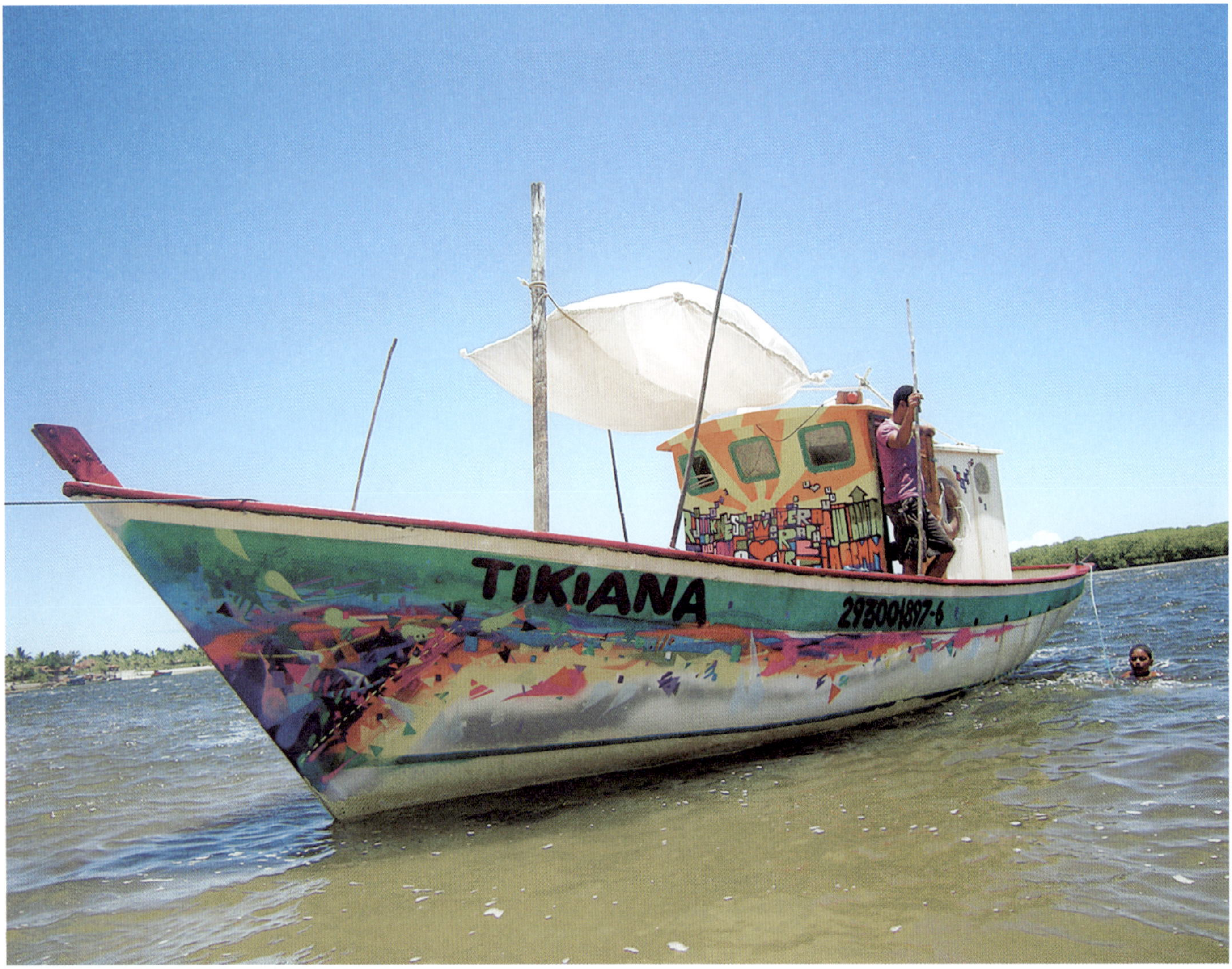

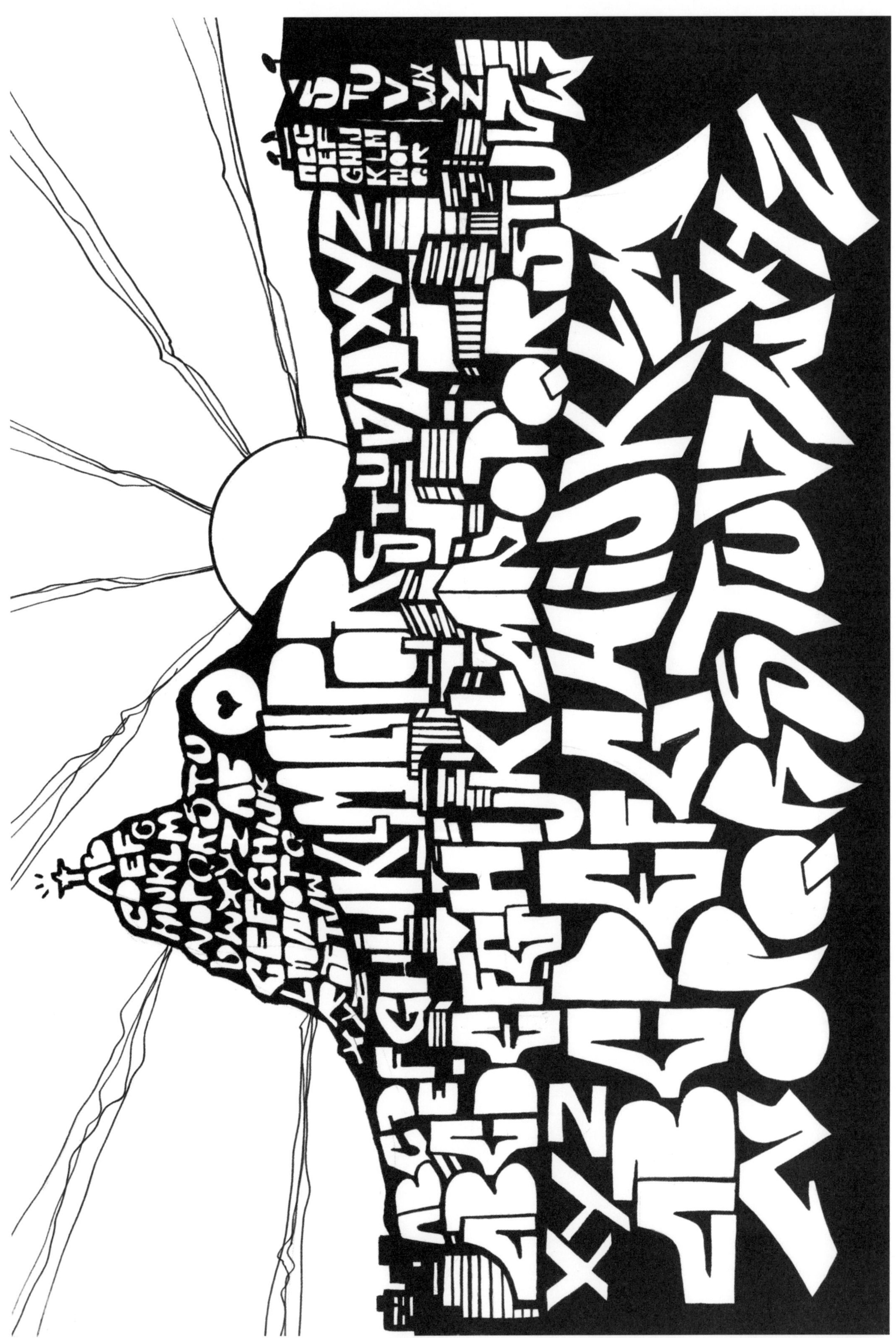

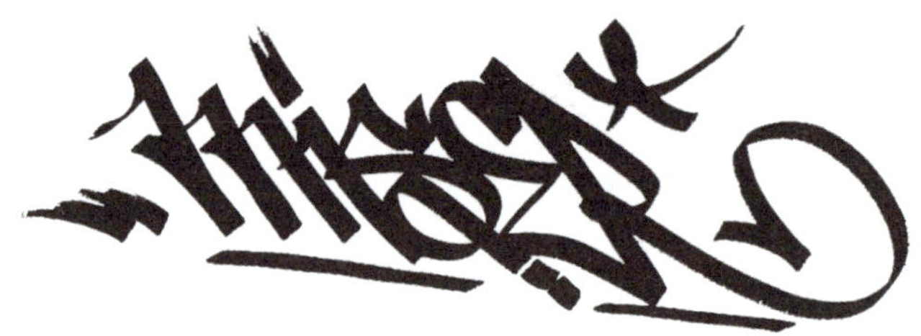

Mise

BOSTON, USA
Crew member of 156, Control, TCS, (T), KTC
Writer since 1990
Favourite letter: E
www.instagram.com/mise_rock

Mise is a tattoo artist by profession. He drew his alphabet in coloured pencil on tracing paper, choosing a simple design to keep the letter structure clear and legible. Mise believes that it's the illegal element of graffiti that keeps it raw and prevents the art from turning into another part of mainstream culture.

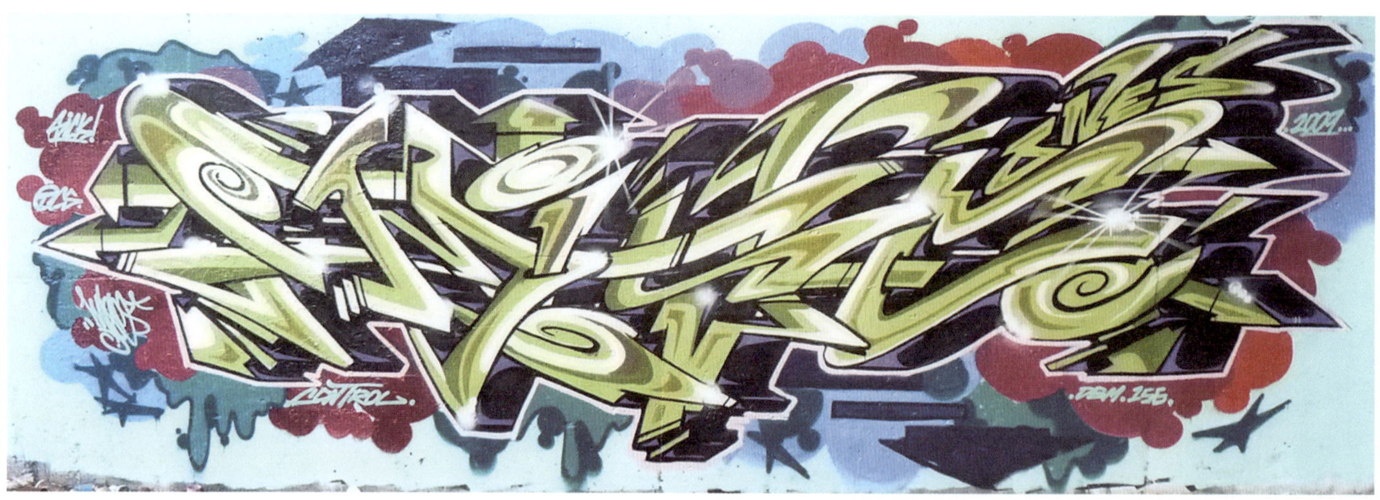

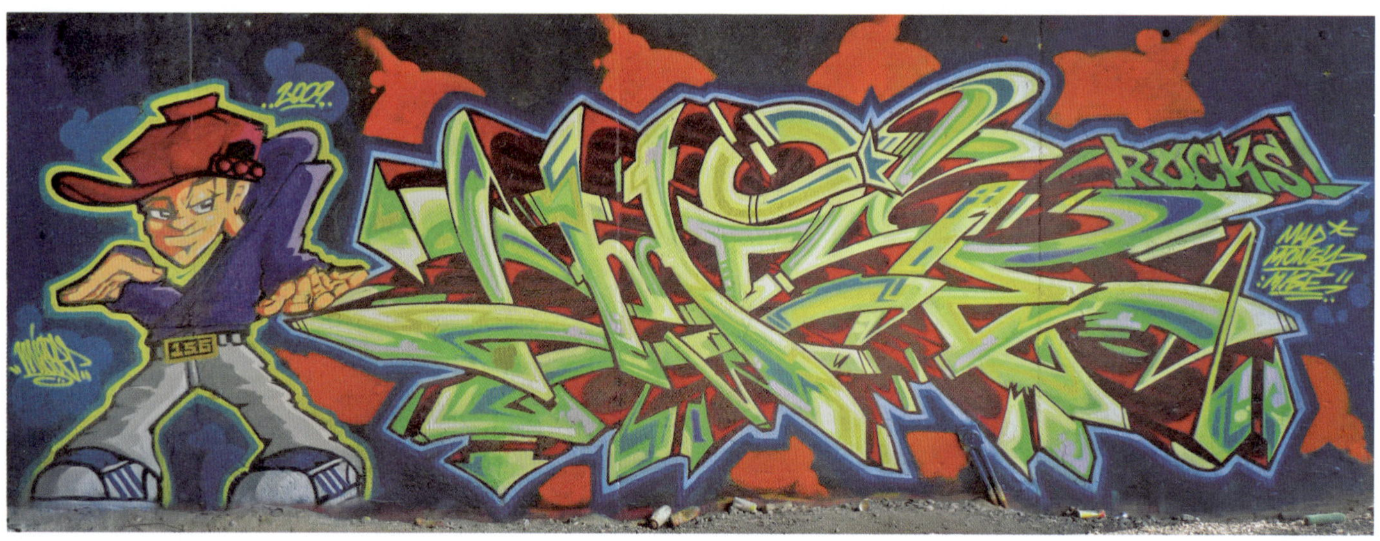

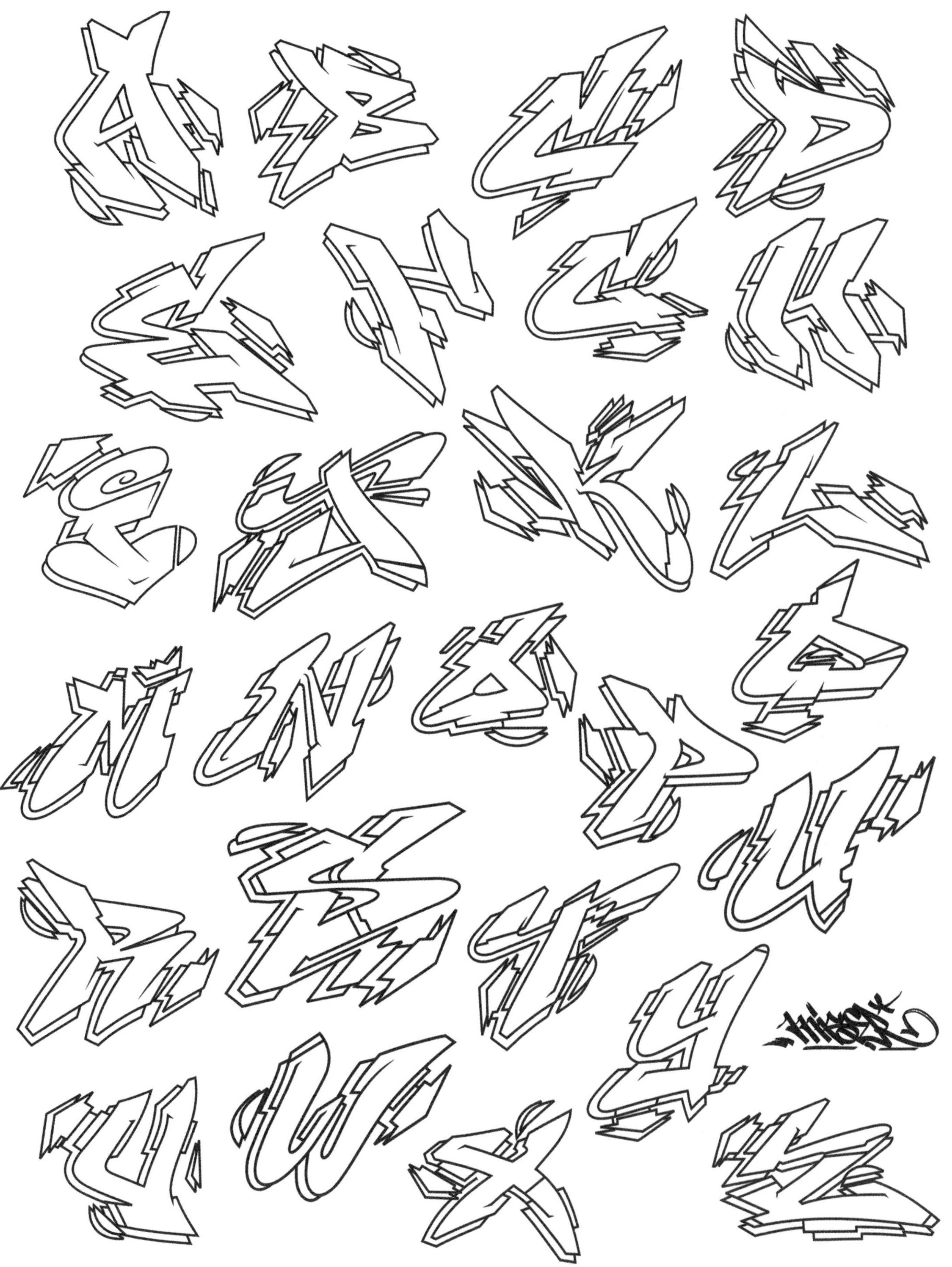

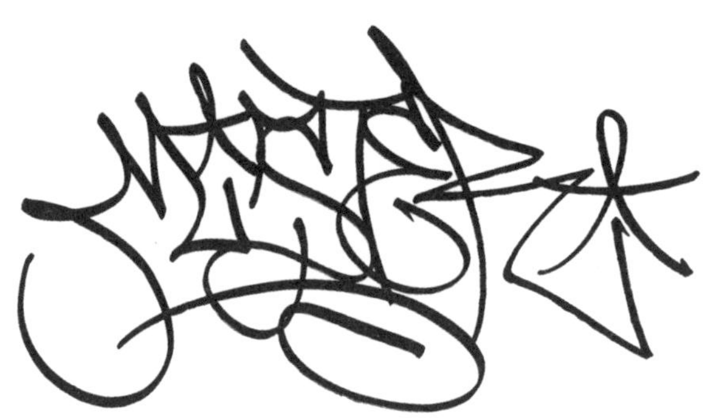

Mister

EINDHOVEN, NETHERLANDS
Crew member of SOL, CFH
Writer since 1988
Favourite letter: B

Mister prefers clear shapes and classic elements. His alphabet is a combination of acrylic paint on canvas and tiles painted with ink. On what it takes to create a good piece, Mister says: 'It's all about the pure form in which nothing is camouflaged.'

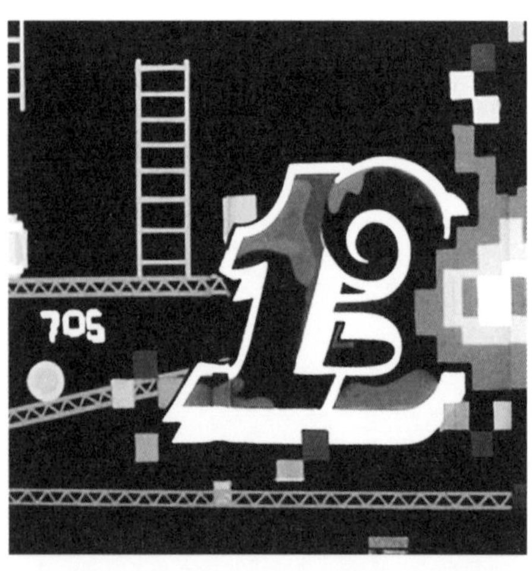

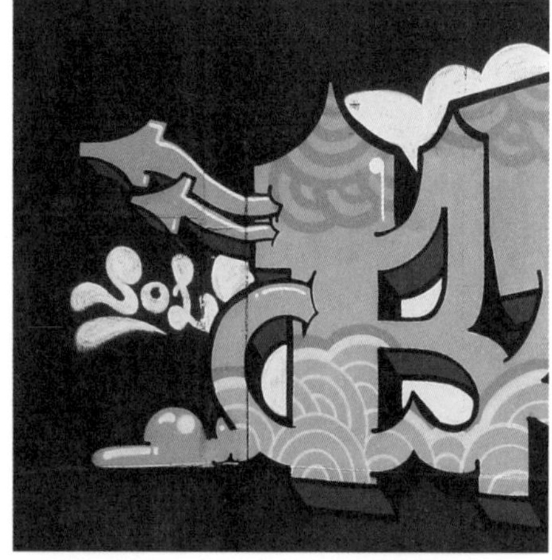

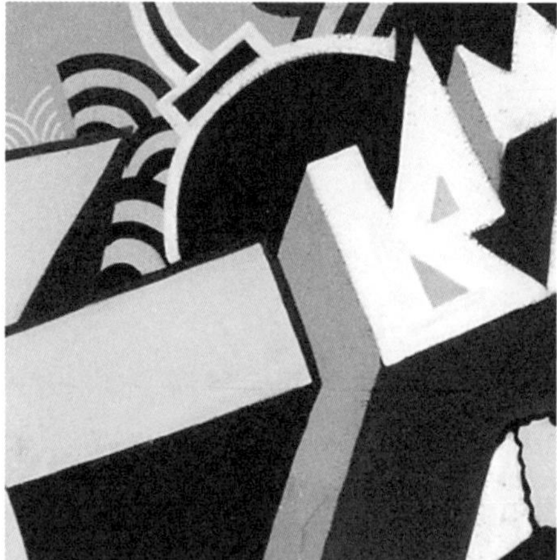

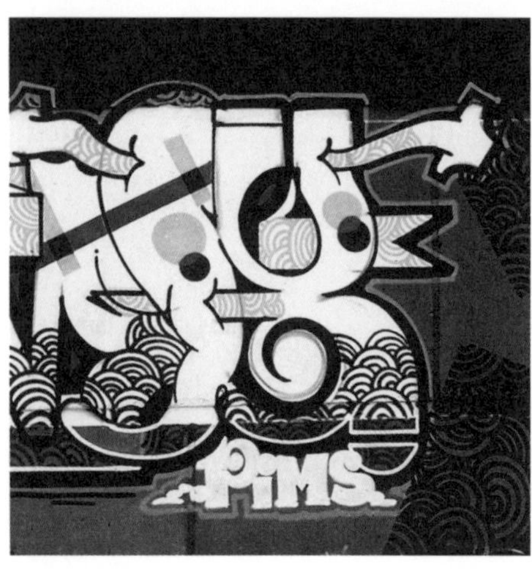

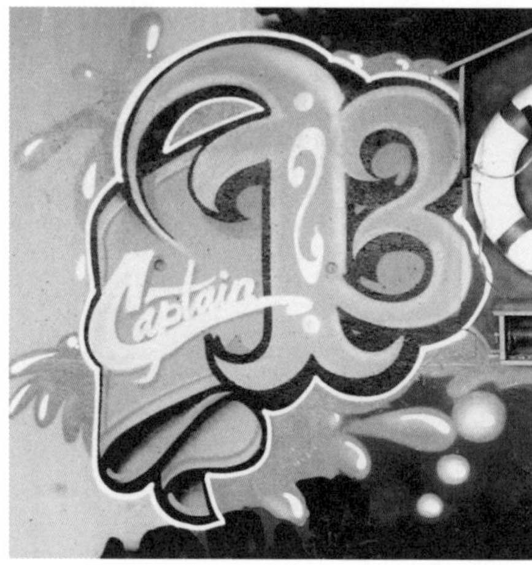

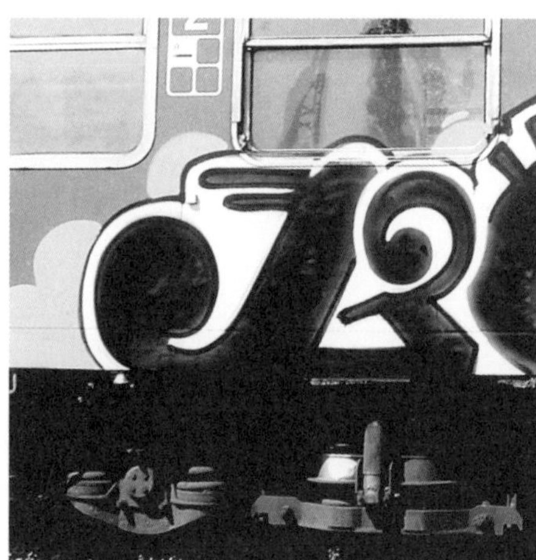

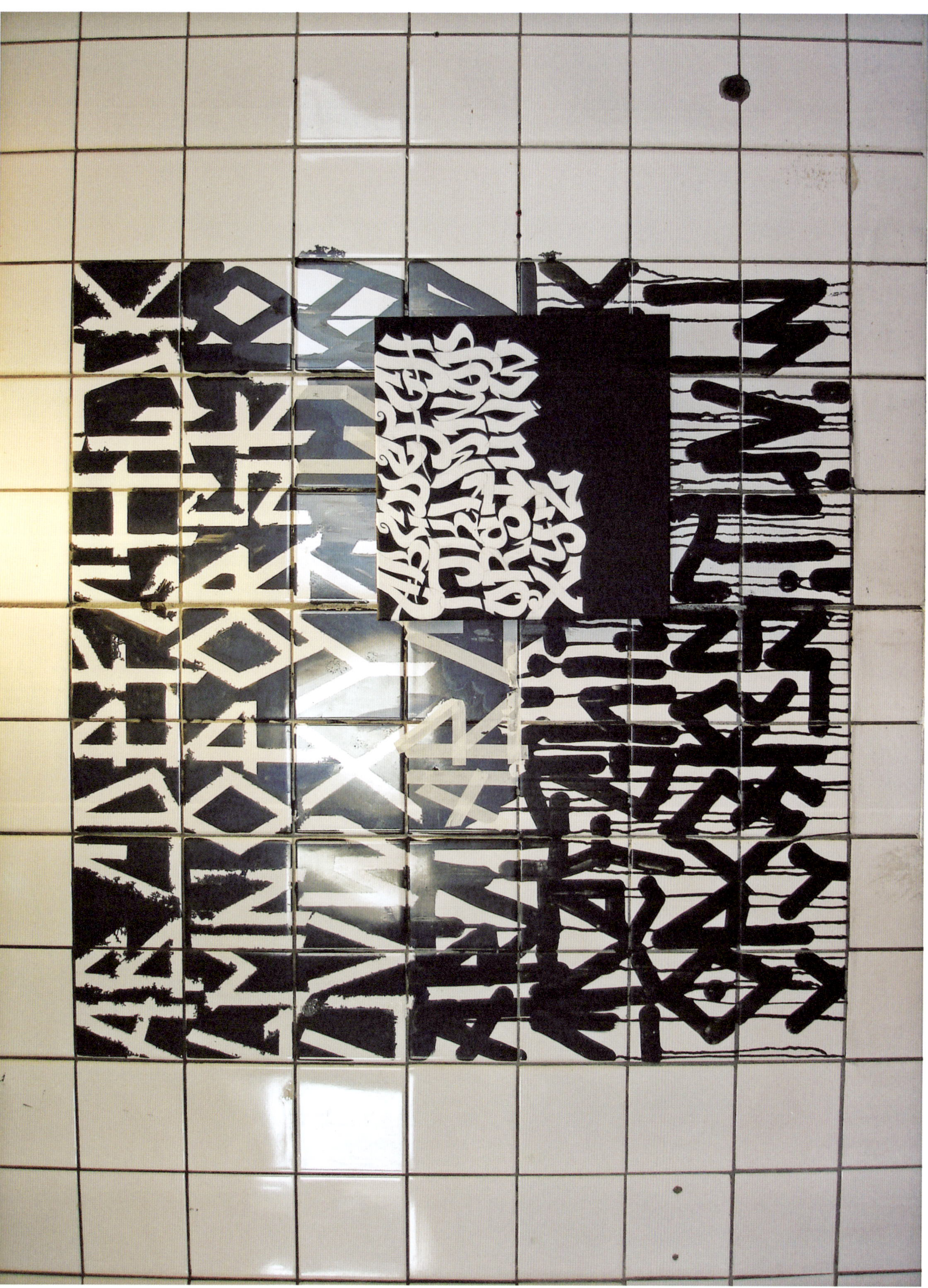

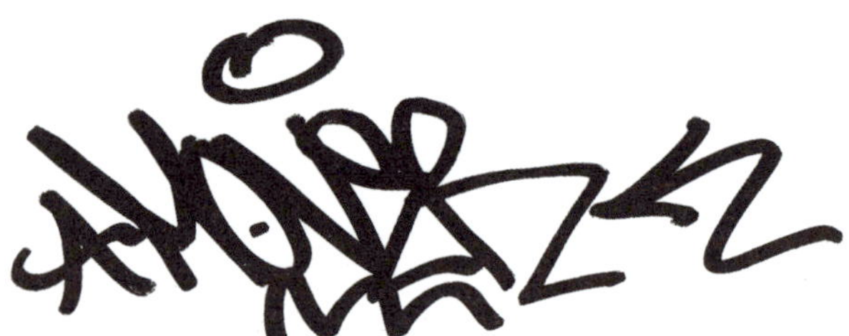

Mover
BENICARLO, SPAIN

Crew member of Loshp, O.K.
Writer since 1991
Favourite letters: M, O, V, E, R
oscart77.blogspot.com

Mover has developed a distinctive style that is accessible and fun. His letters sometimes look a bit like balloon animals, with their twisting lines, round edges and white highlights. Graffiti keeps his inner child alive, Mover says.

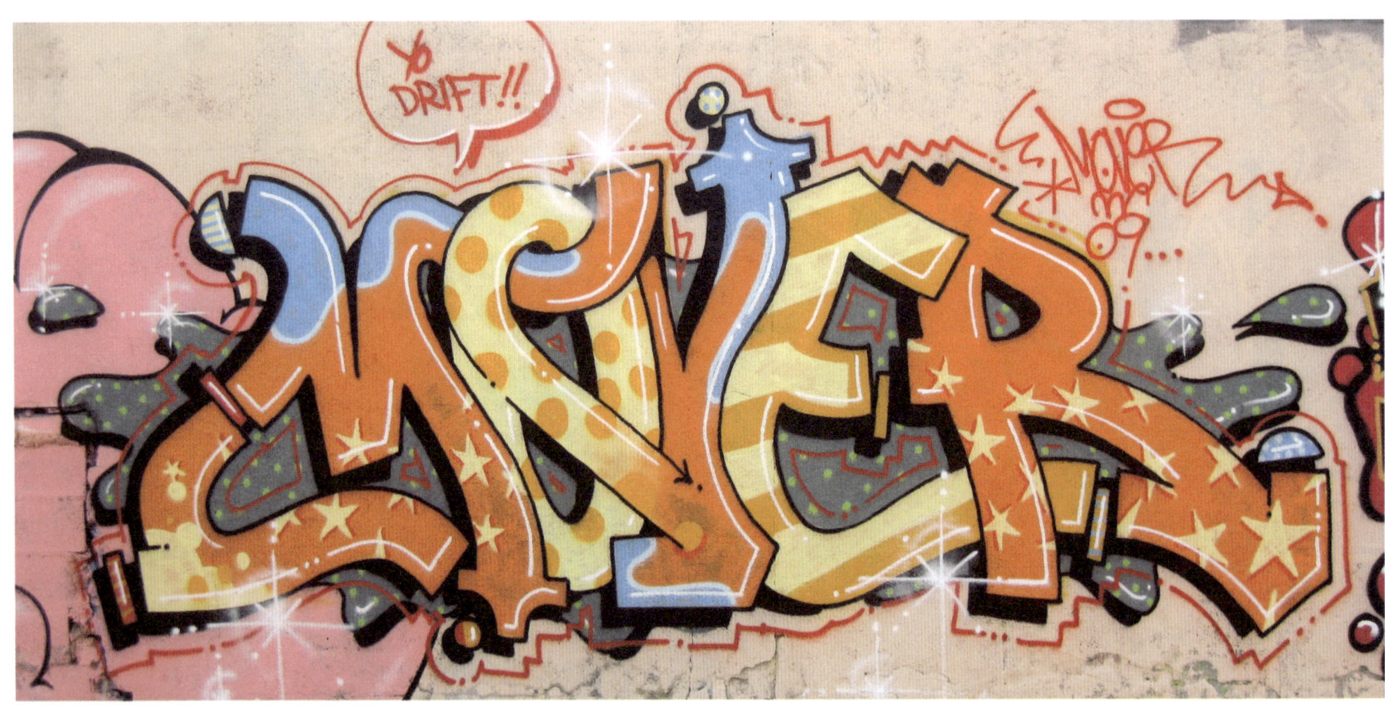

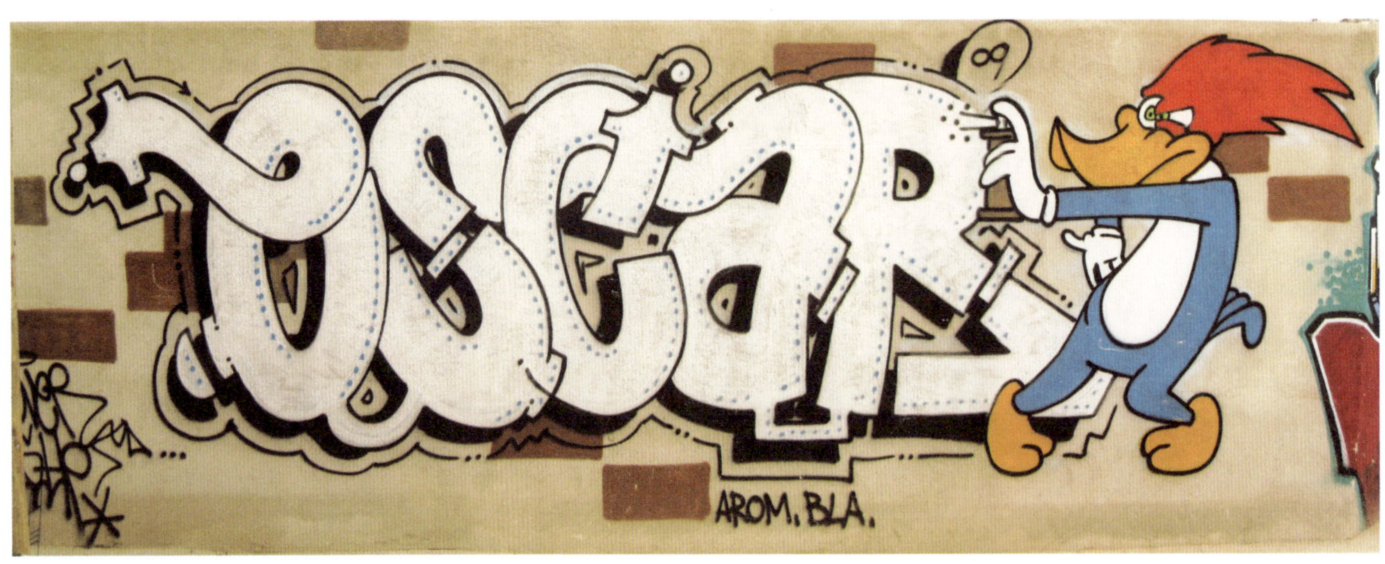

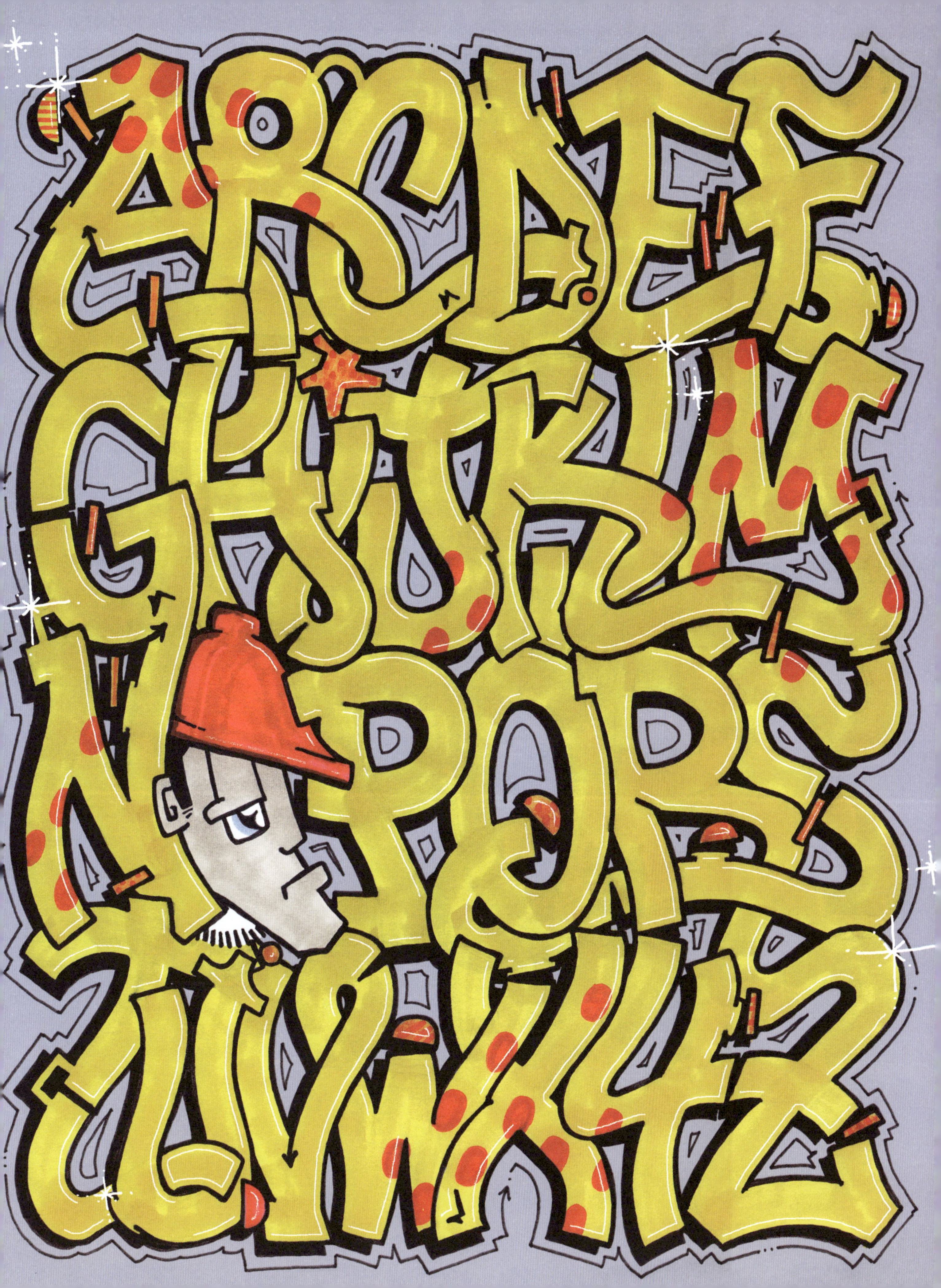

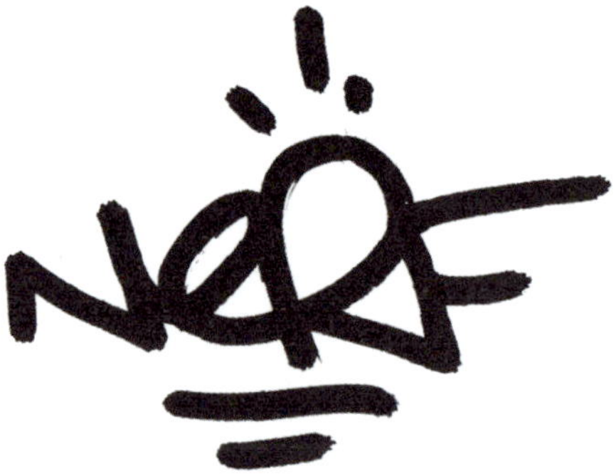

Nerf

BUENOS AIRES, ARGENTINA
Crew member of TBA, FFF, LBD, BA
Writer since 1999
Favourite letter: E
www.flickr.com/nerfff

Nerf has developed his own style of 3D letters based on a cube
system. On the wall his colourful pieces are reminiscent of
children's building blocks. Nerf likes clean styles with a carefully
chosen colour scheme.

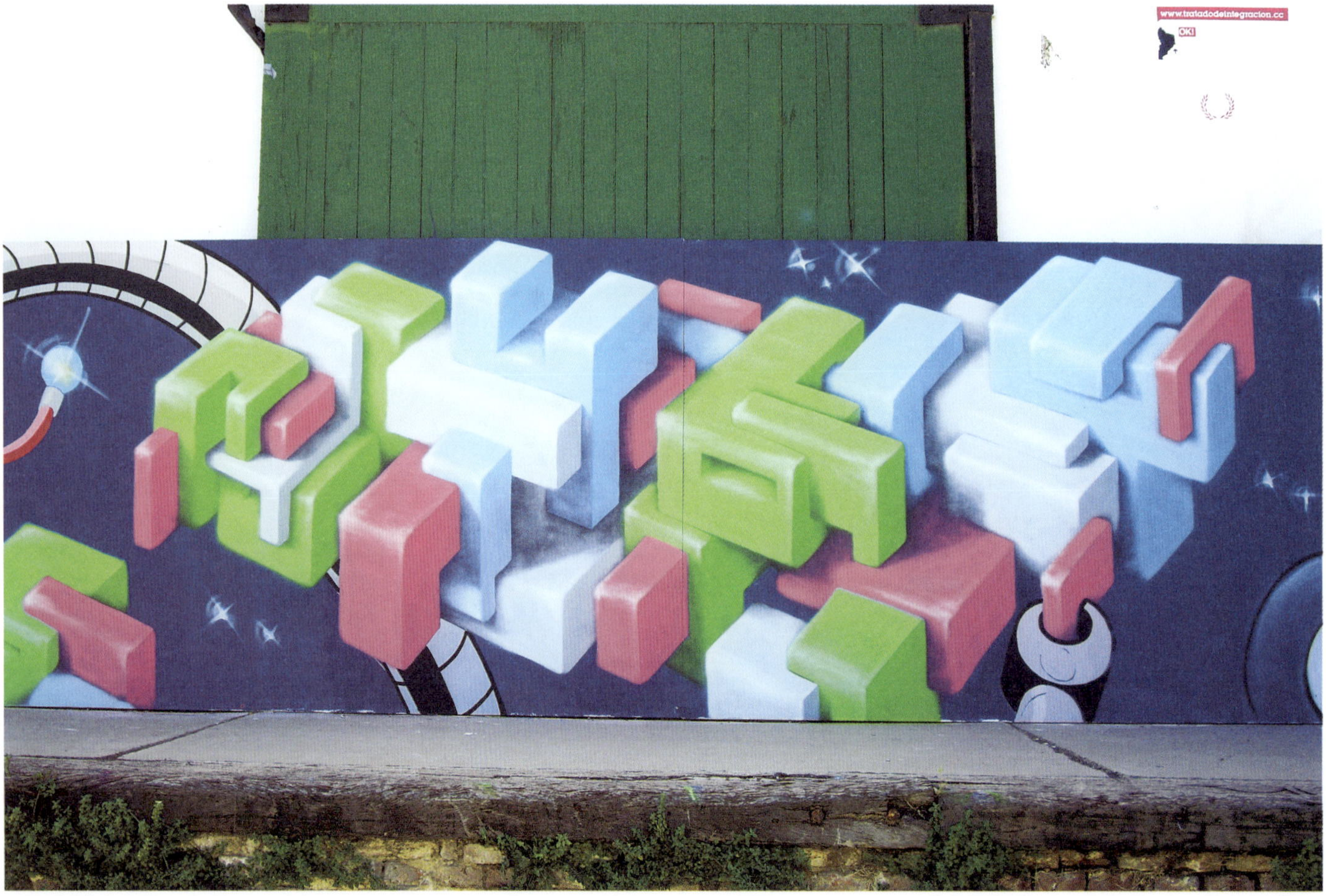

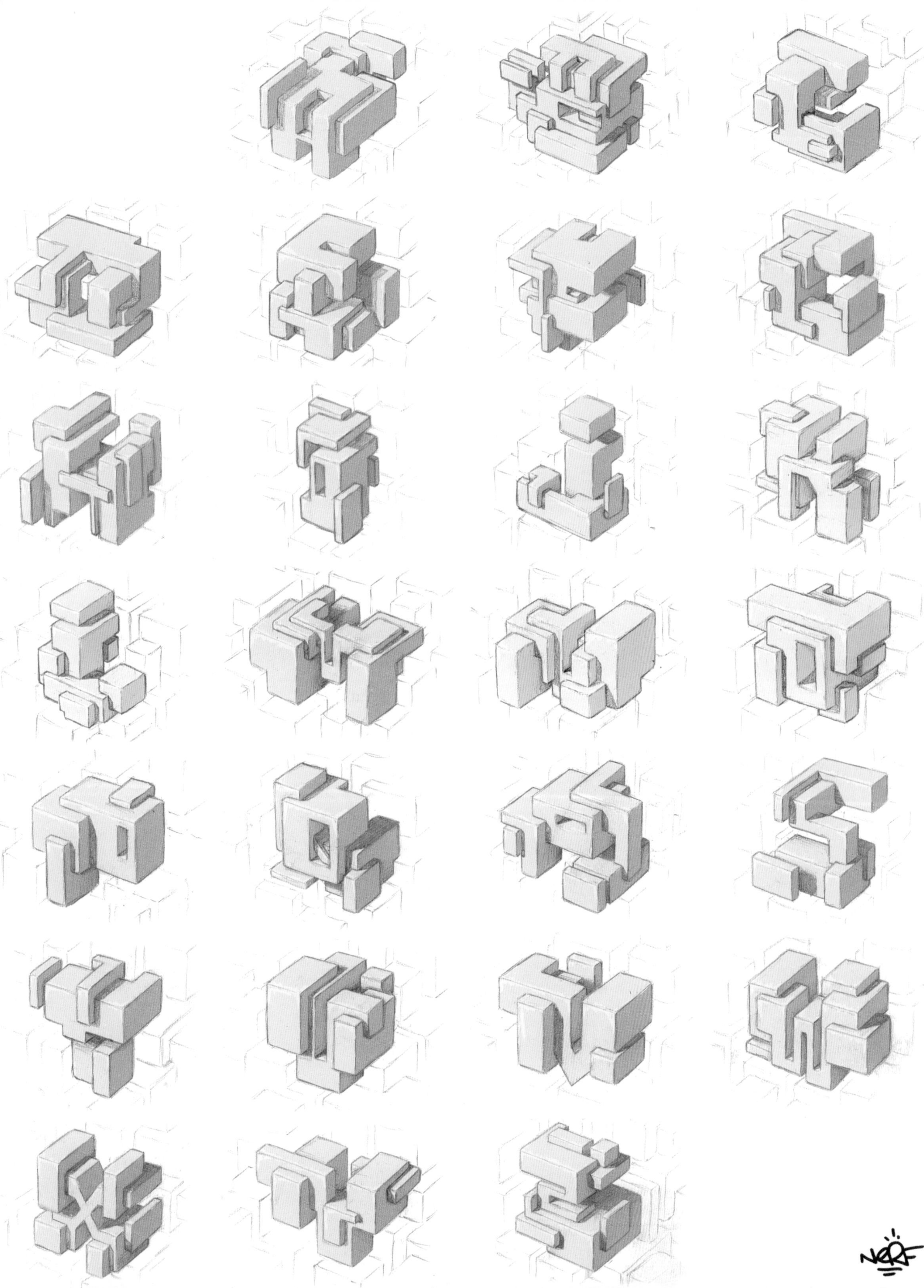

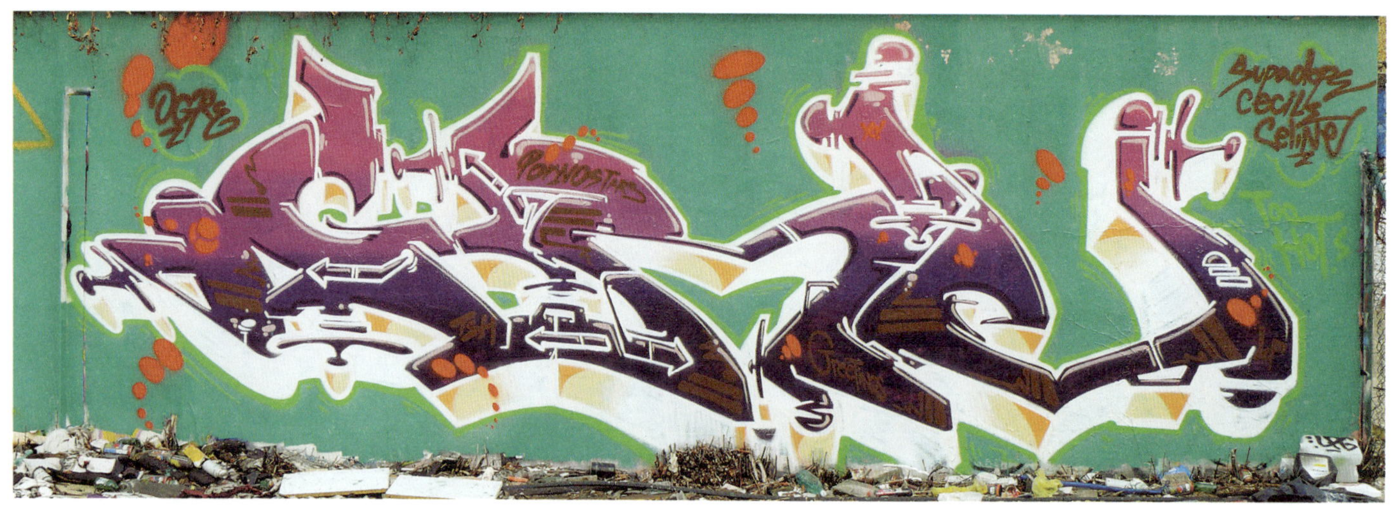

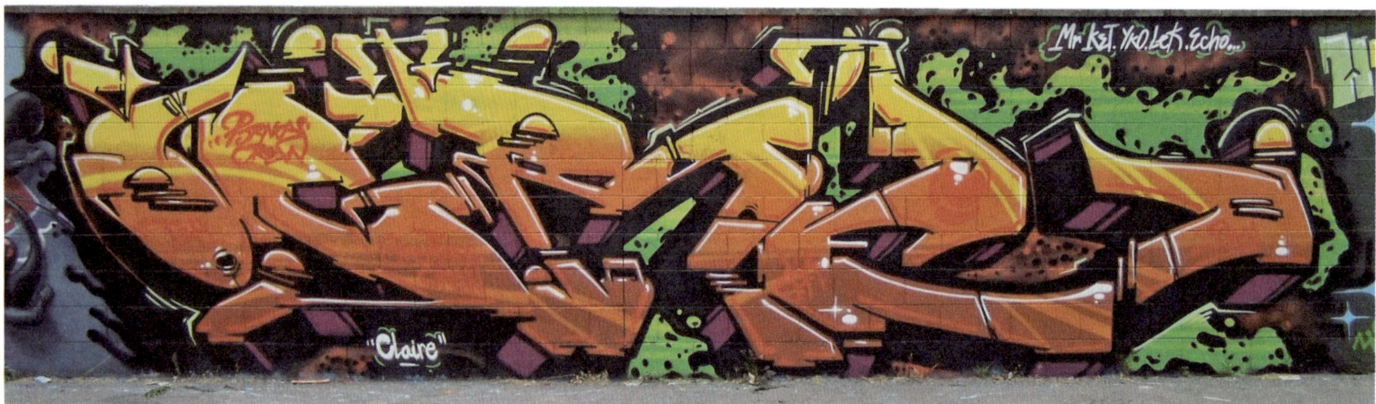

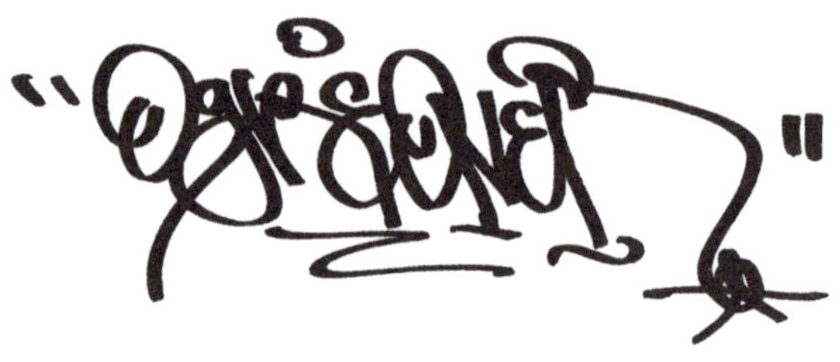

Ogre

LYONS, FRANCE

Crew member of Pornostars, QMJ, TSH, LCF, LBN, Greetings Crew
Writer since 1995
Favourite letters: Z, S, E
www.facebook.com/ogreoner

Ogre is known for his dynamic wildstyles with interesting letter joins, good colour choices and effective details. He painted his alphabet predominantly in different shades of blue on a 24-metre-long wall. To make his name stand out within the sequence, he highlighted those letters in red. According to Ogre, it takes 'flow, balance and a clever colour match' to create a fresh piece.

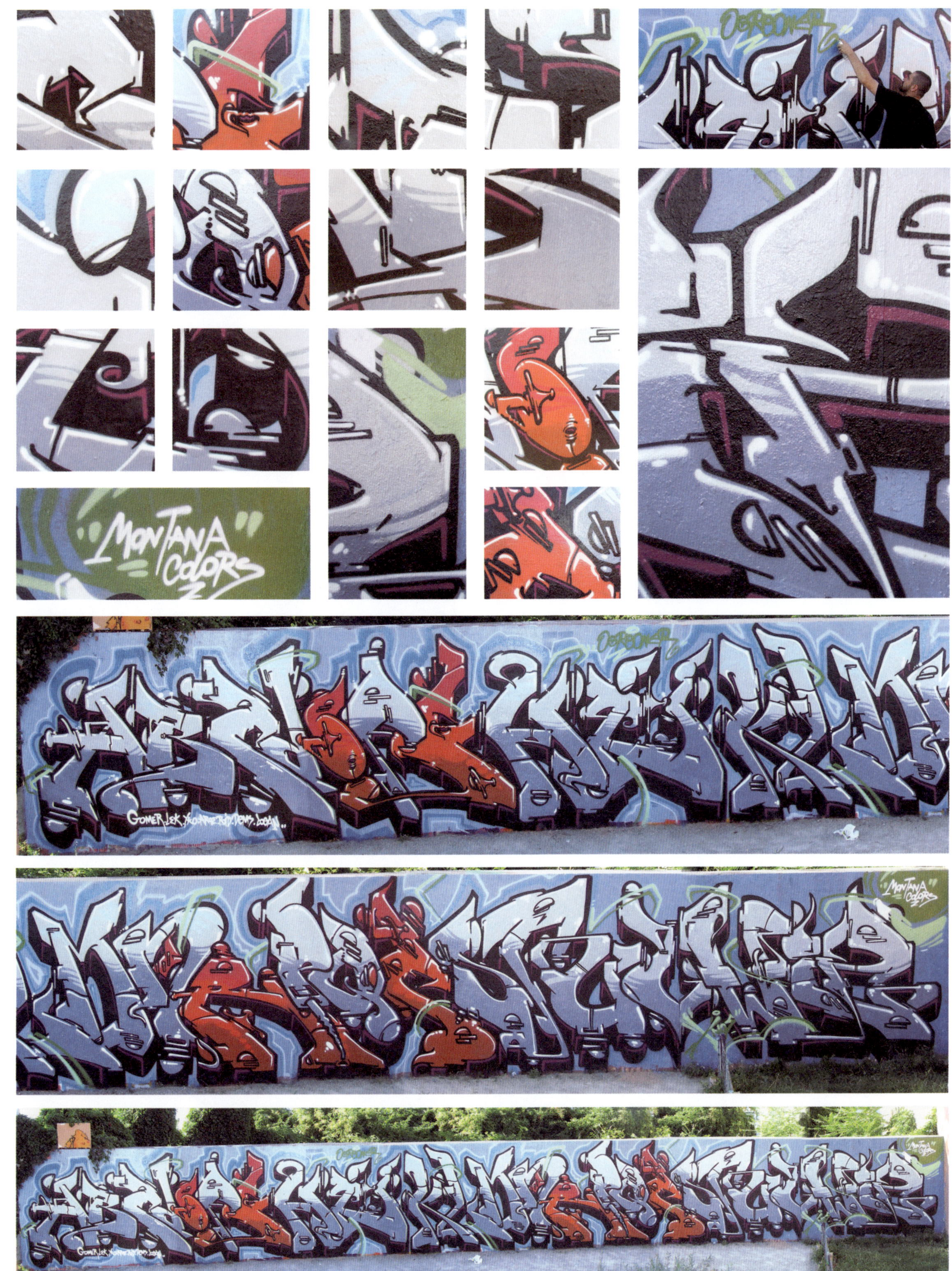

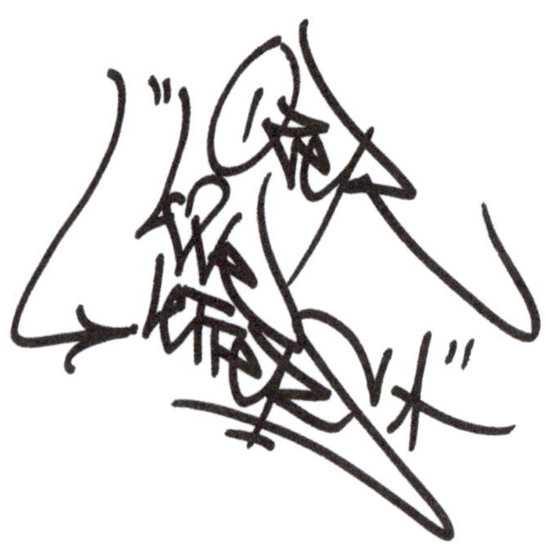

Ozer

PARIS, FRANCE
Crew member of LoveLetters
Writer since 1988
Favourite letter: Z
ozer.ths.free.fr

Ozer's classic, clean, compact and dynamic style is complemented by a bright colour scheme. Well-constructed and well-executed letters are the key to a good piece, he says. Ozer wanted his alphabet to tell a little story, so he deliberately left out the 'O' to wind up the 'Z'.

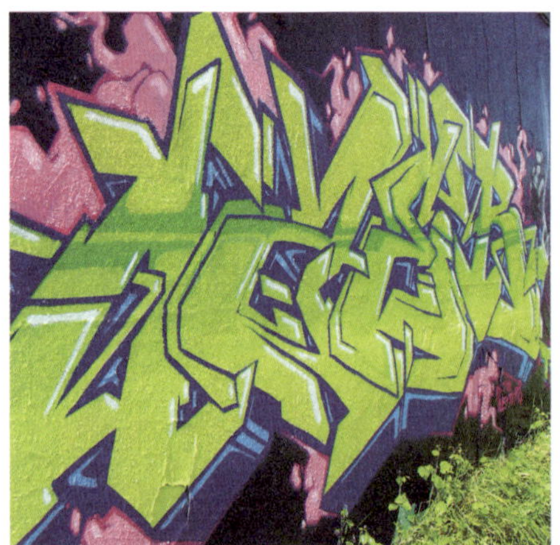

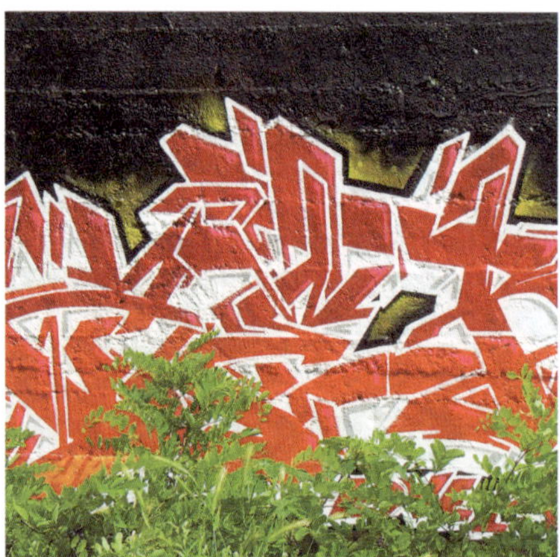

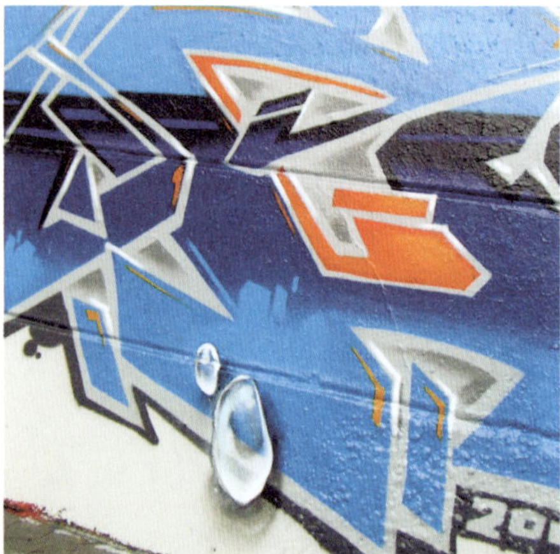

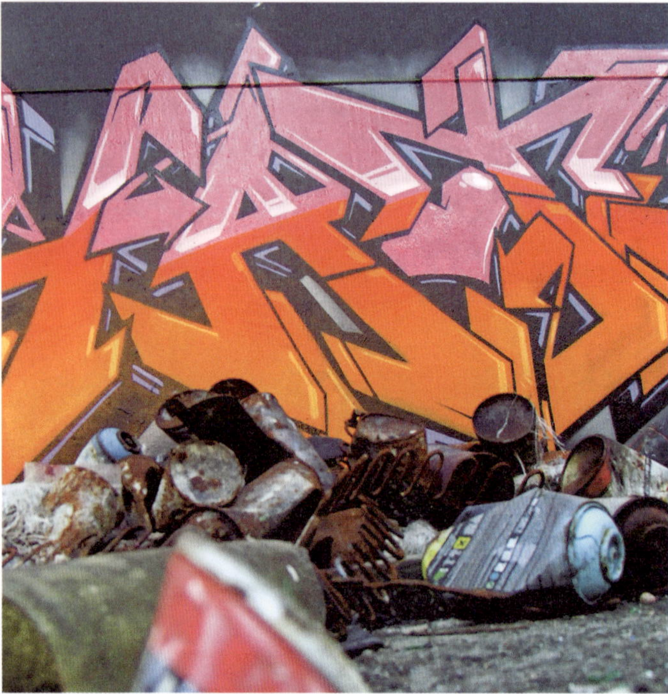

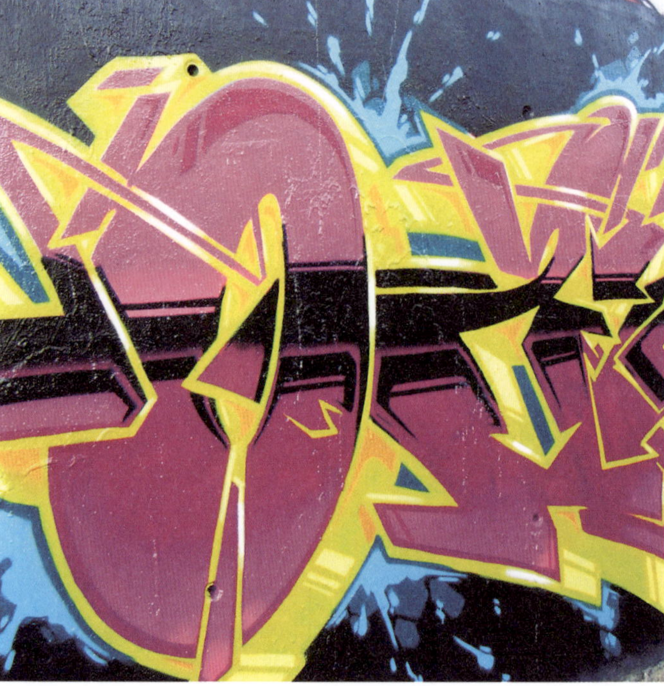

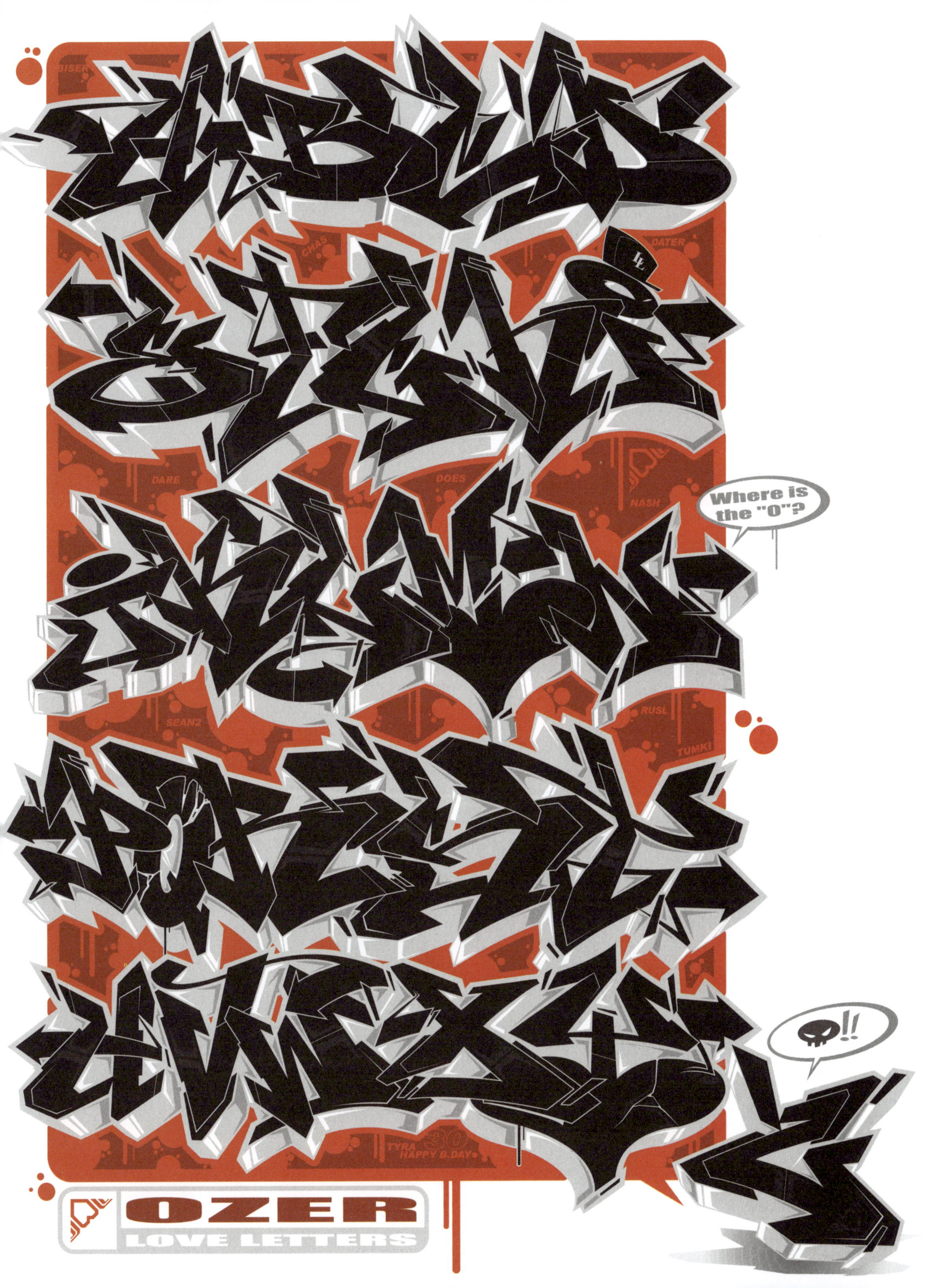

Where is the "O"?

OZER
LOVE LETTERS

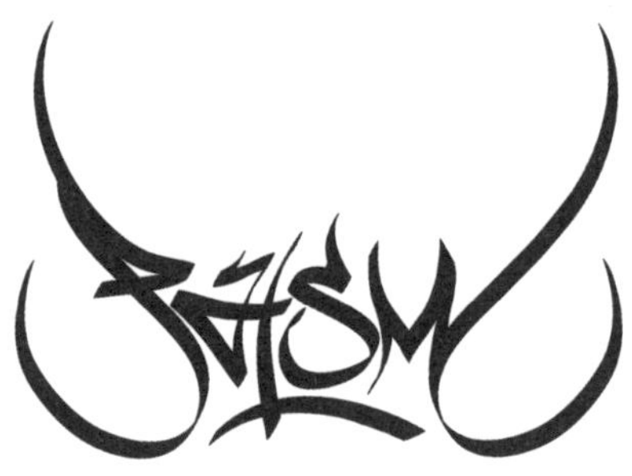

Paism

GRYFICE, POLAND
Crew member of Typoets
Writer since 2000
Favourite letter: P
www.facebook.com/typoets

Paism was always drawn to typography and characters, but his own adventure with letters started in 2000 when he became a writer. He often puts aside the spray can to experiment with other media such as paper and wood. His alphabet, which was constructed on wood using 246 nails and yarn, is a great example of this willingness to experiment. According to Paism, you must open your mind to new things in order to create something remarkable.

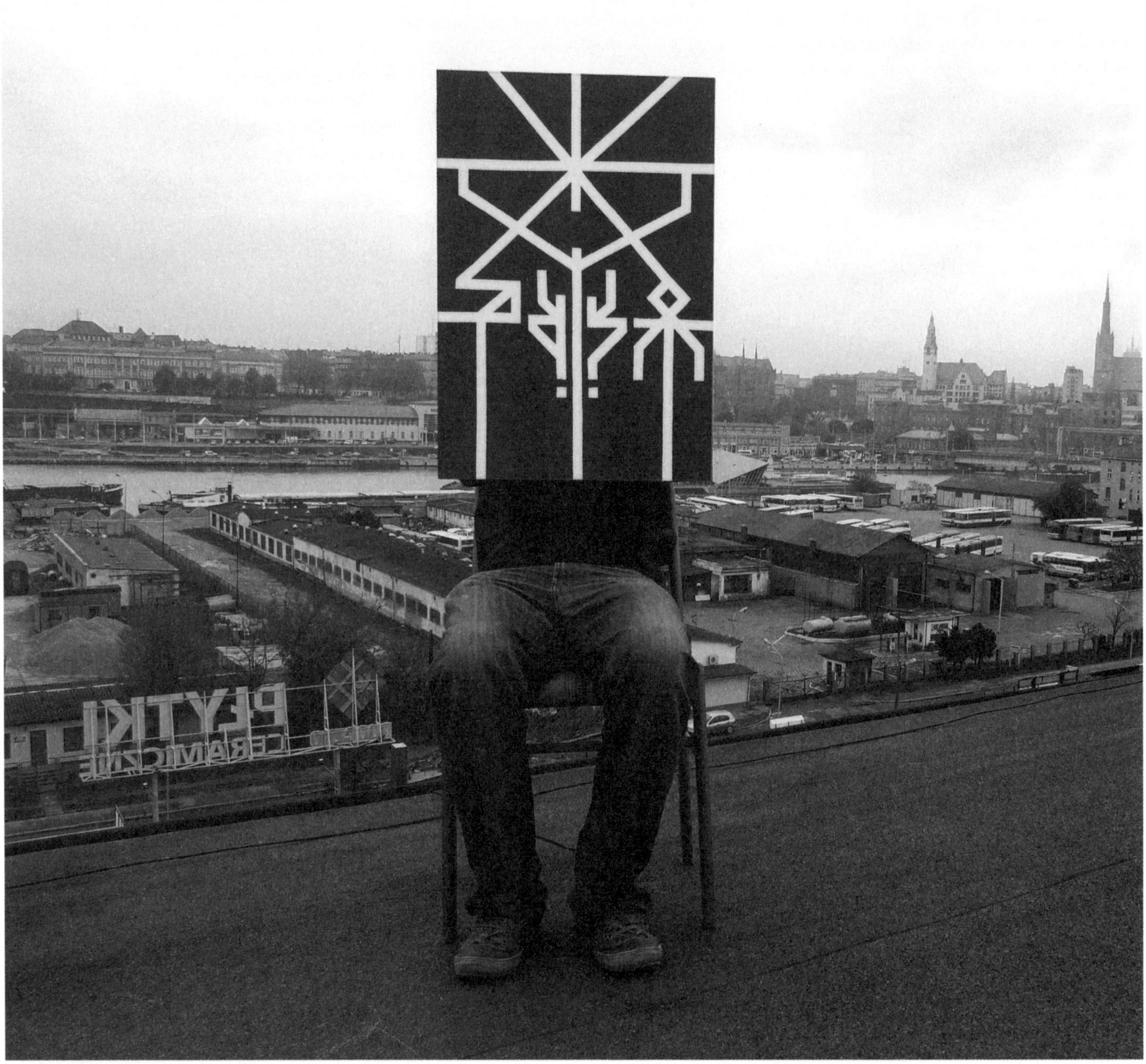

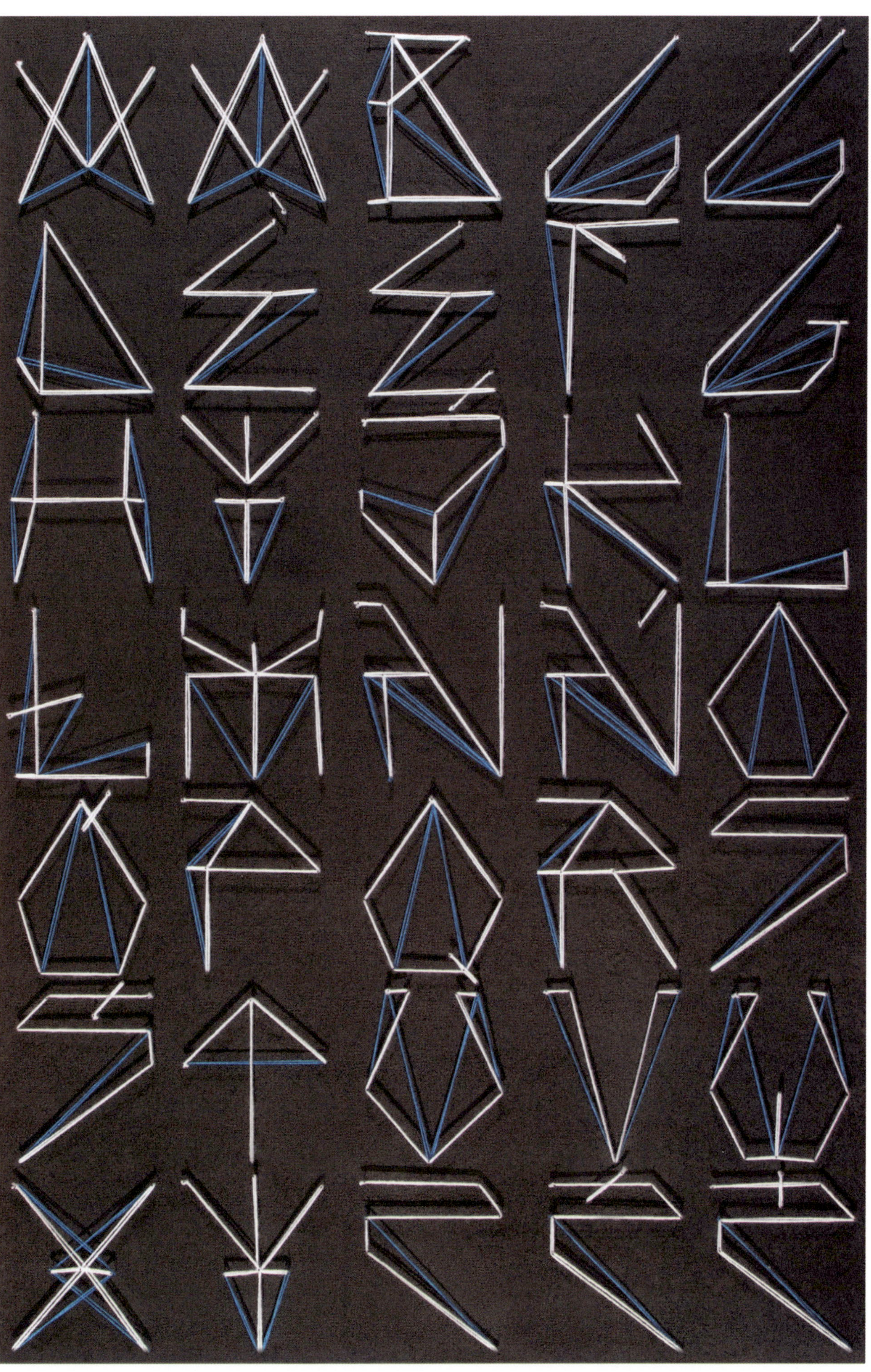

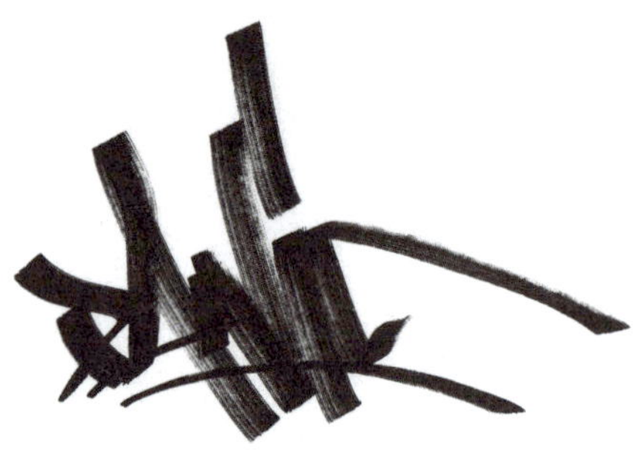

Panic

GRYFICE, POLAND
Crew member of Typoets
Writer since 1995
Favourite letter: P
www.facebook.com/typoets

In the 1990s, when Panic became a writer, spray paint was hard to come by so he usually worked with brushes. He continues to explore various media and letter shapes. The letter 'P' is his favourite because it is all around him – in his forename and surname, his alias as a writer and the name of his native country. Panic says: 'Graffiti opens up your mind and gives you freedom – a word that is very important to Polish people. I wake up and go to bed with letters swirling around my mind. There is nothing I am more addicted to.'

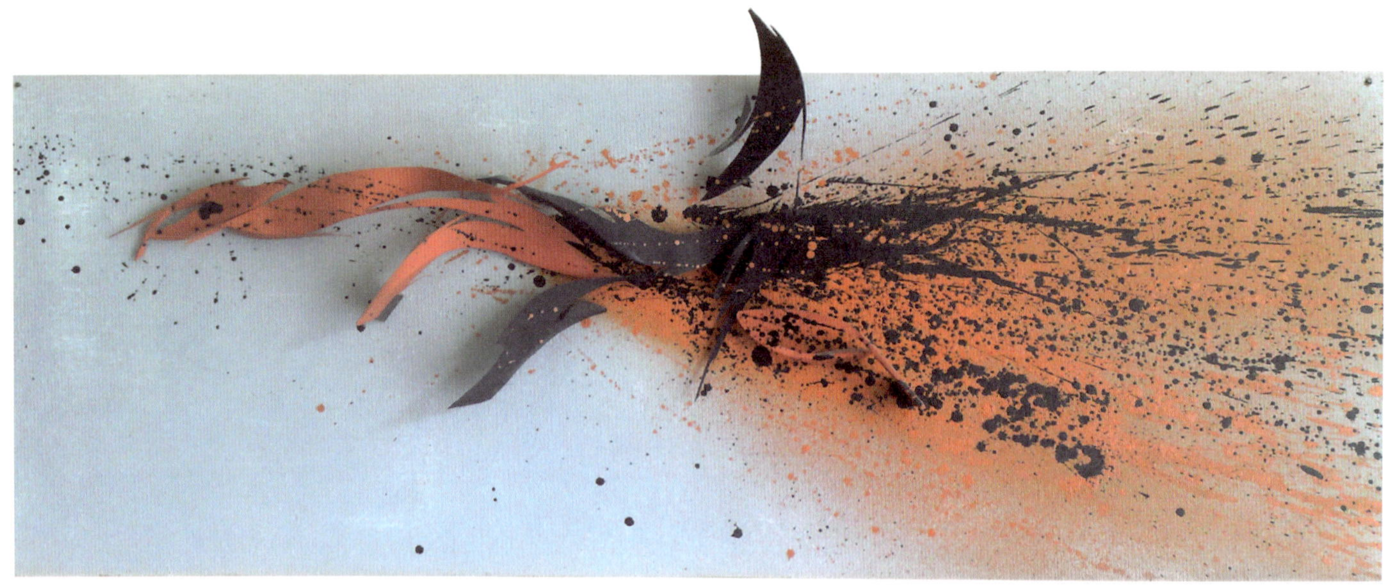

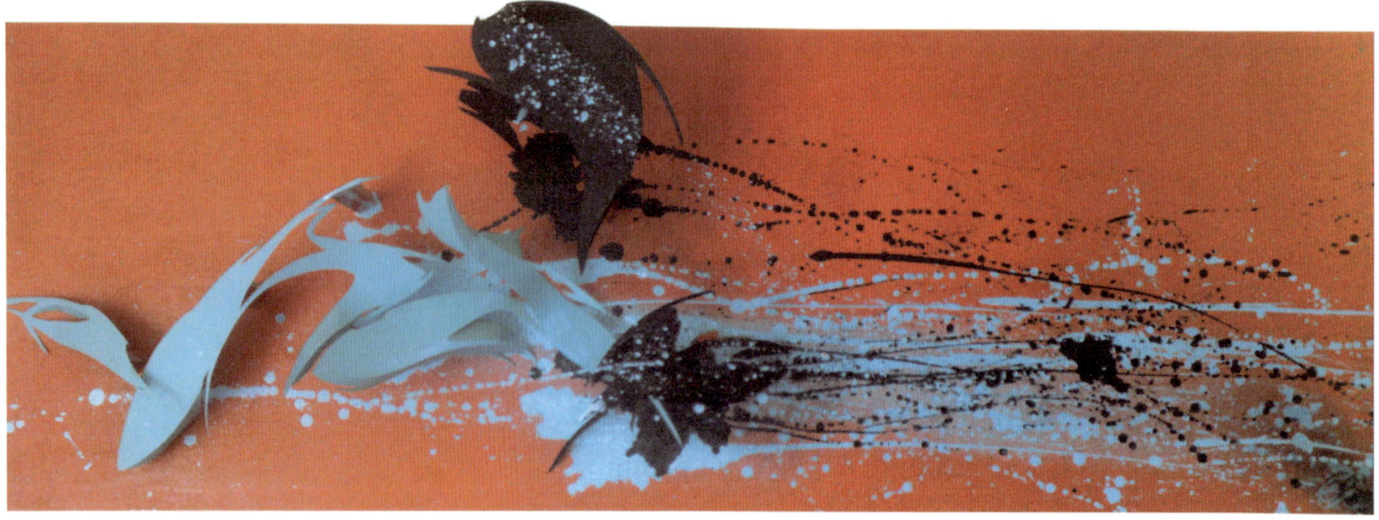

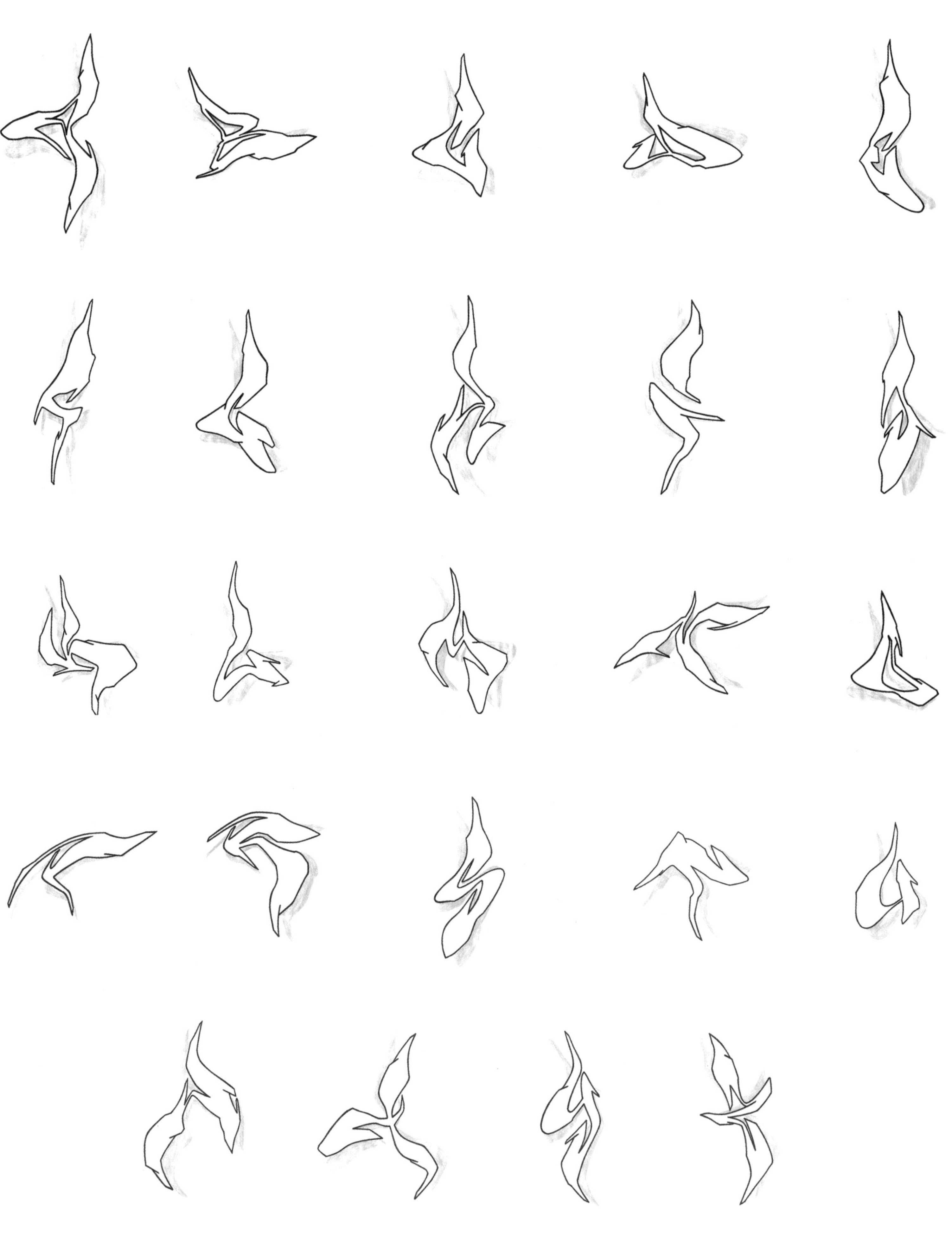

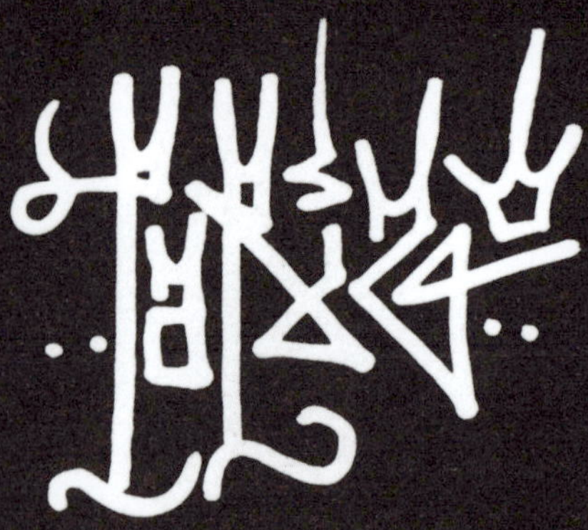

Pariz One

LISBON, PORTUGAL
Crew member of GVS, CSF, VDS, TKO
Writer since 1999
Favourite letter: R
www.pariz-one.com

Pariz One's pieces are extremely colourful. They are also gigantic. Some of the letters in his alphabet are more than 7 metres tall, and none are less than 2 metres in height. Each of the twenty-six letters belongs to a different piece in a different place. Some were done exclusively for this book. Pariz says that his style was influenced by both the New York old school and the European new school, and describes it as 'new old-school style'.

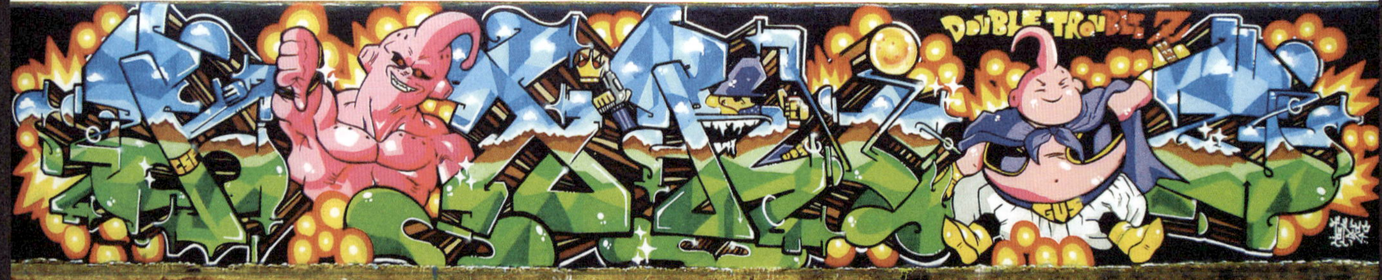

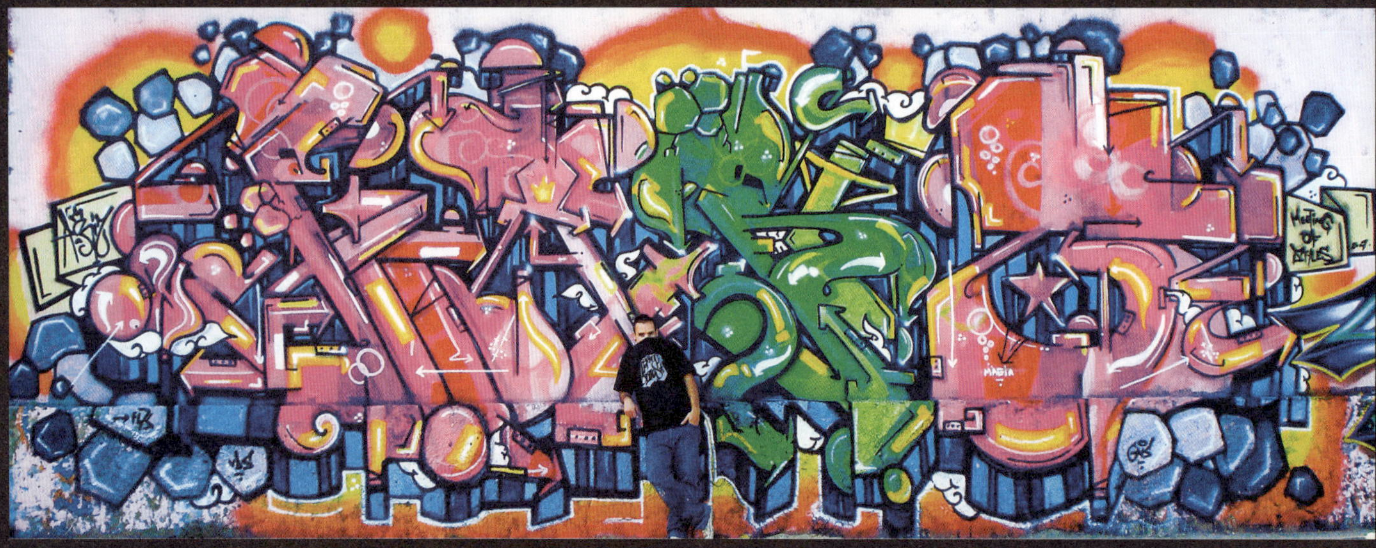

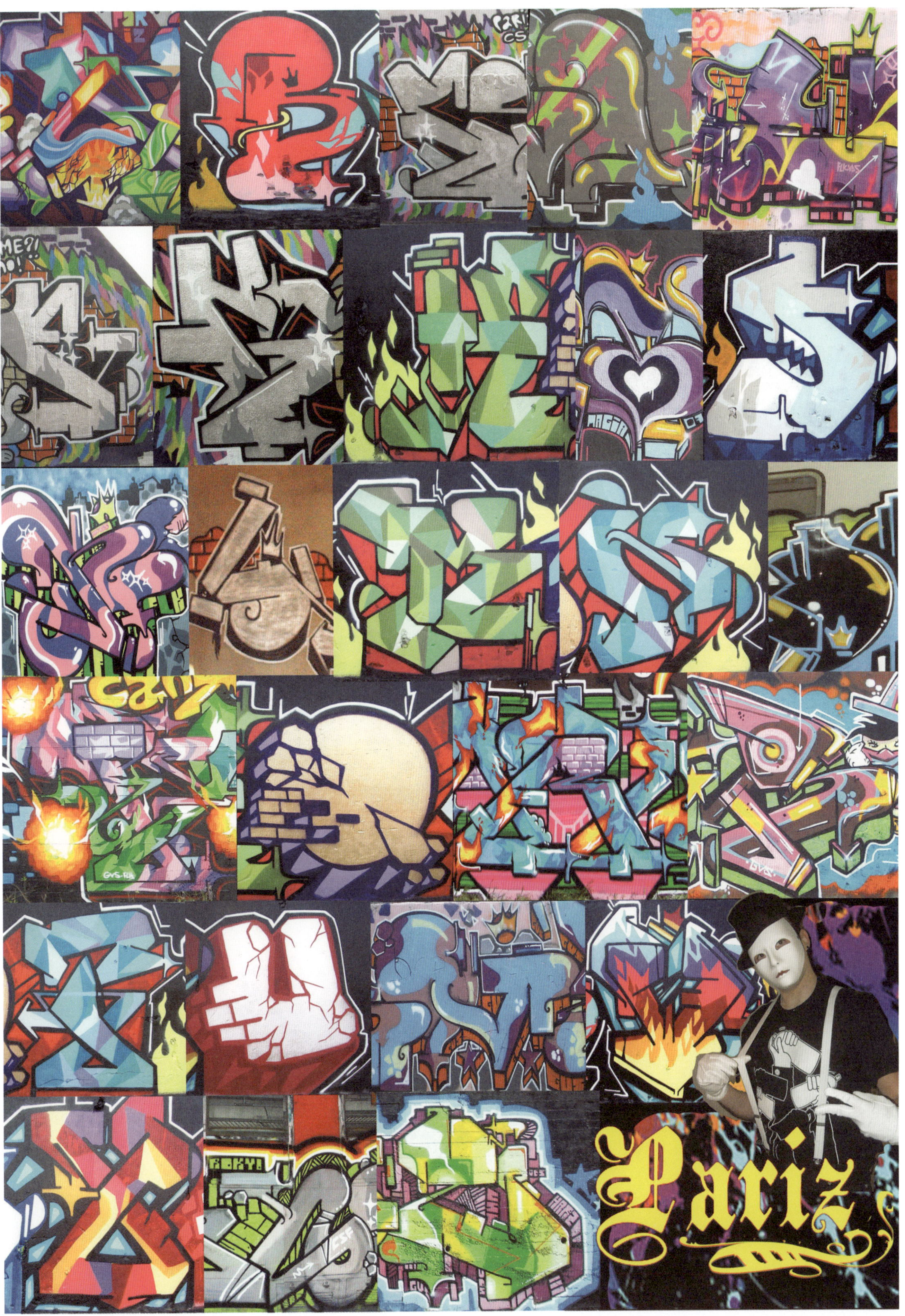
Pariz

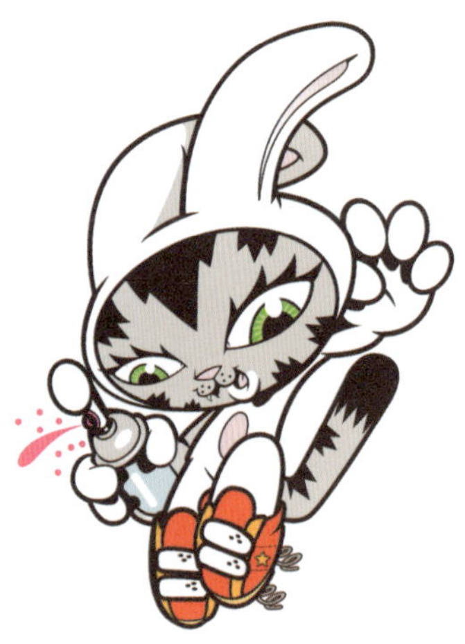

Persue

SAN DIEGO, USA

Crew member of COD, SUK, 7th Letter, TVC, Transcend
Writer since 1988
Favourite letter: P
www.bunnykitty.com

Persue has been working in the action sports industry for over seventeen years. He is not just an aerosol artist but also a skilled graphic designer, illustrator, footwear designer and the mastermind behind Bunny Kitty. Bunny Kitty is a cat with a bunny suit that gives her magical powers. She moves to the city, where a whole world of characters is revealed. The story is constantly evolving and is written both on the streets through Persue's graffiti pieces and in storybook form.

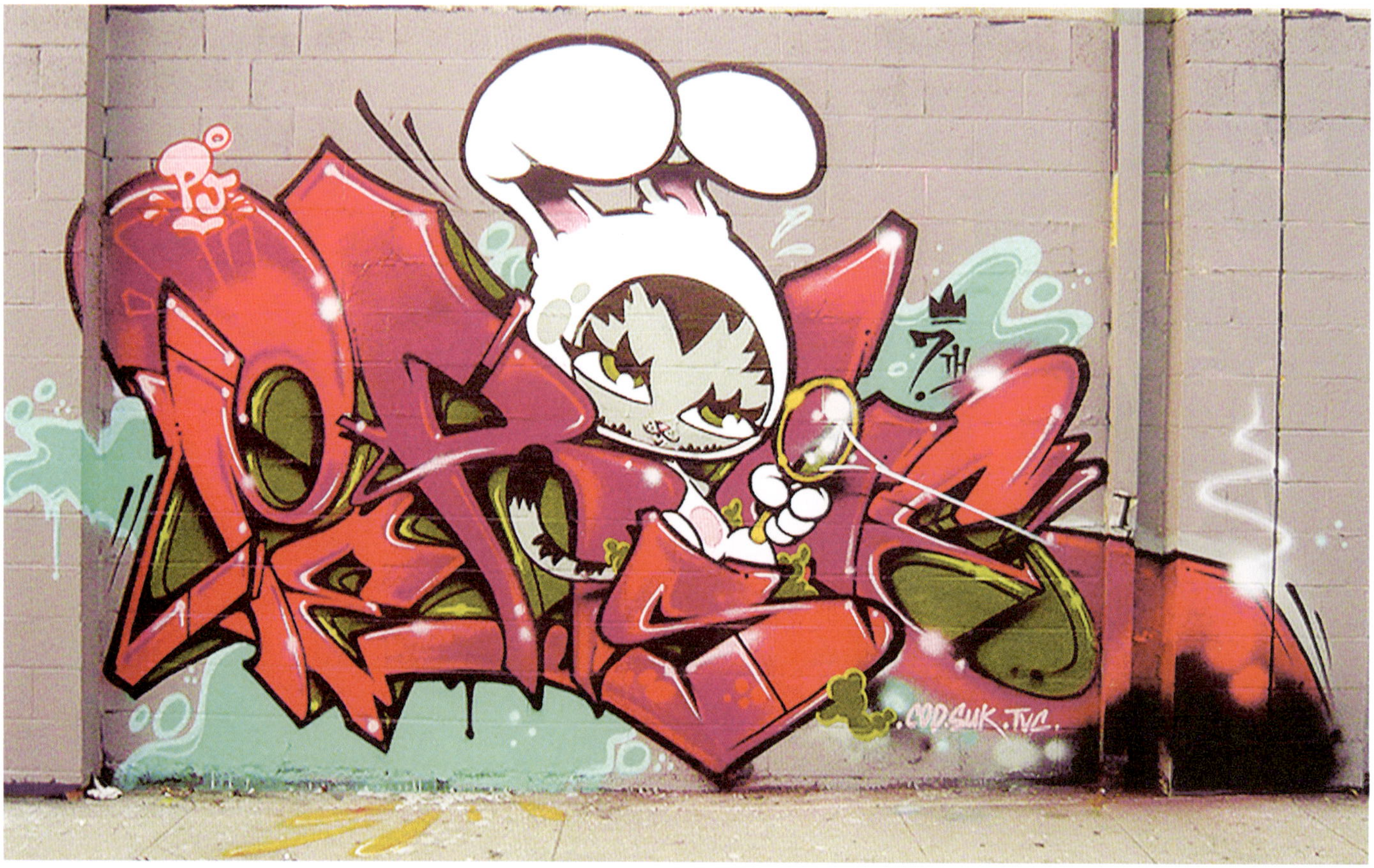

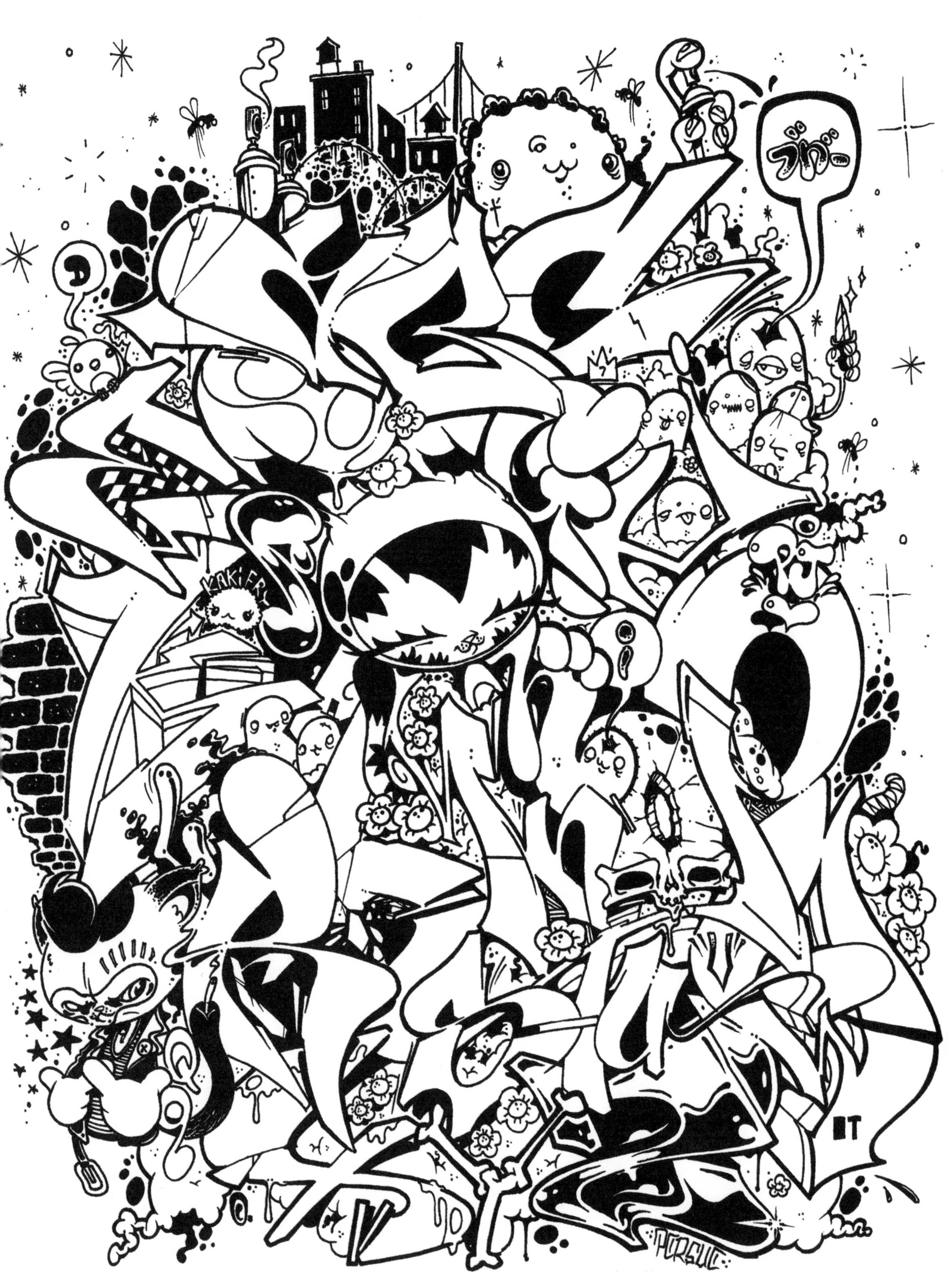

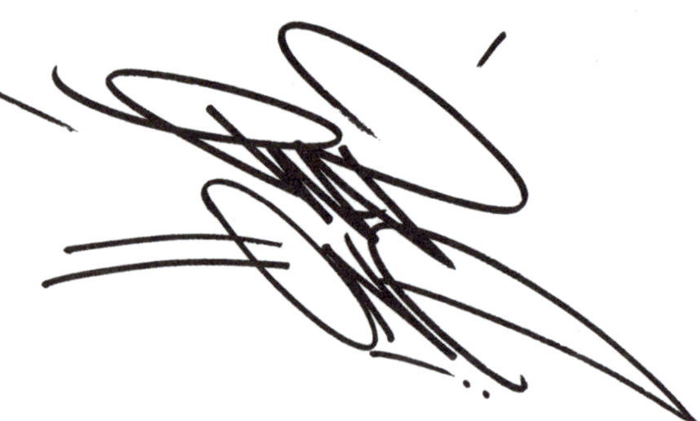

Phat1

AUCKLAND, NEW ZEALAND
Crew member of TMD, SUK, F1C
Writer since 1992
Favourite letter: S
www.flickr.com/therealphat1

Phat1 was inspired by the tags and pieces that he saw on his way to school. He experimented with many different letter forms and even 3D pieces, but he always went back to the classic New York style. He kept the letters of his alphabet simple and accessible because, for him, the letters come first and everything else follows. Discussing his life as a graffiti artist, Phat1 says: 'It's a world in which you have ups and downs, but more ups than downs.'

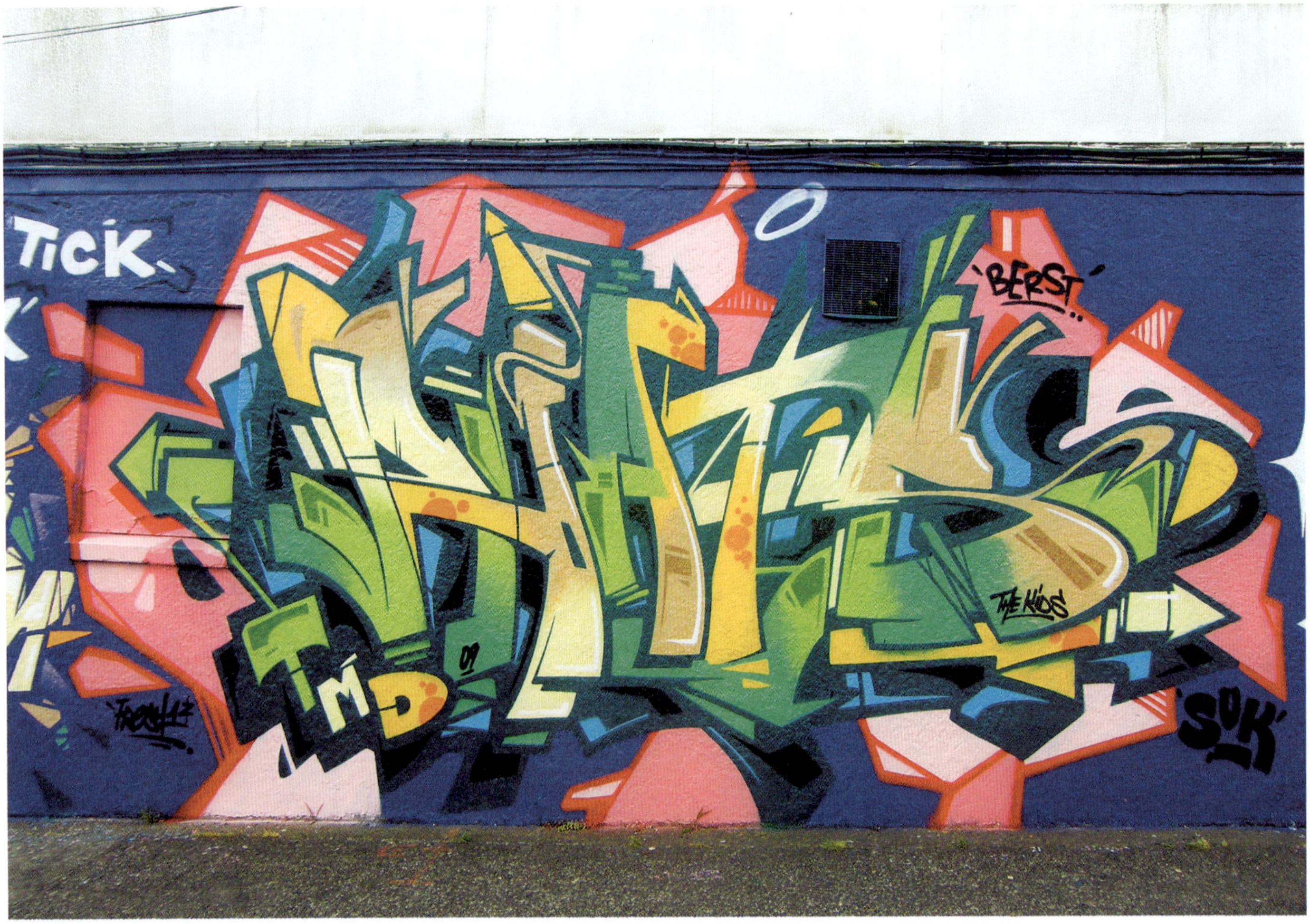

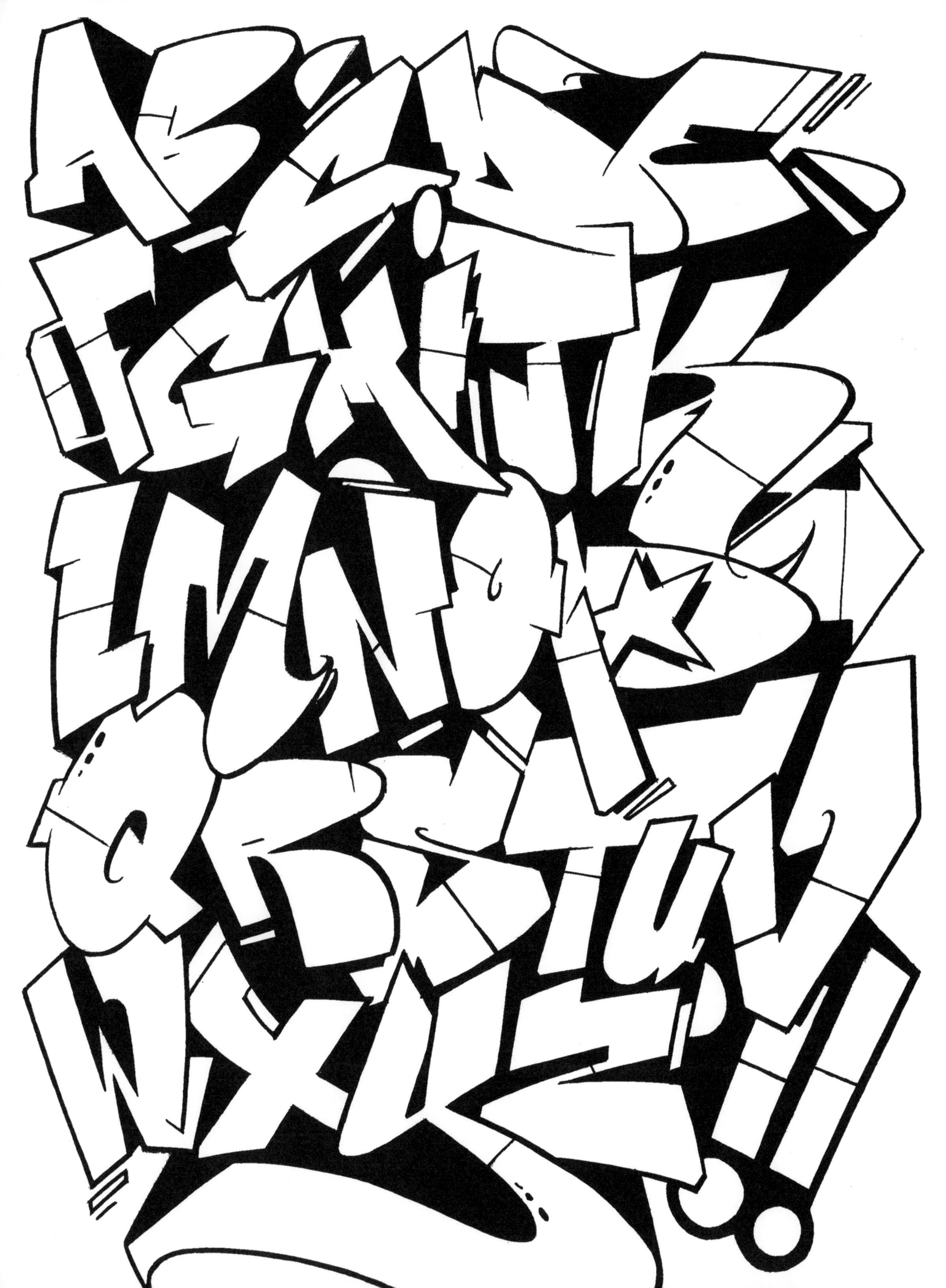

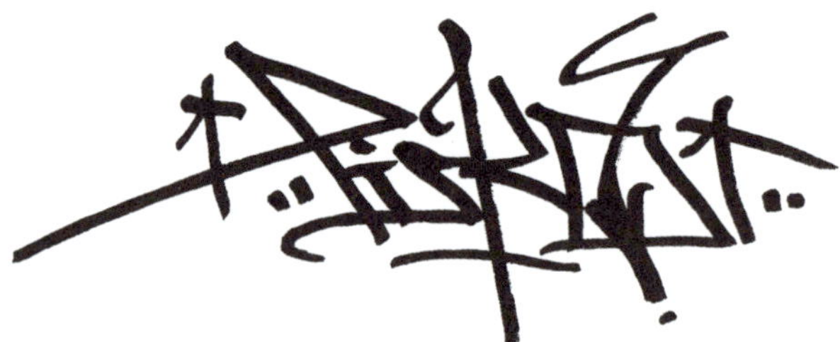

Pisco
STRASBOURG, FRANCE
Crew member of LCP, EC, TWA, MBK
Favourite letters: P, I, S, C, O
www.piscologik.com

Pisco has developed a distinctive wildstyle. Whichever of his three names (Pisco, Pisko or Chile) he chooses to write, his dynamic style is instantly recognizable. Quality letters, suitable colours and a good location are essential in creating a successful piece, he says.

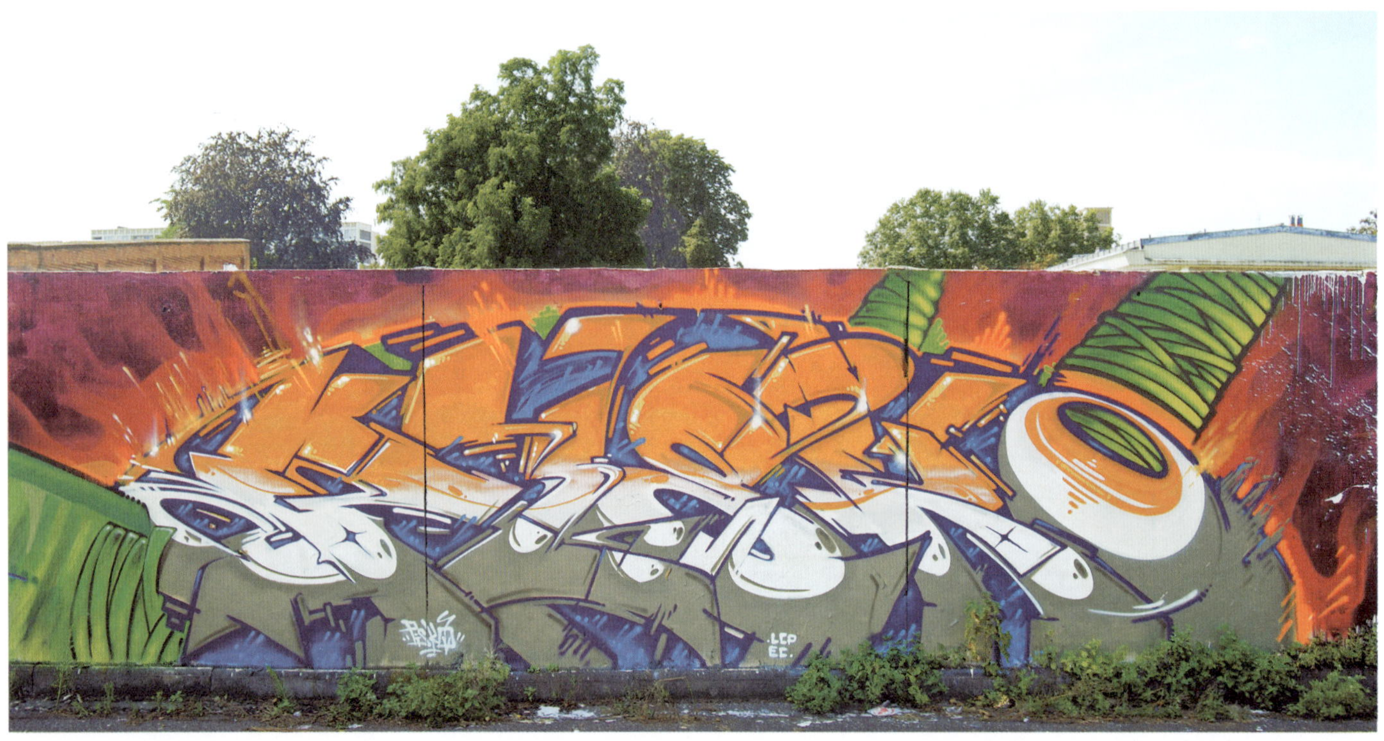

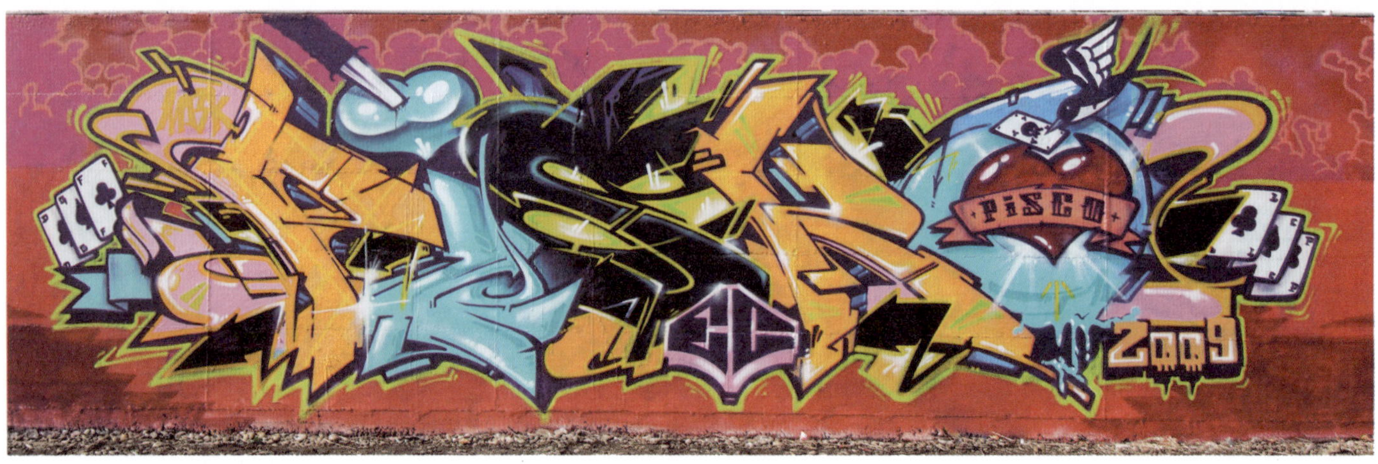

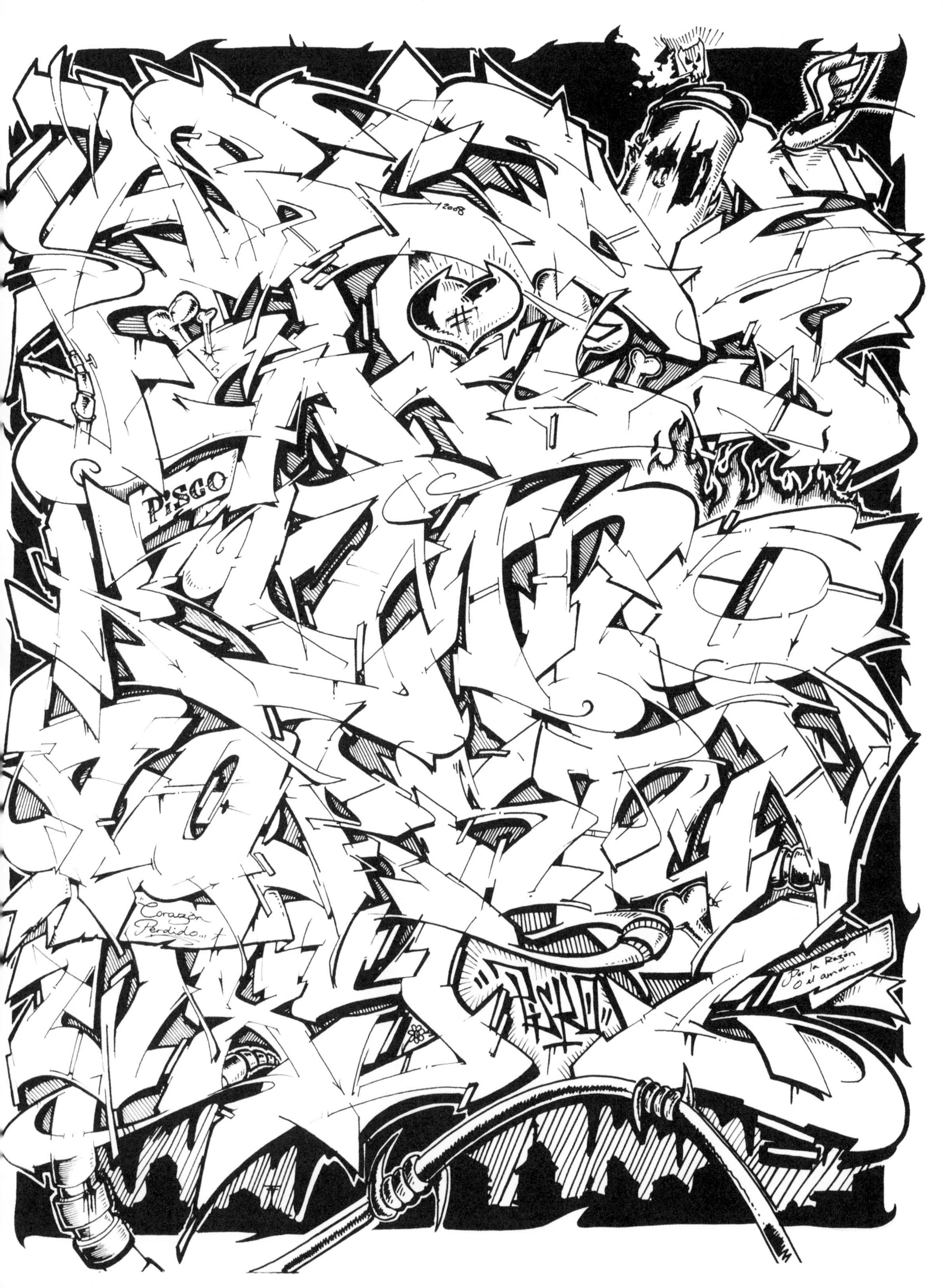

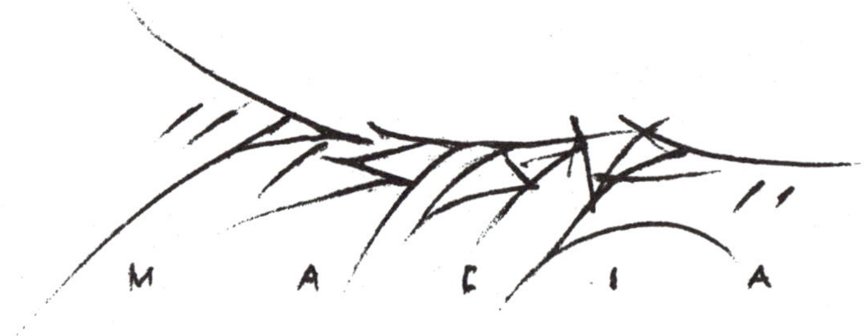

Pistone

STRASBOURG, FRANCE

Crew member of Macia, KMF
Writer since 1996
Favourite letter: 'All of them'
www.macia-crew.com

Pistone's hand-drawn alphabet in ink is a summation of his ten-plus years of experimentation and style development. He broke down the alphabet as if it were a font to emphasize his typical style of heavy vertical strokes. 'A good piece must be complex but legible,' he says, 'with fine detail and the desire to do better.' He likes the way that graffiti allows you to paint any size you want.

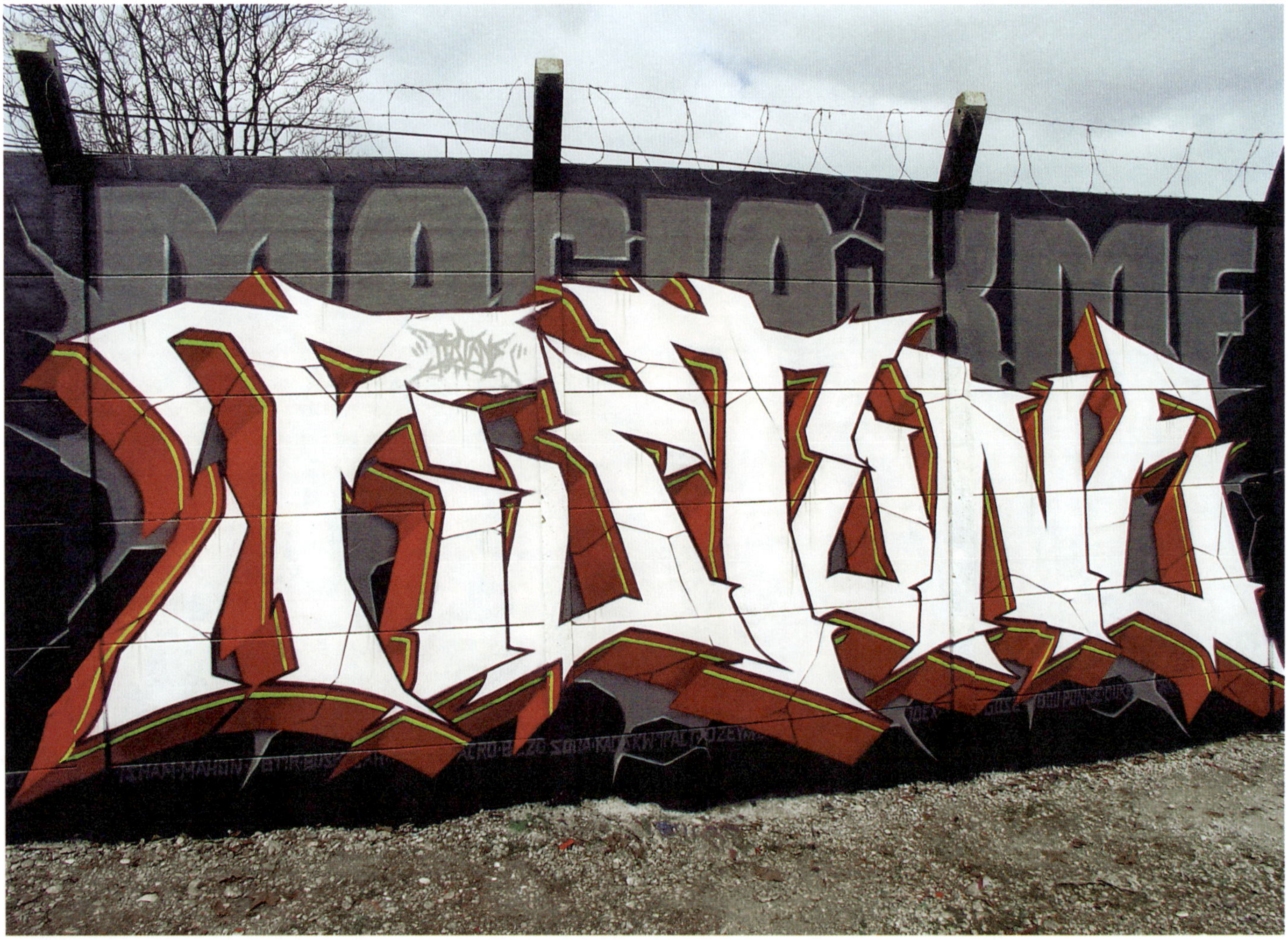

A B C D E

F G H I J K

L M N O P

Q R S T U

V W X Y Z

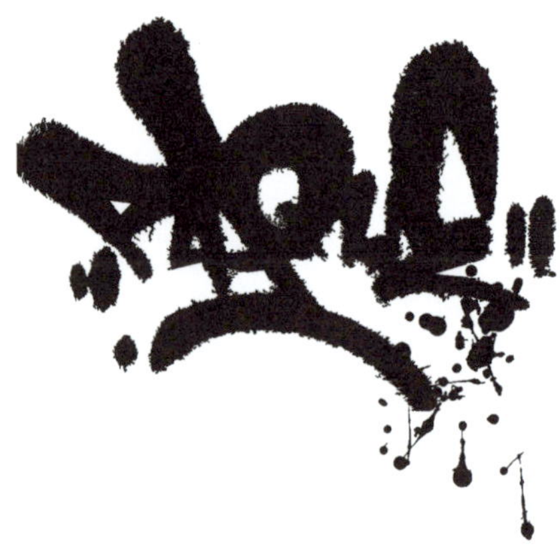

Plaque
COLOGNE, GERMANY
Crew member of Bandits
Writer since 1995
Favourite letters: W, O, K
www.plaqueone.de

Plaque's pieces are harmonious, balanced and neatly executed. He prefers clean-looking pieces, whether it's a throw-up or a wildstyle. The letters of his alphabet share a lot of common features, giving them a unified look. The opportunity to switch between identities is what he likes best about graffiti.

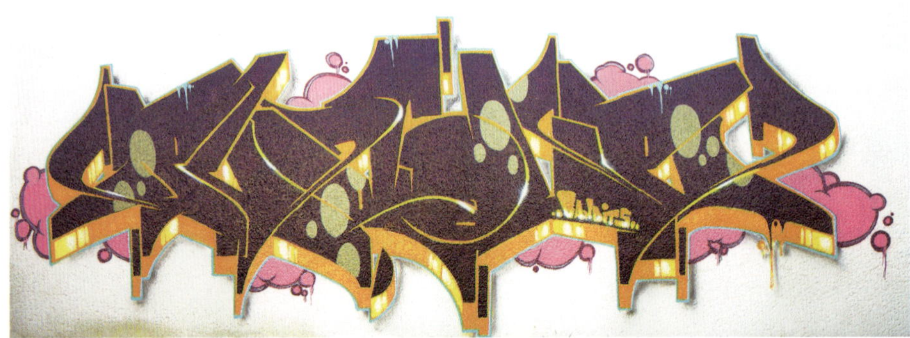

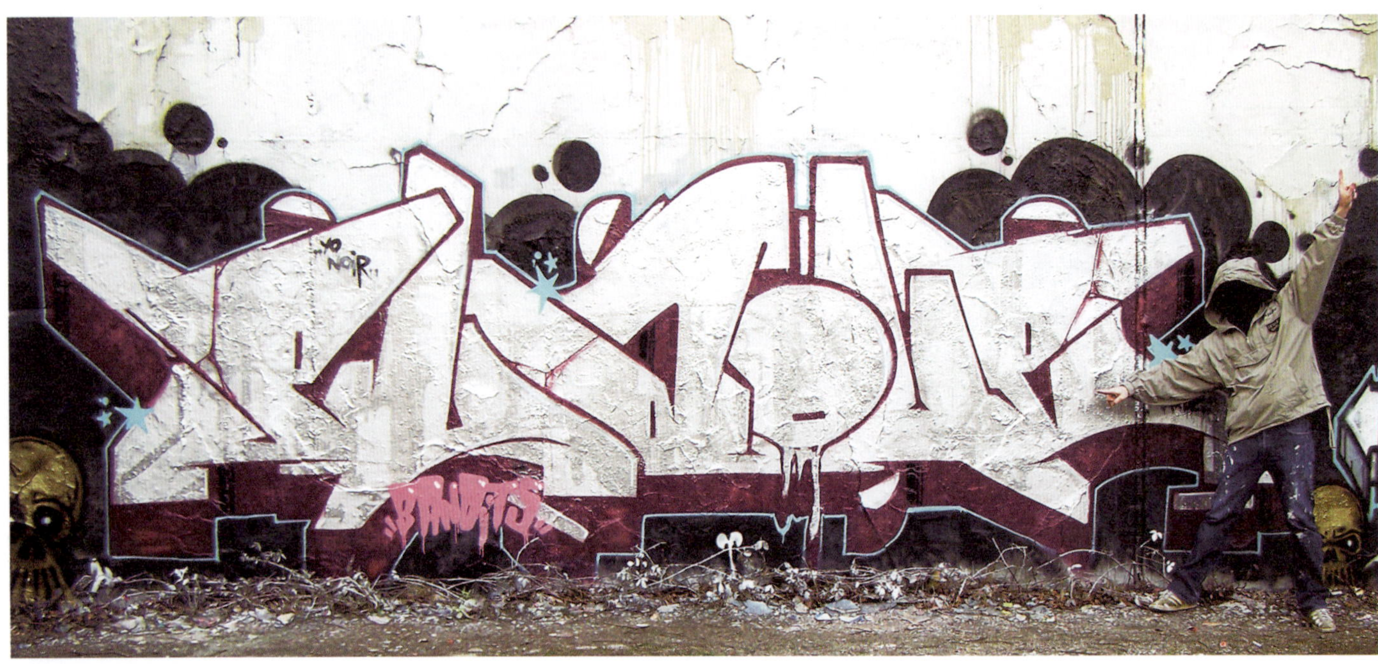

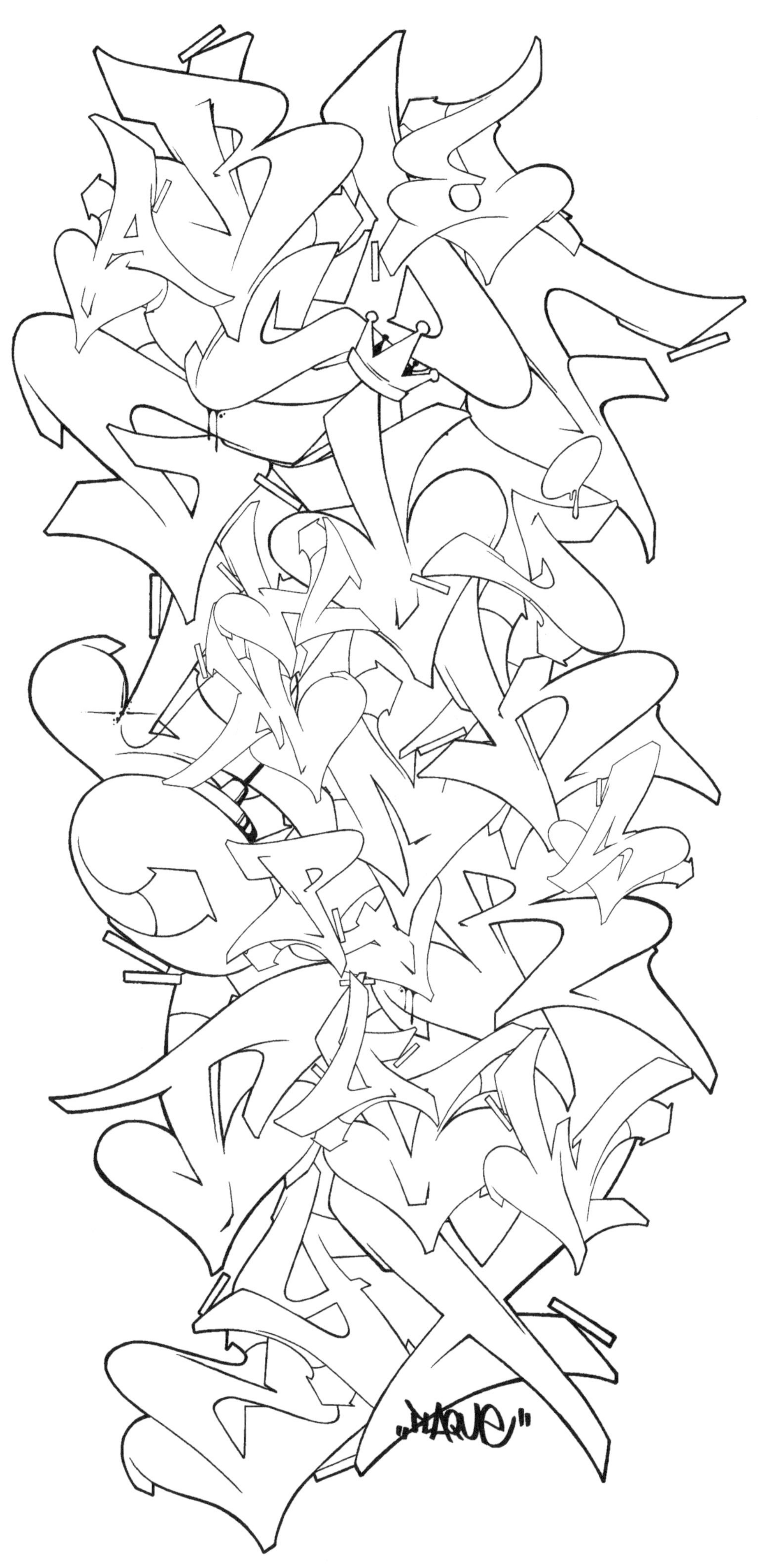

„MAQUE"

Poch

RENNES, FRANCE
Crew member of CP5, P2B, RAW, JNC, WMD
Writer since 1988
Favourite letter: 'No favourite'
www.patrice-poch.com

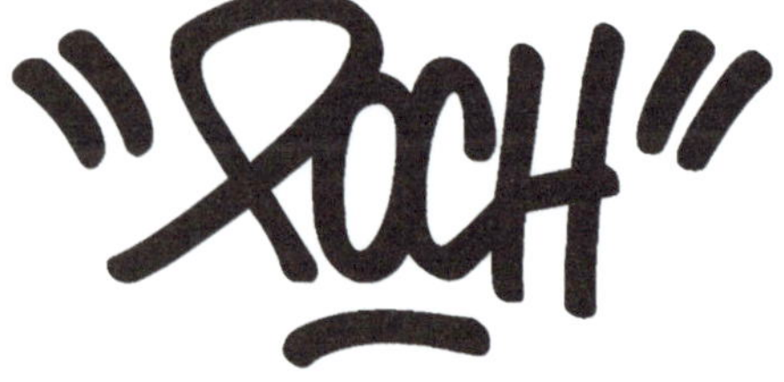

Inspired by French and English rock and punk culture, Poch has been experimenting with different techniques and media such as posters, stencils and spray cans since he got into graffiti in the late 1980s. His distinctive pieces feature clean lines and a limited range of colours.

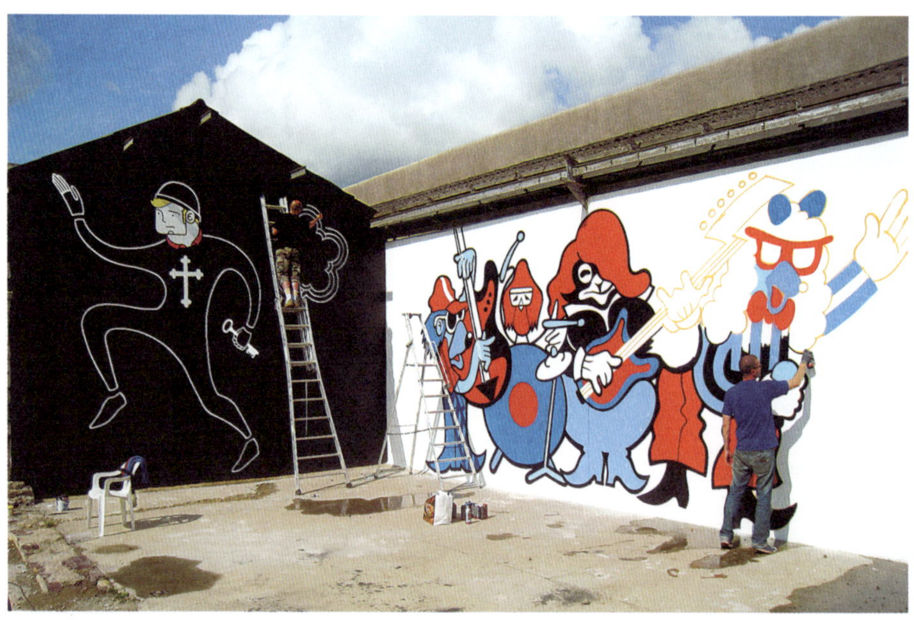

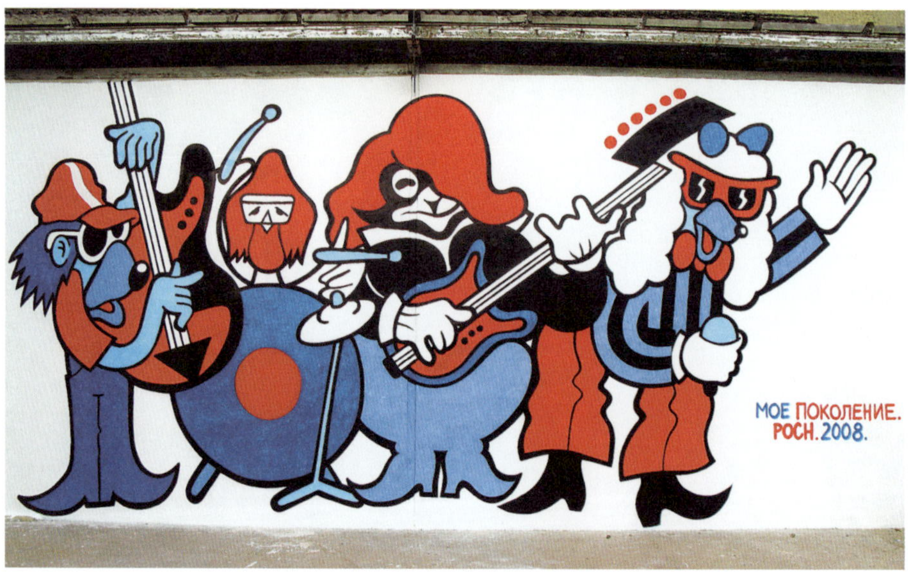

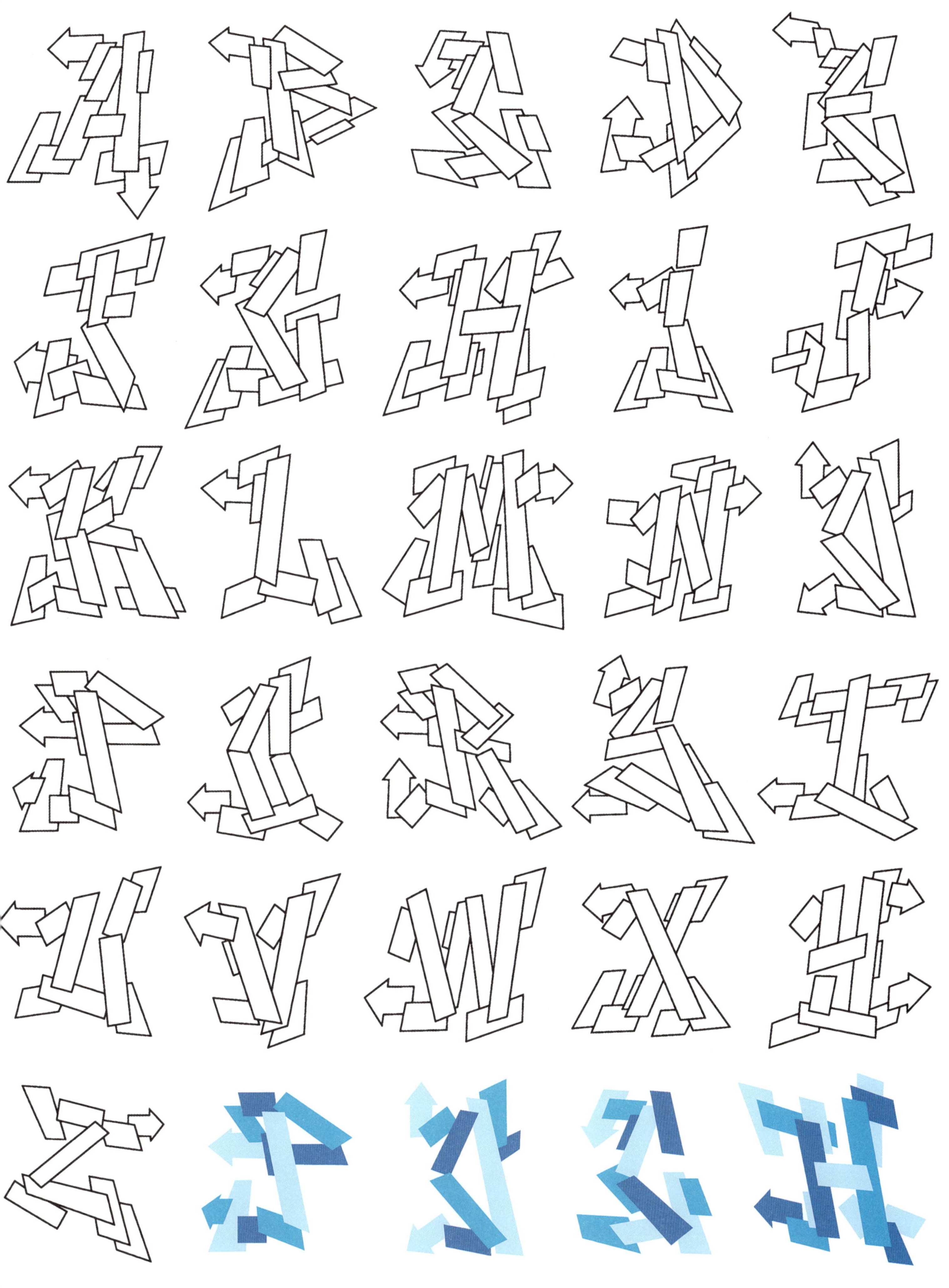

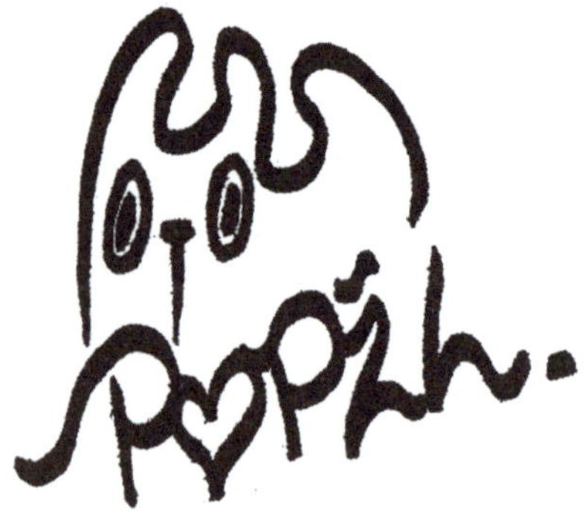

Popil

SHANGHAI, CHINA

Crew member of Quail
Writer since 2005
Favourite letter: P
www.flickr.com/popilcat

The Chinese graffiti scene is still in its infancy, and Popil has developed a unique style that is markedly different from classic New York writing. Using watercolour and colouring pens, she drew a girl in different poses to create the letters of her alphabet. The girl – a character that has evolved over time – has gradually taken on some of Popil's own features. Popil enjoys the sense of freedom that comes with painting in the street, experimenting with size and experiencing the reactions of passers-by.

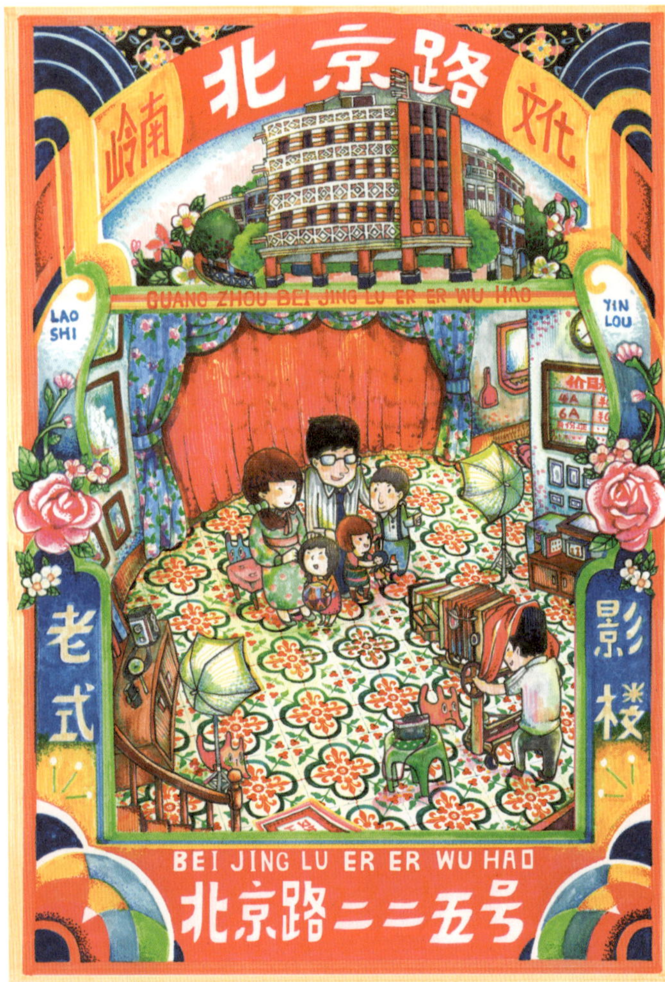

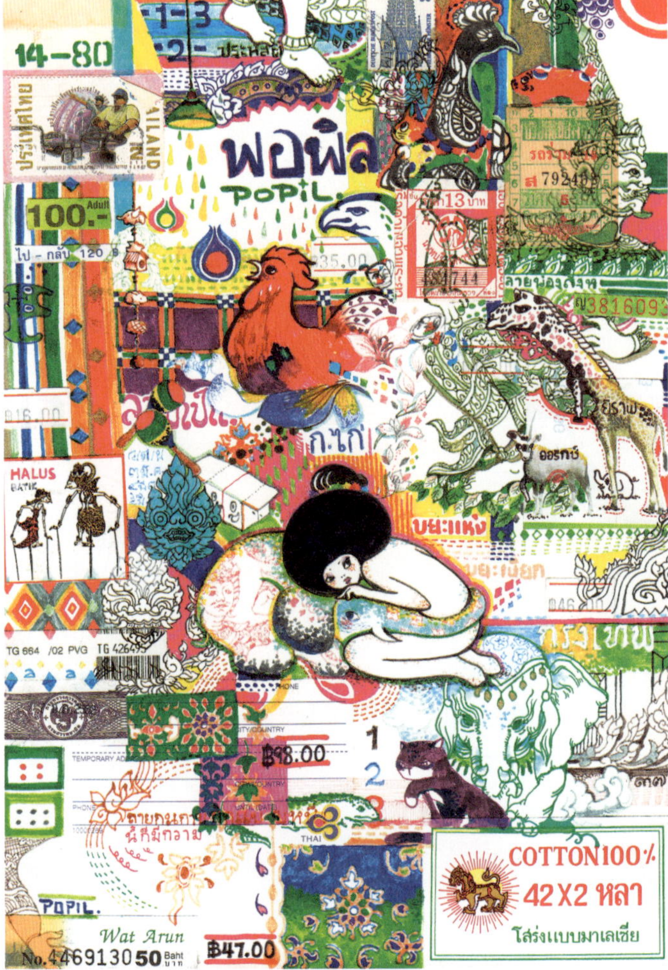

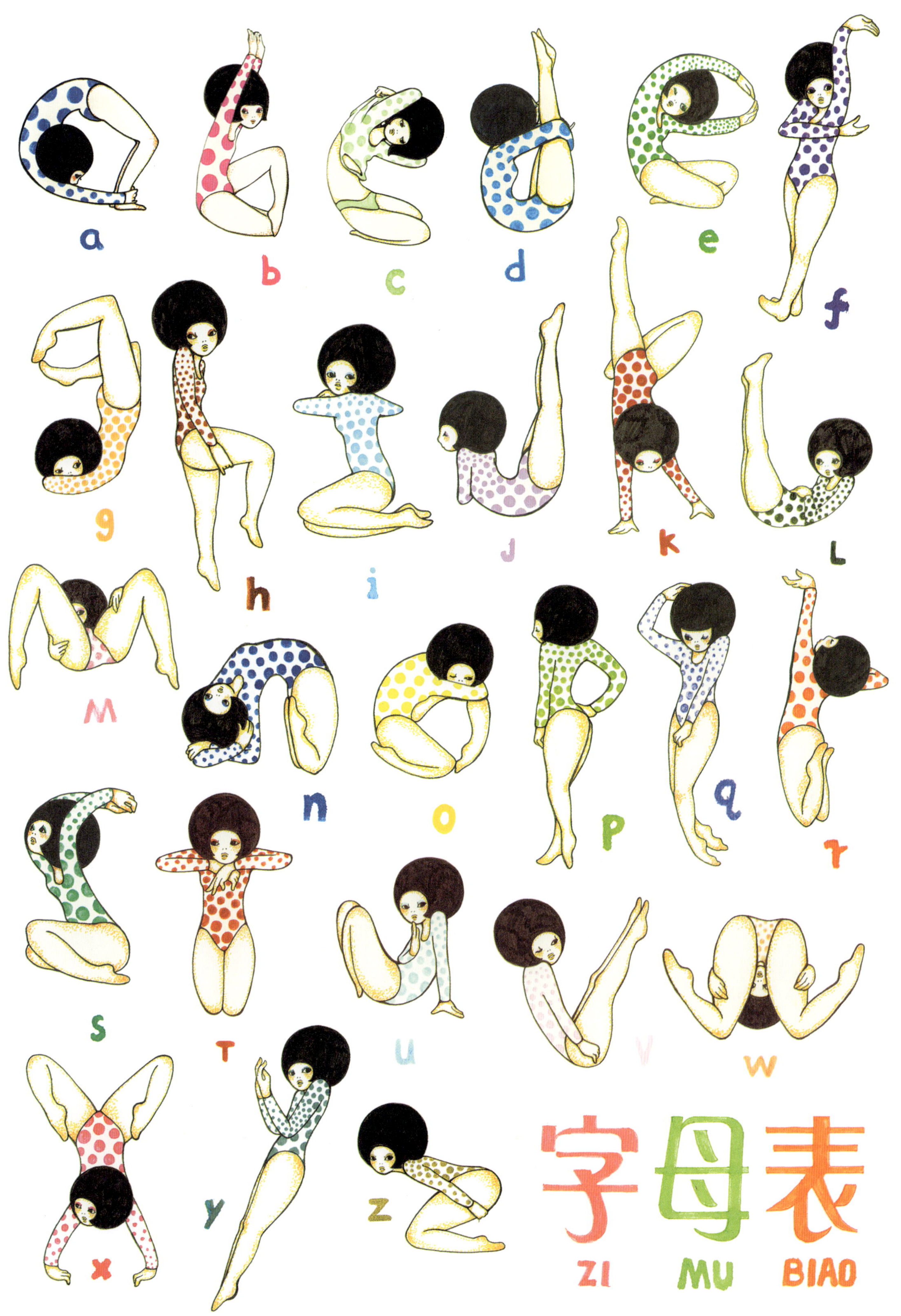

a
b
c
d
e
f
g
h
i
J
K
L
M
n
o
P
q
r
S
T
U
V
W
x
y
z
字母表
ZI MU BIAO

Puppet

STOCKHOLM, SWEDEN
Crew member of NOW!
Writer since 1983
Favourite letter: E
www.puppetindustries.com

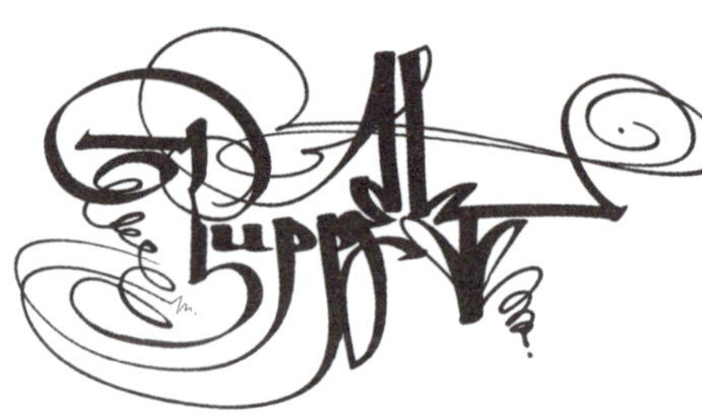

Puppet is known for his 'gridstyles', a unique and eye-catching way of designing his letters like grids. However, he also paints classic pieces and complex murals. His famed 'Dragon Wall' of 1989 was one of his first murals and won him great respect. In addition to his work as a graffiti artist, he now earns a living as an illustrator and graphic designer.

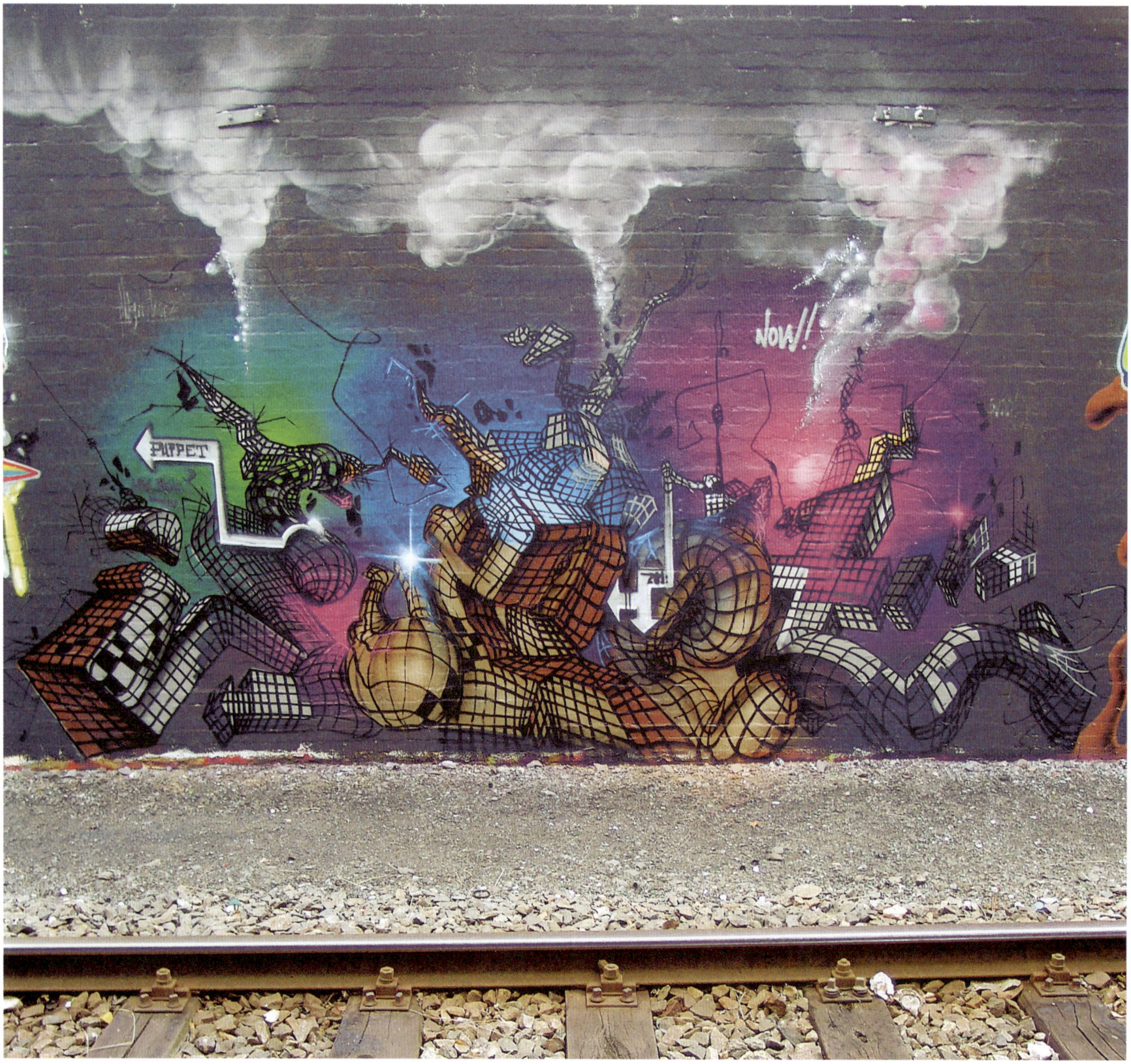

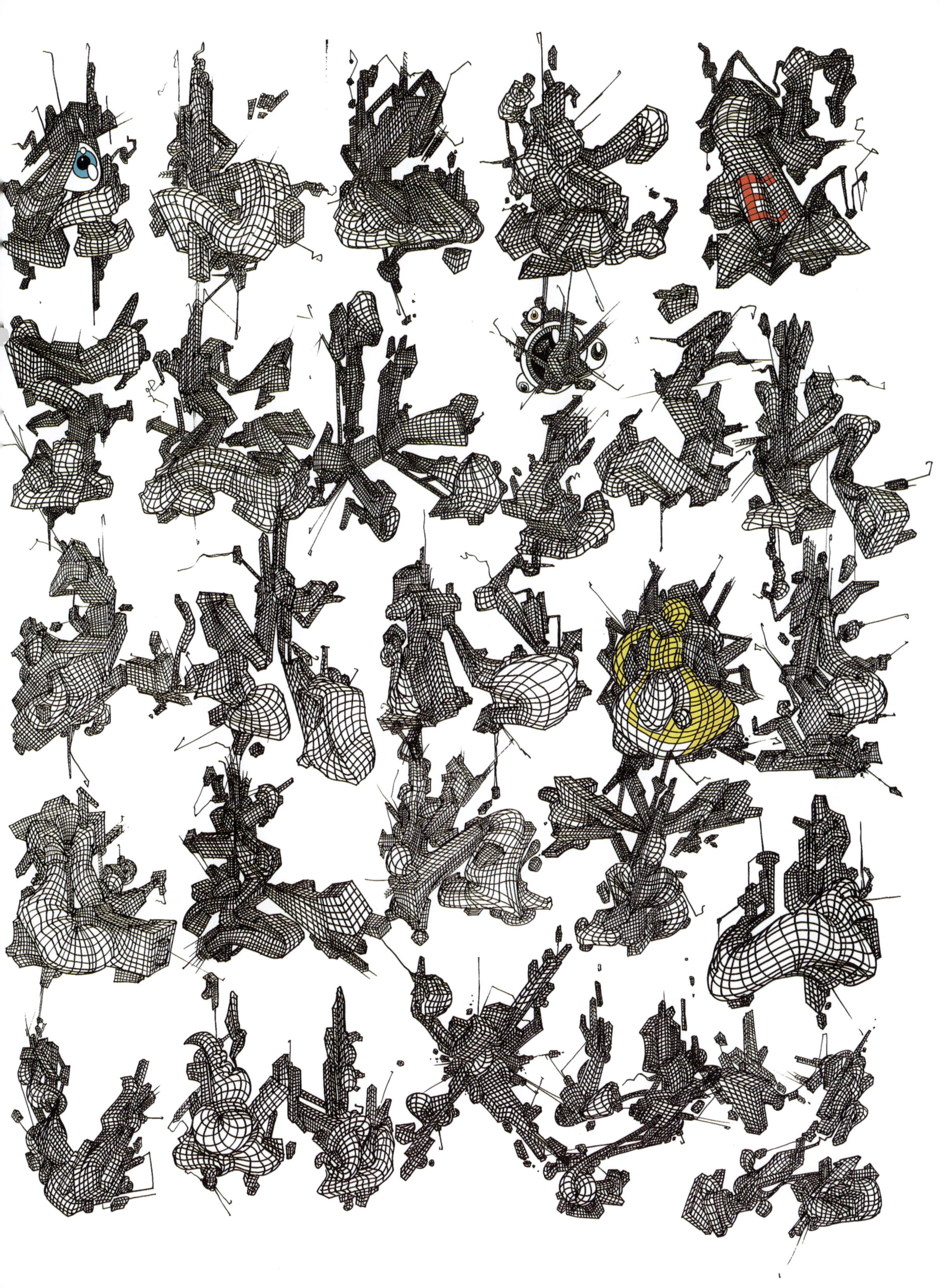

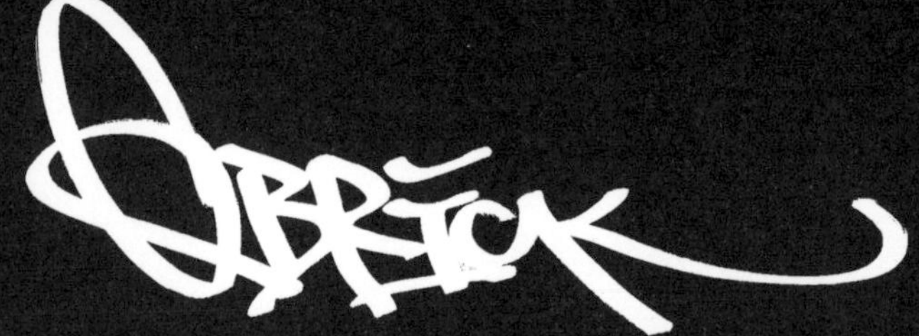

Qbrick
ATHENS, GREECE

Crew member of SKIDS
Writer since 2001
Favourite letter: Q
www.myspace.com/georgehascancer

Greek writer Qbrick is well known for his remarkable one-colour pieces, which are almost always in either black or white. He prefers to paint derelict landscapes, placing his unconventional, raw letters with great sensitivity. When he's finished painting, he takes striking black-and-white photographs of his work to underline the effect. He loves graffiti because 'the journey never ends'.

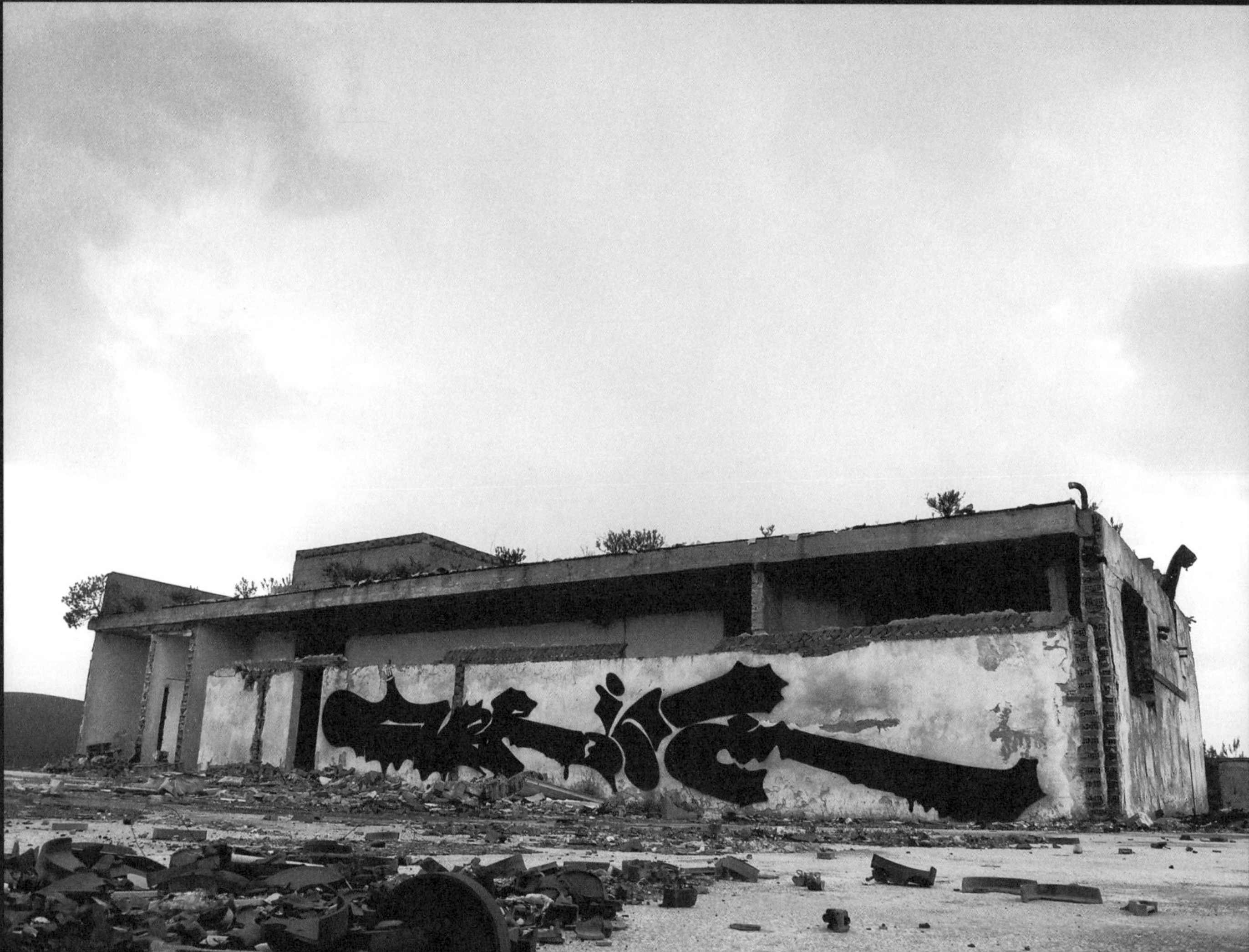

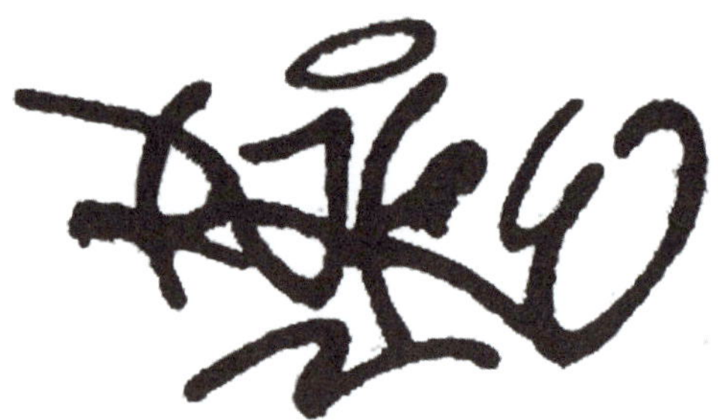

Rake

FRANKFURT, GERMANY
Crew member of Blue's
Writer since 2002
Favourite letters: N, O, P

As one of Frankfurt's twenty-first-century school of writers, Rake says that he is 'on a long journey' in terms of his work. After he had finished the 'F', he decided that it was too boring to simply sketch the whole alphabet in the same format; so he made up the remaining letters using different sketches and painted walls. Rake likes having a home anywhere in the world through graffiti and feeling like he is in *Beat Street*.

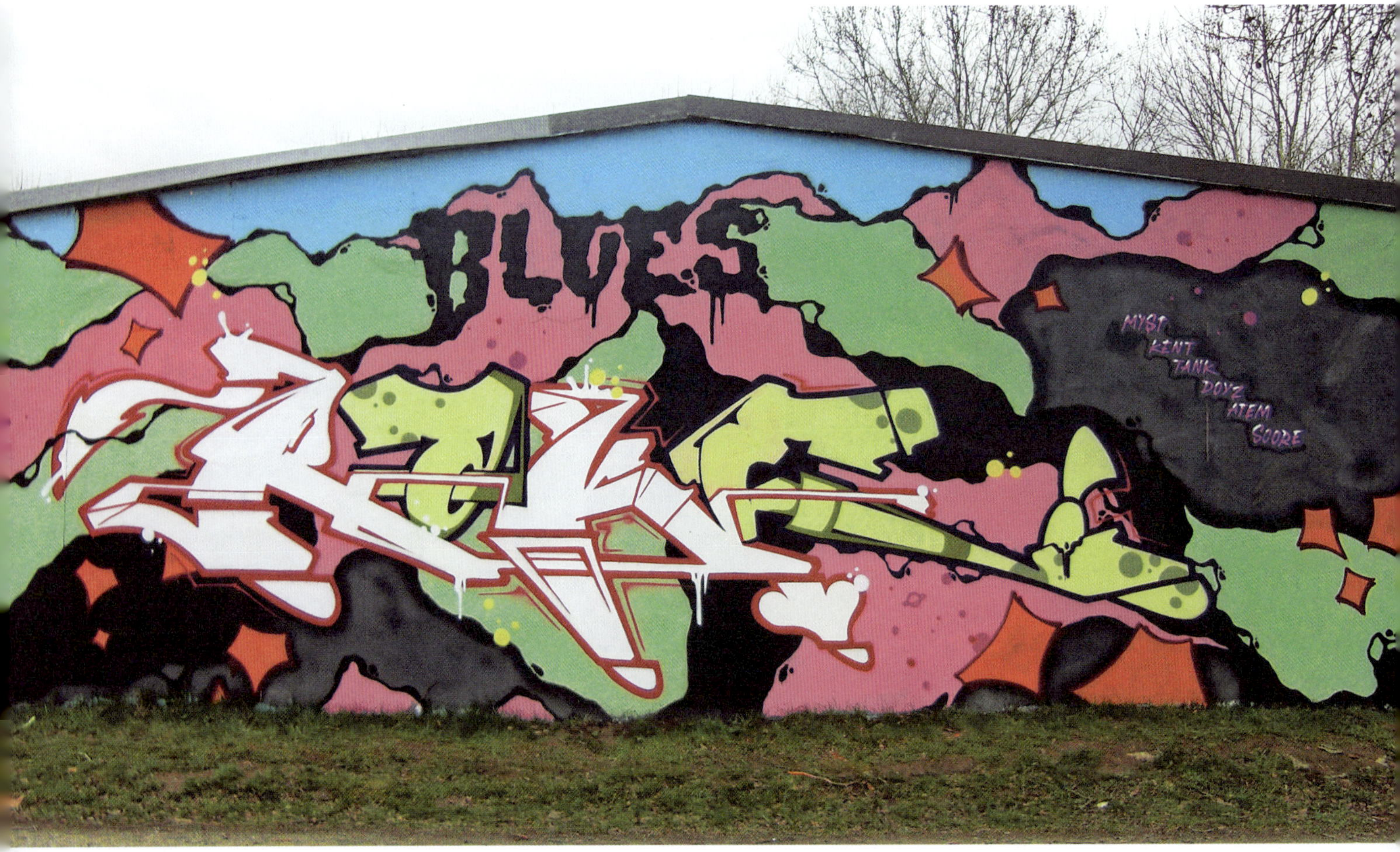

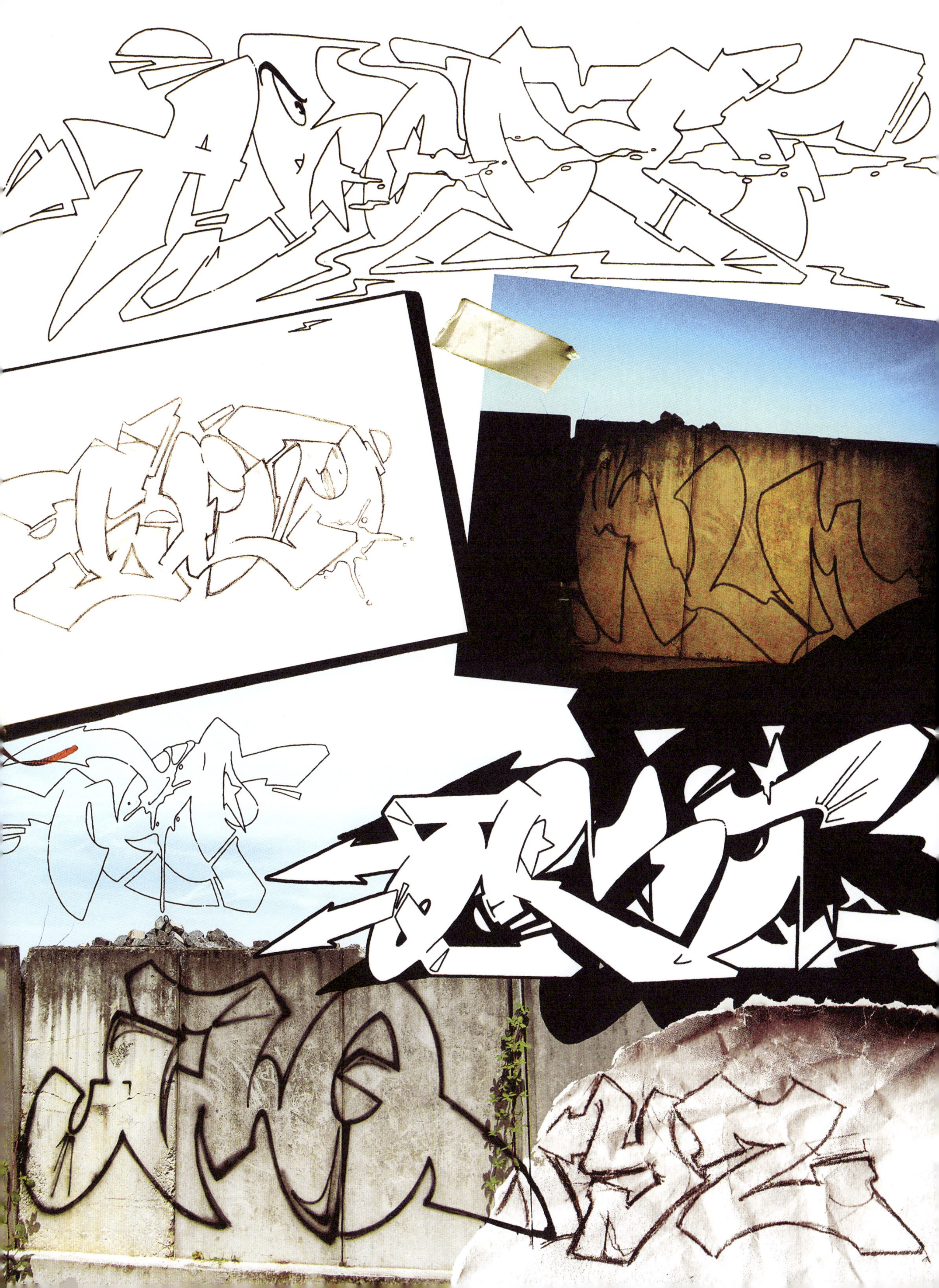

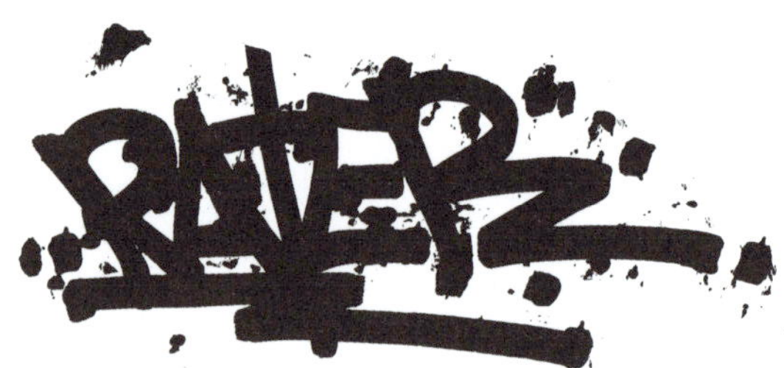

Rater

MINSK MAZOWIECKI, POLAND
Crew member of HOT, VHS
Writer since 1998
Favourite letter: R
www.rater1.com

Rater's pieces can be found all over Poland. With his crew he also travels abroad to paint. His style is characterized by clean straight lines, legible letters and a careful use of colour. 'The best thing about graffiti is the friendships you find through the passion for painting,' he says.

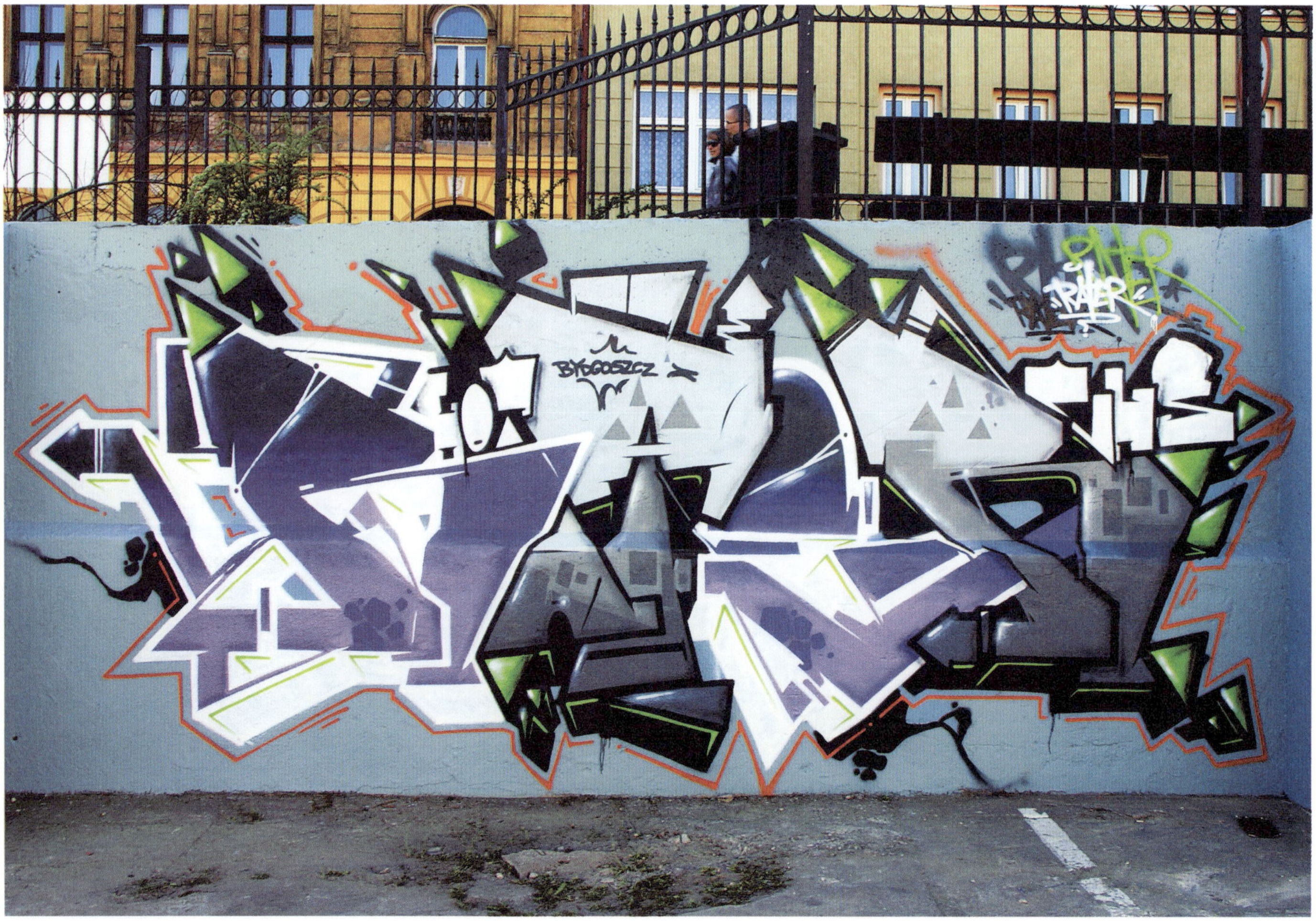

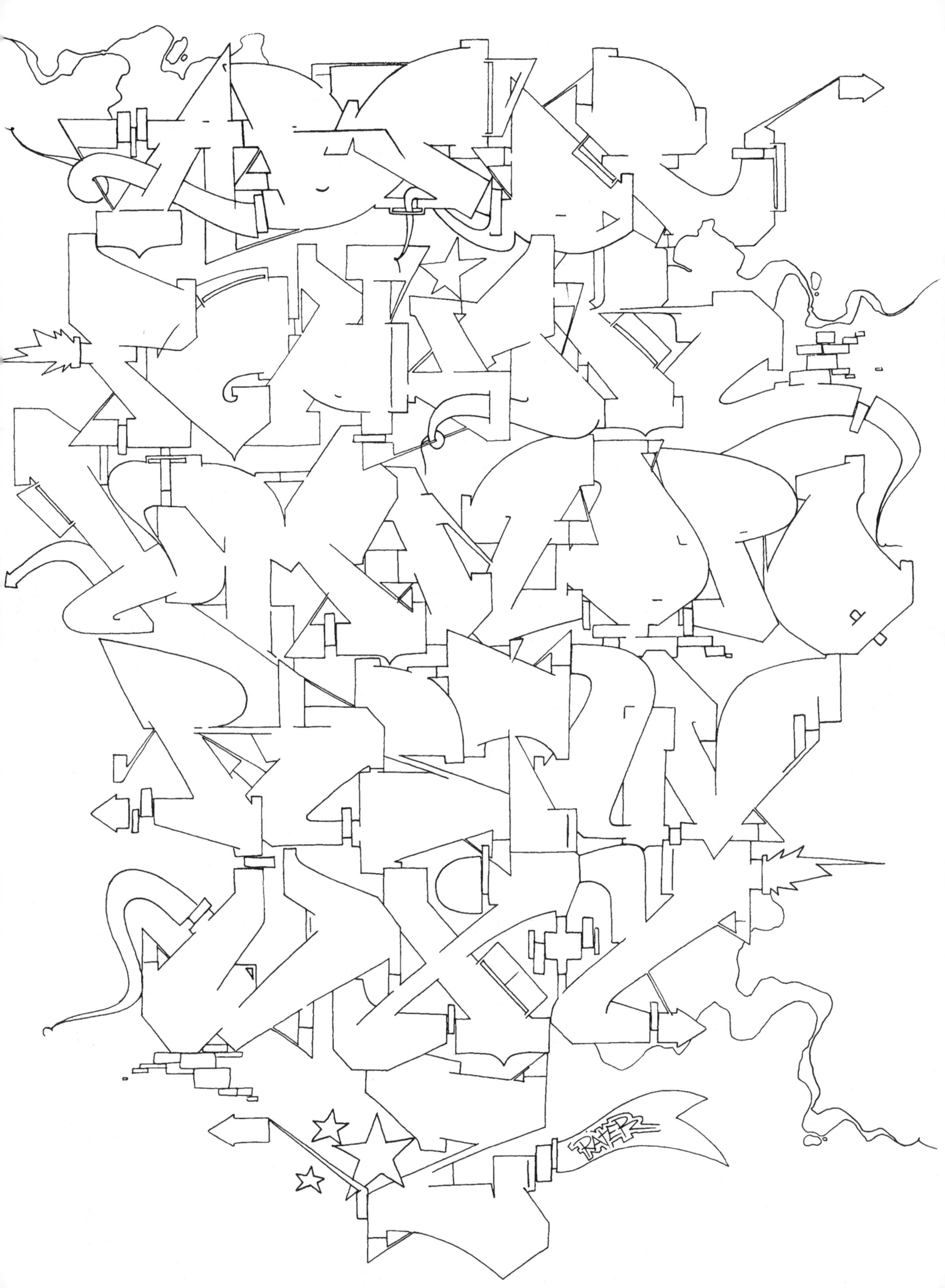

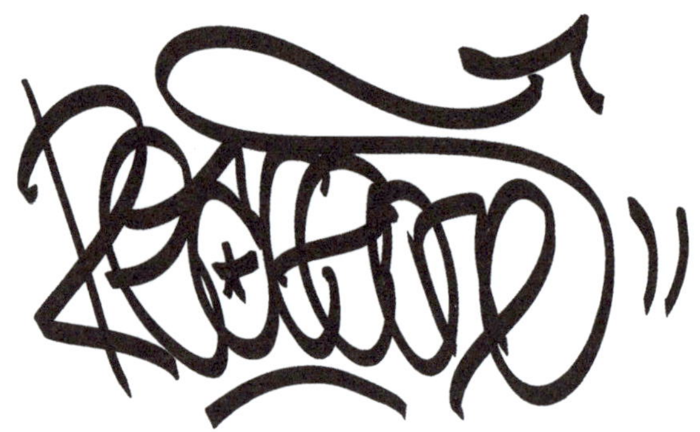

Reece

PIRNA, GERMANY
Crew member of IAC, NYCD, 23, SOX, FOO
Writer since 1995
Favourite letter: E
www.bandits-dresden.de

Reece loves working quickly and spontaneously with simple, raw lines. His throw-ups are found all over Dresden. He describes his style as 'big, small, soft, ugly and pretty'. 'The best thing about graffiti is doing outlines,' he adds.

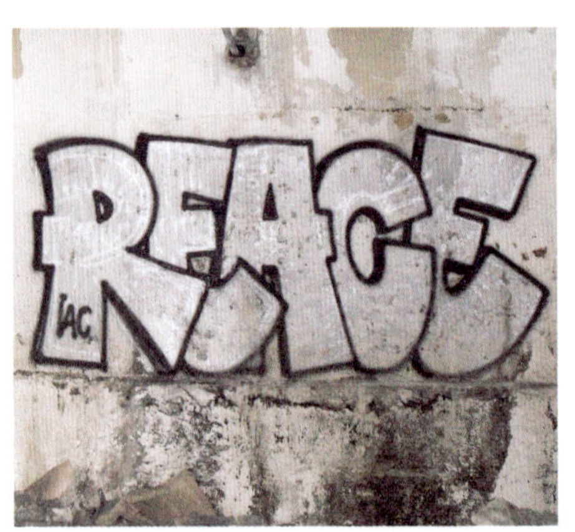

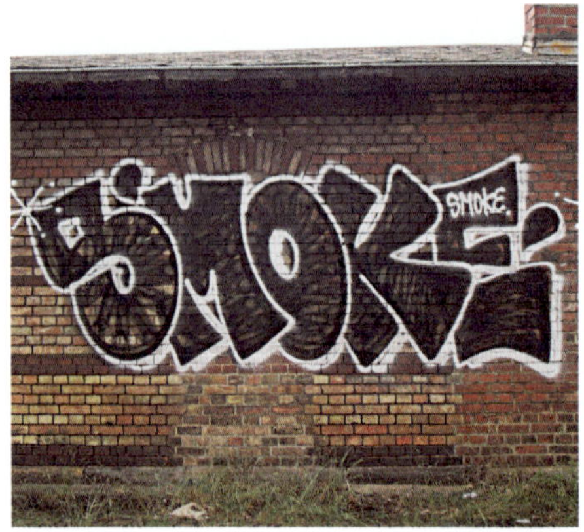

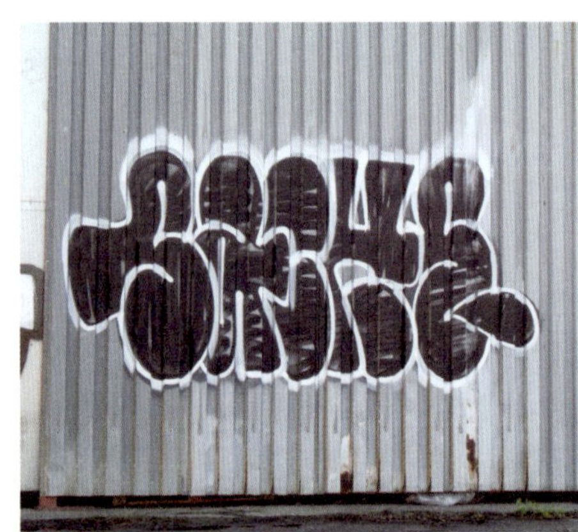

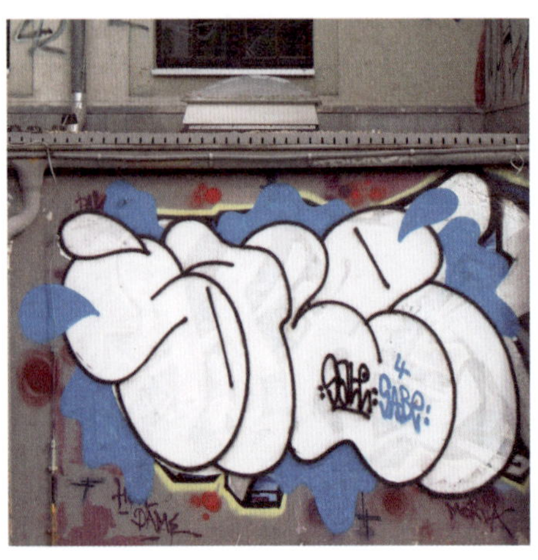

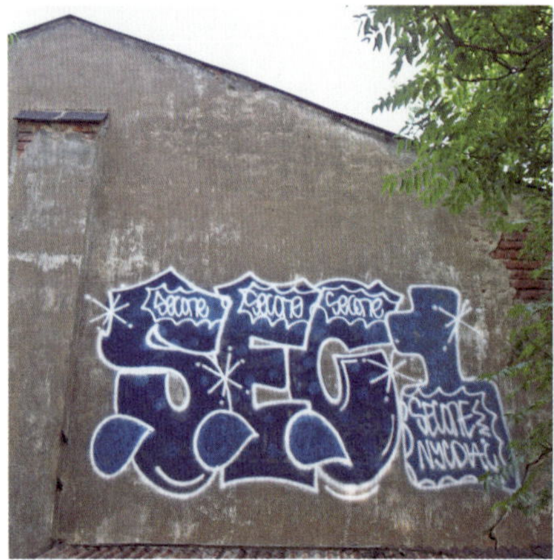

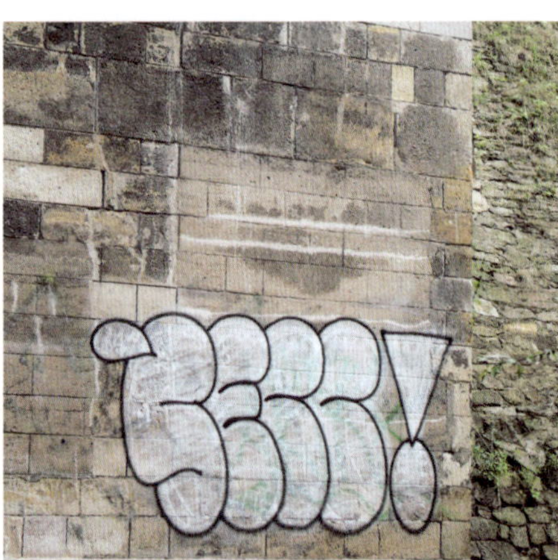

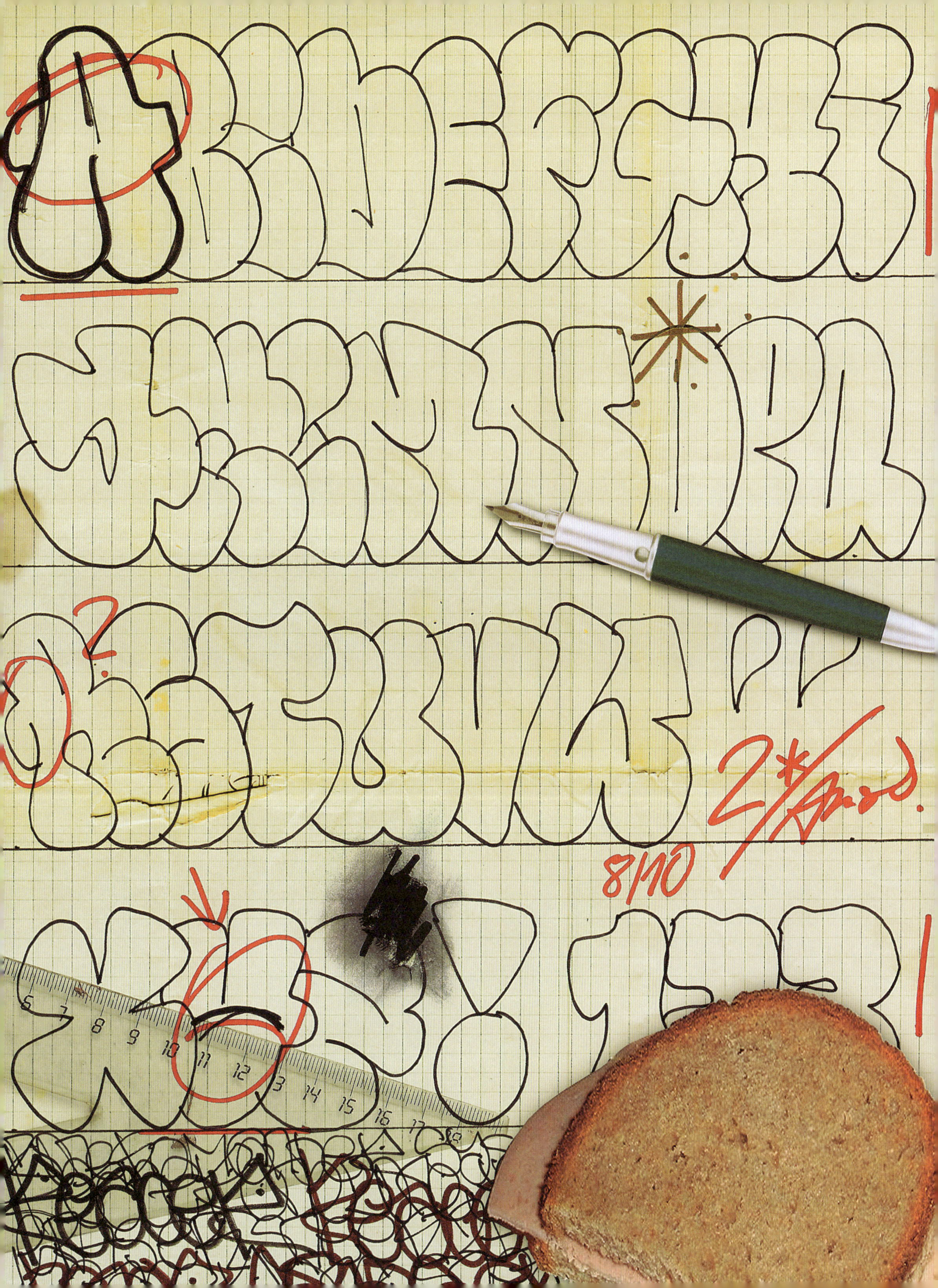

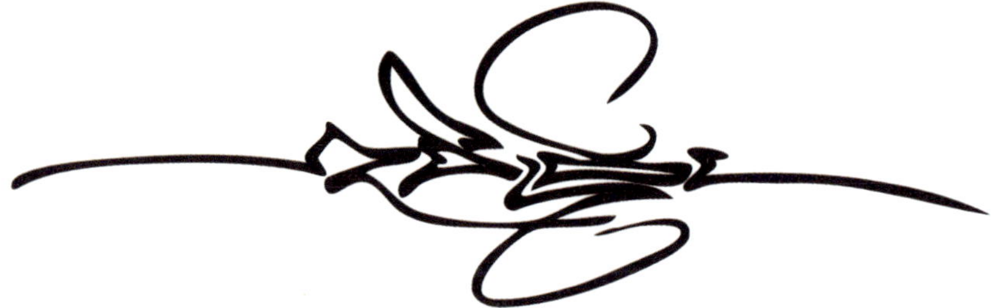

Replete
LEEDS, UK
Crew member of TPN
Writer since 1994
Favourite letter: T
www.repletes.net

Replete is a graffiti artist, graphic designer and animator from Leeds. He has worked for both the computer games and music industries. During his graffiti career he has experimented with spray paint on walls and canvases, sculpture and even animation. His letters are reminiscent of insects and their antennae. Describing his alphabet, he says: 'Imagine a collection of cockroach antlers, hung on the wall like trophies of past successful hunts into the grimy folds of my mind.'

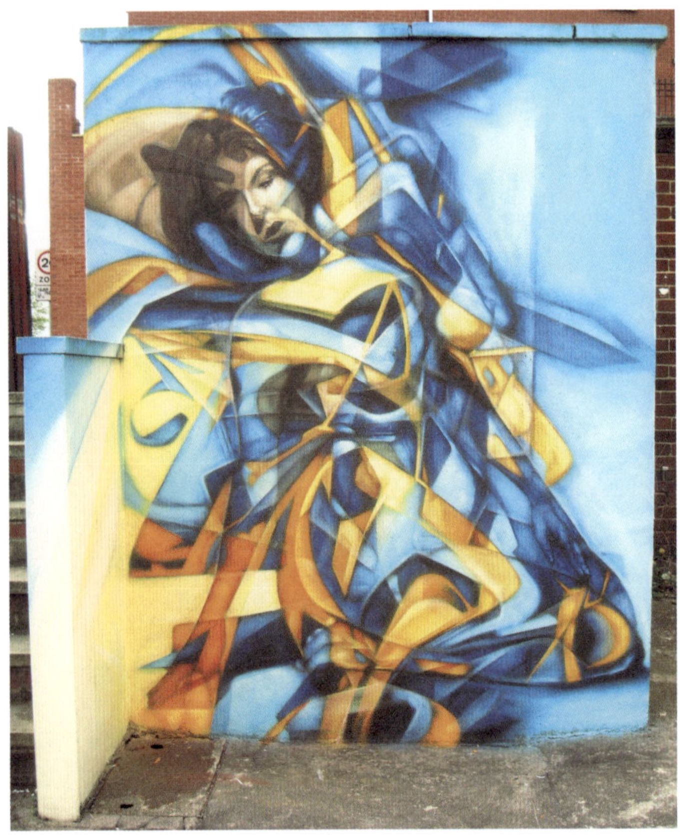

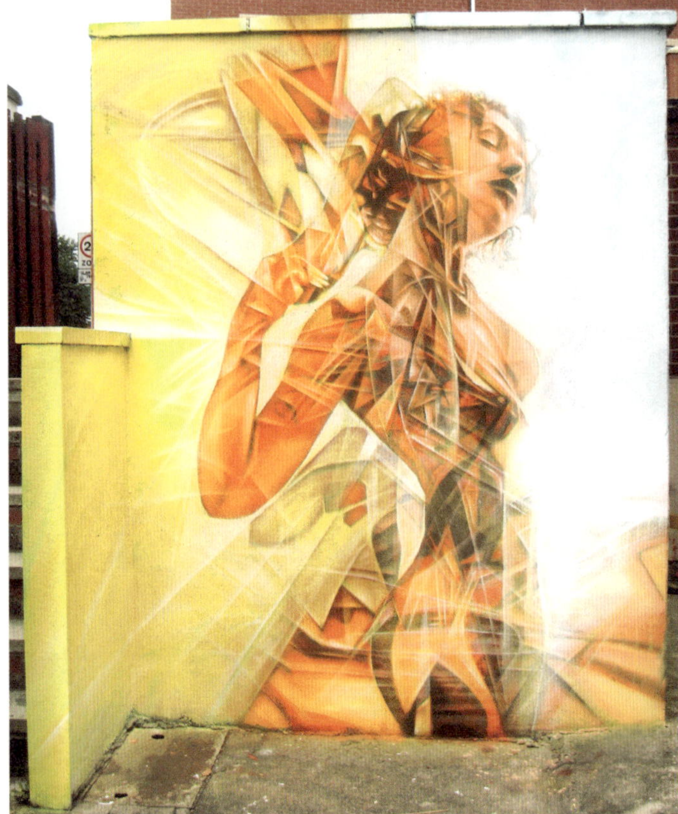

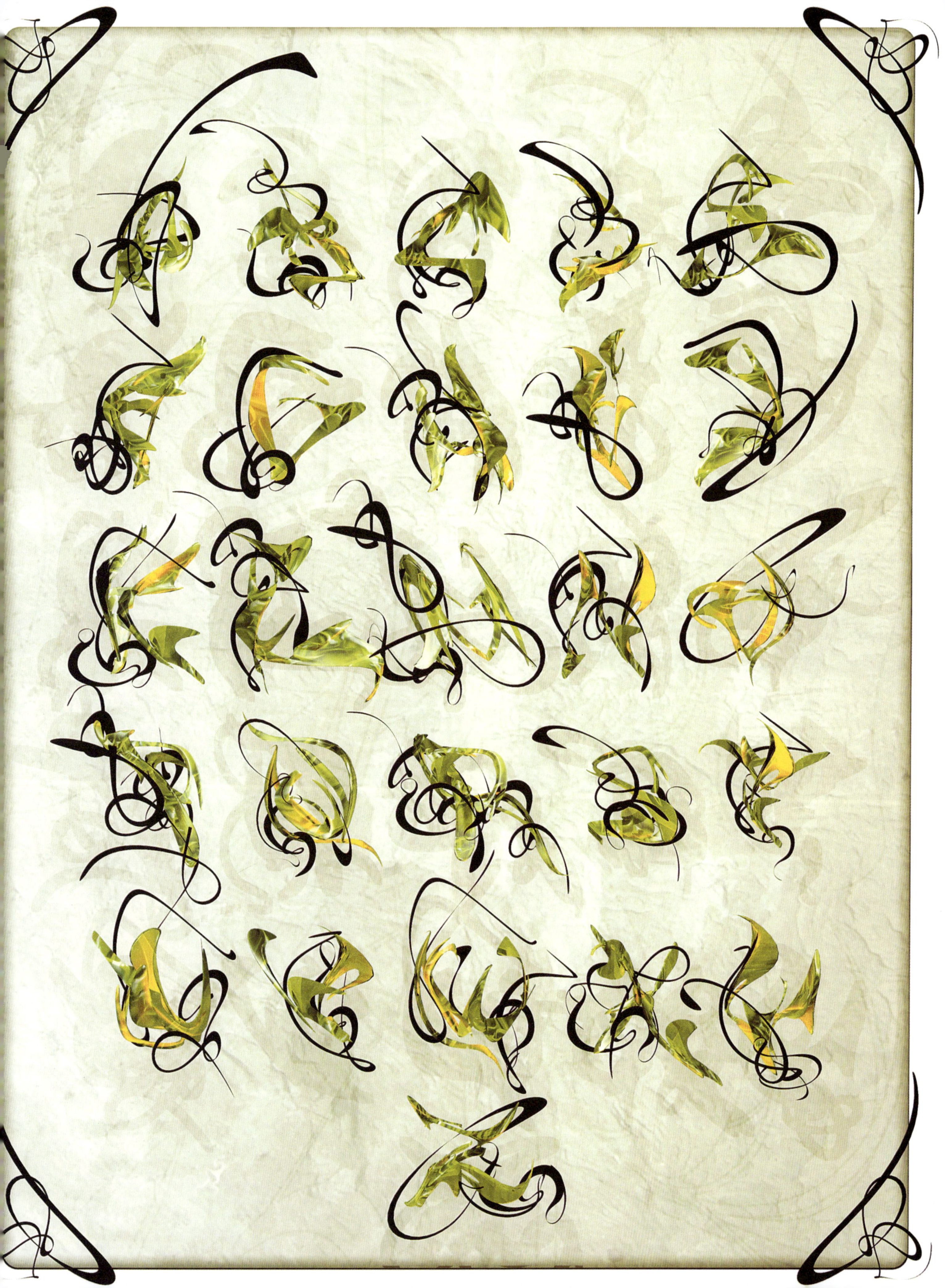

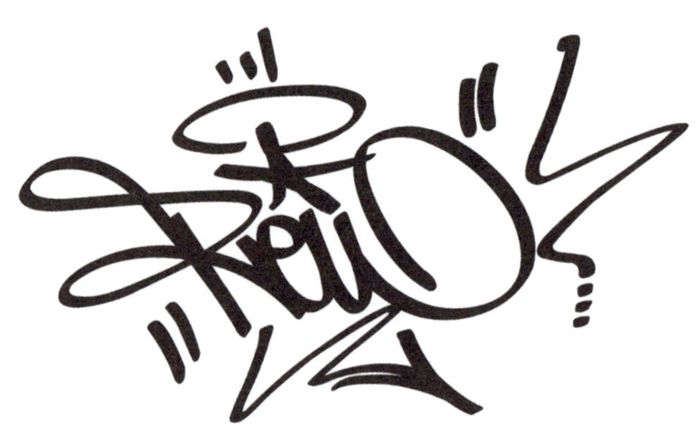

Rew

BERLIN, GERMANY
Crew member of Kreuzberg
Writer since 1988
Favourite letter: 'All of them'
www.myspace.com/rewkreuzberg

Rew started painting in Berlin back in the 1980s. He is still active and never stopped developing his style over his many years of writing. Rew has a passion for tags and explains his alphabet with a quote from Bruce Lee: 'Simplicity is the key to brilliance.'

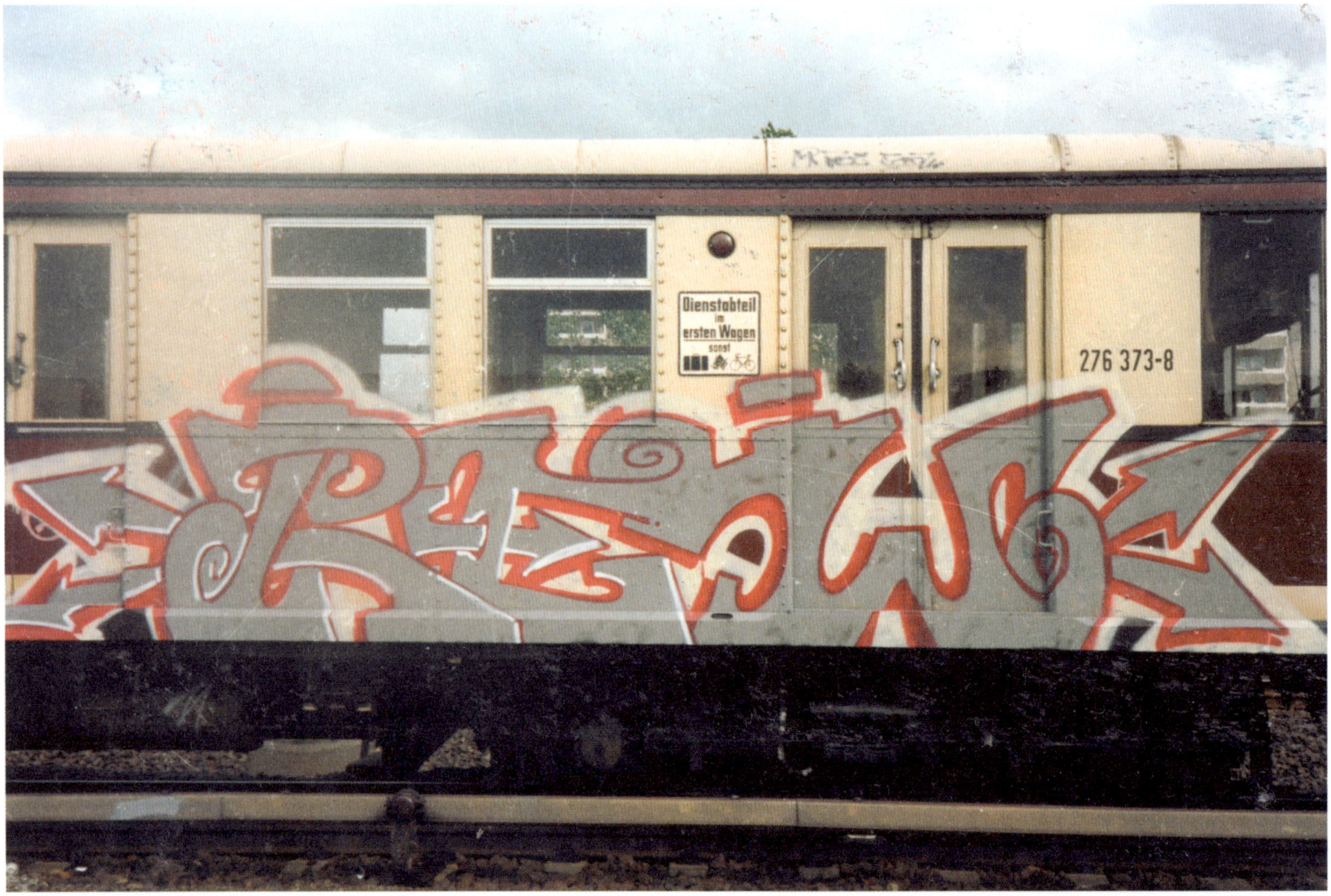

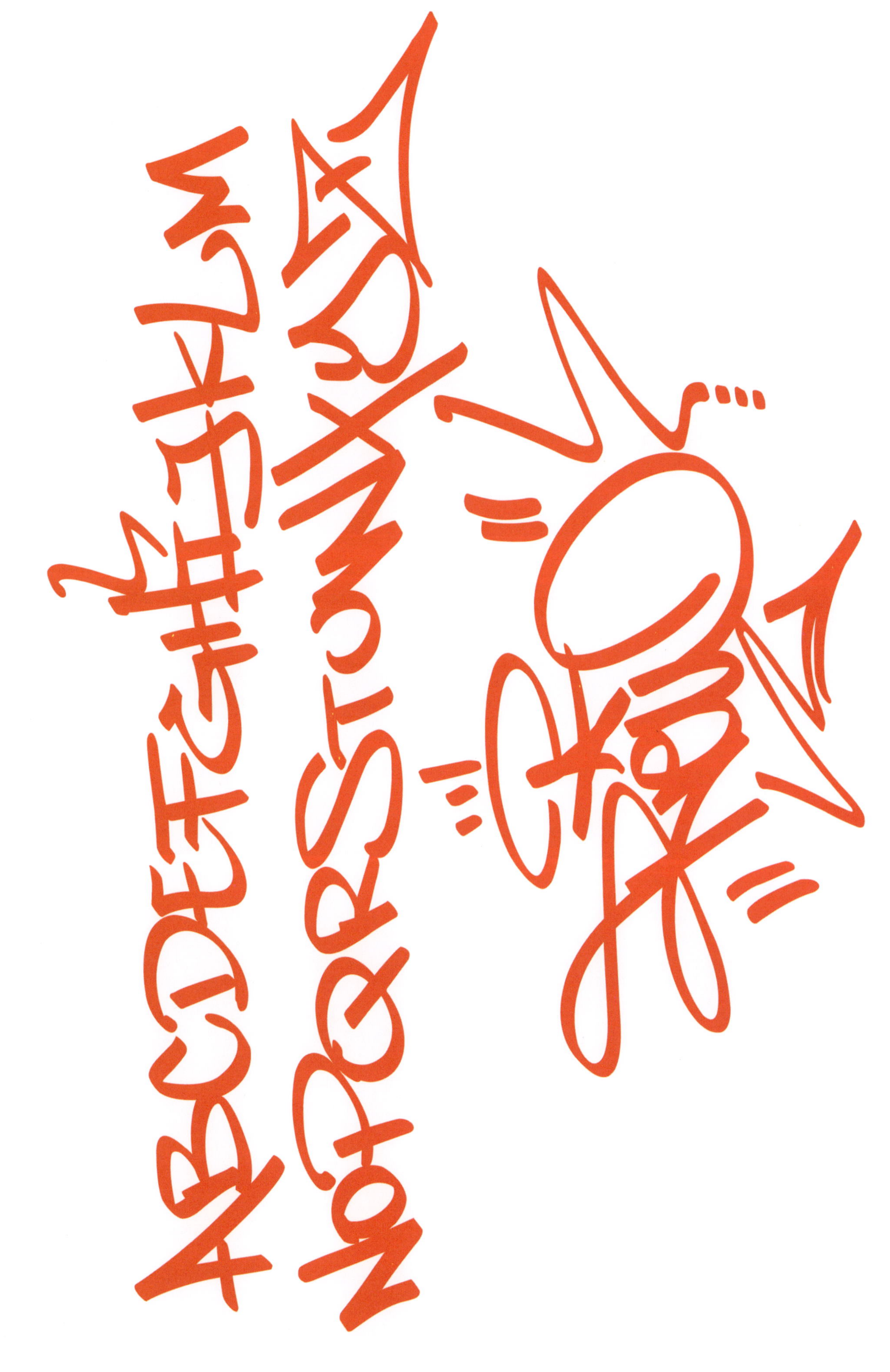

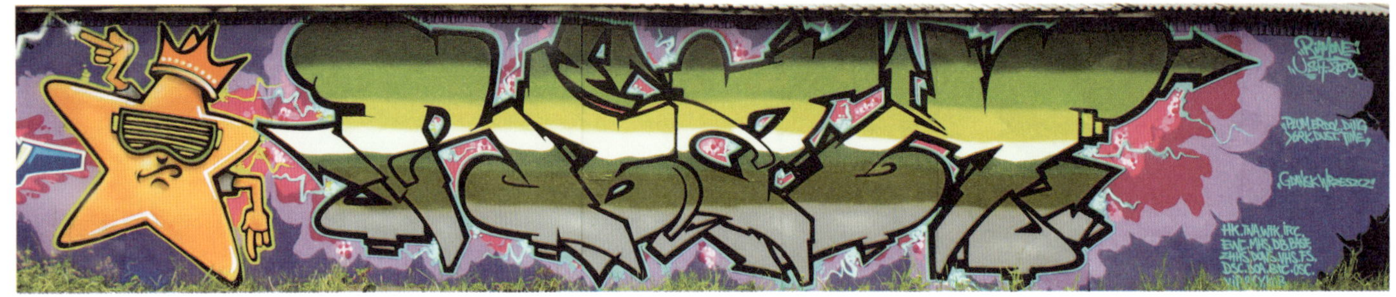

Riam

GDANSK, POLAND
Crew member of USH
Writer since 1996
Favourite letter: R
www.facebook.com/riamone96

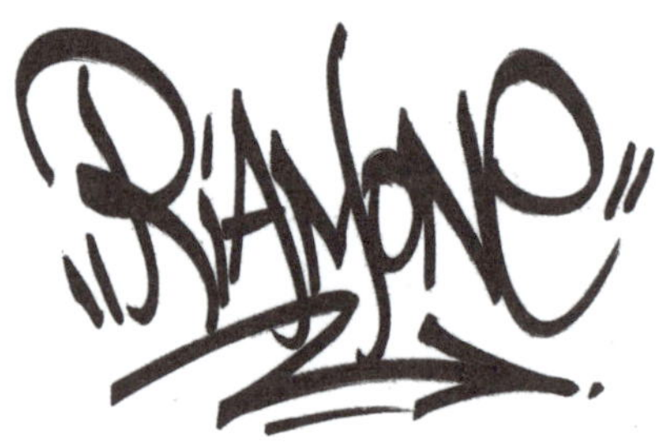

Riam often paints his pieces freestyle. He places a high value on technique and the way a piece is executed, choosing colours that are harmonious and fresh and outline the shape of his letters perfectly. 'The relaxing sound of the spray cans' is what he likes most about graffiti.

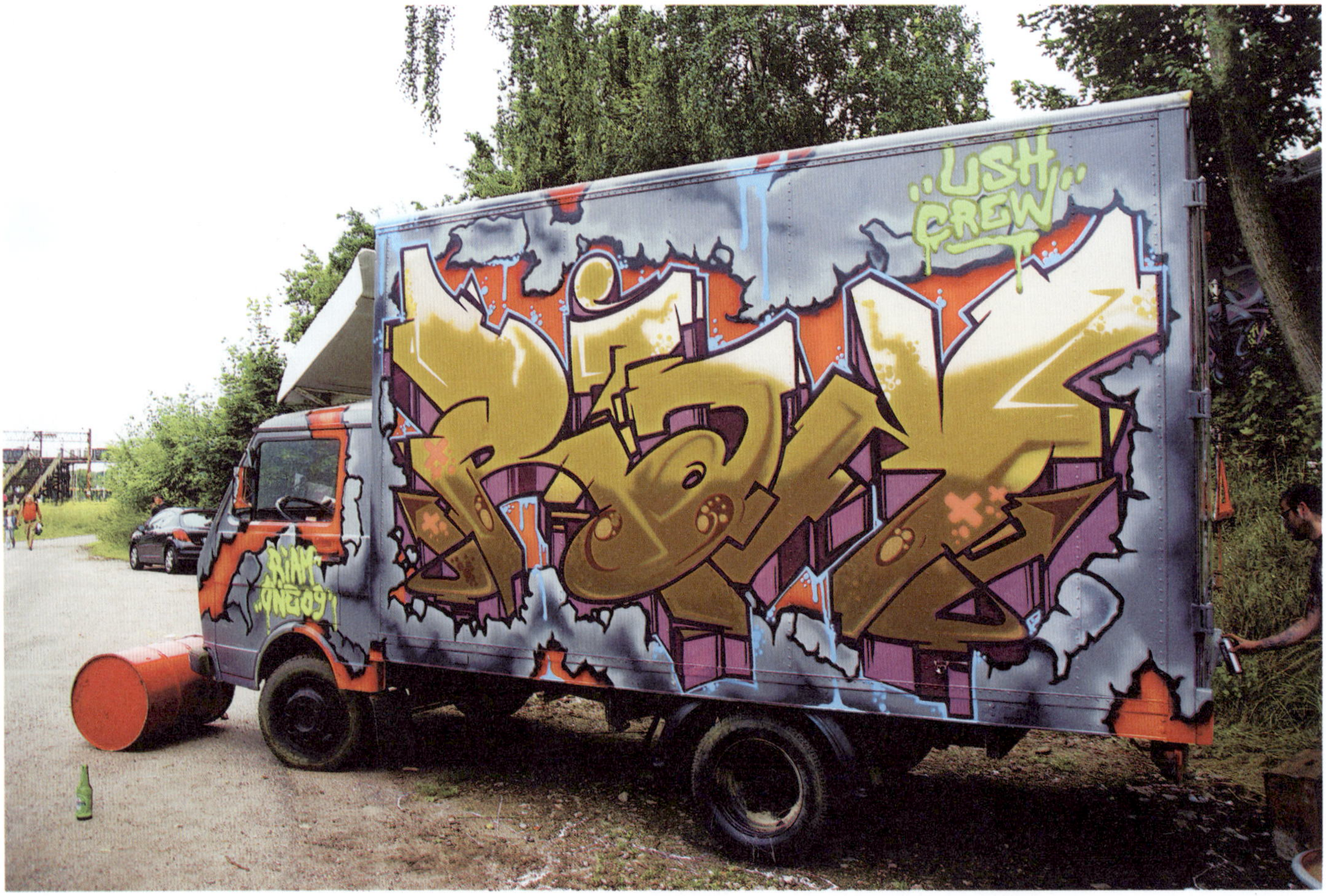

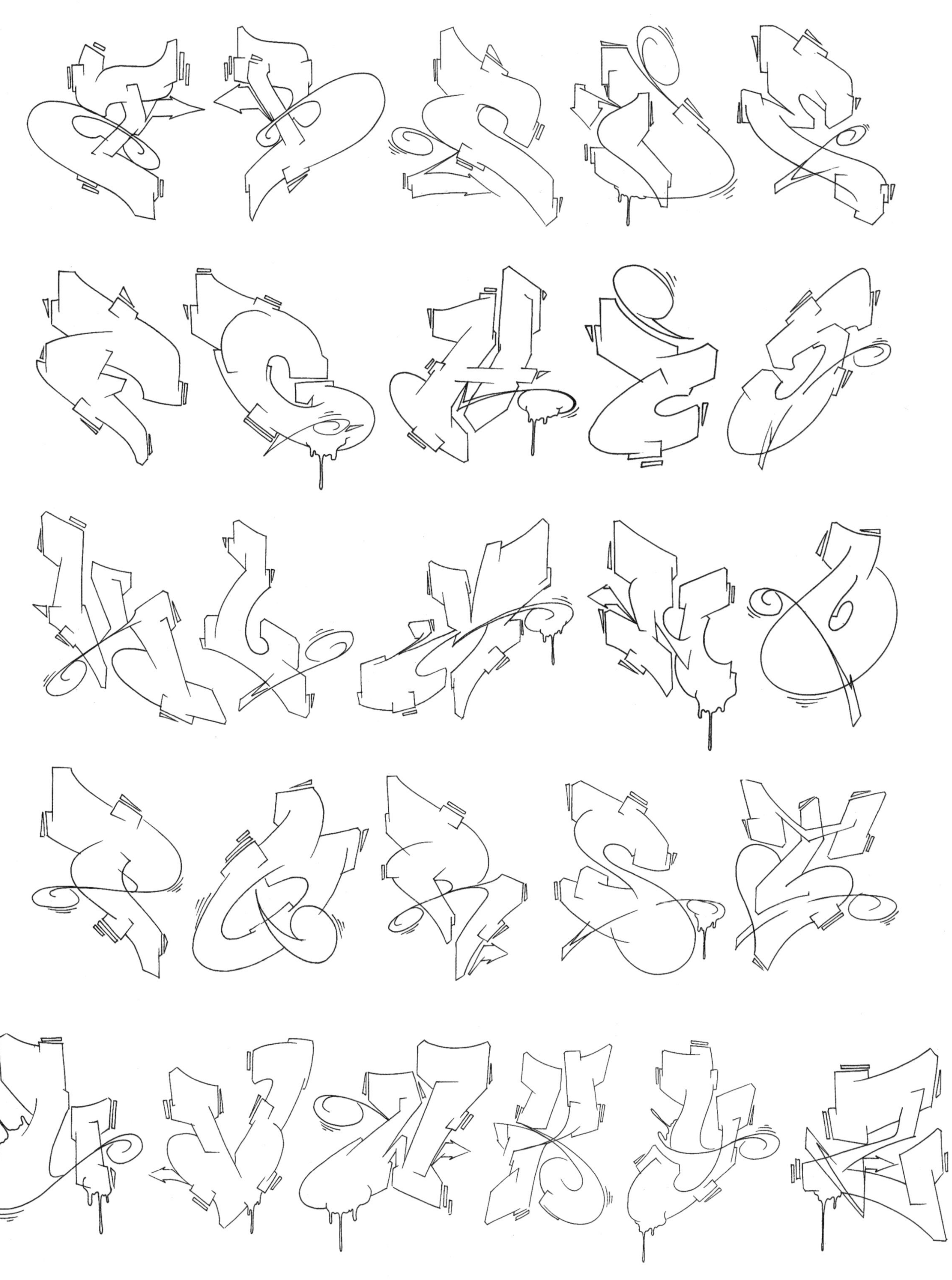

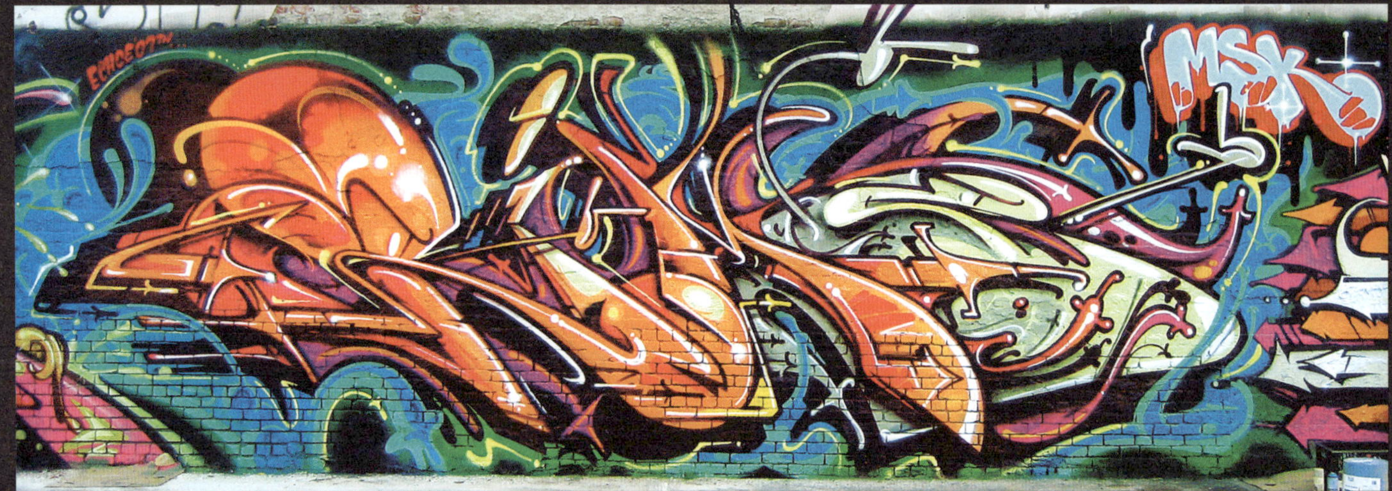

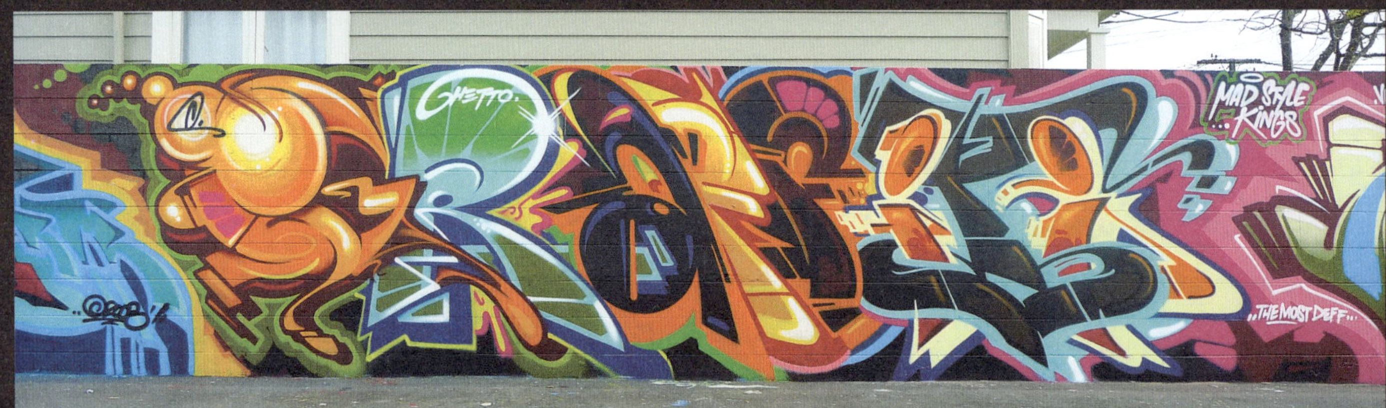

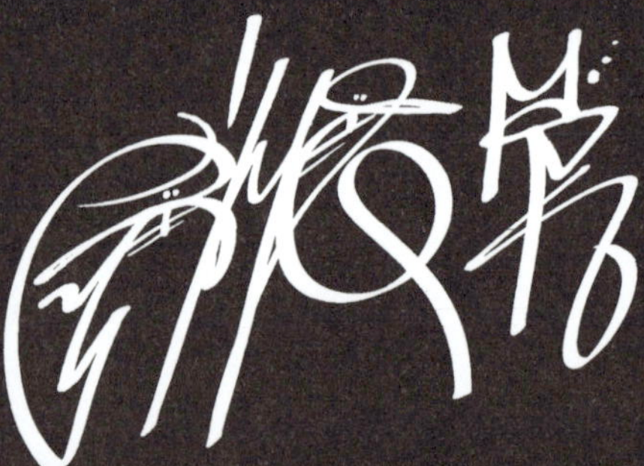

Rime
NEW YORK CITY, USA

Crew member of MSK
Writer since 1991
Favourite letter: E
www.jerseyjoeart.com

Rime is also well known as Jersey Joe. He started writing in New
York City and New Jersey but moved to Los Angeles later in his
career. There, he joined the MSK crew and became part of the
artists' collective known as The Seventh Letter. Rime is also
the mind behind The Exchange Project, an interchange project
among well-known writers. He teaches graffiti art to kids in LA,
is involved in different design projects and shows his work in
galleries. 'Successful art work is usually linked to an emotion,'
he says. 'The better connected something is to the creator, the
more successful the work.'

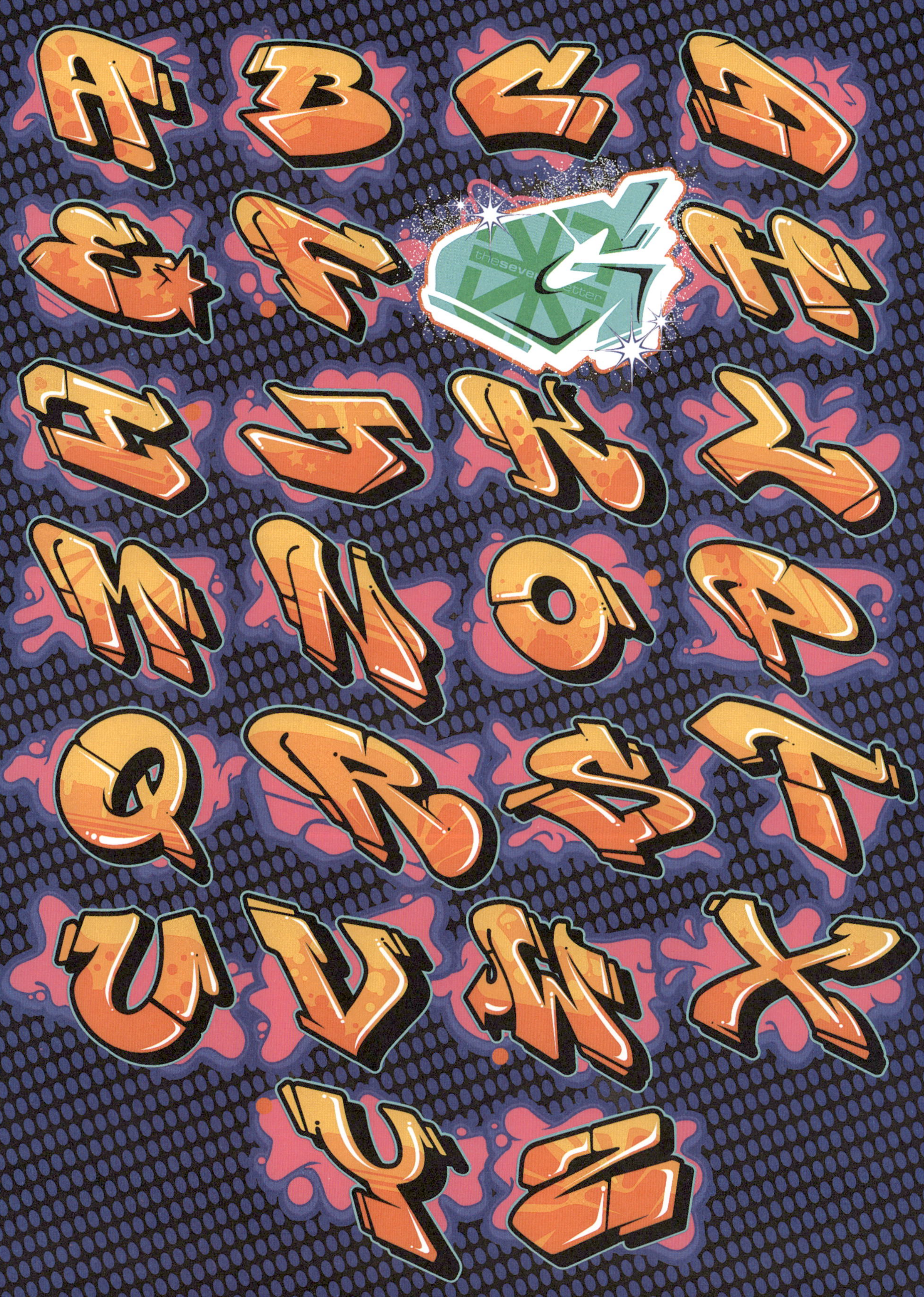

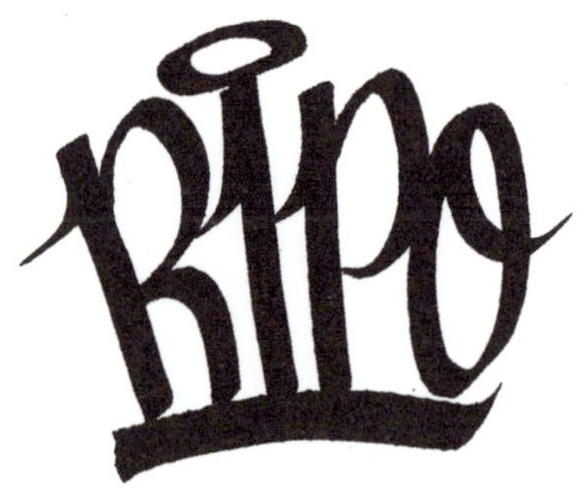

Ripo

NEW YORK CITY, USA
Writer since 1997
Favourite letter: 'All of them'

Ripo is originally from New York City but currently lives in Spain.
He created his alphabet using white enamel paint on mirrors;
he then put up the mirrors on the streets of Barcelona and took
pictures of the reflections. Ripo explains the idea: 'Graffiti usually
fills in the "negative" or forgotten spaces of cities – ignored parts
of signs, doors, walls… I played off this concept by painting in the
negative space of the letters and letting the city fill in the rest.'

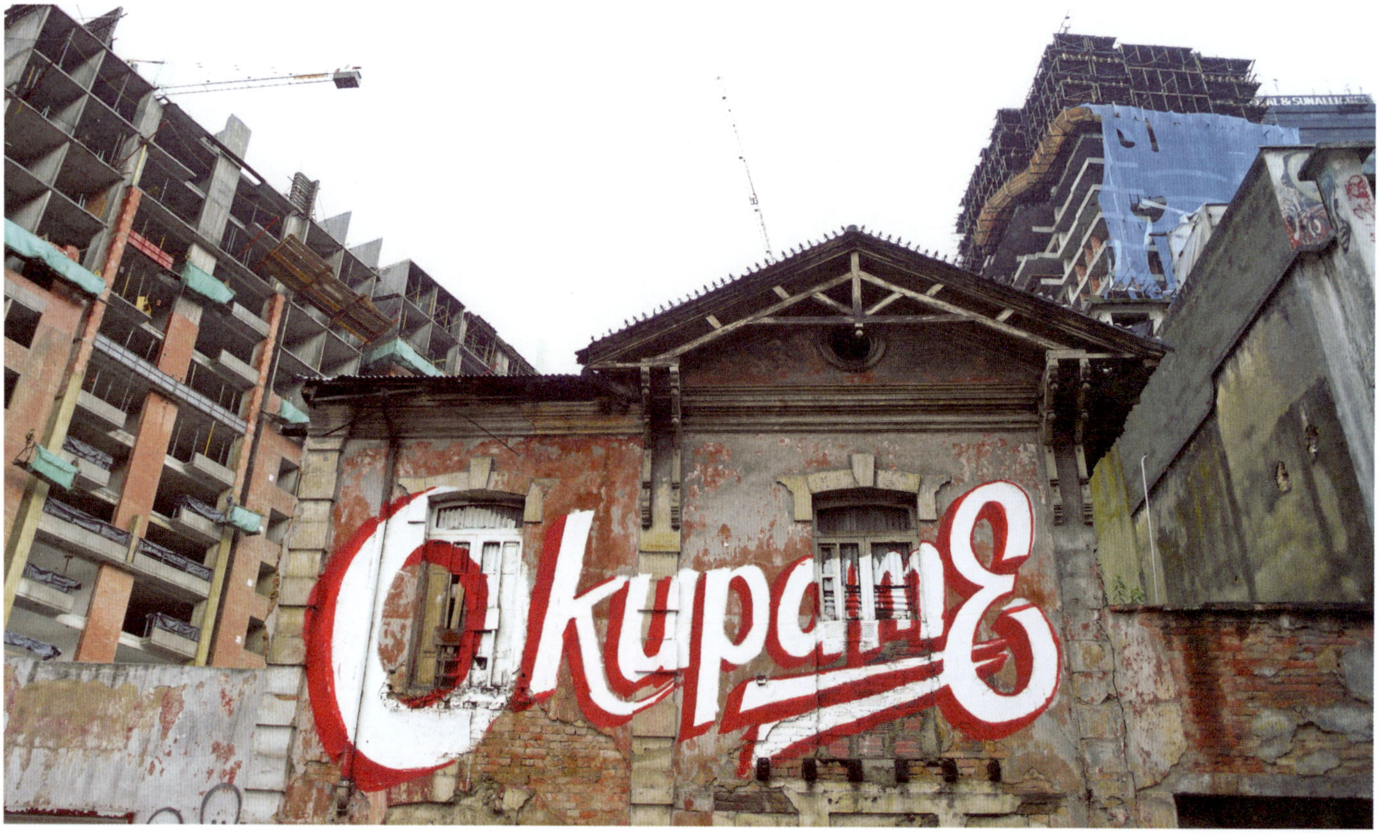

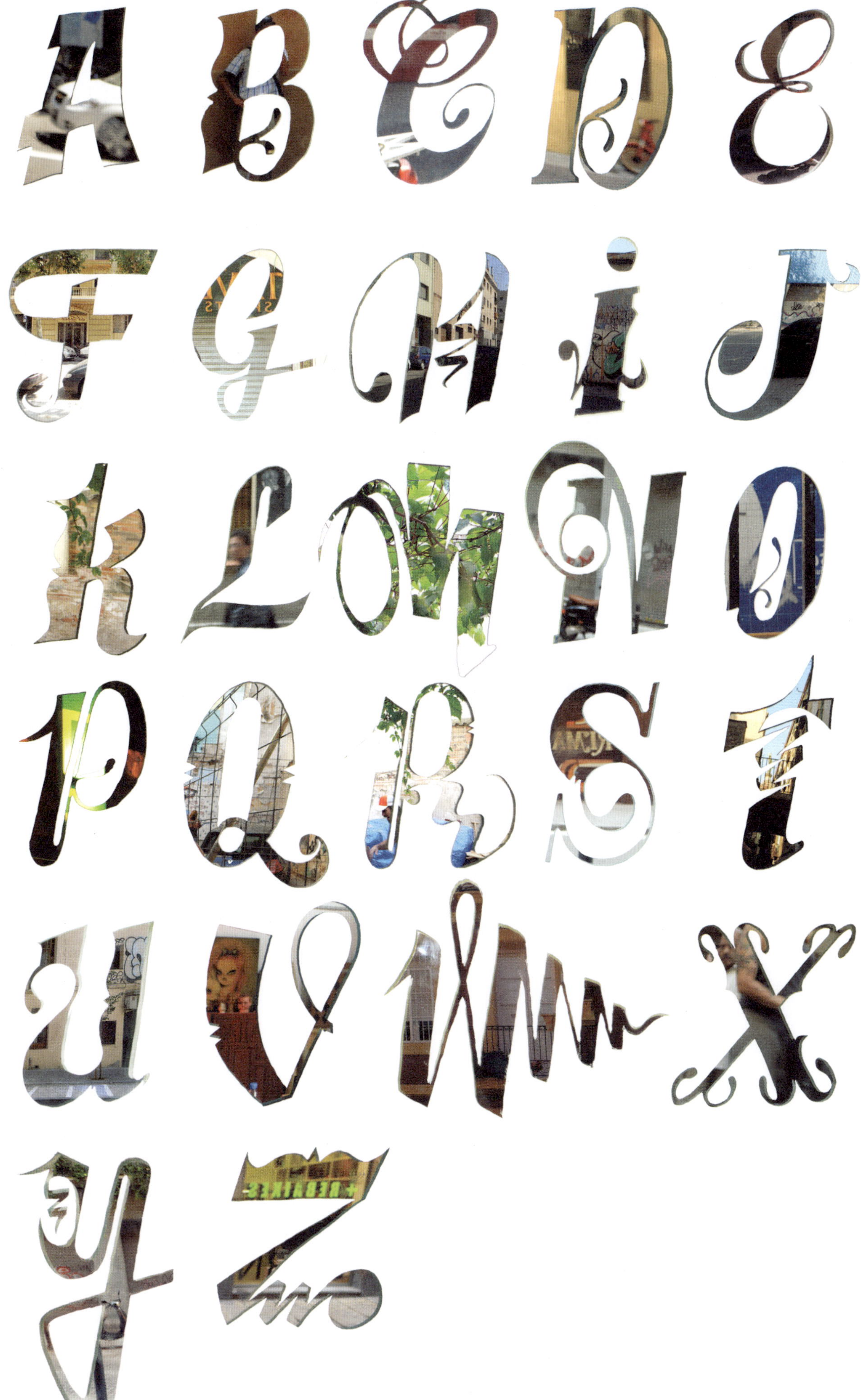

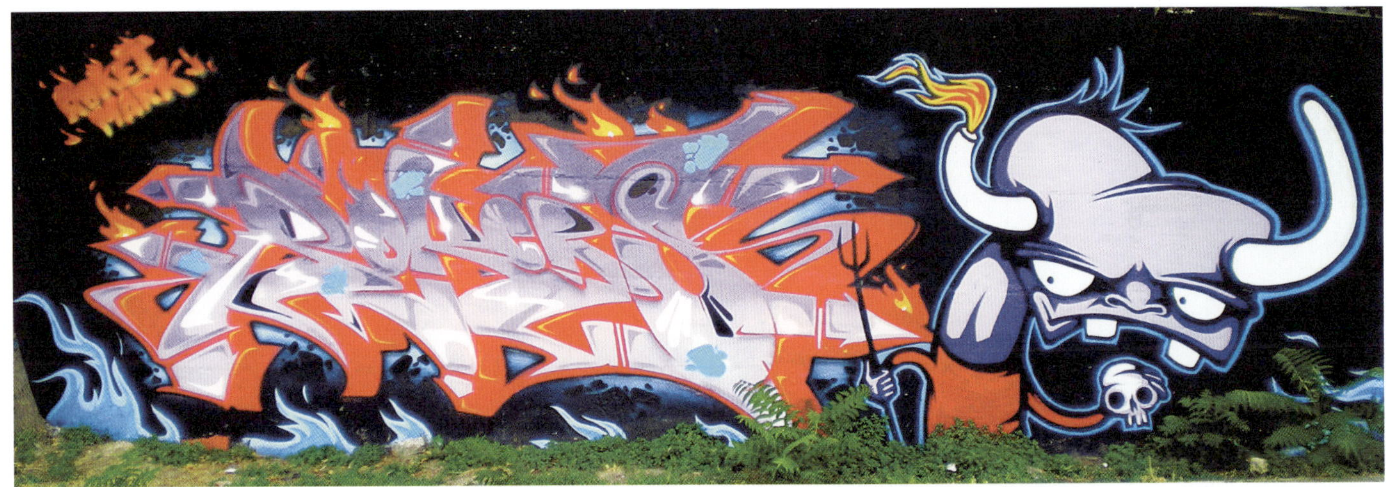

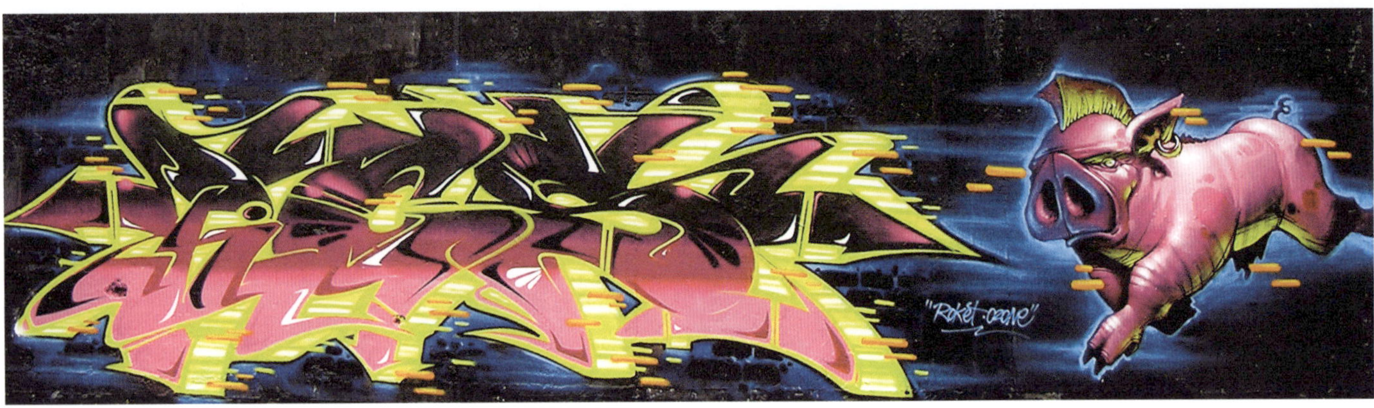

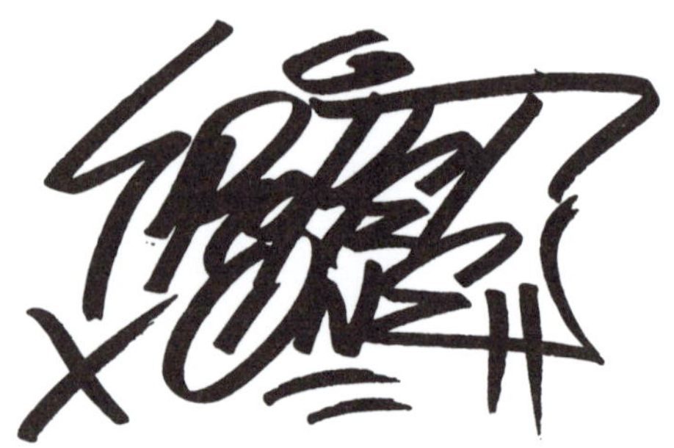

Roket

ATHENS, GREECE

Crew member of TDS, WFC, Pigs
Writer since 1997
Favourite letters: A, L, P, H, A

Roket's style is characterized by clean-cut lines, vivid colours, classic letters and a lot of detail. To reflect this style in his alphabet, he packed his spray cans and went out to paint six separate walls, all similar in size, later putting the results together to make one image. In his opinion, it is most important to act spontaneously while painting a piece. The New York fat cap is his favourite tool for this.

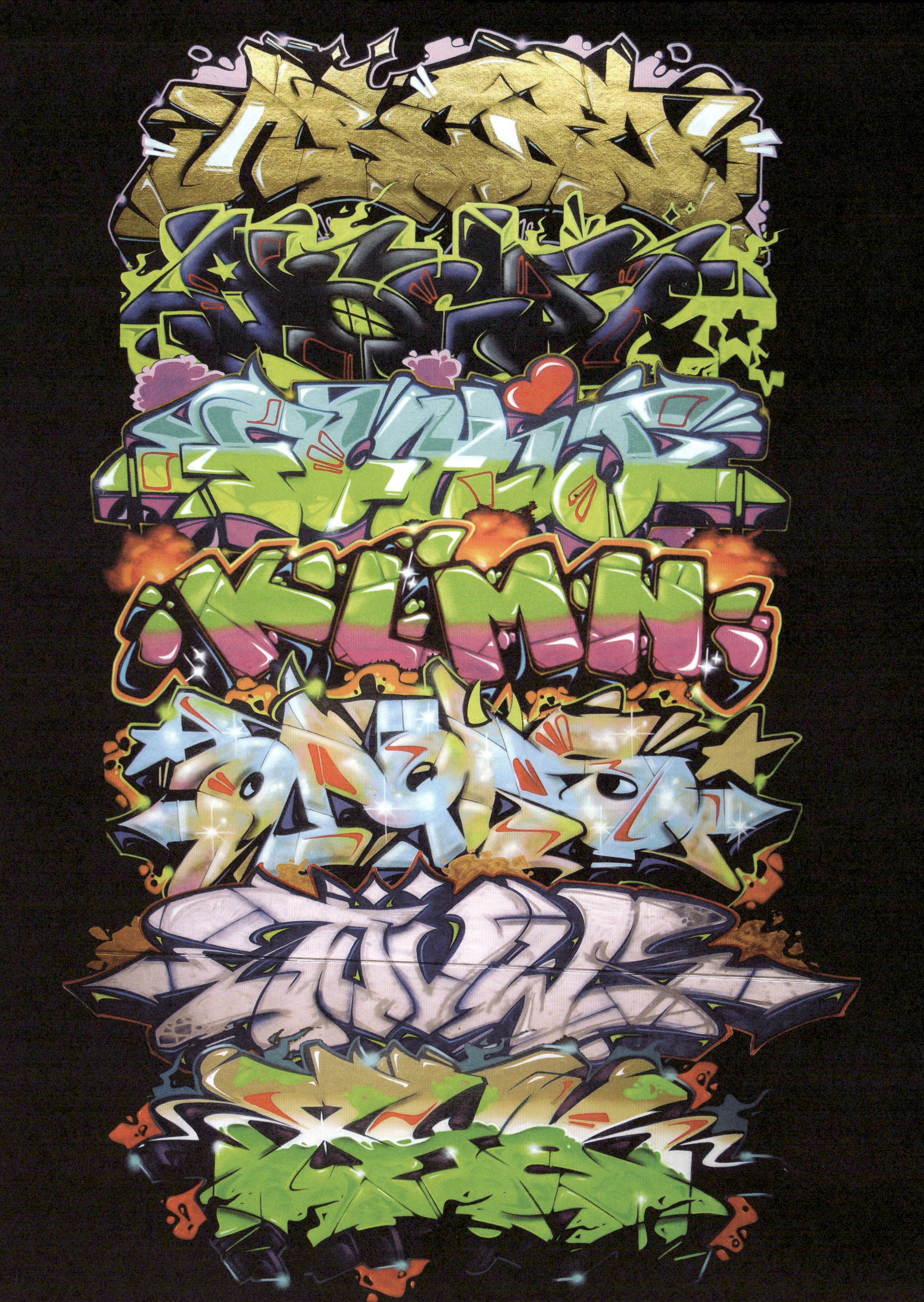

Rosy One
BIEL-BIENNE, SWITZERLAND
Crew member of ONT, Style Animals, DPP
Writer since 1989
Favourite letters: A, B, E, G, K, M, R, S
www.rosyone.com

Rosy One's style – and lifestyle – revolves around 1980s hip-hop culture. She collects old vinyls, ghetto blasters, shoes, hats and all kinds of vintage clothing and is the main force behind the Dopepose project – a growing collection of photos from the 1980s and early '90s in which people are pictured posing against an array of backdrops, from pieces to cars. Rosy One describes her style preferences as follows: 'Readable letters, sparse fill-ins so that the colours don't compete with the letters, and old-school elements like clouds, stars, arrows and funky characters.'

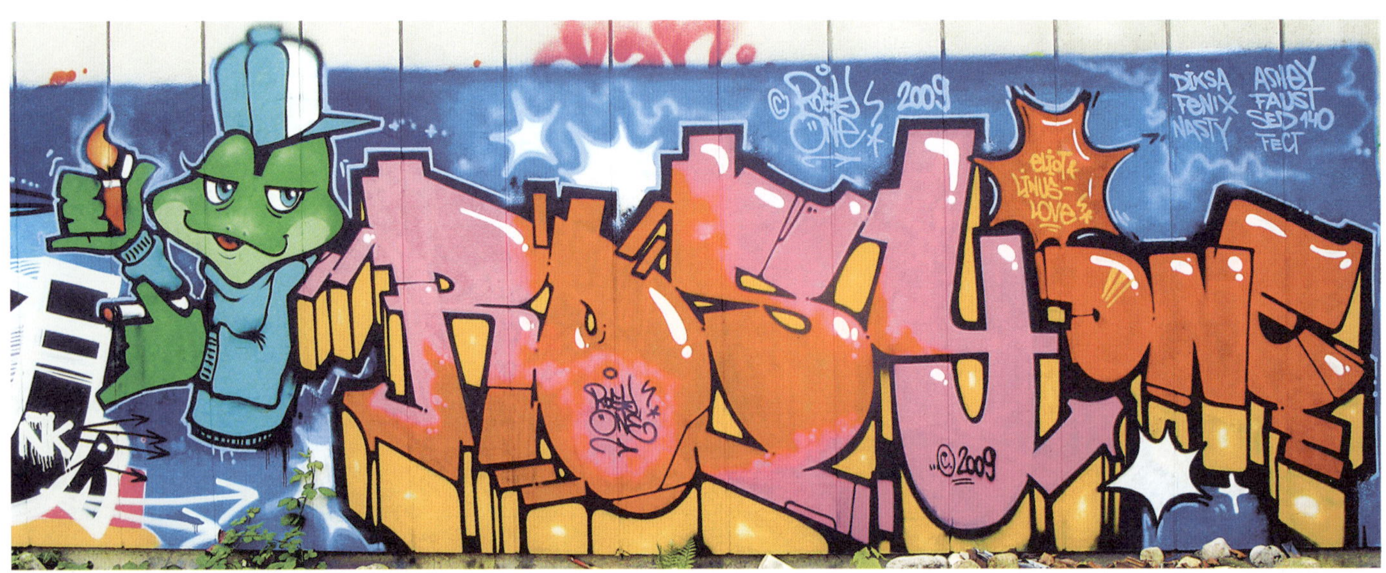

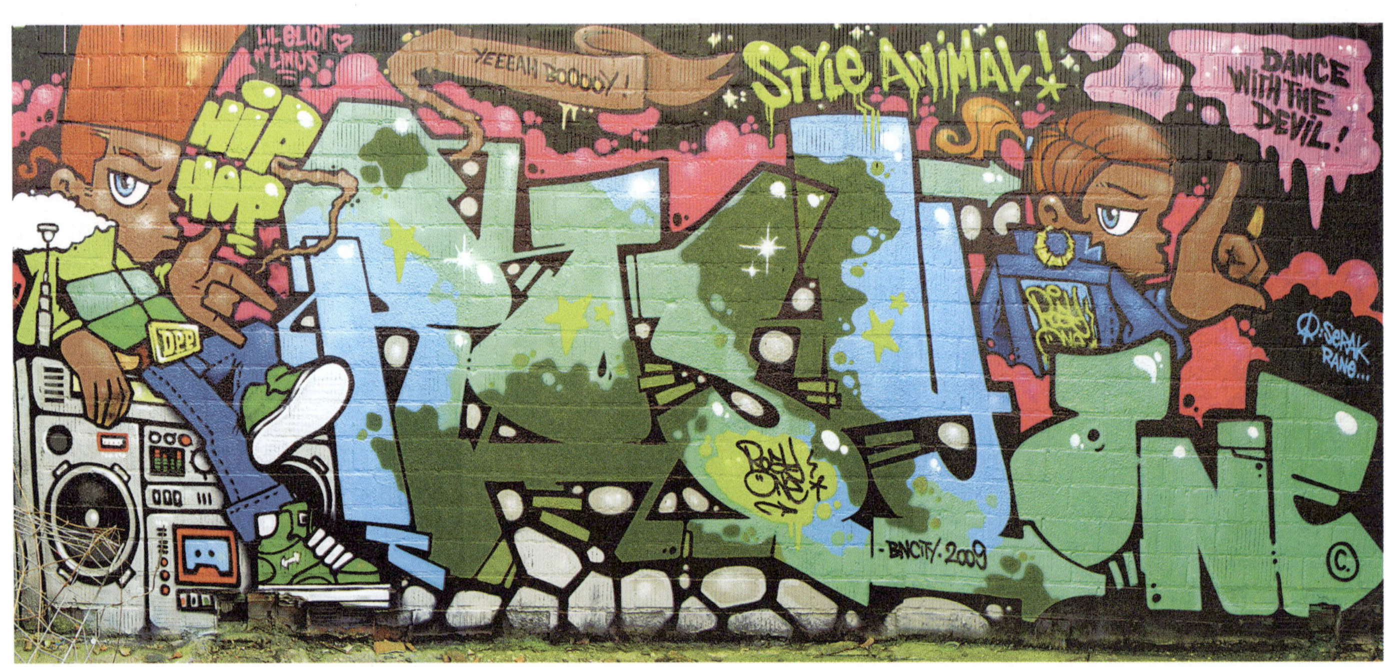

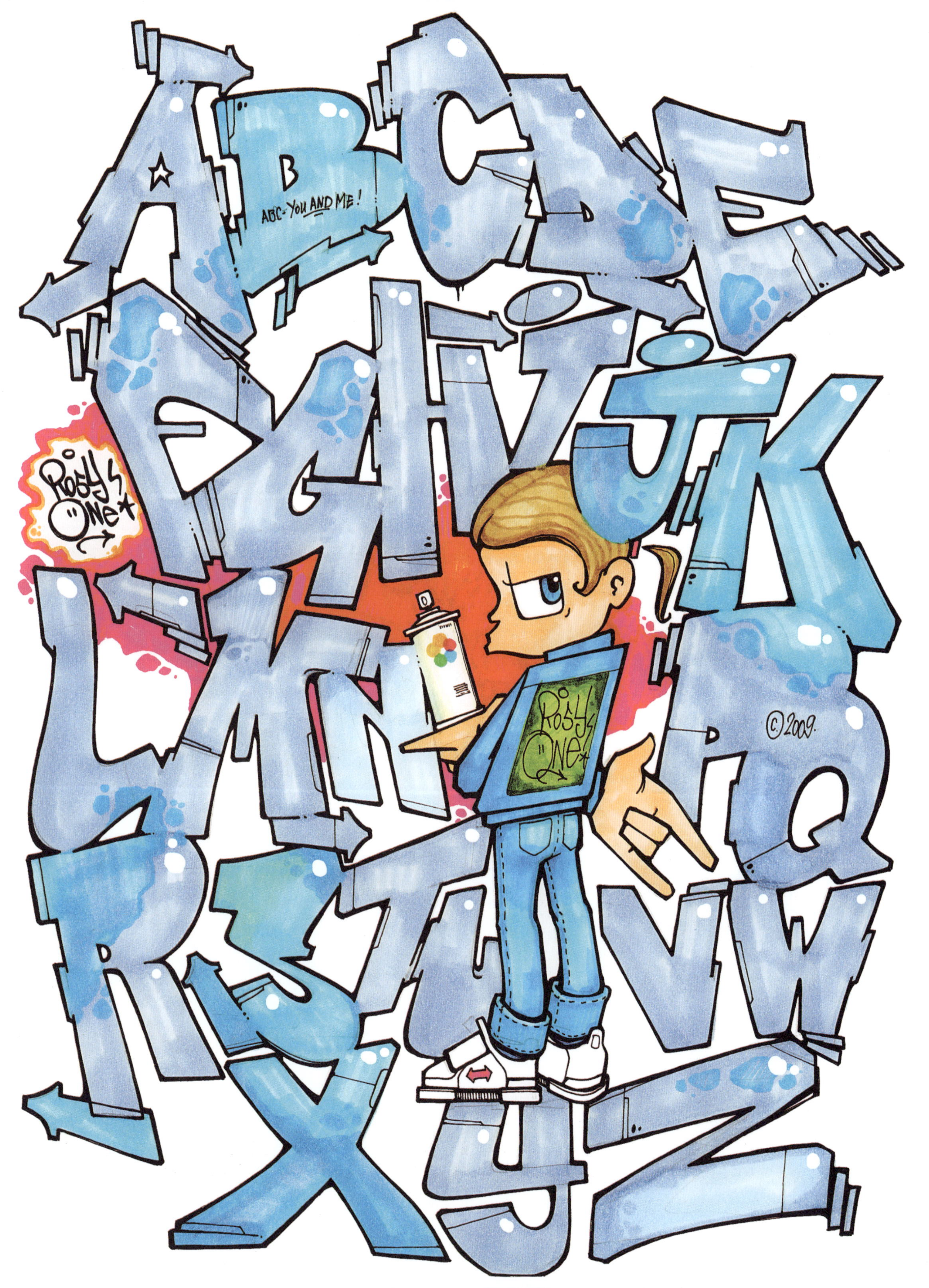

ABC - YOU AND ME!
ROSY's ONE
ROSY's ONE
© 2009.

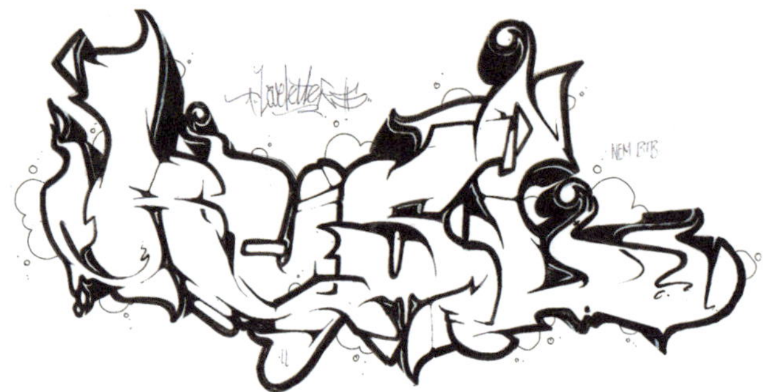

Rusl

STUTTGART, GERMANY
Crew member of LL, NEM, BTB
Writer since 1993
Favourite letter: S
www.rusl1.de

Rusl likes to experiment with different letter forms, techniques and applications. One project has centred around the photographic technique known as 'light graffiti', using a light source and a camera to 'paint' his images at night. In another project, which he calls 'liquid graffiti', he paints the outlines of his pieces as if they have liquefied, thus giving the letters a watery or lava-like appearance. As well as the actual painting process, Rusl appreciates the graffiti network.

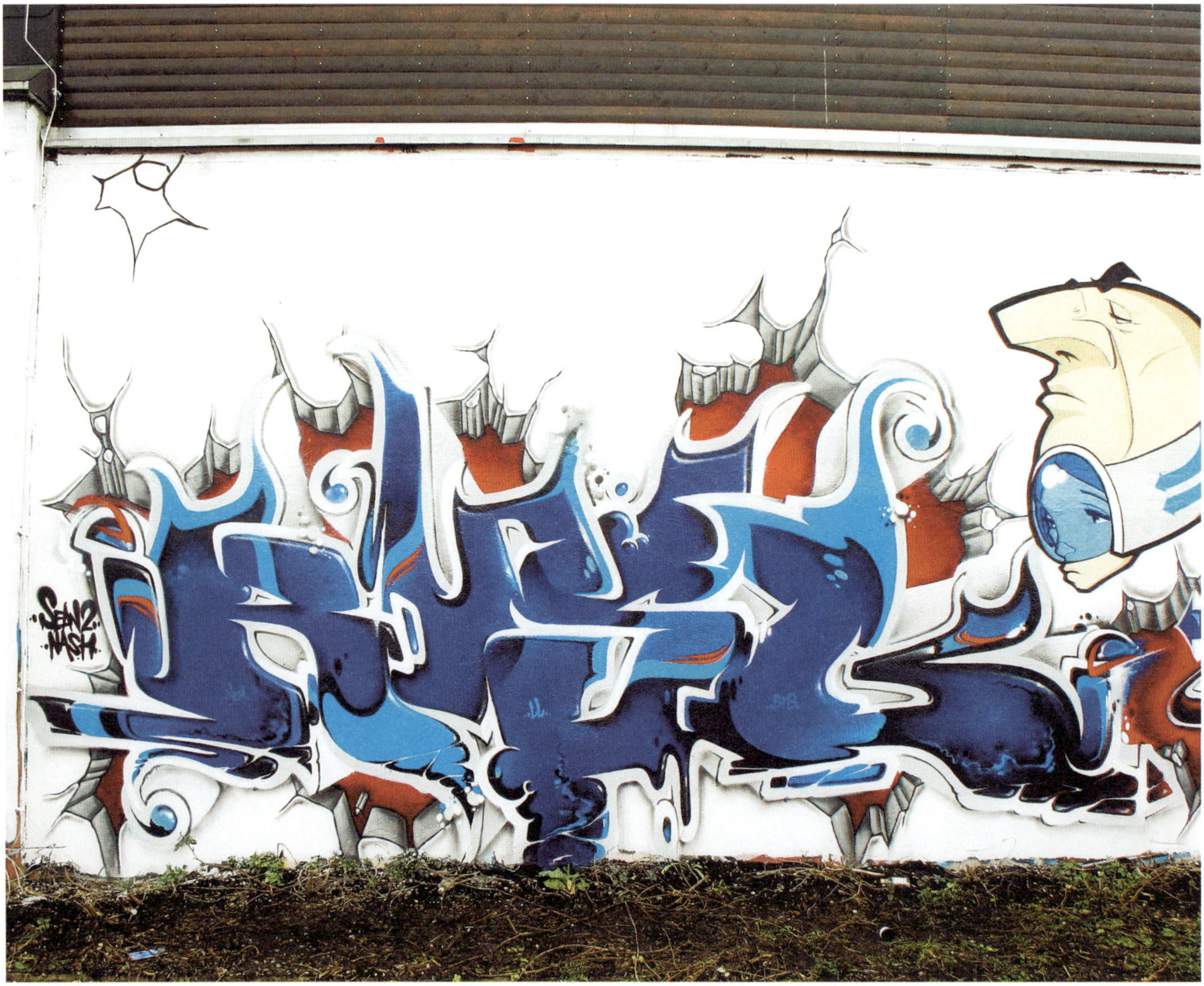

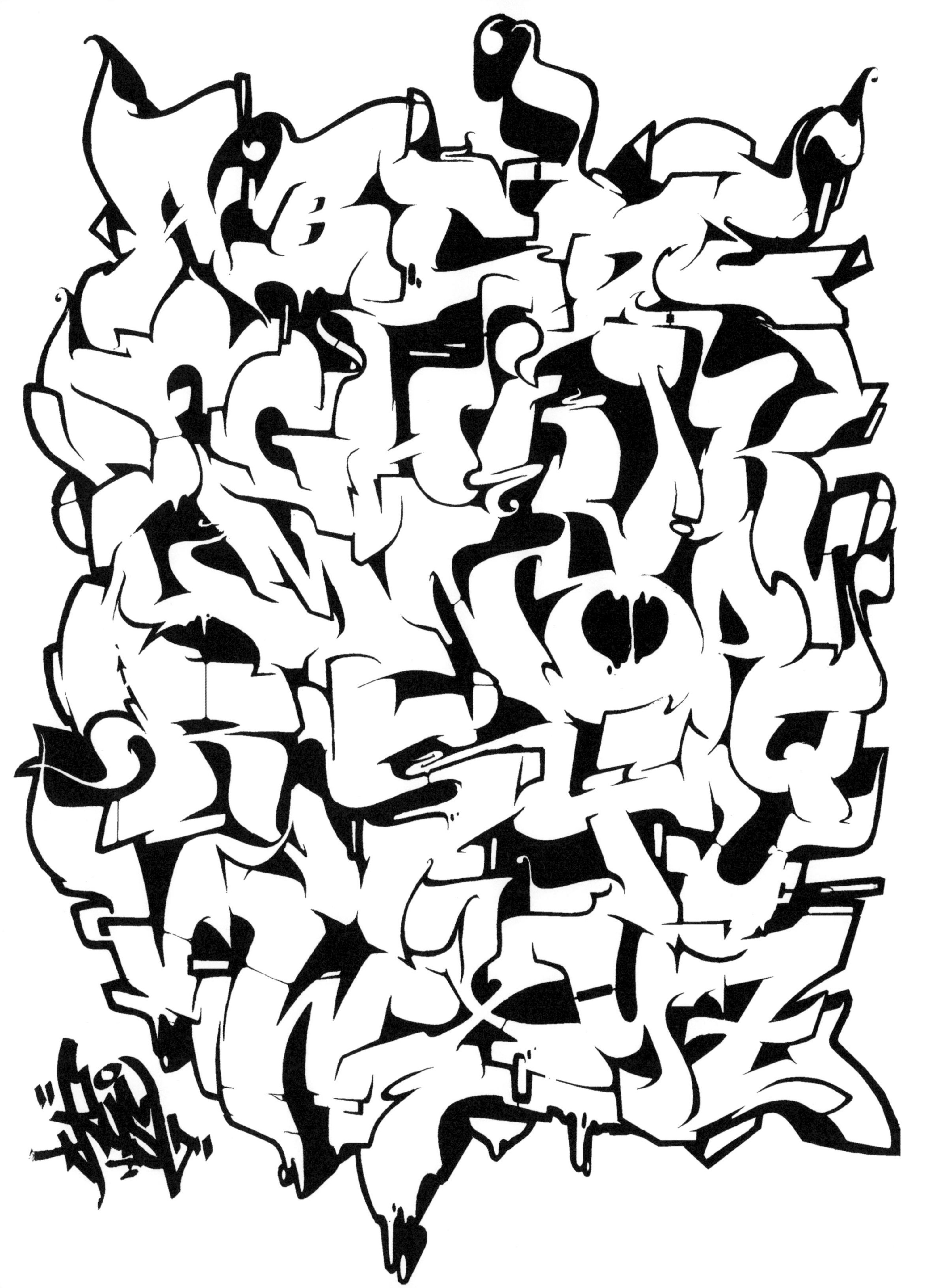

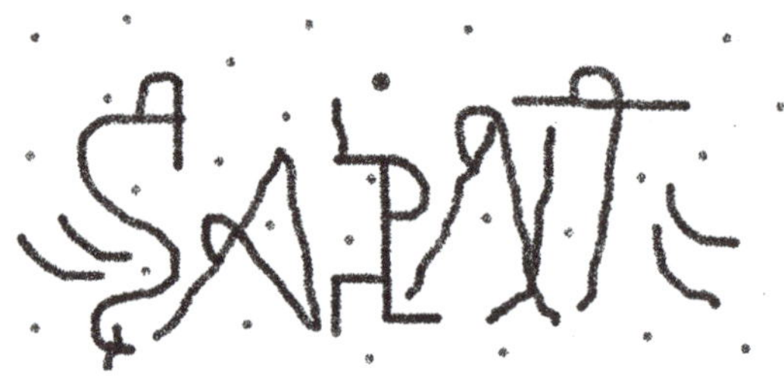

Saint

BUCHAREST, ROMANIA
Crew member of OILERS, LMC, CCTV, BIGOTE ROJO, FTP
Writer since 1999
Favourite letter: S

Saint describes his style as 'dilettante'. He had never designed an alphabet before and wanted a simple but appealing solution. So he took a pair of scissors and some magazines, cut out the individual letters and put them together in a collage.

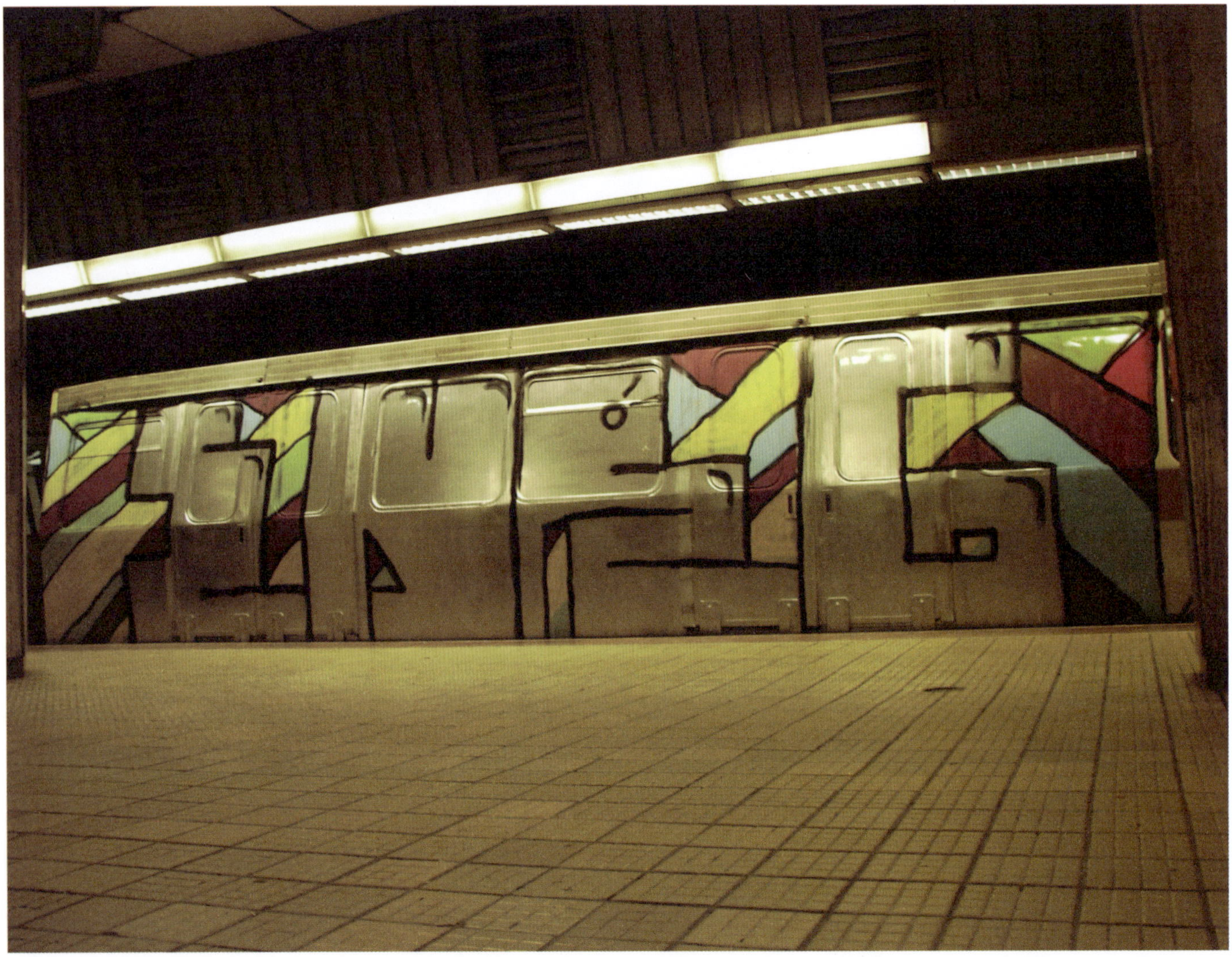

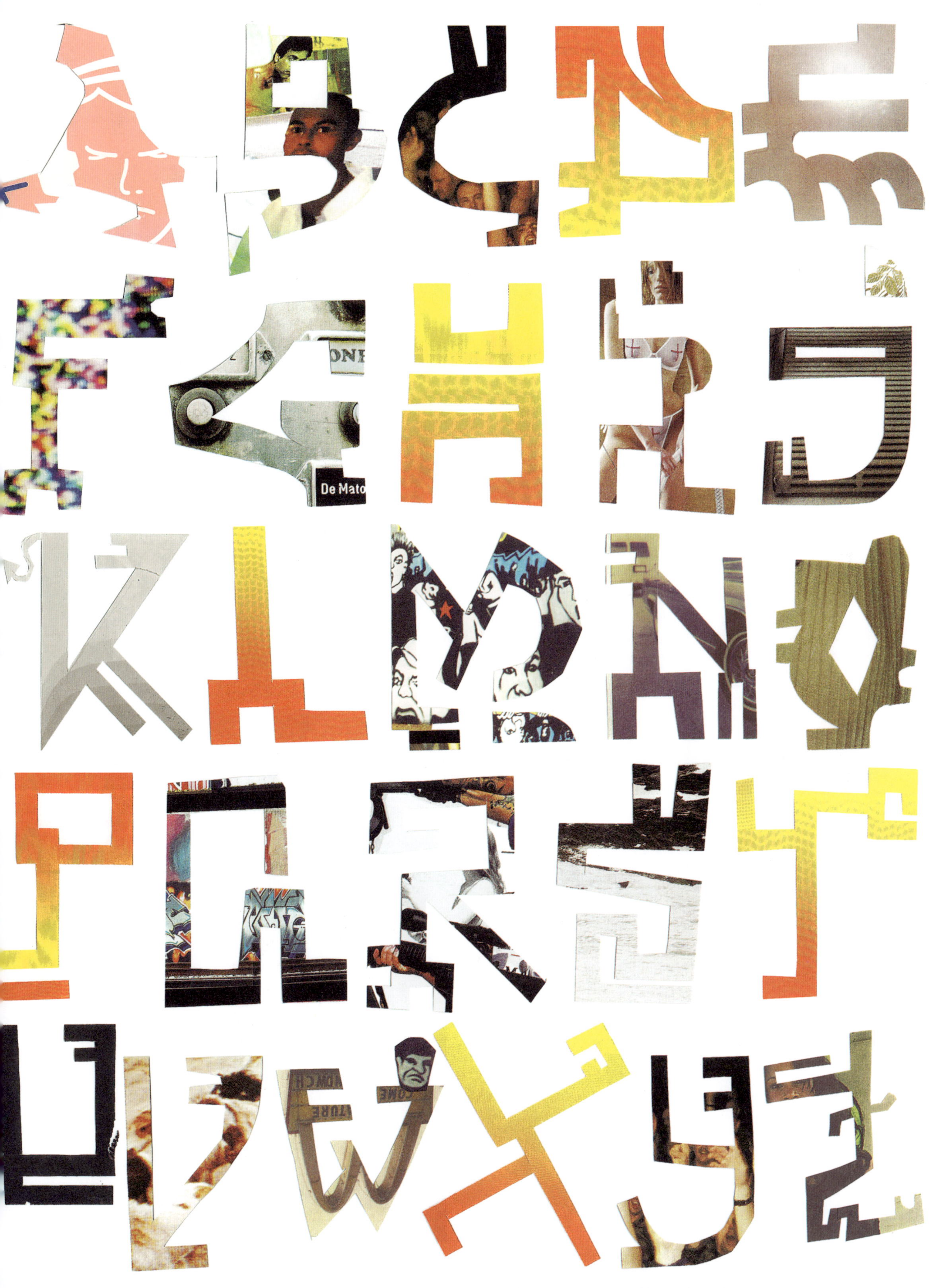

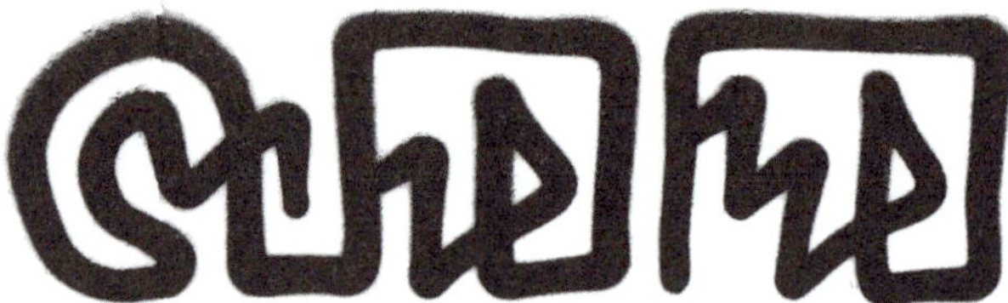

Scheme
MOSCOW, RUSSIA
Crew member of StyleKonstruktor
Writer since 2004
Favourite letter: S
www.stylekonstruktor.com

Scheme is one of Russia's best-known writers owing to his unusual graphic semi-3D style. He had already designed several fonts, but mostly with Cyrillic letters in his native language. 'I always start developing my fonts with the letter "S" and then go from there, using the same elements for all the other letters,' he explains. 'I create the fonts on sketching paper with the help of a special three-dimensional grid.'

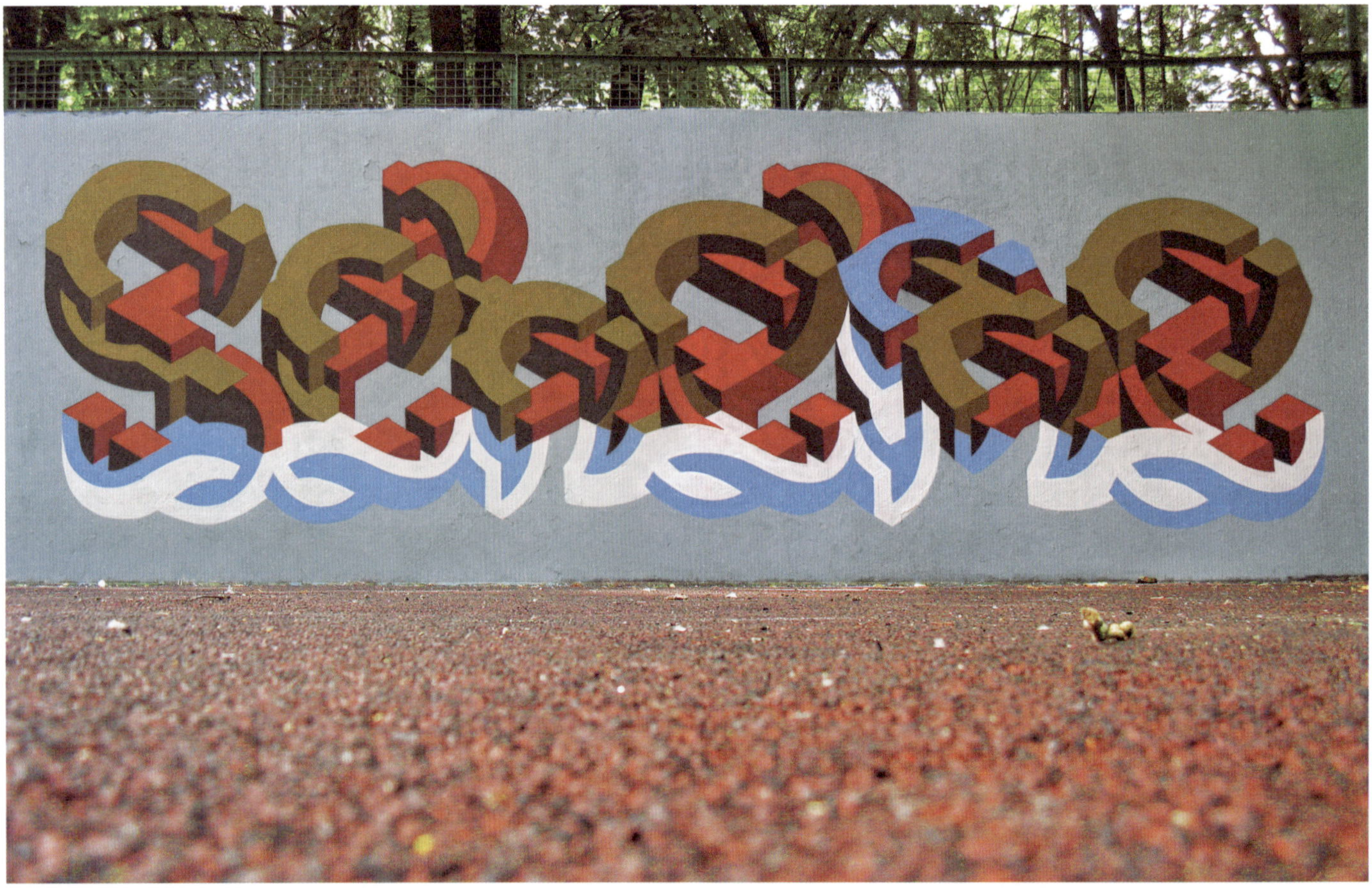

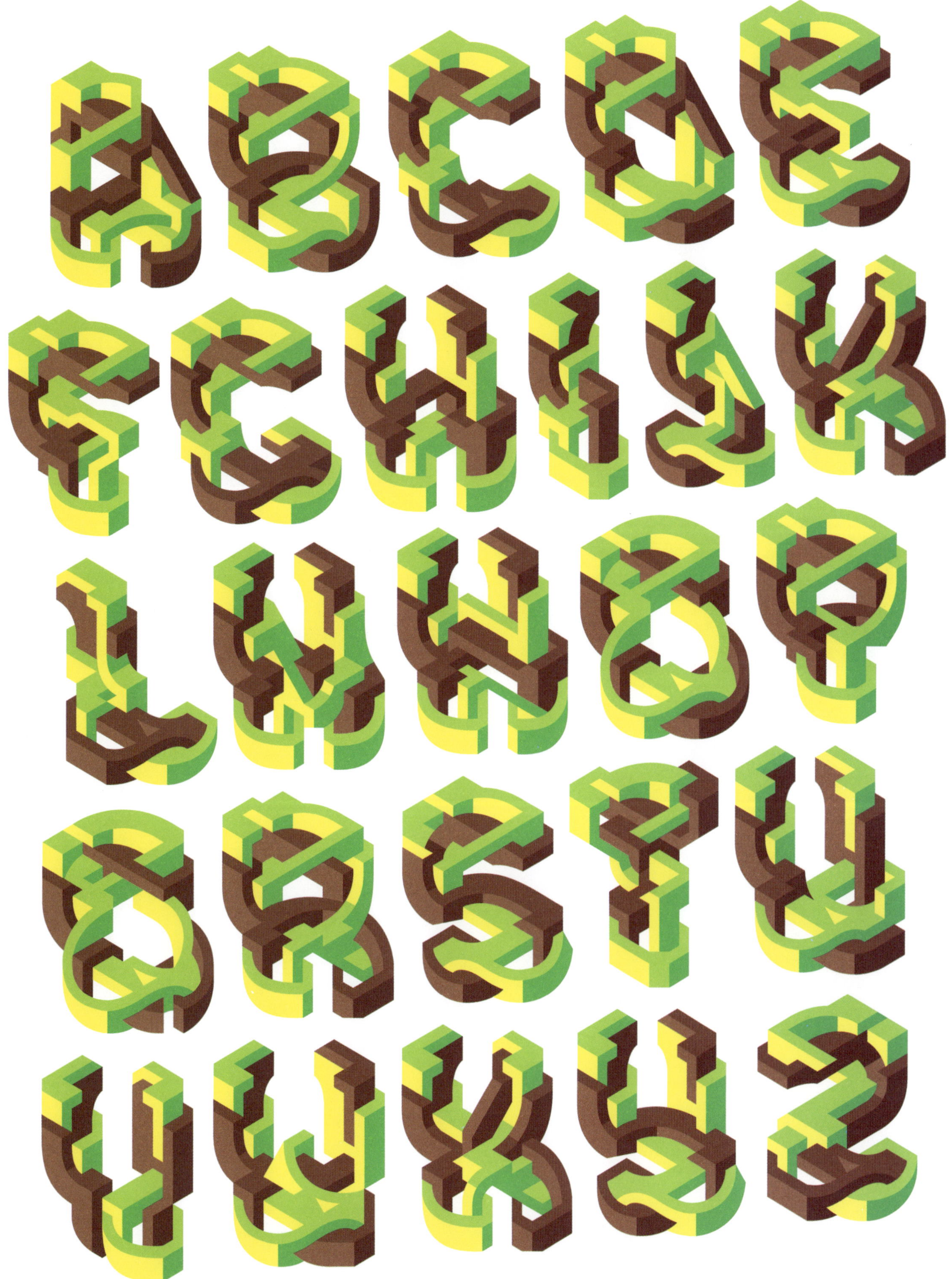

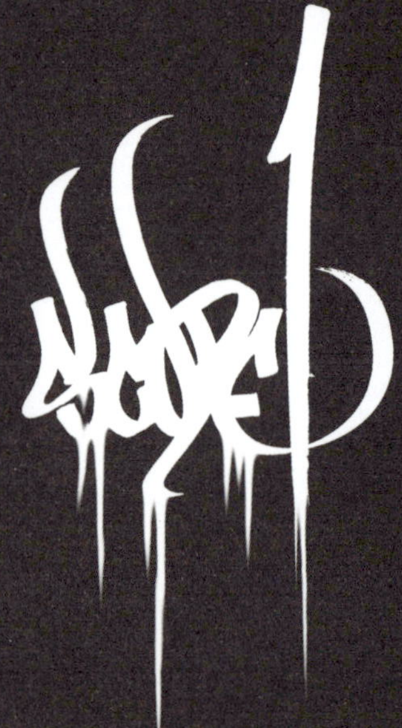

Scope
SINGAPORE

Crew member of OAC, KD, JNC
Writer since 1994
Favourite letters: S, E
www.thekorefoundation.com
www.flickr.com/mrscope

Scope is a member of an artists' collective based in Singapore
called Operation Art Core (ARTKORE). With this collective he
works on different design and art projects. About style in general
Scope says: 'The basic letter structure should be practised first,
before moving on to a more advanced level. Only then can you
produce a good piece.'

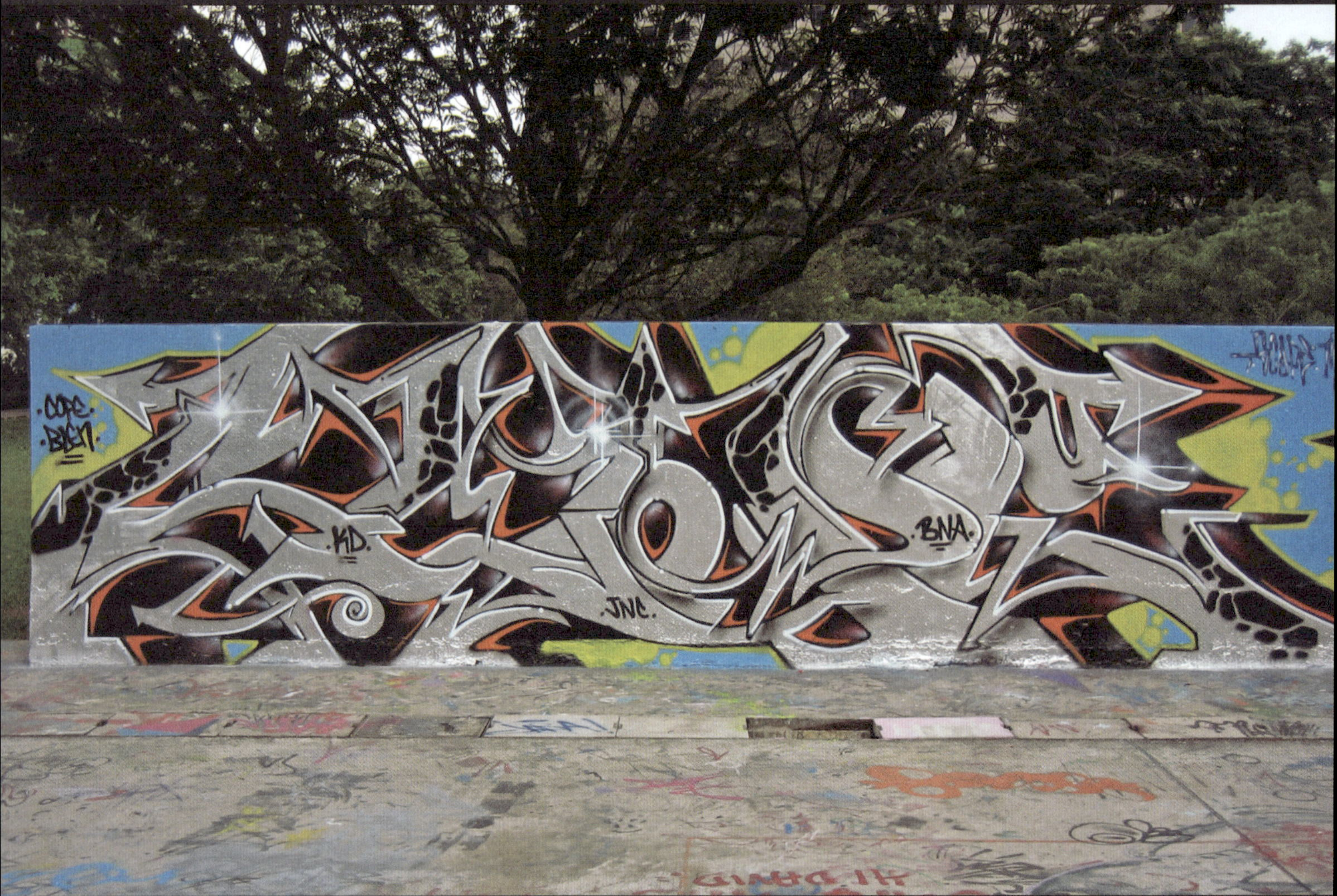

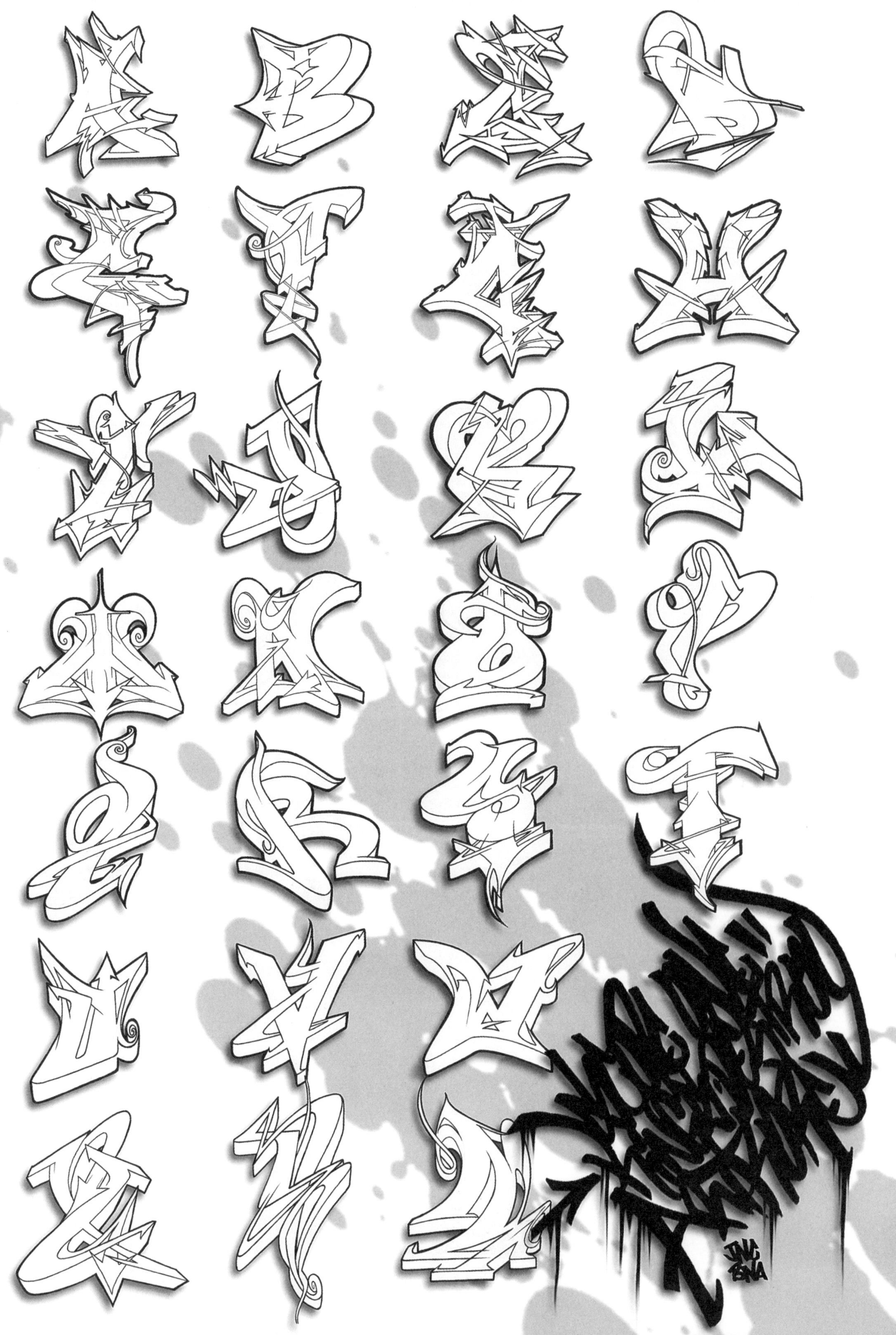

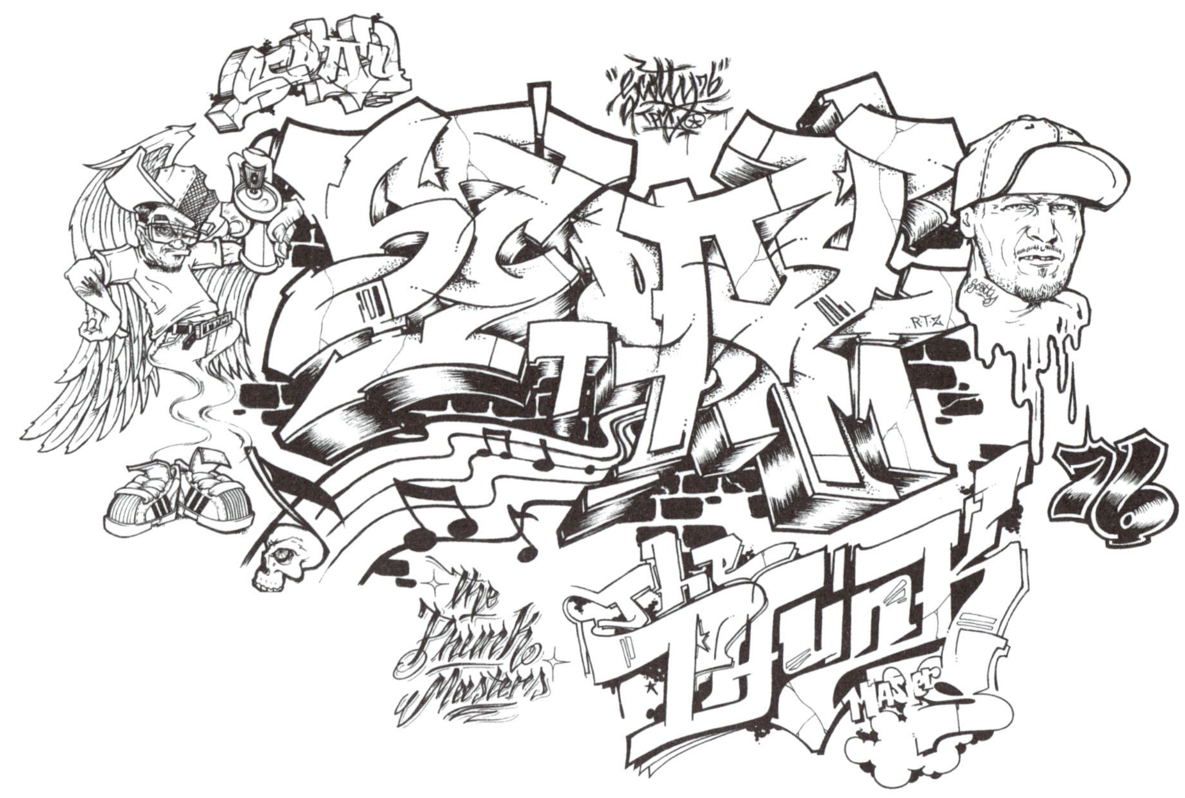

Scotty76

HEIDELBERG, GERMANY

Crew member of TPM, RTZ, T2B, KOT, EDK, 156, EGO
Writer since 1988
Favourite letter: 'Hasn't been invented yet'
www.facebook.com/ScottyTPM

Scotty76 has achieved recognition in more than one discipline. Over the past twenty-plus years he has made a name for himself as a writer, a skilled breakdancer, a tattoo artist and a designer of many music-based projects. Thanks to his many talents, he has travelled the globe. In his opinion, a piece can only be described as 'good' when everything is harmoniously connected – the style, the surface and the surroundings.

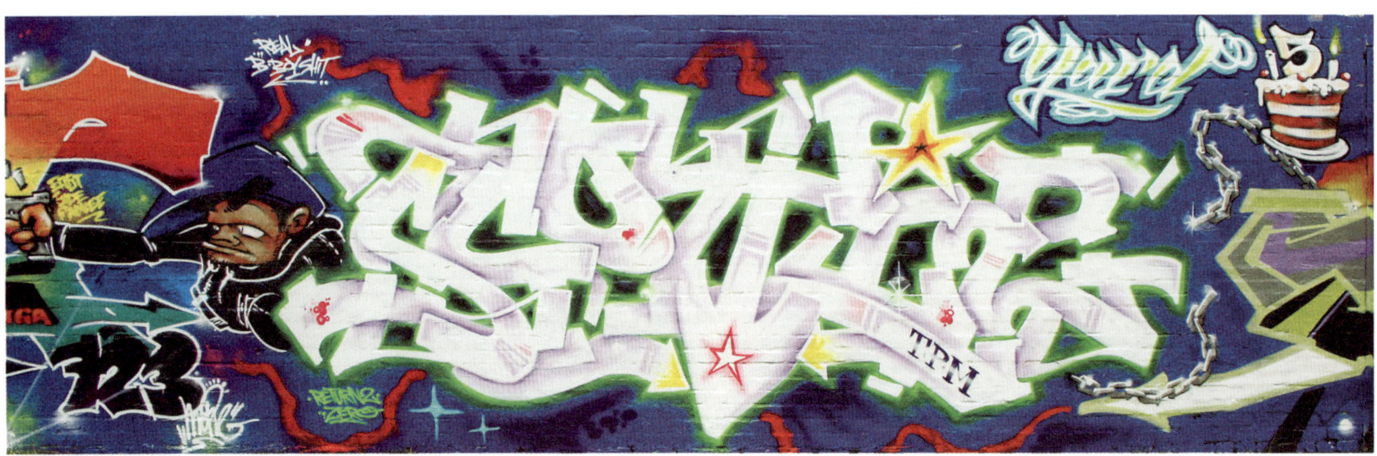

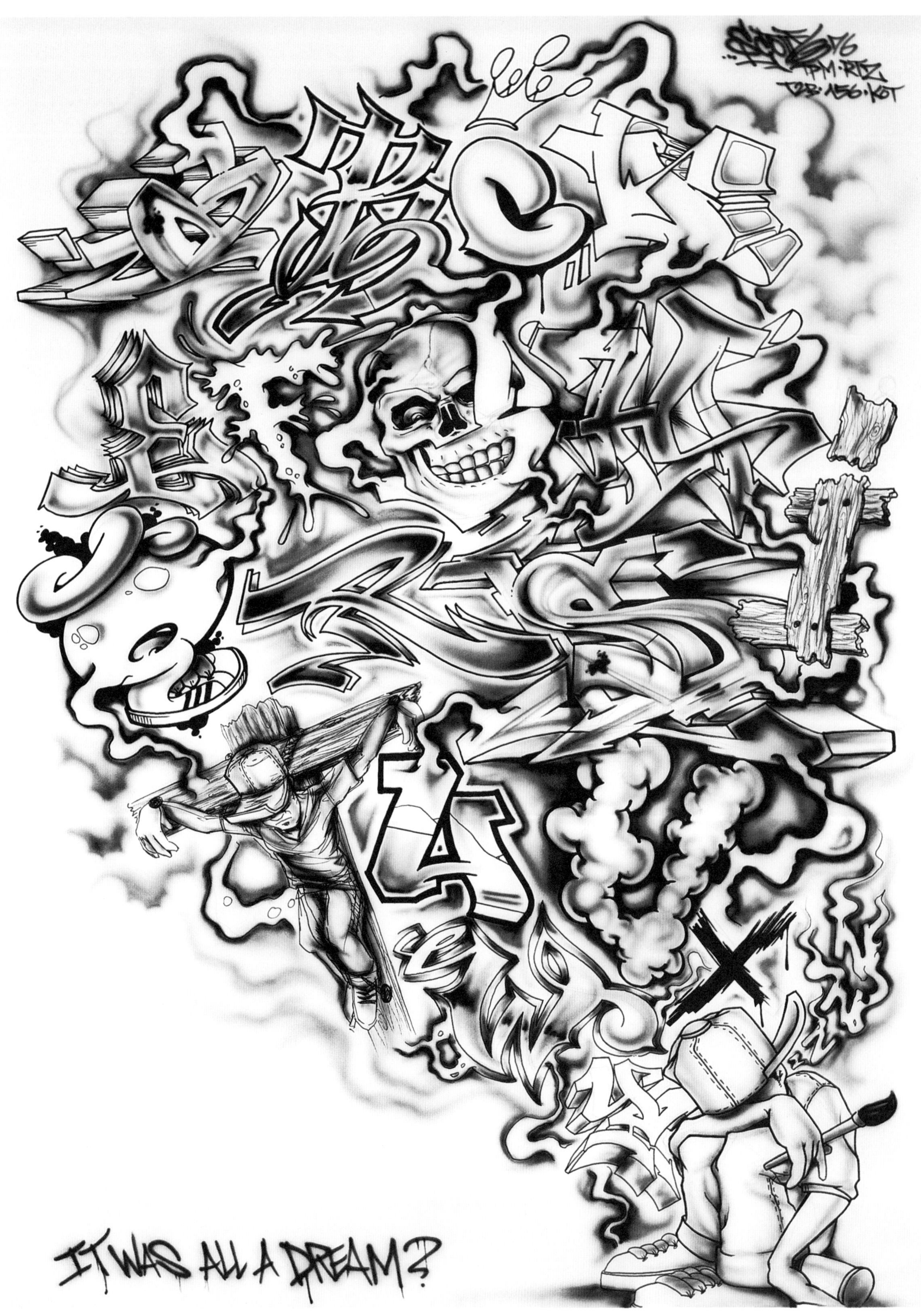

IT WAS ALL A DREAM?

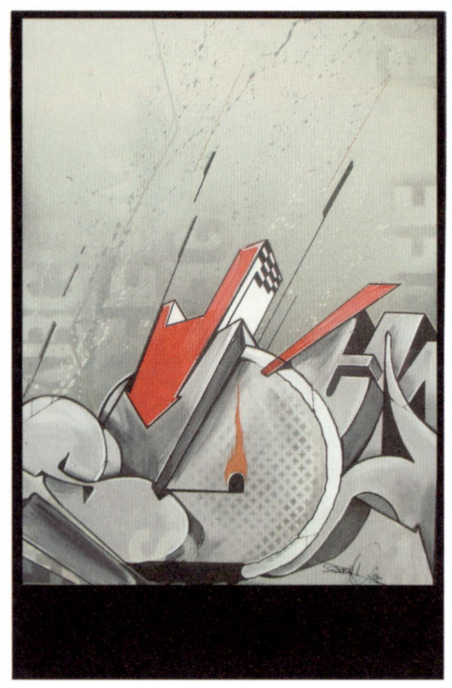
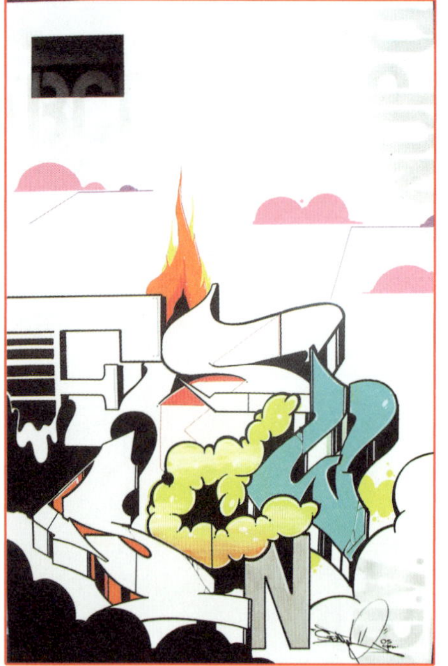
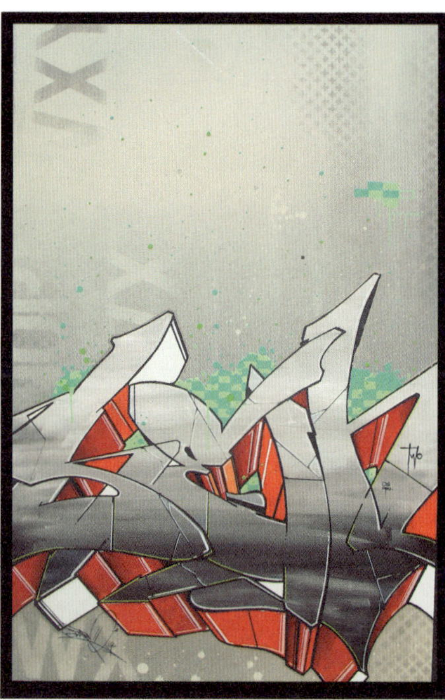

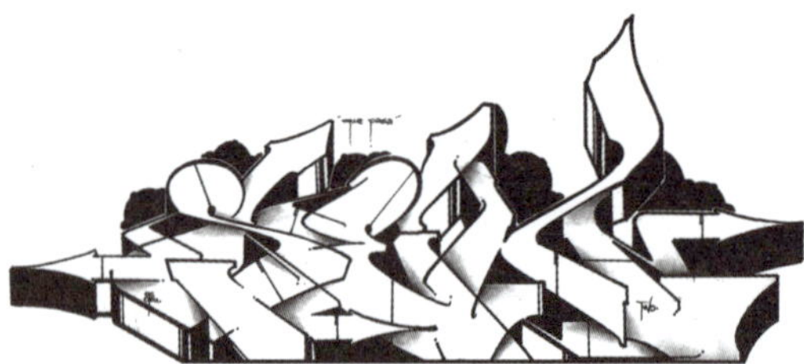

Sen2
NEW YORK CITY, USA
Crew member of Os Cru, Pornostars
Writer since 1986
Favourite letter: S
sen2manystyles.tumblr.com

Sen2 comes from Puerto Rico. He has travelled a lot since starting out as a writer, and his style has developed from wildstyle to a more legible European approach, with careful consideration of backgrounds and colour combinations. He is also the owner of Da Bakery – a graffiti supplies shop and art gallery with a rooftop hall of fame. Since opening its doors in May 2009, the store has become a meeting place for local and international artists.

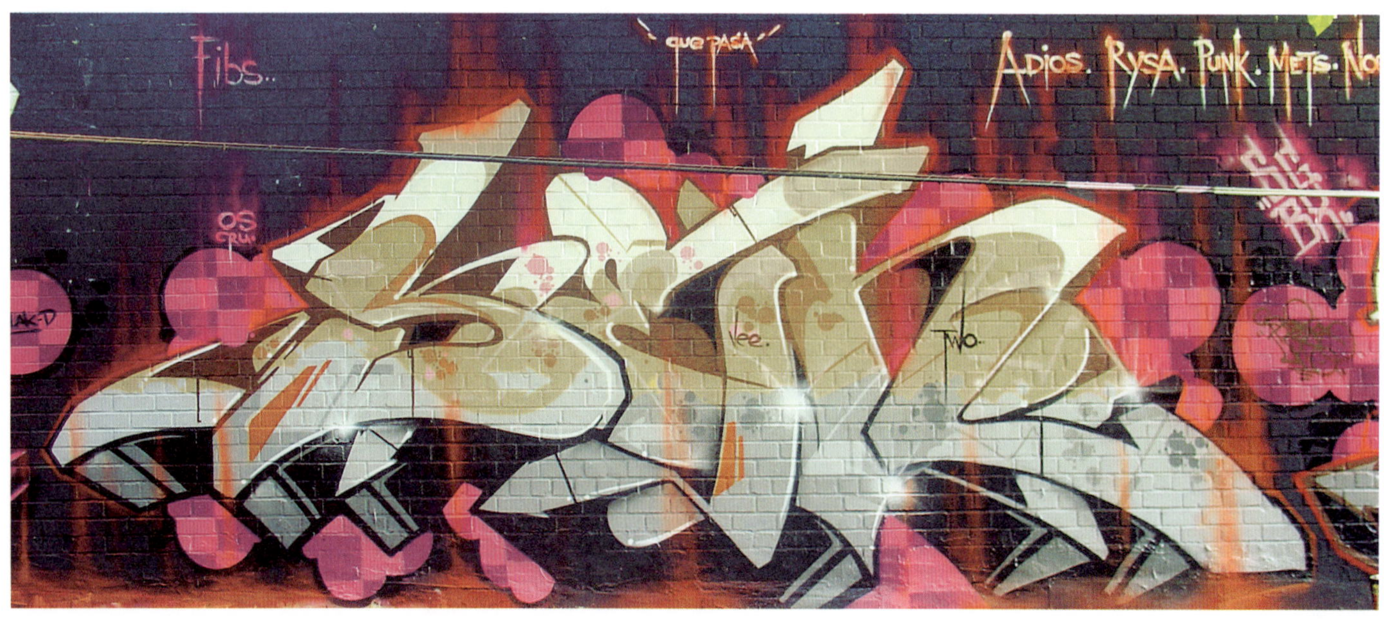

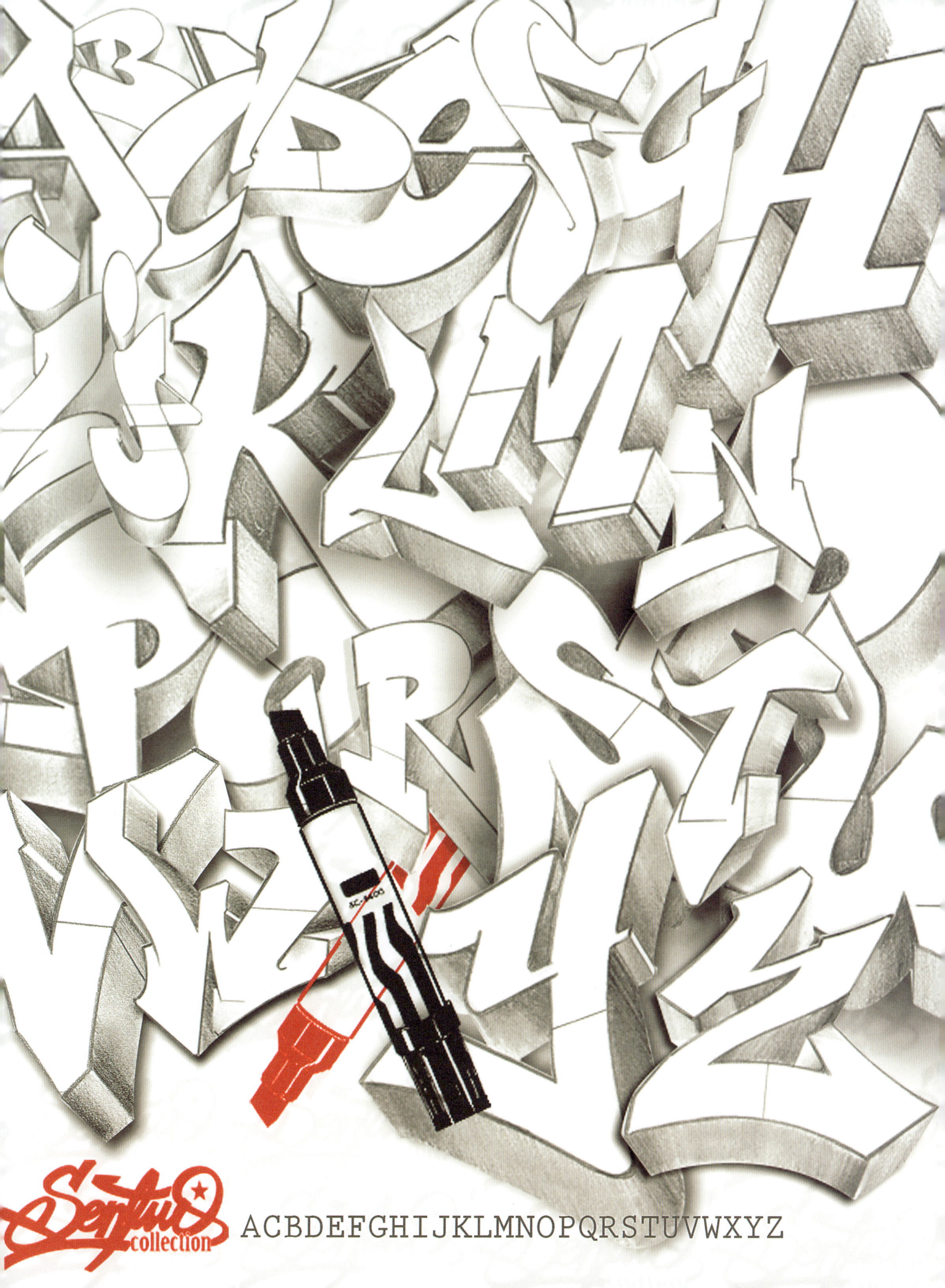

Seytwo collection
ACBDEFGHIJKLMNOPQRSTUVWXYZ

Serch

ZWOLLE, NETHERLANDS
Crew member of FAC, Zwolle's Freshest,
WSU, OK, C2, NES, TDS, TMT, TM7, BYI, SUK
Writer since 1986
Favourite letter: E

Old-school writer Serch is a member of many international graffiti
crews. His pieces are original, legible and well balanced. He says:
'A good piece needs dope lettering and a good balance. Colours
and all that are important, but essentially they are just tools with
which to customize your piece.'

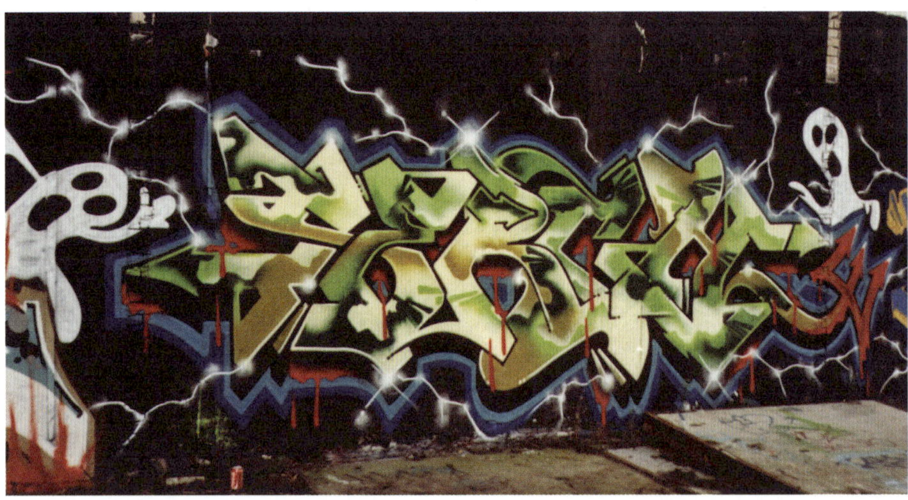

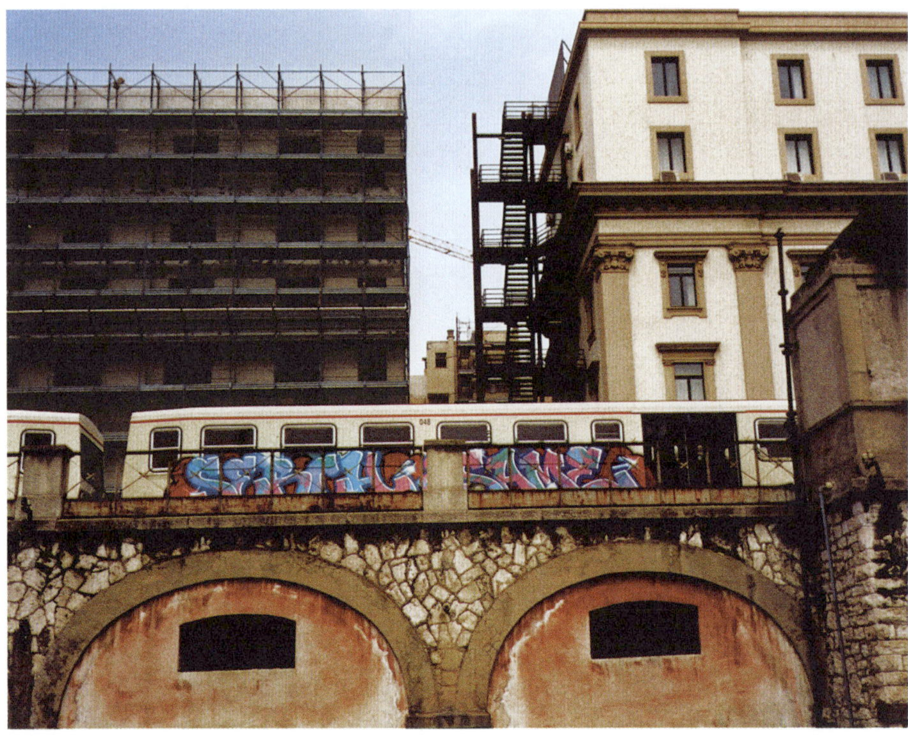

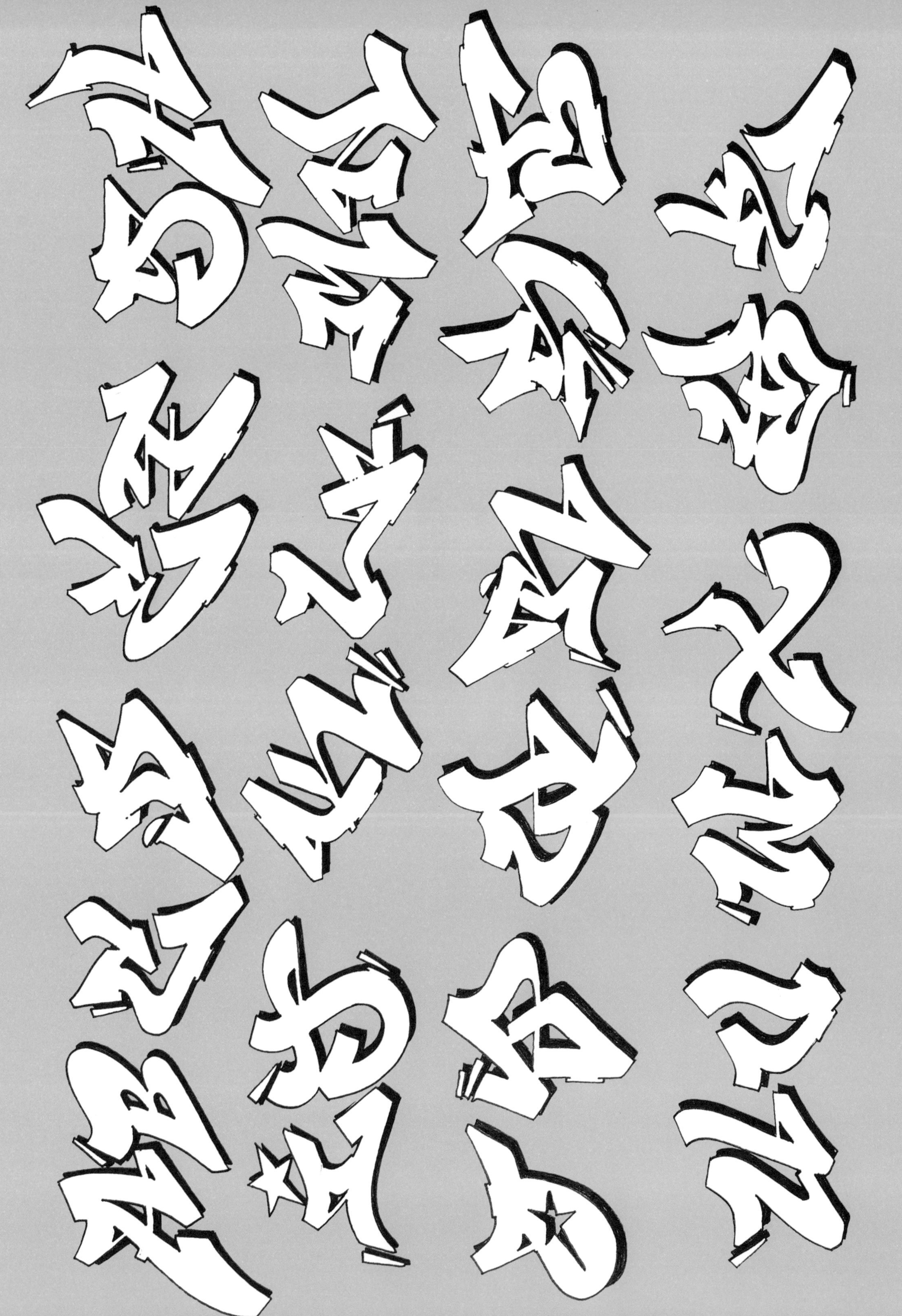

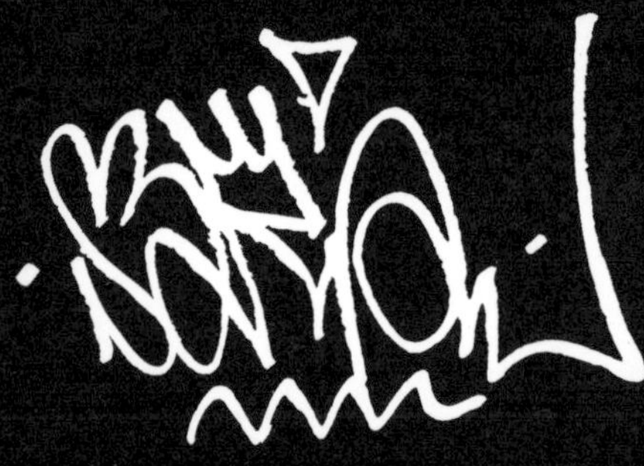

Serial

INOWROCLAW, POLAND

Crew member of Typoets
Writer since 2000
Favourite letter: 'All of them'
www.facebook.com/typoets

Serial likes pieces that have something special and are able to surprise him.
He compiled his alphabet using bicycle parts, tools and other objects he had
found at home. He says: 'Letters are everywhere – just take a closer look.'

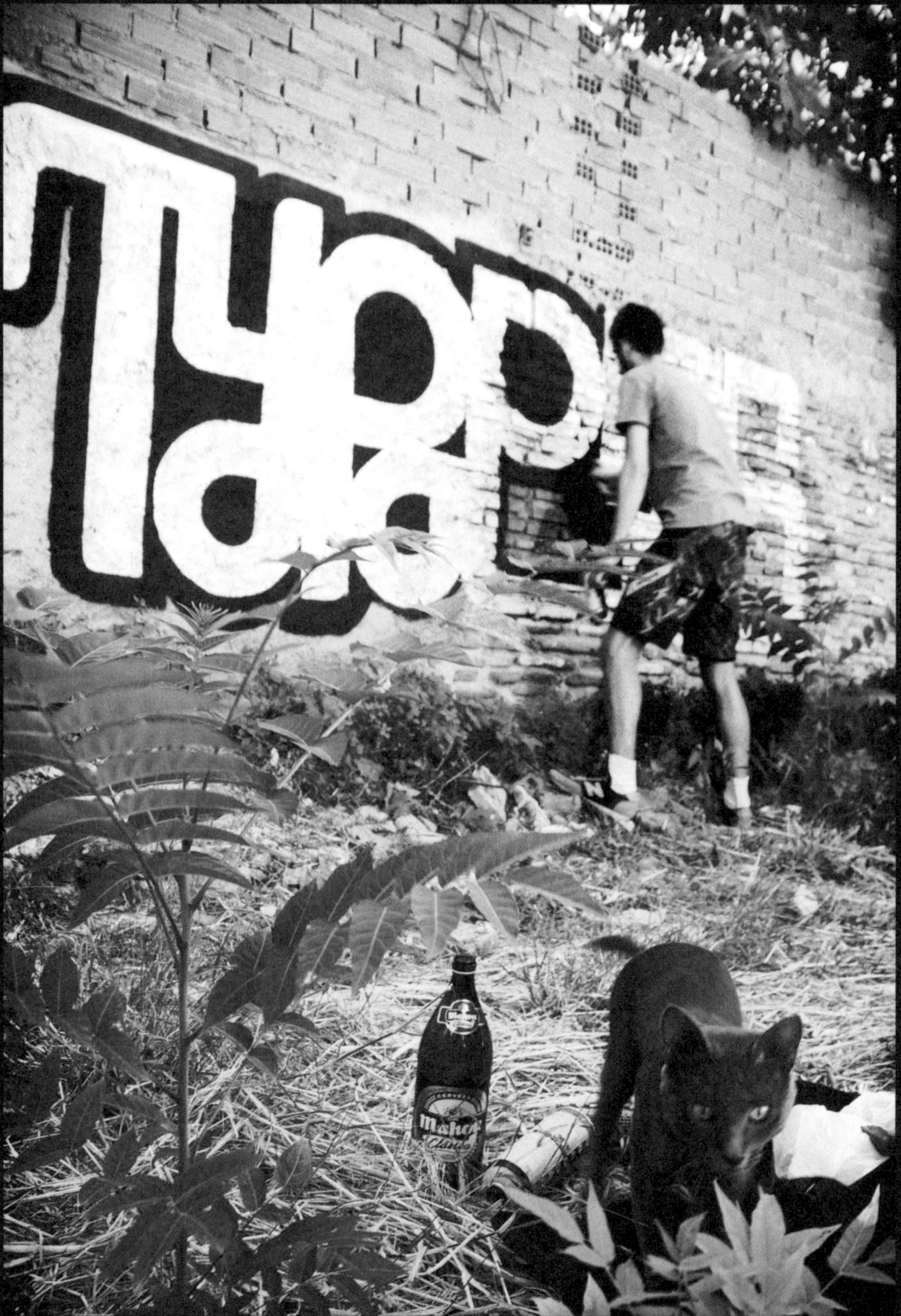

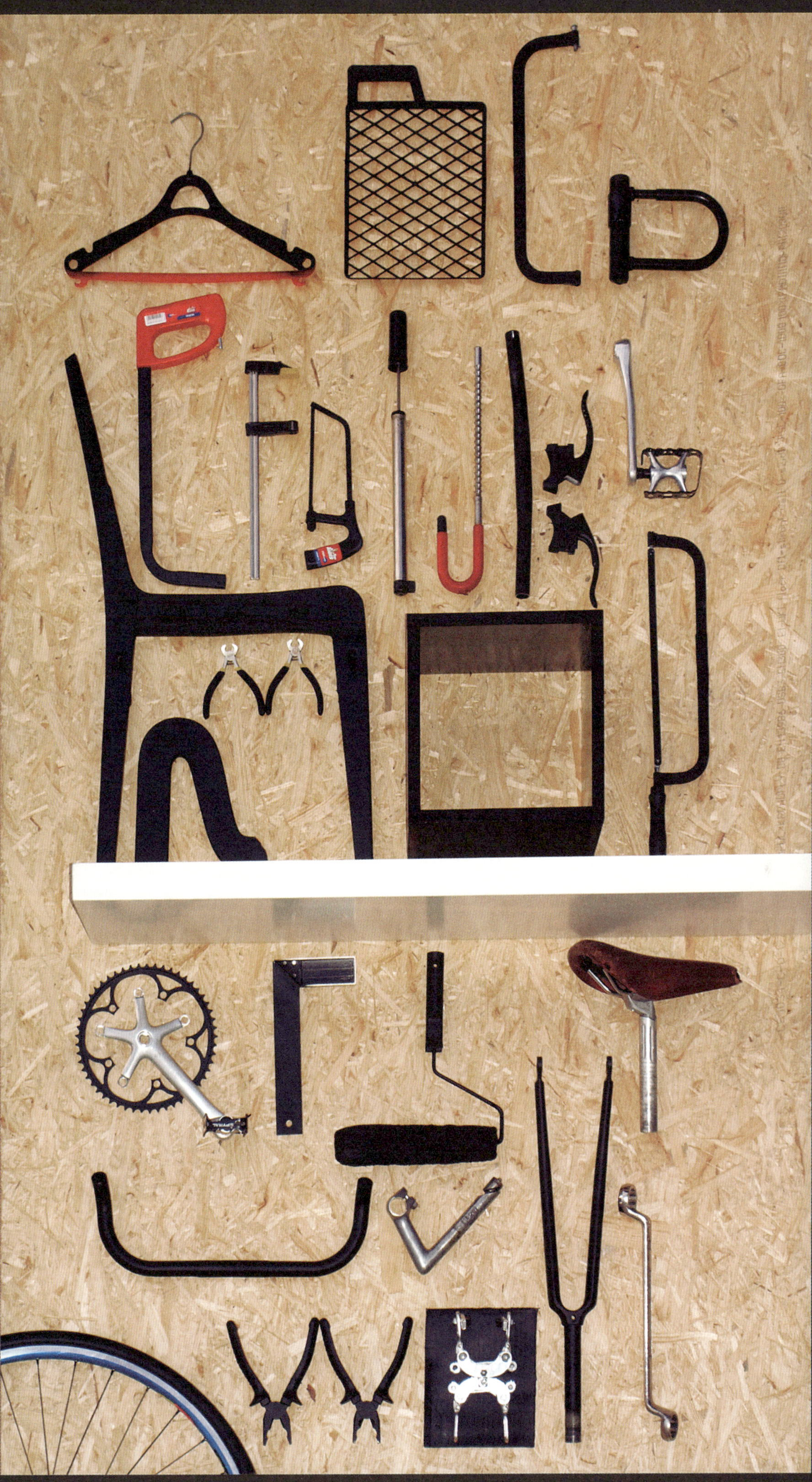

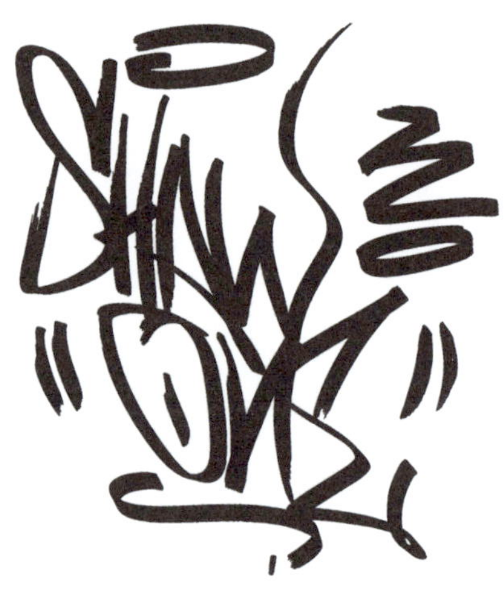

Shaw One
BERLIN, GERMANY
Crew member of Adult Entertainment
Writer since the early 1990s
Favourite letter: S

For Shaw One graffiti is all about freedom. That's why he likes
pieces that 'ignore the mainstream and embrace creativity'. He
designed his alphabet to reflect his passion for trees. 'I just like
them,' he explains. 'From the top to the roots – they are heritage
and future in one. The unstoppable growth of nature combined
with the never-ending possibilities with letters.'

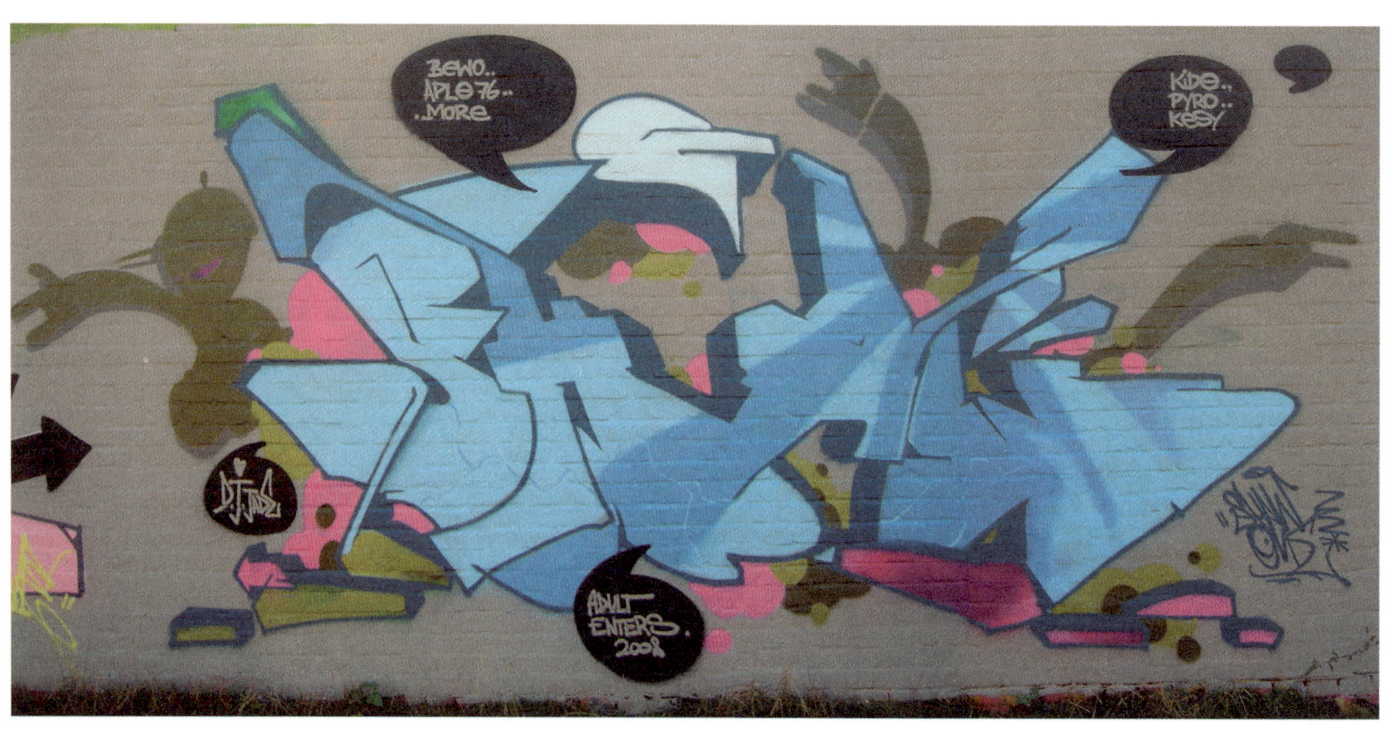

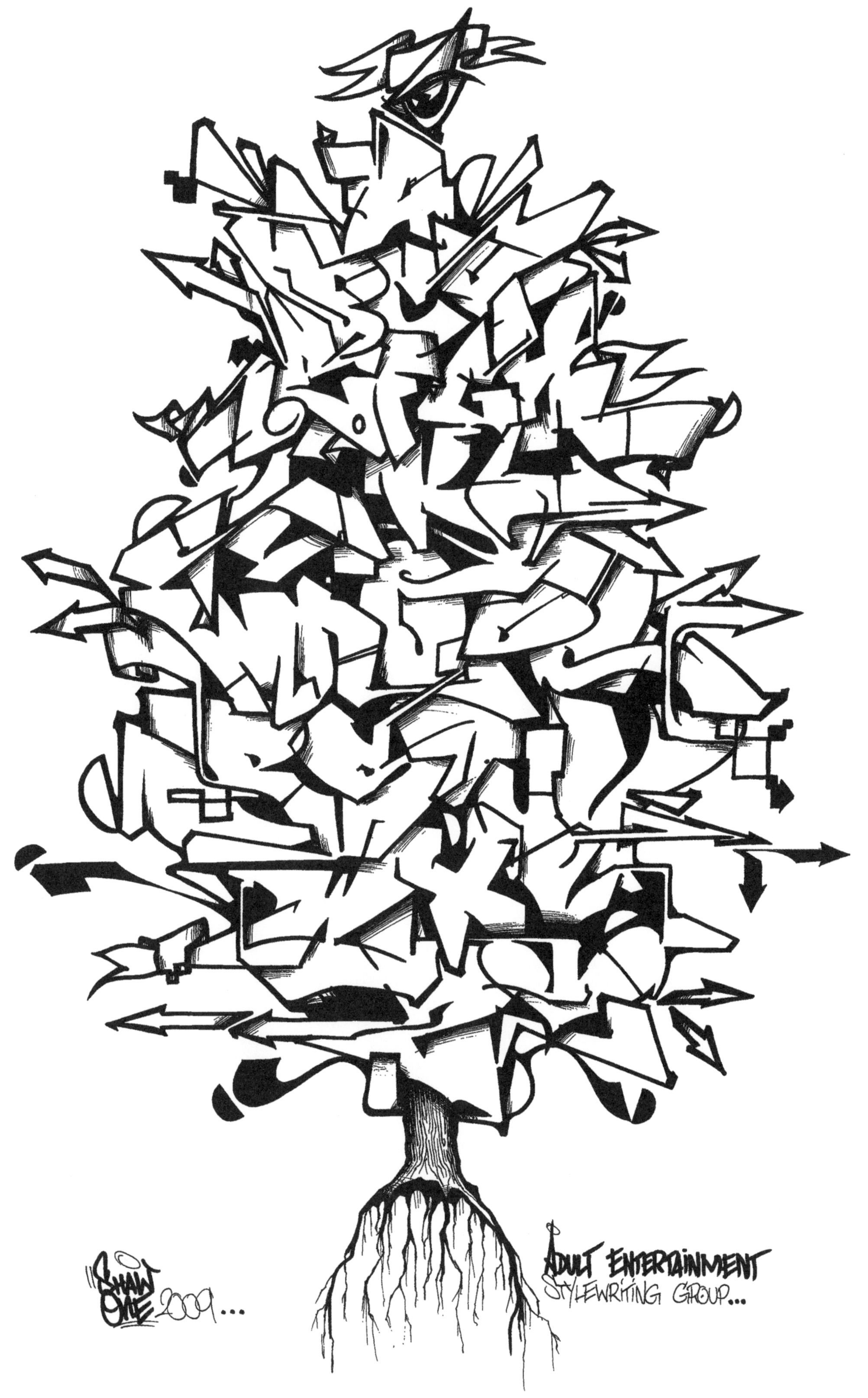

SHAW ONE 2009...
ADULT ENTERTAINMENT STYLEWRITING GROUP...

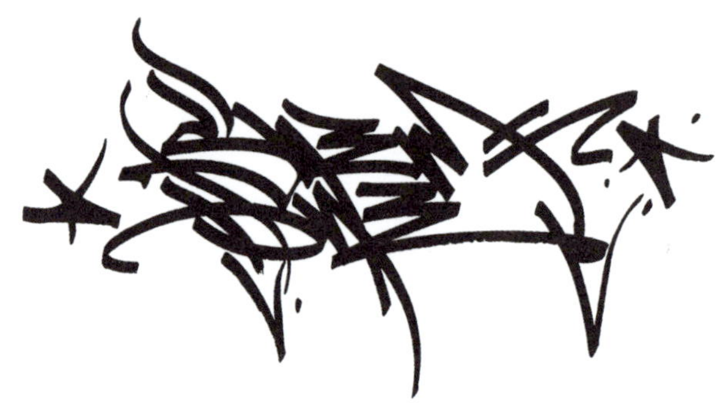

Shem
MELBOURNE, AUSTRALIA
Crew member of Rock Da City, F1C
Writer since early 1987
Favourite letters: S, R

Shem, also known as Reign or Paso, is into traditional wildstyle letters. He painted his alphabet freestyle on a 60-metre wall over seven days. For him it's essential that the letters dance, move and are well proportioned, connected and balanced. There are many reasons why he loves graffiti: 'It can take you away from the stresses of the real world. As well as enabling you to be creative, it can also give you fame, respect, confidence, money, friends worldwide, and', Shem jokes, 'girls love a talented artist!'

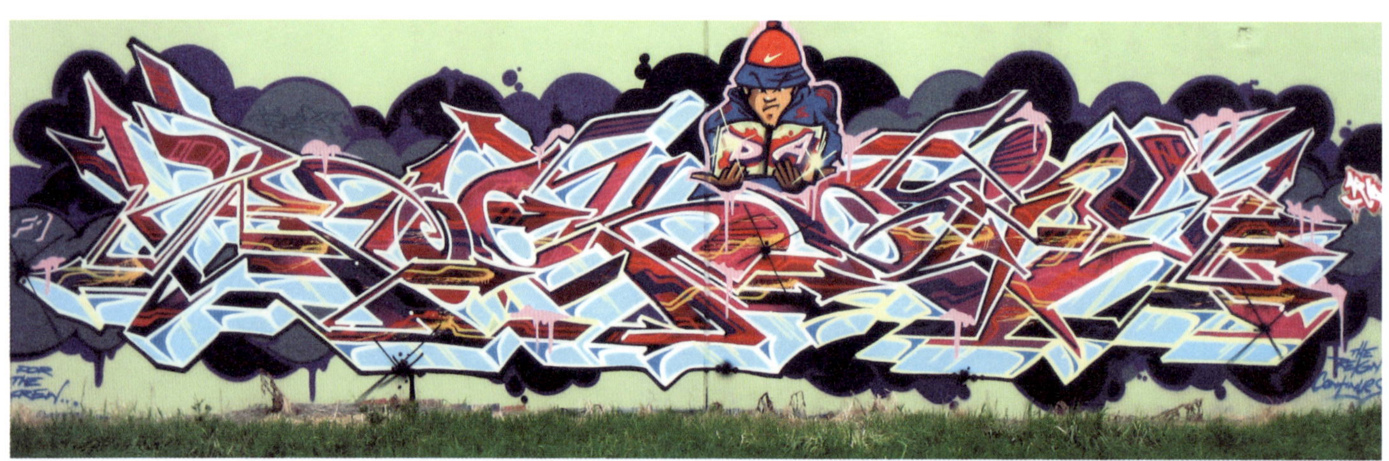

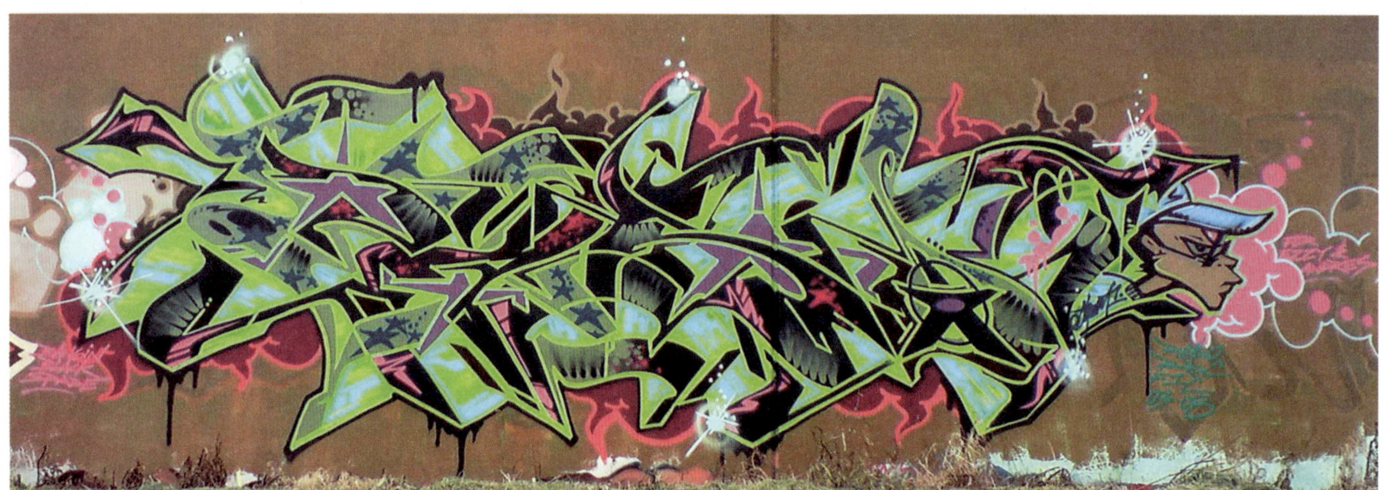

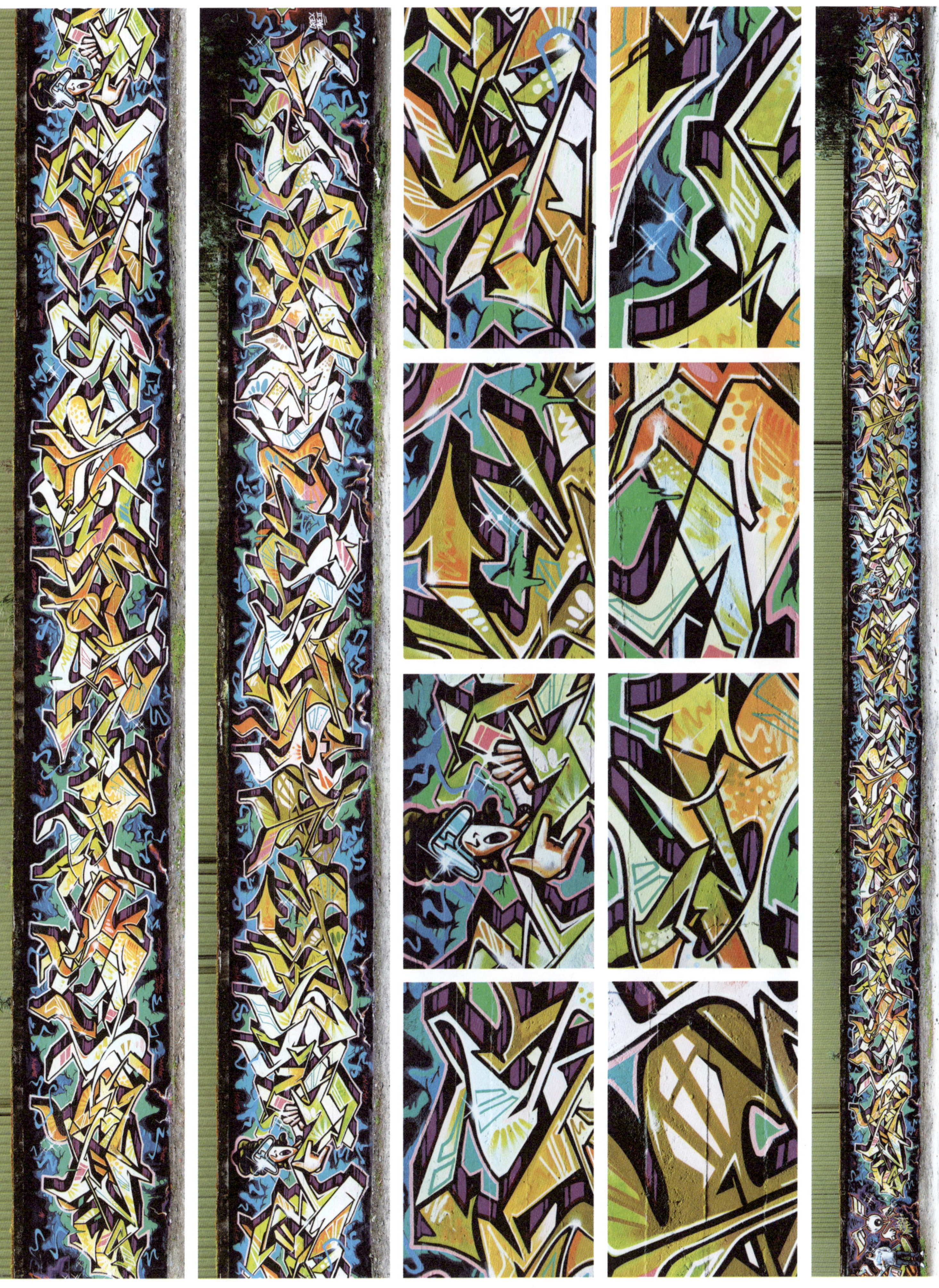

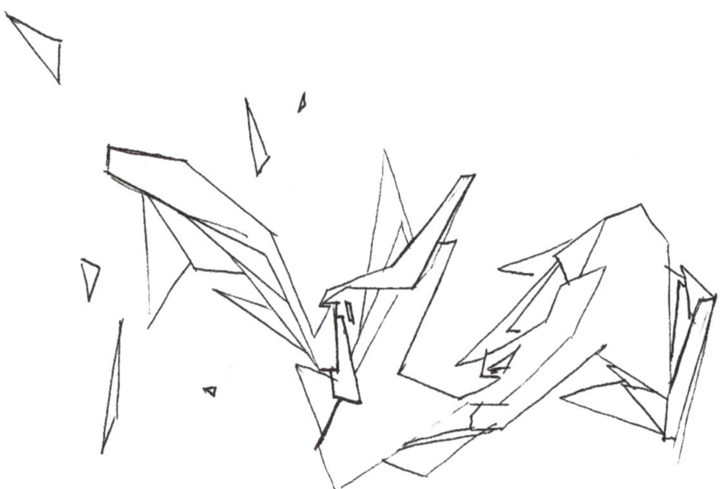

Sign
WIESBADEN, GERMANY

Crew member of Via Grafik
Writer since 1995
Favourite letters: S, K, E, g …
www.sign-portfolio.de
www.vgrfk.com
www.arcademi.com/via-sign

Sign is a member of the widely known artists' collective and design studio Via Grafik and is active in the fields of graphic design, motion graphics and illustration. He describes his style as 'freaky, modern, graphic, flexible and abstract'. For his alphabet he used a graphic triangular style that had recently featured in some of his other pieces. Most importantly a piece should be dynamic and compelling, he says.

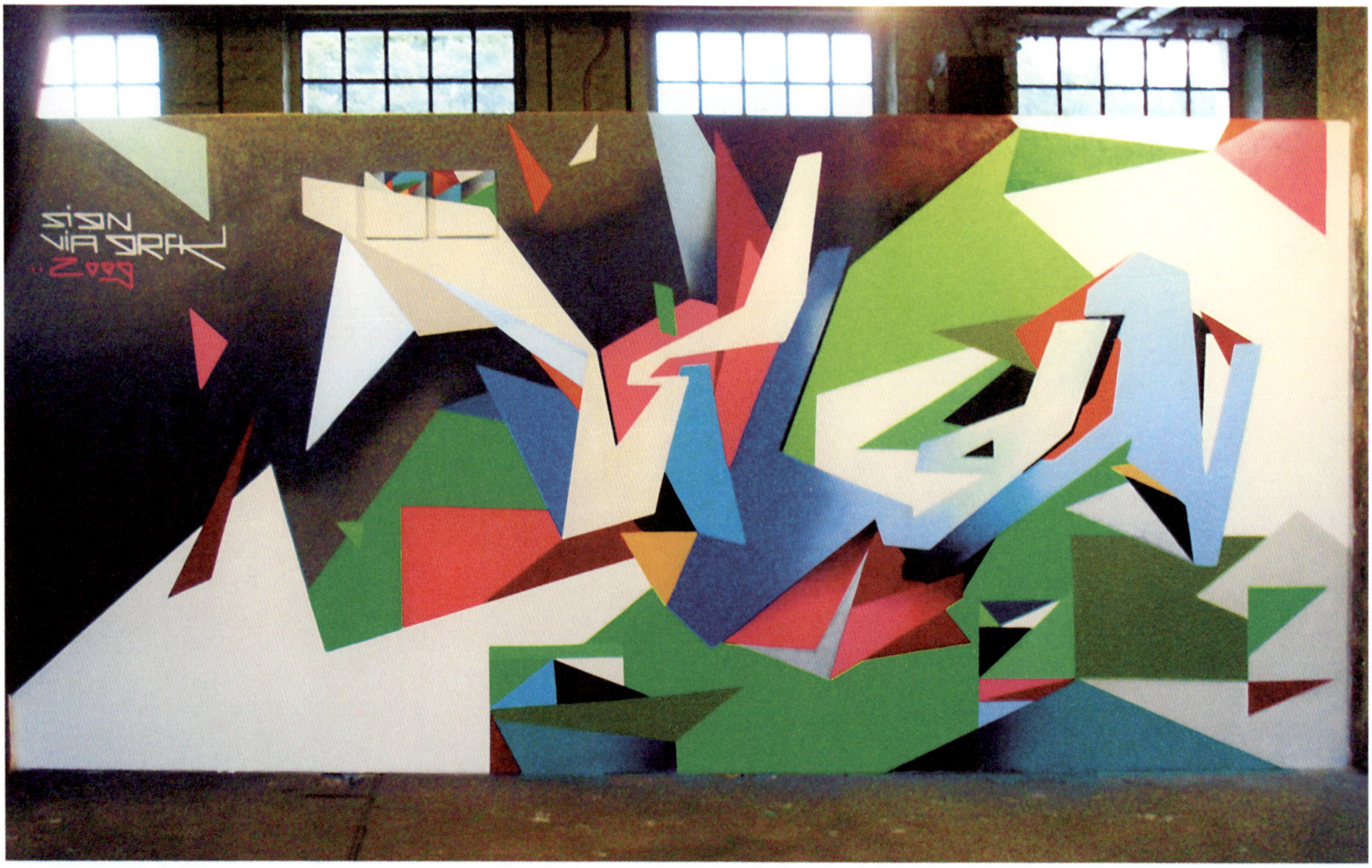

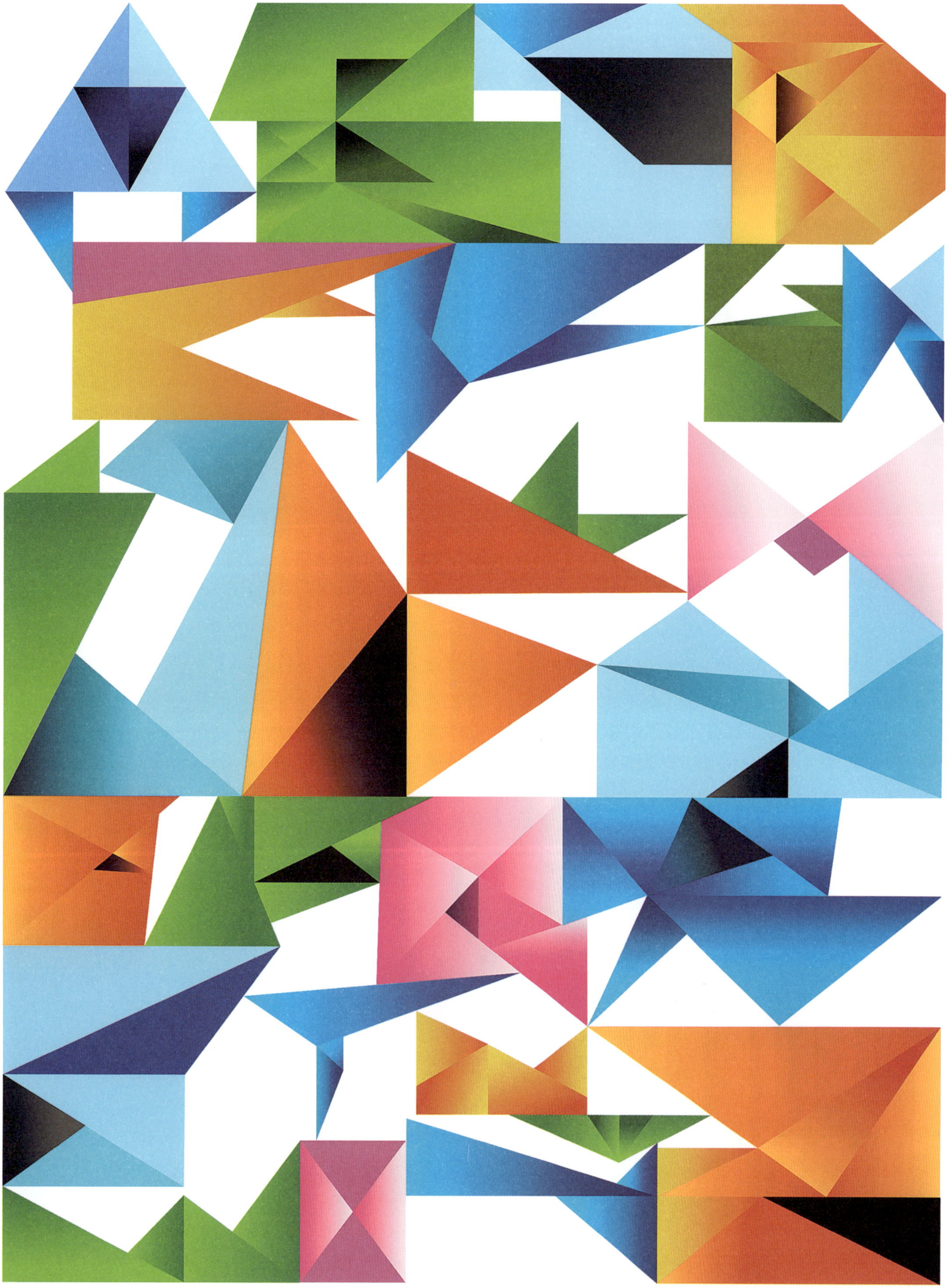

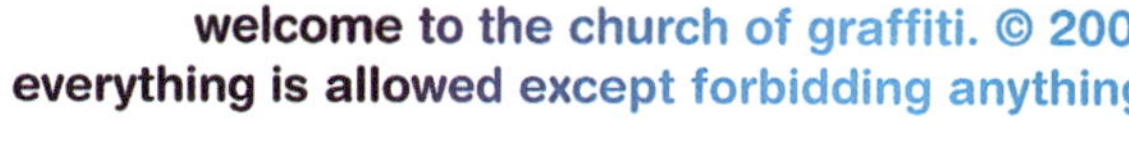

welcome to the church of graffiti. © 2009
everything is allowed except forbidding anything!

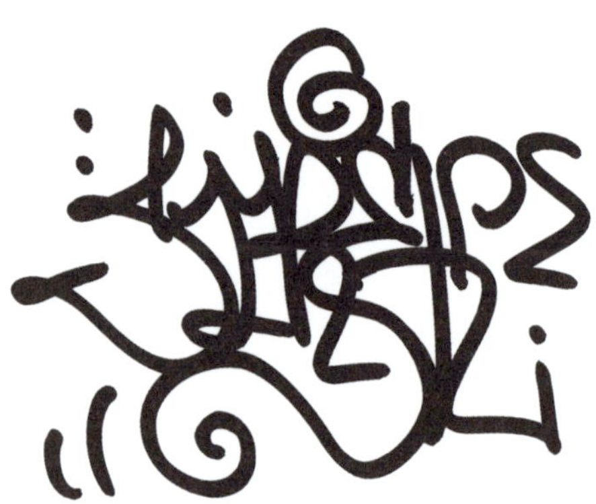

Sirek

VALLADOLID, SPAIN
Crew member of VTM
Writer since 1993–94
Favourite letter: S
www.myspace.com/supersirek

Sirek is influenced by the original New York old-school style.
His pieces are recognizable by their steady outlines, variety of
detail and abundance of colours. Creating his alphabet was like
a 'training session', he says. 'The letter "O" is a self portrait.' The
mix of freedom and discipline is what he likes most about graffiti.

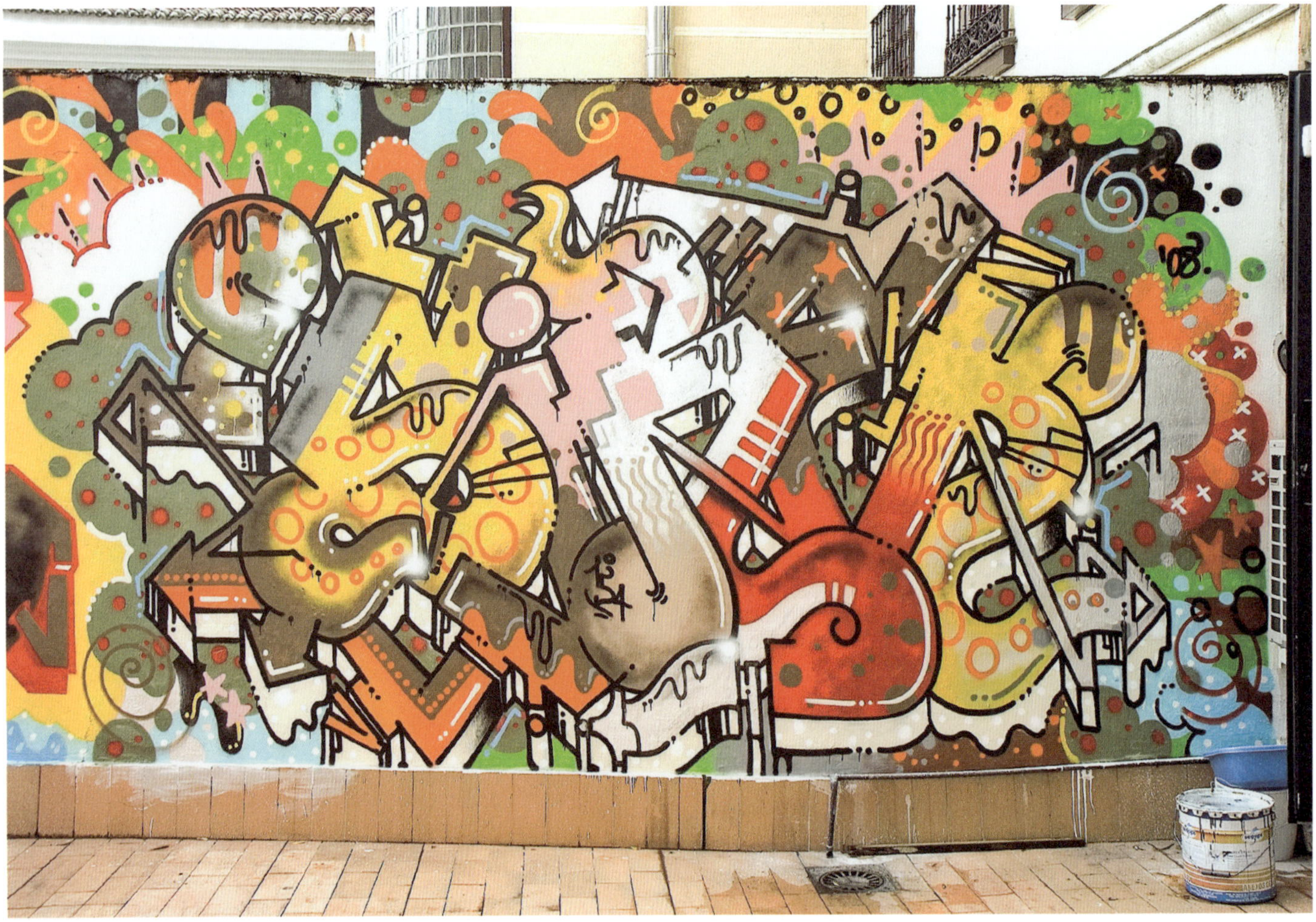

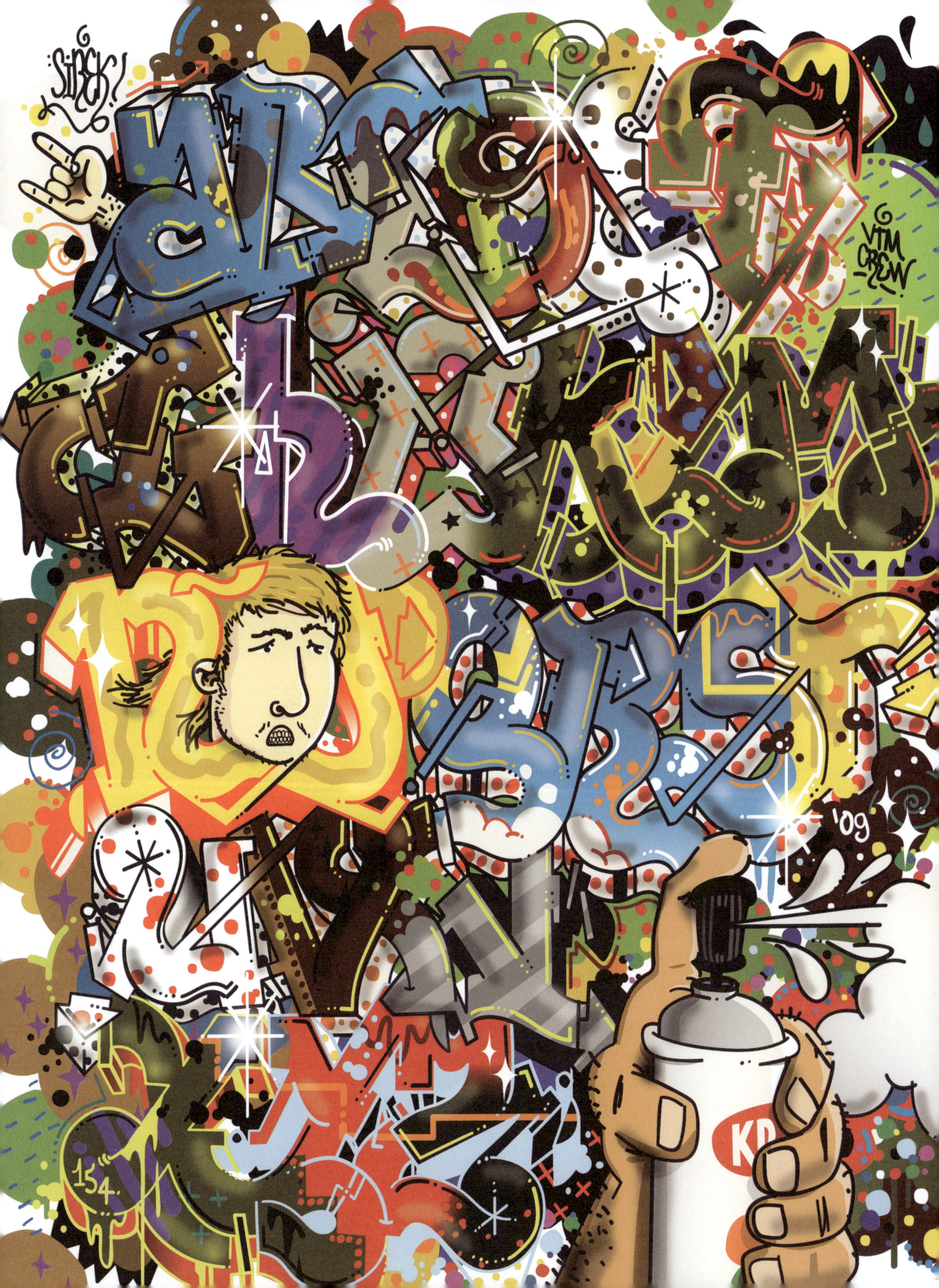

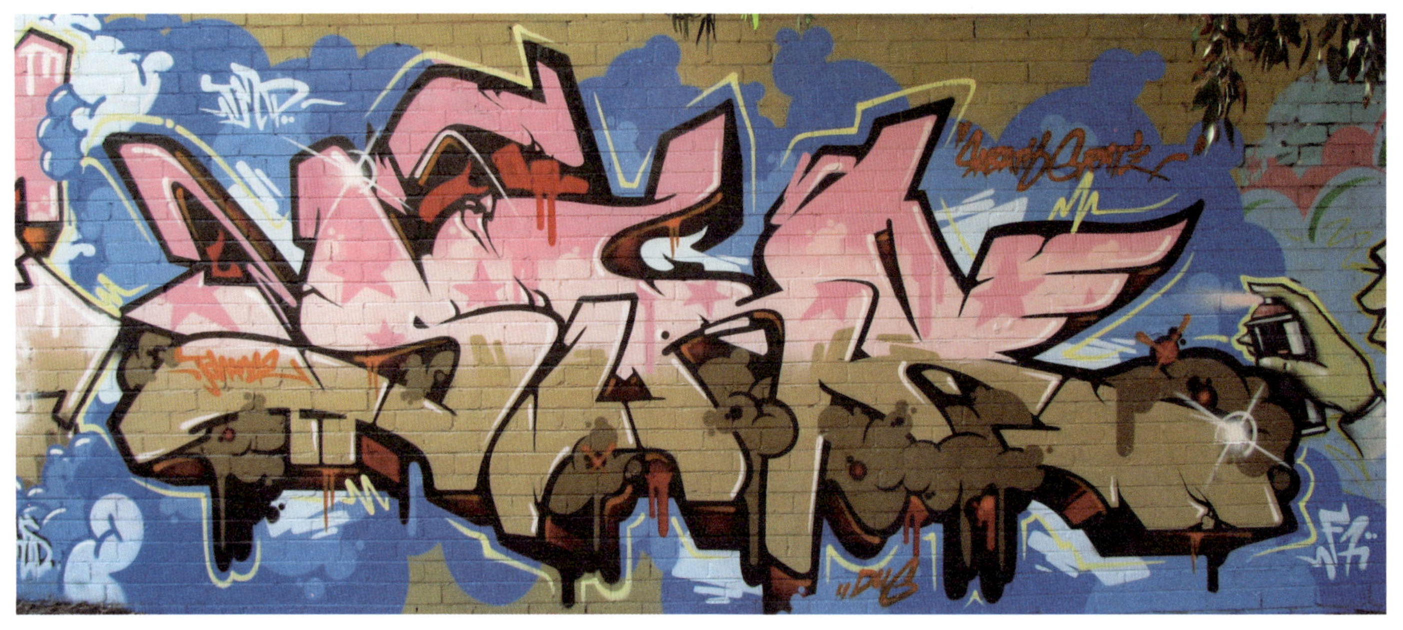

Sirum

MELBOURNE, AUSTRALIA
Crew member of F1, TMD, LBD
Writer since 1995–96
Favourite letter: S
www.komplexgraphix.com

Sirum began his graffiti career as a solo writer, producing many of his works along Melbourne's railway lines. Inspired by comic book illustration and movements such as Pop Art and Art Nouveau, Sirum's pieces are usually bold and very detailed. The idea behind his alphabet was to 'simply focus on the letters and keep the overall look clean, fresh and flowing'.

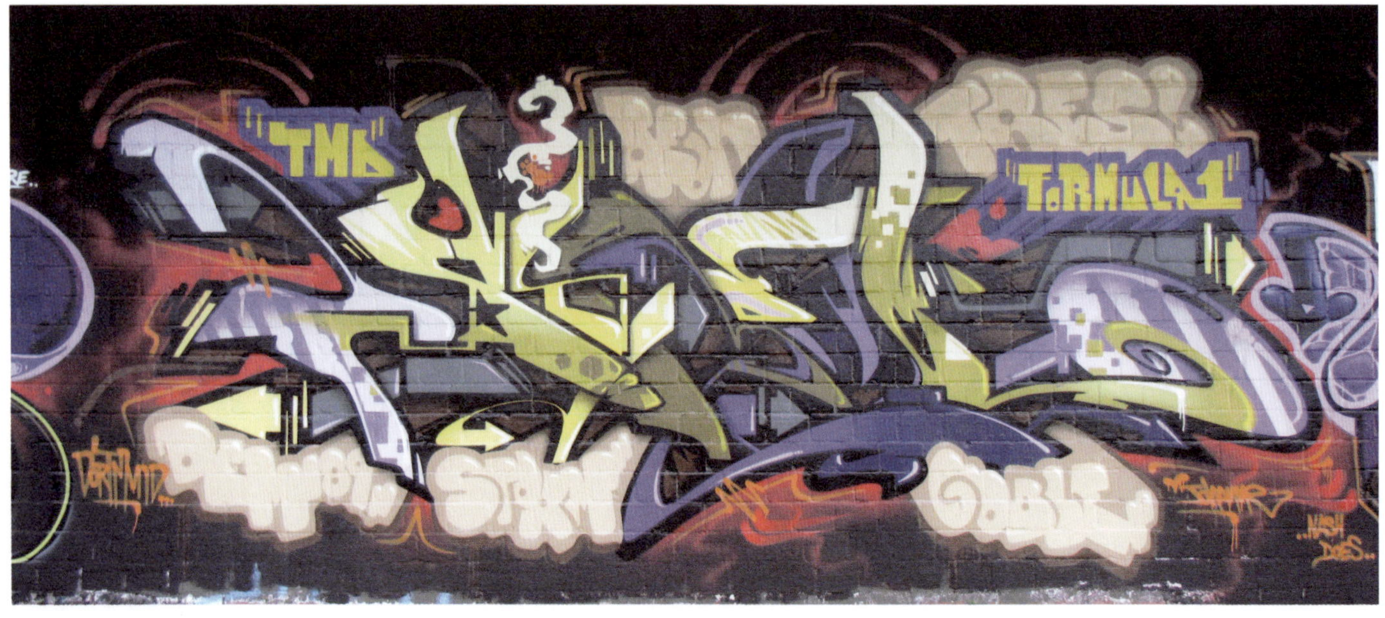

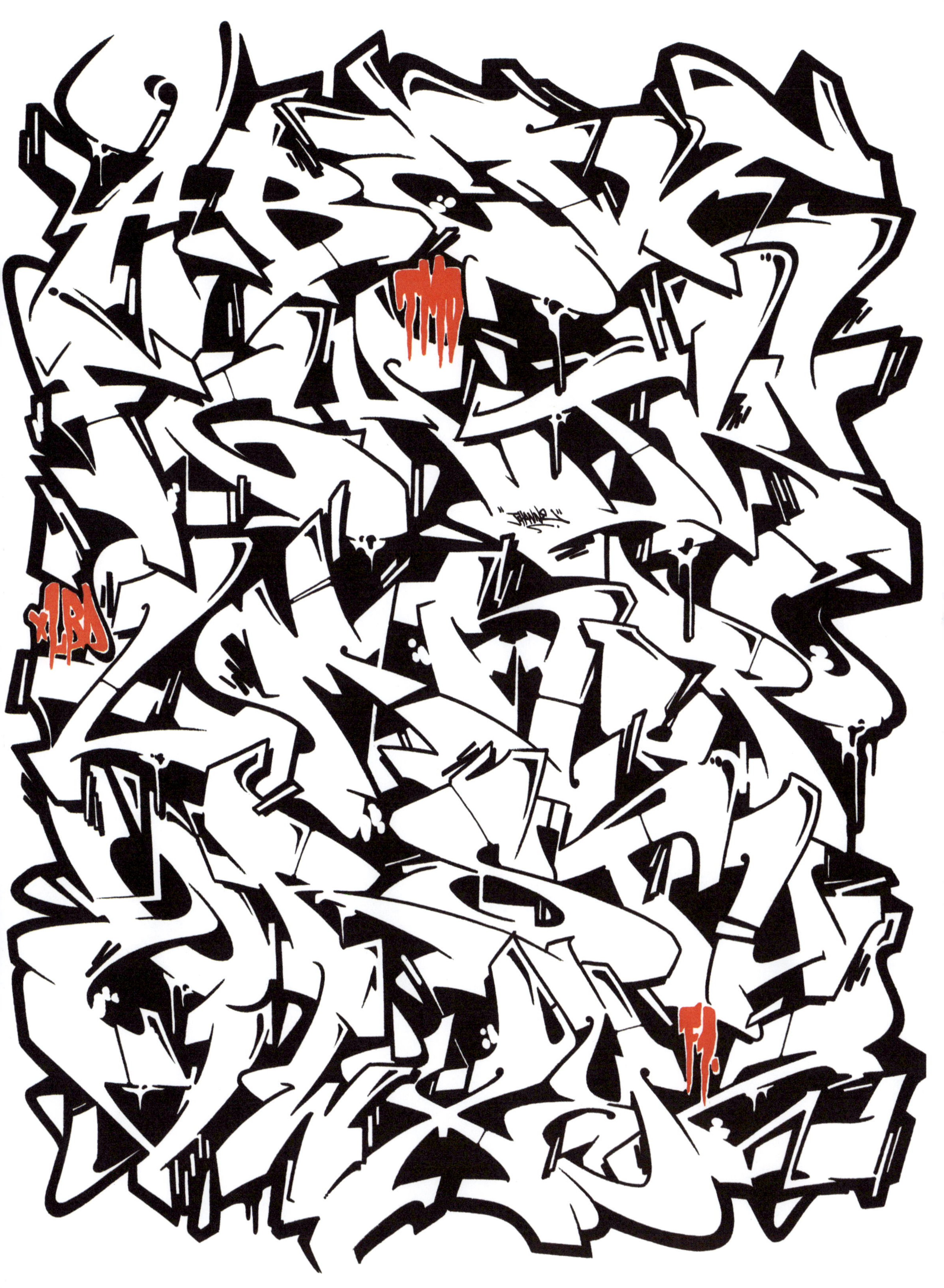

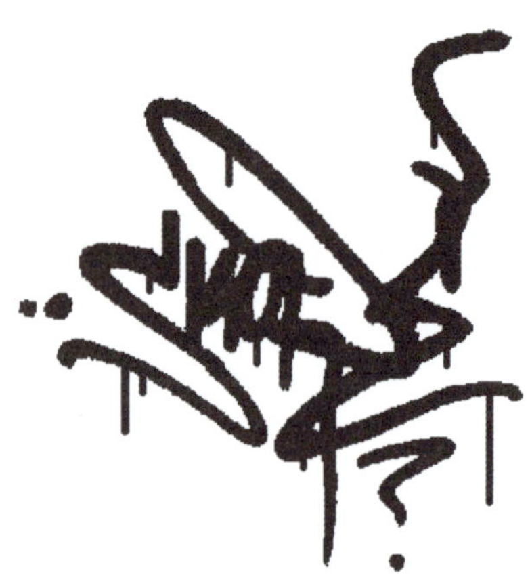

Skore

LONDON, UK
Crew member of TRC
Writer since 1984
Favourite letter: S
www.flickr.com/skoretrc

Skore is an old-school writer from London and still active. His alphabet was hand-drawn and coloured digitally. When it comes to creating a good style, Skore says: 'It takes a perfect balance of five words – flow, funk, flap, fire and flourish. The flow is the way a piece works from left to right, the funk is the flavour, the flap is the human touch, the fire is the passion and the flourish is all those extra bits, the eye-catchers.'

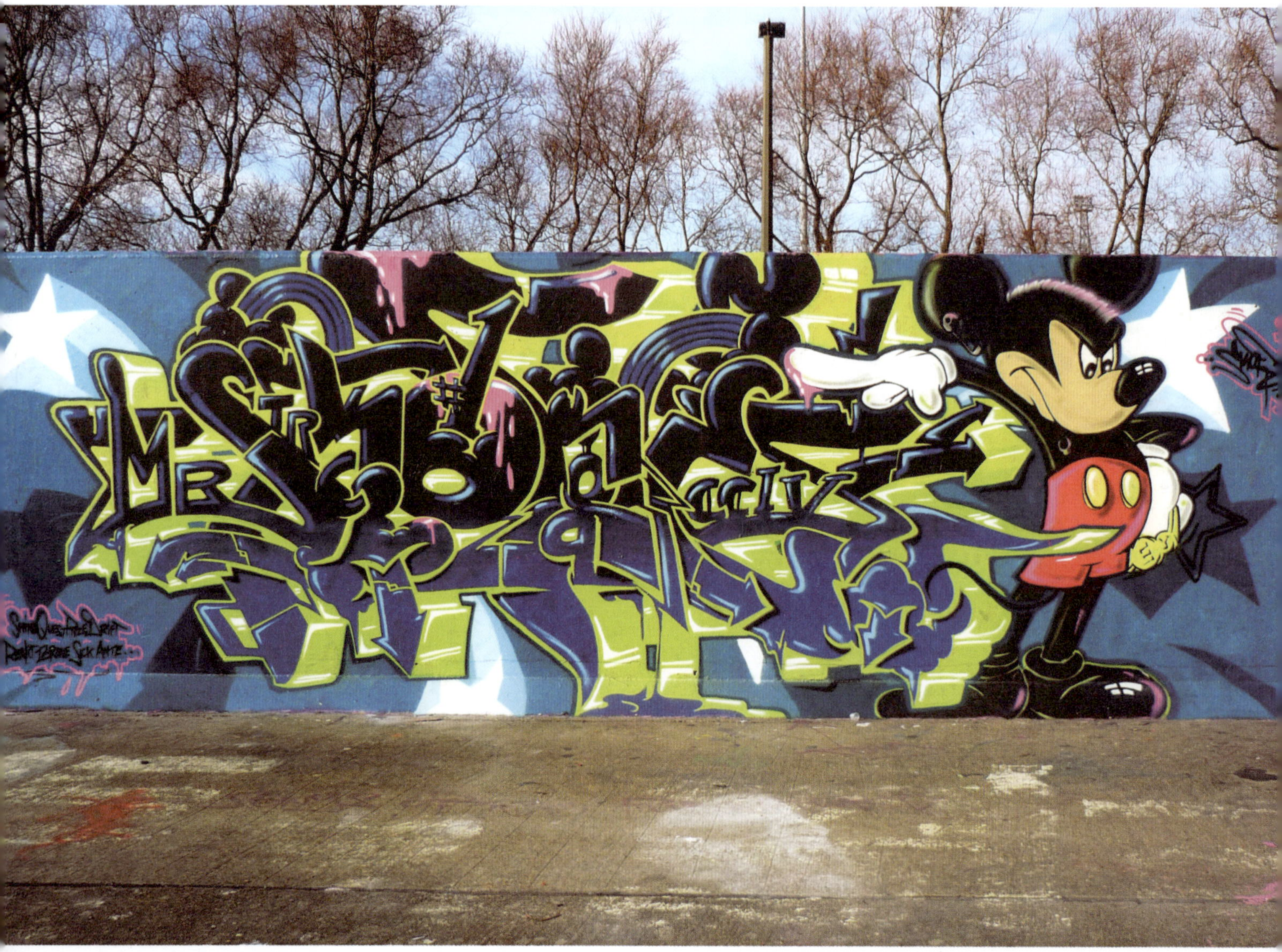

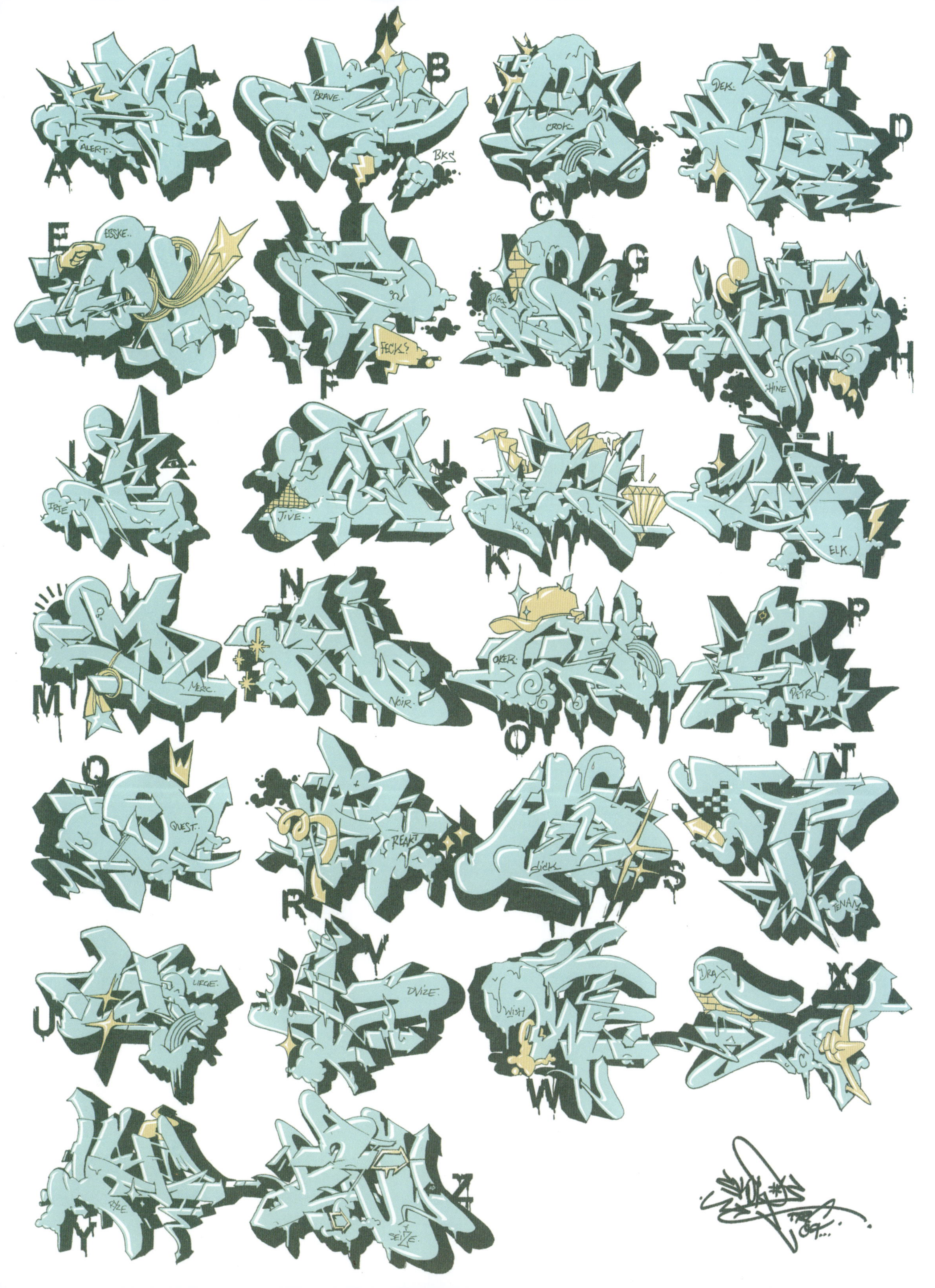

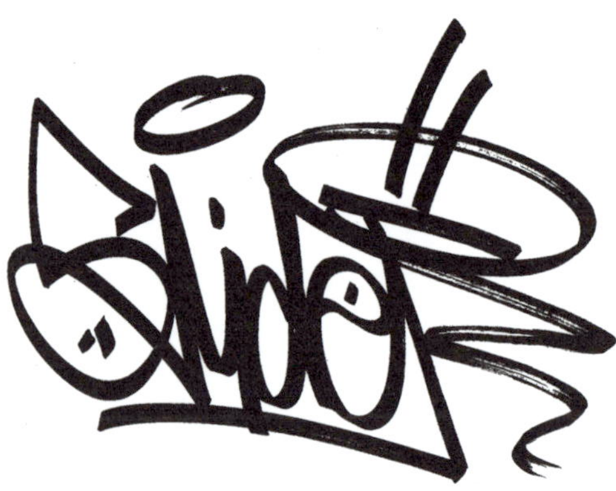

Slider

DRESDEN, GERMANY
Crew member of Bandits, Macia
Writer since 1994
Favourite letter: S
www.bandits-dresden.de

Slider is the founder of Bandits and the main force behind the crew. Over the years he has pushed his style through various training techniques: one is everyday tagging; another, painting nothing but straight lines for a whole year. Slider also tests a vast number of colour combinations without neglecting the legibility of his letters. Passion is what he appreciates most about graffiti.

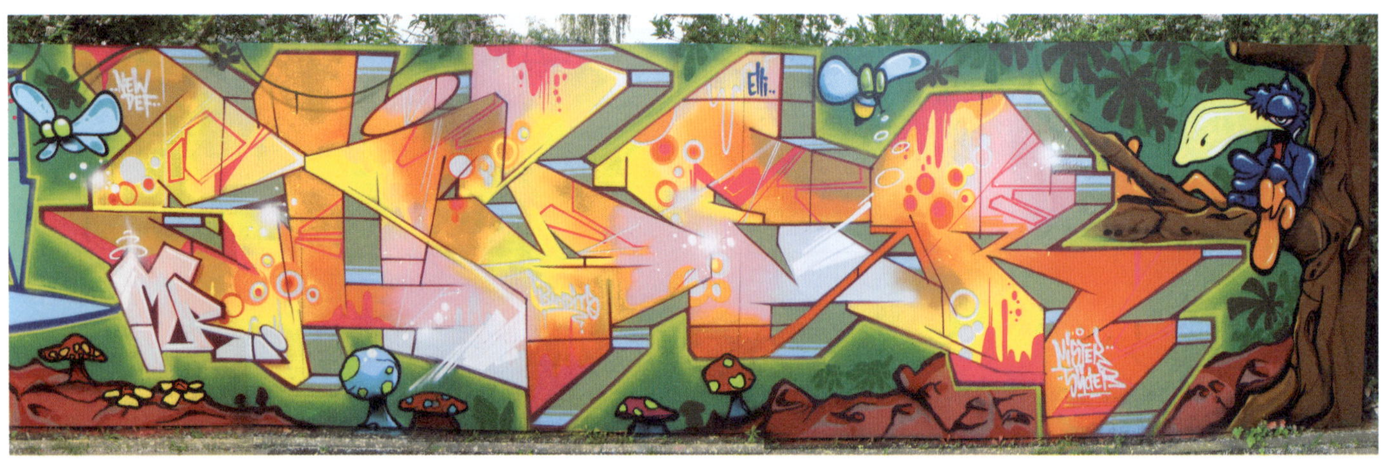

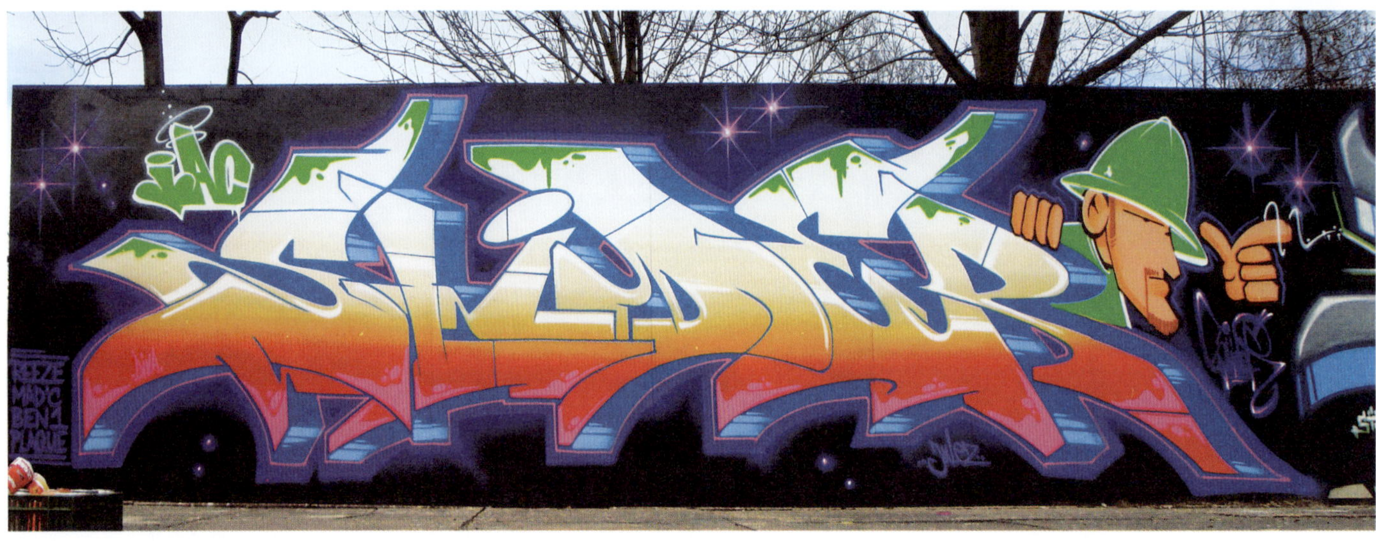

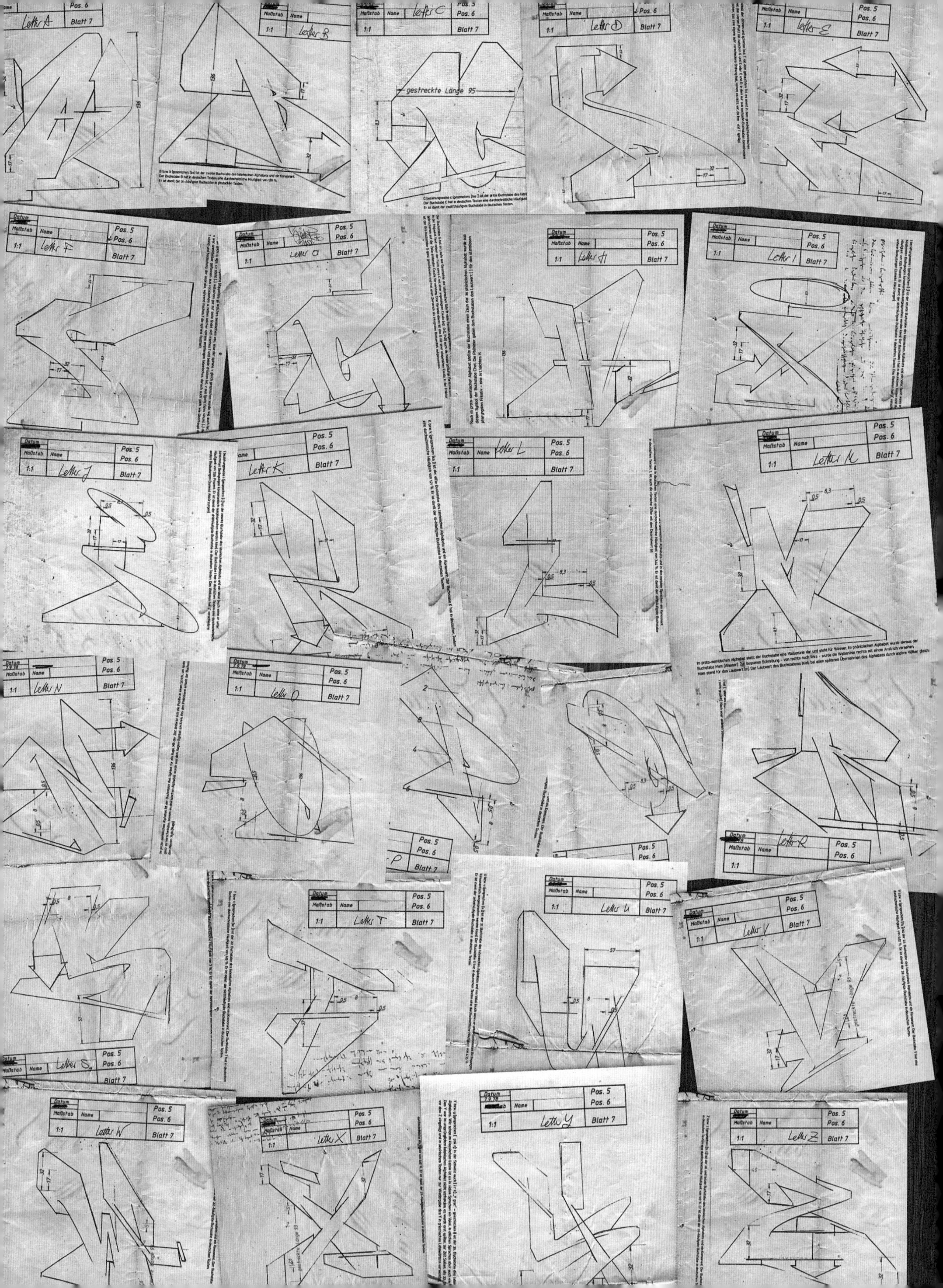

Letter A
Letter B
Letter C
Letter D
Letter E
Letter F
Letter G
Letter H
Letter I
Letter J
Letter K
Letter L
Letter M
Letter N
Letter O
Letter P
Letter R
Letter S
Letter T
Letter U
Letter V
Letter W
Letter X
Letter Y
Letter Z
gestreckte Länge 95
Datum
Maßstab
Name
Pos. 5
Pos. 6
Blatt 7
1:1

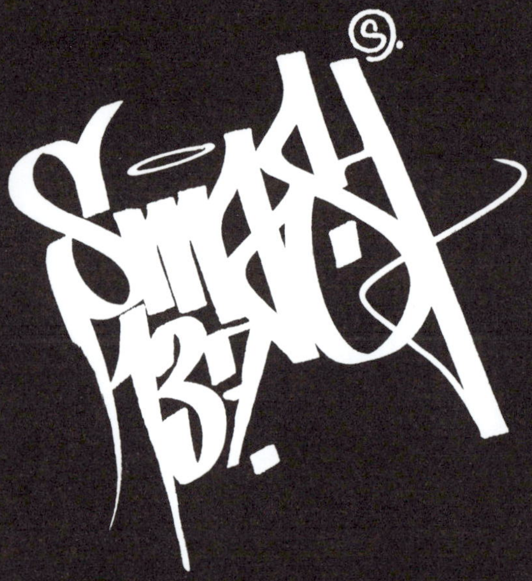

Smash137
BASEL, SWITZERLAND
Writer since 1990
Favourite letter: S
www.smash137.com

Smash137 has made a considerable mark on the graffiti scene over the past decade. He continually pushes his style and has successfully mastered the transition from the streets to the art gallery without losing the energy of his outdoor work. His graffiti is solely based on letters, which he describes as 'swinging, attractive, legible, proud and honest'. He says of his alphabet: 'I agree that the single letter has to work by itself, but writing is about words and the art of making individual letters work together in harmony.'

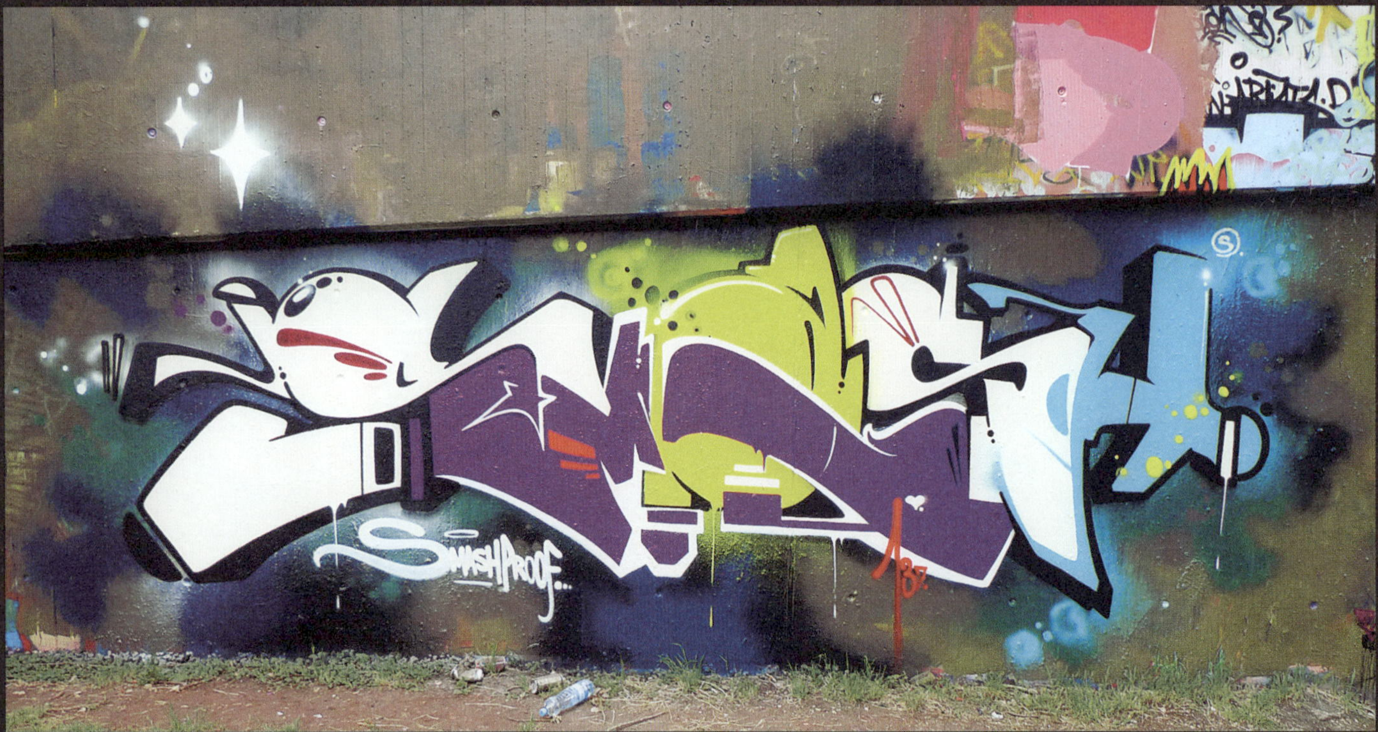

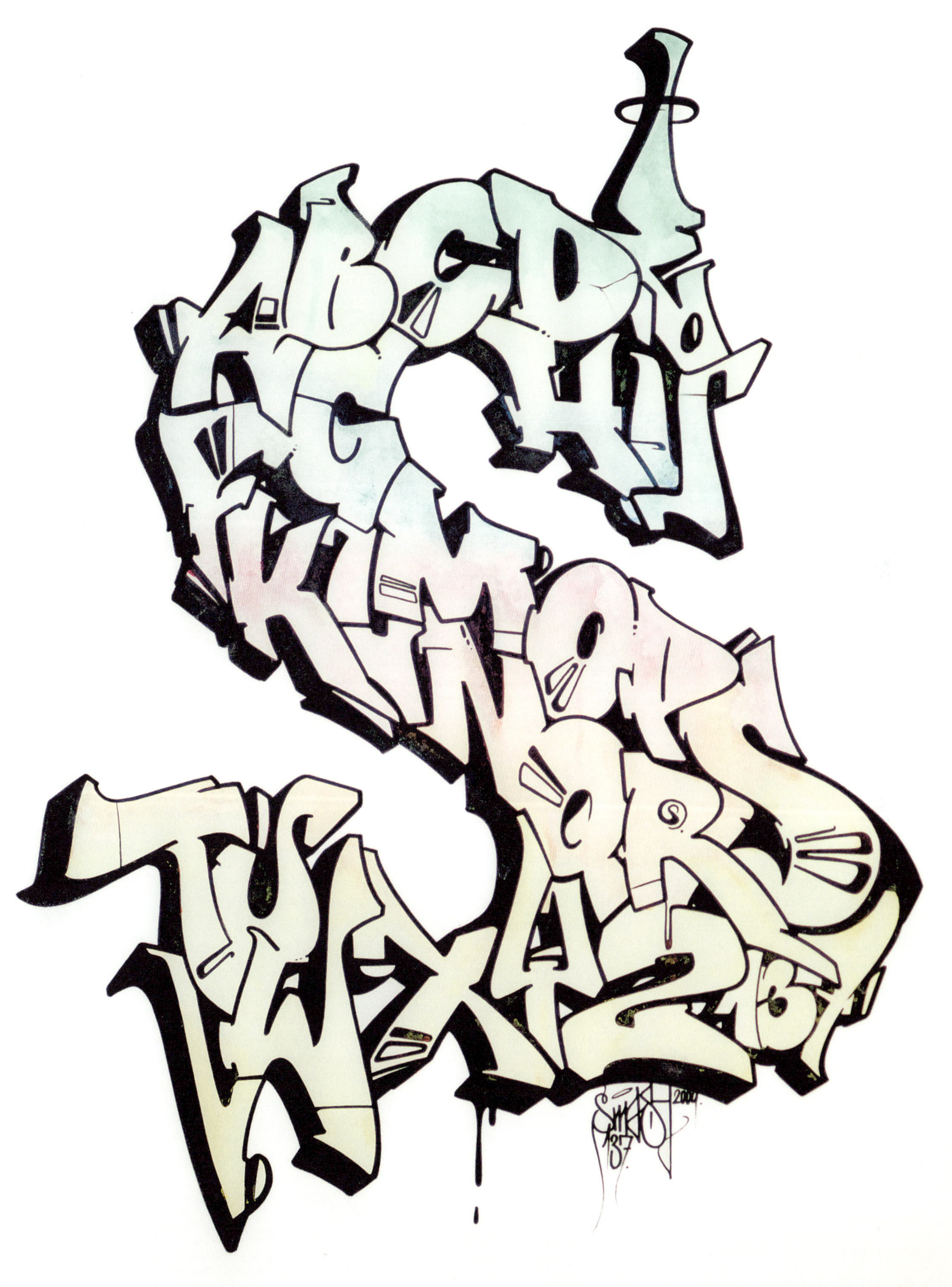

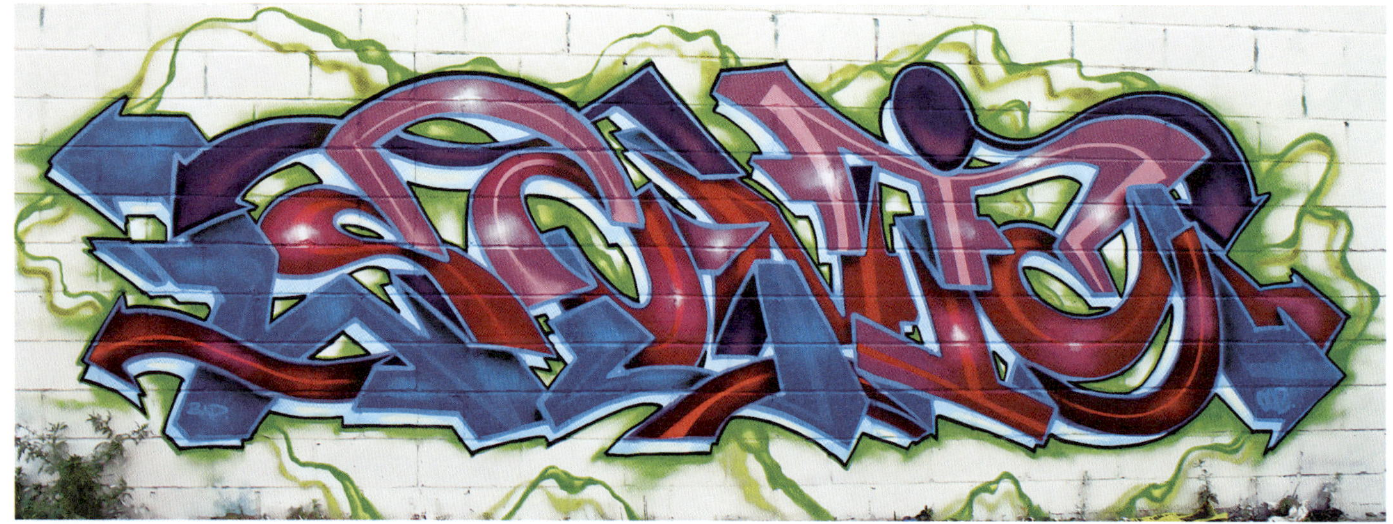

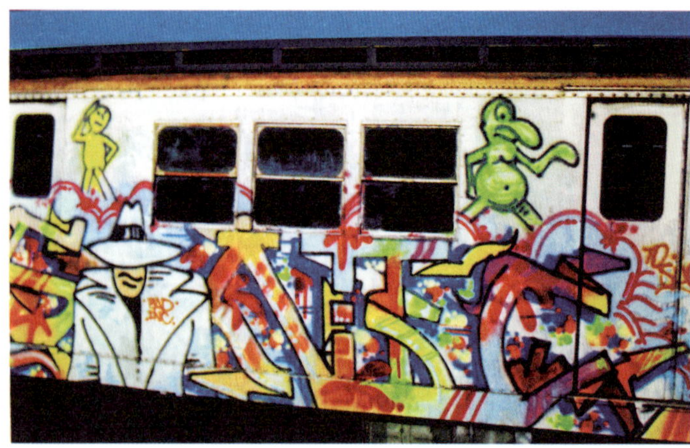

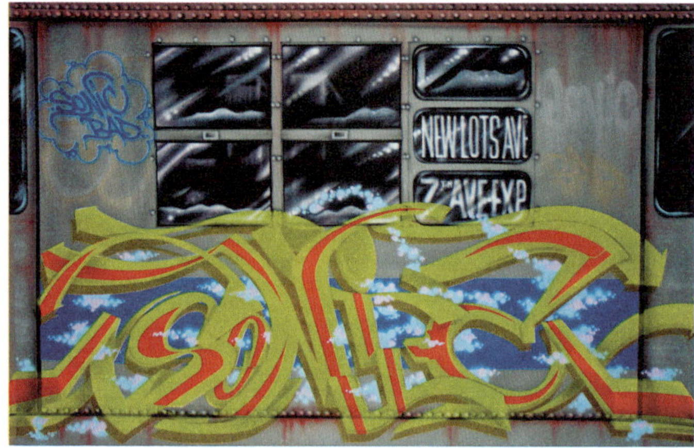

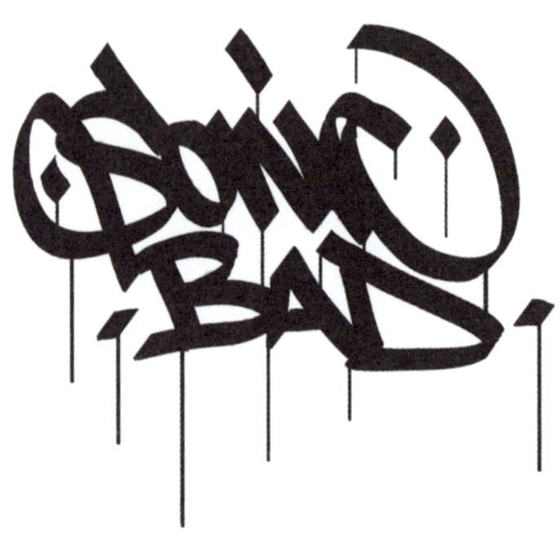

Sonic

NEW YORK CITY, USA

Crew member of BAD, MAC
Writer since 1973
Favourite letters: S, O, N, I, C
www.myspace.com/sonicbad

Sonic is one of New York's old-school writers. He has never stopped developing his style, which he describes as 'original, unique and folding letters'. He based his alphabet on the folding letters he used in the early 1970s, saying: 'The letters are thirty-six years of style made simple.' Some of Sonic's best memories are graffiti ones: 'Memories of running the underground subway system in NYC, spray-painting trains until the early morning light, trying not to get killed by passing trains and the electrified third rail track. Staying ahead of the vandal squad, all while making masterpieces. This is and always will be the best thing about graffiti. It's mine and no one can take it from me!'

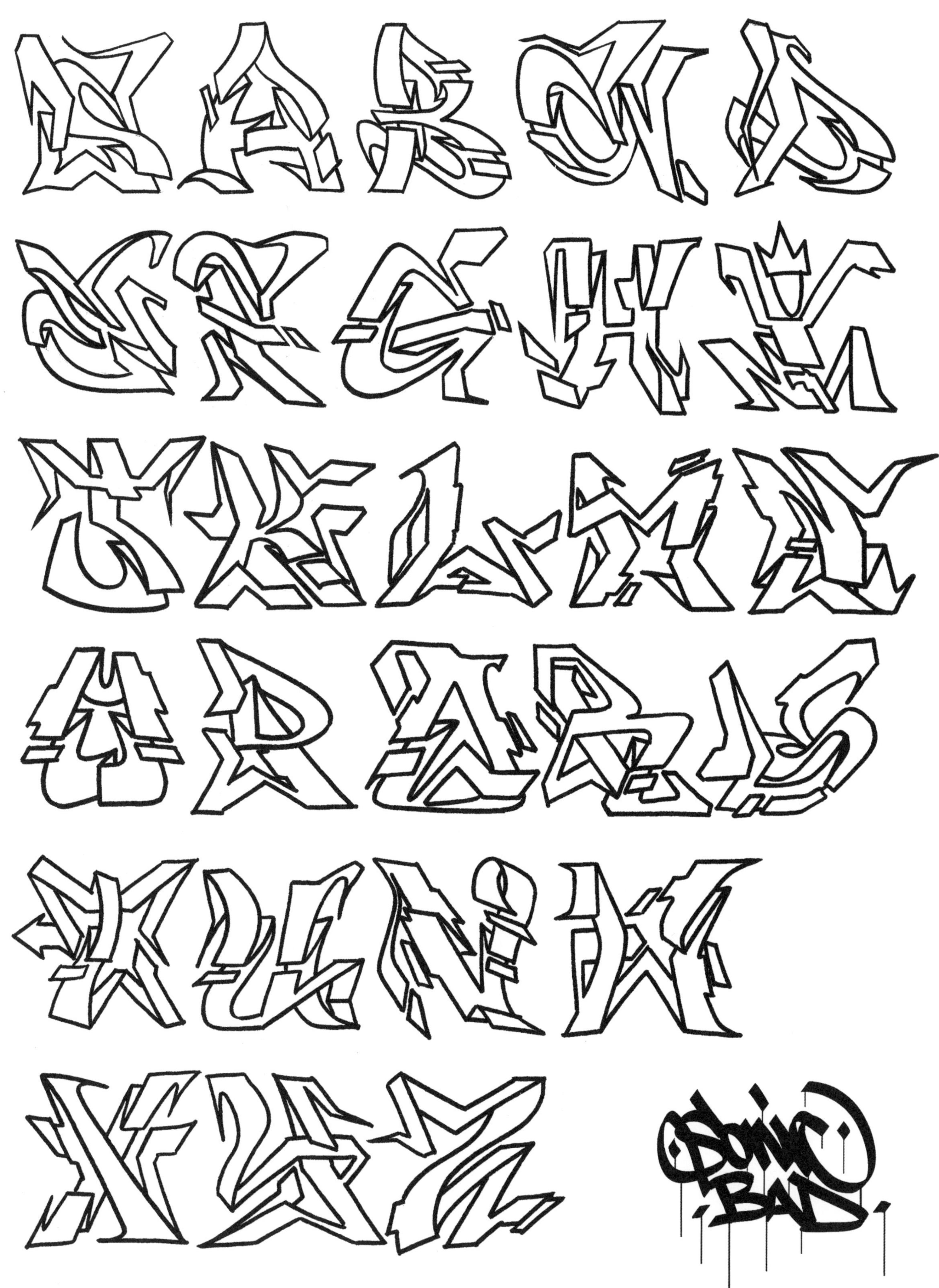

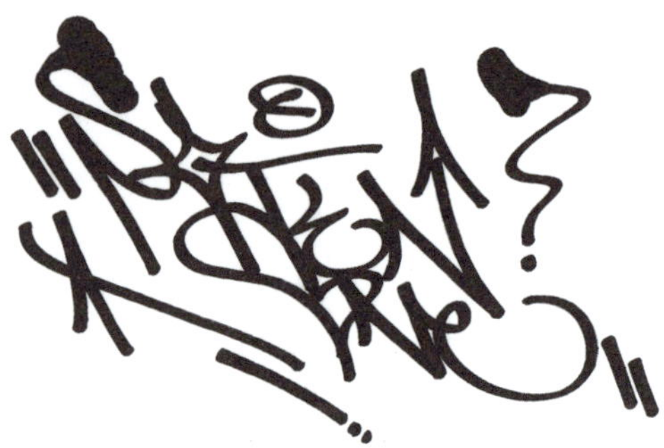

Soten

COPENHAGEN, DENMARK
Crew member of SSH
Writer since 1997–98
Favourite letter: S
www.ilovegraffiti.de/soten

Soten belongs to Copenhagen's active new generation of writers. He travels a lot and leaves his name on walls and trains all over Europe. His pieces are distinguished by dynamic letters, a vivid choice of colours and an eye for quality. A good piece has 'aggressive letters, swing and something that makes it stand out from the wall', Soten says. Nothing else matters when you paint – this is what he appreciates most about graffiti.

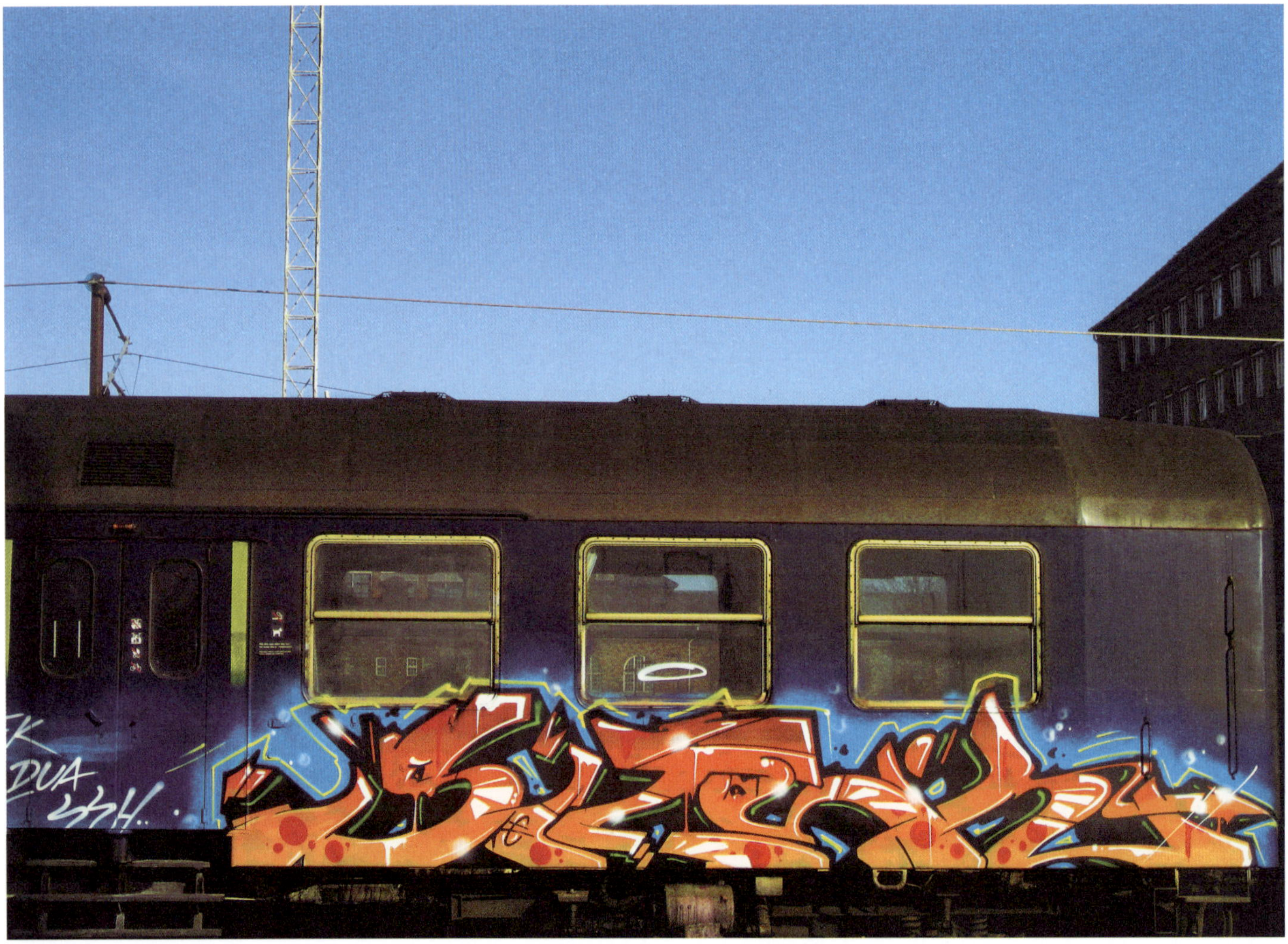

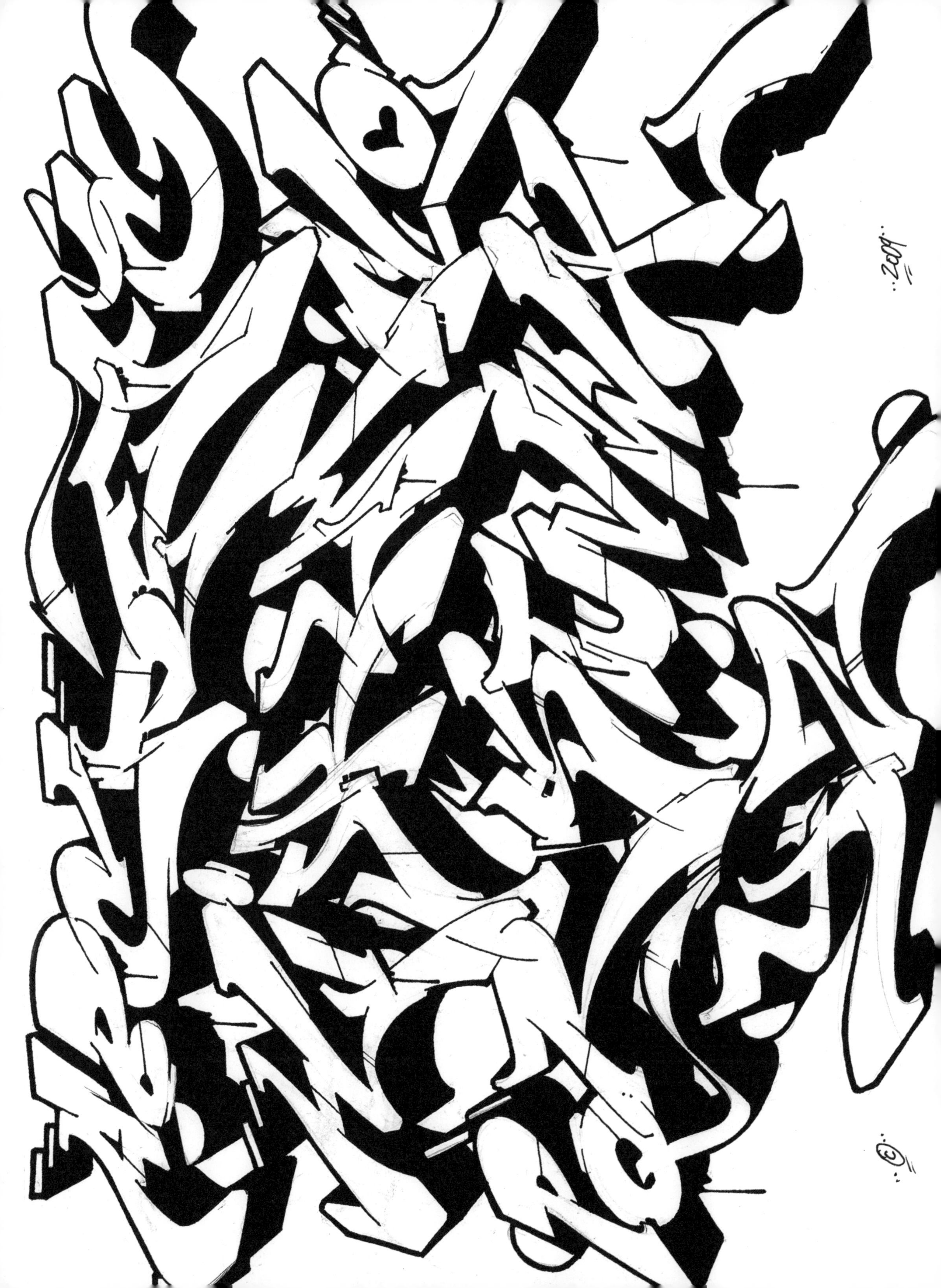

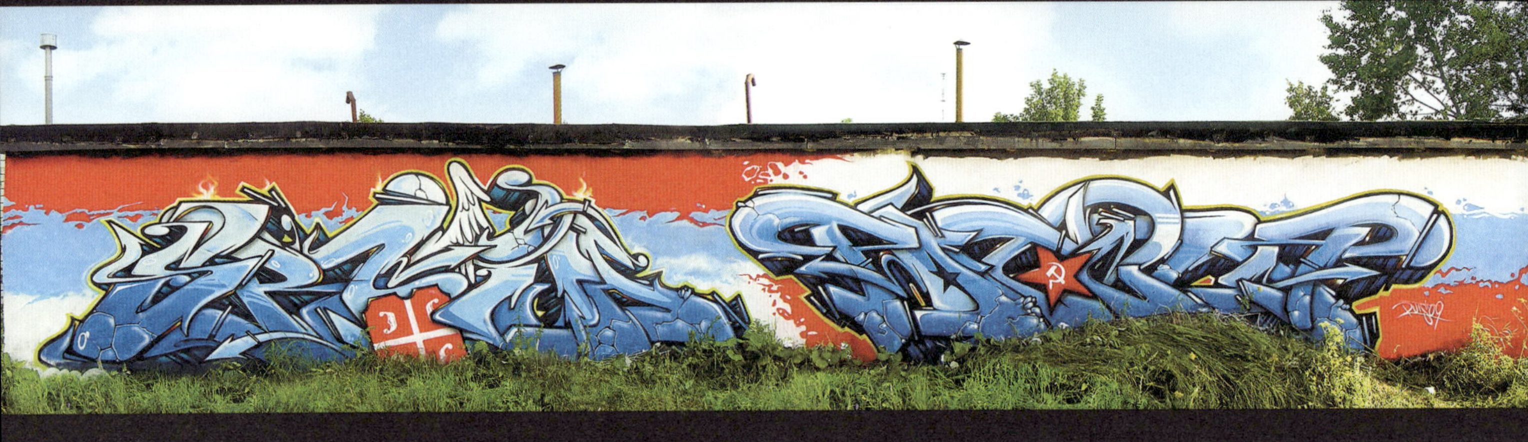

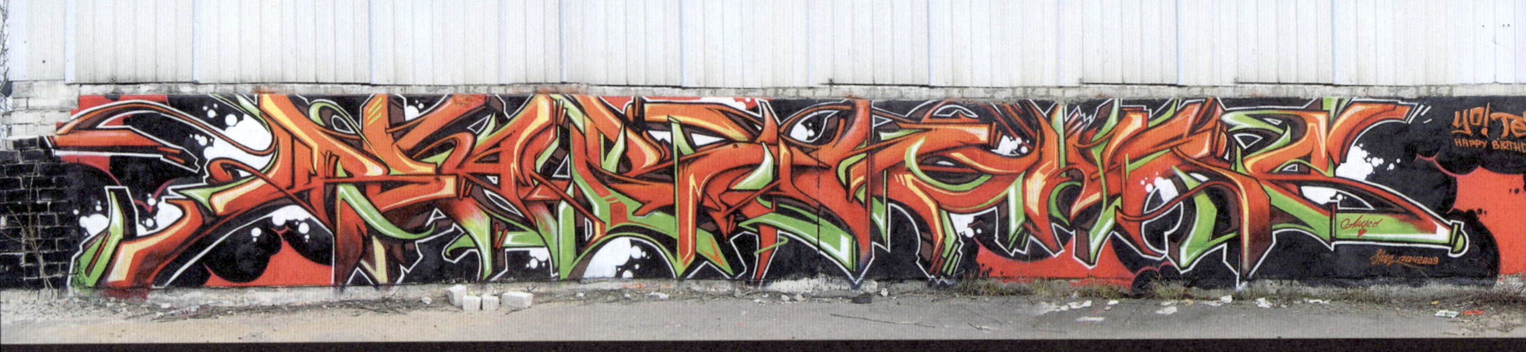

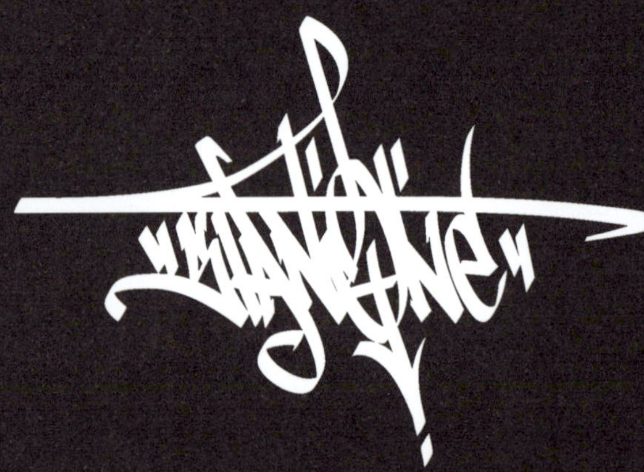

Stan

NIZHNIY NOVGOROD, RUSSIA

Crew member of 4R, Urban Roots

As a Russian writer, Stan wanted to represent his native language in this book, so he designed a Cyrillic alphabet. Some of the letters resemble letter forms in the Latin alphabet, but Cyrillic letters

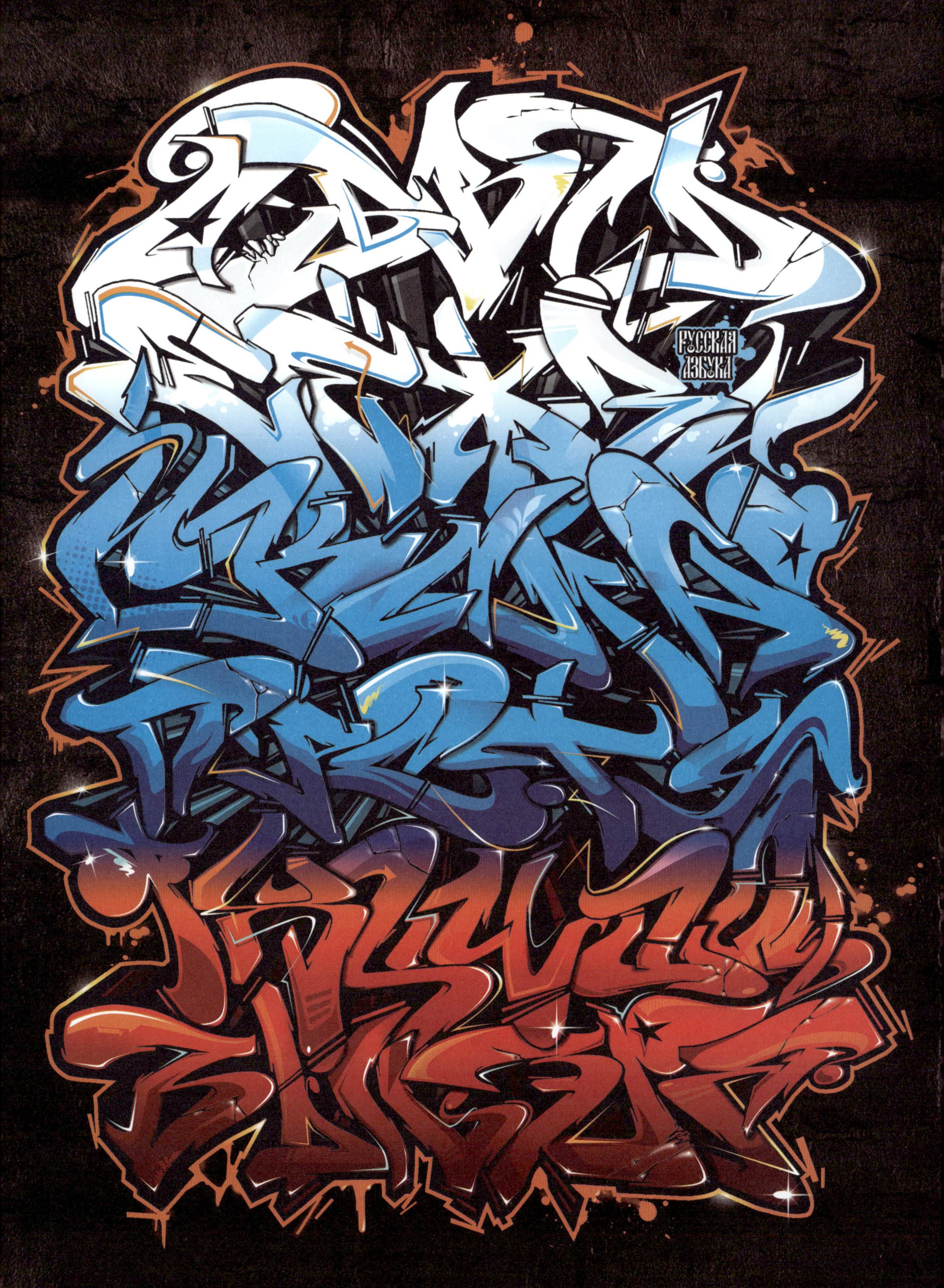
РУССКАЯ
АЗБУКА

Staynice

BREDA, NETHERLANDS

Writers since 1997
Favourite letter: 'All of them'
www.staynice.nl

Staynice is a successful design team which focuses on graphics and typography. The members have their roots in graffiti and are still active on walls. Their alphabet was designed digitally like a font. With graffiti they create something that didn't exist before, which is what they like best about the culture.

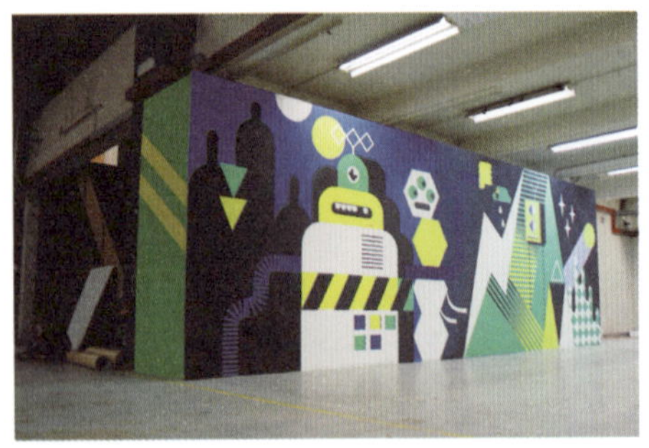
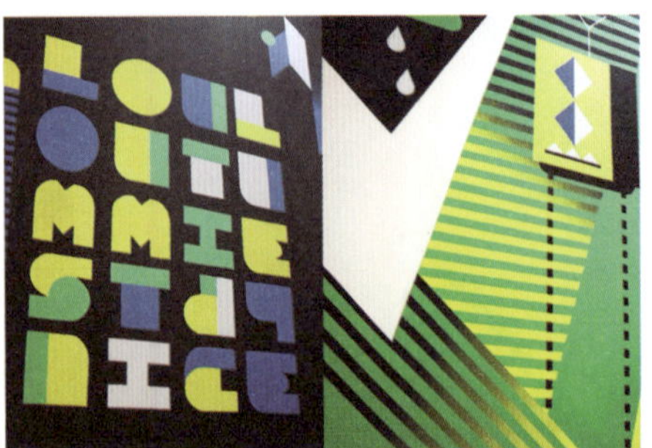
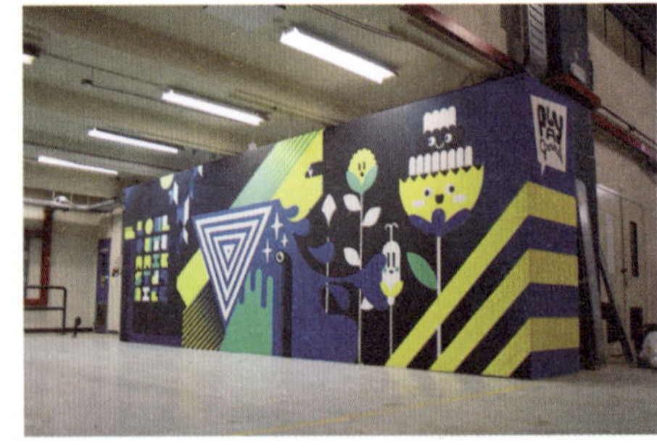
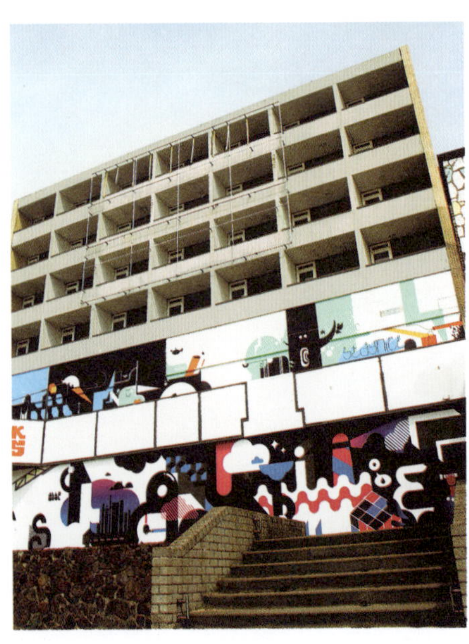
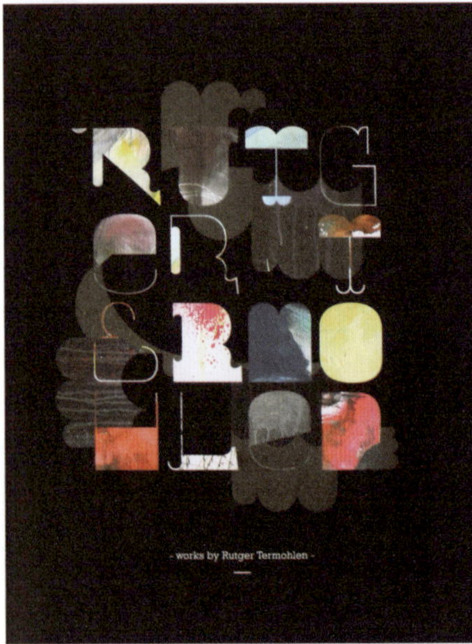

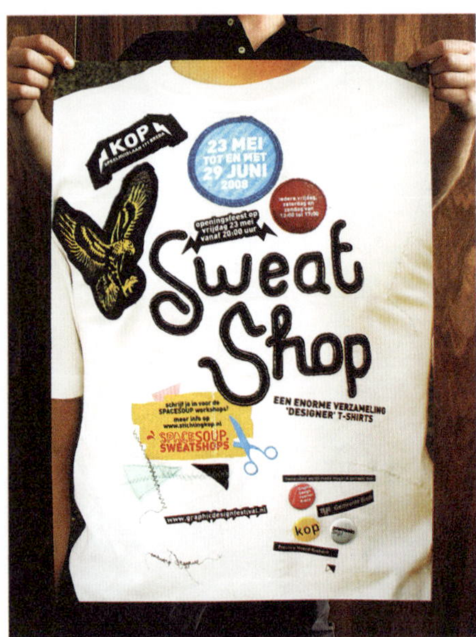

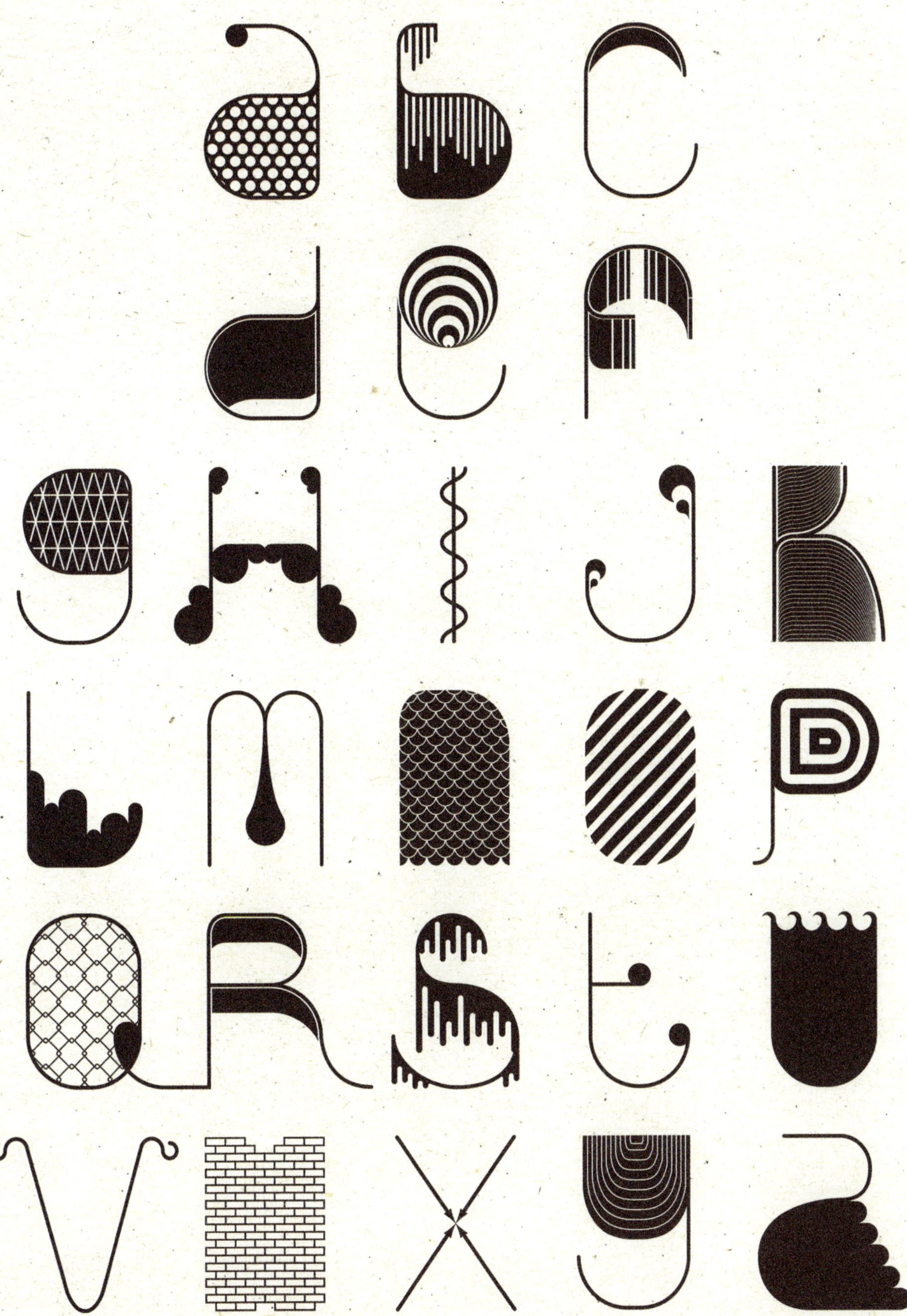
staynice

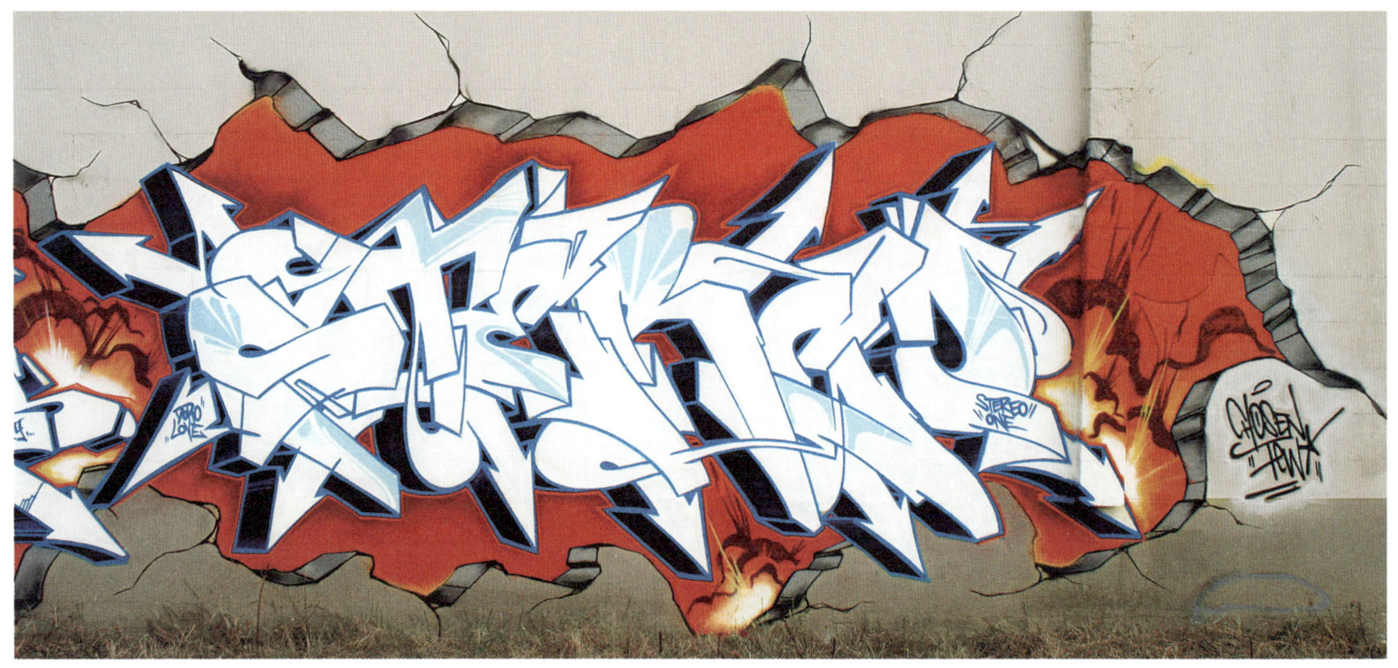

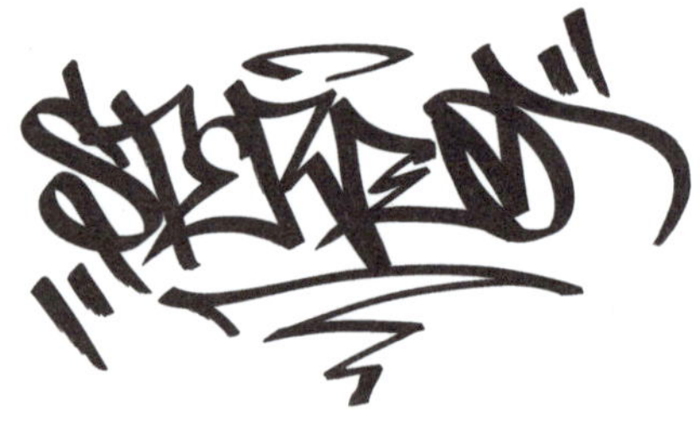

Stereo
HAMBURG, GERMANY
Crew member of Chosen Few, BSE
Writer since 1991
Favourite letter: E
www.funkjood.com

Sketching was Stereo's introduction to graffiti, but he soon progressed to a variety of disciplines – tagging, bombing and piecing. His pieces are classic and diverse. 'A good piece has to be well proportioned,' he says. 'It needs swing in the single letters and a fresh flow throughout the whole piece.' Stereo associates graffiti with many things, including 'travel, watching your own and others' progress, and having a good time with some of your closest friends.'

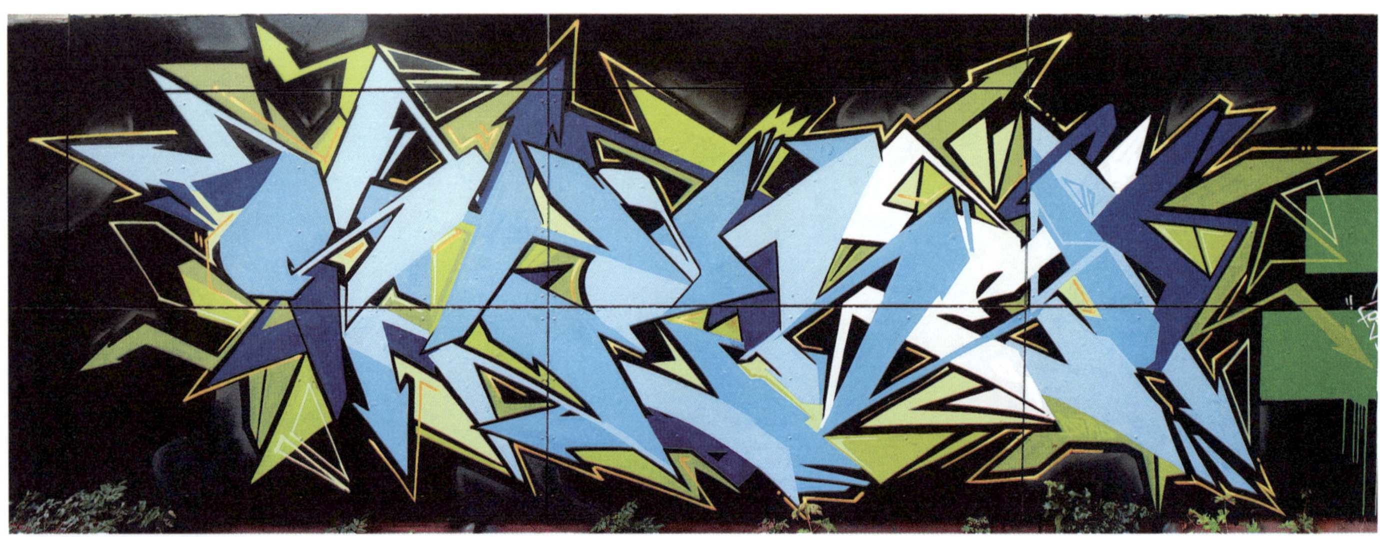

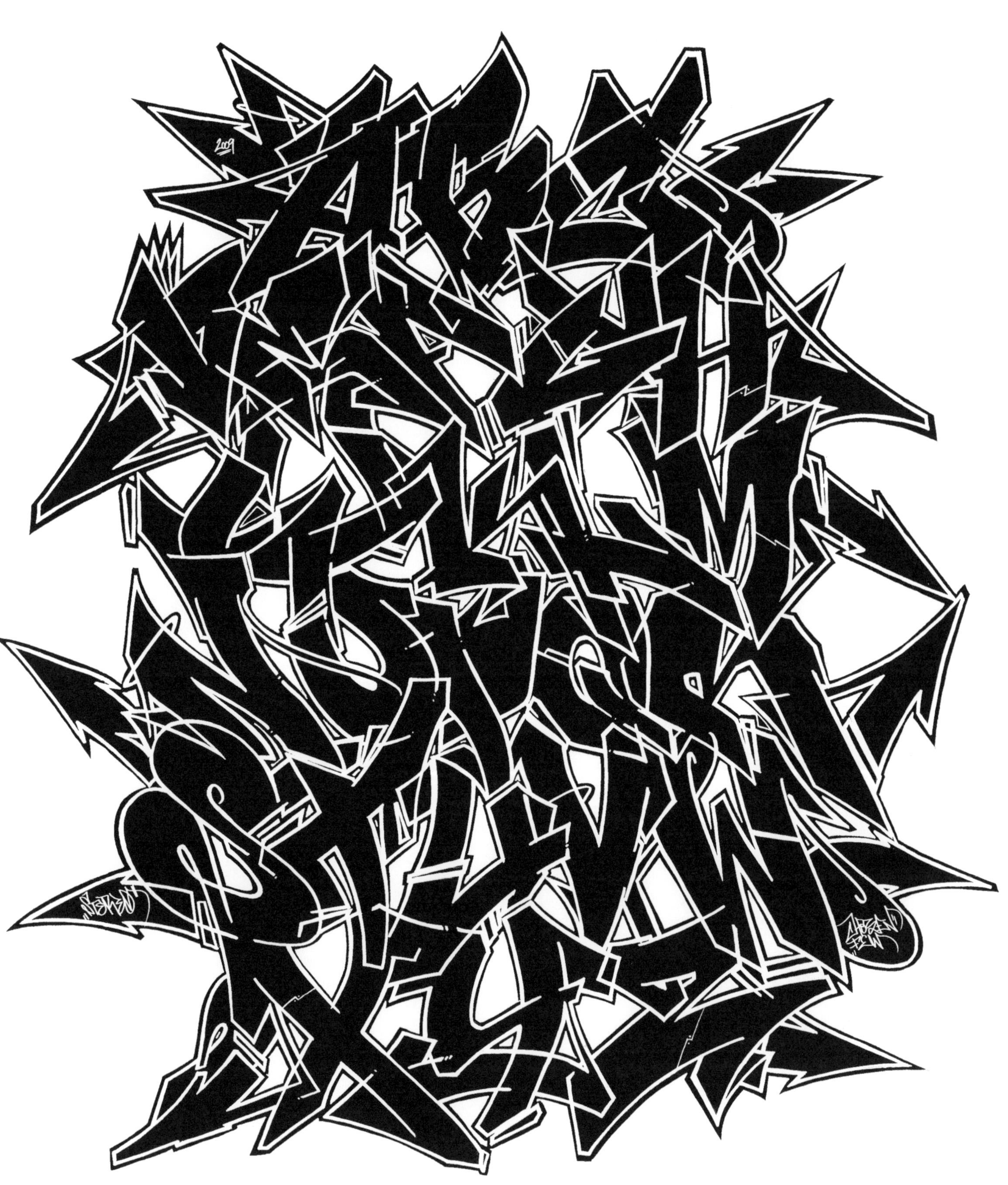

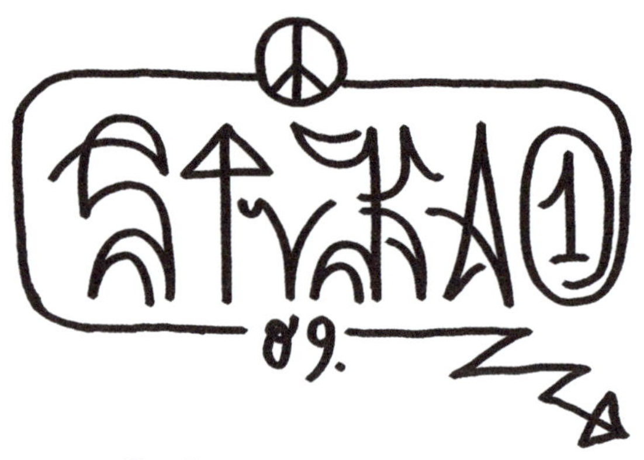

Stuka

BRAUNSCHWEIG, GERMANY
Crew member of BSC, BürolBüro, ASP, ES
Writer since 1991
Favourite letter: S
www.stukabazooka.com

Stuka is well known for his letter forms. To get his alphabet done
he needed a lot of coffee and cigarettes, good music, fun, pigment
ink, a ballpoint pen, marker, watercolour paint, potato prints,
paper, a computer and a pair of tiger/leopard/zebra-print leggings.
He describes the resulting style as 'intergalactic poptastic soft ice
cream'. He values the friendships he has made through graffiti
above all.

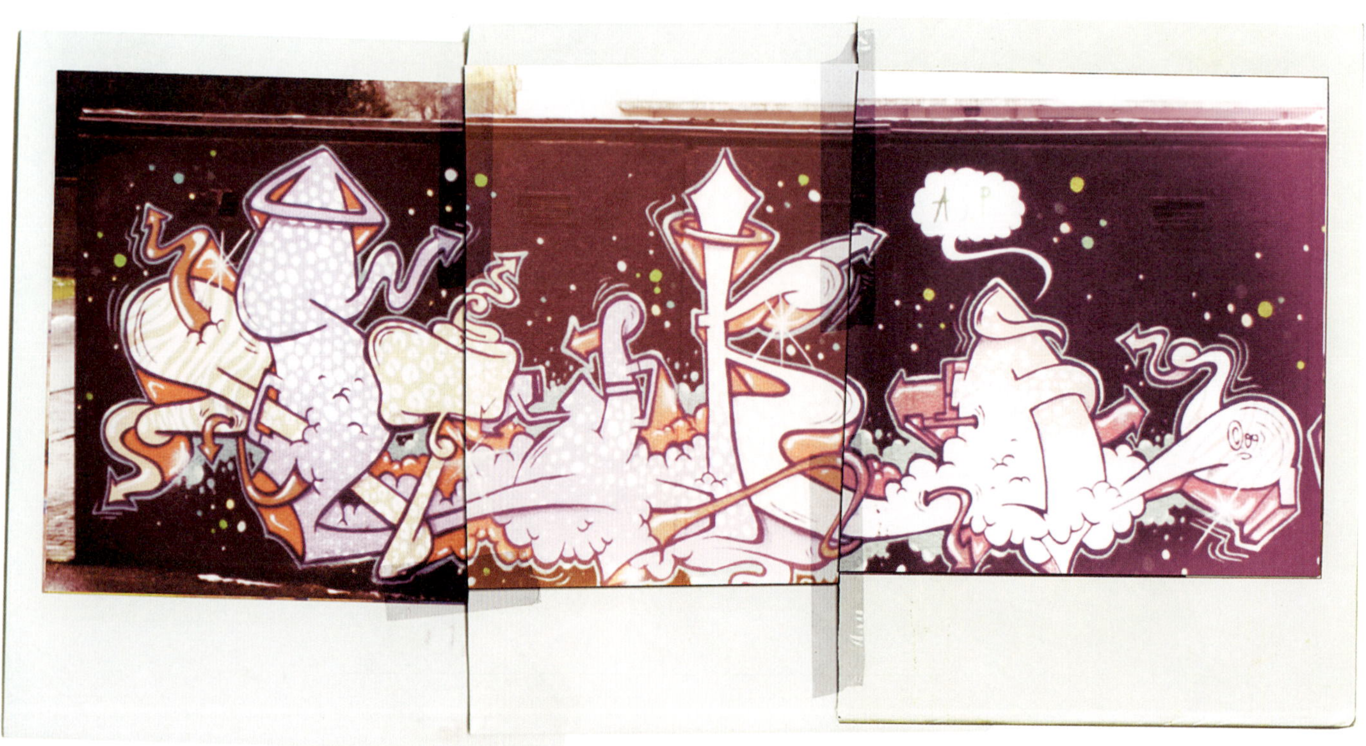

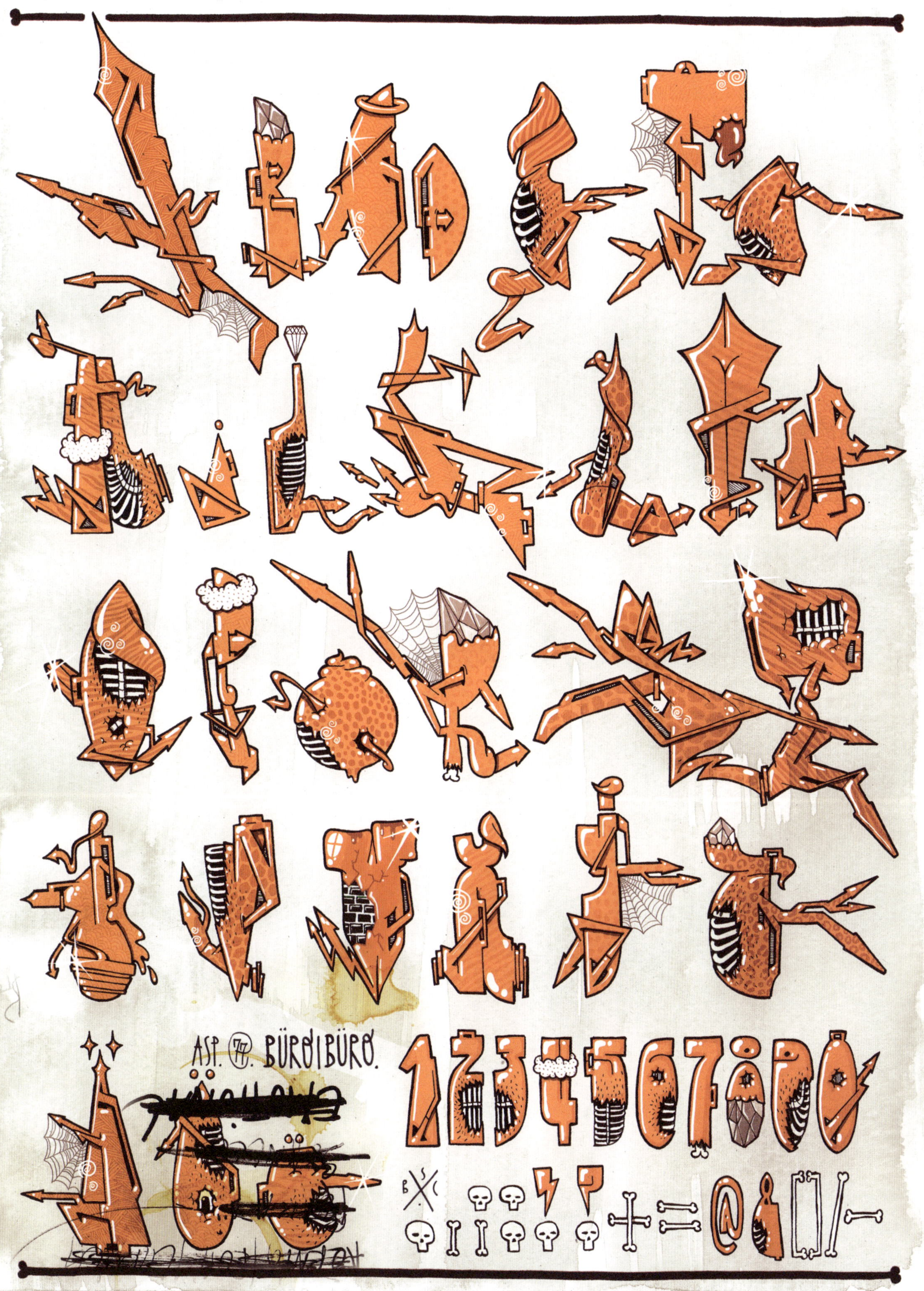

ASP. BÜROIBÜRO.
1234567890

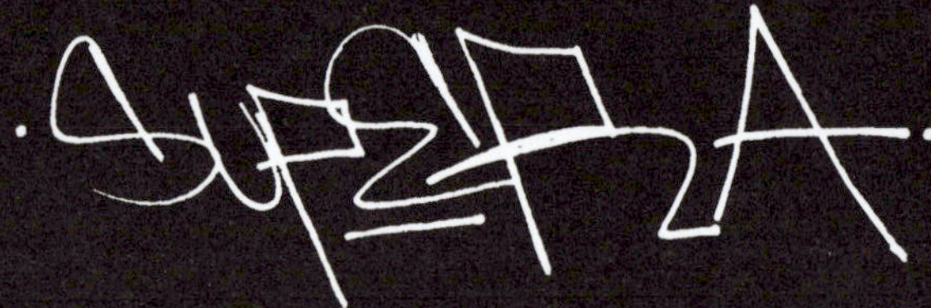

Super A
GOES, NETHERLANDS
Writer since 1994
Favourite letter: A
www.super-a.nl

Super A wanted to create his alphabet in a novel way. Armed with spray paint and stencils, he headed over to his chosen location. 'As I climbed over the edge of the bridge, a car approached and parked right under me,' he says. 'While I was waiting for it to leave, a second car approached – it was the cops. I was hanging under the bridge, hoping they wouldn't look up. The cops checked the other car and left. And I carried on with my mission.'

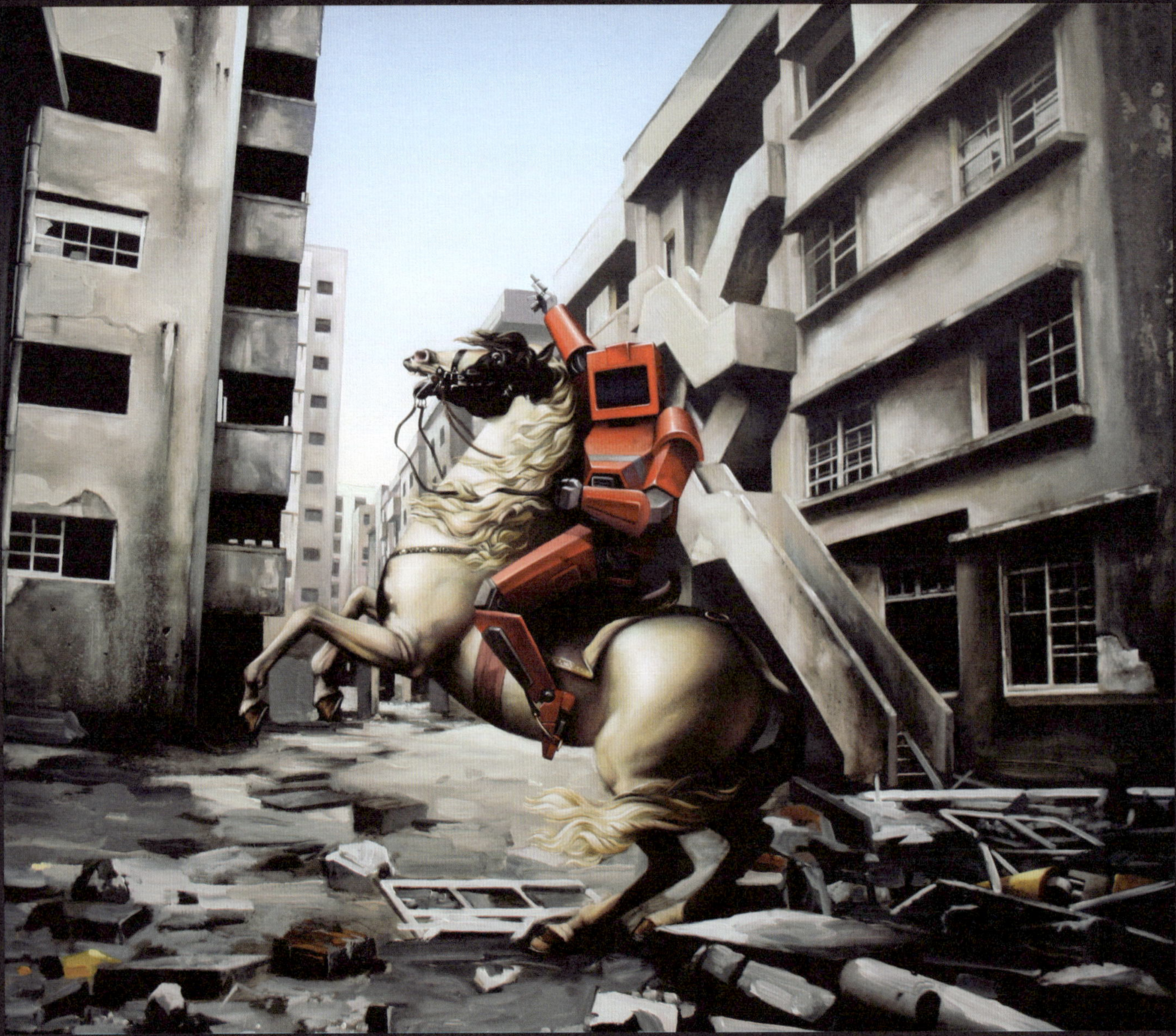

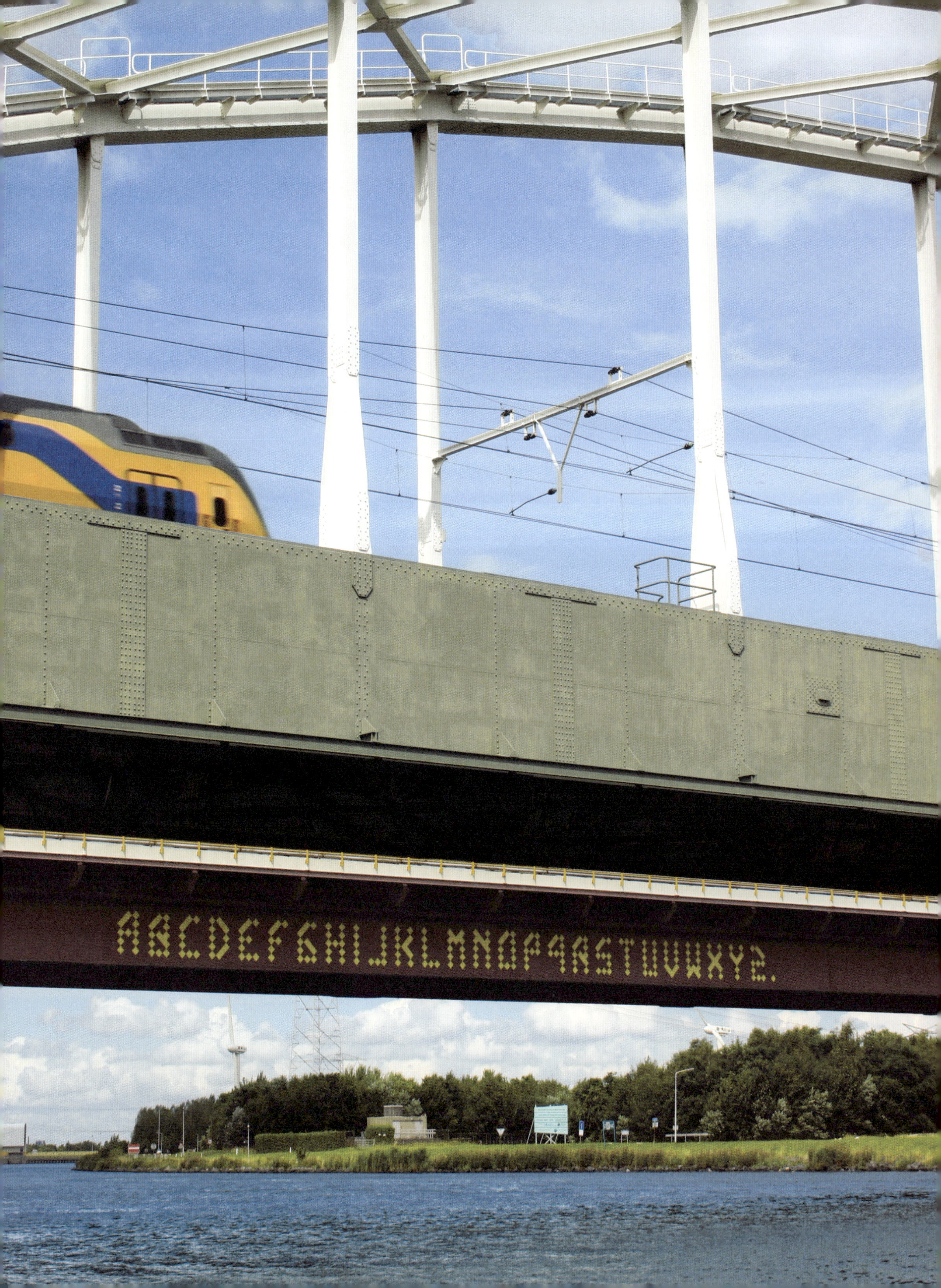

ABCDEFGHIJKLMNOPQRSTUVWXYZ.

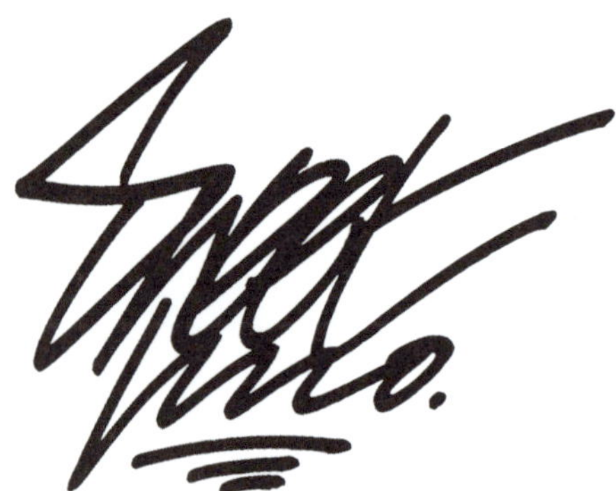

Sweetuno

BASEL, SWITZERLAND
Crew member of ASS, WAF
Writer since 1990
Favourite letter: S
www.sweetuno.net

Sweetuno grew up in Basel but currently lives in Heidelberg, Germany. He is known for spontaneous, funky, raw, original pieces and fresh throw-ups. However, he chose light graffiti for his alphabet, swapping spray paint for an LED-glowstick and a camera. After three nights and twenty-six different locations, his alphabet was complete.

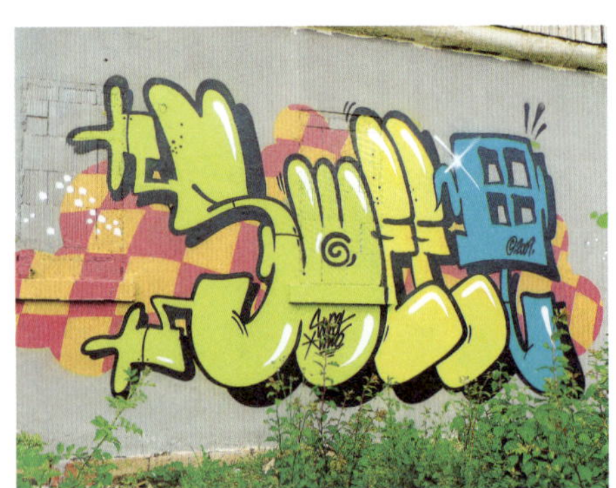

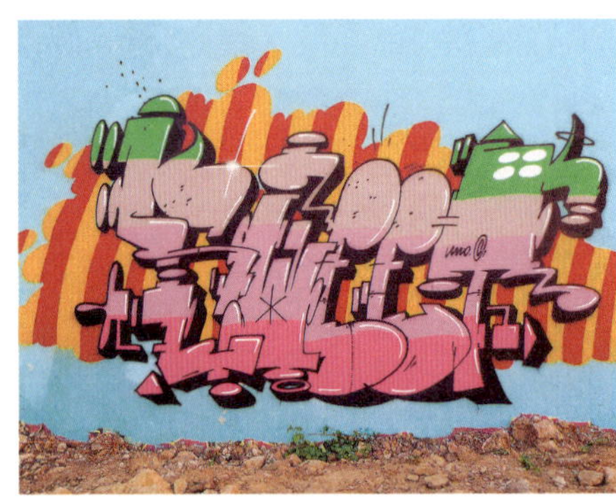

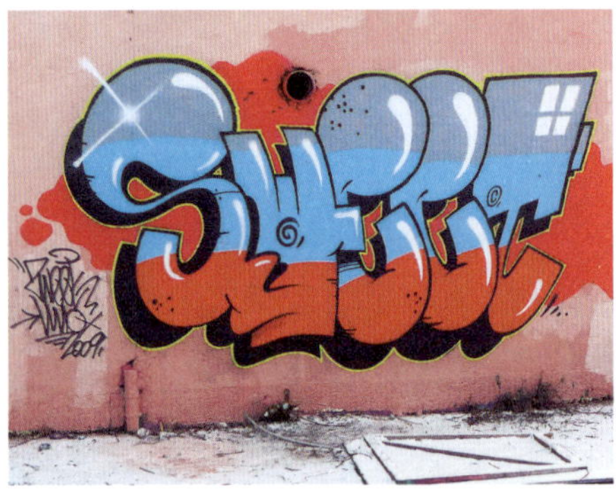

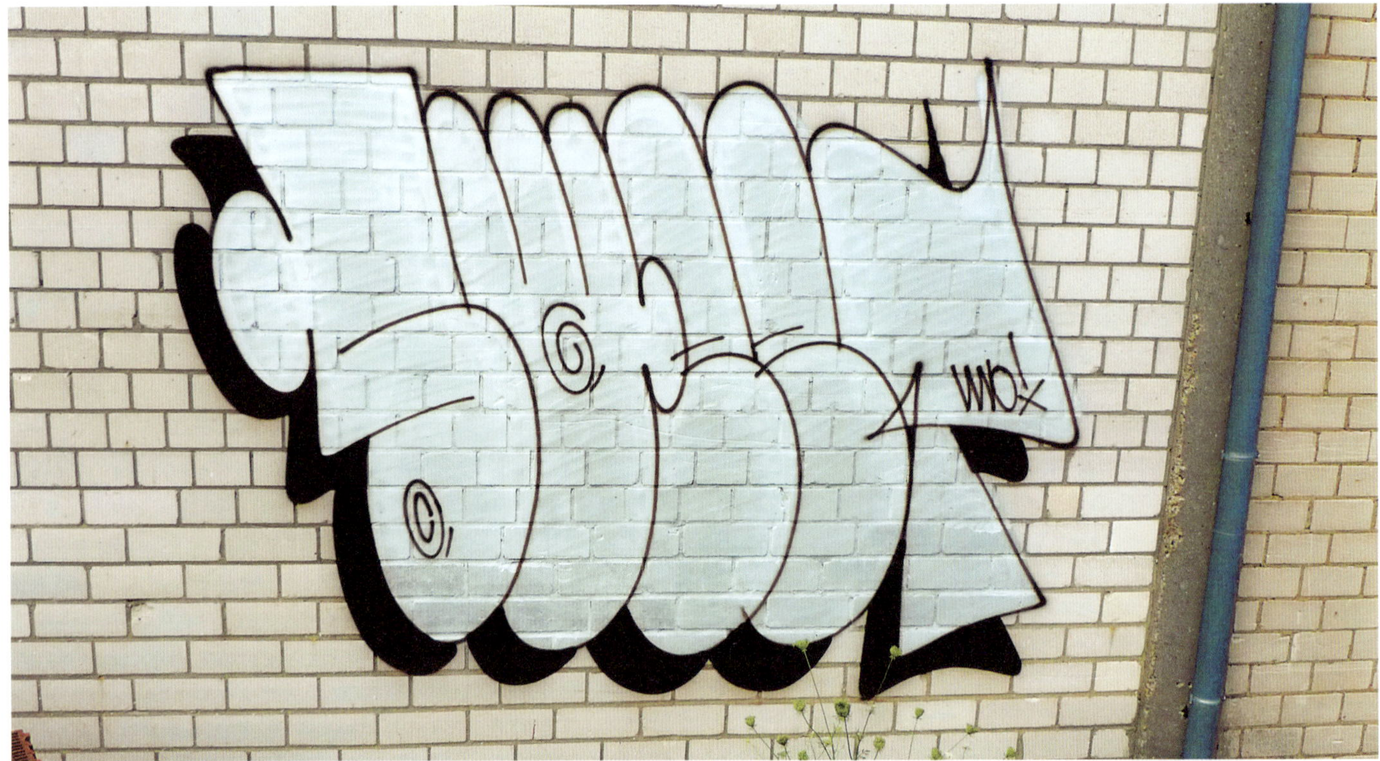

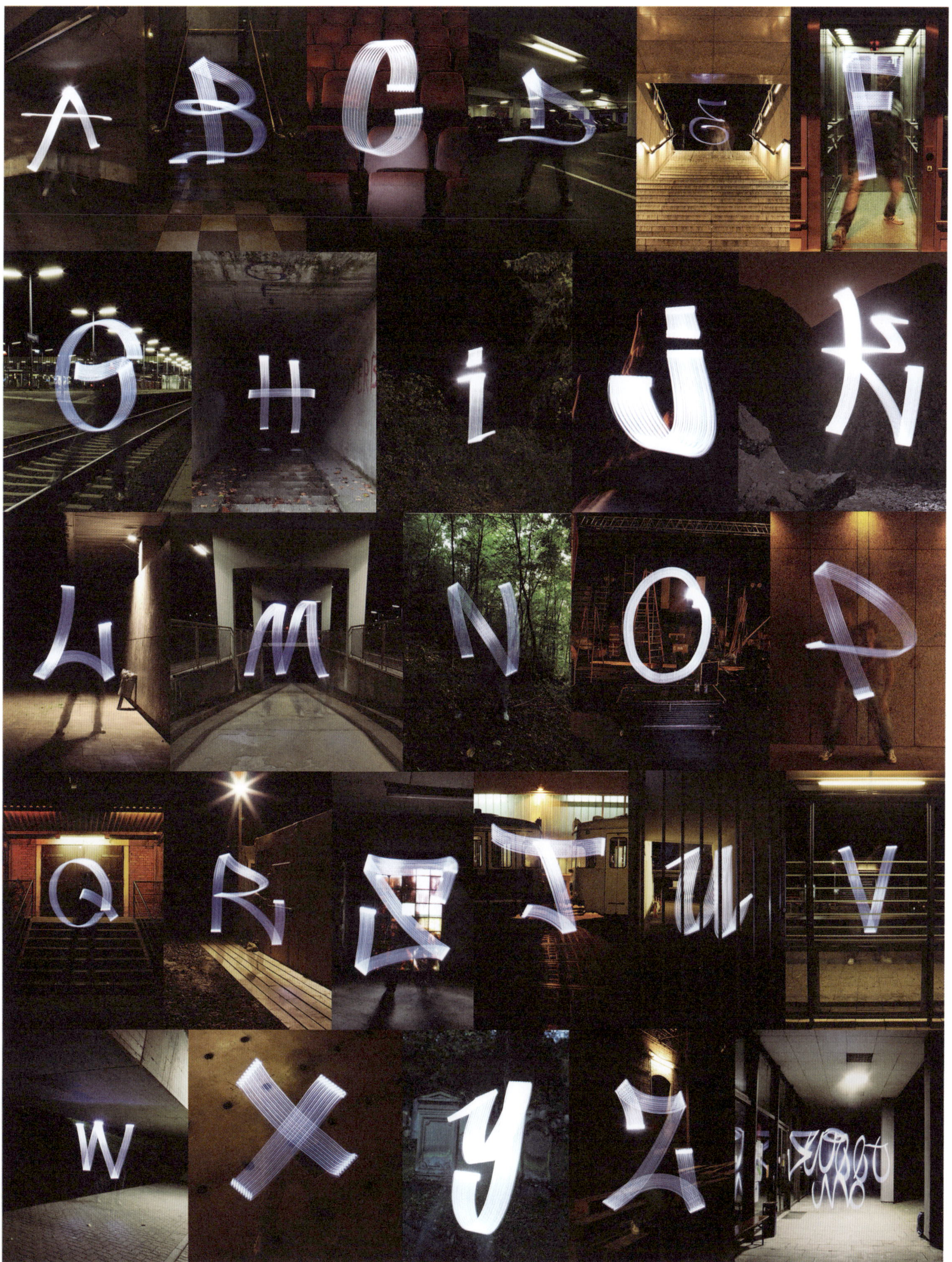

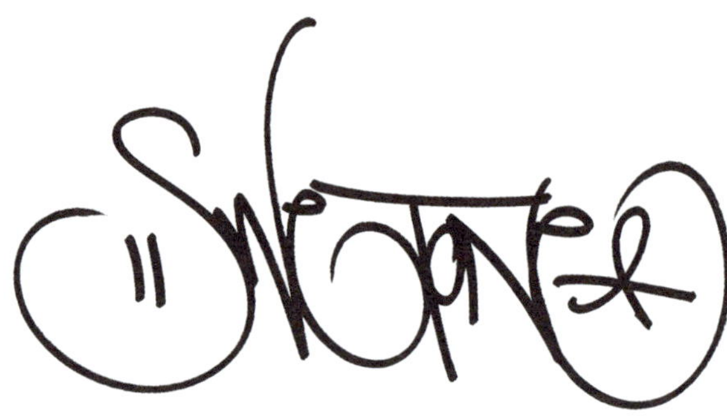

Swet

COPENHAGEN, DENMARK
Crew member of TWS, Fatboys, QAD
Writer since 1985
Favourite letters: S, W, E, T

As writers get older, and life's responsibilities catch up with them, they tend to go out painting less and less or stop writing altogether. Swet is an exception. He does well over 200 pieces a year and continually pushes his style of letter construction. He has mastered a variety of styles, but his pieces always bear his hallmark. He summarizes his approach perfectly with the following statement: 'It don't mean a thing if it ain't got that swing.' To do his alphabet he got up at 5 am one beautiful summer morning, packed his high-pressure cans and fat caps, painted his twenty-six letters and then went to work.

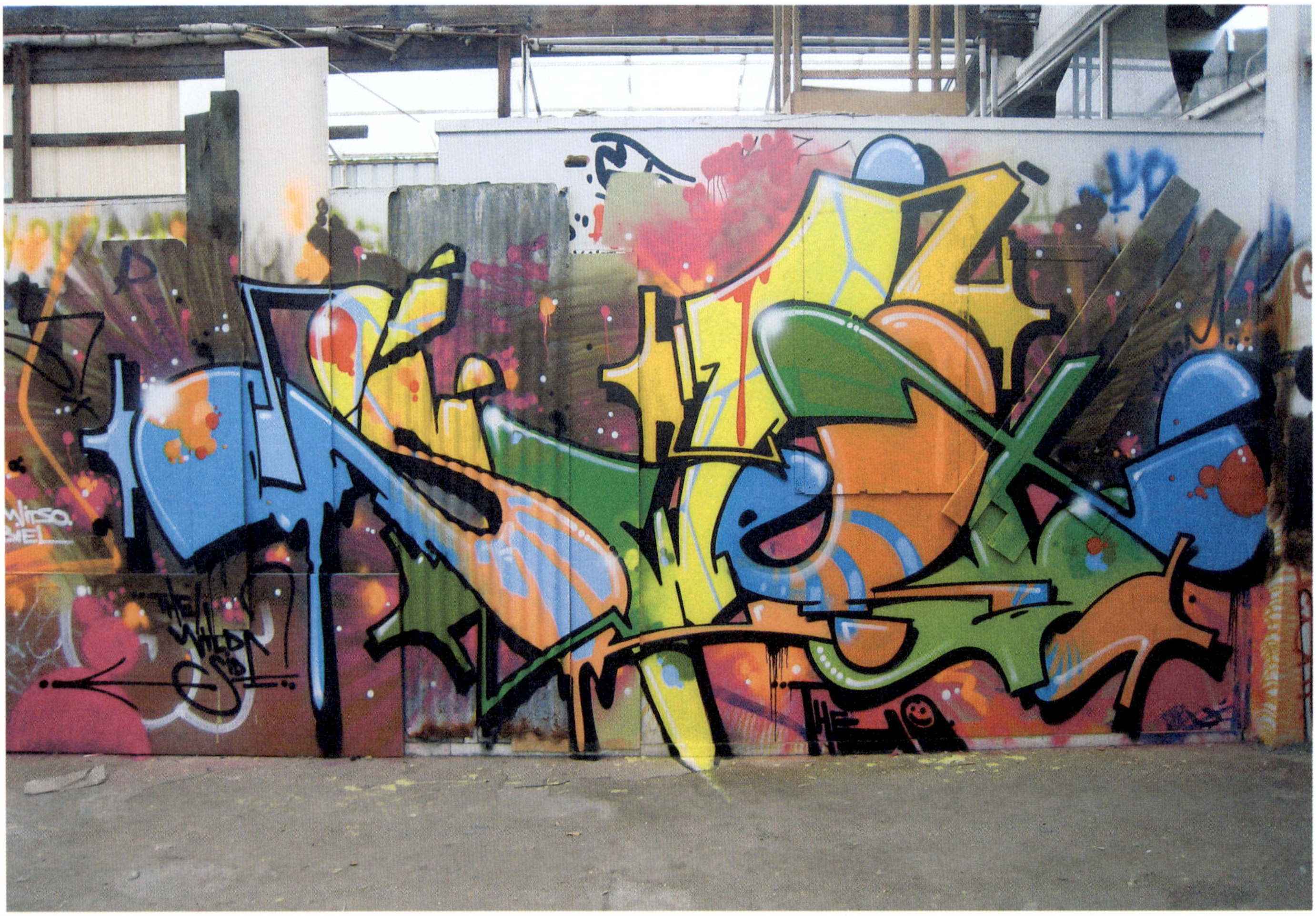

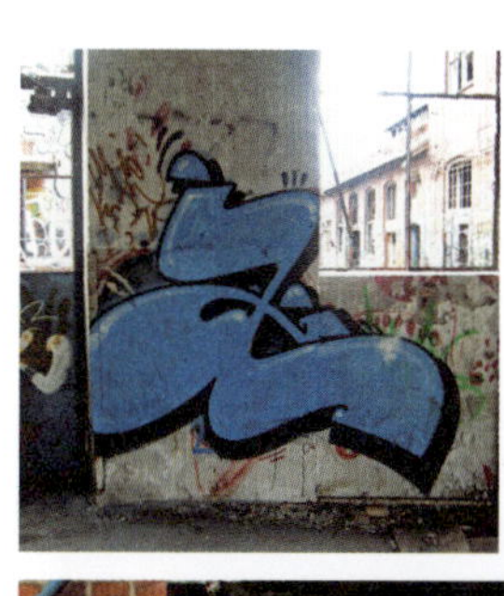
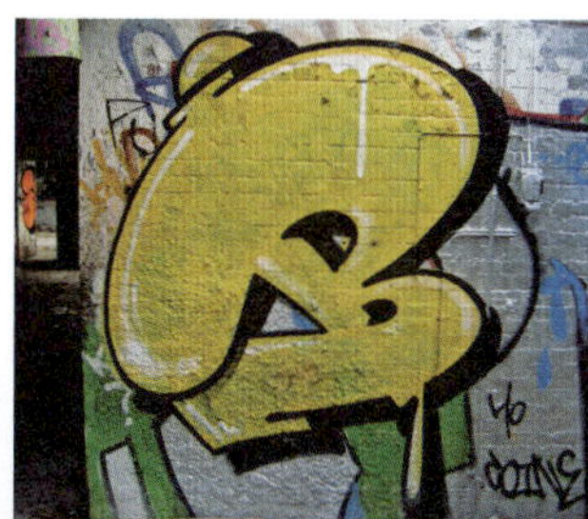
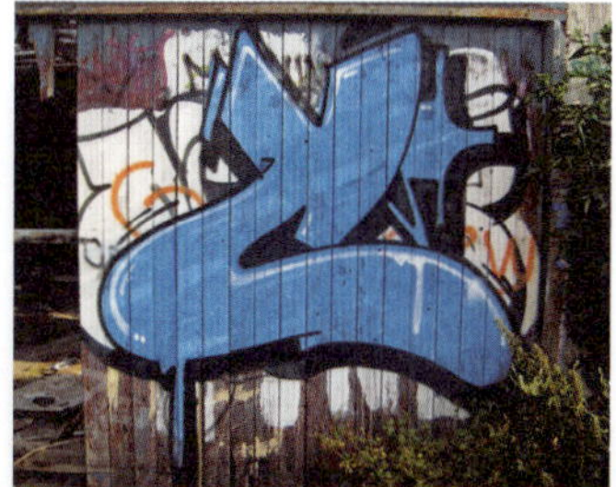
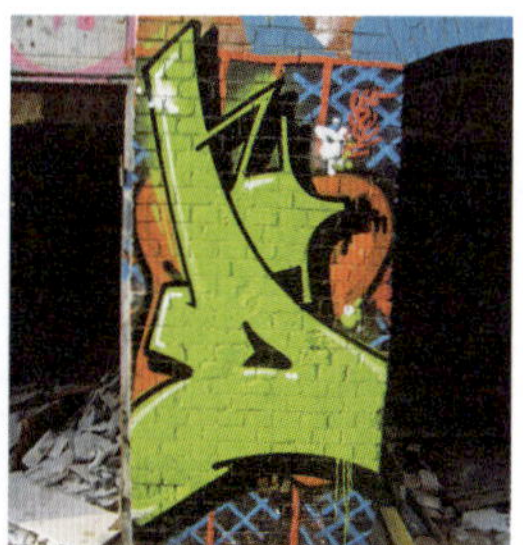
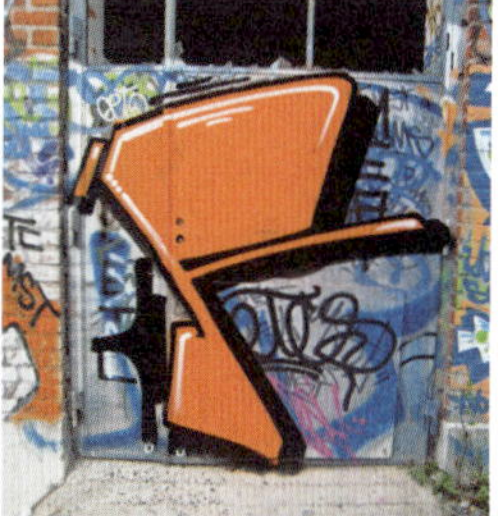
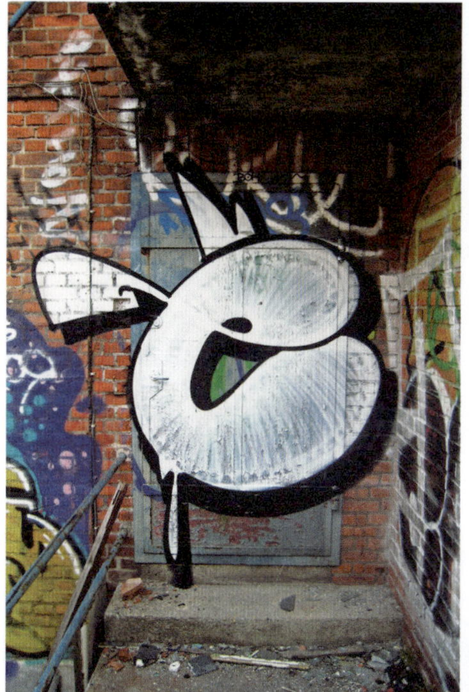
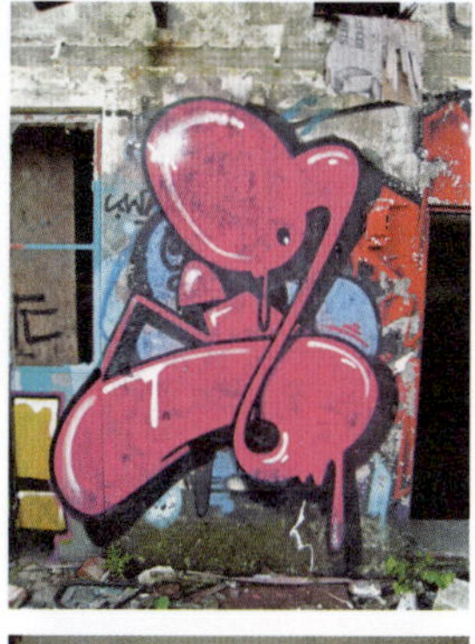
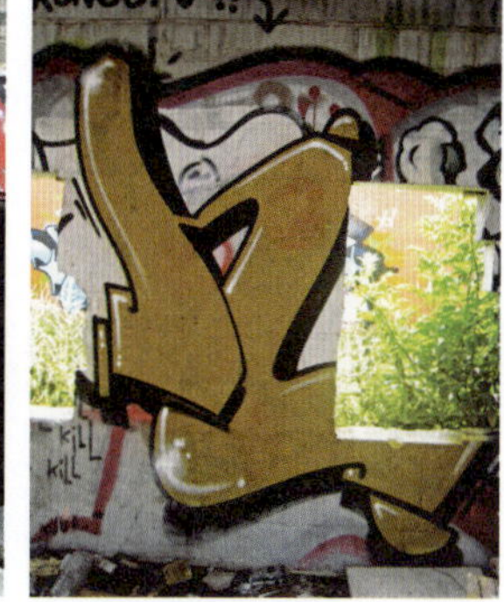
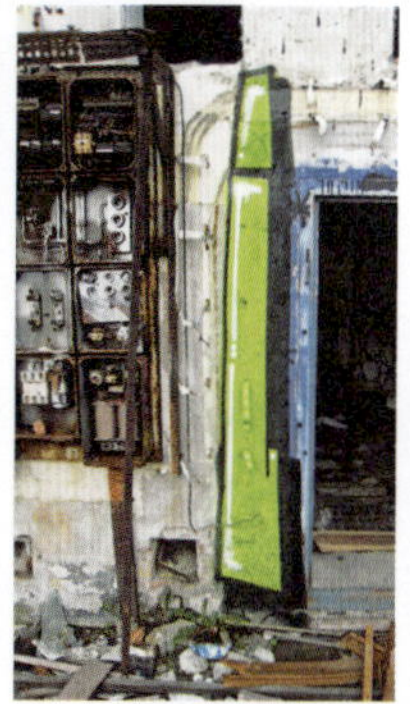
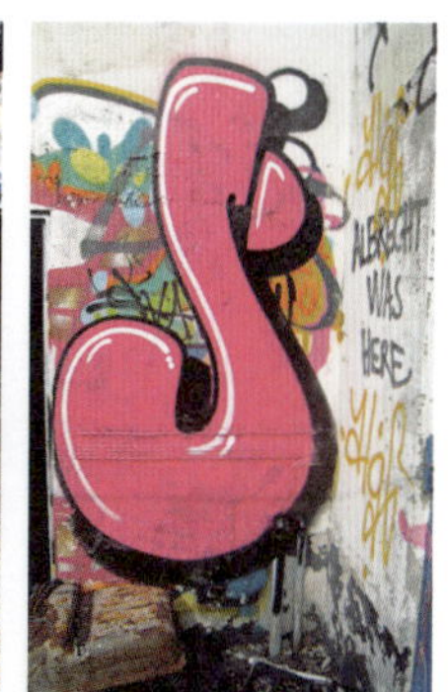
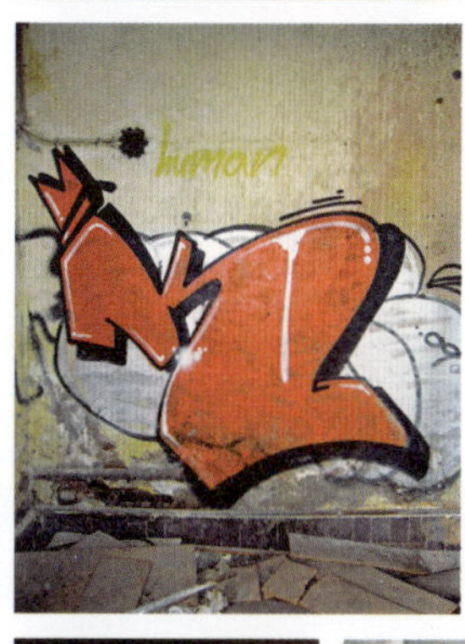
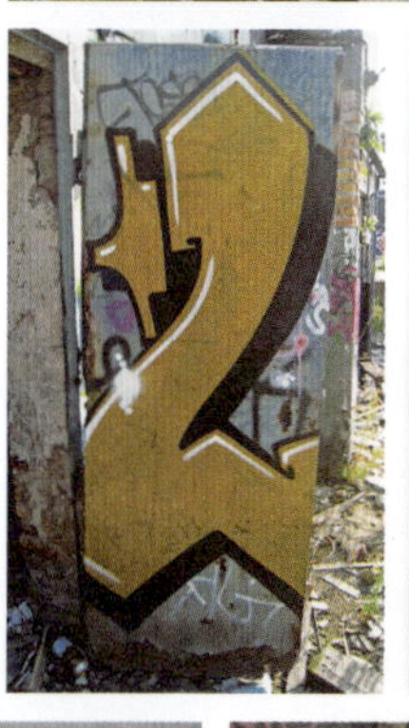
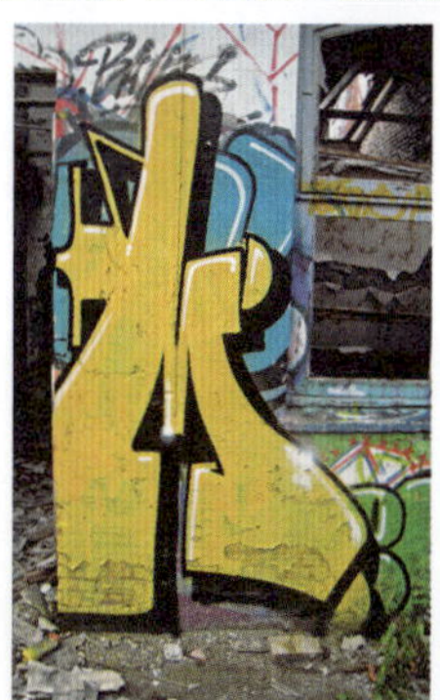
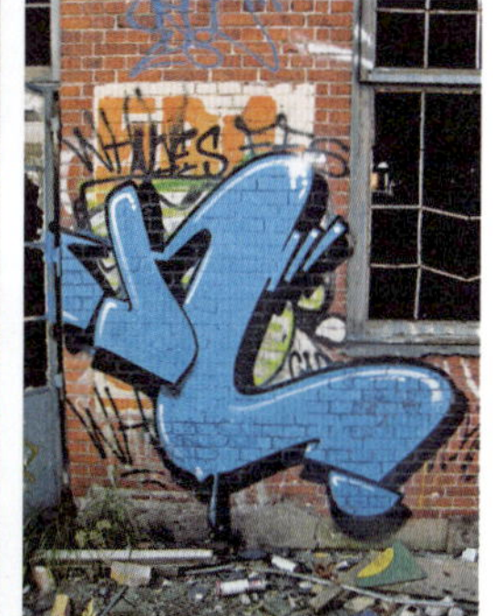
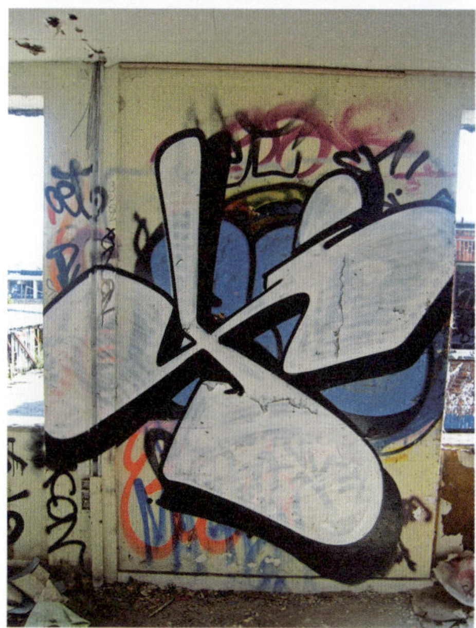
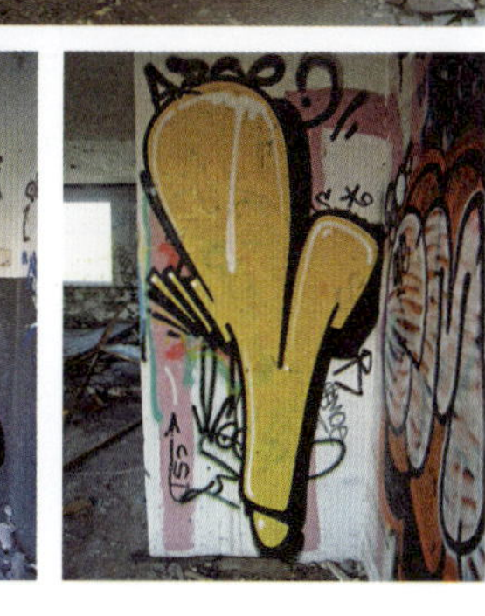
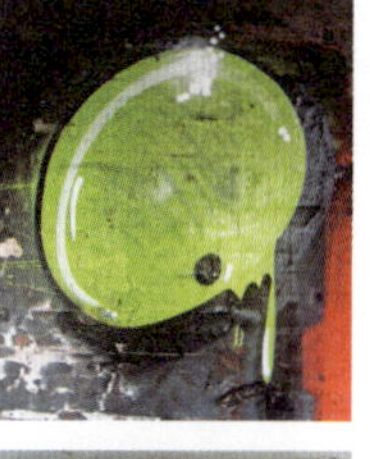
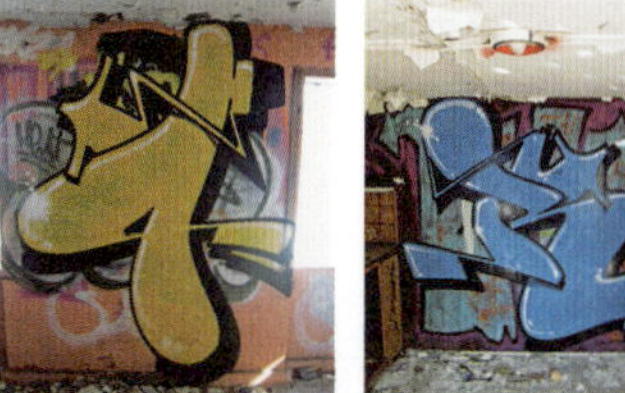
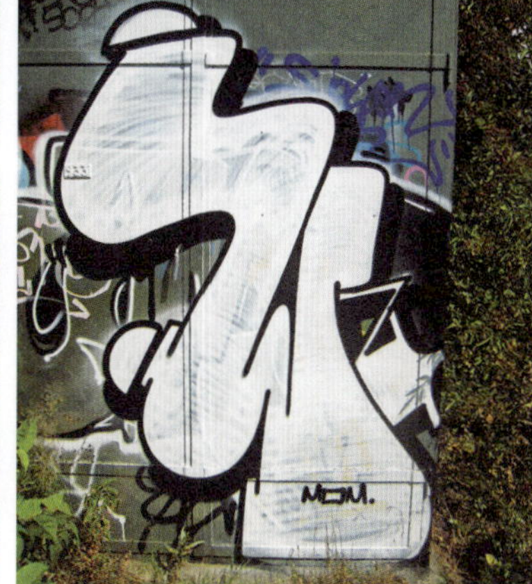
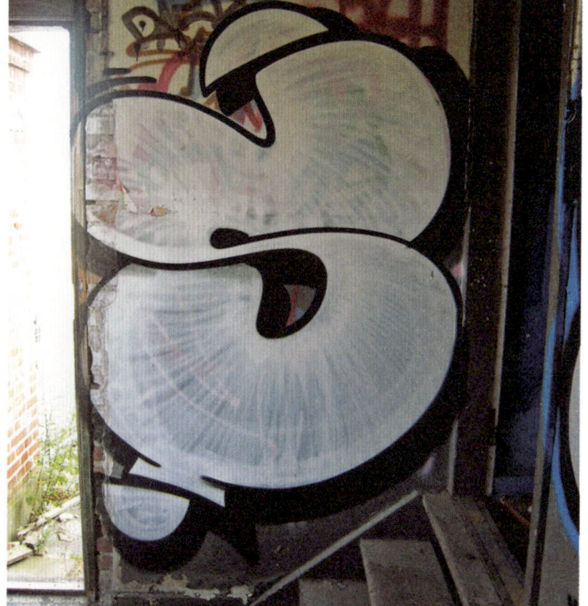
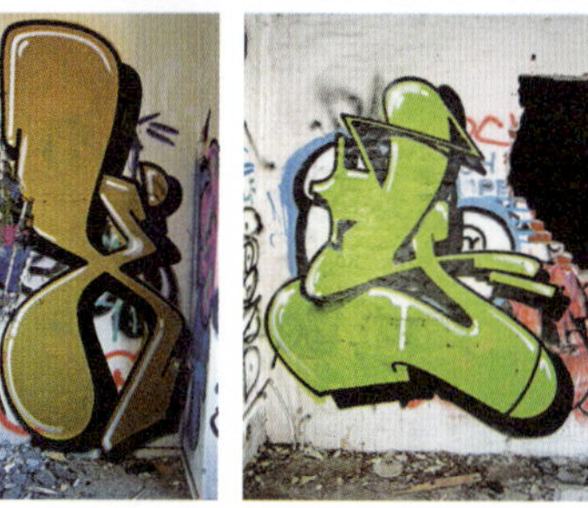
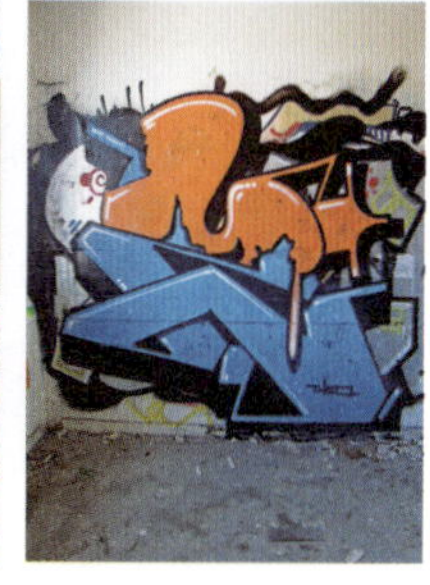

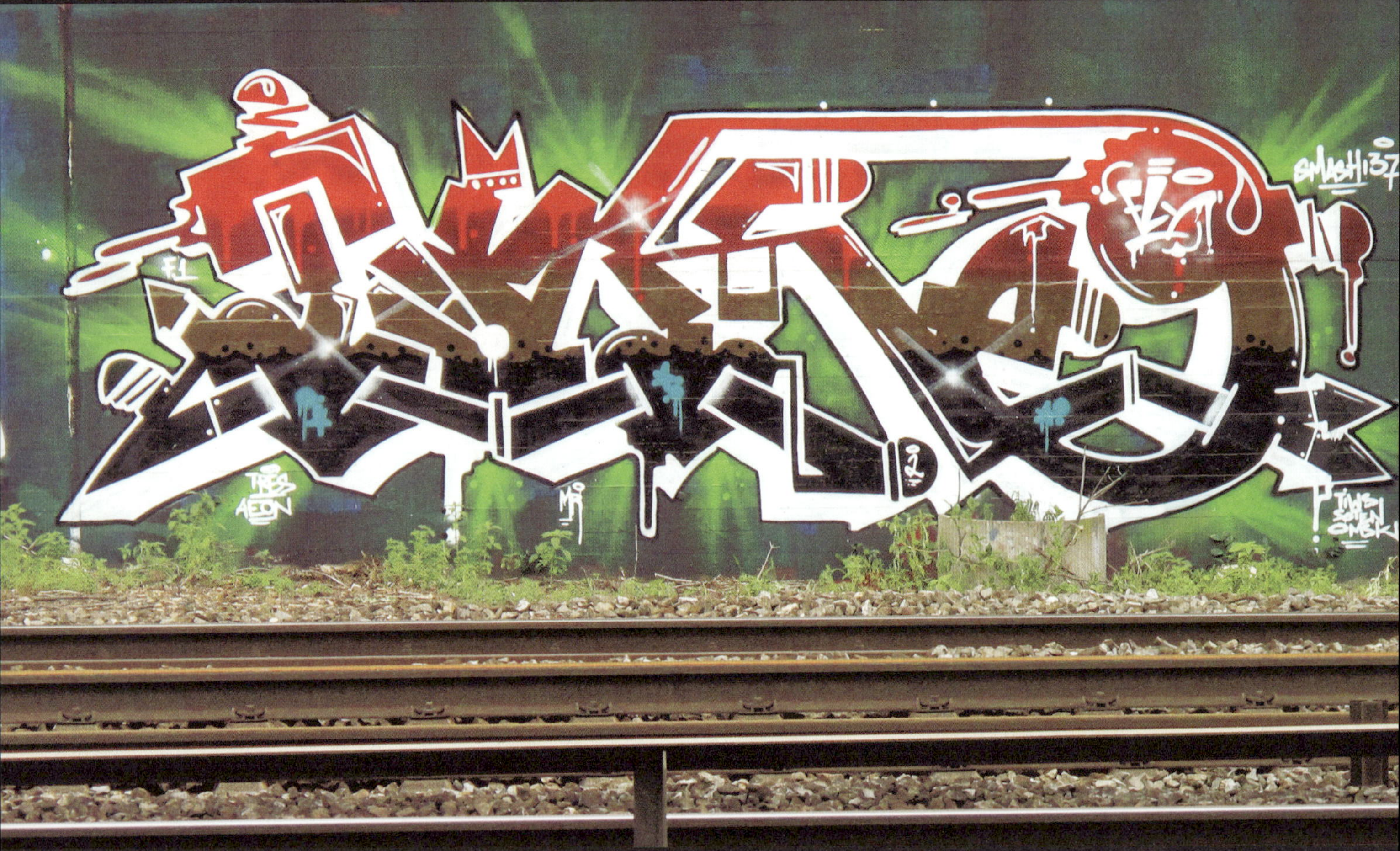

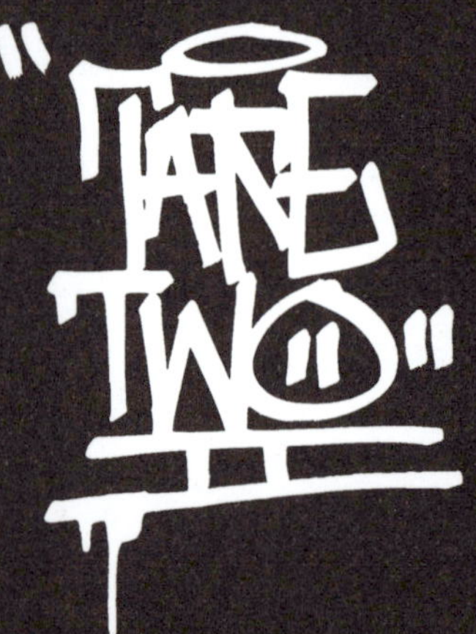

Take2

MELBOURNE, AUSTRALIA
Crew member of FLY, MR, F1, DB, STC
Writer since 2004
Favourite letter: 'I like them all!'

Take2 only started writing a couple of years ago but has already developed a fresh personal style. His pieces are rooted in old school but have a contemporary flavour. In 2009 he travelled around Europe, the USA and Japan to paint and built up his skills a lot during this period. A quality style, he says, is about 'good letters above all, then colours and the placement of the piece'.

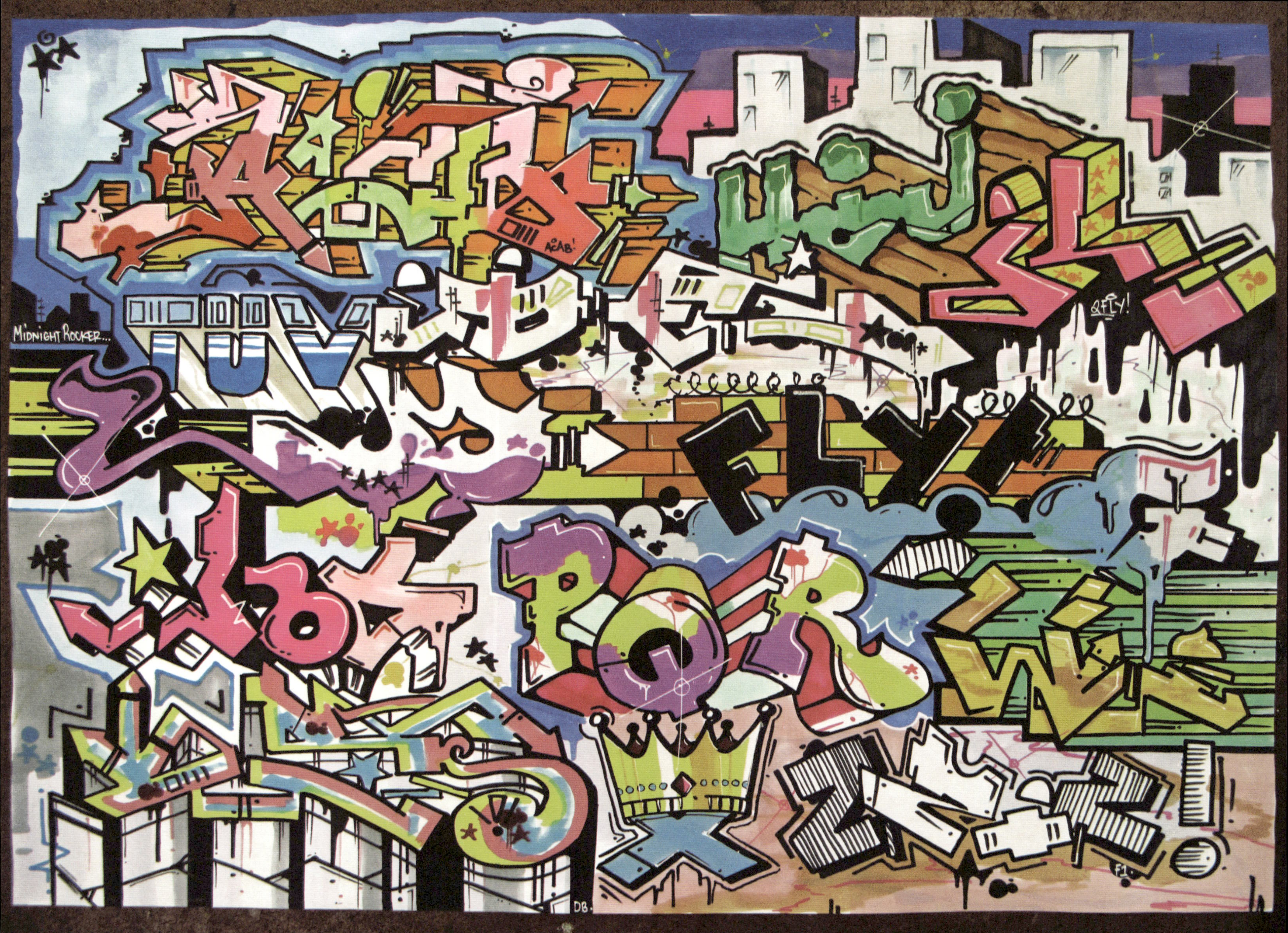

MIDNIGHT ROCKER...
ACAB!
QFLY!
FLY!
TUV
POR
WX

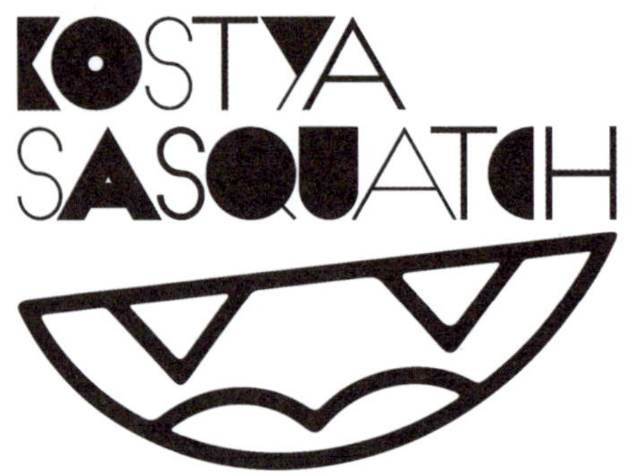

TAKECARE
MOSCOW, RUSSIA
Crew member of In the Buddka
Favourite letter: Δ
www.thelocalgenius.com

Kostya Sasquatch, also known as TAKECARE, works as an artist and graphic designer in Moscow and is passionate about typography. 'With my alphabet I just wanted to make something very simple and clear without a lot of visual effects,' he says. 'I care about composition and shape, and try to avoid complexity when it is not really necessary.' Kostya appreciates the opportunities afforded by graffiti: 'Nowadays people don't have much opportunity to shape the reality they live in – their streets, their houses, the local shop, etc., were all designed and built by others. Graffiti is a chance to take some control back.'

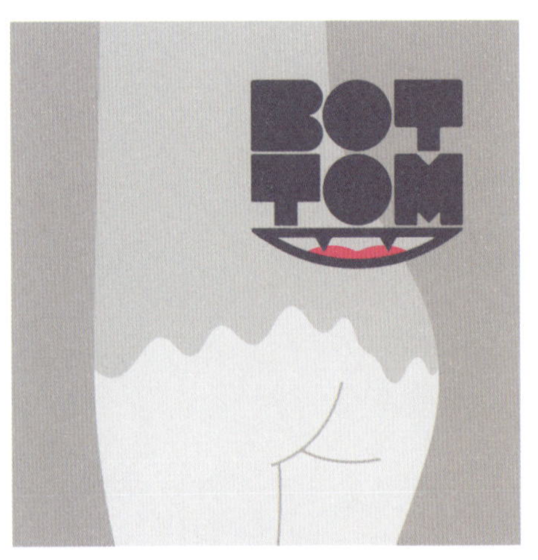

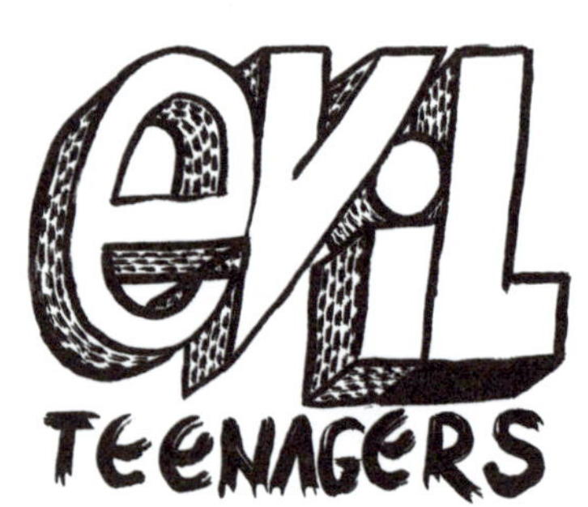

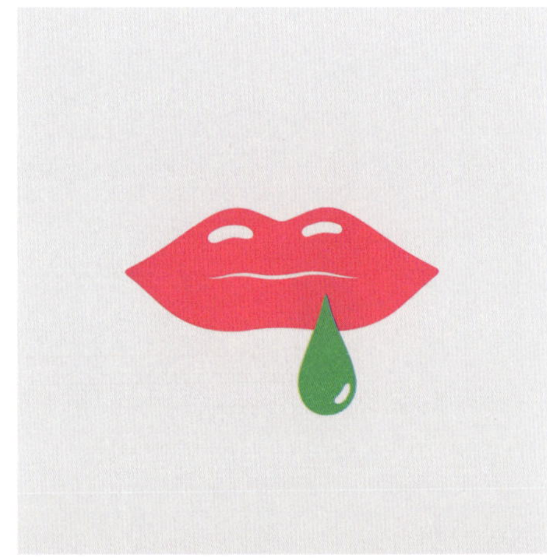

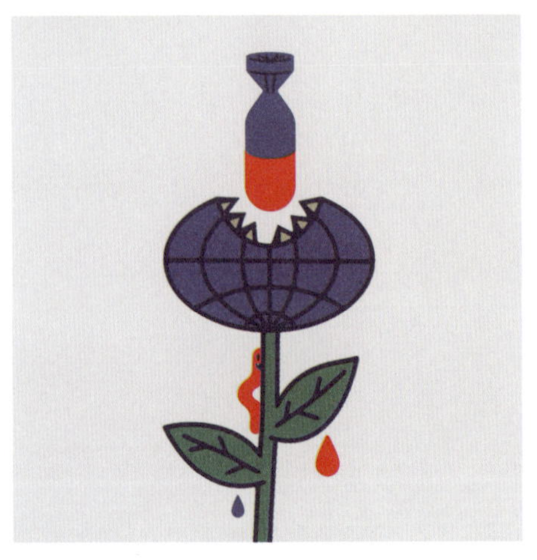

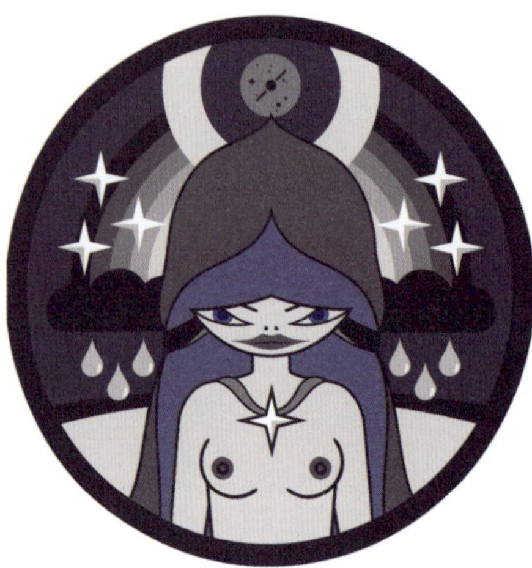

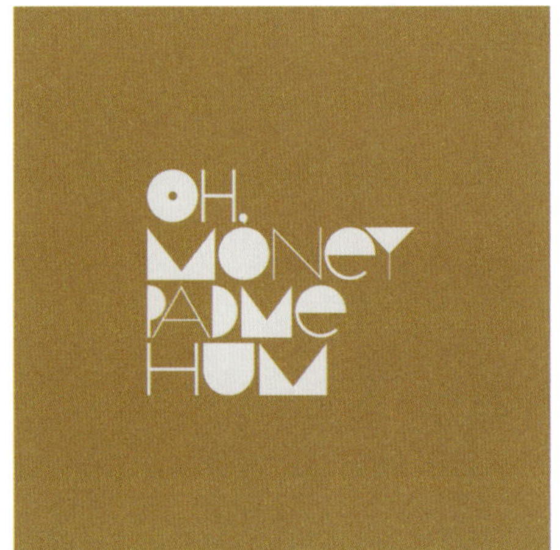

ABCDEFG
HIJKLMNO
PQRSTU
VWXYZ

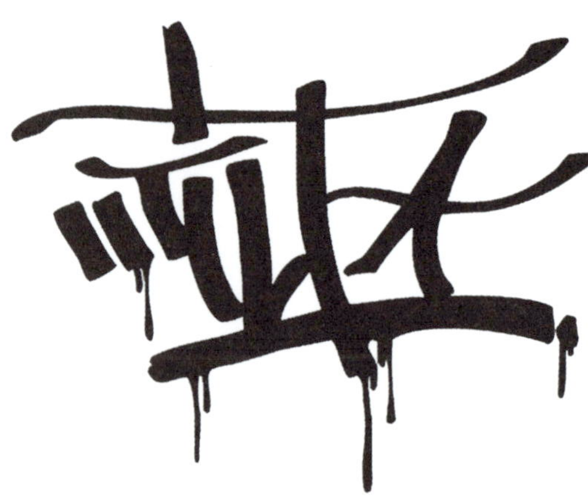

Tilt

TOULOUSE, FRANCE
Crew member of BAD, KD
Writer since 1988
Favourite letter: R
www.graffitilt.com

Tilt travels around a lot to paint and is well known for his vibrant, simple bubble pieces and body art. He has recently been focused on letters and has designed a lot of alphabets. Tilt executed the alphabet opposite in paint on plexiglas and displayed it in an old French frame. He deliberately left out certain letters and added a Tilt piece instead. You need love and passion to create a good piece, he says, and sometimes also nerve.

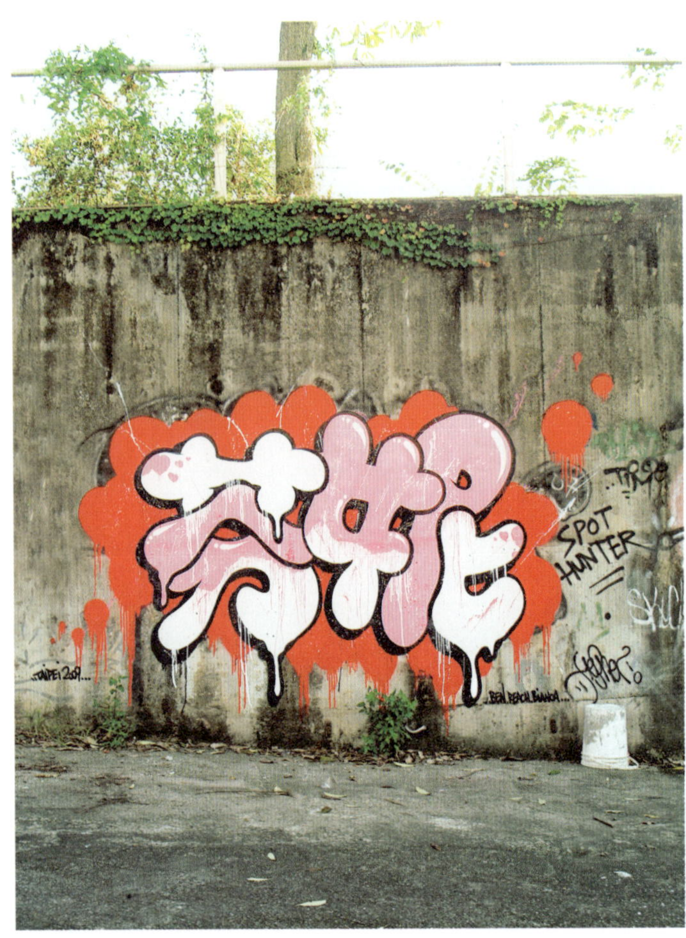

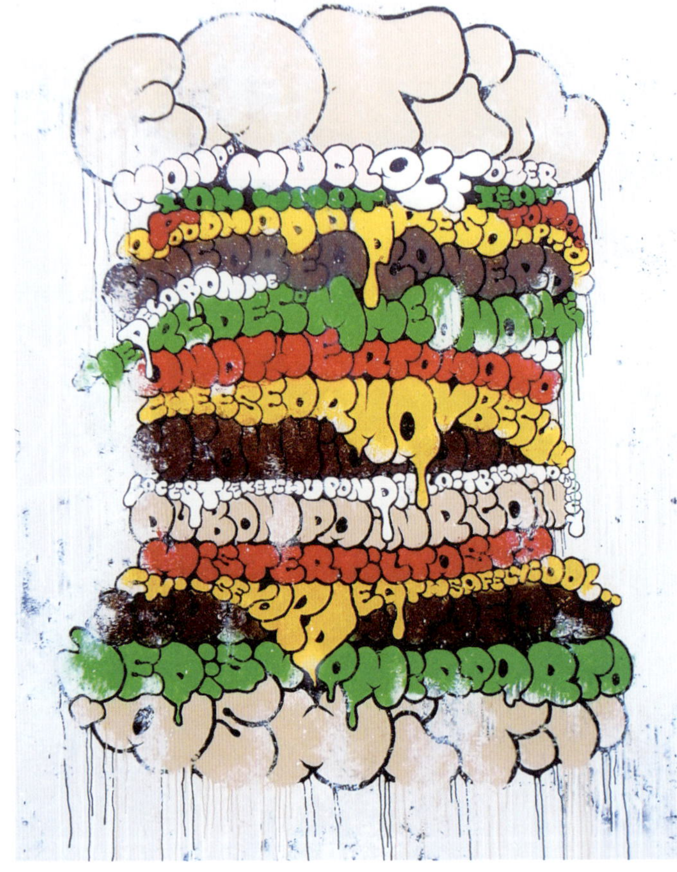

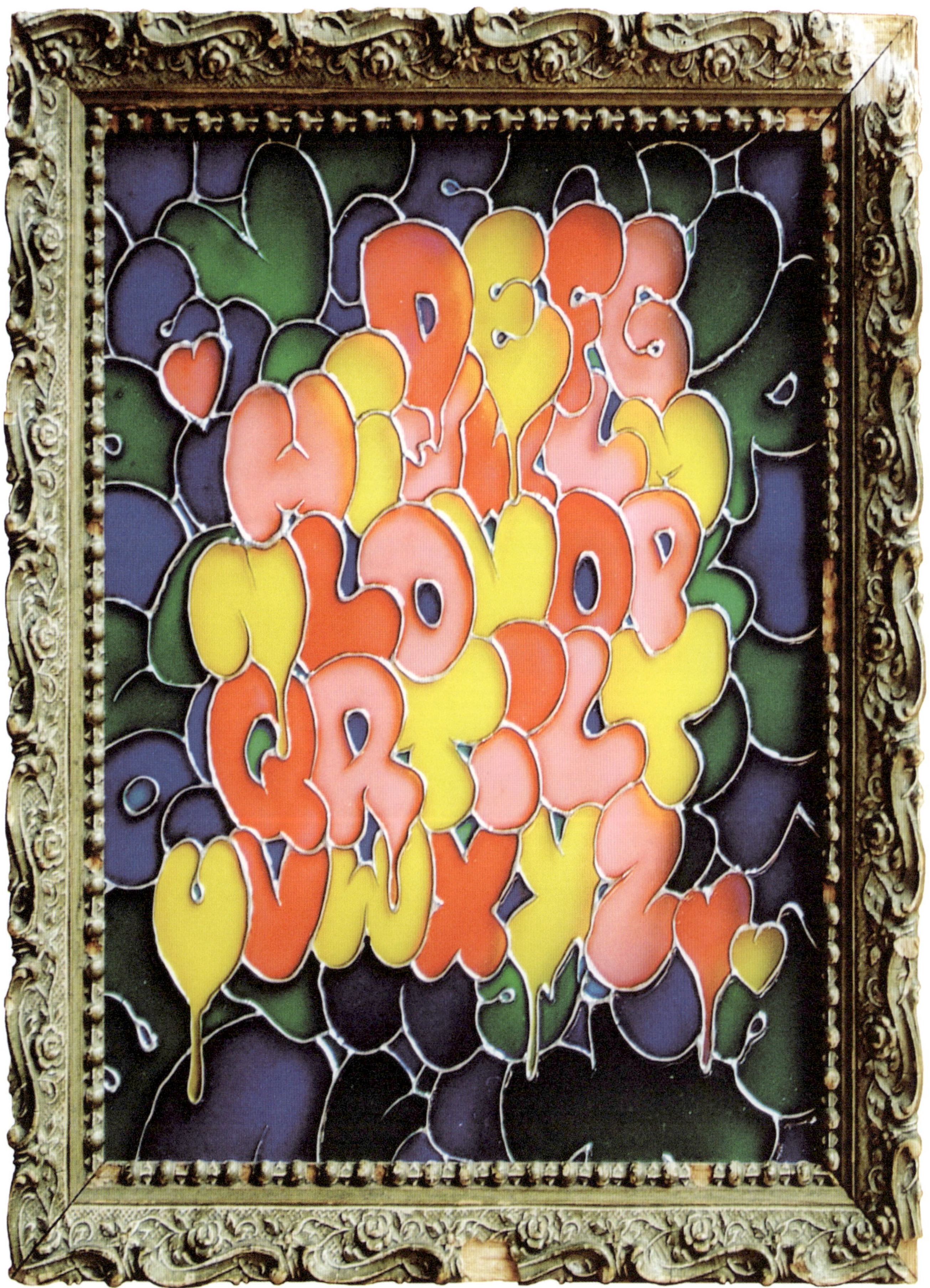

ABCDEFG
HIJKLMN
OPQRS
TUVWXYZ

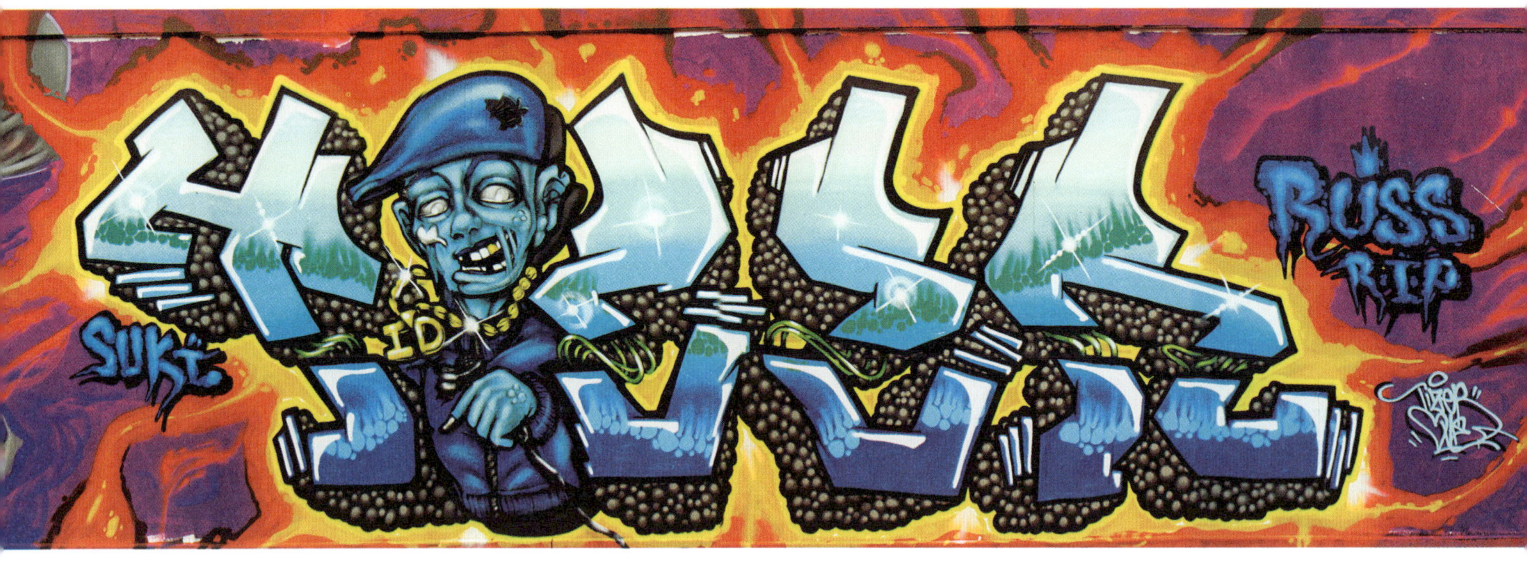

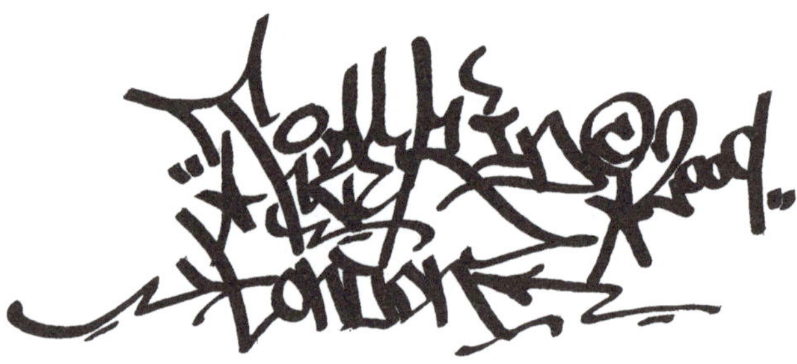

Tizer

LONDON, UK
Crew member of Ivory Dukes, SDM
Writer since 1988
Favourite letter: Z

Tizer's pieces are experimental, spontaneous and humorous. The calligraphy of his alphabet is based on old South London handstyles. According to Tizer, the most fascinating aspect of graffiti is 'seeing how different people can create amazing art work out of a can of paint'.

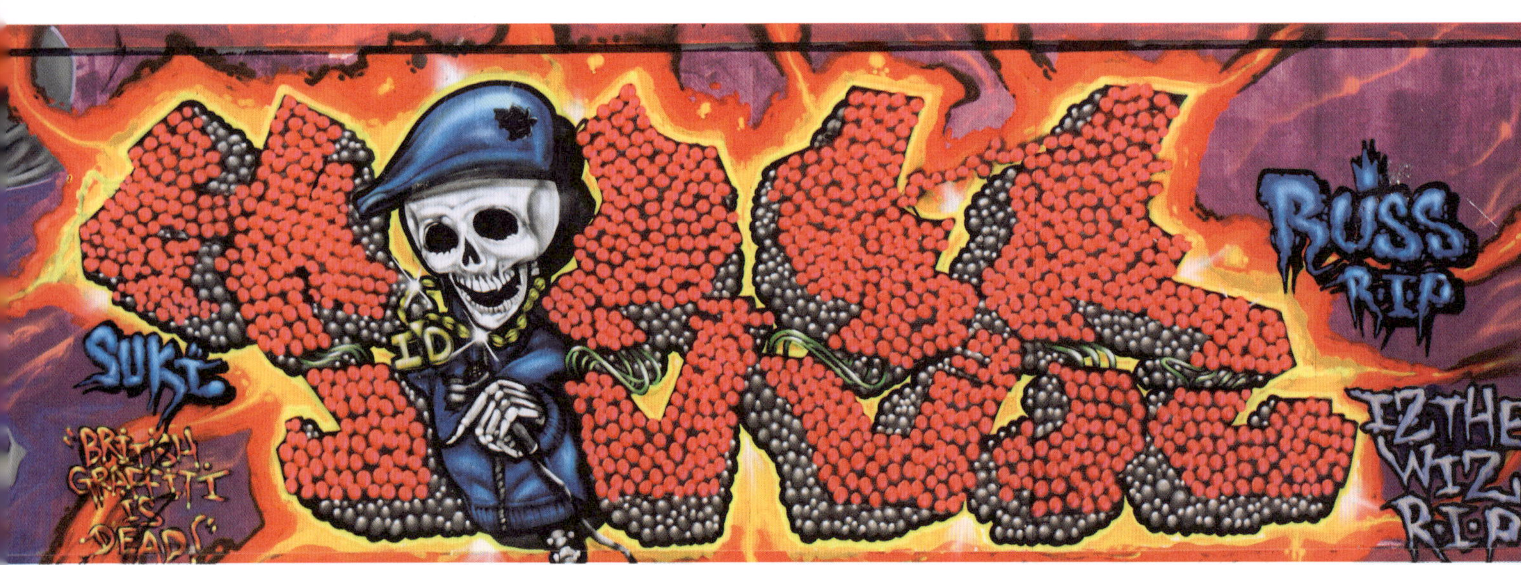

ABCDEFG
HIJKLMN
OPQRSTU
VWXYZ

abcdefghijklmn
opqrstuvwxyz

ʤastonE

Toast One
ZURICH, SWITZERLAND
Crew member of TWS
Writer since 1990
Favourite letter: E

Graffiti artist Toast has achieved international recognition in several disciplines. He is an exceptionally talented graphic designer and illustrator, as his Pyrochimps series shows to great effect. His unusual letter sculptures and canvases are exhibited in respected galleries, but he is equally adept at spray-painting letters and characters on walls. He prefers working in black, or black ink (which is also the title of his book). According to Toast, all it takes to create a good piece is 'a good idea'.

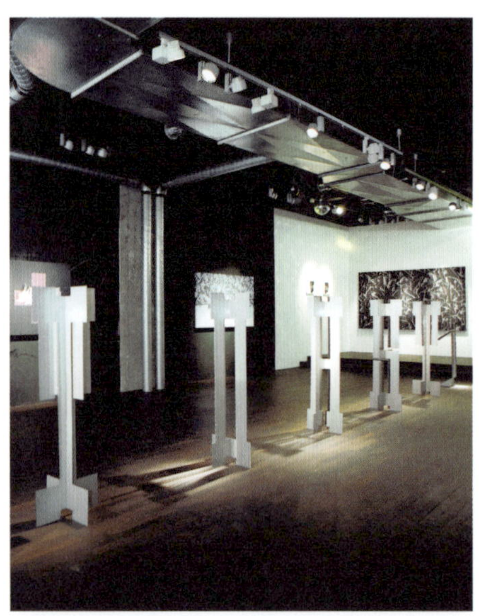
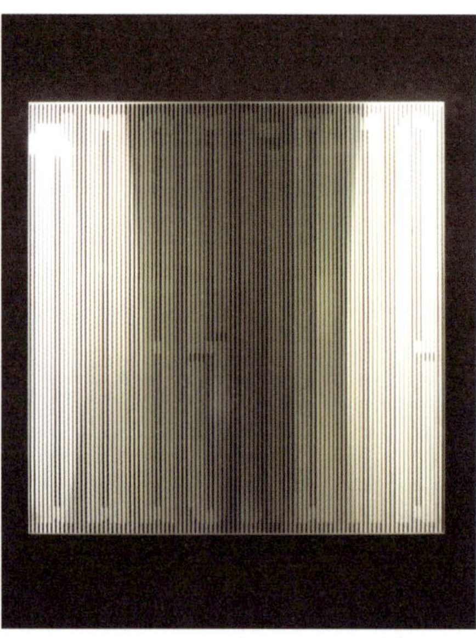
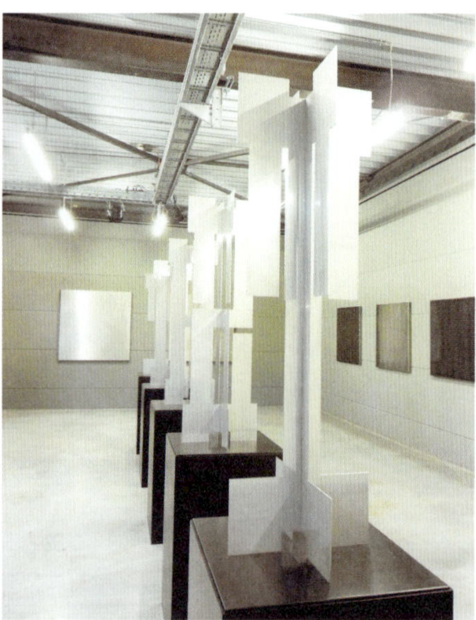
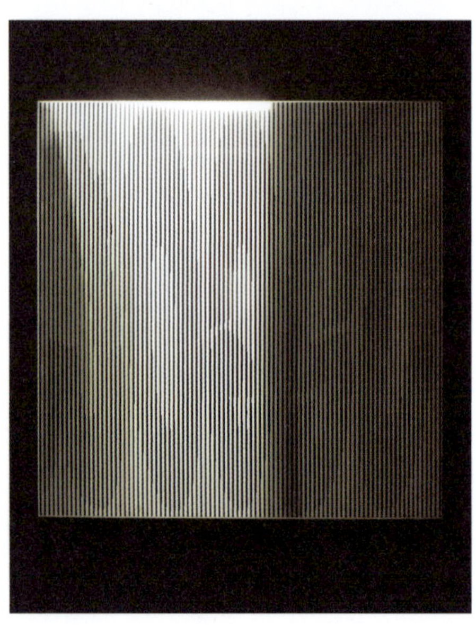
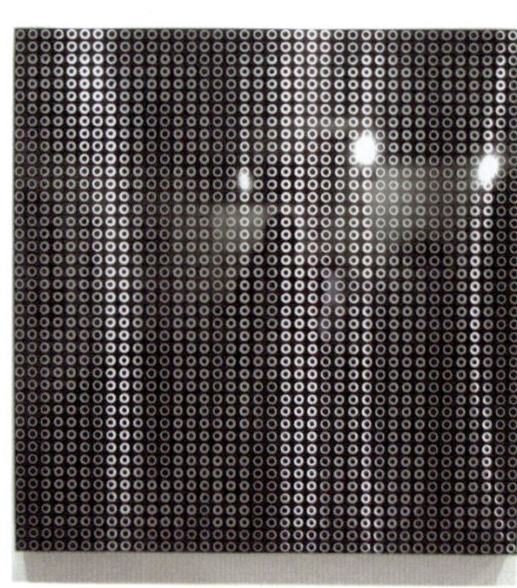
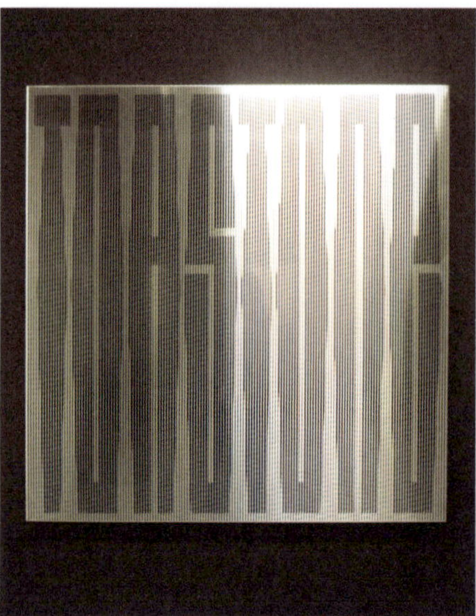

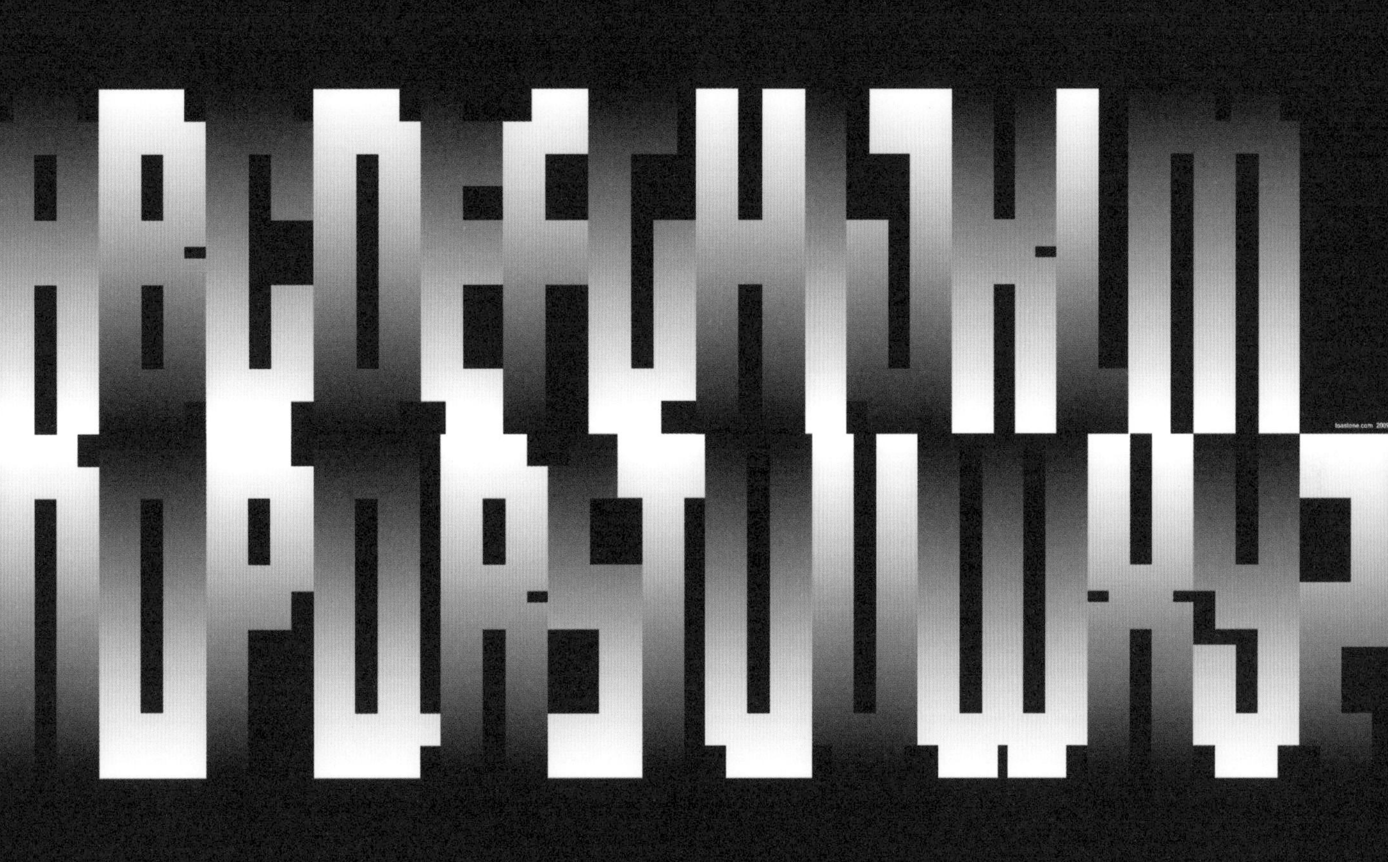

toastone.com 2009©

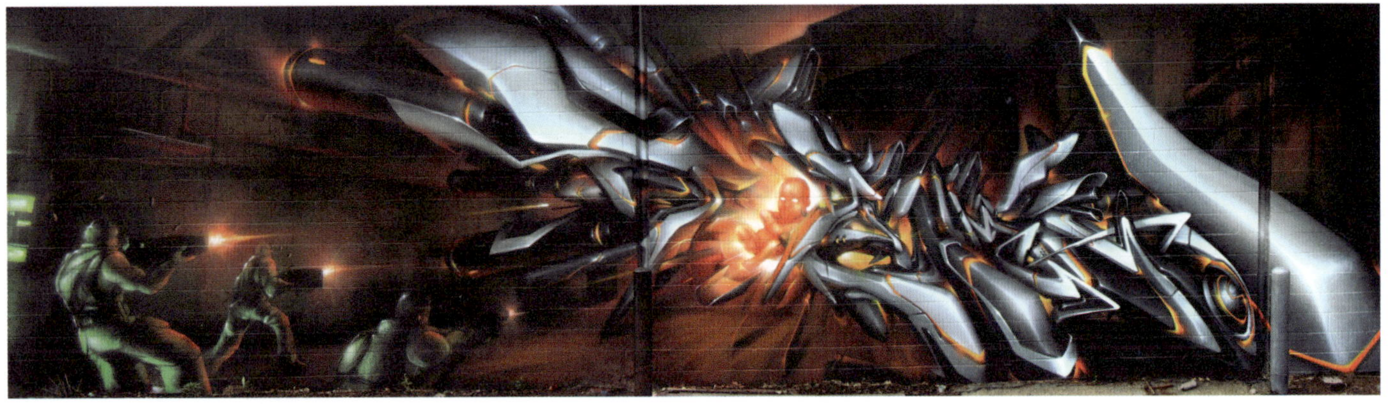

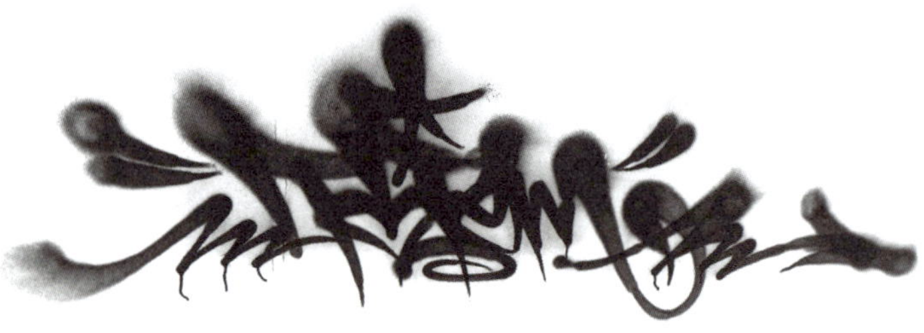

Totem

ATLANTA, USA
Crew member of TATS,
3A, BU, TGE
Writer since 1990
Favourite letter: E
www.mr-totem.com

Totem came to prominence in the graffiti scene through his unusual mix of aggressive, almost robotic 3D letters and characters – a style that he calls 'The Mechanical Battle Serif'. Many well-known companies have commissioned work from him, including Coca-Cola, Shell, BBDO, Nike and Sony. In order to create a good piece, you need to 'train and study current and historical, archetypal graffiti lettering, then apply your own thesis when mastering the basics', Totem says.

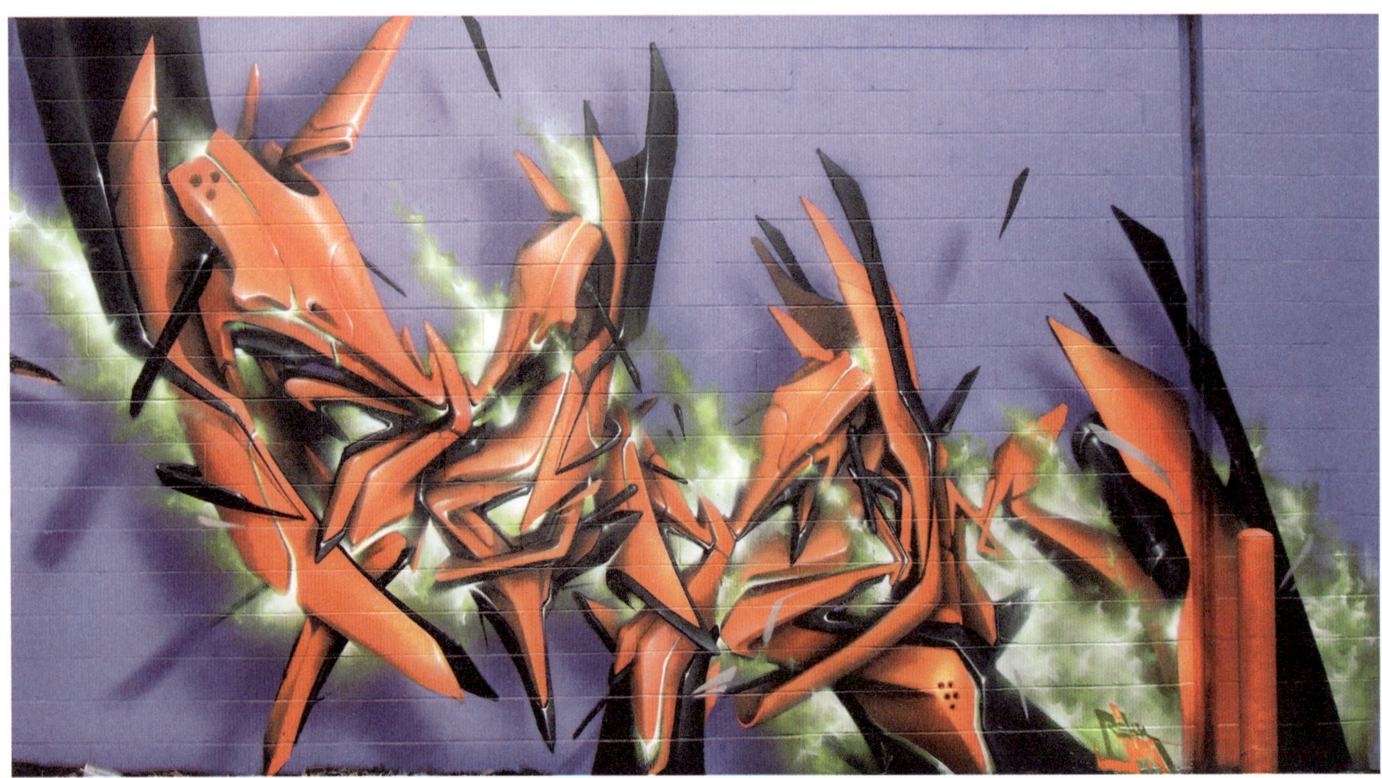

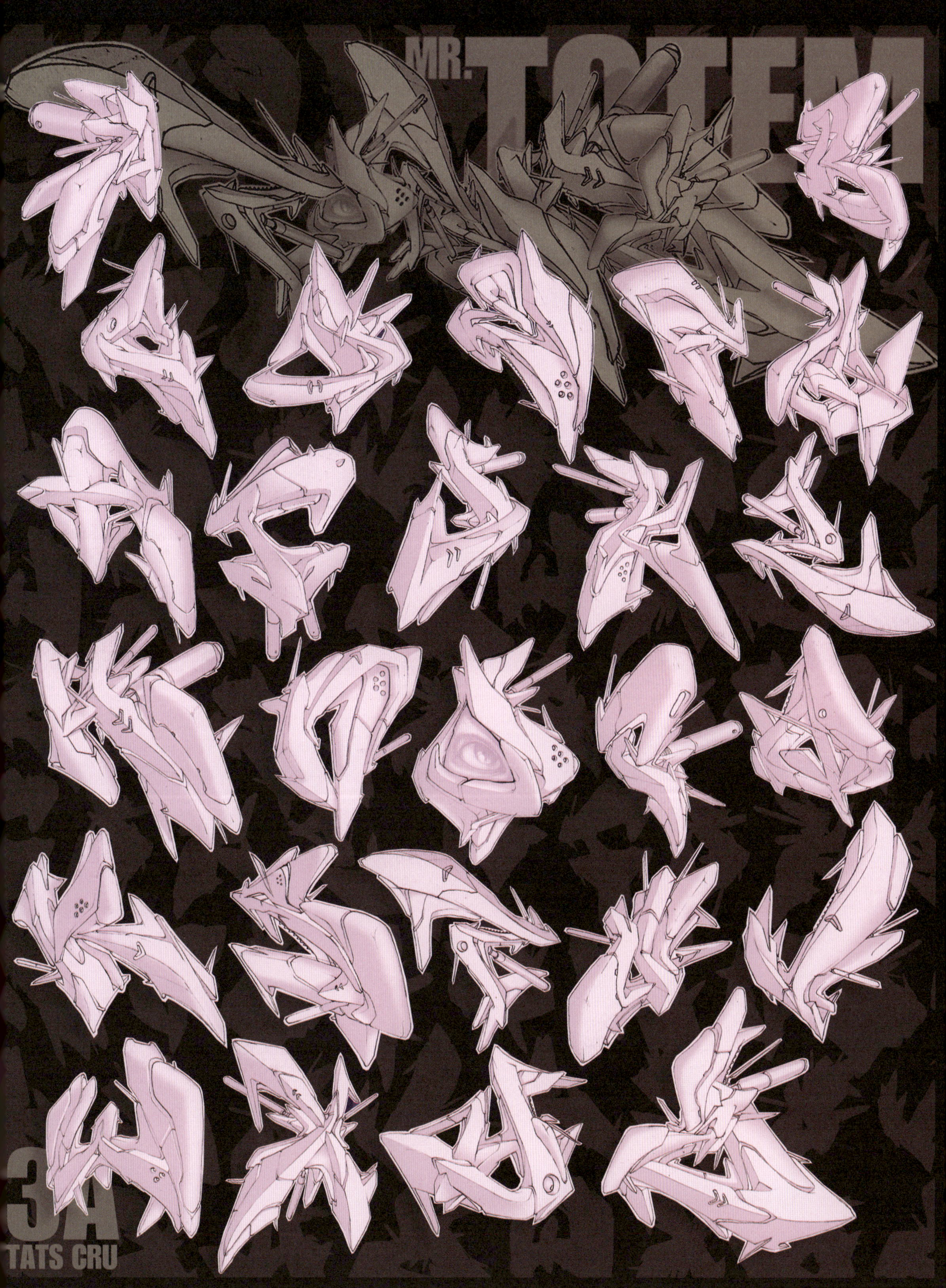

MR. TOTEM
3A
TATS CRU

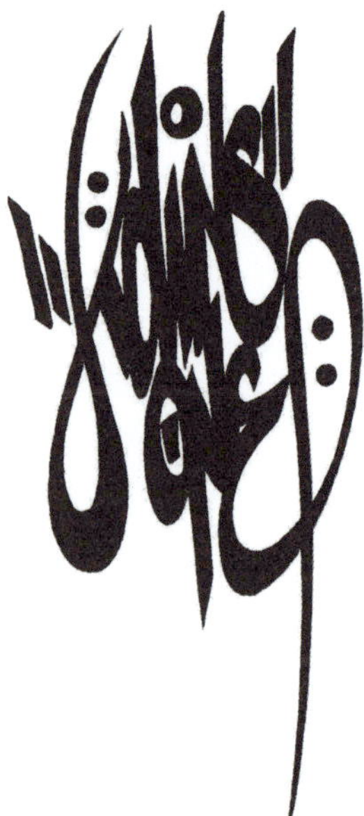

Towns

LONDON, UK
Crew member of RT
Writer since 1999
Favourite letter: S

Towns has travelled extensively with his Represent London crew, creating high-quality wall productions and highlighting the English contribution to the international graffiti scene. He is putting a lot of energy into honing his style and technique, although he thinks that 'it's impossible to create the perfect style because you will always be lacking in a certain area'. For him, it's all about building well-structured letters and creating something that he likes.

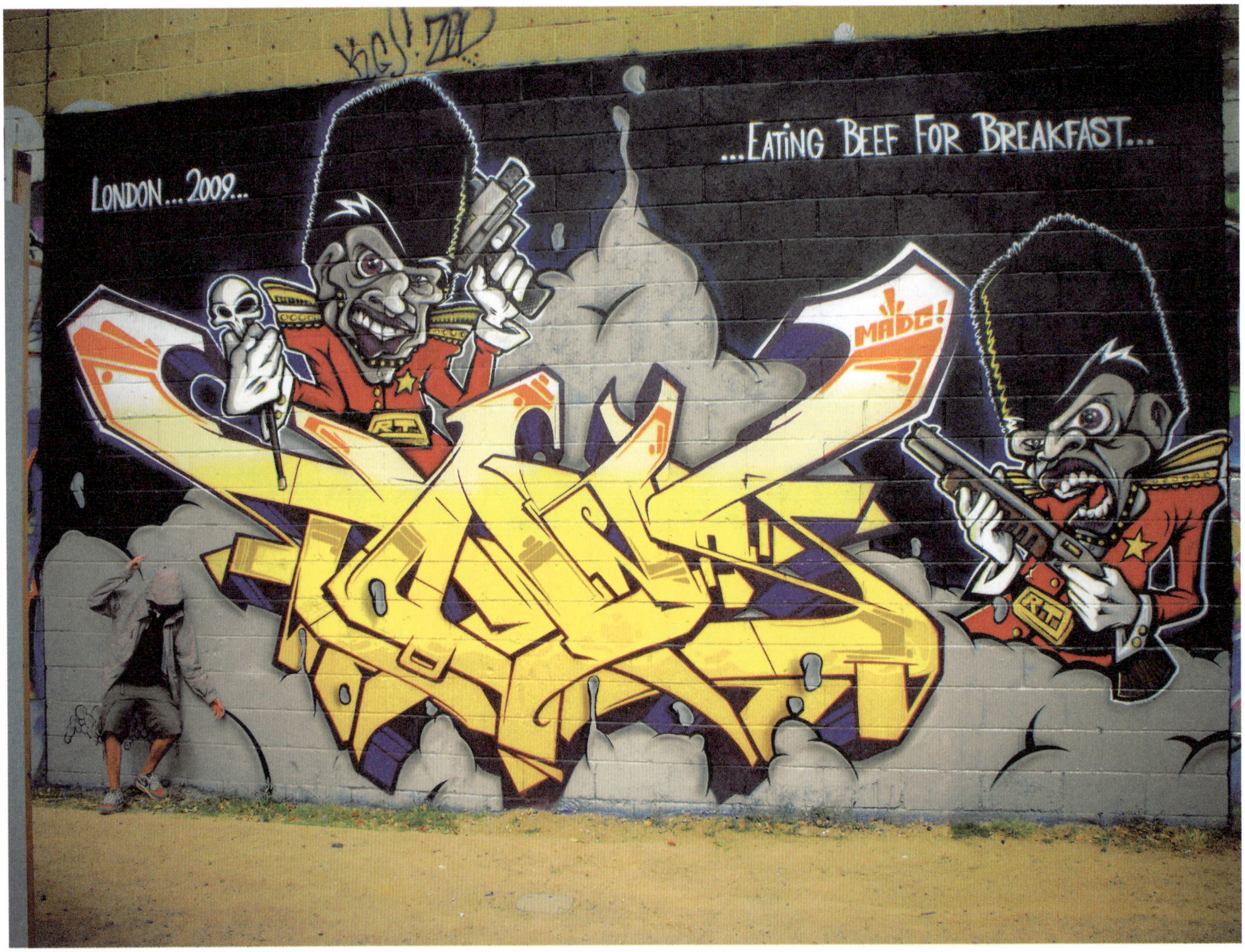

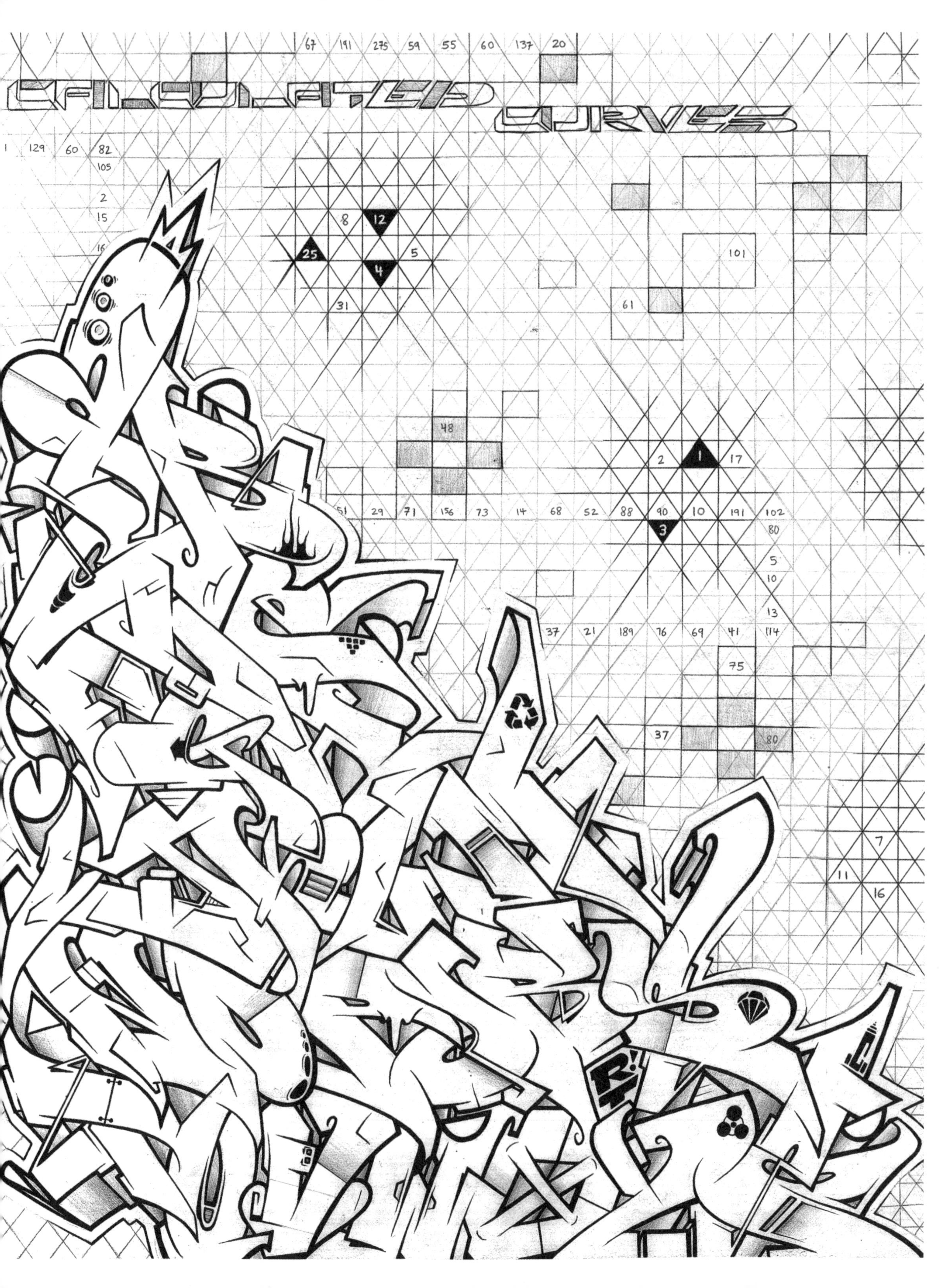

CALCULATED CURVES

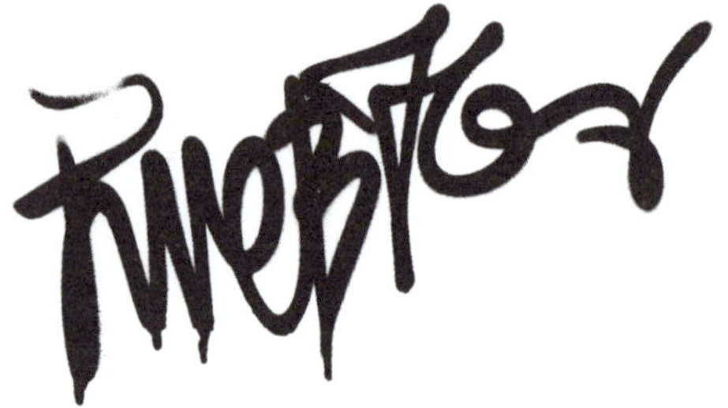

Tweb76
COPENHAGEN, DENMARK
Crew member of The South Side Crew, Clicks
Writer since 1992
Favourite letter: E
www.tweb76.com

Tweb76's pieces are an interesting combination of solid but fluid lines, rounded elements and limited colours. He has designed his twenty-six letters like a font to illustrate his typical style: 'To me it's all about personalizing your letters. Simple colour combinations and technique are nice, but a strong personal style is essential to keep your letters alive.'

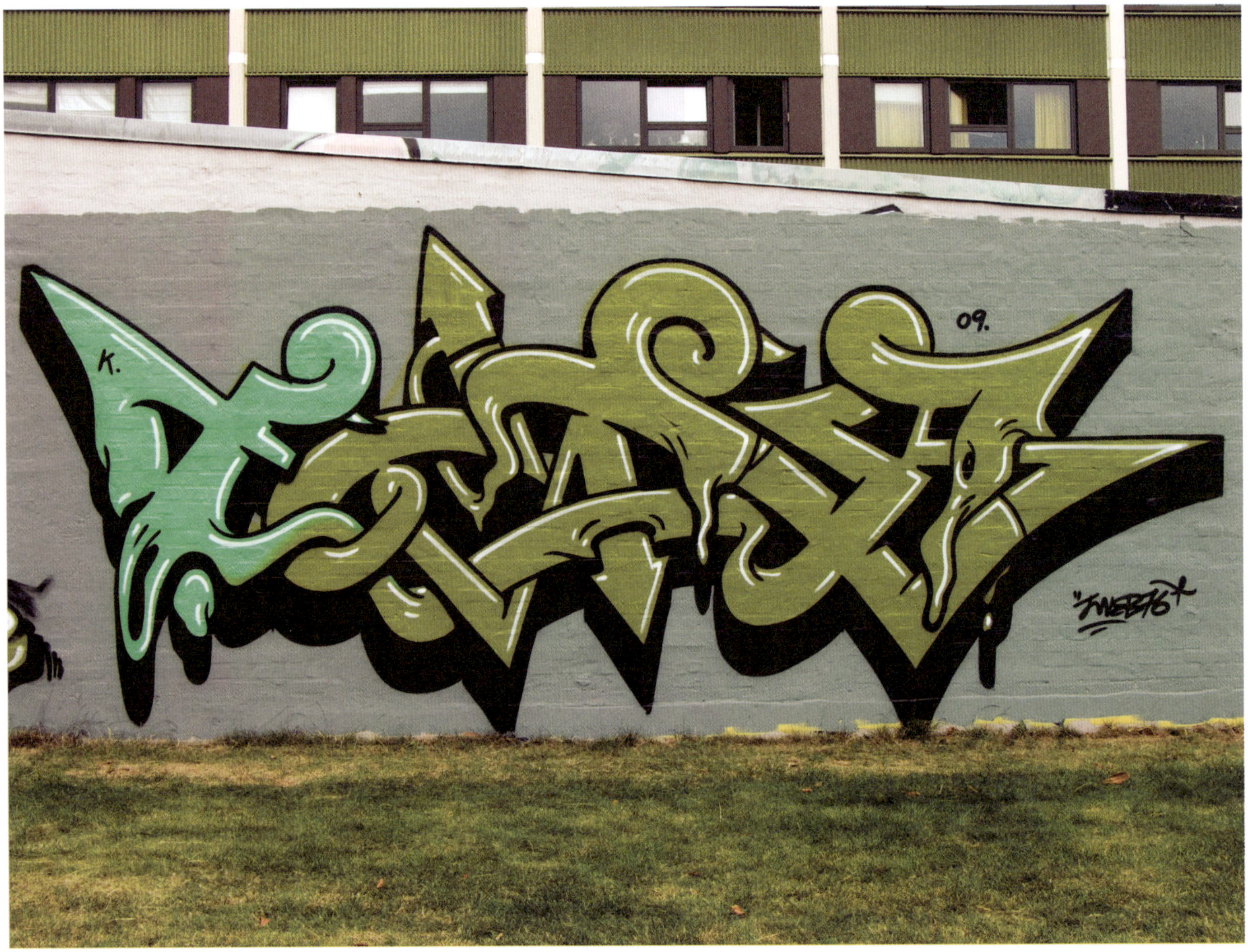

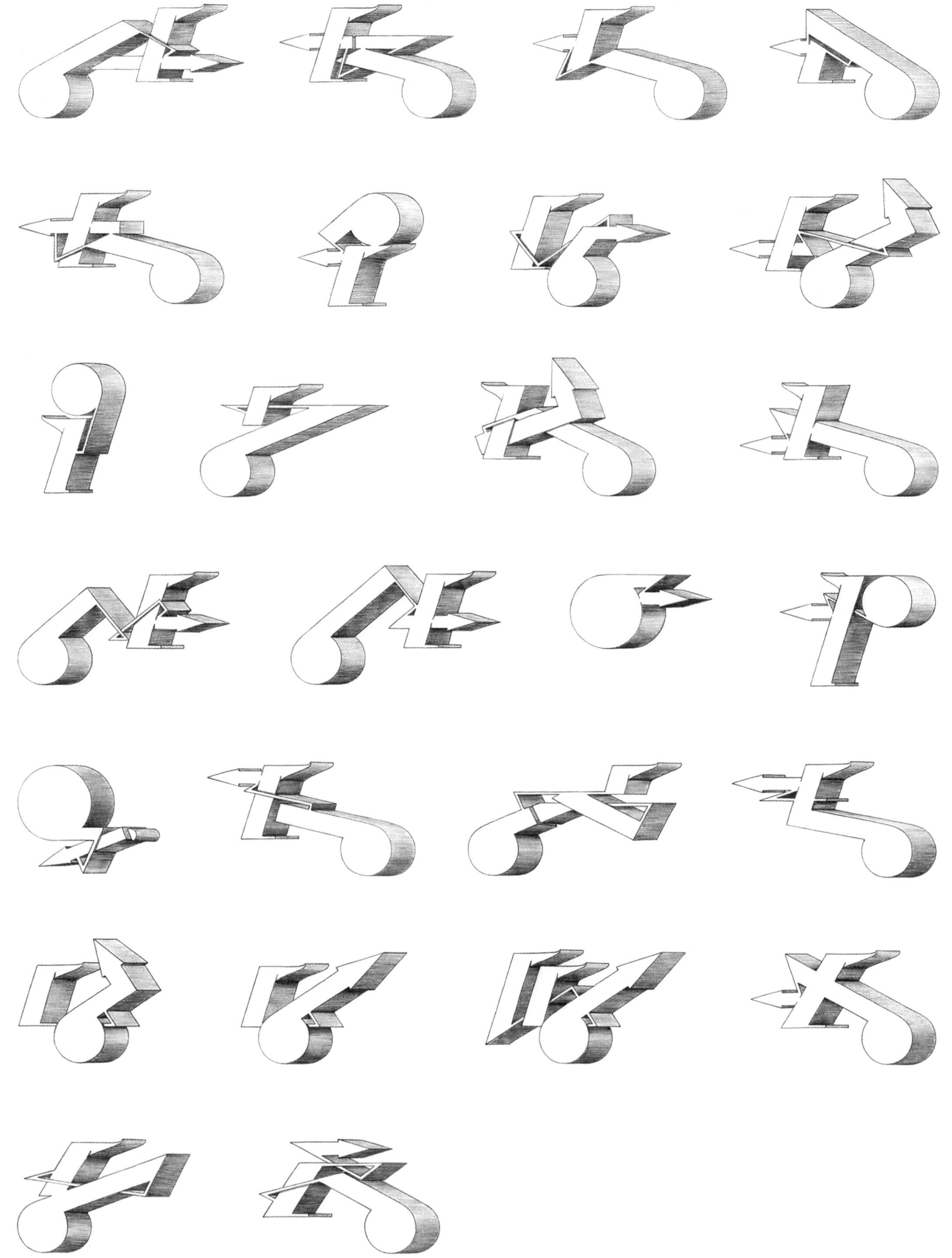

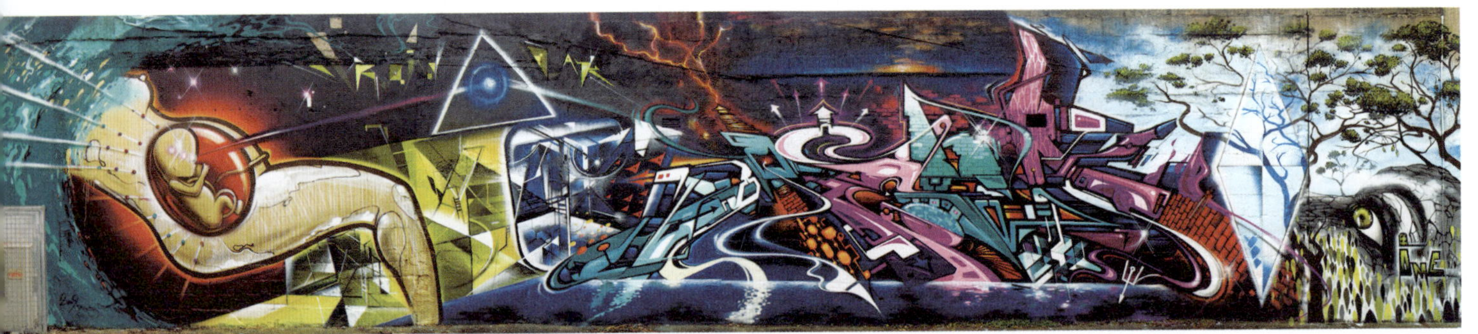

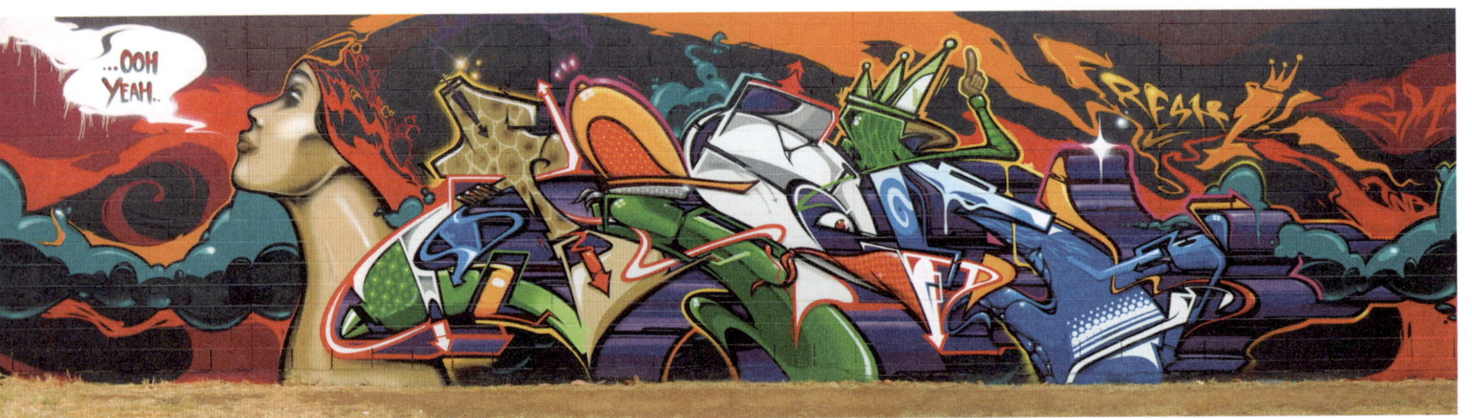

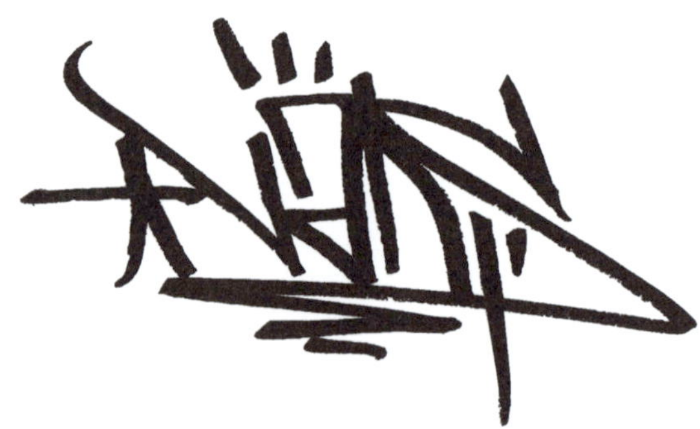

Vans The Omega
ADELAIDE, AUSTRALIA
Crew member of F1, GM, TNB, 1SA
Writer since the late 1980s
Favourite letter: E
www.instagram.com/vanstheomega

When Vans The Omega first started to express himself artistically, he used an airbrush pistol, crayons, shoe polish, markers and pastels. In 1990 he painted his first piece with aerosols. He loves writing for many reasons, including the paint-stained hands, the sound of the paint being expelled from a can, being immersed in colour theory, finding a new shape or meeting like-minded people while travelling the globe. He calls graffiti his 'constant love affair'.

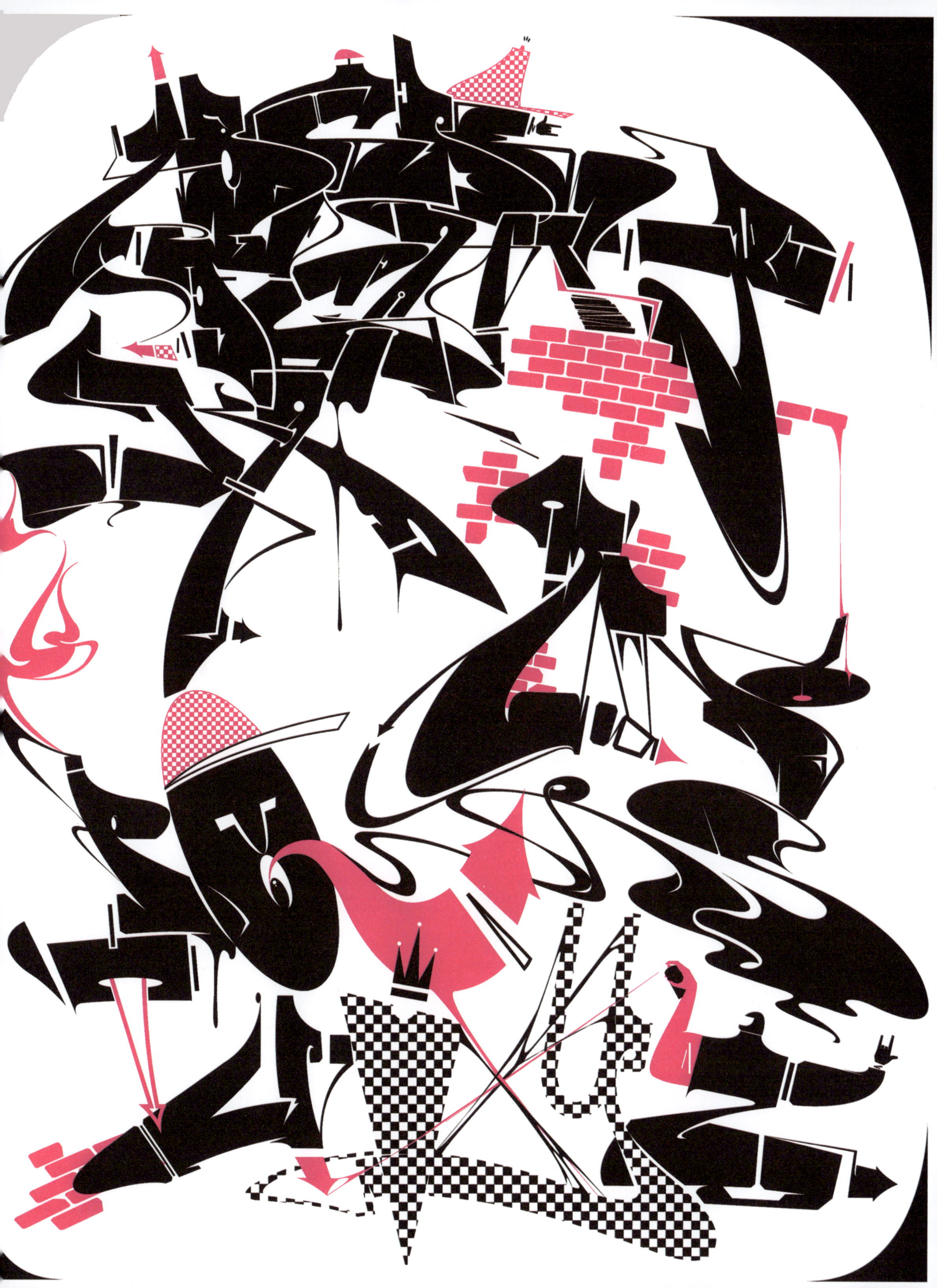

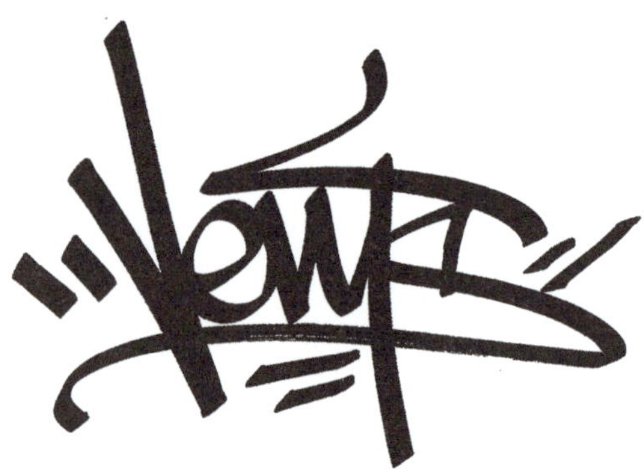

Vents

AUCKLAND, NEW ZEALAND
Crew member of RTR
Writer since 1996
Favourite letter: E

Vents' original plan was to paint each letter of his alphabet individually using a range of different techniques and colours. In the end he decided to do one single wall to represent his style. Vents feels most comfortable when he can work freestyle with a spray can on a wall. 'This way I can never be sure of the finished outcome, and maintain a level of spontaneity in my work,' he says.

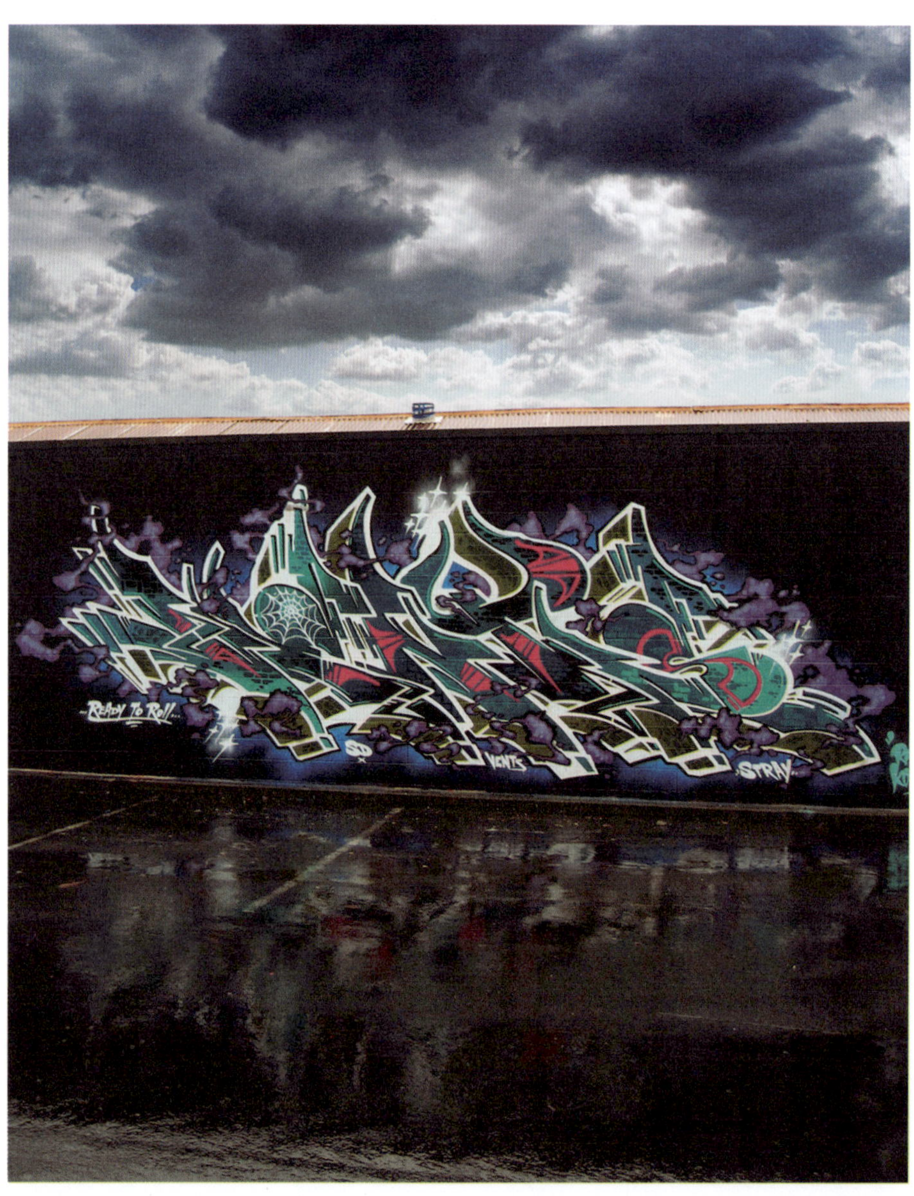

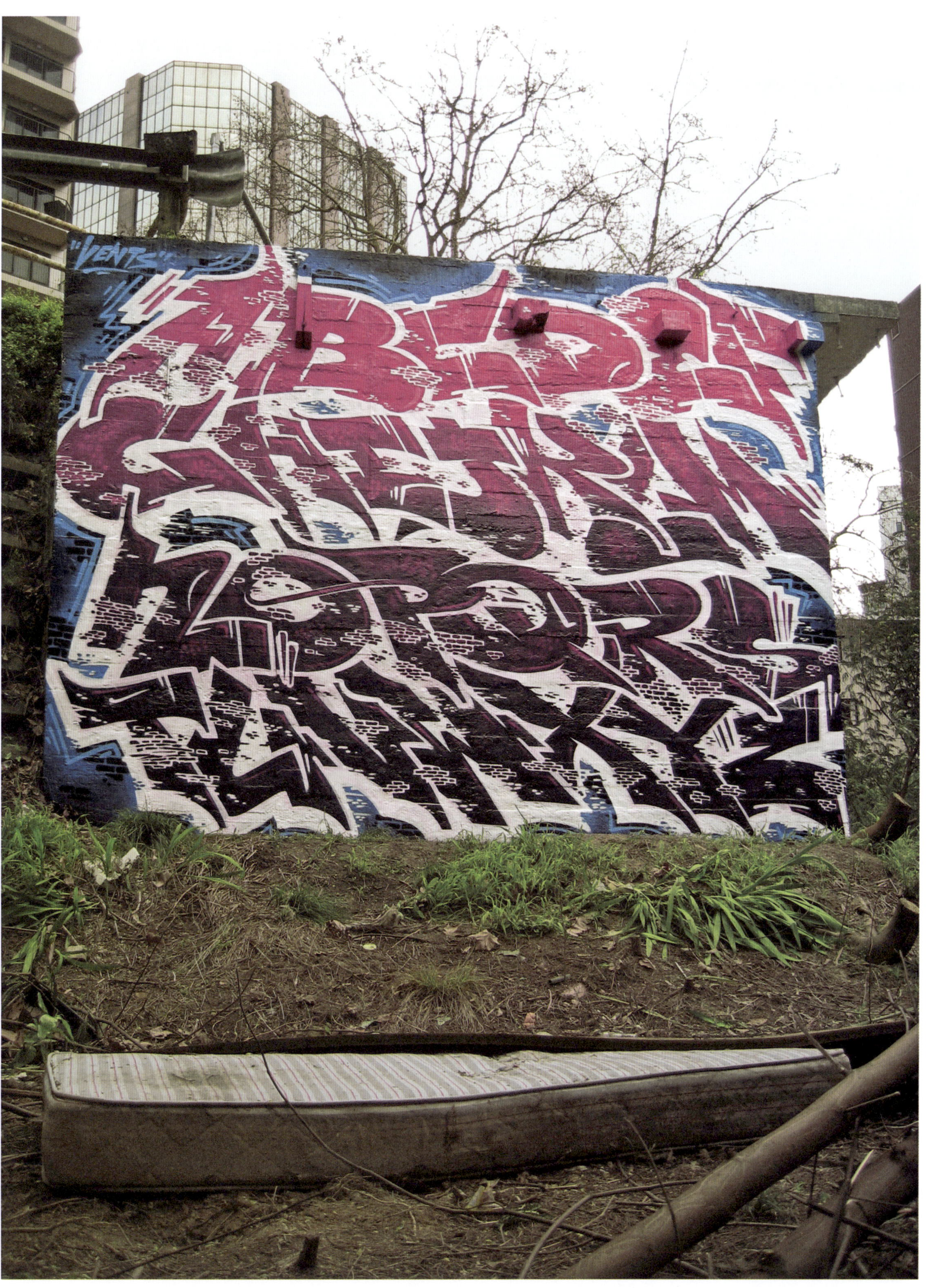

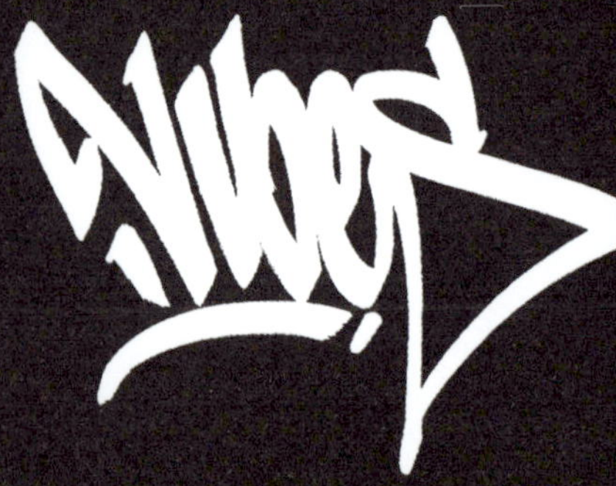

Vibes

LONDON, UK
Crew member of RT
Writer since 1997
Favourite letter: S
www.instagram.com/vibes_ldn

Vibes describes his style as 'natural, aggressive and London'. He doesn't focus on letters alone, but also creates characters on walls and canvases. 'I think to create a good-looking piece, flow and of course style within the letters are most important. I like a piece that looks like it can stand its ground.'

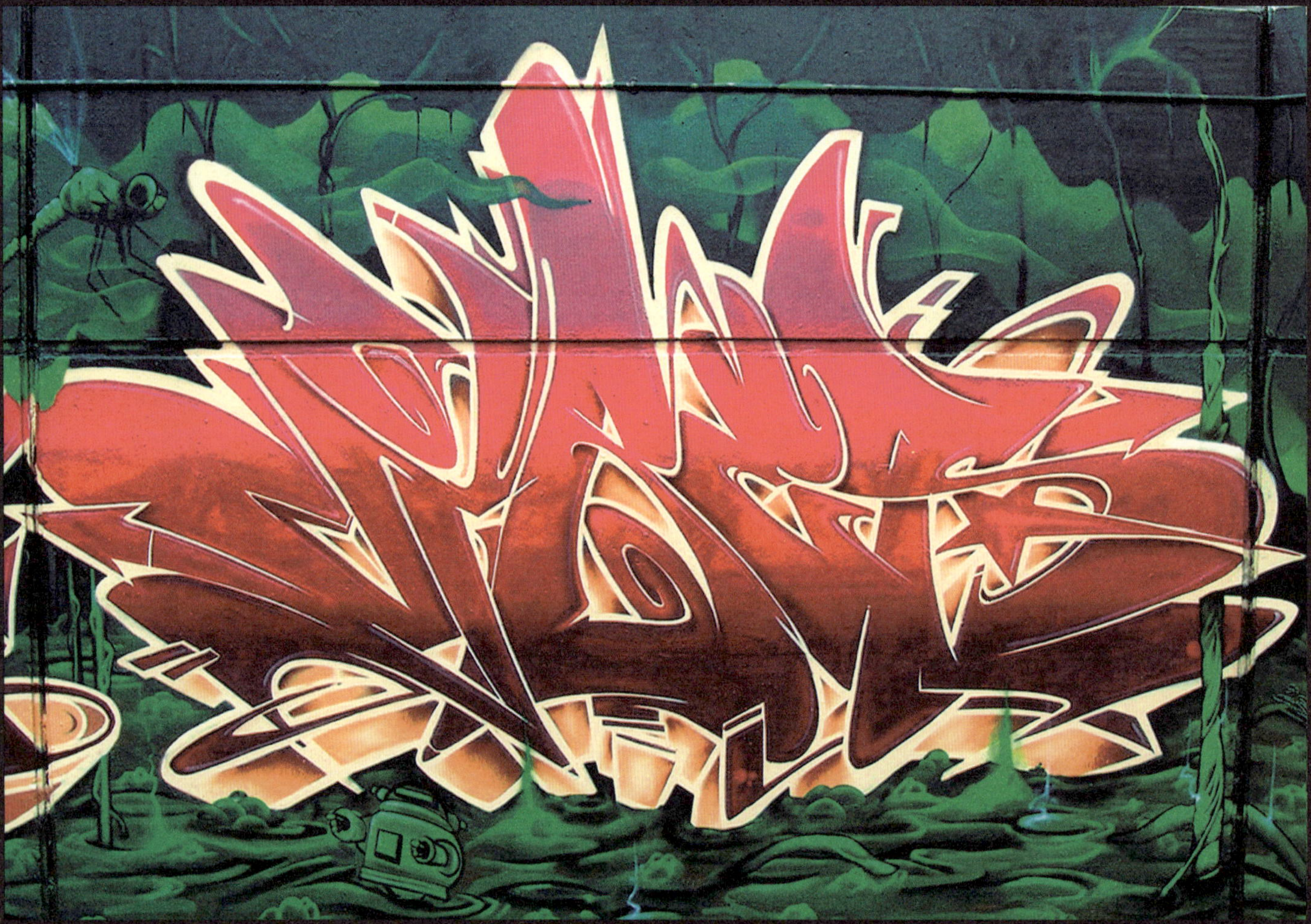

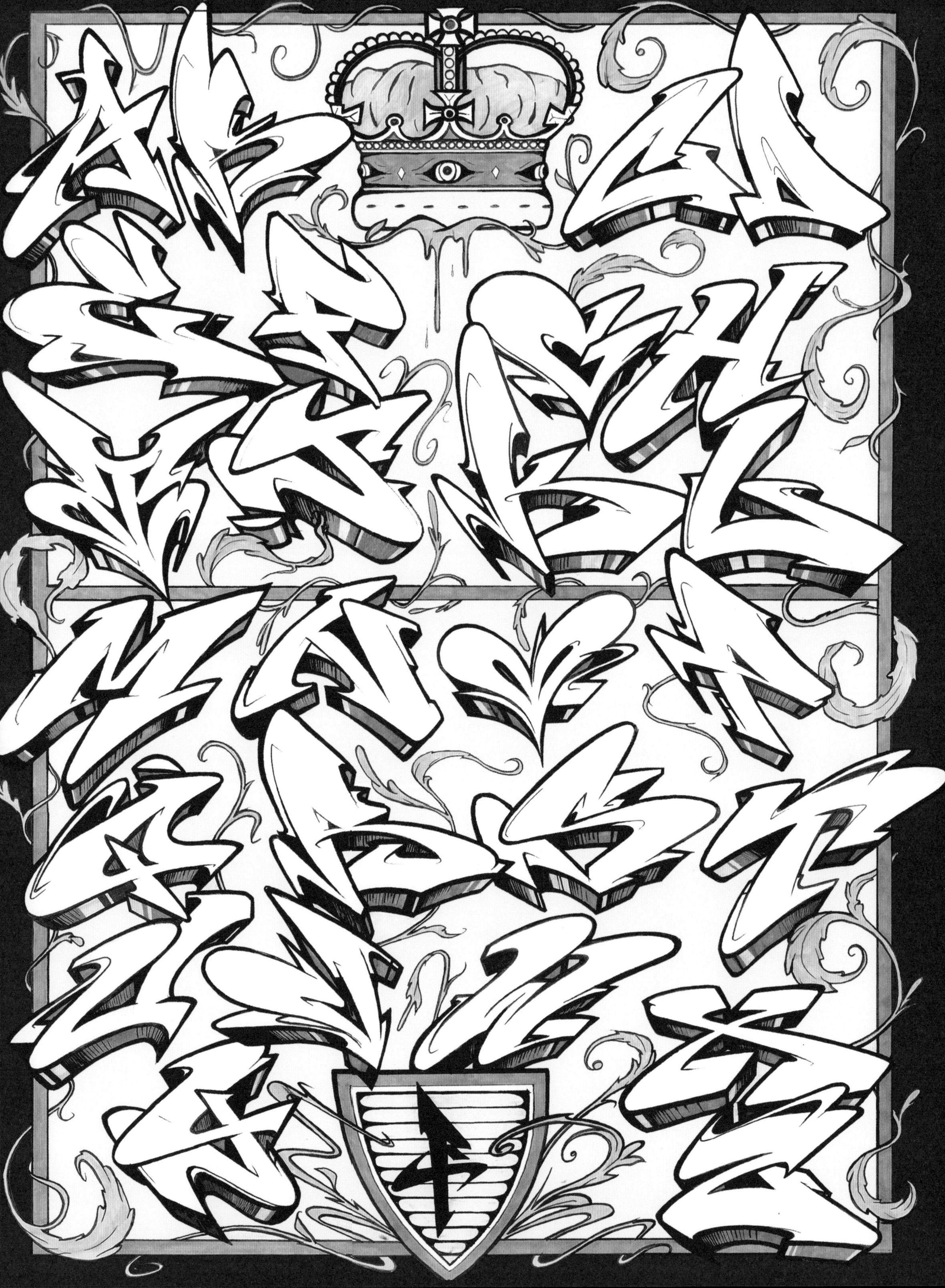

Vision

PARIS, FRANCE

Crew member of OC, MCZ
Writer since 1985
Favourite letter: S
www.myspace.com/bombuntildeath

Vision keeps his letters simple but vibrant, and his colourful, classic pieces immediately catch your eye. He chose to paint his alphabet with spray cans and caps on a 2 × 6 metre wall. Graffiti is his favourite way of being creative, meeting different people while travelling, and for him it's the best way to have a good time with friends.

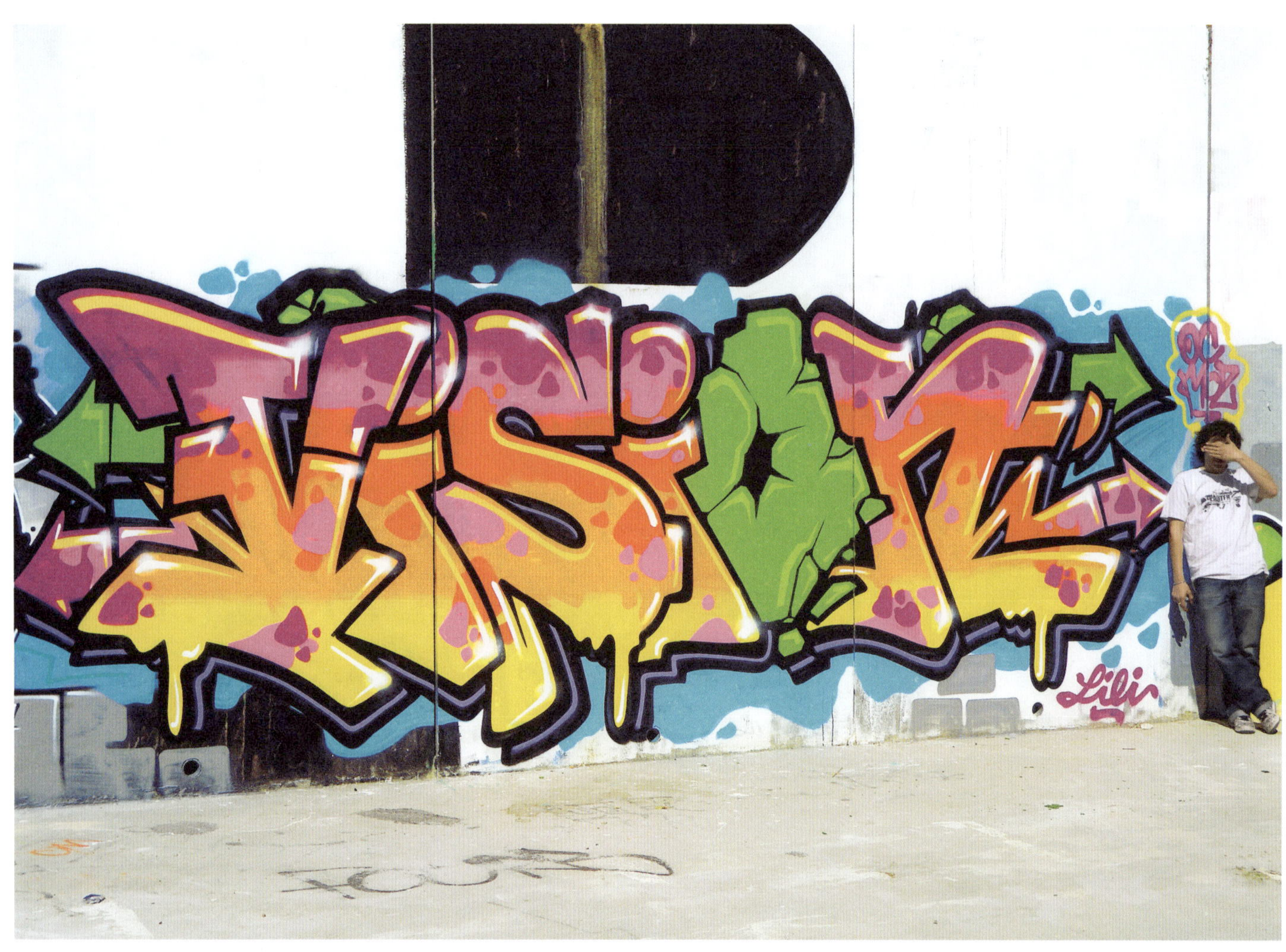

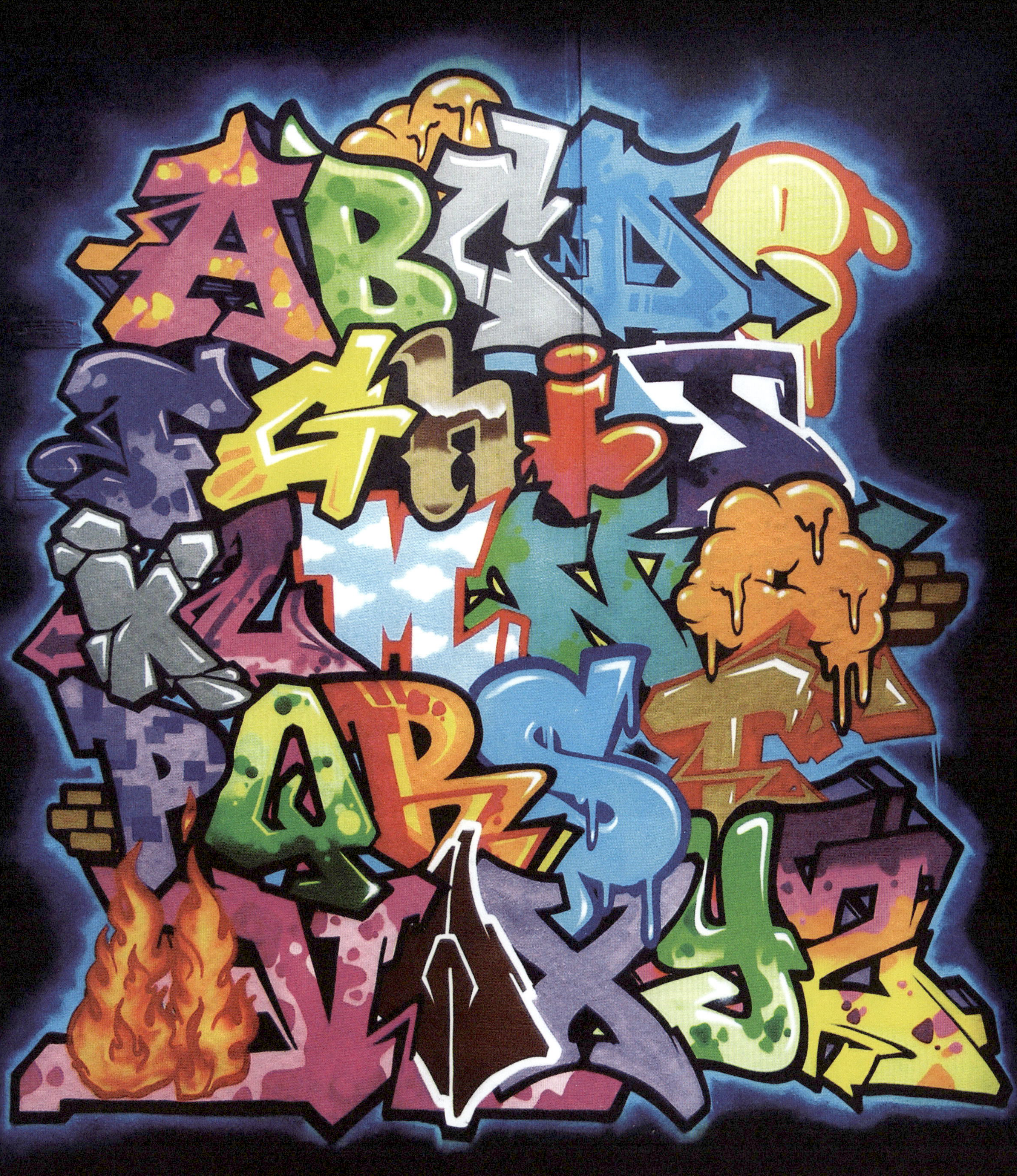

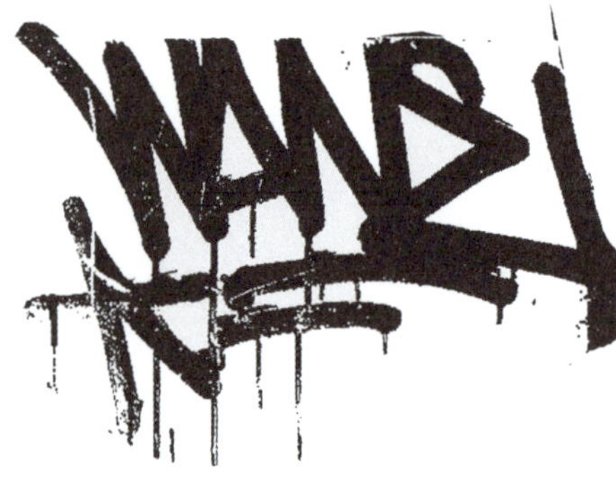

Wane

NEW YORK CITY, USA
Crew member of TC-5, FBA, FC, IBM, COD, AOK, AND, RIS, 156
Writer since 1983
Favourite letter: K
www.waneone.com

Wane, also known as Knows, has a classic New York style with an unorthodox twist. He develops his own unique style of lettering using unconventional joins, for example. Wane created four versions of his font to represent his style. 'My alphabet is inspired by legends like Chain3, Seen TC5, Skeme, Shame and West,' he explains, adding: 'Graffiti is a world of its own. Only writers and artists can understand how it works and they will do anything to keep it alive.'

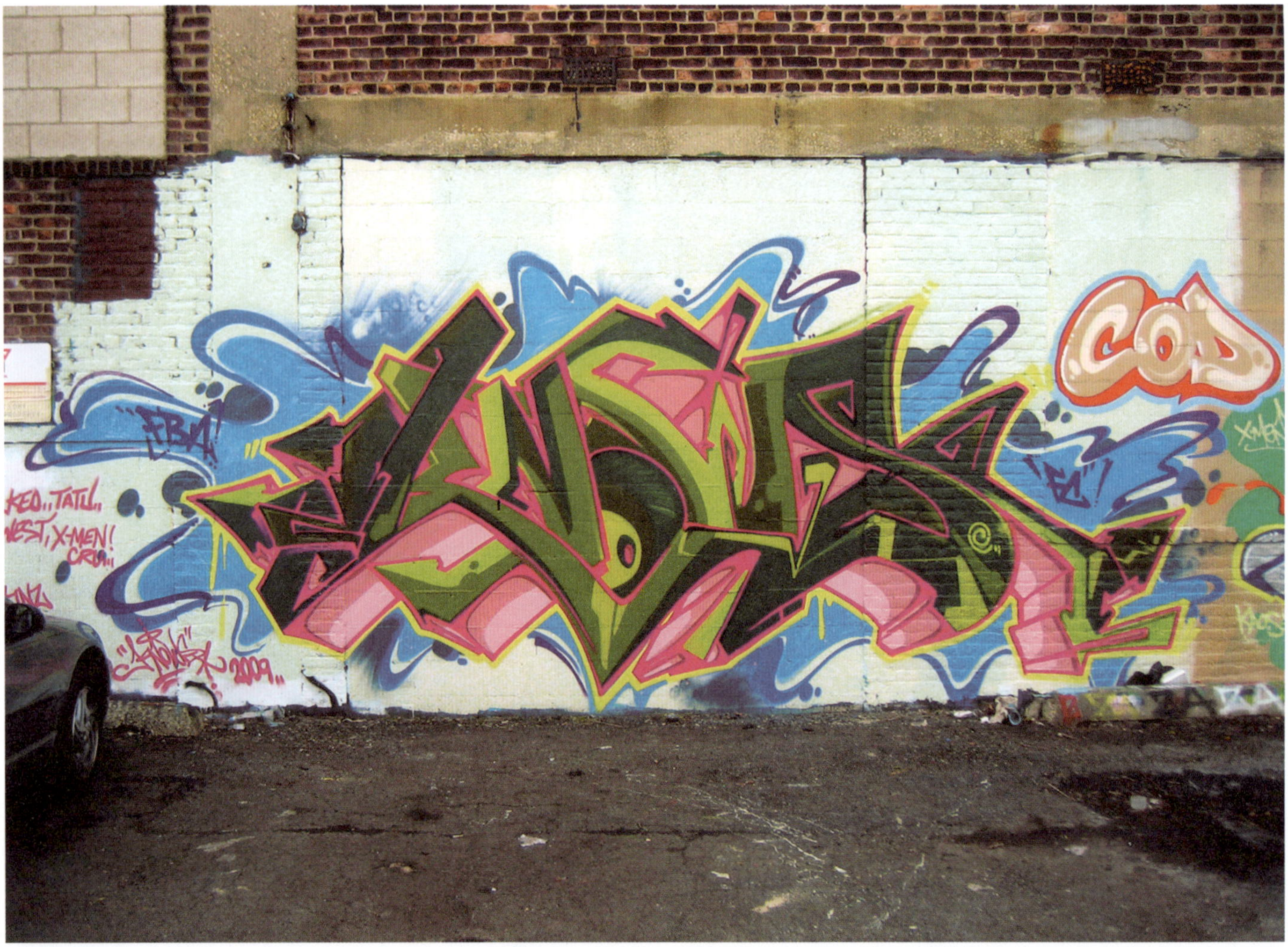

ACKNOWLEDGED STYLE ®

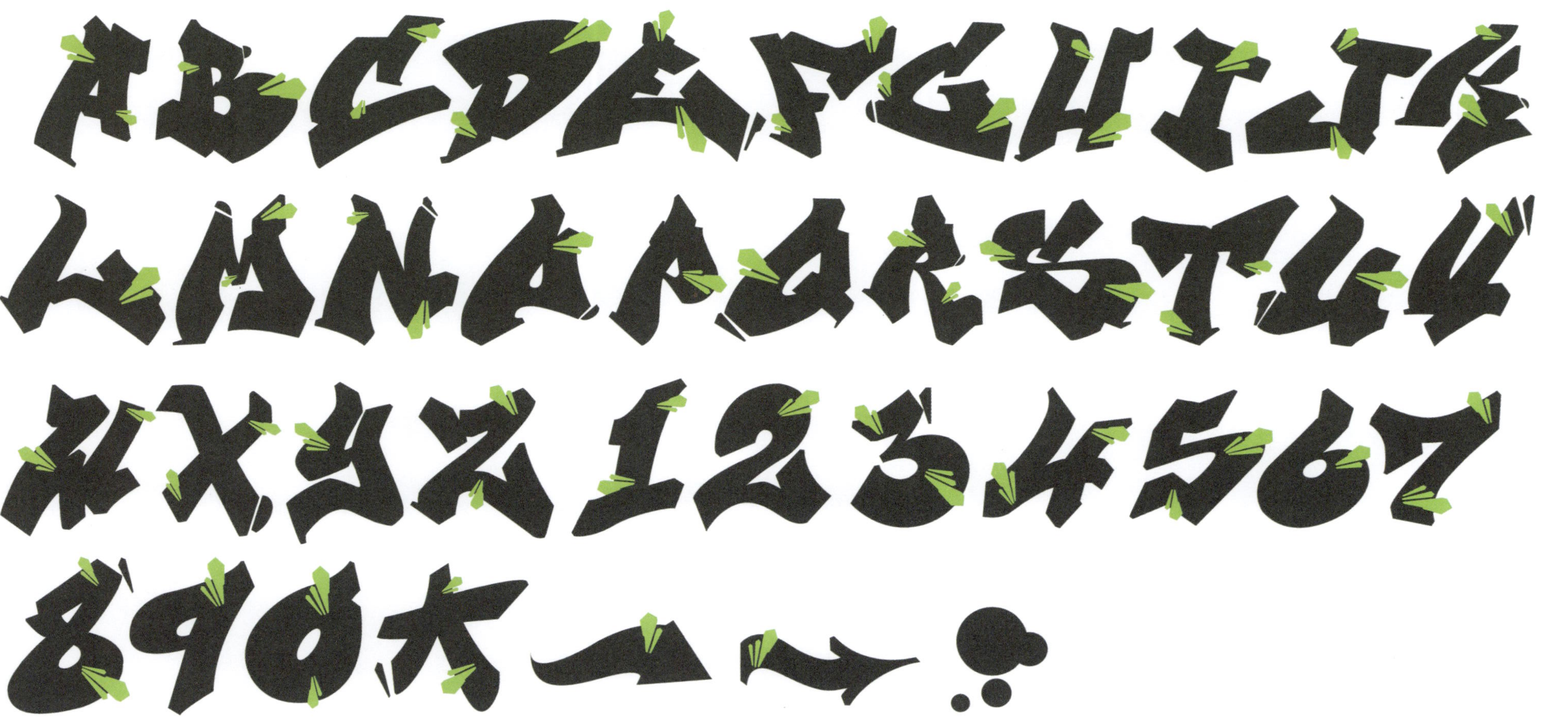

ACKNOWLEDGED OPEN LETTERS ®
ACKNOWLEDGED LETTERS ®
ACKNOWLEDGED ERODEDRIPS ®

Mr. Wany

MILAN, ITALY

Crew member of Heavy Artillery, PDB, PUF
Writer since 1990
Favourite letter: 'I love all letters'
www.wanyone.com

Mr. Wany is well known for his distinct characters and flowing pieces. He makes a living from advertising and design projects and has worked with brands like MTV, D&G, Eastpak, Adidas and Nike. For Wany, being proficient in as many fields as possible is key: 'It's important to know how to do tags, bombing, lettering, backgrounds and characters with originality.'

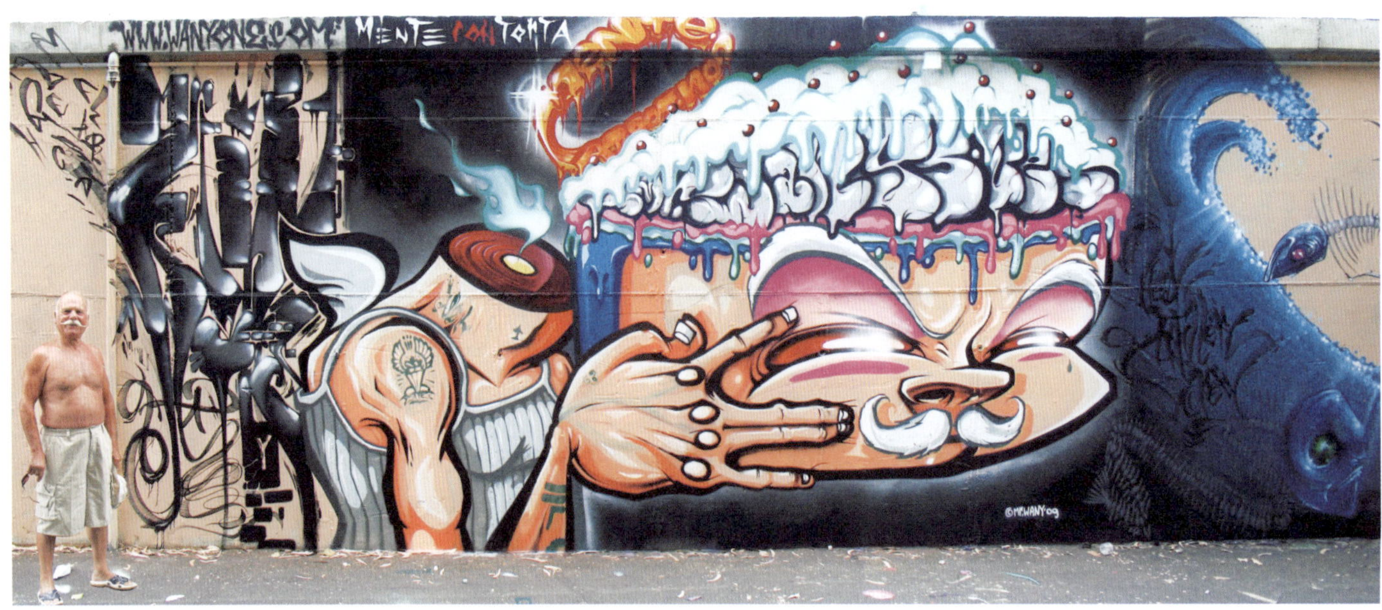

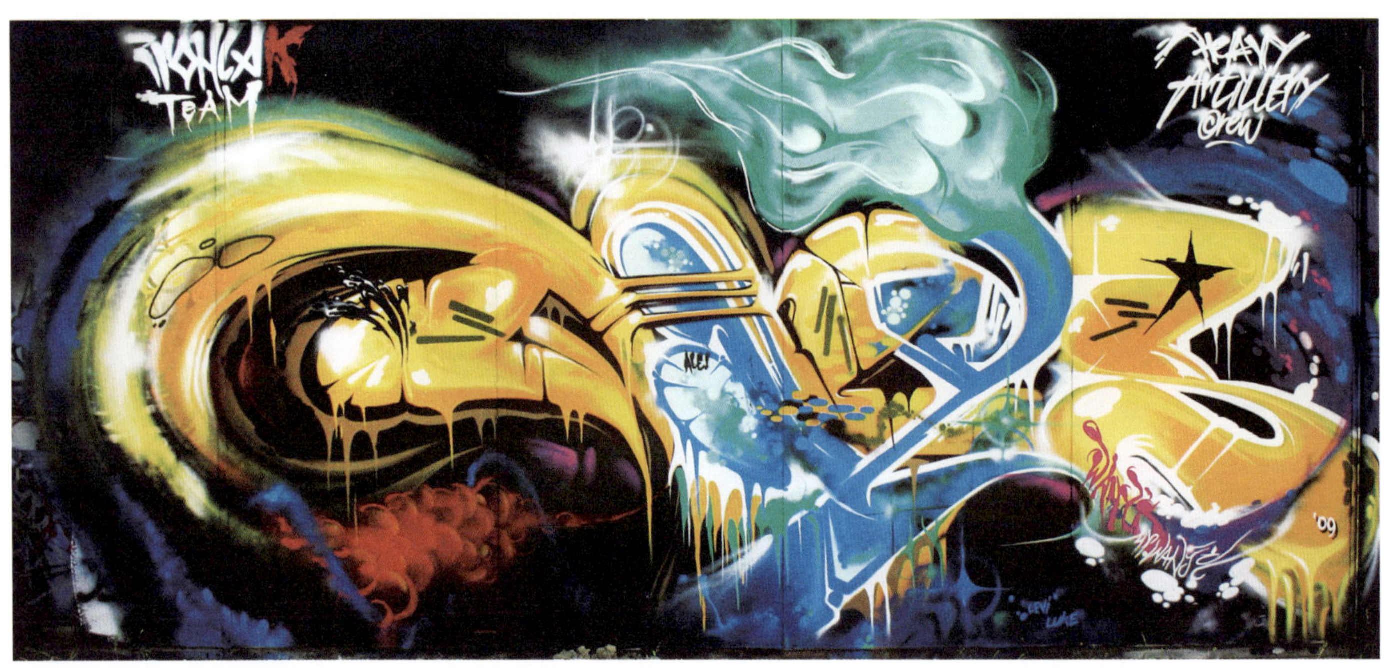

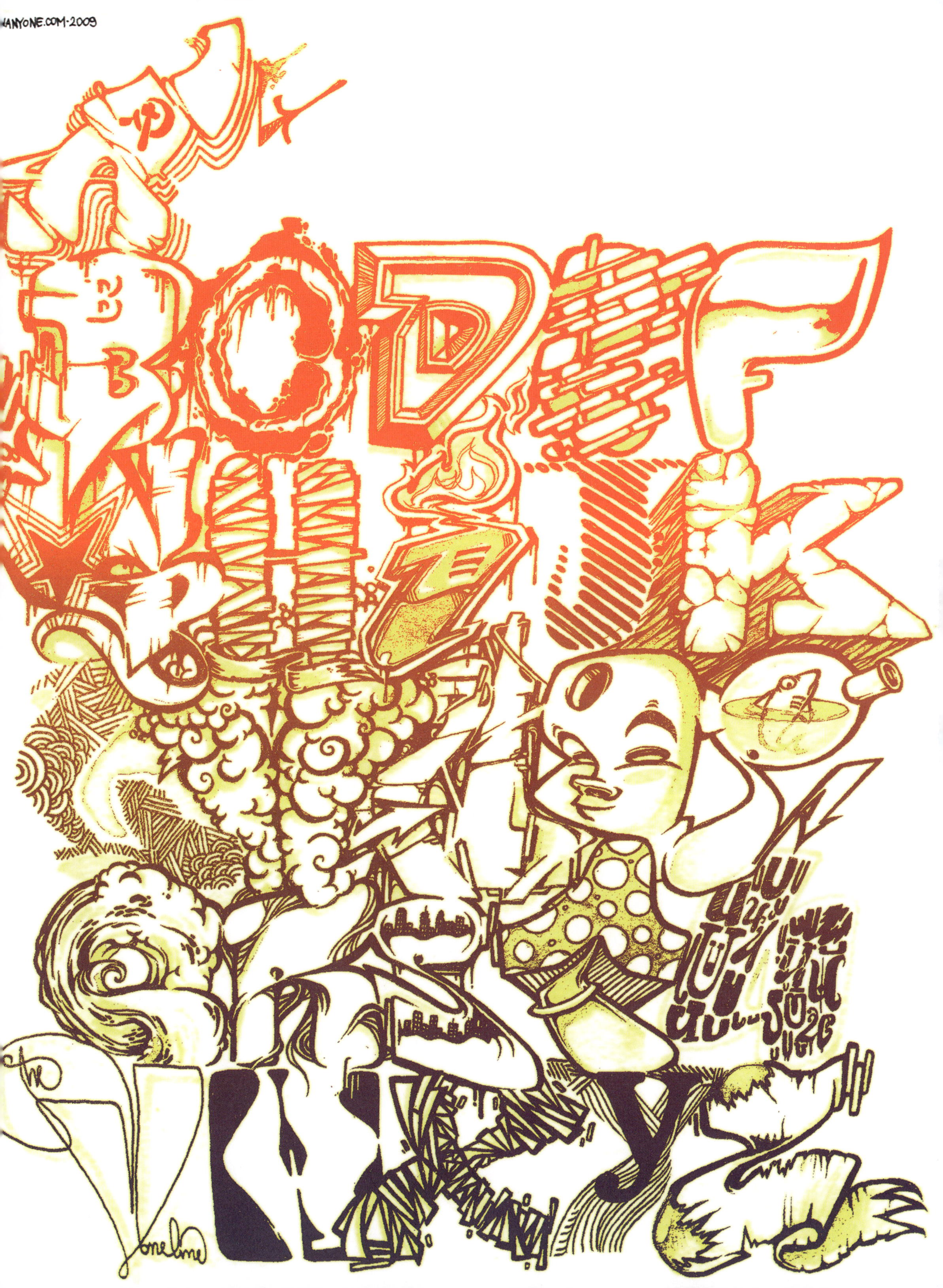
ANYONE.COM-2009
BODY
OF
WHAT
WORK

Wert

BARI, ITALY

Crew member of Nsis
Favourite letter: W
www.myspace.com/wert80

Wert likes to skew and stretch his pieces to give them energy and flow. He decided to paint his alphabet freestyle at the Bari line on a 30-metre-long wall. 'A good piece is when the letters and fill-ins melt together like cheese on a pizza,' he says.

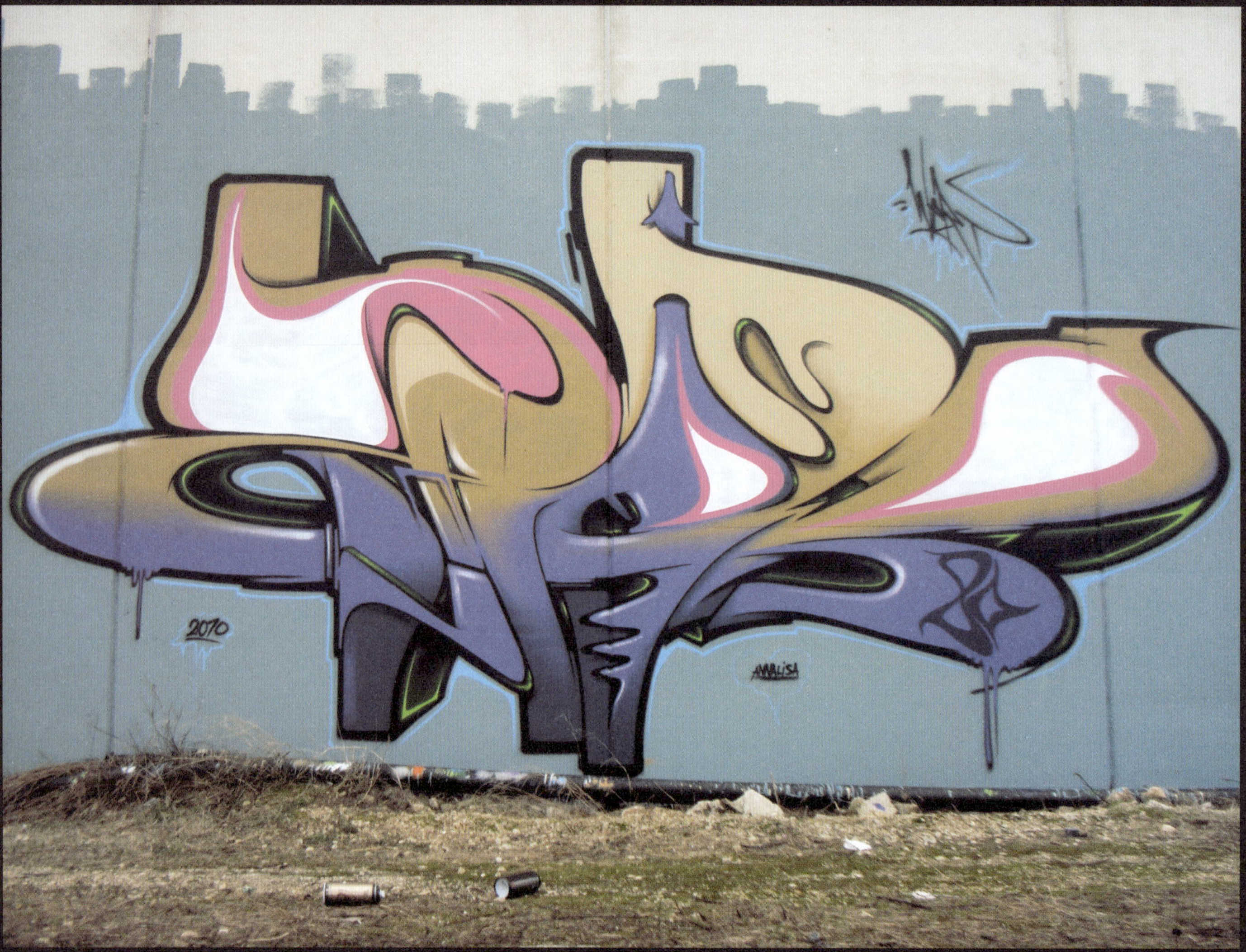

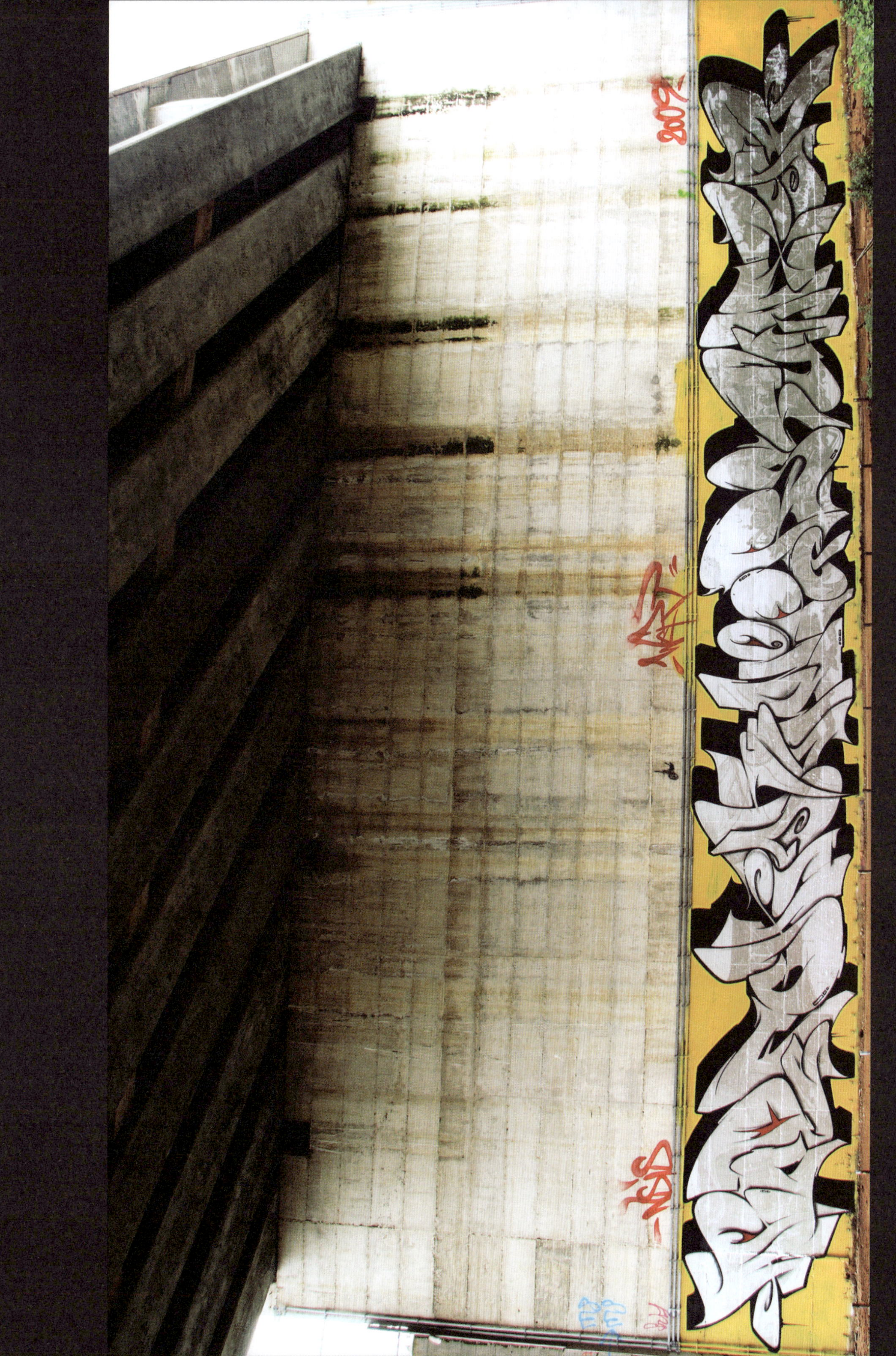

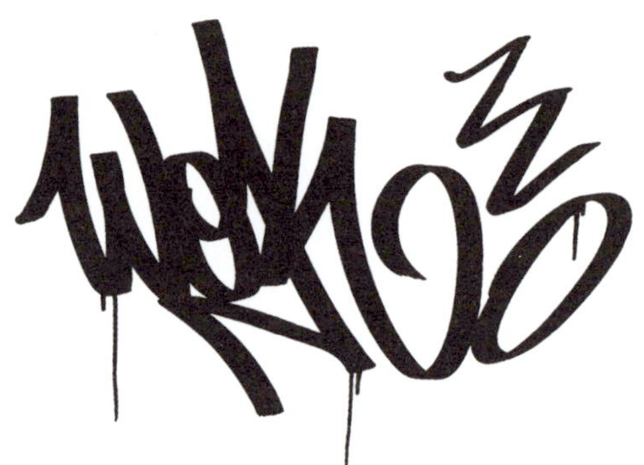

Wok

DRESDEN, GERMANY

Crew member of Bandits, Macia, 104
Writer since 1997
Favourite letters: M, A, Z
www.worldwildwok.com

Wok has a passion for massive pieces with straight lines, distinct 3D blocks and a brave choice of colours. He likes dirty fill-ins and backgrounds, which he cleans up with a sharp and fresh outline. In his hometown of Dresden he is also known as the rapper Courage, and his lyrics often refer to his life as a graffiti artist and the difficulties it brings. In Wok's opinion, all you need is 'straight letters, a good spot and four spray cans' to create a nice piece.

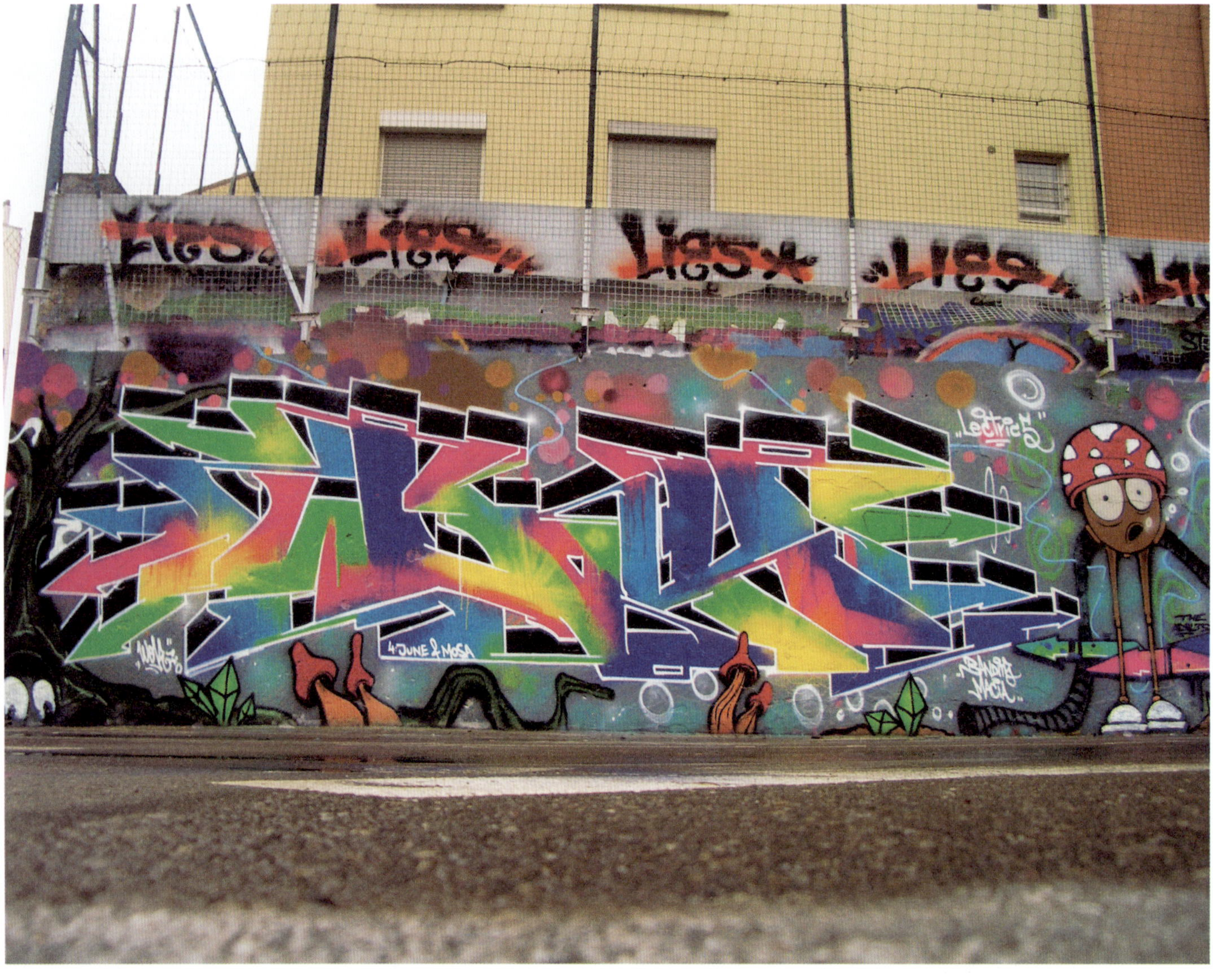

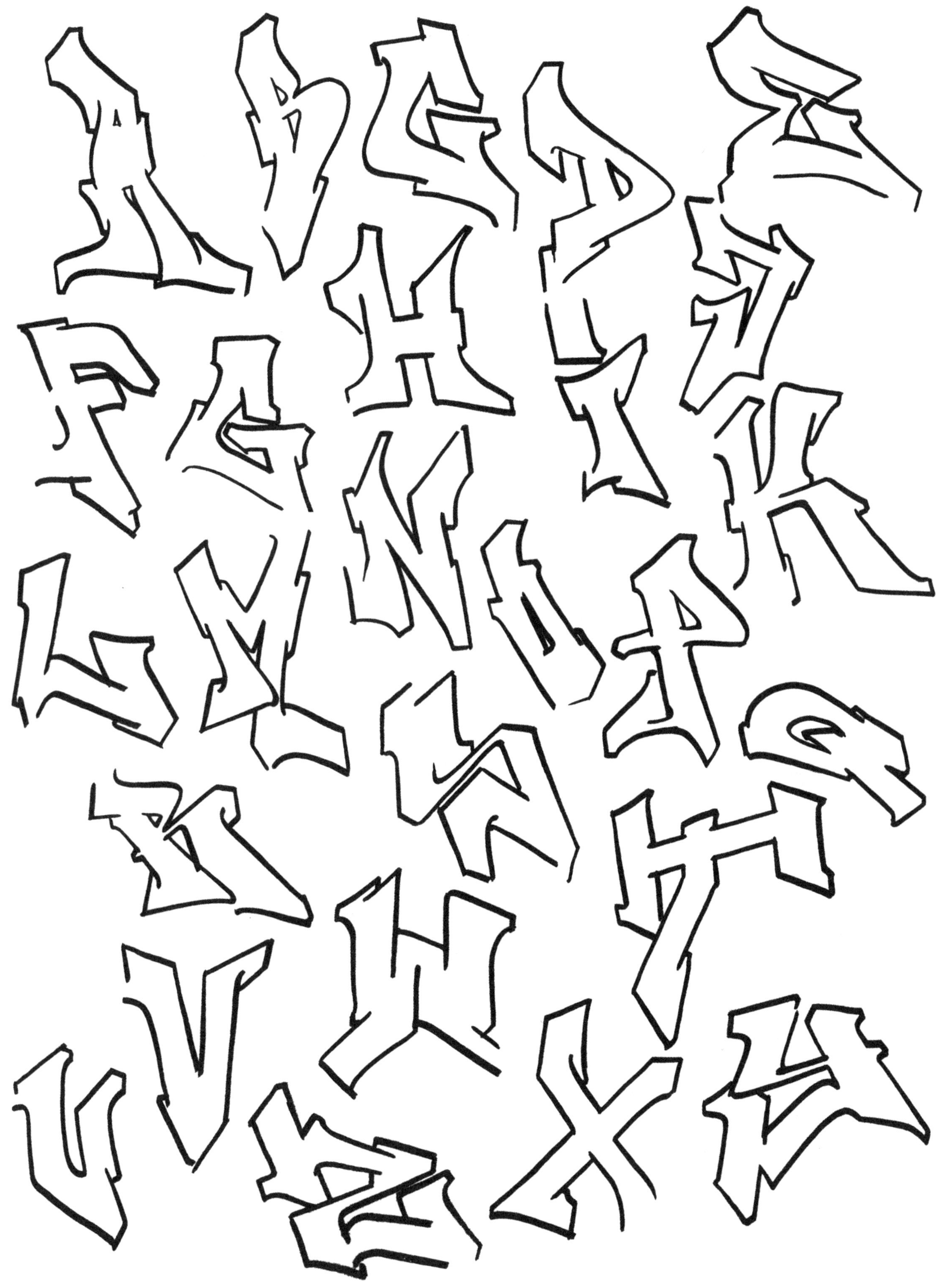

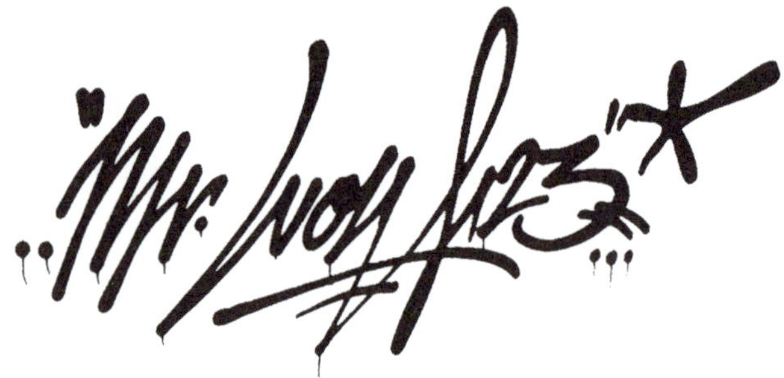

Wow123

BREMEN, GERMANY
Crew member of TMD, SUK
Writer since 1988
Favourite letter: E
www.markus-genesius.com

Wow123's signature style is clean, angular and complex with a lot of fine detail. However, he also tries his hand at simpler styles, bubble letters and 3D pieces. 'Having my own signature is the most important thing for me,' he says. 'There are too many copies out there.' The artist, who is also known as Bed74, earns a living from his work on canvas and from commissions to paint walls.

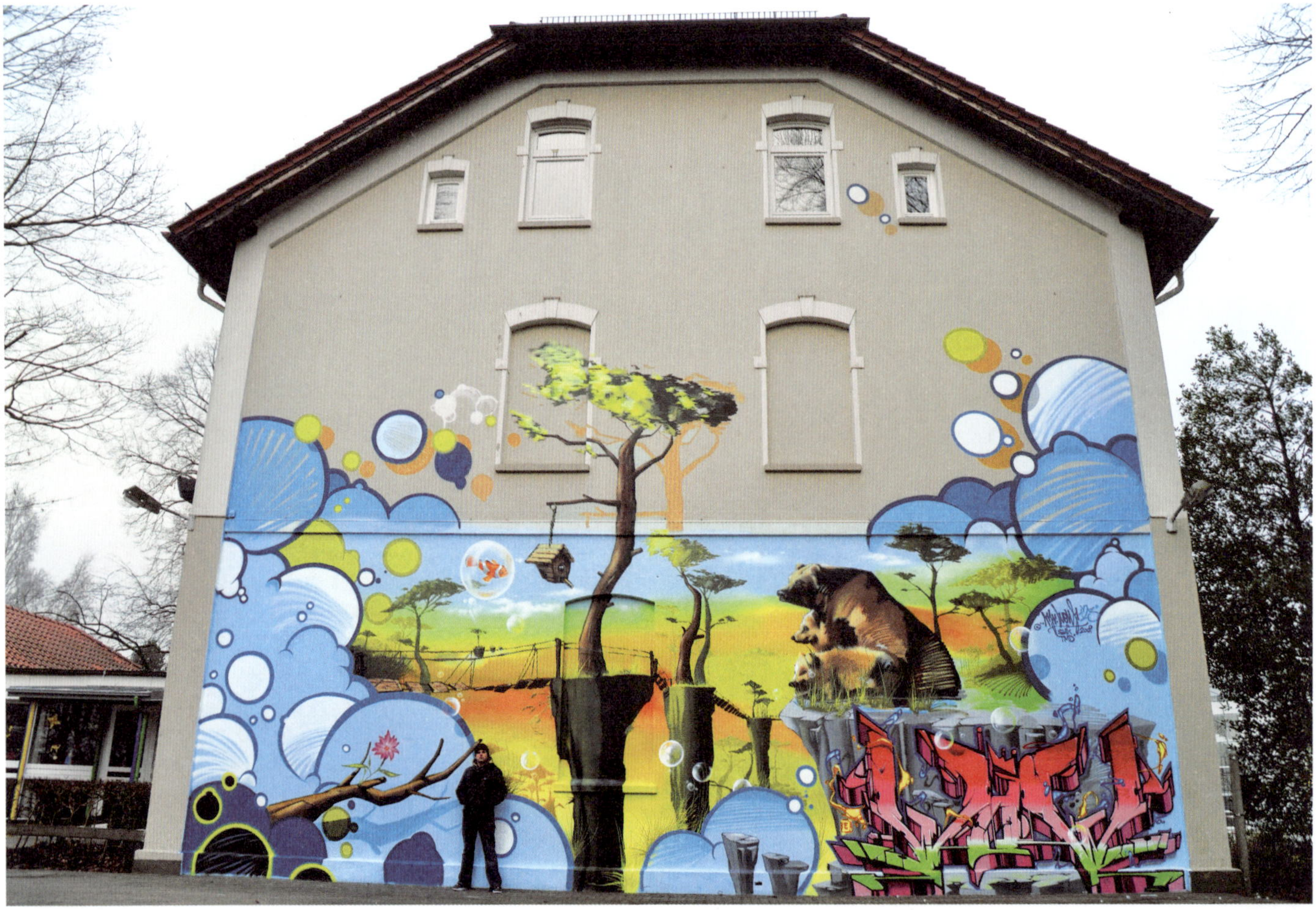

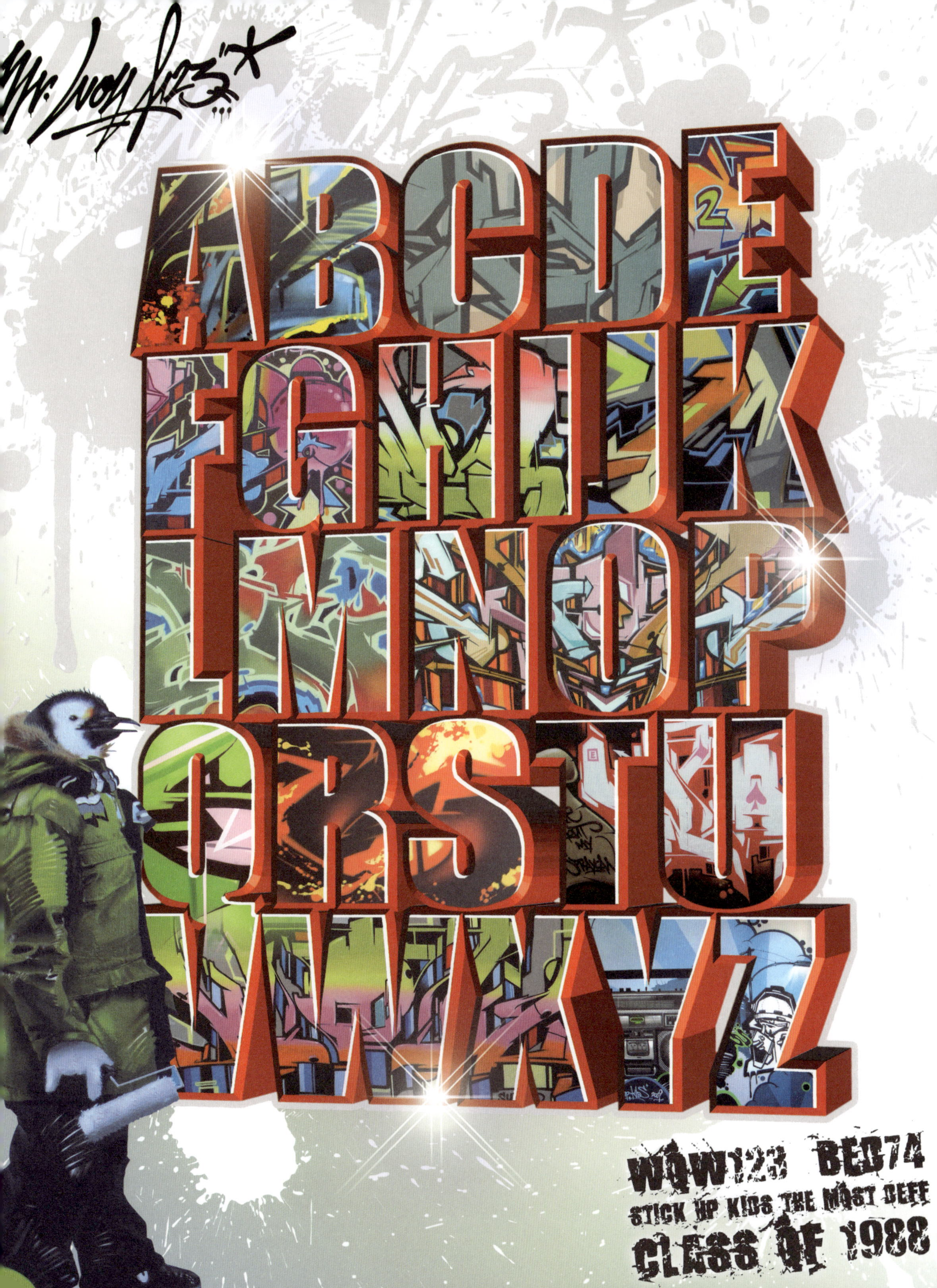

A B C D E
F G H I J K
L M N O P
Q R S T U
V W X Y Z
WQW123 BEO74
STICK UP KIDS THE MOST DEFF
CLASS OF 1988

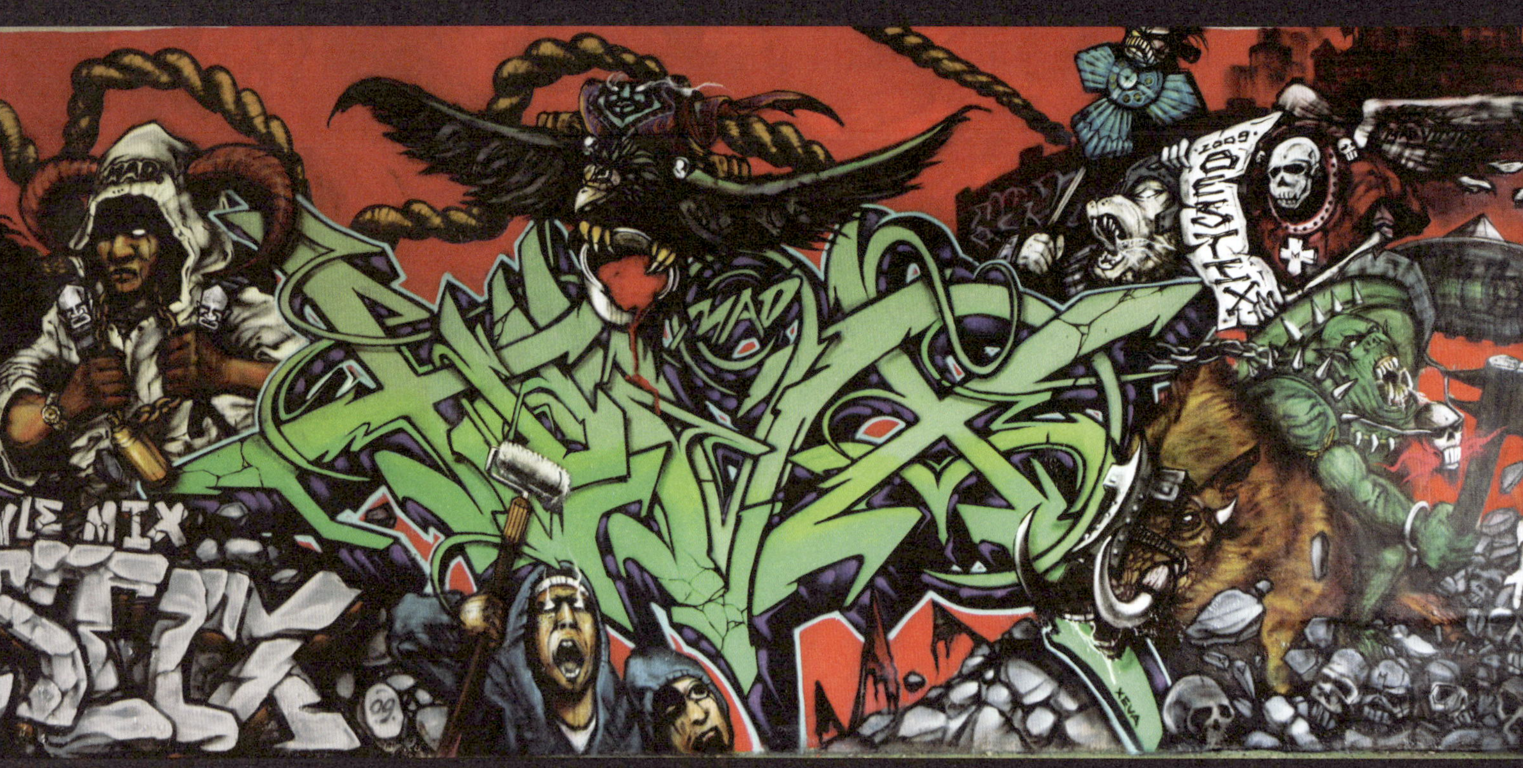

Xeva
SEOUL, SOUTH KOREA

Crew member of Mad Victor
Writer since 1999
Favourite letter: X
www.madvictor.com

The South Korean graffiti scene is still quite small and the local style is reflected in Xeva's work. Like other writers from his hometown, Xeva has mastered both letters and characters. Even though his native language is based on a different system, it is important to him to experiment with letters from the Latin alphabet according to graffiti tradition and to keep them legible.

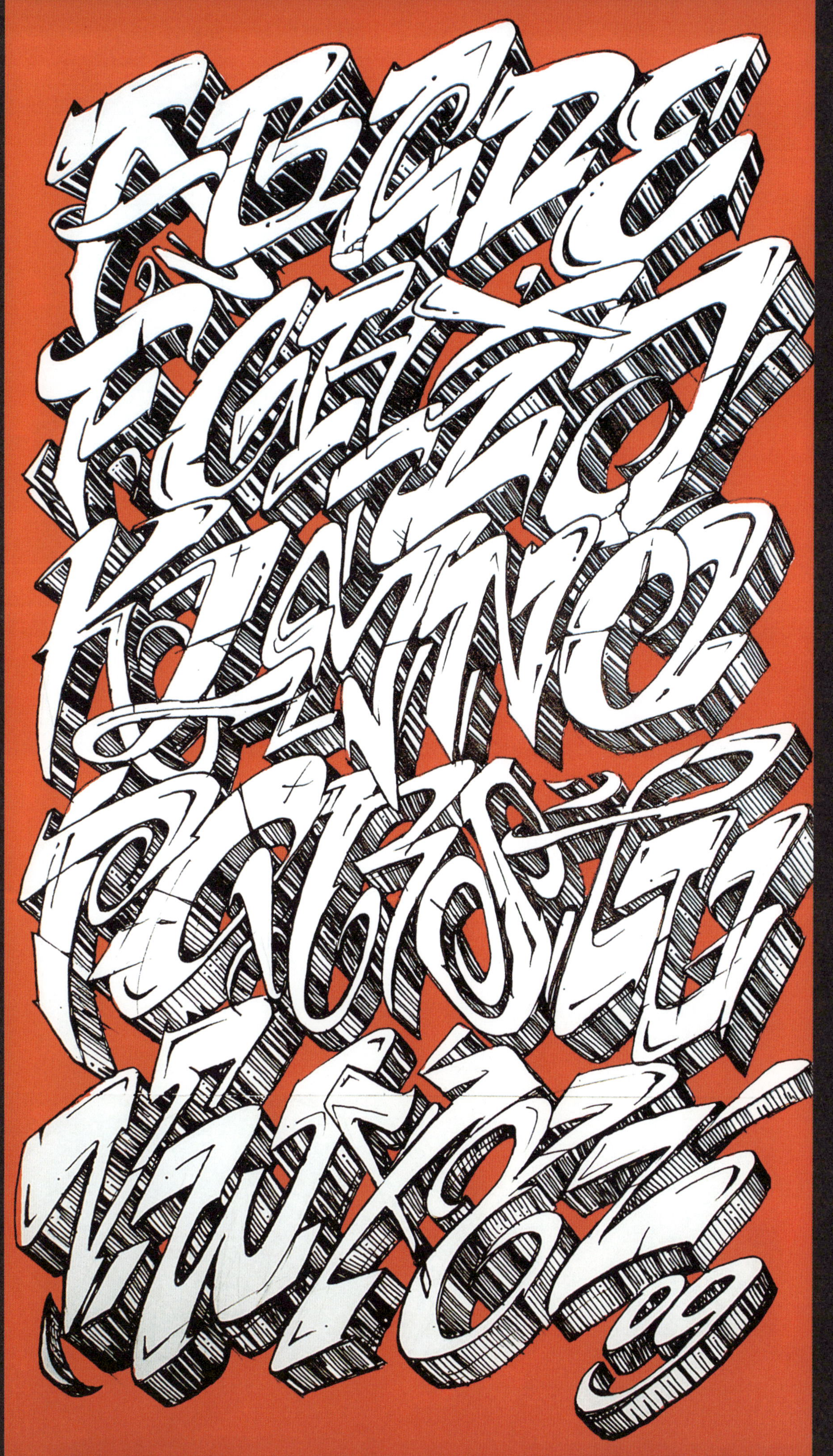

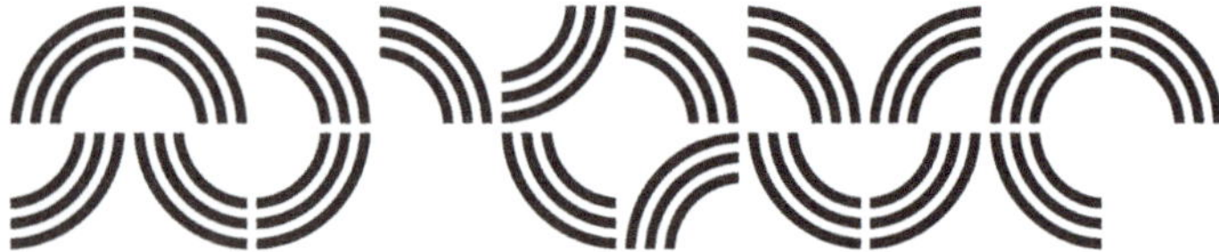

Xpome
SOFIA, BULGARIA

Crew member of Rock
N Rollers, Typoets
Writer since 2001
Favourite letter: X
www.flickr.com/xpome

Xpome likes to branch out from classic graffiti to find alternative solutions. His alphabet reflects his style, which is geometric, graphic, symmetrical and simple. He drew the alphabet in white pencil on black cardboard. 'Through graffiti you meet loads of nice and crazy people who share the same passion, and you never have to pay for accommodation again,' he says.

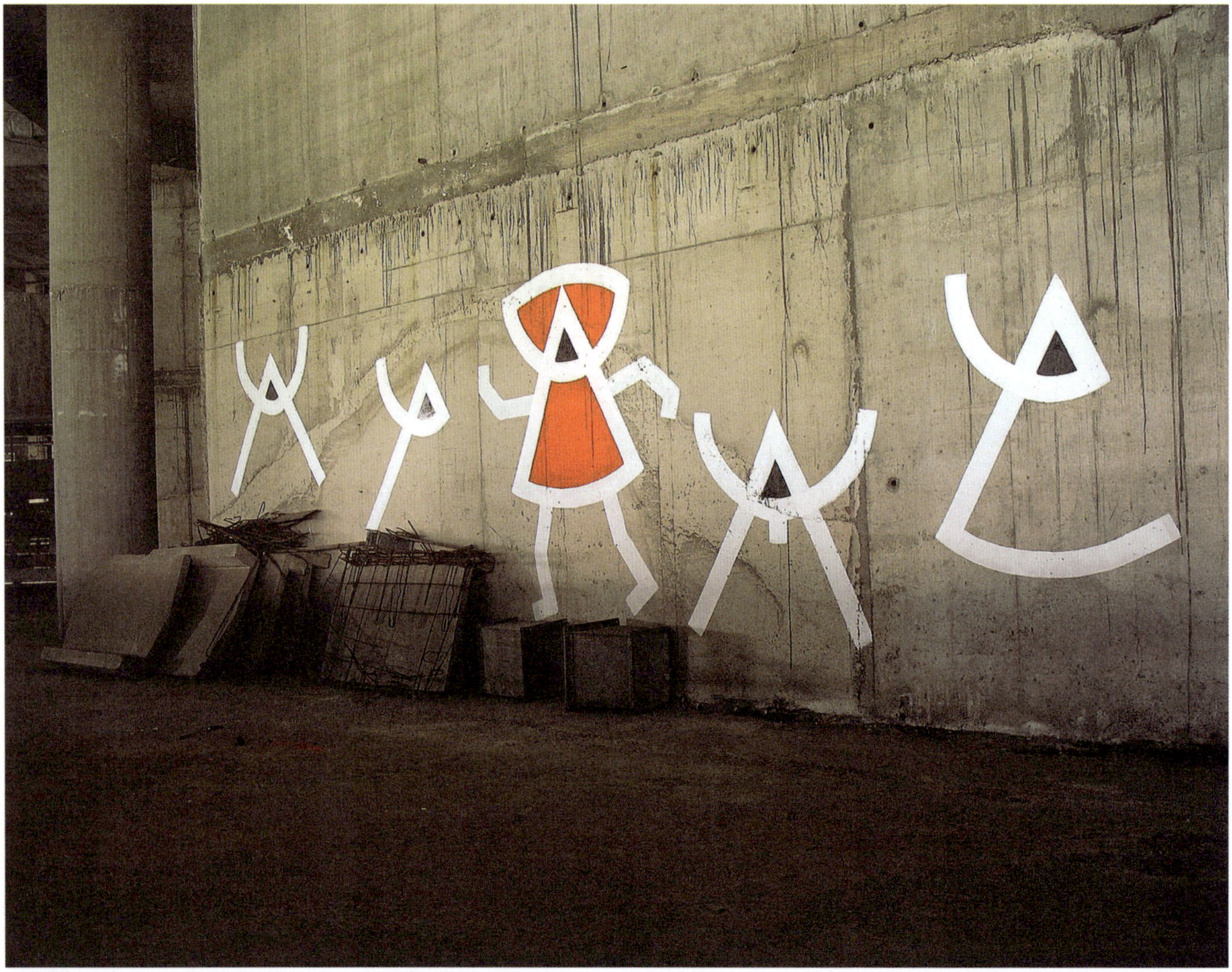

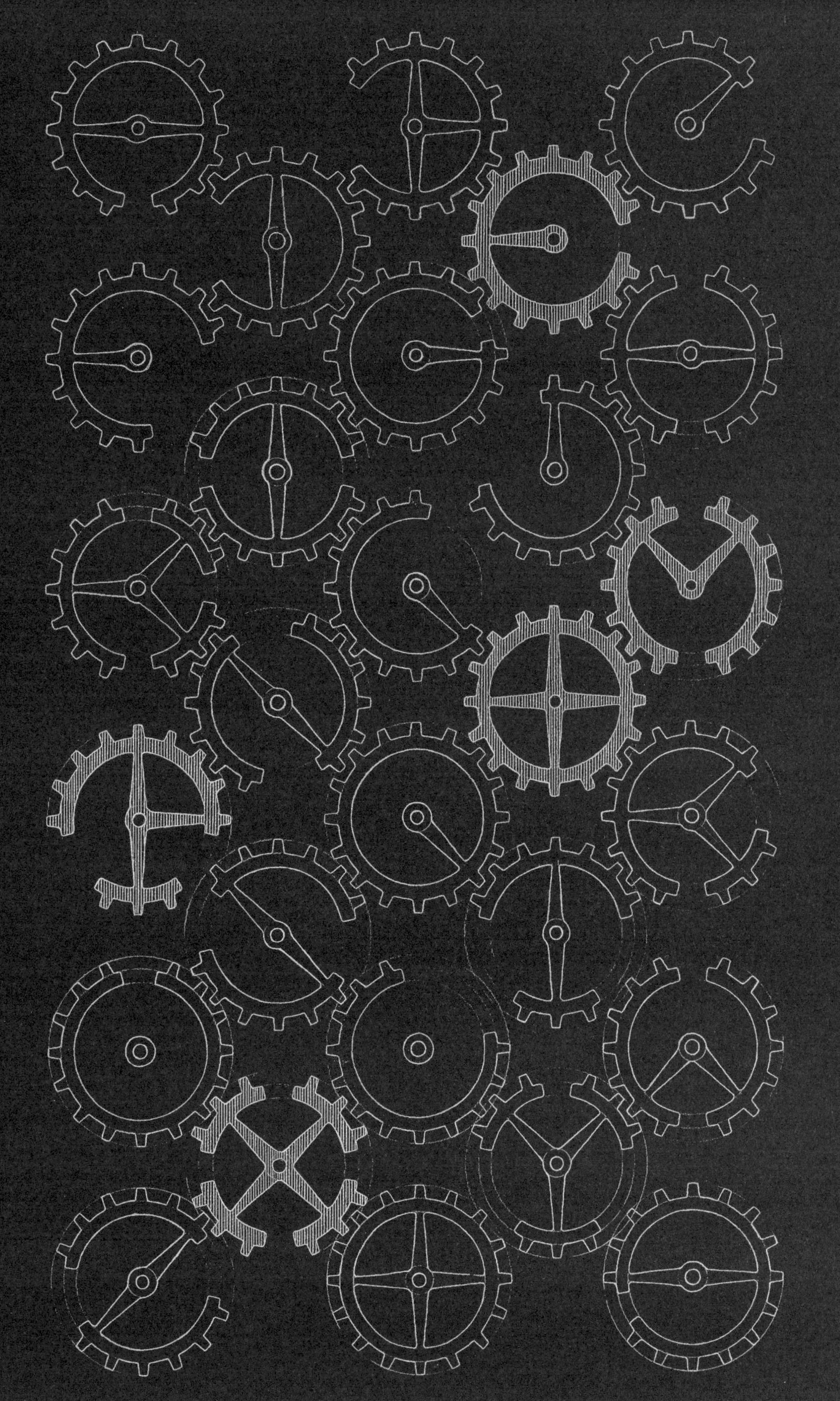

Zedz

AMSTERDAM, NETHERLANDS
Crew member of Incontrol, Mad Posse, Dope Style Kings,
Clowns From Hell
Writer since the mid-1980s
Favourite letter: Z
www.zedz.org

Zedz is famous for his bold and stylized 3D letters, which are reminiscent of
modern architecture. When he first started out as a writer he painted simple
pieces, but his letters have gradually become more and more experimental
and abstract over the years. In his current 3D designs, the individual letters
are hard to make out. A good piece needs 'the right mix of inspiration and
originality', according to Zedz.

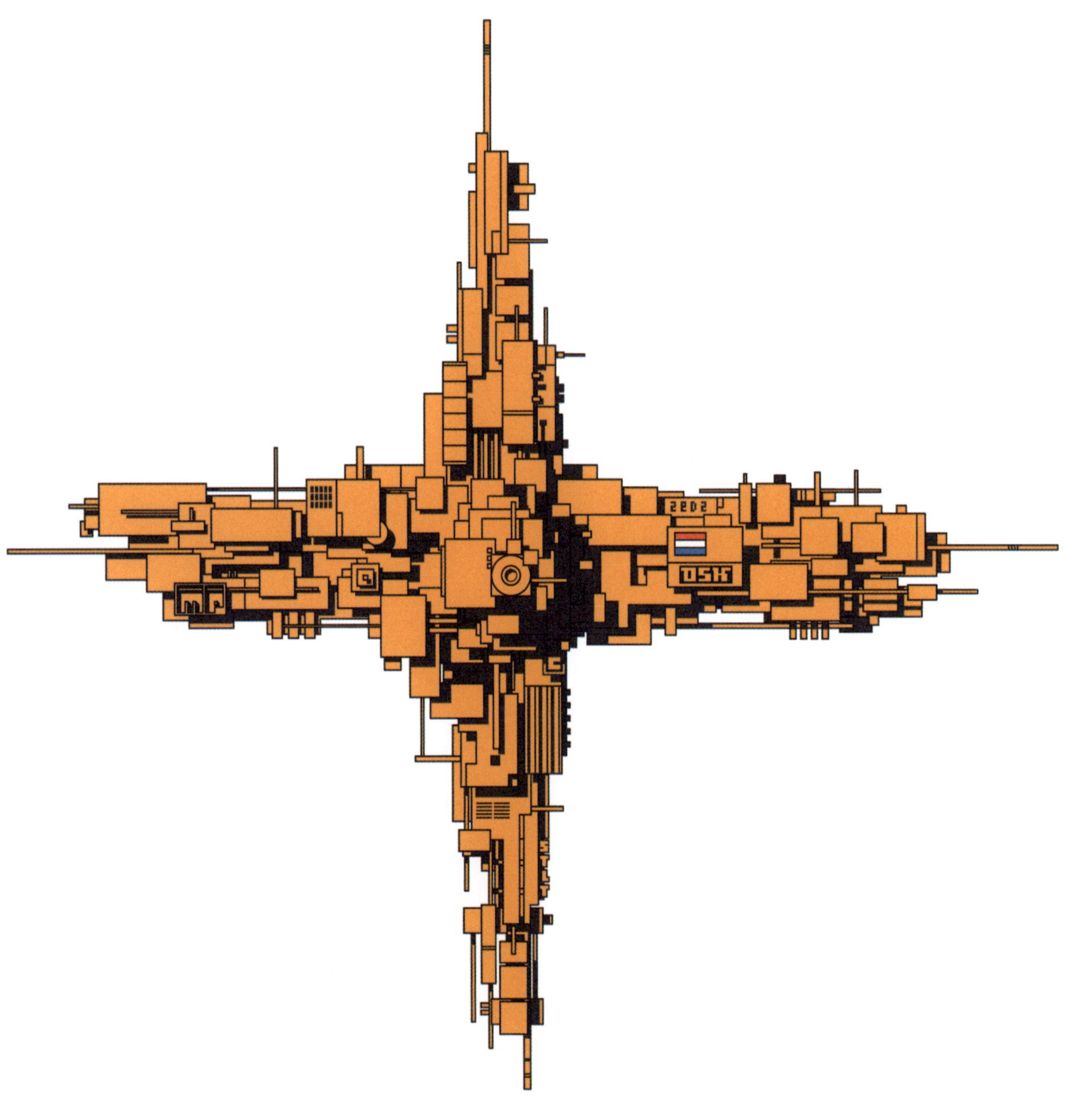

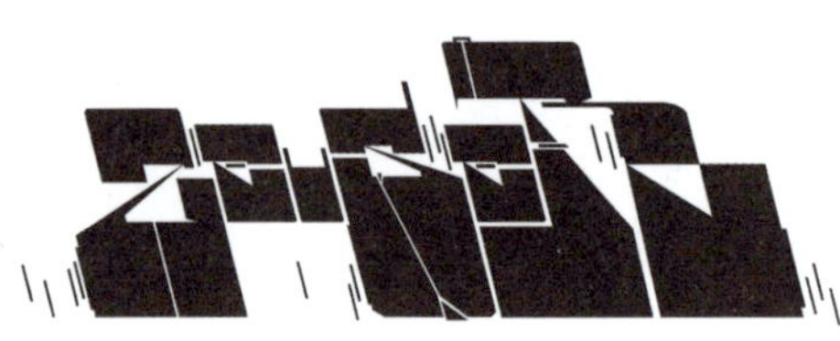

Zeus40

NAPLES, ITALY
Crew member of Wildboys
Writer since 2000
Favourite letter: E
www.flickr.com/zeus40

Zeus40 and his Wildboys crew are known for their well-executed styles and characters, and striking wall productions. Personality – and a style that reflects this – is all that is needed to create a good piece, says Zeus40. Above all, he values the freedom to be himself through graffiti.

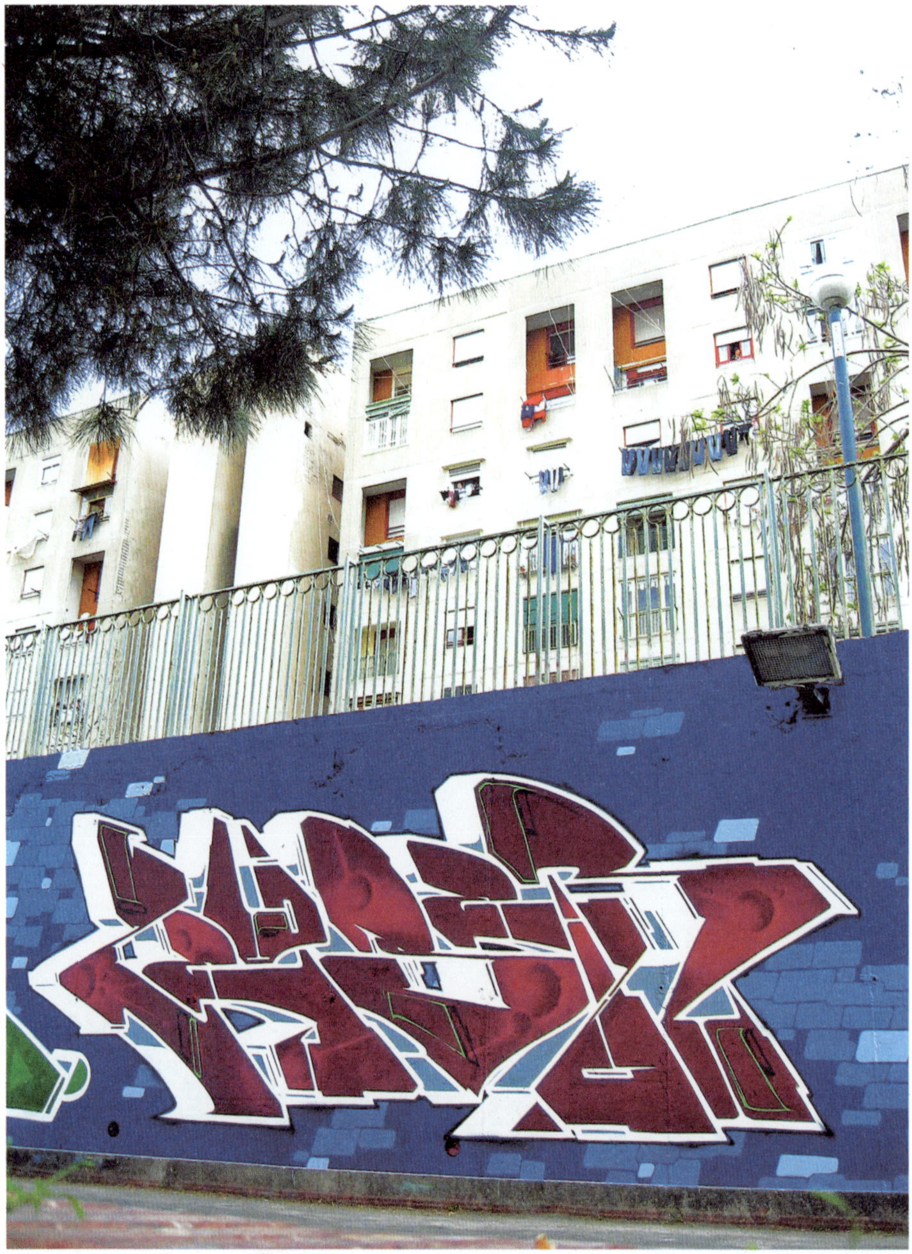

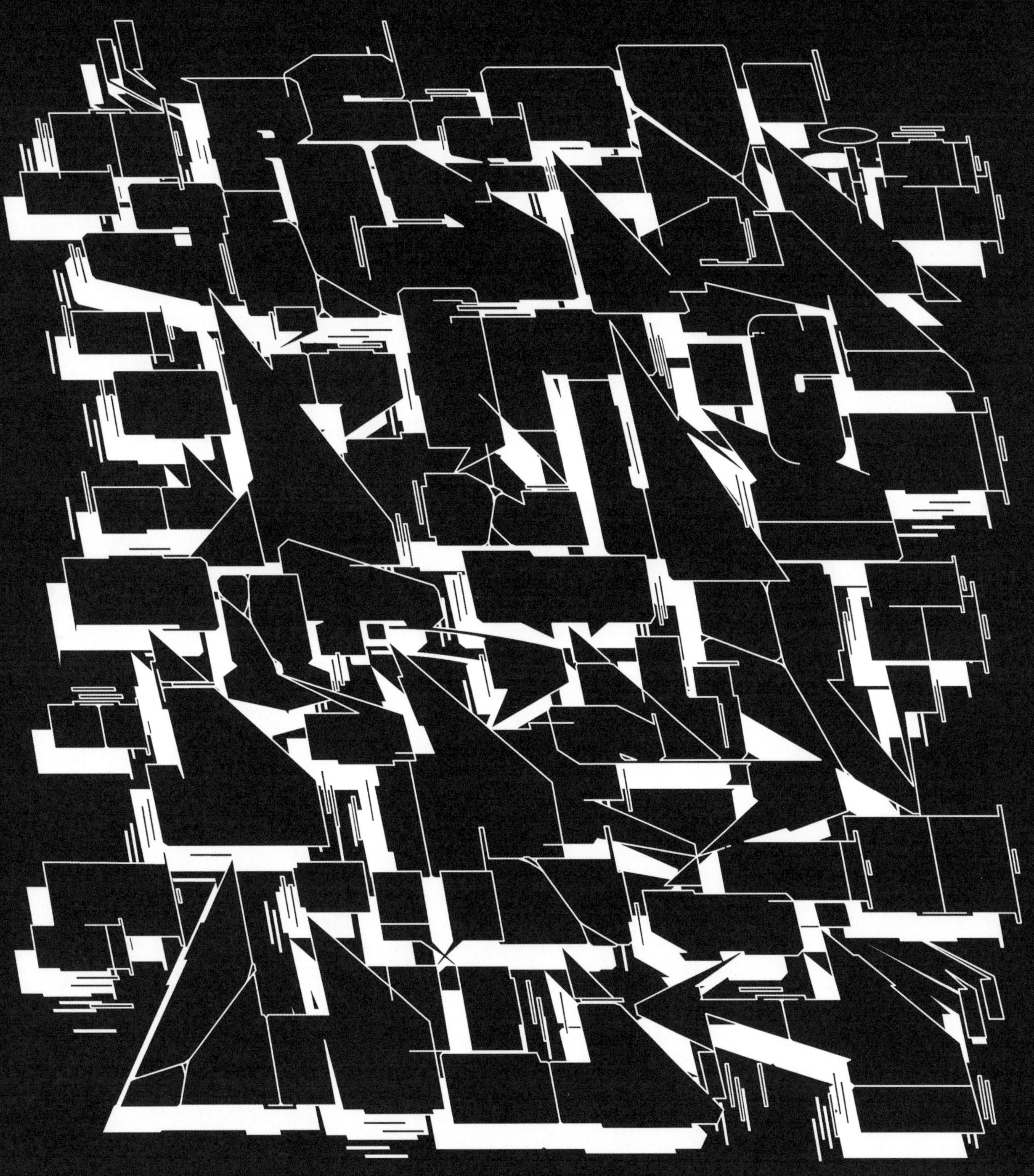

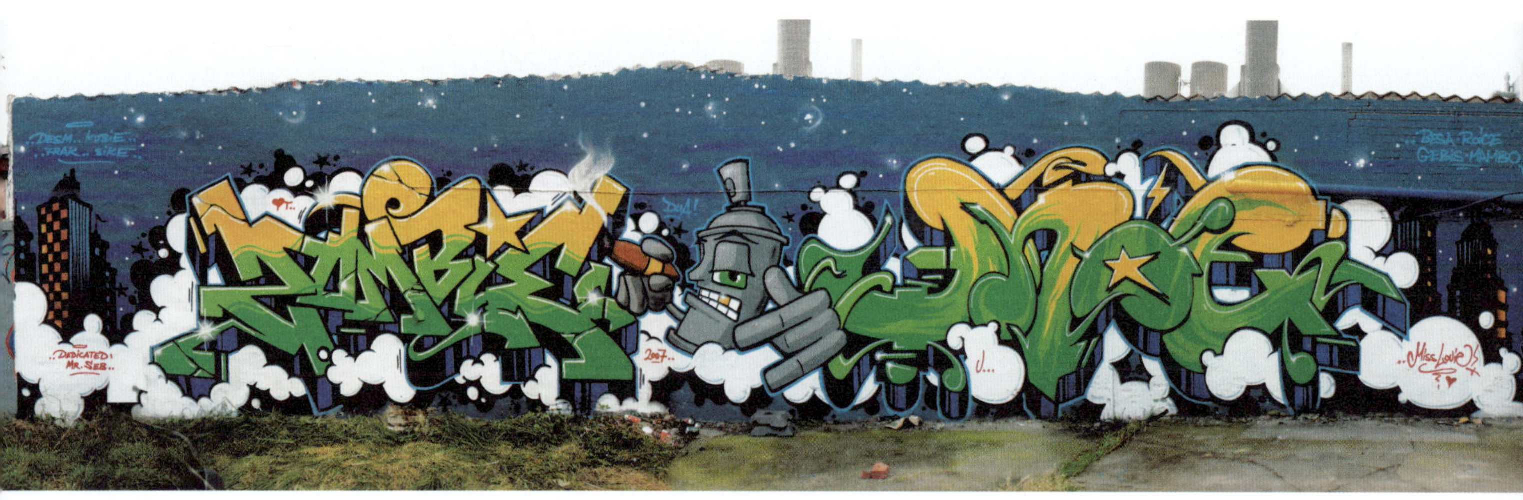

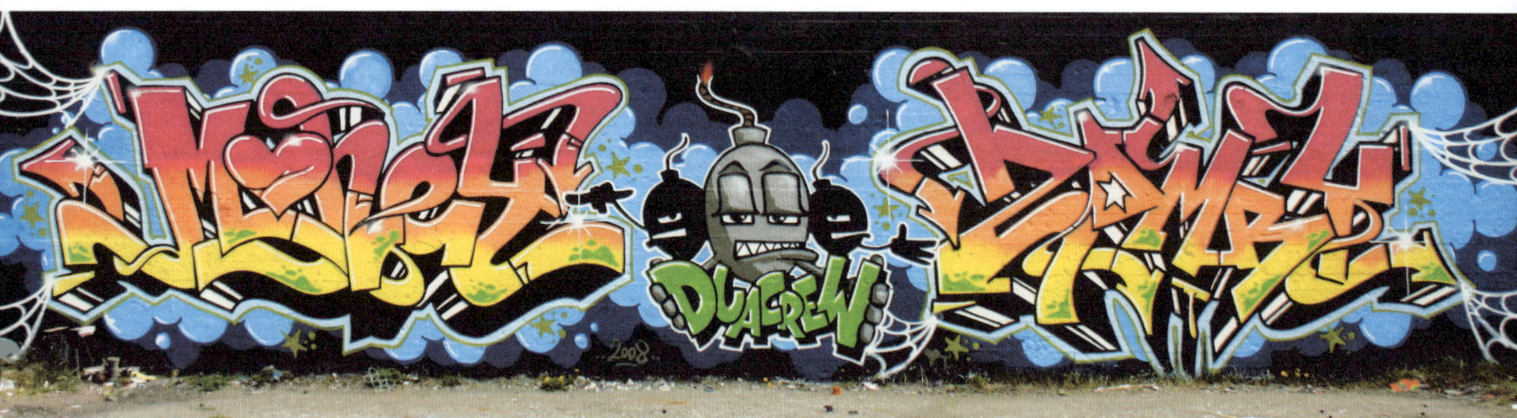

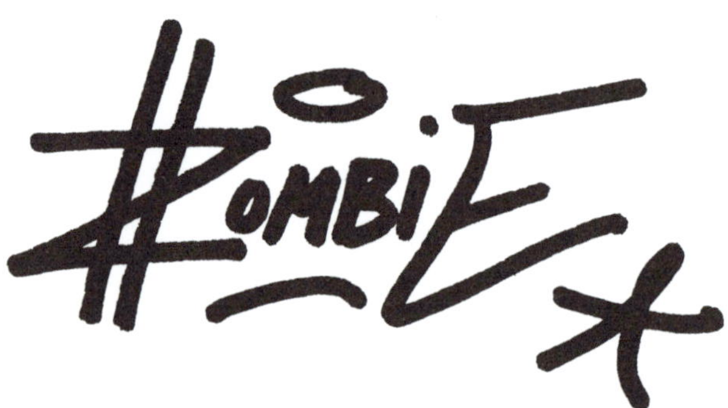

Zombie

COPENHAGEN, DENMARK
Crew member of DUA
Writer since the late 1980s
Favourite letter: M

Zombie likes classic letters and characters with a strong cartoon influence. His pieces always feature vivid contrast-rich colour schemes and steady outlines. 'When I look at pieces, I always look at the basic letter construction,' he explains. 'How would the letters look without all the colours and effects? A good piece works without all that. And I love to see the raw lines of a fat cap – I think it gives a piece a special energy.'

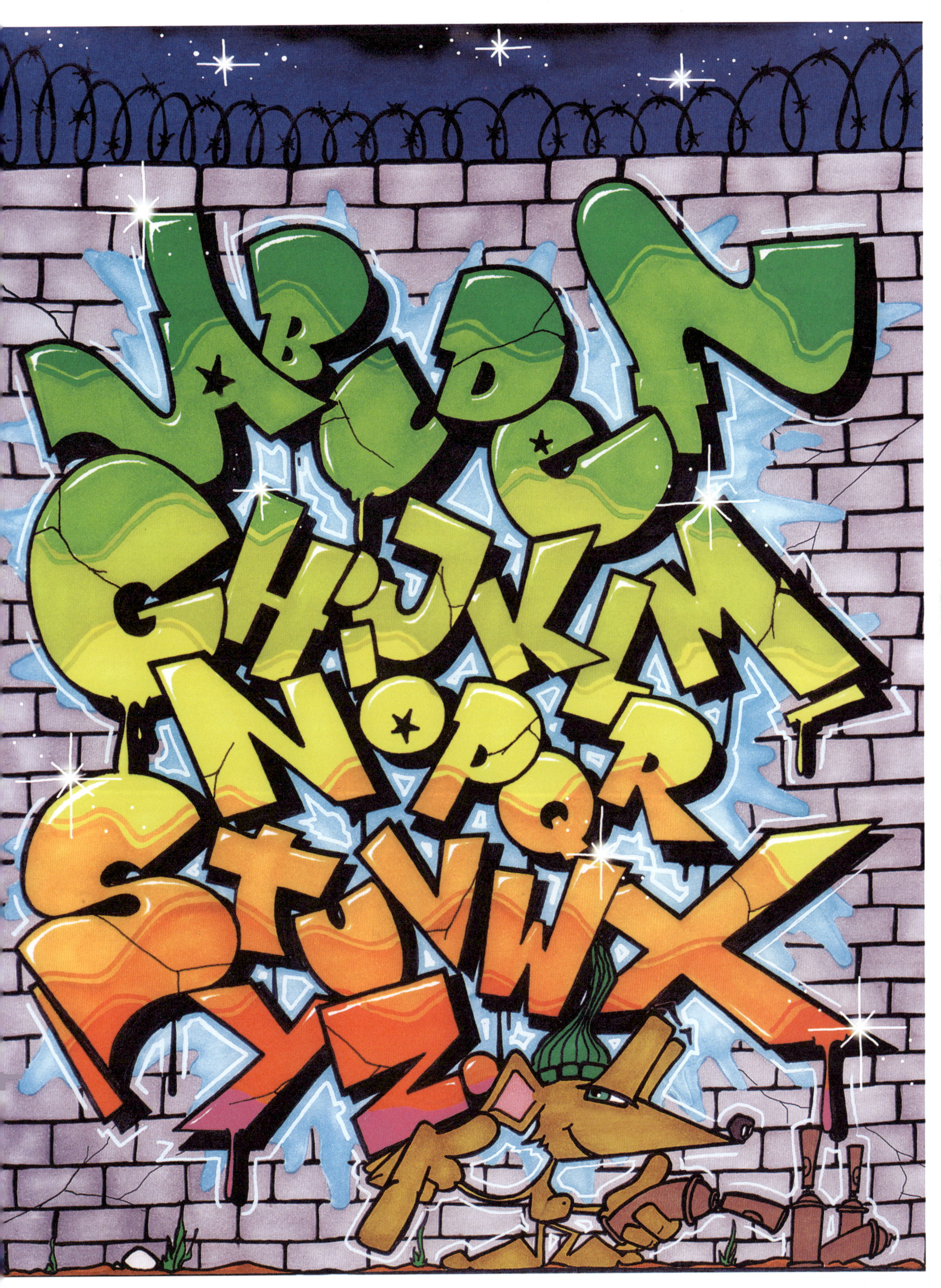

A B C D E F
G H I J K L M
N O P Q R
S T U V W X
Y Z

Websites

www.123klan.com
www.44flavours.com
www.a76.fr
www.alexeykio.com
www.apashoner.com
www.artimejoe.com
www.ashesgang.blogspot.com
www.askew1.com
www.aventuresextraordinaires.fr
www.bandits-dresden.de
www.beet74.com
www.cantwo.com
www.cmpspin.com
www.crashone.com
www.dare.ch
www.digitaldoes.com
www.faith47.com
www.flying-fortress.de
www.funkjood.com
www.graffitilt.com
www.herakut.de
www.hesoe.com
www.hooker1.com
www.ilkilkilk.com
www.ilovegraffiti.de
www.jabaone.com
www.jay-flow.com
www.jdemsky.com
www.jeremyville.com
www.jeroo.de
www.jerseyjoeart.com
www.jinsbh.com
www.jordae.com
www.klub7.de
www.komplexgraphix.com

www.latlas.net
www.lectrics.fr
www.loomit.de
www.macia-crew.com
www.madc.tv
www.madvictor.com
www.marceloment.com/br
www.markus-genesius.com
www.megaceet.com
www.michel-cren-pietsch.de
www.mr-totem.com
www.onepoint.cz
www.patricepoch.com
www.piscologik.com
www.plaqueone.com
www.puppetindustries.com
www.rater1.com
www.repletes.net
www.rosyone.com
www.rusl1.de
www.sicksystems.ru
www.sign-portfolio.de
www.smash137.com
www.staynice.nl
www.stukabazooka.com
www.sweetuno.com
www.super-a.nl
www.thelocalgenius.com
www.tmdcrew.com
www.tweb76.com
www.urbanroots.ru
www.viciousstylescrew.com
www.wanyone.com
www.worldwildwok.com
www.zedz.org

Picture Credits

All illustrations on a particular artist's spread are by that artist.
Additional picture credits and captions are given below:

6 Atom One

74 Photo: gentrifried

216 'Okupame' ('Occupy Me'), Bogotá, Colombia

276 LEFT Chinese lettering, Fanny, Bubble Girl piece, Taipei,
Taiwan, 2009
RIGHT The Burger (The Scorpio Collection courtesy of
Phillips de Pury & Company), spray paint and acrylic
on canvas, 180 × 150 cm

304 'Catch me if you can', Delmenhorst, Germany, 2009;
Photo: Axel Stock

319 Rosy One

Acknowledgments

A massive thank you to all the artists around the world who contributed with such dedication. Special thanks to all those people who have helped and inspired me along the way. I would like to thank the following people in particular for their support:

Amok
Can Two
Chas
Darco
Dare
Thomas Deichsel
My family
Jürgen Feuerstein
Klark Kent
Lady Pink
Letruc
Annelies Maenhout

Mare139
Mogi
Newkon
Omsk167
Marco Prosch
Reno Rössel
Seen UA
Slider
Smith
Swet
Stephan Walde

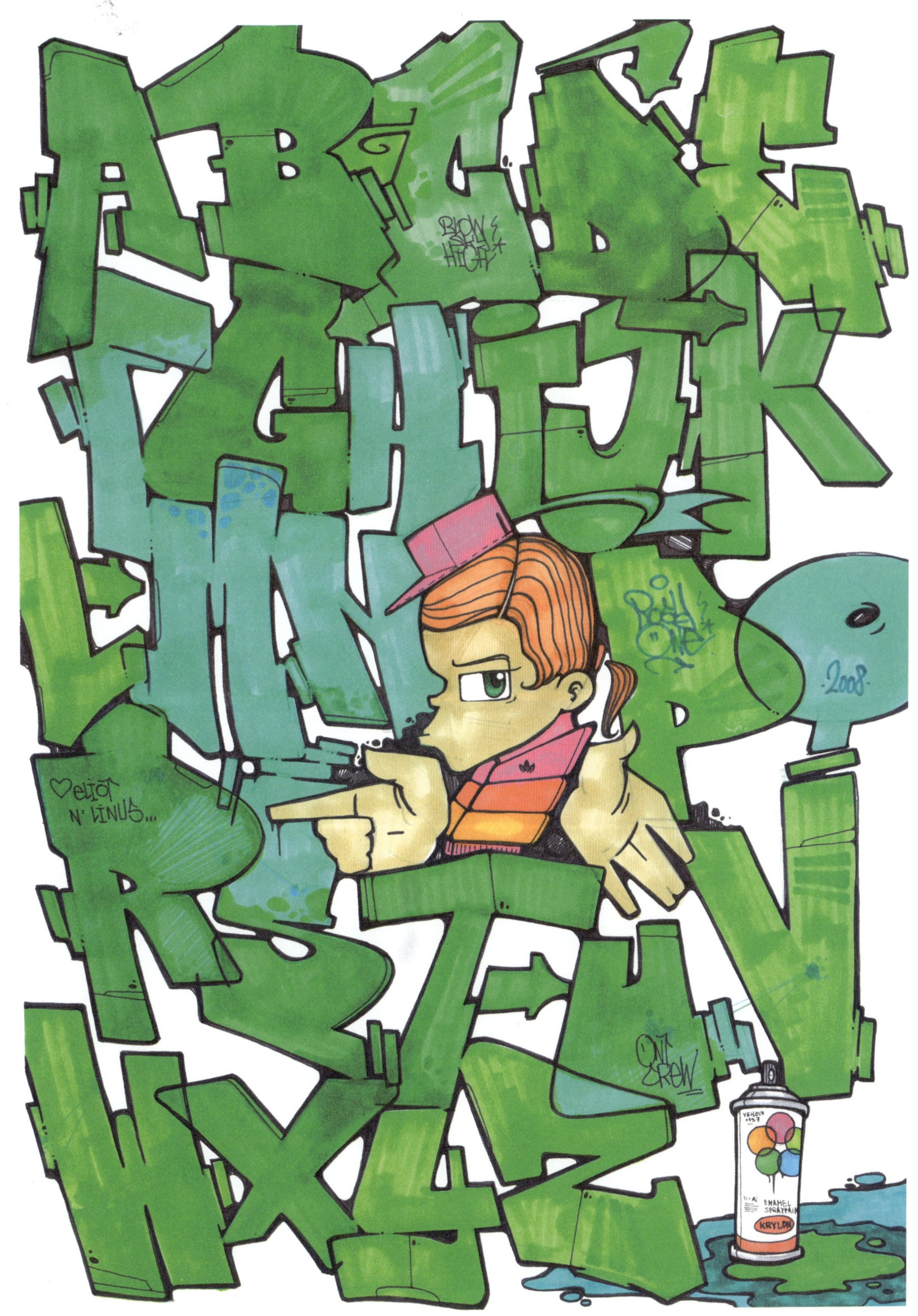

BLOW &
HIGH
ELIOT
N' LINUS...
2008
KRYLON
ENAMEL
SPRAYPAINT

First published in the United Kingdom in 2011
as *Street Fonts* by Thames & Hudson Ltd,
181A High Holborn, London WC1V 7QX

First published in the United States of America in 2011
as *Graffiti Alphabets* by Thames & Hudson Inc.,
500 Fifth Avenue, New York, New York 10110

First paperback edition published in 2018
Reprinted 2024

Street Fonts | Graffiti Alphabets © 2011 and 2018 Claudia Walde

Cover design by MadC

All Rights Reserved. No part of this publication may be
reproduced or transmitted in any form or by any means,
electronic or mechanical, including photocopy, recording
or any other information storage and retrieval system,
without prior permission in writing from the publisher.

British Library Cataloguing-in-Publication Data
A catalogue record for this book is available
from the British Library

Library of Congress Control Number 2010936748

Street Fonts ISBN 978-0-500-29416-1
Graffiti Alphabets ISBN 978-0-500-29429-1

Printed and bound in China by Toppan Leefung Printing Limited

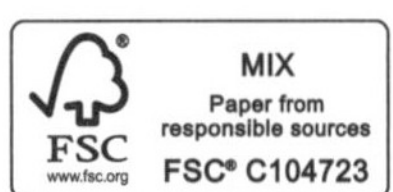

Be the first to know about our new releases,
exclusive content and author events by visiting
thamesandhudson.com
thamesandhudsonusa.com
thamesandhudson.com.au